Ashes Diary 2005

Ashes Diary 2005

Ricky Ponting
& Brian Murgatroyd

HarperSports
An imprint of HarperCollins*Publishers*

Harper*Sports*

An imprint of HarperCollins*Publishers* Australia

First published in Australia in 2005
by HarperCollins*Publishers* Australia Pty Limited
ABN 36 009 913 517
www.harpercollins.com.au

HarperCollins*Publishers*
25 Ryde Road, Pymble, Sydney, NSW 2073, Australia
31 View Road, Glenfield, Auckland 10, New Zealand
77–85 Fulham Palace Road, London, W6 8JB, United Kingdom
2 Bloor Street East, 20th floor, Toronto, Ontario M4W 1A8, Canada
10 East 53rd Street, New York NY 10022, USA

National Library of Australia Cataloguing-in-Publication data:

Ponting, Ricky.
  Ashes diary.
  ISBN 0 7322 8152 0.
  1. Ponting, Ricky – Diaries. 2. Cricket captains – Australia –
  Diaries. 3. Cricket players – Australia – Diaries.
  4. Test matches (Cricket) – Australia – History.
  5. Cricket – Tournaments – Australia. I. Murgatroyd, Brian.
  II. Title.
796.358092.

Cover photography by Phil Hillyard/© News Limited
Cover design by Stuart Horton-Stevens, Geeza Design
Statistics compiled by Ross Dundas
Internal design adapted from original by Christa Moffitt by HarperCollins Design Studio
Typeset in Sabon 11/17 by Kirby Jones
Printed and bound in Australia by Griffin Press on 79gsm Bulky Paperback

5 4 3 2 1   05 06 07 08

Acknowledgments

There are numerous people I need to thank for helping me record the past 15 months, my third diary as captain of the Australian cricket team.

First of all, thanks to my beautiful wife, Rianna, who has supported me throughout this amazing journey. You are my inspiration, my love, and I am so proud to have you in my life. No matter what happens on the field, as long as I have you beside me then I know everything in the world is right.

Thanks, too, to my family and Rianna's family for your constant love and support, and also to my manager, Sam Halvorsen. Sam, you are a fantastic friend and I could not wish for anyone better to look after my interests.

To all my team-mates and the team's support staff, thanks for your hard work, friendship and encouragement. I am especially grateful to Jock Campbell for his help in getting me in great shape for the Ashes tour, and Jonathan Rose, our media manager. As ever, Jono, this diary could not have been written without your assistance.

Brian Murgatroyd has once again helped get my thoughts down on paper, a massive job given the amount of cricket we played over the period of time covered in this diary. As ever, it has been a pleasure to work alongside you. Thanks should also go to Brian's wife, Aarti Singh Dabas, and his family and friends for allowing him to focus on this project so completely.

The staff at HarperCollins have once again excelled themselves, getting this diary ready in a remarkably short time after the Ashes tour, and have remained amazingly calm despite the deadline pressures. Thanks to everyone there, especially Alison Urquhart, Ali Orman, Sophie Hamley, Graeme Jones, and Sarah Shrubb and Nicola O'Shea.

Others who deserve special praise for their help and assistance are all the staff at Cricket Australia, Barney Francis of Sky Sports, Ross Dundas for his sterling work on the statistics, the Gayleard family — John, Jennifer, Jessica and Jack — Garry Rainford and the Catherine Hill Bay Bowling Club. Thanks to you all for helping to make this book possible.

Contents

THE SPIRIT OF CRICKET

WRITTEN BY CRICKET AUSTRALIA
CONTRACTED PLAYERS, OCTOBER 2003

In 2003, Cricket Australia's contracted players wrote a code that represents the spirit in which they seek to play the game. It reads:

As cricketers who represent Australia we acknowledge and embrace 'The Spirit of Cricket' and the laws of our game.

This Players' Spirit of Australian Cricket serves as a guide to the shared standards of behaviour that we expect of ourselves and of the values we hold.

Our on-field behaviour

We play our cricket hard but fair and accept all umpiring decisions as a mark of respect for our opponents, the umpires, ourselves and the game.

We view positive play, pressure, body language and banter between opponents and ourselves as legitimate tactics and integral parts of the competitive nature of cricket.

We do not condone or engage in sledging or any other conduct that constitutes personal abuse.

We encourage the display of passion and emotion as a sign of our enjoyment and pride in the game, as a celebration of our achievements and as a sign of respect for our opponents.

Our off-field behaviour

It is acknowledged that we have a private life to lead but understand our off-field conduct has the potential to reflect either positively or adversely on us as individuals and also on the game of cricket.

We consider off-field conduct that may be likely to warrant legitimate public criticism to be unacceptable conduct.

Our team

We take pride in our sense of the importance of the team and acknowledge the role of the team captain and our direct support staff. We demonstrate this by displaying loyalty and compassion to each other, by accepting our role as mentors and by supporting each other to abide by these values.

We value honesty and accept that every member of the team has a role to play in shaping, and abiding by our shared standards and expectations.

We strive to be regarded as the best team in the world. We measure this by our on-field achievements and by exploring ways in which we might continue to 'raise the bar' in respect of our own professionalism.

We acknowledge and follow the traditions of our game while encouraging and accepting experimentation that will enable us to create our own traditions and history. We do this in the expectation that we will leave the game in a better shape than it was before we arrived.

Our opponents

We acknowledge and respect that our opponents may hold different cultural values and beliefs from our own, and value the diversity and richness this adds to the game.

By treating our opponents with dignity and forging bonds of mutual respect, we will overcome any cultural barriers.

Our supporters

We value our supporters and acknowledge those who support our opponents and the game of cricket. We demonstrate commitment to our supporters by always giving our best and demonstrating leadership in everything we do.

Our family

We value the contribution and sacrifices of our families that enable us to meet these expectations.

Respect

We respect the governing bodies of the game, our support teams in every capacity and our players' association. We demonstrate this respect by seeking and offering frank and open communication in accordance with the Players' Spirit of Australian Cricket.

Part 1:
Top End Tour 2004

SRI LANKA IN AUSTRALIA

Muttiah Muralitharan is named in Sri Lanka's squad for the Top End Tour. There had been speculation that he would not tour after being no-balled for throwing on two previous trips, and following concerns about an injury and reported remarks by the Australian Prime Minister about tests of his bowling action.

Sri Lanka's squad: Marvan Atapattu (captain), Russel Arnold, Upul Chandana, Tillakaratne Dilshan, Dilhara Fernando, Rangana Herath, Sanath Jayasuriya, Mahela Jayawardene (vice-captain), Romesh Kaluwitharana, Farveez Maharoof, Lasith Malinga, Muttiah Muralitharan, Thilan Samaraweera, Kumar Sangakkara, Chaminda Vaas, Nuwan Zoysa.

Wednesday 9 June

Australia names a 13-man squad for the two-Test series: Ricky Ponting (captain), Adam Gilchrist (vice-captain), Jason Gillespie, Matthew Hayden, Michael Kasprowicz, Simon Katich, Justin Langer, Darren Lehmann, Damien Martyn, Glenn McGrath, Shaun Tait, Shane Warne, Brad Williams.

The squad basically picked itself, but a major point of interest will be the form of Glenn McGrath.

He has taken a long time to get back to his best and regain rhythm after his long-standing ankle injury, and the selectors have put him on notice, letting him know that they expect results from him. Glenn has always thrived on lots of bowling to gain his rhythm; the injury, and the fact that the season ended just as he got back to full fitness, meant he was not able to get that bowling before he toured Zimbabwe in May, and the results that followed were correspondingly disappointing.

Glenn's strengths as a bowler have always been his high action, which allows him to generate extra bounce, together with a wrist position that ensures that the seam stays upright on its way down the pitch. All that appears to be in order, but the extra bit of zip he always used to have was missing in Zimbabwe, maybe because he still lacks a bit of confidence in his ankle so is not pushing himself as hard as he can — understandable after a long-term injury.

I have chatted with the selectors about Glenn and there is no question, at this stage, of his being left out. I think we are all waiting, expecting the old McGrath magic to reappear any minute, but on the other side of the coin, he is not getting any younger and there are bound to be doubts, even in his own mind, about whether he can come back after around 9 months out of the game at an age when most fast bowlers are hanging up their boots.

His boots are big ones to fill — as was shown last summer, when we struggled to bowl India out twice during our home Test series — and the squad the selectors have named here does include other fast bowling options. Shaun Tait — who clanged me on the head with a very rapid bouncer in the nets in Colombo back in March, when he was called up to replace the injured Brett Lee — covers for Brad Williams, who left the tour of Zimbabwe with a sore back. Lee is still not fit, after surgery on his ankle.

Friday 11 June

Shane Warne breaks a bone in his left hand while playing in a first-class match in the United Kingdom for Hampshire against Essex. The injury makes him a major doubt for the Top End Tour, with the series set to start in less than 3 weeks' time.

Sunday 13 June

Warne is given a 50/50 chance of being fit in time for the series with Sri Lanka after consulting a hand specialist in the United Kingdom. Cricket Australia's medical officer, Dr Trefor James, confirmed that Warne's injury — a broken metacarpal bone — does not require surgery.

Tuesday 15 June

Muttiah Muralitharan pulls out of the series in Australia for 'personal reasons'. Muralitharan was reported for having a suspect bowling action at the end of the home series against Australia in March. Sri Lanka team manager Ajit Jayasekera said Muralitharan's team-mates fully support the player's decision to miss the tour.

I am disappointed Murali will not be touring Australia, for several reasons.

From a personal point of view, I was looking forward to locking horns with him. As a player you want to compete against the best, and his record shows that he falls into that category, whatever the rights and wrongs of his bowling action.

I have always enjoyed our battles, and have been lucky enough to score a few runs against him in the past, and those runs are some of the most satisfying of my career. Murali poses problems — through the massive spin he generates — that other, orthodox spinners simply cannot match, and his absence will put a big dent in Sri Lanka's bowling resources.

I would be very disappointed if Murali's 'personal reasons' were related to concern about the type of reception he might get in Australia. He has been barracked a fair bit in this country in the past, but I can vouch for the fact that you get abuse yelled at you as an international cricketer whenever you are abroad. Some of it can be personal and unpleasant but it happens to us all; you just have to be professional enough to block it out and get on with the job in hand. If that is one of the reasons Murali is not touring, then all I can say is if he was one of my players and did the same thing then I would not be very impressed and do not think the selectors would be too impressed, either.

He did take plenty of wickets against us in the recent series in Sri Lanka, but overall I thought we played him pretty well, something he confirmed to me when we had a drink together after the final Test of the tour. I wonder if our skill in dealing with his threat in Sri Lanka had any bearing on his decision, especially as Darwin and Cairns are unlikely to be as spin-friendly as Colombo, Galle or Kandy. His absence does give Shane Warne — fitness permitting — the chance to catch him at the top of the list of Test wicket-takers, so I am sure it is not a decision he made lightly.

No replacement has been named. This could be a positive for Sri Lanka, in that the other bowlers will now get the chance to show they have what it takes to fill Murali's boots.

Wednesday 16 June

Brad Williams is ruled out of the Top End Tour after failing to recover sufficiently from the back injury that forced him home early from May's tour of Zimbabwe.

Former Australia fast bowler Dennis Lillee labels Muralitharan's absence 'a pathetic decision and a real cop-out'.

Monday 21 June

Muralitharan's manager, Kushil Gunasekara, confirms that the player will be visiting Australia during the upcoming Test series after all — for promotional work.

Shane Warne is expected to be available for selection for the first Test in Darwin, starting on 1 July, after his injured left hand was examined by leading hand surgeon Greg Hoy.

Stuart MacGill is called up to the Australian squad as a replacement for the injured Brad Williams. 'Given we already have four fit fast bowlers in the squad, Stuart gives us some added flexibility,' said Chairman of Selectors Trevor Hohns.

Sri Lanka captain Marvan Atapattu sits out his team's match ahead of the first Test with a back injury.

Tour match, Darwin, day 1: Northern Territory Chief Minister's XI 7–364 (Langer 151, Bowden 75) v the Sri Lankans.

Tour match, Darwin, day 2: Northern Territory Chief Minister's XI 419 (Langer 151, Bowden 75, Treumer 65) lead the Sri Lankans 5–304 (Sangakkara 163*, Jayasuriya 64) by 115 runs.

Tour match, Darwin, day 3: The Sri Lankans 7–378 declared (Sangakkara 203*, Jayasuriya 64) and 1–6 require another 181 runs to beat Northern Territory Chief Minister's XI 419 and 9–145 declared.

Tour match, Darwin, day 4: The Sri Lankans 7–378 and 5–187 (Dilshan 66*) beat Northern Territory Chief Minister's XI 419 and 9–145 declared by 5 wickets.

I was at the airport in Sydney on Sunday, about to board a flight to Brisbane en route to Darwin, when I got a call from home that Auntie Annette, my father's only sister, had become very ill.

Annette had been suffering from terminal cancer for quite a while, so everyone in the family knew this terrible time would come eventually, but it was still a shock to get the call that she was deteriorating rapidly.

---

* not out

I flew home straightaway and got into Launceston around 6 o'clock in the evening, with a view to visiting her first thing on Monday morning, but after a restless night I got another call from my father, at about 5 o'clock in the morning, saying that Annette had passed away during the night.

It was devastating news for us all: no one expected her to pass away so suddenly. I knew Annette very well because we kids — me, my sister Renee and brother Drew — spent lots of time with her and her husband Michael during school holidays when we were growing up. At least I have very happy memories of the time I spent with her, but that is not much comfort right now.

My initial plan had been to visit Annette and see what the doctors said; if there was a suggestion that she would not make it through the week I would pull out of the Test. But even though she passed away far more quickly than any of us expected, I had no thoughts of leaving my family and heading up to Darwin.

The match was to be my first as Test captain on Australian soil, but that sort of landmark was the furthest thing from my mind while I was with my family. I hope I will have plenty more opportunities to play for and captain Australia, but I only have one family, and it was important for me to be with them — not only for my father, but also for my grandparents, both of them now faced with the fact that they had outlived their daughter. The decision not to play in Darwin was an easy one. I have no regrets about it, and would make it again in an instant if presented with similar circumstances.

Tuesday 29 June

Ricky Ponting pulls out of the first Test against Sri Lanka after the death of his aunt. Adam Gilchrist is named as captain in place of Ponting, with Darren Lehmann stepping up to the vice-captaincy.

Victoria's Matthew Elliott is named as Ponting's replacement in the squad.

Sri Lanka captain Marvan Atapattu is passed fit for the Test.

Although I am not playing in the Test I have still been in close contact with several of the players in Darwin to discuss options and tactics for the match.

Even before I pulled out I chatted with Justin Langer, who captained the Northern Territory Chief Minister's XI in Sri Lanka's warm-up fixture, and he brought some encouraging news about Glenn McGrath.

According to Langer, McGrath bowled beautifully: he said no one should have any concerns about McGrath going into the Test match. McGrath bowled 38 overs in the match, and though he managed just 1 wicket in each innings, he only conceded 87 runs. Langer said that on another day, and with a little more luck, McGrath would have enjoyed a much better haul.

Later, I chatted with Adam Gilchrist about McGrath's role in the Test. There has been some speculation about whether or not he will take the new ball — after all, Michael Kasprowicz and Jason Gillespie did very well with it in Sri Lanka — but both Gilchrist and I agreed that McGrath should get that chance. He has never let us down in that role, and he will ensure that the batsmen are under pressure straightaway; besides, in Kasprowicz we have a bowler who is equally at home with the older ball. Also, giving McGrath the new ball will be just the boost he needs. Even though he is an experienced campaigner, this match is still his first Test in a year. Even top players get nerves, especially when they are coming back from a serious injury.

The selectors' decision to go with Matthew Elliott as my replacement was straightforward, even though there was a case for picking Martin Love. Love has been on the fringes of the squad for a while, and scored a hundred against Bangladesh in the Top End series of last year, but he has not played any cricket lately. Elliott, on the other hand, is back in the country after a successful spell with county side Glamorgan and a superb summer for Victoria — he is match-sharp, and deserves his chance.

Gilchrist and I also discussed Shane Warne's fitness. Warne has done everything asked of him in the build-up to the match and Gilchrist has no doubts he is fit to play. The only dilemma is where he should field. It might be a risk for him to stand in his normal first slip position — no one wants to see him get another blow on the hand. We agreed to be guided by Warne on that one.

Thursday 1 July

First Test, Darwin, day 1: Sri Lanka 3–43 trail Australia 203 (Lehmann 57, Vaas 5–31) by 160 runs.

I could only watch the match on television, but it was still pretty obvious that batting conditions were not easy. The ball swung and seamed around, and the bounce was variable. Although our total does not look very impressive, we still appear to be in control.

The key was our opening stand of 72, from Justin Langer and Matthew Hayden. Its importance was shown later, when Sri Lanka claimed the last 7 wickets for just 30 runs. That partnership, together with contributions from Damien Martyn and Darren Lehmann, ensured that we have a competitive score.

Amid the clatter of wickets it was impossible not to feel sorry for Matthew Elliott. Called up at the last minute, circumstances have dictated he is on a hiding to nothing. The pitch is a poor one, he knows no matter how well he does he will probably have to give up his spot to me for the next match, and as he was not expecting to play his cricket gear is still in the United Kingdom, so he is using borrowed equipment. Without even a pair of batting shoes, he had to wear a pair of borrowed running shoes rather than spikes. And although he came in after that fine opening stand, conditions were far from easy and he lasted just 8 balls before edging Chaminda Vaas into the slips.

Watching the television coverage gave me a chance to take a close look at the new Sri Lanka quick bowler, Lasith Malinga. He is a small man but has an amazing slingshot, round-arm action and his arm is so low that the ball is in front of the umpire's chest at the point of release. He looked impressive, and along with Vaas formed a useful new ball combination.

Our new ball combination was equally effective and with Glenn McGrath justifying the faith shown in him to take two of the three Sri Lanka wickets to fall before the close, we look in control.

Friday 2 July

Australia names its provisional 30-man squad for the ICC (International Cricket Council) Champions Trophy that will take place in England in September: Ricky Ponting (captain), Andrew Bichel, Nathan Bracken, Michael Clarke, Adam Gilchrist (vice-captain), Jason Gillespie, Brad Haddin, Ian Harvey, Nathan Hauritz, Matthew Hayden, Brad Hodge, Brad Hogg, Michael Hussey, Michael Kasprowicz, Simon Katich, Justin Langer, Brett Lee, Darren Lehmann, Jimmy Maher, Damien Martyn, Glenn McGrath, Jonathan Moss, Marcus North, Andrew Symonds, Shaun Tait, Dominic Thornely, Shane Watson, Cameron White, Brad Williams, Damien Wright.

First Test, Darwin, day 2: Sri Lanka 97 (McGrath 5–37) require 312 runs to beat Australia 207 and 201 (Gilchrist 80, Lehmann 51).

Although Sri Lanka's target of 312 looks achievable, on a pitch of variable bounce and excessive movement, it is the equivalent of 600 to chase.

The approaches of Adam Gilchrist and Darren Lehmann summed up the surface. Both were almost reckless at times. They obviously though it was best to look to score as many runs as quickly as possible because if they just looked to hang around that would not achieve very much. Sooner or later on a pitch like this a ball would have their name on it.

Glenn McGrath carried on where he left off last night, and marked his comeback Test with a 5-wicket haul. From what I saw, his form looked excellent. He swung the ball, and when he bowled bouncers he really appeared to hurry up the Sri Lanka batsmen — both very good signs.

Saturday 3 July

First Test, Darwin, day 3: Australia 207 and 201 beat Sri Lanka 97 and 162 (Kasprowicz 7–39) by 149 runs.

I arrived in Darwin soon after tea, just as the celebrations were starting following a convincing win.

As expected, Sri Lanka never got close to the victory target and Michael Kasprowicz made the lives of the visiting batsmen a nightmare. He bowled with plenty of aggression and had the uncanny ability to hit one particular spot on the surface. The spot in question was on a decent length and every time he hit it the ball flew through. It made him an unpleasant prospect to face and he ended up with a well-deserved 7 wickets.

There was general agreement after the match that the pitch was unsatisfactory, but I was asked by the media whether it was the surface or poor technique that had led to so many low scores among the batsmen. The argument was that batsmen had been so spoiled by so many easy batting tracks in the recent past that now, faced with tougher conditions, they did not know how to cope.

There may be some truth in that. Stephen Waugh always spoke to us about the importance of 'ugly runs', the need to graft as a batsman when conditions are not in your favour. Having said that, I still think our batsmen were well enough prepared for this Test. The squad practised hard in Brisbane but, although everyone was prepared, they were not prepared for conditions quite as tough as this.

I did say to reporters that a positive result is much better than a boring draw on a flat pitch. That has been taken as a defence of the surface here in Darwin but it is not meant to be. I did not play in the Test so it would be wrong for me to shoot my mouth off about the pitch, and in any case the scores say it all: the match finished in 3 days and there were only three scores of 50 in the entire match.

My point is that what everyone should be looking for is an even contest between bat and ball. The pitches we played on against India last summer went to the opposite extreme — they were too good for batting — and now we have a surface which is far too heavily weighted in favour of the bowlers. What is needed is a happy medium.

Thursday 8 July

The day before the second Test, and when I spoke to the media I came out in favour of Cairns and Darwin as international venues. Plenty has been said against these matches taking place, with reports of Cricket Australia losing money on the series and suggestions that it is cricket overkill, but I am in favour of these Top End tours.

The International Cricket Council's (ICC's) international program means we have to play matches against all the other Test teams and without these series it would be impossible to do that. On top of that, I think Australia's players enjoy playing home Tests at this time of year.

The facilities — apart from the pitch at Darwin — are excellent, the venues give us a chance to get away from the usual big city routines we have around Tests in the domestic summer and offer a chance for players to do some sightseeing or fishing in some really beautiful spots. My wife, Rianna, is taking the chance to experience this part of the world and has joined me for this match.

This will be my first home Test as captain but that sort of milestone is not something I will dwell on. I obviously value the captaincy very highly but the most important thing to focus on is our performance. Milestones are nice but they will look after themselves as long as the team is successful.

Our pre-match team meeting did not cover Shane Warne's attempt on Muttiah Muralitharan's world record for Test wickets. He needs 8 wickets to pass Murali's mark of 527 but the meeting glossed over the subject, as we did in Galle earlier this year, when he sat on the brink of 500 wickets. Media and public expectation ensure there is enough pressure on Warne without us adding to it; he knows he is close to the mark and he also knows that his best approach will be to go about his work as normal. If he does that then wickets are likely to come, and if they do we will all celebrate with him after the event.

There was a suggestion in the media that we might look at playing five bowlers, but that is not in the equation. The surface has been prepared by Kevin Mitchell junior, the curator at The Gabba in Brisbane, and it looks similar to that pitch: hard, flat and with a good grass cover that should ensure it will allow a fair contest between bat and ball. If our four bowlers perform to their usual standards then including a fifth bowler would be overkill.

Despite that, we do have an extra bowler with us — Brett Lee. Coming back from the ankle injury that cut short his tour of Sri Lanka, this Test is the perfect opportunity to get him back around the squad, allow him to work with fitness coach Jock Campbell and give him the chance for a first outdoor bowl since the injury in March.

It is still relatively soon after Annette's death but all my family are very keen for me to play in this match and so I am happy to respect those wishes. They are all in my thoughts but now it is time to get back to business.

Friday 9 July

Second Test, Cairns, day 1: Australia 2–370 (Langer 159*, Hayden 117, Martyn 56*) v the Sri Lankans.

We are in a commanding position already thanks to Matthew Hayden and Justin Langer. On a pitch expected to help the quicker bowlers, they set out to dominate and put together their sixth double-century opening stand in Tests, a mark never before achieved in the history of the game.

It was no surprise that Marvan Atapattu asked us to bat first when he won the toss. With a covering of grass on the pitch, the last thing he wanted — after the hiding his batsmen took in Darwin — was to expose them to another examination at the hands of McGrath, Gillespie and Kasprowicz on a fresh pitch, as conditions were likely to suit the pace bowlers, at least for the first couple of hours.

Things still worked in our favour. The pressure on the Sri Lanka bowlers to justify Atapattu's decision, together with the pressure Hayden and Langer put on the bowlers, combined to ensure we got away to a flying start.

If your side decides to bowl, as Sri Lanka did here, then a long opening stand can be utterly dispiriting but it can also be tough on the batsman due in next, in this case me. Sitting around and waiting for your chance can be almost as tiring as being out in the middle. You can find yourself watching every ball, half getting up from your chair every time there is a close call, and by the time you eventually get to the crease you can be mentally worn out.

It is obviously necessary to watch the game to see who is bowling and what they are trying to do in order to be well prepared when your turn comes, but it is also important to be able to switch off, maybe chat about other things with team-mates or those around you, and just make sure you stay as relaxed as possible.

I managed that today but although I started well once I got in I was not able to go on and get a big score. I cruised to 22 before, facing Lasith Malinga for the first time, I was deceived by his unusual slingshot round-arm action. The delivery that dismissed me was a driveable length but because he bowls with such a low arm the angle of release took the ball further away from me than I expected. I ended up playing away from my body, was not over the ball when I hit it, and although it came off the middle of the bat it went straight to the fielder at cover.

Saturday 10 July

Second Test, Cairns, day 2: Sri Lanka 2–184 (Atapattu 75*, Sangakkara 74) trail Australia 517 (Langer 162, Hayden 117, Martyn 97, Lehmann 50, Chandana 5–109) by 333 runs.

On paper it looks as though we batted recklessly today. From 3–454 we slipped to 517, but although we would have liked a few more runs I am not too concerned.

Our aim was to get as many runs as we could in the first innings but also to give ourselves the maximum time to take 20 wickets on a pitch few of us expect to deteriorate very much. That approach means we will always look to play positively and we got out playing exactly that way.

Sri Lanka also bowled well, with the leg-spinner Upul Chandana finding some spin in the surface, something that will encourage Shane Warne. Chandana never looked like he was going to run through us but bowled steadily in his best display against Australia. He is one player who seems to have benefited from a greater level of responsibility in the absence of Muttiah Muralitharan.

We were not at our best when we bowled today and Marvan Atapattu and Kumar Sangakkara took advantage to get Sri Lanka off to an excellent start, with Atapattu showing what a classy player he can be. We dismissed him several times on the recent tour of Sri Lanka, bowled between bat and pad, but there was no hint of a repeat of that failing today as he played beautifully.

We looked to be more attacking than we were in Sri Lankan conditions, with a greater emphasis on the slip cordon because of the extra bounce available here, but things did not click for us. There was no lack of effort from the bowlers so maybe it was one of those days when you have to give credit to the batsmen for playing well.

Sunday 11 July

Second Test, Cairns, day 3: Sri Lanka 5–411 (Atapattu 133, Sangakkara 74, Samaraweera 53*) trail Australia 517 by 106 runs.

Today was hard labour for the bowlers. Any previous life in the surface has now more or less disappeared so it was a case of rotating the fast men while trying to tie up an end with Shane Warne at the other. The fate of the match is now likely to depend upon how much the pitch deteriorates and whether or not the weather causes too many more interruptions as we lost 21 overs today to bad light and rain.

The wearing of the pitch will be a key factor if Warne is to get close to Muttiah Muralitharan's world record. He bowled steadily today, adding the wicket of Tillakaratne Dilshan to the one he picked up on day 2 when he removed Kumar Sangakkara.

Our first task is to get the five remaining Sri Lanka wickets and then look to build a lead before there is any prospect of Warne being able to weave his magic in the final innings. We have got too far ahead of ourselves in trying to set up matches before, most recently against India at Adelaide last December, and paid the price for it. This whole player group is aware of that and it is not a mistake I expect us to repeat.

Monday 12 July

Second Test, Cairns, day 4: Australia 517 and 2–194 (Hayden 68*, Martyn 52*) lead Sri Lanka 455 (Atapattu 133, Sangakkara 74, Samaraweera 70) by 256 runs.

We speak about what we want to do as a team before every day's play and today our emphasis was on aggression, something we were able to put into practice very effectively when play resumed after more rain washed out the first session. There have been plenty of times in the last few years when teams have reached a position like the one Sri Lanka found themselves in after the third day and given themselves a pat on the back for competing with us rather than realising they have to play just as hard for the remaining two days of the Test.

Sri Lanka was in that comfort zone and we exploited it by rattling through the last 5 wickets in quick time before setting about establishing a target for our bowlers in the fourth innings.

The plan up to the close was to consolidate, move the lead to a decent level and then press on without doing anything stupid, and we managed that pretty well. We want to give ourselves as long as possible to bowl Sri Lanka out a second time but at the same time there was no point in just throwing wickets away tonight. That is the recipe for a collapse and we are well aware Sri Lanka has plenty of players capable of chasing a fourth innings target.

When Justin Langer was out, I emphasised the point to Matthew Hayden and at first we ensured we did little more than see off the new ball. Once we did that and I felt settled at the crease I said to Hayden that it was time one of us looked to press on and I was happy for it to be me. We were still not entirely secure and if both of us had looked to accelerate and then got out, it would have made it tough to press on with two new batsmen at the crease.

My mind-set was to play as I would in a one-day game, looking to be positive and try to score from every ball, but in the first over with that new mind-set I got out. I slashed Nuwan Zoysa straight off the middle of the bat but straight to Sanath Jayasuriya in the gully, another frustrating dismissal as, once again, I got myself in only to fall without going on to make a big score.

Thankfully Damien Martyn filled my role and played a lovely innings up to the close, including a massive straight six over the commentary boxes off Upul Chandana, and we are in a prime position to put our foot flat to the floor when play resumes tomorrow.

Tuesday 13 July

Second Test, Cairns, day 5: Australia 517 and 9–292 declared (Hayden 132, Martyn 52, Chandana 5–101) drew with Sri Lanka 455 and 8–183 (Sangakkara 66).

Although I was happy with the way we bowled today, a combination of the excellent pitch, time lost earlier in the match because of bad weather and our failure to take our chances meant we had to settle for a draw.

The pitch did offer some turn to Shane Warne and he bowled well, managing to equal Muttiah Muralitharan's world record in the process, but in the end Nuwan Zoysa and Chaminda Vaas held out until it became too dark to continue.

The draw and the fact Warne did not claim the record outright did lead to a sense of disappointment and anti-climax but I could not question anyone's effort, and if we play like this in every Test we are going to win far more than we draw or lose.

The plan at the start of the day was to score runs as quickly as possible to give ourselves the maximum time to bowl Sri Lanka out a second time. At the same time I did not want to give them a hint of a chance to win the game. By removing that option from the game by setting a massive target we could maintain attacking fields all day and also test their mental resolve. We presented them with a similar challenge in Colombo in March and several of their players did not know how to cope. Some, like Thilan Samaraweera, simply tried to block almost everything and that took all the pressure off the bowlers. Others, like Tillakaratne Dilshan, tried to attack but although that challenged the bowlers it also increased the risk of a mistake, something we were just as happy about. In the end Sri Lanka failed to hold out and I knew that would be in the back of their minds.

Hindsight says we batted on 20 minutes too long but if we had taken all the chances and half-chances on offer we would still have won. We missed catches from Upul Chandana, Kumar Sangakkara and Nuwan Zoysa — I spilled the last one, at a nice catchable height, at second slip off Jason Gillespie — and in the end those misses were the key reason for our failure to win.

Chandana was a central figure in the action for a couple of reasons. He took another 5-wicket haul as we looked to press on in the morning, finishing with 10 wickets for the match, and then became Warne's record-equalling 527th wicket.

If you had said before this Test that Chandana would take 10 wickets I would have laughed at you, especially when I looked at the pitch. He is a steady bowler but his record is very modest at Test level. But although you could argue that some of his wickets were the result of batsmen looking to hit out, he still deserved his haul because he bowled with good control and summed up the conditions well, bowling the ball quite quickly so the batsmen always struggled to get down the pitch at him.

The longer the match went on, the less the pitch offered the quicker bowlers, so Warne became our best wicket-taking option. I was happy to keep him going and that strategy also gave him the chance to claim the record outright.

Warne's intensity was excellent and although the record was on the line, I thought he kept his focus very well. Even when Adam Gilchrist whipped off the bails and began celebrating Chandana's dismissal the emphasis among everyone, even Warne, was still on winning the Test rather than any individual achievement, pleased though we were for him to equal the mark.

One black mark against us today was the 25 per cent fine handed out to Glenn McGrath for swearing after he had an appeal turned down early in the Sri Lanka innings. But on a positive note we were able to calm him down quickly so he could regain his focus.

When umpire Aleem Dar turned down McGrath's lbw appeal against Sanath Jayasuriya, the bowler could not believe it. He put his head between his legs and swore loudly and I could see he was losing control.

McGrath is at his best when he is calm, and when he gets annoyed or upset he can lose that focus that makes him such a great bowler. We saw that when he bowled poorly after his row with Ramnaresh Sarwan during the Antigua Test of 2003 and when he gets in that zone he seems to forget about the cameras, the television viewers and how his actions might appear. As captain it was vital I made sure he did not slip into that trap again.

It was the end of the over and as he headed off to his fielding position, still reflecting on the decision, I ran over to him, gave him a pat of encouragement and also said to him 'Remember *the Spirit of Cricket*.' That is our agreement as players for how we want to play the game, and that includes accepting umpiring decisions without complaint. McGrath acknowledged that straightaway. He knew he had done the wrong thing and he was right back to business in the next over he bowled. McGrath's attitude after the incident was even praised by both umpires during the hearing and that helped to lessen the fine.

Part 2:
County Cricket for
Somerset

Thursday 15 July 2004

Twenty20 Cup, Taunton: Somerset 5–211 (Trescothick 56) beat Northamptonshire 5–207 (van Jaarsveld 61, Sales 60*) by 4 runs.

Two days after the Test in Darwin I found myself almost 20 000 kilometres away playing my first-ever game of county cricket, and it has been an amazing experience.

The reason it was so amazing is that my debut for my new team, Somerset, came in the new shortened version of the game, Twenty20 cricket, with each side having just 20 overs to bat. It left me breathless as the ball flew to all parts of the tiny Taunton ground, and with only 75 minutes to get each set of 20 overs in and new batsmen expected to be ready to face up just 90 seconds after the fall of the previous wicket, there was no time for anyone to relax.

Before I write too much about the game, it is worth explaining how I have ended up at Somerset. The idea began when I got a call from my Tasmania team-mate and good friend Jamie Cox, who has been an overseas professional here for several years. He asked if I would be interested in going over for a short spell during the season, and after thinking about it and chatting with him again we agreed it would be a good idea for both of us. It gives Jamie a break during an always busy county season and at the same time it allows me the chance of good quality outdoor practice in English conditions ahead of the Champions Trophy in September.

I have always said I wanted to play county cricket once I was established in the Australia side, and now that I am and my personal life is also settled, it made perfect sense for me to slot in this time. Rianna has flown to New York for a holiday and will join me in a couple of weeks' time.

Taunton is the venue where I first captained Australia, in a county match on the 2001 Ashes tour when Stephen Waugh and Adam Gilchrist both rested. That match is not my greatest memory in cricket, even though I got a century and we won. We did so with a very limited bowling attack as McGrath, Lee and Gillespie were all resting and we wrapped things up on the last afternoon thanks to Simon Katich's wrist-spin.

I chose to play on the day I arrived from Australia, having landed early in the morning. My view is that Somerset has gone to the trouble to contract me so I want to repay that faith by doing the right thing by the county. The last thing I want to be seen to be doing is just taking whatever money they pay me and coasting. I wanted the club and my new team-mates to see that straightaway.

Cox met me at the airport, drove me to Taunton and we went straight to the ground and met the coach, Kevin Shine, the former Middlesex and Hampshire fast bowler, and some of the players. Then it was off to my new home for the next month, a small flat about 2 minutes' walk from the ground owned by the county's Chief Executive Peter Anderson, a short rest then back to the ground to play the game, which started in late afternoon. That is another innovation of Twenty20 cricket, the idea of using the long summer evenings in England, as playing matches then gives working people more chance to watch them.

That idea certainly seems to have been successful. This was the county's last match in the competition this year and it had not won before today, yet the ground was packed and it was great to see so many children among the crowd. Anderson told me that 75–80 per cent of the turnout was people who do not normally come to watch county cricket, so this new format is introducing a new audience to the game.

The experience of walking into a dressing room full of people I barely knew was a very strange one. I had played against two of the squad's England players, Marcus Trescothick and Ian Blackwell, at international level, and Michael Burns, the captain, is a good friend of Cox and has played club cricket in Tasmania, but otherwise it was a case of walking onto the field never having met most of the squad before today. That may be one reason I managed to be involved in two run-outs in our innings.

I found myself asking lots of questions of my team-mates before the start as I had no idea how to approach my innings, never having seen a game of Twenty20: should I look for boundaries straightaway or spend a few balls playing myself in? And do we keep wickets in hand to accelerate late on or press right from the start?

The fact Taunton is such a small ground answered those questions as both sides scored at more than 10 runs per over throughout, providing the fans with more than 400 runs and a last over finish. Our win turned out to be Somerset's first in any competition for as long as anyone could remember and that meant it was the perfect chance to get to know my team-mates a bit better after the match.

Twenty20 cricket is a big hit in the United Kingdom, but whether it will work in Australia is another matter. One thing in its favour in the UK is that the first stage of the tournament takes place on a regional basis with each county playing its neighbours, but that would not work in Australia because of the vast distances involved. Also, I would not like to see the existing competitions reduced just so Twenty20 cricket can be slotted into the program, because both the Pura Cup and ING Cup in their present form are excellent breeding grounds for quality cricketers to emerge.

On the other hand, anything that gives our state cricketers the chance to perform in pressure situations in front of decent crowds would be a positive. I like the idea behind the concept but still need to be convinced it is right for Australia.

Wednesday 21 July – Saturday 24 July

County Championship, Scarborough, division 2: Somerset 451 (Ponting 112, J Francis 109, Burns 74, Blackwell 73) and 0–6 beat Yorkshire 296 (Lehmann 90*, Wood 59, McLean 6–79) and 160 (Wood 66, McLean 5–45) by 10 wickets.

My first championship match for Somerset and we came away with our first win of the campaign, after 3 months of the season.

It is hard to believe that a side can go as long as that without a victory, but now we have ended that drought — I hope I can play a small part in keeping whatever momentum we have established.

My first impression of the first-class game in the United Kingdom was pretty favourable. The standard was pretty good, as you might expect when you look at the two sides in this match, with Yorkshire including Ian Harvey and Darren Lehmann as well as three England players in Chris Silverwood, Richard Dawson and Anthony McGrath. We had England one-day all-rounder Ian Blackwell and West Indian fast bowler Nixon McLean, and both sides had plenty of young home-grown talent as well.

The pitch was okay to play on, and although one end offered a little extra bounce, which meant I took a couple of deliveries on the gloves, it allowed me to get my Somerset career off to the perfect start with a century. That was a relief because I was nervous, even though this was no Ashes Test match at Lord's; I was desperate to do well, desperate to make a good impression on my team-mates and the county that was employing me, and desperate for us to break our duck.

The overall intensity of the match was good too, in contrast to some of the stories I have heard about county cricket with players coasting at 70 per cent because of the long and grinding nature of the season. I will admit there were some players who gave me the impression they would prefer to be in the dressing room rather than playing, but there was a good feeling around the side, helped no doubt by finally nailing a win.

My plan is to bring runs and also attitude to the dressing room. I may be Australia captain but I am not going to come in and say 'this is how we must play', although I will provide input if asked.

I will train, prepare and play as I always do, show I love a contest and enjoy the game, and hopefully that will rub off on my new team-mates. As one of the veteran players, Peter Bowler, said when we got together: 'If we cannot lift with the Australian captain around then we never will.'

We celebrated the win in style. The Somerset players were due to have dinner with the county chairman on Friday night, the third evening of the match, and as we wrapped the match up that day it turned into a very good dinner that gave me another chance to get to know my new team-mates away from the dressing room.

We had another match against Yorkshire, this time a one-day game, at the same venue on Sunday so, with an unexpected day off, a few of us went to nearby York for a race meeting on Saturday. I backed the first two winners and ended up all square for the day and it was a relaxing way to cap off a very satisfying few days.

Sunday 25 July

National League, Scarborough, division 2: Yorkshire 4–255 (Lumb 71, Gale 70*, Wood 56) beat Somerset 6–252 (Ponting 113) by 6 wickets (Duckworth-Lewis method).

I got my first glimpse today of why we have been performing so poorly this season. Our bowling was awful and we ended up losing a game we should have won comfortably.

We did not have the best of the conditions as there were rain delays when we batted that prevented us gaining momentum. We saved Ian Blackwell, a massive hitter of the ball, for a late onslaught and he made 22 from 12 balls but the rain reduced his effectiveness by chopping 4 overs from our innings.

We still had a competitive total though, which required a Yorkshire side without the injured Darren Lehmann to score at better than a run a ball from the start of its innings, and when we got rid of Ian Harvey in the first over we should have coasted to victory, but it didn't happen; we used seven bowlers, but we were never able to exert any control. It was a disappointing display but I hope we can learn from it.

National League, Taunton, division 2: Worcestershire 225 (Solanki 122) beat Somerset 191 (Ponting 46) by 34 runs.

I am starting to understand some of the realities of life as a county cricketer. After yesterday's defeat at Scarborough we jumped into the car at 8 o'clock and drove the 480 kilometres south to Taunton, getting home at 2 o'clock in the morning, and then up again today for another match starting just after lunch.

Admittedly this is not an everyday occurrence — today's match was rescheduled from earlier in the season — but it is hardly ideal preparation for elite athletes. Michael Burns and I were driving late into the night after a tiring game, stopping for dinner at a fish and chip café on the motorway, and then back into action the next day with little chance for rest or recovery. Maybe it is no wonder players get injured or disillusioned with the life and pray for rain to grant them some respite. It is also a surprise there are not more road accidents among players who are forced to drive between venues after a hard, physical day of work.

I am lucky as I have come in fresh and excited midway through the season and after today I have a few days off, heading to Paris to meet with Rianna. But for some of the players there is the prospect of another match, this time against a touring side, in this case Sri Lanka A. With such a grinding season there is an obvious need to rest most of the senior players for a match that will have no significance in the county's season, but several of them are expected to play and are not looking forward to the prospect.

Given our very limited preparation for today's match we did okay, but did not ram home our advantage. The team spoke after the Yorkshire one-day game about players taking responsibility to win a match rather than leaving it up to others and today we failed to do that, myself included, as we were unable to reach a modest target.

National League, Taunton, division 2: Sussex 9–274 (Goodwin 50, Cottey 50) beat Somerset 9–268 (J Francis 79, Ponting 56, Parsons 54, Cottey 5–49) by 6 runs.

Back from a few days in Paris but no change in the problem that is infecting our season: a failure of players to finish matches off. We faced a stiff chase but although four players passed 30, none of us went on to see the side to victory.

The standard was again pretty good with Sussex, last year's county champions, having a bit of attitude and aggression. And as well as Murray Goodwin, the former Zimbabwe batsman who plays for Western Australia, they also had Pakistan leg-spinner Mushtaq Ahmed, who bowled very well.

But the Sussex destroyer turned out to be Tony Cottey, a small man who bowled some flat off-spin and ended up with 5 wickets as we pressed the panic button and self-destructed.

Rianna is now with me after we linked up in Paris following her holiday in New York. I caught the Eurostar train that goes under the English Channel to meet her and we had a great time for a few days as neither of us had been to the French capital before. I did not attempt any French, something that seemed to upset the locals, but thankfully I was able to rely on Rianna. She is a great planner and made sure she studied a phrase book before getting there.

Monday 2 August

Australia names its 14-man squad for the Videocon Cup against India and Pakistan, and the ICC Champions Trophy. It is: Ricky Ponting (captain), Michael Clarke, Adam Gilchrist (vice-captain), Jason Gillespie, Ian Harvey, Matthew Hayden, Brad Hogg, Michael Kasprowicz, Brett Lee, Darren Lehmann, Damien Martyn, Glenn McGrath, Andrew Symonds and Shane Watson. Brad Haddin will replace Adam Gilchrist for the Videocon Cup.

Brett Lee is a special talent with his ability to swing the ball both ways at high pace and I will always want him involved whenever possible, so it is a pleasure to welcome him back to the squad after the injury nightmare he has endured over the past year. For Lee and everyone else involved, the Videocon Cup in the Netherlands should be the perfect opportunity to blow away the winter cobwebs in match conditions ahead of a tournament we have never won. That is especially important as we have made a habit of starting slowly in one-day tournaments in recent years.

Adam Gilchrist is staying back in Australia for the birth of his second child but I have no worries about that. Brad Haddin is a more than capable stand-in, and although Gilchrist will come into the Champions Trophy without any match action, I know he is professional enough to still be working hard back home, and his batting has always been about instinct rather than hours and hours of repetitive net sessions.

We have named just one specialist spinner in Brad Hogg, which may raise a few eyebrows as the ICC tournament is taking place in late summer in the UK, traditionally a time for worn pitches that favour the slower bowlers. But I am confident Andrew Symonds, Darren Lehmann and even Michael Clarke can do an effective job if called on, with Lehmann especially proving himself a reliable bowling option over the past 2 years, someone who never goes for many runs. Between those four we can usually be guaranteed 15 to 18 overs of spin if necessary.

Tuesday 3 August – Thursday 5 August

County Championship, Taunton, division 2: Somerset 394 (Ponting 117, Blackwell 98, Bowler 86, Jones 5–94) and 2–164 (Bowler 55, J Francis 54, Ponting 18*) beat Glamorgan 262 (Elliott 103, Thomas 54, S Francis 5–42) and 294 (Elliott 85, Wallace 70, Thomas 52, Blackwell 7–90) by 8 wickets.

Another win for us in the county championship, the United Kingdom's equivalent of the Pura Cup, and after 3 months without a single success in this competition we are suddenly on a roll.

It does not take a genius to work out why our fortunes have turned around. In our two wins we have posted decent totals, and had bowlers capable of taking 20 wickets. In the last match at Scarborough, Nixon McLean returned from injury to claim 11 wickets, and Simon Francis found some rhythm and bowled beautifully in the first innings before Ian Blackwell's left-arm spin did the damage when Glamorgan batted again.

There were a few more points of interest in the match for me. Matthew Elliott played beautifully for Glamorgan in the best display of batting I have seen since I arrived in this country. His defence looked solid, there were no rash shots, but he was quick to pounce on any loose ball and he looked a class act.

The match gave me the chance to catch up with Elliott and Glamorgan's other overseas player, Michael Kasprowicz, and I also got my first look at Simon Jones since he injured his knee in that horrific accident at The Gabba in November 2002. He picked up 5 wickets, bowling tidily enough, but he did not seem to have quite the pace or control I remember him showing in his brief outing in that Ashes Test. Maybe that is no surprise after such a serious injury.

National League, Chester-le-Street, division 2: Somerset 4–147 (Ponting 83*) beat Durham 9–162 (Hamilton 66*) by 6 wickets (Duckworth-Lewis method).

This was an odd match in a couple of ways. To start with, it took place on the slowest pitch I have ever played on. I caught Durham's opening batsman, Nicky Peng, at second slip off opening bowler Richard Johnson, who is not the slowest bowler in the world, and yet I was only a few yards from the bat. The only time I can ever remember standing as close in that position was in Barbados against the West Indies last year.

The slowness of the pitch contributed to the low totals and I experienced it first-hand when I batted. On a couple of occasions I tried to play square cuts but was through the shot so early that I ended up hitting the ball back down the pitch. It was bizarre.

The other odd feature of the match was that the second innings took place in some of the eeriest conditions I have experienced. The match was a day–night game and finished in a combination of mist and drizzle that enveloped the ground. After I got back to the dressing room the Somerset players said that despite the floodlights they could barely see what was happening out in the middle because of the mist.

County Championship, Chester-le-Street, division 2: Durham 231 (S Francis 5–75) and 6–85 drew with Somerset 8–400 declared (Johnson 101*, Laraman 66*, Ponting 50).

This was my last match in county cricket, at least for this year, and despite the loss of two whole days to rain we almost managed to win due to an amazing innings by our opening bowler, Richard Johnson.

With only two days to play when the match began, our plan was to bowl Durham out as quickly as we could, try to get a lead, then have another go at bowling them out. Durham managed to bat on longer than we would have liked and by the time Johnson came into bat at number ten we were just 12 runs ahead.

His response was a remarkable display of hitting that brought him his hundred from just 63 balls and suddenly left us with half a chance of forcing a win, and we managed to take 6 wickets in just over 37 overs before time ran out.

Johnson took full toll on South Australia's Shaun Tait, who was making his debut for Durham. It was a match Tait will want to forget as quickly as possible. Tait was the bowler who hit me on the head in the nets in Colombo in March, but he has played very little cricket since then — and it showed.

He only played because of the rain, which gave him an extra 2 days to get over his jet lag, but off the back of a winter break he had no rhythm at all and he bowled a 15-ball over to me full of no-balls. At one stage his front foot at the point of delivery was so far over the front line that it landed in the bowlers' follow-through marks.

Tait was bewildered about the problem, turned to his captain, Jon Lewis, and said, 'I'm sorry but I have no idea what's happening,' not the ideal thing you want to hear from your new overseas fast bowler. He was in disarray as he told me afterwards nothing like that has ever happened to him before.

Durham coach Martyn Moxon approached me later and asked if I had ever seen Tait have problems like that in the past, but I said whenever I had seen him he'd had no such difficulties. We wondered if it was just a case of the new player trying too hard, but I put it down to the fact he has not bowled in the middle for a few months. Whatever the reason for the problem, Moxon said he had just one day to cure it with Tait before the next match.

Tait's problem and the lack of time to put things right before the next game sums up county cricket in one sense, at least from my limited perspective. There are too many teams, too many games and not enough time between those games to correct technical flaws and rest. And in 2005 there will be even more matches as each county will play its local rivals home and away in the Twenty20 Cup.

With such a full program of matches, one of the things players and coaching staff must do is try to keep players fresh and stop any staleness from setting in. From what I saw at Somerset that does not always happen, and I told coach Kevin Shine as much when we chatted over my time with the county.

When players turn up for practice there are two nets set up and three bowlers operate in each net, meaning that at any one time only eight players are involved in the session while the rest of the squad, instead of working on their fielding, are sitting around doing nothing. That is a waste of everyone's time, as is the squad often arriving for a one-day game soon after breakfast even though it starts at lunchtime. County cricketers do an awful lot of sitting around rather than relaxing away from the game.

With such an intense program of matches there is an obvious temptation for players to save themselves for the long haul rather than going flat out in every game, but during my time with Somerset I did not see too much evidence of that. Shine told me that my presence may have helped to remove that. After the first fielding drill I took part in, he told me: 'That is the best workout the players have put in this season. You have had an effect already because everyone wants to show the Australian captain they can play.'

As to whether overseas players are the right way to go in county cricket, everyone has their views. Some are in favour of two per county, some prefer one, and others reckon a system closer to Australia, where overseas players are rare, would be best.

No overseas players at all would be the wrong option, because as England's best players are centrally contracted and rarely play county cricket, the absence of foreign stars would severely weaken the game in the UK. I favour a slightly more controversial idea, with players joining counties on short-term contracts, as I did. One of the problems with county cricket is that the workload of playing, travelling and then playing again eventually wears out even the best players, but a short-term deal removes the threat of that happening while, at the same time, bringing an injection of fresh energy into a dressing room. And as a crowded international schedule means the top overseas players are rarely available for a full county season any more, the idea of short-term contracts would mean counties could once again sign the best players, as they did 20 years ago.

There is a risk that overseas players could become mercenaries, touting themselves round to the highest bidder and not giving much back in return, but if counties select their overseas stars properly and look for players who will bring energy and commitment with them then I think the idea would work.

I would certainly like to play county cricket again but I am not sure I would want to do it for a whole season. And I would be happy to go back to Somerset, which is a batsman's paradise. I had a good time, made some good friends at the county and hope I gave something back to the club in return for its faith in me.

Apart from the pitch at Durham, I found conditions pretty good and the standard of play was okay as well, but I could have done without the driving, especially as my previous experiences of the UK have involved being driven around on a team coach. Of all the home-grown players I saw, the innings that impressed me most was one by Vikram Solanki, who batted intelligently for his one-day hundred against us at Taunton, while our opening bowler, Simon Francis, bowled better and better as my month with the county went on.

I did not miss captaincy. It was a nice break from having to make all the decisions, but I still offered suggestions to Michael Burns when he asked me and always tried to keep thinking like a captain, as I have done right through my career, even before I took charge of the Australia team.

Part 3:
Videocon Cup

Tuesday 17 August 2004

The ICC announces the nominations for its awards dinner, to be held in London ahead of the Champions Trophy. Ricky Ponting and Matthew Hayden are nominated in all three categories they are eligible for: one-day international player of the year, Test player of the year and cricketer of the year. The nominations were decided by a five-man panel made up of chairman Richie Benaud, Ian Botham, Sunil Gavaskar, Michael Holding and Barry Richards.

It is nice to be recognised in this way, especially as honours like this are not the reason you play the game and it is also rare to be recognised for individual achievement in a team sport. It is flattering to be nominated and the fact six Australians are up for awards is a testament to how well we have done this year. However, without wanting to downplay an awards ceremony that carries the mark of cricket's world governing body before it has even taken place, I would not be surprised if the issue of who wins what will be forgotten pretty soon after the ceremony. What happens on the field is all most players care about, and awards that come from that are a nice bonus if they happen but nothing more.

Thursday 19 August

India bowlers Harbhajan Singh and Ashish Nehra are both ruled out of the opening match of the tournament suffering from viral fever.

No-balls will be called by the third umpire rather than the umpires in the middle during the tournament as an experiment using television technology.

Saturday 21 August

India's Sachin Tendulkar is ruled out of the Videocon Cup because of a persistent elbow injury. No replacement is named and Tendulkar still hopes to be fit for three one-day internationals against England and the Champions Trophy that follow this tournament.

Videocon Cup, Amstelveen, match 1: Pakistan 6–192 (Malik 68) beat India 127 by 66 runs (Duckworth-Lewis method).

Despite more bad weather this morning, the tournament got under way, and although we did not see any of the match we heard the scores. It sounds like the pitch is going to be a tricky one to bat on. The Pakistan spinners took 7 of the India wickets to fall and ran out very comfortable winners in a contest reduced to 33 overs per side. It means India has to beat us in the next match to retain its interest in the competition as the format is that each side plays the other just once before the top two sides contest a final. Such a short course is not ideal, especially for the side that misses out on the final.

With the India–Pakistan match going on we trained at a club ground a short drive from our hotel, and the facilities turned out to be modest as, with all the rain around, it has not been easy for anyone to prepare decent practice pitches.

I had a nasty shock as soon as I opened my bag at the start of the session as I discovered two of my favourite bats were stolen in transit from Taunton. One of them was the bat I made my 257 with against India in Melbourne last December, and although it is not the end of the world, it is still very frustrating.

Although most leading players will have maybe five or six bats at any one time, usually of identical weight, most will also have a favourite that for some reason feels a little better than the rest, and that bat will get used and used in matches until it is not fit to hit another ball. Speaking personally, if I get a bat I really like I will save it for matches while breaking in others in net practices. The bat I used in Melbourne was a real favourite for me but now I will have to get on with life without it.

Sunday 22 August

India seam bowler Ajit Agarkar is ruled out of Monday's match against Australia because of a side strain; Ashish Nehra is still unfit with a viral fever but Harbhajan Singh has recovered enough to be considered for selection, and batsman Mohammad Kaif is doubtful for the match with a sore shoulder.

We attempted another practice session ahead of tomorrow's match but a combination of the weather and disappointing facilities — caused partly by the rain — meant it was almost a complete waste of time. Today's session was always optional in any case, as it is the day before a match and also the day before the start of a pretty intense period of action, so the idea is for players to conserve as much energy as possible.

Team manager Steve Bernard, vice-captain for this tournament Darren Lehmann and coach John Buchanan joined me for our regular pre-series meeting with the match referee, Chris Broad, and the umpires, and the use of the third umpire to call no-balls was explained to us.

In principle the idea sounds excellent as it will allow the standing umpires, to concentrate on the business end of the pitch, instead of having to look down at where the bowler is planting his front foot then quickly re-focus on what is happening as the batsman tries to play the delivery.

But I am not sure the whole issue has been thought out properly here. There are two side-on cameras level with the stumps, one at either end, but that means the umpire's view of the front line could be obscured if a fielder or batsman gets in the way, and without the option to switch to a camera on the other side of the field it means he could miss no-balls. And I am surprised the umpires will be trialling the system for the first time in a match as they have not trained with it beforehand. I am in favour of technology for line decisions but if it is going to be used it should be done properly or not at all.

The weather forecast is not great for the next few days but we still picked our sides for the two matches against India and Pakistan on the basis that both matches will happen. We will rotate the quicker bowlers to ensure everyone gets some sort of workout and the decision was that Jason Gillespie will miss out tomorrow.

Monday 23 August

Videocon Cup, Amstelveen, match 2: Australia 7–175 v India, match abandoned.

A frustrating day, but even though we did not get close to finishing the match, we now have one foot in the final. All we have to do in our final group match on Wednesday is avoid losing as heavily to Pakistan as India did and we will face Pakistan again in the final.

That may be bad luck on India as today's rain gave them no chance to make up for their defeat on Saturday, but you can never have too much sympathy for the opposition in professional sport, and if the roles were reversed I am sure India would be delighted to see us effectively out of the tournament given our recent record against it.

Even if the match had run its course today — and after morning rain it had already been reduced to 32 overs per side — we were in a strong position to win on a really poor pitch.

Maybe as a result of being covered for so long over the past few days, the pitch was dry, abrasive on the ball and had no pace at all. With the ball not coming onto the bat it was very difficult to play shots with any conviction and we only got momentum at two stages in our innings.

The first time was when we set off at a decent pace, trying to take advantage of the fielding restrictions and the hardness of the new ball as we brought up 50 inside 9 overs. Then Michael Clarke gave us some acceleration, with 42 from 28 balls, before the rain returned. Clarke played a gem of an innings. He was innovative, moving around the crease to disturb the bowlers' rhythm, and he managed to find the boundary thanks to some powerful shots.

I scored 26 from 28 balls as part of our early push for runs, before I got what I thought was a poor decision from Steve Bucknor. Lakshmipathy Balaji bowled me a good length ball that nipped back as I pushed forward and flicked my back thigh on its way through to wicketkeeper Rahul Dravid. I thought Dravid was appealing for a catch but Balaji seemed to go up for lbw and Bucknor agreed with him. It was not Bucknor's only mistake of the day as he also gave Andrew Symonds out, caught behind cutting at Anil Kumble's leg-spin when he did not hit it.

India performed steadily as the pitch suited their style of bowling, with several of their players delivering slower balls and cutters as the ball gripped in the dry surface. As a batsman you never really feel settled at the crease because you are liable to get a ball that misbehaves. From that point of view, with the likelihood of two more games to play at the venue, today's shortened match was a useful learning experience for us.

Tuesday 24 August

More rain today, but even if it had been a fine day I would have been unable to practise. I needed some treatment from physiotherapist Errol Alcott after waking up with some uncomfortable tightness around my hips.

It is a regular problem I have and a result of tightness I suffer in my lower back. This bout may have been caused by all the driving I did during my spell of county cricket and the remedy was Errol Alcott's elbows and fingers working on my hip flexor muscles, which is very unpleasant.

With no cricket to write about, the media spoke to me about the tour of India to come and what I thought about Shane Warne's role on that tour. Warne has not done well in India in the past but I put that down to his lack of fitness on his two previous Test tours. On the first trip he was on the brink of a finger operation and on the second he had just come back from a broken finger. Now he has no such problems, is physically fitter than ever before and also fresher thanks to his 12-month drug ban.

Also, he now has a better idea how to bowl in Indian conditions. The key is patience, rather than searching for a wicket with every ball, because India's batsmen love to hit boundaries. The crowd feeds off a high scoring rate and that, in turn, feeds the India batsmen's approach. If the home side gets on top in that situation the match can run away very quickly. The key for Warne, and the rest of us, will be to starve the Indians of scoring opportunities. If we do that the wickets should come.

Wednesday 25 August

Videocon Cup, Amstelveen, match 3: Australia v Pakistan, match abandoned.

More rain meant no play but there was intrigue behind the scenes as the administrators tried to get us to reschedule the tournament.

The three cricket boards have apparently lost lots of money from television revenue because of the washouts and to help offset that, the initial plan was to get us to agree to play our match against Pakistan tomorrow.

It meant two matches in three days ahead of the Champions Trophy, but the players were happy to agree if it meant some time in the middle, as a few of us are fed up of all the hanging about.

However, there was then a proposal we should also replay our match with India. The argument was that, by only agreeing to reschedule our match with Pakistan, it left India at a disadvantage. The other issue is that India is where many of the sponsors and television revenue comes from, so a tournament with India in the final is a lot more attractive than one where they do not qualify.

Cricket Australia Chief Executive James Sutherland pleaded with us to agree to rescheduling both matches, but we refused. Our stance had less to do with our rivalry with India and more to do with what would be expected of us. Under that plan we would play India on Thursday and Pakistan on Saturday with the final on Sunday, making three matches in four days if we qualified.

Under negotiations for the new Memorandum of Understanding between the players and Cricket Australia, we are trying to move away from back-to-back matches to improve the quality of cricket by giving us extra rest and recovery time between games, so agreeing to this would hardly be consistent with that stance. And such a hectic schedule, which would mean arriving in England a day later than planned, would not be in the interest of our main goal, the Champions Trophy.

In the end we got our way and, with the organisers reluctant to reschedule our match with Pakistan and not India, we now have just one more match left, against Pakistan in the final on Saturday. Our stance might seem selfish as it deprives the viewers at home and the fans here of the chance to watch more cricket in this tournament, but our priority has to be the Champions Trophy and doing what we think is best to help us win that tournament. If we do not win that tournament because we are without a player who got injured as a result of playing three matches in four days in this tournament, we would be doing ourselves a disservice.

Thursday 26 August

It is announced Australia has rejected a proposal to reschedule its matches against India and Pakistan.

Sachin Tendulkar, Rahul Dravid and Shoaib Akhtar are all suffering from viral fever.

Friday 27 August

We picked the side for the final today and decided to leave Michael Kasprowicz out of the starting line-up, opting for Brett Lee and Jason Gillespie to back up Glenn McGrath in a three-man pace attack. Our thinking is that Kasprowicz has played plenty of county cricket this northern summer and so needs the run-out less than the other bowlers.

Tomorrow's opponents are Pakistan and deep down I think we would prefer to play them rather than India in the final. Both sides can be dangerous but India has been the more consistent one-day side in the recent past and we know they can raise their game against us. Pakistan is more of an unknown quantity but that does not mean we will be treating them lightly.

The ICC announces the results of a survey it conducted with international captains on the use of technology. There was broad approval of it, although Ricky Ponting felt most decisions should be left to the on-field umpires.

Videocon Cup, Amstelveen, final: Australia 7–192 (Hayden 59) beat Pakistan 175 by 17 runs.

We have some more silverware for the trophy cabinet but I am sure this tournament will not live long in the memory, even for those of us who played in it.

The weather and a very poor pitch meant that what looked to be a perfect lead-up to the Champions Trophy has been a damp squib. The bowlers benefited from a run-out today in match conditions, and it allowed us to get the squad together well ahead of the tournament in England but otherwise it has been a waste of time. Even the three cricket boards involved have not generated the revenue they were hoping for.

The main problem apart from the weather was the pitch, which was shocking. I am sure some of that is due to the rain and the fact that it remained covered for such a long time, but when the covers came off the surface was not good enough for international cricket.

Originally the idea was to have two pitches prepared, one on which the three round-robin matches would be played and one for the final, but the rain meant there was no time to prepare the second pitch so we used the original pitch for today's match and it bordered on dangerous. Every second delivery was breaking the surface and when you have Shoaib Akhtar and Mohammad Sami bowling at 150 kph that is not much fun to face.

We got out of jail today but we did it because we are battle-hardened and have faith in our ability to win after so much success in recent years. That faith means that when the match can go either way we tend to take the initiative ahead of other sides, and that was what happened today. Pakistan, in sight of victory, lost its last 5 wickets for 21 runs.

I also made the news today for my stance on the use of technology in the game. The ICC surveyed all international captains and I hit the headlines as the man most strongly against any move away from the authority of the on-field umpires.

I have no problem with line decisions being referred to the third umpire. But I cannot agree with the school of thought that says we use replays for bat–pad catches and Hawkeye for lbw decisions. I have even heard one suggestion that sides should be allowed a certain number of appeals to the third umpire in every innings if one of the on-field umpires turns down an initial appeal.

I do not want to lose the human element in the game. Call me old-fashioned, but getting a bit of luck from an umpire's decision has been part of the game for more than 100 years and I cannot see why that has to change now. Of course, it cuts both ways. You may get lucky with a decision one day but then you cannot complain when one goes against you. That is cricket.

Another innovation to be trialled at some Champions Trophy matches is giving umpires earpieces that are connected to sound picked up by stump microphones. The idea is to help them pick up the noise of edges more easily. I am happy to see how that experiment goes, especially after talking with Australian umpire Simon Taufel, who is all in favour of the idea and feels it will help, especially in noisy stadiums.

Part 4:
ICC Champions Trophy

One-day international, Lord's, London: Australia 6–269 (Symonds 104*, Hayden 52) beat Pakistan 259 (Youhana 88, Inzamam 72, Kasprowicz 5–47) by 10 runs.

This may have been billed as a practice match for both sides but it was a full-blooded contest that we just shaded, thanks to that extra bit of belief at certain times during the day.

We recovered twice, first from a shaky display from most of the top order thanks to Andrew Symonds and Michael Clarke, and then again when Inzamam-ul-Haq and Yousuf Youhana threatened to win the match for Pakistan with a partnership of 162.

Symonds was at his awesome best, much as he was against Pakistan in the World Cup match in Johannesburg in February 2003. I do not believe anyone in world cricket can hit the ball as hard as Symonds did in the closing overs as he reached his second 50 from just 37 balls.

Symonds's innings helped cover up an undistinguished display by several of us at the start of the innings. We could hide behind the excuse of poor preparation in the Netherlands but that does not wash really, because we had a week of practice at our Champions Trophy base in Southampton before this match. I was deceived by a slower ball from Mohammad Sami and trapped on the crease before I got the chance to establish myself.

One thing I was pleased about today was our fielding. We looked sharp and it was the difference between the two sides. Symonds was dropped twice and they turned out to be costly misses — a straightforward chance to Rana Naved at long on and a slightly harder one to Youhana at third man.

We again opted to give one of our fast bowlers a rest day ahead of the Champions Trophy and this time it was Glenn McGrath who sat out the match. He did not seem too unhappy as it meant he could climb into the legendary Lord's lunch, but looking ahead to the tournament I do not envy the selectors' task. They are likely to have to leave out one of Michael Kasprowicz, Brett Lee, Jason Gillespie and McGrath, unless we opt to play all four fast bowlers.

Kasprowicz sealed today's win while Lee bowled with real pace but also had a problem with no-balls. Because of its slope from one side of the ground to the other, Lord's is not always the easiest place to bowl, but in Lee's defence he is just coming back after a long injury lay-off so hopefully he will have benefited from this workout and be able to come to terms with the problem. Adam Gilchrist also arrived today after the birth of his second child and spent the second half of the day in the dressing room. He looked fit and well and it goes without saying that it is great to have him here.

After the match I headed for the museum at Lord's, just behind the pavilion, to speak to the media but on my way I had an honour that very few Australians have ever experienced — I got to hold the real Ashes urn. The urns you see Allan Border, Mark Taylor and Stephen Waugh holding in various photos down the years are all replicas as the real one is reckoned to be too fragile to travel, and as a result a large crystal replica was presented when we won the last three series. I got the chance to hold the real deal for a Marylebone Cricket Club video on the subject and it was the thrill of a lifetime, but I did not try to see just how fragile the urn really was by giving it a squeeze.

Tuesday 7 September

Today was a pre-India training session. Jock Campbell, our fitness coach, took us for a workout in the gym dressed in full tracksuit. The idea is to get us used to working our bodies in hot conditions and it was no fun at all, but we have adopted this technique before, in Perth ahead of our last trip to India, for the TVS Cup in October 2003, and it worked then, so hopefully when we get there in a few weeks' time we will feel the benefit.

This evening was the ICC's awards dinner and, although the concept is good, perhaps future events could give greater thought to the needs of players in what turned out to be a long, warm and — we noted — fairly dry evening. All the teams gathered for an official photo before heading into the foyer of the venue to mingle ahead of the ceremony itself, before sitting down for the meal and presentation. Perhaps the organisers thought they were looking after the fitness needs of elite athletes by offering only water! The event was covered by television which meant it was very warm because of the lighting.

It was flattering to be selected to captain both the Test and ODI sides of the year, especially as I have only led Australia in four Tests, and pleasing, too, that Jason Gillespie, Adam Gilchrist and Matthew Hayden were also selected for one or both of the sides. Every player selected received a presentation cap in a display case.

Australia names its squad for the Test tour of India that follows the Champions Trophy. It is: Ricky Ponting (captain), Michael Clarke, Adam Gilchrist (vice-captain), Jason Gillespie, Matthew Hayden, Nathan Hauritz, Michael Kasprowicz, Simon Katich, Justin Langer, Brett Lee, Darren Lehmann, Damien Martyn, Glenn McGrath, Shane Watson, Shane Warne, Cameron White.

Champions Trophy, The Oval, London, Pool A: New Zealand 4–347 (Astle 145*, Styris 75, McMillan 64*) beat the USA 137 (Oram 5–36) by 210 runs.

Champions Trophy, Edgbaston, Birmingham, Pool D: England 5–198 (38 overs, rain stopped play, Solanki 62) v Zimbabwe.

India fast bowler Laksmipathy Balaji is ruled out of the tournament with an abdominal injury; he is replaced by Amit Bhandari.

Champions Trophy, Edgbaston, Birmingham, Pool D: England 7–299 (Collingwood 80*, Solanki 62) beat Zimbabwe 147 by 152 runs.

Champions Trophy, Southampton, Pool C: India 4–290 (Ganguly 90, Laxman 79) beat Kenya 192–7 by 98 runs.

I spoke to the Australian media today before our match against the USA on Monday, and after the way they played against New Zealand, the USA's inclusion in this tournament was at the top of everyone's agenda. They may play a lot better against us, but I doubt it very much, and I have to say that I do not agree with the inclusion of the smaller (in cricketing terms) nations in this tournament.

To my mind, the fact that few — if any — of the so-called minnows are competitive cheapens the event. This is what we saw in Sri Lanka in 2002, when the Netherlands was thrashed. Having one lesser side in each group means that at least half the matches in the first part of the tournament are one-sided, irrelevant and a poor spectacle, which cannot be a good thing for the game.

I accept the need to grow the game, but qualification for a tournament like this should be far tougher than it was here: the sides in the next tier played off against each other and the best team in that event won through. That format means that whichever team plays the best cricket over a short tournament gets through to this tournament, which is a prestige event. All that has done in the recent past is ensure that we get different sides — Scotland, the Netherlands and now the United States — appearing in recent major tournaments. They get thrashed, learn nothing, then slip back into the pack. Those lesser sides should only be admitted to the top tier if they prove themselves to be the best from that level over a prolonged period of time, maybe three or four years. The ICC seems to be getting to grips with that through its new Intercontinental Cup, but it is too late for this tournament and that is a real shame.

Sunday 12 September

Champions Trophy, Edgbaston, Birmingham, Pool B: South Africa 1–94 beat Bangladesh 93 by 9 wickets.

Monday 13 September

Champions Trophy, Southampton, Pool A: Australia 1–66 beat the USA 65 by 9 wickets.

Today was as near a waste of time as you can get in this game. We turned up and totally outclassed a side wholly ill-equipped to be at this tournament without breaking a sweat. The fact that most of us headed to the gym afterwards tells you everything you need to know about how much we took out of ourselves playing the match.

I asked our players beforehand to take an approach the same as in Zimbabwe earlier this year: to try to win the game as quickly as possible by playing to the full capacity that is expected from an Australian side. 'Play it as tough and hard as we can and if we can finish it in one or two hours then let's do it,' I said.

There was also the issue of making sure our net run rate was better than New Zealand's, just in case our match against it was washed out on Thursday. The best way to do that was to bowl first, knock the USA over in double-quick time, then score the runs we needed as quickly as we could. It meant that I was delighted to win the toss and bowl, and after dismissing the USA for 65 we knew we had to score our runs in 11.5 overs to overtake New Zealand's rate. We strolled there with 4 overs in hand.

Matthew Hayden's view of events was shown by the way he approached his innings. He attempted a few wild slogs before eventually getting out and he hated every minute of his time in the middle. He would much rather have spent an hour on a bowling machine than batting against an attack that bears no relation to anything we will see either in this tournament or for a long time to come.

Seeing the USA team at close quarters, my biggest disappointment was that most of them seemed to be the wrong side of 30, with several of them former first-class cricketers from the Caribbean. I understand the argument that if they played lots of USA-born younger players they may not have qualified for the event in the first place, but at least a group of young players will have a chance to learn and develop. The likelihood is that most of this group will not be playing the next time a major tournament comes around, so anything the squad may have learned from their two beatings in this event will be meaningless.

Tuesday 14 September

Champions Trophy, The Oval, London, Pool D: Sri Lanka 6–195 beat Zimbabwe 191 (Chigumbura 57).

Champions Trophy, Edgbaston, Birmingham, Pool C: Kenya v Pakistan, no play, rain.

Wednesday 15 September

Champions Trophy, Southampton, Pool B: West Indies 3–269 (Gayle 99, W Hinds 82) beat Bangladesh 131 (Dillon 5–29) by 138 runs.

Champions Trophy, Edgbaston, Birmingham, Pool C: Pakistan 3–95 beat Kenya 94 (Afridi 5–11) by 7 wickets.

Thursday 16 September

Champions Trophy, The Oval, London, Pool A: Australia 3–199 (Symonds 71*, Martyn 60*) beat New Zealand 9–198 by 7 wickets.

This was a clinical performance, especially after New Zealand made a decent start, and the sort of workout we needed ahead of a semi-final.

We will now face either England or Sri Lanka, but we do not care which as we feel we can beat either of them.

The most encouraging aspects of our display were the performances of Glenn McGrath, Andrew Symonds and Damien Martyn, and for McGrath it was an especially significant effort. He proved why he should never be left out, bouncing back from an early mauling to take 2 wickets in an over, and we were always in control from that point. That mauling may have prompted some captains to take him off, but after playing alongside him for a decade I have total confidence in him, and he repaid that faith today.

Symonds was brutal, he took to Chris Harris and Daniel Vettori and with Martyn at the other end, taking few risks, and just getting by on solid accumulation and dispatching the bad ball, we cruised home. With Darren Lehmann and Michael Clarke not required we have a solid look to our line-up.

One disappointing aspect of the day was the behaviour of a section of the crowd. Staging the match in London meant there was a large percentage of fans from both Australia and New Zealand in the ground, as the city is a base for many young people travelling from Australasia to the UK. A few of those people had too much to drink and insisted on charging onto the ground, then as we left the venue abuse and items were thrown at the team bus. There are no perimeter fences at the venues for this tournament and I would not like to see them, but I just hope today was a one-off because it was a match between traditional rivals, as some of the scenes were not very pleasant.

Friday 17 September

Champions Trophy, Southampton, Pool D: England 3–118 (32 overs, rain stopped play, Trescothick 64*) v the Sri Lankans.

Saturday 18 September

Champions Trophy, Southampton, Pool D: England 7–251 (Flintoff 104, Trescothick 66) beat Sri Lanka 5–95 by 49 runs (Duckworth-Lewis method).

Champions Trophy, The Oval, London, Pool B: South Africa 6–246 (Gibbs 101) v West Indies 0–20 (6 overs, rain stopped play).

Champions Trophy, The Oval, London, Pool B: West Indies 5–249 (Sarwan 75, Chanderpaul 51*) beat South Africa 6–246 (Gibbs 101) by 5 wickets.

Champions Trophy, Edgbaston, Birmingham, Pool C: Pakistan 7–201 (Youhana 81*) beat India 200 (Dravid 67) by 3 wickets.

Australia spinner Brad Hogg breaks down with a serious hamstring injury during practice at Edgbaston ahead of the semi-final with England.

Champions Trophy, Edgbaston, Birmingham, first semi-final: England 4–262 (Vaughan 86, Trescothick 81, Strauss 52*) beat Australia 9–259 (Martyn 65) by 6 wickets.

This has been a disastrous day. Not only have we failed once again to progress in this tournament, but I have injured my left thumb and I am really worried that it is going to restrict my role in the upcoming tour of India.

The thumb injury happened when I dived forward from second slip to try to grab an edge from Michael Vaughan off Michael Kasprowicz's bowling. The ball bounced just in front of me, hopped up off the turf and hit right on the top tip of the thumb. It hurt straightaway but luckily the weather in Birmingham was so bitterly cold that it helped deaden the pain.

The blow felt different from a simple knock that aches for a while before settling down, and I said to Adam Gilchrist, 'I'm in trouble here.' I called physiotherapist Errol Alcott on at the end of the over to have a look at it and already the tip of the thumb had gone black and was swollen. I could have gone off but we had a semi-final to win and it did not enter my head to leave the field. I asked Alcott to tape up the injury and he could then have a better look at it later.

The reality of the situation only hit me after the match. If the thumb is seriously damaged, I could have risked further injury by staying on the field, although that did not happen and I did not take another blow during England's successful run chase. The closest shave was when Vaughan cracked a ball to my right at cover point. I dived to stop it and, as I did, my left hand came over my body and slapped against the ground. That hurt.

As for the match itself, it was just one of those days when we were below our best and England was good enough to take advantage. The pitch was slow and maybe we could have done with having a spinner of Brad Hogg's quality in our line-up; maybe, too, we could have done with Ian Harvey's changes of pace. But I am not sure either player would have made much of a difference. On the day England just played better than us. At the halfway stage I said to John Buchanan that I thought we were 30 runs short of a winning score and that figure proved about right in the end.

The figures suggest we bowled poorly and, to an extent, that may be fair. But I think it is also worth giving England's batsmen some credit. They played well and maybe it was a case of them not allowing us to bowl well by putting pressure on us.

A major disappointment was the lack of a crowd at the venue. I played in the Test match of 2001 at Edgbaston and then the ground was buzzing with a full house making plenty of noise. Today it was freezing cold and the ground was comfortably less than half full. It had all the atmosphere of the moon and sums up the way this tournament has gone, with too many poor matches ahead of the climax of the event surely playing a part in reducing the interest of fans.

My thumb kept throbbing, even when I put it in a cup of ice to try to reduce the swelling. I am booked to have an X-ray tomorrow morning and already fear I will miss the start of the India tour. And, to cap off a bad day, there was the added frustration of having to hang around after the match to do a drugs test after my name was pulled out at random to take the test.

Wednesday 22 September

Champions Trophy, Southampton, second semi-final: West Indies 3–132 (Sarwan 56*) beat Pakistan 131 by 7 wickets.

This morning's X-ray confirmed my worst fears and I am flying home to Australia rather than off on tour to India. My thumb is fractured in three places, and while the rest of the side is looking forward to playing in the series that everyone seems to be talking about, I will be watching from a distance.

The bad night's sleep I had was yet another indicator that something was seriously wrong. With my thumb down by my side I felt a constant throbbing, so I ended up trying to sleep with my hand above my head on the pillow in an attempt to stop the blood flowing to that area quite so easily. It sounds stupid but I was so restless and in a fair degree of pain that I was happy to try anything.

Errol Alcott came with me to the hospital and I told him of my lack of sleep. He has been the team's physiotherapist for 20 years so he has been through this with players many times before, and I am sure he knew what my symptoms meant but he preferred to wait for the results of the X-ray before passing too hefty a judgment on my condition.

Those results left me shattered and the first question I asked Errol was, 'How long does this mean I will be out for?' I was desperate to go with the rest of the squad, even though I knew I would not be fit for the first Test, but Errol quickly quashed that thought. 'I know what you're like, Punter,' he said. 'You will be itching to get involved, the thumb will get a knock and you will put the healing process back. Go home, see a surgeon and see if surgery can help speed up the process of healing.' After that, he said, we will all have a better idea of how long I will have to wait before playing again.

I have had a few finger injuries, mostly bruising, but this is the first time I have suffered a break. I have known players who play through breaks too as, if there is little danger of further injury, it is simply a case of how much pain you can bear. But in my case that is impossible. I cannot move the thumb at all and you do not realise how important the thumb is until you get in this sort of situation. To add to the frustration, I cannot even play golf during my lay-off as I need the thumb to grip the club.

A whole host of thoughts have been racing through my head as I have tried to come to terms with missing the start of the trip. Chief among them is that, as captain, I will not be with the team, especially on a tour that means so much to me. A lot has been made of our failure to win a series in India since 1969, and the chance to be part of putting that record straight is a massive motivating factor for me and the other players. And on top of that there is my poor record on the last tour of India, when I made 17 runs in three Tests. I am desperate to show I can score heavily there.

Rianna was just as upset as me when I told her and not just because she knows how much I want to be part of this tour. She was looking forward to going to India as she has never been before. The main reason she stayed with me for the past two months rather than heading home was so she could go with me at the start of the tour, but that idea has now gone out the window.

We had a team meeting where I wished the lads all the best and then Rianna and I headed down to London — not to catch the flight to India but to head back to Sydney.

Part 5:
Australia in India

Thursday 23 September – Friday 24 September 2004

Brad Hodge is drafted into Australia's squad for the tour of India in place of Ricky Ponting; Adam Gilchrist will captain the side and Darren Lehmann will act as vice-captain.

The only bonus of missing the start of the India tour is that I get to spend time in my new house. I have only seen it once before, for two hours between the end of the Cairns Test match against Sri Lanka and leaving for the United Kingdom to play for Somerset, so it will be nice to settle in for a while with Rianna, albeit in far from ideal circumstances.

The last time an Australian captain flew home from the United Kingdom with an injury was when Stephen Waugh developed deep vein thrombosis because of a torn calf muscle, so I am hoping something similar does not happen to me this time, especially as I am allergic to aspirin, something that is often used to thin the blood and prevent clotting during flights.

I discovered the allergy a few years ago. Errol Alcott often gives out aspirins at the start of a flight but after I took one my head started itching. On another occasion, when I took a painkiller after injuring my hip in the West Indies in 2003, I broke out in blotches and had to take antihistamine tablets to stop the reaction.

Saturday 25 September

I visited the specialist today and discovered that I do not need surgery on the fractured thumb and that I have a chance of being fit for the third Test.

I was happy to have an operation if it meant speeding up the healing process, and we discussed it, but the specialist said it would not make any real difference. Any surgery would be extremely difficult as the screws required to hold the fracture in place would be tiny, only a couple of millimetres wide.

It is only when you suffer an injury like this that you realise how much you use your thumbs in everyday life and how many times during the day you knock a thumb. Normally I would not notice the knocks but it is now very painful and sensitive so, to protect the thumb as it heals, we are having a couple of guards made. They will fit over the top, be held in place by Velcro and will allow me to bend the thumb at the bottom joint, which is not affected by the fracture.

Wednesday 29 September – Tuesday 5 October

5 October: Sachin Tendulkar is ruled out of the first Test after failing to recover from the elbow injury that sidelined him for the Videocon Cup and the Champions Trophy.

30 September – 2 October, Mumbai, tour match: Australia 7–302 declared (Katich 71*, Hayden 67) and 2–207 (Langer 108, Clarke 52) drew with Mumbai 255 (Muzumdar 52).

I have spent the last few days staying in touch with the lads in India, texting and phoning on a regular basis, and also working on my fitness. The main point of discussion has been who will fill my spot at number three. My first thought was that Damien Martyn, Darren Lehmann and Simon Katich should all move up one place, allowing Michael Clarke to slot in at number six, but as I chatted with Adam Gilchrist, John Buchanan and other senior players and selectors, it turned out there were other ideas floating about.

Martyn feels settled at number four and when I chatted to him he said he preferred to stay at four. The other options at three are either Gilchrist or Katich. Gilchrist was keen to bat there, allowing him to settle against the quicker bowlers when he first went in. In 2001 he struggled when he went into bat against spin bowling, and while he was confident he could deal with that if required, he felt he could be better used at three. He did a great job for us there at Kandy against Sri Lanka earlier in the year when I was injured and was confident he could do it again.

Gilchrist coped with extreme heat in that Test to come straight from keeping wicket to score a match-turning hundred, but this time he will have the added burden of captaincy so we agreed it was too much to ask of him. Also, if he batted at three it would mean Clarke would bat at seven and, in his debut series, it would mean he might have to bat with the lower order. Gilchrist is experienced at doing that so that was another reason to keep him down the order.

In the end it was an easy decision to slide Katich in at number three. He is a fighter, a tough character, and he has proved very adaptable. He played spin very well in Sri Lanka in March but he is another player who would probably prefer to get the chance at

* not out

establishing himself against the new ball, and this promotion will give him that chance.

During my calls to India we also confirmed the game plan we will be using during the Test series. In the past we may have been guilty of over-attacking but on this tour our aggression will come from the idea of putting pressure on the India batsmen to score runs by keeping things tight.

That approach helped in selection of the side for the first Test. Gilchrist said Brett Lee bowled well against Mumbai and, like McGrath and Kasprowicz, he also offers the option of a bowler who can reverse-swing the ball, an important quality in the hot, dry conditions. But with our game plan, McGrath, Kasprowicz, Jason Gillespie and Shane Warne are our best attack to keep things tight, especially as Lee can be prone to leak runs if his rhythm is not perfect.

Wednesday 6 October – Sunday 10 October

First Test, Bangalore: Australia 474 (Clarke 151, Gilchrist 104, Katich 81, Langer 52, Harbhajan 5–146) and 228 (Harbhajan 6–78) beat India 246 and 239 (Dravid 60, Pathan 55) by 217 runs.

Although it was tough for me not being there for this win, I still shared in the joy of it in more ways than one. I not only watched most of it on television but I also got a call from the lads once the match was over.

That call was a really nice touch. I was about to go to bed after we wrapped up the match on the final day when the call came through, and it helped ease my frustrations at not being there to share in a really important win. To go 1–0 up in a series like this, which has been built up to such a huge level, is a superb achievement and if we can maintain the discipline we showed in this Test then we will be very hard to beat.

The batsmen all coped well with the conditions, and although Harbhajan Singh took 11 wickets in the match, a lot of those wickets were lower order players. Our top order coped pretty well with him, as was the case when we played against Muttiah Muralitharan in Sri Lanka earlier this year.

Our focus was best shown by the performances of Adam Gilchrist, Michael Clarke on his debut and all our bowlers. Given all the circumstances — Test debut, foreign conditions and the pressure of replacing me in the side — I think Clarke may never play a better innings than this one throughout the rest of his career.

I spoke to him before the opening tour match against Mumbai, told him to use that match to work out a batting game plan and then stick to it, and he clearly did that. On the 2001 tour I worked out a way to play but then tried to alter my approach when I saw the ball turning and bouncing in the first match of the series. Rather than trust my instincts and plans I started doubting my ability to cope with conditions and my game fell apart. Michael backed himself here and benefited from that decision.

Having Gilchrist scoring so freely at the other end took the pressure off Clarke. Gilchrist does that naturally, as his 104 from 109 balls shows. And although Gilchrist's effort may have been overshadowed by the debutant's hundred, it was still a special innings which also showed the wisdom of keeping him at number seven in the order. His role in shepherding Clarke along cannot be overstated.

We did not enforce the follow-on, but it was another sign we have learned from 2001 when we did enforce it in Kolkata, only to see VVS Laxman and Rahul Dravid bat us into submission. Not making India bat again now was simply a case of realising which approach gave us the best chance to win the match. Batting again gave our bowlers a rest, gave the pitch a chance to deteriorate further and also effectively shut India out of the match. The home side was left with only a draw to play for when it batted again and that is a tough mind-set to adopt. The India batsmen did not know how to approach the task and perished.

My routine was to watch the match from the start then slip out during lunch for an hour or so and head to nearby Tonkin Oval, where I did some fitness work. Our fitness coach, Jock Campbell, has given me some work to do, mainly sprinting and running between 30 and 200 metres at a time, the idea being to replicate game situations as much as possible.

Thursday 14 October

Second Test, Chennai: India 1–28 trail Australia 235 (Langer 71, Hayden 58, Kumble 7–48) by 207 runs.

I was ruled out of the third Test today after another appointment with Ian Hargreaves, the Sydney specialist.

It is a bitter pill to swallow but also hardly a surprise. I have been wearing the guard on my thumb over the past two weeks and have not done anything with the thumb in the hope of allowing the healing process to start. And although an X-ray showed that the process is under way, the thumb is still a long way from being right.

When I first saw Ian he said that once the healing process began, the fracture would repair very quickly, but in some ways that was the worst thing he could have said. Ever since then I have woken up every day hoping to find my thumb is back to normal, but it has not worked out like that.

That was proved with a pinch test to find out how much strength I have in my thumbs. I was able to exert 15 kilograms of pressure with my right thumb but only half a kilogram of pressure with my left and even that effort brought pain.

The test made me decide to get rid of the guard. It has protected the thumb but also meant it has stiffened up through lack of movement. I cannot expect to take the guard off and just start playing again, so it is coming off now and I am starting to mobilise the thumb whenever I can. I cannot make large bends at the joint but that will come with time and use.

Today's play was frustrating to watch as we lost our way after a great start from Matthew Hayden and Justin Langer. Three of our players walked rather than waiting for decisions to be made by the umpires, and although one of them was Adam Gilchrist, a known 'walker', I was surprised to see Jason Gillespie and Michael Kasprowicz follow suit. I was not aware it was team policy to walk and neither Gillespie nor Kasprowicz has a reputation for being walkers. I sent a text to find out what was going on but never got a reply.

Friday 15 October – Monday 18 October

Second Test, Chennai: India 376 (Sehwag 155, Kaif 64, Patel 54, Warne 6–125) and 0–19 drew with Australia 235 and 369 (Martyn 104, Kumble 6–133).

Rain ruined this Test when the final day was washed out with the match fascinatingly poised. India was definitely the favourite to score the 210 further runs it required for the win, but there was no way the result was a foregone conclusion and we can take plenty from the match.

Top of the list was the way we fought back from a very tough position at the start of day 4. At that stage we were, in effect, 4–9 but Damien Martyn and Jason Gillespie played superbly and batted through the first 4 hours of the day.

LEFT Unhappy returns! Matthew Elliott played his first Test in five years when I dropped out of the Darwin match against Sri Lanka. Here dismissed by Chaminda Vaas, he made 1 and 0 before making way for my return in Cairns.

RIGHT Happy returns. Glenn McGrath, fit again after a long-term ankle injury, took 10 wickets in two Tests against Sri Lanka in July 2004. He also earned a 25 per cent fine for his reaction after this lbw appeal against Sanath Jayasuriya in Cairns was rejected.

LEFT 527 reasons to smile. Shane Warne acknowledges the applause of his team-mates and spectators in Cairns after equalling Muttiah Muralitharan's world-record haul of Test wickets.

LEFT Coming my way?
I wait for a mistake from
Glamorgan's Matthew
Elliott during my month as
Somerset's overseas
professional in 2004.

Stu Foster / © 2004 Getty Images

Adrian Dennis / AFP / Getty Images © 2004 AFP

ABOVE Ball watching. I look for leg-side
runs during our Champions Trophy clash
with England in September 2004, a match
in which our hopes of silverware and my
left thumb were both shattered.

Renee Nowytarger / © Newspix

LEFT Thumbs down. I face the media in
Sydney on 14 October after finding out
my fractured digit is not healing quickly
enough to let me play in the third Test
against India.

RIGHT The next generation. Michael Clarke, who took my place in the Test line-up at the start of the India series, is congratulated by Adam Gilchrist after reaching his hundred in Bangalore, only the 17th Australian to score a century on debut.

Indranil Mukherjee/AFP/Getty Images © 2004 AFP

Hamish Blair/ © 2004 Getty Images

LEFT Mucking in. I made myself useful by performing twelfth man duties after arriving in India in time for the third Test in Nagpur.

RIGHT High fives. Back in the side for the final Test against India in Mumbai, I celebrate with debutant Nathan Hauritz after he dismissed VVS Laxman.

Hamish Blair/ © 2004 Getty Images

Hamish Blair/ © 2004 Getty Images

LEFT The final frontier. The squad celebrates after our victory in Nagpur, which made us the first Australia side to win a Test series in India for 35 years.

ABOVE Michael Clarke in action against New Zealand in Brisbane in November 2004, where he made a hundred on his first Test appearance in Australia to go with his debut hundred in India.

ABOVE RIGHT Face off. New Zealand's Craig McMillan and Adam Gilchrist agree to disagree over the issue of walking after the Brisbane Test.

RIGHT Going to a happy place. Jason Gillespie marks his maiden Test 50, against New Zealand in Brisbane, in unorthodox style. Glenn McGrath, who also passed 50 in a record 10th-wicket stand of 114, looks on.

LEFT Down and out in Melbourne. Michael Kasprowicz is brought to his knees by New Zealand's match-turning assault on his bowling at Telstra Dome in December 2004.

LEFT Shoaib me the way to go home. Pakistan fast bowler Shoaib Akhtar points Matthew Hayden to the dressing room after dismissing him in Perth in December 2004. The gesture cost Shoaib a 40 per cent fine.

Hamish Blair/ © 2004 Getty Images

RIGHT Eighth wonder. Glenn McGrath celebrates another victim on the way to a career-best 8–24 in the Perth Test against Pakistan.

Ryan Pierse/ © 2004 Getty Images

Tim Carrafa/ © Newspix

LEFT Santa Claus is coming to town. Brett Lee and I clown around during Christmas celebrations at Melbourne's Crown Casino. The look on the face of Darren Lehmann's son Ethan suggests we should stick to cricket.

RIGHT Brothers in arms. Brian Lara and I enjoy the atmosphere of the Melbourne Cricket Ground after playing in the match staged to raise funds for tsunami relief. Batting with him was a highlight and an education.

ABOVE AND RIGHT Double trouble. Outstanding fast bowling by Brett Lee and Glenn McGrath was the key to our success in the 2005 VB Series against Pakistan and the West Indies. Lee was man of the series and McGrath was man of the match in the second final, against Pakistan in Sydney.

ABOVE Back to the future. The format was new but the styles were distinctly retro when we played our first-ever Twenty20 international, against New Zealand in Auckland in February 2005.

ABOVE Sorry, mate! Brett Lee apologises to New Zealand's Brendon McCullum after bowling him a beamer in Auckland during the one-day international series.

LEFT The rescuers. Adam Gilchrist (foreground) and Simon Katich in action during their match-turning partnership of 212 in the first Test against New Zealand in March 2005. New Zealand's James Franklin is the suffering bowler.

ABOVE Punting pair. Jason Gillespie and Glenn McGrath relax in Christchurch after bowling us to victory in the first Test against New Zealand.

ABOVE RIGHT Crossing over. Hundreds by Damien Martyn (running towards camera) and Adam Gilchrist (back to camera) helped create a winning position for us in Wellington before bad weather had the final say.

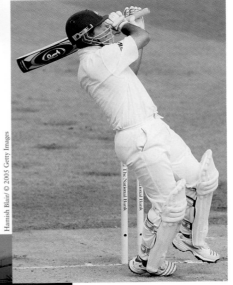

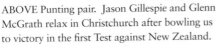

ABOVE Pulling out all the stops. I watch the ball sail over the boundary during the third Test in Auckland, on the way to my 22nd Test hundred.

LEFT Trophy time. Man of the series Adam Gilchrist and I celebrate after we completed a 2–0 Test series win over New Zealand with victory in Auckland.

Shane Warne's 6 wickets were another big plus for us and, in better shape than ever before, he went past Muralitharan's world record for Test wickets and took his first 5-wicket haul in Tests in India. Hopefully it will mean he goes from strength to strength for the rest of the series.

Now the players have a well-deserved break ahead of the next Test, starting in Nagpur on 26 October, with some of the squad heading to Singapore. The break was requested when the itinerary was planned because we felt four back-to-back Tests would be a tough assignment and India's players, much more used to the conditions, would find it easier to cope.

Tuesday 19 October

I am on my way to India. Today's X-ray shows that the bone is healing and although I am not fit for the third Test in Nagpur, I am travelling with a view to being ready for the fourth and final match of the series, in Mumbai starting on 3 November.

From the moment I took off the guard five days ago I have been picking up my bat but I have not yet been able to grip it properly. The plan is for me to work with the squad during the third Test but I will train with the guard on my thumb. Even now, another knock will put me out of commission for that Mumbai Test and may even jeopardise my start to the domestic summer. It is just a case of being careful and also building up confidence in my own mind.

Friday 22 October – Friday 29 October

Third Test, Nagpur: Australia 398 (Martyn 114, Clarke 91, Lehmann 70) and 5–329 declared (Katich 99, Martyn 97, Clarke 73) beat India 185 (Kaif 55, Gillespie 5–56) and 200 (Sehwag 58) by 342 runs.

We have done it. We have crossed what the media christened 'the final frontier', becoming the first Australia side to win in India since 1969. Many people questioned our right to be included in a list of truly great sides down the years without a win in this country, but now we have achieved it — a huge monkey off our back.

It was a very emotional time for me, made more so because I have not played a shot in anger. And a mix of relief, frustration and pride at the performance of the rest of the squad caused me to break down and cry when we all got together as a group in the dressing room after the match.

Justin Langer, in charge of our team song whenever we win a Test match, got up on a table in the dressing room and called everyone together. Then, in turn, he called on each player to join him and explain what the Test and series win meant to him. He called me up and I was pretty much lost for words. All I managed was, 'I can't explain what it means to be part of it but I can explain what it means to be part of this group . . .' and at that point I started to cry.

A lot of us had been through the heartbreak of the narrow series loss here in 2001 so to win this series is extra special, especially after India came to Australia last summer and held us to a drawn series. I think a lot of us see this series win as a payback for those two series and that makes it doubly satisfying.

Not playing here was frustrating but it was the right decision, as I was not fit. In the lead-up to the Test I had some throw-downs and batted against spin, and a couple of the players thought I looked so assured in the nets that I should put myself up for selection. But just a few deliveries from the seamers, with the ball thudding into the splice of the bat and jarring my thumb, convinced me I was nowhere near fit. I could not play cross-bat shots as I was unable to roll my wrists over the ball as I cut and pulled because of pain from the thumb, and I even had to take a break from practice on the second day of the Test because the pain was too intense. I was a little concerned that I might have damaged it again but physiotherapist Alex Kontouri assured me it was simply my thumb's way of telling me to take it easy. My natural enthusiasm for action meant I overdid it when I arrived and this was a sign to rest.

Apart from the second day, when I did not bat, my days were pretty full. I would have a gym session morning and evening to ensure I was properly fit, get to the ground to have practice with the other non-players in the squad — Nathan Hauritz, Brad Hodge and Cameron White — once those players involved in the Test had finished with the nets, and then act as thirteenth man during the day, running on drinks and gloves to players and ministering to players' needs when they came off the field. After the match Adam Gilchrist made a point of thanking me for my efforts during the match but it was just what every non-player in a squad is expected to do. A few of our squad commented they did not see India's injured captain, Sourav Ganguly, doing the same thing, but that was no concern of ours.

I am hopeful of being ready for the final Test, and the hamstring injury suffered by Darren Lehmann while batting during this match means that if I am ready then the selectors do not have a potentially ticklish decision to make over who to leave out for me. Everyone in the middle order has made some sort of contribution to this series win and so it was not a decision I would have wanted to make myself.

The win was especially sweet for Glenn McGrath as it has come in his 100th Test. There must have been a time not so long ago when he was wondering if he would ever reach the landmark, but he is there now and a series win in India is a fitting reward. On the eve of the match we all gathered to pay tribute to him, with manager Steve Bernard composing a poem to mark the occasion, and Langer and Shane Warne also saying a few words. Warne played his 100th Test in Cape Town and ended it as man of the match when we won the series in South Africa. He said a very wise thing too: 'Everyone says enjoy the match but don't get caught up in things, just go out and do your job.' McGrath did that as well, and finished with 5 wickets.

Sachin Tendulkar was back for India, but I could see from the sidelines that he was nowhere near fit. I guess India was hoping his presence would have a galvanising effect on the team, but the injury to his left elbow meant he produced no power in his top hand to drive the ball, and every time he mishit a delivery his top hand came off the bat, a sign to me that he did not have any power in his elbow or arm. It was a gamble that didn't pay off.

Monday 1 November

New Zealand announces a 14-man squad for its Test tour of Australia: Stephen Fleming (captain), Nathan Astle, Ian Butler, James Franklin, Hamish Marshall, Chris Martin, Brendon McCullum, Kyle Mills, Jacob Oram, Mark Richardson, Mathew Sinclair, Scott Styris, Daniel Vettori, Paul Wiseman.

Tuesday 2 November

Shane Warne fractures his right thumb batting in the nets and will miss the fourth Test; Nathan Hauritz is drafted into the squad in his place.

Although Shane Warne has been ruled out — and we will miss him on a pitch that even before the start of the match is dry and devoid of grass — I am fit to play. I did everything asked of me in practice, batting and fielding with no serious pain. There was still some discomfort when I played cross-bat shots in the nets, but nothing compared with the pain I had in Nagpur. I am not 100 per cent fit but

I am fit enough to play without being hindered when I bat. I will not be fielding in the slips, especially as very few balls carry through at a comfortable height here in India; I will probably station myself at mid-off. My biggest fear is a ball reaching me on the half-volley or bouncing awkwardly, but I cannot allow that to affect me and I have no major doubts about playing. I just want to ensure that we finish the tour on the right note: a 3–0 series win, something I feel we deserve. I do not feel India deserves a Test win from this series, so, as I said to the players today, we have to make sure that does not happen.

Wednesday 3 November

Fourth Test, Mumbai, day 1: India 2–22 v Australia.

My return to Test cricket was a frustrating one, with just 11 overs possible because of bad light and rain. But even in that time it was clear that this is a very poor pitch.

India won the toss and batted on the basis that the surface will just get worse and even in the play that was possible it was clear to see that is exactly what is likely to happen. The ball seamed around, burst the top of the pitch, we saw variations in bounce and with humidity around it also swung.

We quickly got on top and so it was frustrating when umpires Aleem Dar and Rudi Koertzen took us off for bad light. I spent a long time in the middle talking with them about that decision and I did not agree with it. It was a dull, overcast day with drizzle around and we made the decision to start the Test under lights. After 11 overs I could not see how conditions had changed but the umpires suddenly felt the light had got worse, offered the batsmen the chance to go off and they took it. But although I could not agree with the decision, I know I would have accepted the offer to go off if I had been batting, so I guess I cannot complain too much.

Thursday 4 November

Fourth Test, Mumbai, day 2: India 104 and 0–5 trail Australia 203 (Martyn 55, Kumble 5–90) by 94 runs.

We are in a strong position, but on a surface that continues to deteriorate we cannot afford to let India get any sort of a lead to bowl at in the fourth innings. One way or another I think there will not be much left of this match tomorrow night.

We could be accused of reckless batting, as several of us got out playing attacking shots. There was no team policy but we all agreed it is the type of surface where simply occupying the crease is a waste of time. Sooner or later there will be a ball with your name on it, so you should try to get as many runs as you can before that ball comes along and also put some pressure on the bowlers. That helps explain why Anil Kumble not only picked up 5 wickets but also conceded 90 runs from just 18 overs.

I was one of his victims and felt I was a bit unlucky. I went for a pull shot but mistimed my swing and was struck on the back hip. When I saw the replay in the dressing room it looked close, but I thought it deserved the benefit of the doubt about whether it would have gone over the top of the stumps.

Friday 5 November

Fourth Test, Mumbai, day 3: India 104 and 205 (Laxman 69, Tendulkar 55, Clarke 6–9) beat Australia 203 and 93 (Harbhajan 5–29) by 13 runs.

We have ended the tour on a low after losing a tight Test in a thrilling finish. The only consolation is that it does not affect the series result and we have regained the Border-Gavaskar Trophy.

This match has been a lottery and a travesty of the way Test cricket should be played, and I said as much not just to the media after the match but also to match referee Jeff Crowe before play today. James Sutherland echoed my thoughts to Crowe and hopefully he will take them back to the ICC.

International cricket should be played on the best possible surface so it can be not only a true contest between bat and ball but also one that allows the best players to display their skills. On this pitch there was no way you could bat properly because balls kept misbehaving, and the fact that our part-time spinner, Michael Clarke, took 6–9 sums up conditions.

There has to be some sort of penalty for producing a substandard surface like this. It is not possible to hold the home team responsible for the preparation of the pitch, but this is not the first time the surface in Mumbai has been too poor for Tests. Surely the ICC must look at imposing some sort of sanction on venues where pitches are consistently below par. The best way would be to remove a ground's Test status unless the surface improves, but I am not sure that will happen, especially in the glow of today's thrilling finish.

We should still have won this Test. We let India get too far in front and then batted recklessly in pursuit of the target. I have to take the blame myself for the first issue as, in hindsight, I should have bowled Clarke sooner. I delayed bringing him on because I backed our frontline bowlers, but we bowled too many bad balls and gave India some momentum. When Clarke did come on he bowled quickly enough to prevent batsmen getting down the pitch at him and, as he was also able to get turn from the surface, the Indians could barely lay a bat on him.

Clarke's performance showed the Indian spinners what pace they needed to bowl to succeed — quick and flat — and that was the type of delivery that Murali Kartik dismissed me with. His first ball to me was on a perfect length, had me wondering whether to go forward or back, exploded off the surface, took my outside edge and gave slip a comfortable catch.

We could again be accused of reckless batting, especially as we only needed 107 to win, but there was no team plan to go out with all guns blazing. Nathan Hauritz, Gillespie and Kasprowicz all played sensibly and squeezed 35 runs from the last 3 wickets, and if we had all sold our wickets as dearly as those three we would have won.

Part 6:
New Zealand home series

Australia announces a 12-man squad for the first Test against New Zealand. It is:
Ricky Ponting (captain), Michael Clarke, Adam Gilchrist (vice-captain), Jason Gillespie,
Matthew Hayden, Michael Kasprowicz, Justin Langer, Brett Lee, Darren Lehmann
(subject to fitness), Damien Martyn, Glenn McGrath, Shane Warne.

I was able to slot into the side in Mumbai without the need to drop
anyone because of Darren Lehmann's hamstring injury, but with
Lehmann now expected to be fit the selectors have opted to recall him
and leave out Simon Katich.

When I was asked for an opinion by the selectors I said that
Katich should be retained. I do not think mentioning that here is
being disloyal to Lehmann because it is well known how much of a
fan of his I am. He is a superb player and has been a great help to me
during my time as captain, but my preference for Katich here is based
on the job he did in India and, to an extent, Sri Lanka. He was
uncomplaining in Sri Lanka when, after a superb double of 125 and
77 not out against India in January, he was left out for the next two
Tests. Then, when he was recalled, he played a crucial innings in
Colombo that helped us secure a 3–0 series win.

Fast forward to the India tour and when I was injured Katich
did a great job, averaging over 40. I felt that after an effort like that
he deserved the reward of further inclusion, but the selectors felt
otherwise and, given Lehmann's series in Sri Lanka earlier this year
when he scored two crucial hundreds, that is equally understandable.

It does not upset me when my views on a selection issue like this
are asked for then overlooked. My job is to captain the side and the
selectors' job is to pick it. I do not envy them that task, given the
amount of quality players around, and there are always going to be
plenty of disappointed players. It is nice to have my views considered
but even when I do not get my way, as is the case here, I still know
that the 10 other players I walk onto the field with are all top quality,
whoever they are.

Thursday 11 November

Tour match, Sydney, day 1: New South Wales 1–26 trail the New Zealanders 213
(Sinclair 88) by 187 runs.

Tour match, Sydney, day 2: New South Wales 8–278 (Thornely 59, Krejza 54) lead the New Zealanders 213 by 65 runs.

Tour match, Sydney, day 3: New South Wales 286 and 0–25 need another 104 runs to beat the New Zealanders 213 and 201 (Sinclair 79, Richardson 50).

Time to forget cricket for a day — my sister Renee got married today and I was able to be there. She planned the date around my availability and everything worked out well, including the weather, which was vital as it was an outdoor wedding. The wind blew and the temperature was chilly, but the rain stayed away and Rianna and I had a great time.

Tour match, Sydney, day 4: New South Wales 286 and 1–129 (Jaques 70*) beat the New Zealanders 213 and 201 by 9 wickets.

Darren Lehmann is passed fit to play in the Test and Brett Lee is named 12th man. Lee will be released after day 2 of the match to go and play an ING Cup match for New South Wales against Victoria on Sunday.

First Test, Brisbane, day 1: New Zealand 7–250 (Sinclair 69, Oram 63*) v Australia.

We can be pretty satisfied with our work today. Although there was some decent bounce and a little seam and swing for the quicker bowlers, conditions were still batsman-friendly, so to restrict New Zealand to less than 3 runs per over and take 7 wickets was a good return for us.

The main issue of the day was the catch I took to get rid of Mathew Sinclair. The whole issue would never have arisen if Stephen

Fleming, the New Zealand captain, had agreed to my suggestion before the match that players should accept the word of fielders on whether or not catches have been taken cleanly. We agreed to do that with Sri Lanka and it worked well, but Fleming would not agree as he said some of his players preferred to wait for the umpire's decision.

In one sense I can understand that position. I am not a walker and always wait for the umpire's decision if I have nicked a catch behind, but the issue of whether or not a catch has carried is different. In that case it is not a question of whether or not you have hit the ball but, more than that, it is a case of accepting the word of another player, something I am very keen we get back to.

We have looked to use technology for these sorts of things, but in many cases that technology is not good enough to show an incident conclusively and that, in turn, has provided an invitation for players to bring the game into disrepute. Players can stand at the wicket even when they know they are out, in the hope that the incident is referred to the television umpire. More often than not, a replay will not show conclusively that a catch has been taken cleanly, so the batsman gets the benefit of the doubt.

New Zealand's failure to accept the agreement would have worked in its favour today if replays had proved inconclusive, but the side-on angle showed I grabbed the edge a couple of centimetres from the turf and Sinclair was on his way.

Now, New Zealand needs to be aware their stance on this matter will cut both ways. I will have no problem with one of my batsmen waiting for an umpire's decision even if a New Zealand fielder says he caught a catch cleanly. If the replays are then inconclusive and our player is reprieved then Fleming's refusal to accept our offer really will backfire for them.

Friday 19 November

First Test, Brisbane, day 2: Australia 4–197 (Martyn 59*, Ponting 51) trail New Zealand 353 (Oram 126, Sinclair 69) by 156 runs.

Today's plan was to take the last three New Zealand wickets quickly then set about building a large first innings, but we were set back first by some great hitting from Jacob Oram — who made an outstanding, unbeaten maiden hundred — and the loss of 4 wickets before the close.

Oram hit cleanly but we bowled poorly at him. He hits out in a slightly unusual way, closing the face of the bat, which means a lot of balls go through mid-on and midwicket, but we fed that strength by bowling too straight at him rather than making play through cover and square of the wicket on the offside. Next time we need to bowl at him with more width.

Oram's hitting knocked us off our stride and caused some controversy. Shane Warne was trying to restrict him by bowling at his pads, but allowed a couple of deliveries to slip down the leg-side and Aleem Dar, the umpire, called them as wides. That did not impress Warne and he debated the subject with the umpire, something picked up over the stump microphones and broadcast on ABC Radio.

Most of the fielders, myself included, were on the boundary as we tried to stem the flow of boundaries so I was not able to intervene, although there was no way I could have foreseen what was going to happen anyway. Warne was bowling that leg-stump line to avoid getting whacked about, but we all know the laws about negative bowling, so the umpire's call was fair enough. Warne and Dar had a frank exchange of views but I have not heard any more about that after play.

I did not play very well, even though I got 51. I felt very rusty, never settled and middled very few balls before trying to pull a Chris Martin delivery, spooning it up from the toe-end of the bat. I am not fully fit and my thumb is still causing me discomfort but I cannot blame that for my dismissal.

The day ended in a minor controversy when Michael Clarke and Damien Martyn came off the field with most of the ground in shadow but the far side of the field still in sunlight. It did not look good as conditions were hardly unplayable, but Stephen Waugh always told me that, whenever possible, you should try not to bat in anything other than perfect light. New Zealand was on top here and another wicket could have made our position even more fragile, so although there was no order from the dressing room, the batsmen in the middle assessed the situation and decided of their own accord to come off.

Saturday 20 November

First Test, Brisbane, day 3: Australia 9–564 (Clarke 141, Gilchrist 126, Martyn 70, McGrath 54*) lead New Zealand 353 by 209 runs.

An amazing day, and one most of us never thought we would see, with Glenn McGrath making a Test match 50. That contribution, along with Jason Gillespie, helped rub salt into New Zealand wounds after Michael Clarke and Adam Gilchrist made superb hundreds to turn the match in our favour.

Soon after McGrath went into bat most of the rest of the squad went to get into their whites as, despite his best efforts, he rarely lasts very long at the crease. After a few overs he and Gillespie were still there, and Darren Lehmann came to me and said, 'This is going nowhere so do you think we should declare?' I said I would let it run for a little longer and I am glad I did.

The longer our last wicket pair stayed at the crease, the more excitement there was in our dressing room and viewing area, and there were blokes leaping about and shouting like crazy as McGrath and Gillespie started to hit some boundaries. Our mood changed from fun and disbelief to real excitement, especially when McGrath not only hit his first 6 in Tests but also reached his first Test 50.

The last wicket stand took the game right away from New Zealand, taking its deficit from just over 100 to more than 200, and humiliating its players as well. As the stand continued, that was definitely a factor in my resisting the temptation to declare.

McGrath is always a great one for the one-liner and, sure enough, he came up with a priceless one after leaving the field. His bat is named after Michael Bevan, and McGrath said he was going to ring Bevan and see if Bevan was interested in using a bat named after him.

The excitement was almost enough to make us forget the contributions of Clarke and Gilchrist — without them we would have been in real trouble. Both of them played beautifully, with Clarke achieving an amazing double: a hundred in his first Test in Australia to go with his debut hundred in India. He overcame some early nerves and played beautifully, and he and Gilchrist did exactly what the earlier batsmen, myself included, should have done yesterday — cashed in on an excellent batting surface.

Sunday 21 November

First Test, Brisbane, day 4: Australia 585 (Clarke 141, Gilchrist 126, Martyn 70, McGrath 61, Gillespie 54*, Chris Martyn 5–152) beat New Zealand 353 and 76 by an innings and 156 runs.

After our lacklustre start to this Test I was a bit worried that the players were still feeling the effects of the India tour, but at the end of this Test I think we have started to look as sharp as ever, both individually and collectively.

With the ball, our attack learned lessons from the first innings. All the fast bowlers looked to up their levels of aggression and hit the pitch hard and that allowed us to exploit the variations in bounce that developed as the surface cracked. There was one crack running just outside the line of off stump at one end and Michael Kasprowicz and Jason Gillespie hit it regularly, causing the ball to nip back very effectively.

One such delivery from Gillespie dismissed Brendon McCullum. We — the players and umpire Steve Bucknor — all thought McCullum got a massive edge onto the ball but replays showed he missed it by some distance and just clipped his foot with his bat. The deviation we all assumed was off the edge was from the pitch and so that was unlucky for McCullum.

To show how these things often even themselves out, Craig McMillan got a huge slice of luck, when he edged Gillespie through to Adam Gilchrist but was given not out. A few of us let McMillan know we thought he had been lucky, but his reply was, 'Not everyone's walking, Gilly.' Justice was done next ball when he was dismissed but then Gilchrist and McMillan had a further chat out on the ground straight after the match.

The suggestion coming from the New Zealand camp is that Gilchrist is following some sort of 'crusade' to clean up cricket and the New Zealand players are not happy with that idea, preferring to play the game their way rather than being told what to do. That last part is fair enough but I am not happy with criticism of the way Gilchrist plays his cricket. It is up to him how he goes about things, as long as he is within the laws and spirit of the game. And as far as I am aware, Gilchrist has not told McMillan or anyone else they should walk; today he was merely venting his frustration at McMillan's good fortune to get the decision in his favour, and if McMillan or anyone else edges a catch, stays put and gets given not out then he should expect to get a bit of chat from the fielding side. I was also not happy with the two players trying to sort out their differences so publicly on the field as I think that should have been done over a beer after the game, but hopefully both men now know the other's point of view and that should be an end of it.

That was a sour note on the day but there was humour too, with Gillespie reaching his maiden Test 50. His celebration was unique as he put his bat between his legs and rode it down the wicket in homage to a scene in the Adam Sandler film *Happy Gilmore*. He promised his club mates back in Adelaide and then the Australian team he would do it if he got to 50 — he was as good as his word, and with his long hair flowing as he galloped down the pitch it looked very funny.

Sometimes players can go over the top in celebrations and maybe this was one example of that, but let us also remember that one of the reasons we play the game is to have fun and without that element it would be a boring life.

Monday 22 November

Pakistan names a 17-man squad for its three-Test tour of Australia. It is: Inzamam-ul-Haq (captain), Asim Kamal, Abdul Razzaq, Danish Kaneria, Imran Farhat, Kamran Akmal, Mohammad Asif, Mohammad Khalil, Mohammad Sami, Rana Naved, Salman Butt, Shahid Afridi, Shoaib Akhtar, Shoaib Malik, Yasir Hameed, Younis Khan, Yousuf Youhana.

Wednesday 24 November

New Zealand names a 14-man squad for the three-match one-day series against Australia for the Chappell-Hadlee Trophy. It is: Stephen Fleming (captain), Andre Adams, Nathan Astle, Ian Butler, Chris Cairns, Chris Harris, Hamish Marshall, Brendon McCullum, Craig McMillan, Kyle Mills, Jacob Oram, Mathew Sinclair, Scott Styris, Daniel Vettori.

Friday 26 November

Second Test, Adelaide, day 1: Australia 3–327 (Langer 144*, Hayden 70, Ponting 68) v New Zealand.

My good fortune to win the toss and a superb unbeaten hundred by Justin Langer have put us in charge of this Test already.

Langer took the attack to New Zealand's bowlers right from the start, hitting James Franklin's first four balls of the day for four and did the same again when Franklin returned with the second new ball late in the day. It all formed part of his 20th Test hundred, an amazing achievement for a player who was written off during the Ashes tour of 2001 when I took his spot at number three.

Langer's fluency today does raise the question of whether he should be in the one-day team, but his problem is there are not many spots on offer and it would be a brave selector who dropped Adam Gilchrist down the order or Matthew Hayden out of the side to give

Langer a chance. The positive for us is that, because he only plays one form of the game for Australia, he retains his freshness — and he has shown plenty of that this year.

I made 68 before I was deceived by Daniel Vettori, lured down the pitch and smartly stumped by Brendon McCullum. It was yet another missed opportunity to score a hundred this year, something I am yet to do in Tests in 2004. That fact does not play on my mind too much, as I feel I have been playing pretty well, but I have been asked about it a few times lately by the media and so it is impossible to dismiss completely. I have felt in good form for most of the year but there have been some good balls, some poor shots and a few missed Tests, and it has all added up to a moderate return by the standards I set in 2003, when I averaged 100 in Tests.

I was maybe guilty of looking to be too positive against Vettori, but it was all part of my game plan. It was roasting hot today and so I knew the quicker bowlers would only bowl short spells while the spinners would be used as stock bowlers to keep the scoring rate down and the quick men rested. I figured if I could hit the spinners out of the attack it would give Stephen Fleming a real headache, and for a while my plan worked, until Vettori dismissed me.

I came in when Hayden was caught and bowled by Paul Wiseman, a decision that was referred to the third umpire when Hayden stood his ground, apparently believing he had hit the ball into the turf. The umpires referred the matter to the television official and replays showed he was clearly out. Langer told me afterwards there was a large double noise, like bat hitting ground, that may have caused confusion in the middle, but the replay made the dismissal look so obvious that match referee Mike Procter called me in for an informal chat after play and asked me to explain why one of my players had stood his ground for such an apparently clear-cut dismissal. My reply was simple: 'If it was so clear cut, why did the on-field umpires feel the need to refer it to the television official?' Procter did not have an answer for that.

Saturday 27 November

Second Test, Adelaide, day 2: New Zealand 2–56 trail Australia 8–575 declared (Langer 215, Lehmann 81, Ponting 68, Warne 53*, Gilchrist 50, Vettori 5–152) by 519 runs.

Justin Langer's double hundred, together with some other useful contributions down the order, made this another very good day for us.

Langer relished the roasting hot conditions and showed his ruthless streak in reaching 200. His determination and desire to keep batting is a great lesson to young players not to give it away, even when they score a hundred. He cashed in here, knowing that conditions — good pitch, limited New Zealand attack, hot weather, good form — will not always be so favourable.

It was pleasing, too, to see Darren Lehmann do so well in front of his home crowd. He has not played many Tests in Adelaide and I know everyone was willing him to reach three figures this time, especially as this is the first Adelaide Test since the death of his mentor David Hookes. It was not to be but his innings has certainly eased the pressure on him after his failure in Brisbane.

Shane Warne also enjoyed himself, reaching 50 before I declared. After Glenn McGrath and Jason Gillespie reached half-centuries in the last Test, it was the perfect response to suggestions Warne should slip down the order. He showed today what a dangerous player he can be.

Sunday 28 November

Second Test, Adelaide, day 3: Australia 8–575 declared and 0–57 lead New Zealand 251 (Fleming 83, Astle 52) by 381 runs.

We bowled New Zealand out after tea this evening but I chose not to enforce the follow-on.

Although it gave us a chance to win the game quickly if everything went our way, it also meant our bowlers would be back in the field in hot conditions, and if New Zealand managed to make a decent fist of their second innings it would condemn us to bat last. There is no sign the pitch will break up, but if it does I want us to be able to exploit that, not New Zealand.

Stephen Fleming, the New Zealand captain, returned to form today and played well. He is a good man, I get on well with him and we were able to have a laugh out in the middle today.

We have spent some time together over the last few weeks, filming a series of commercials for Rexona. The idea is to play up the trans-Tasman rivalry in a humorous way, and in one of the commercials I have to slap some of their product on Fleming's face. He then takes revenge by directing me to the women's toilet in a nightclub by covering up the 'Wo' on the sign with his hand.

The close-up shots meant I needed a manicure, something Fleming reminded me of today when I dived for a catch after he swept a ball from Shane Warne onto his pad. I dived full length across the pitch from silly point and scraped my hand over the pitch as I did so. As I lay slumped on the ground after just failing to pull off the catch, Fleming said, 'How's the manicure looking now?'

Monday 29 November

Second Test, Adelaide, day 4: New Zealand 251 and 5–149 require another 315 runs to beat Australia 8–575 declared and 2–139 declared (Hayden 54).

We have come in for some heavy criticism thanks to our approach today, but I could not care less. We added 78 in the first two hours of play and have been labelled dull and boring, but that criticism fails to see why we played that way.

It would have been more entertaining if we had gone into bat and started to try to slog the ball around in search of quick runs towards a declaration, however that approach risked not only losing wickets but also giving New Zealand something positive to take into its innings. We wanted to give them nothing, and our approach did exactly that.

They left the field flat and that was reflected in how they batted later in the day. It looked for a while as though we might be able to wrap up the match in four days but the onset of bad light forced us to rest our frontline fast bowlers, rely on some overs from Darren Lehmann, and New Zealand were able to scramble to the close 5 wickets down.

Tuesday 30 November

Australia names a 14-man squad for the three-match one-day series against New Zealand for the Chappell-Hadlee Trophy. It is: Ricky Ponting (captain), Michael Clarke, Adam Gilchrist (vice-captain), Jason Gillespie, Matthew Hayden, Brad Hogg, Michael Kasprowicz, Simon Katich, Brett Lee, Darren Lehmann, Damien Martyn, Glenn McGrath, Andrew Symonds, Shane Watson.

Second Test, Adelaide, day 5: Australia 8–575 declared and 2–139 declared beat New Zealand 251 and 250 (Vettori 59) by 213 runs.

After we won just after lunch the media asked me whether we were being challenged enough and whether winning is becoming boring.

I will never find winning boring. It is still hard work to win a Test match, as one look in our dressing room during any evening after play will tell you: players are treated for aches, pains, cuts and blisters.

It is up to the other countries to try to catch us up rather than for us to slip back to the field in order to make matches less one-sided. We set our own standards, we enjoy the success that comes from that, and the only way the world game will get better and more attractive is for other sides to aspire to match us. That is their challenge; ours is to maintain our standards, not let them drop back.

A sign we are on the right track at the moment came when the New Zealand players arrived in our dressing room for an end-of-series drink after play. Stephen Fleming told me that he could not remember the last time he faced bowling as good as ours in this Test. He said the line and length of the bowlers was immaculate and he felt like he was never going to get a bad ball.

New Zealand did win something today when Mark Richardson beat Darren Lehmann in a race on the ground after play. Richardson, who is so slow his nickname is Riga (as in rigor mortis), challenges the slowest person in every Test side to a race at the end of a series and he ended up winning this one by 15 or 20 metres. The whole thing turned into quite an event, with live commentary on ABC Radio and quite a fair number of spectators staying on to watch it. Lehmann was so nervous he even had a couple of drinks beforehand to calm his nerves, but even though he lost there was a plus side, as both players raised a decent amount of money for charity, thanks to Travelex, who sponsored the race.

Wednesday 1 December

Tour match, Perth, day 1: The Pakistanis 7–235 (Khan 132*) leads Western Australia second XI 158 (Ronchi 66) by 77 runs.

Thursday 2 December

Tour match, Perth, day 2: The Pakistanis 257 (Khan 142, Coetzee 5–66) and 6–44 requires another 50 runs to beat Western Australia second XI 158 and 192 (Simmons 65, Kaneria 7–45).

Tour match, Perth, day 3: Western Australia second XI 158 and 192 beat the Pakistanis 257 and 83 (Coetzee 5–23) by 10 runs.

Chappell-Hadlee Trophy, Melbourne, first match: New Zealand 6–247 (Astle 70, Marshall 50*) beat Australia 9–246 (Gilchrist 68, Lehmann 50) by 4 wickets.

I am furious we lost this game after making key, basic errors. When we batted, several of us got starts without going on to make a big score, then Michael Kasprowicz conceded 22 runs in the 48th over.

Kasprowicz's boil-over was a real shock, as before that over he was superb, but he lost his line early in the over, the batsmen improvised well and we then had to start altering our plans to try to stem the run-flow in accordance with where the New Zealand batsmen were hitting the ball rather than sticking to our original plan. It did not work.

This was always going to be Kasprowicz's last match before he took a break, missing the next match in Sydney to have a few days with his family in Brisbane, before linking up with us again for the third match in his home city. Given the way he was hit around, I spoke to him afterwards to see if he wanted to alter that plan, stick with the squad and try to get that last over out of his system. He was still happy to have the time off and so we stuck with the original idea. I made it clear to him and the media that he has been rested, not dropped. Thankfully he is a vastly experienced bowler who has seen it all before and I know he will bounce back from this without too much trouble.

My frustration included my dismissal as given out lbw, even though I got a healthy edge on the ball as I attempted to sweep Daniel Vettori. Umpire Rudi Koertzen sent me on my way, and although I was frustrated there was no point in waving my bat at the umpire or remonstrating. I saved my frustrations for the privacy of the dressing room.

One positive out of the game was Brett Lee's bowling. He was very fast, swung the new ball and it was not only the batsmen who struggled to cope with him as a result. I dropped Mathew Sinclair off him at second slip, a regulation catch that beat me for pace, hitting my hands very hard before going to ground.

Tour match, Perth: The Pakistanis 9–256 (Salman Butt 115) beat Cricket Australia Chairman's XI 213 (Rogers 61, Ronchi 51) by 43 runs.

Chappell-Hadlee Trophy, Sydney, second match: Australia 7–261 (Gilchrist 60, Lehmann 52) beat New Zealand 244 (Cairns 50) by 17 runs.

We won, but we also made hard work of it thanks to some brave batting by New Zealand's lower order and, perhaps, my tactics.

The pitch was slow and dry, and after we reduced the Black Caps to 6–86 I kept the slow bowlers going rather than returning to my frontline fast bowlers at both ends. I thought New Zealand would have to keep coming hard at us to try to salvage the game, and they would find that hard to do against spin. They did come hard at us but it paid off for them, with Kyle Mills giving us a real fright thanks to some bold hitting.

It became a bit scary, but once we got last man Chris Harris in, I knew we would win. He had dislocated his shoulder in the field and could barely hold a bat, so there was no way he could sprint between the wickets and rotate the strike enough to ensure Mills could win the game for New Zealand.

When we batted we owed a great deal to Darren Lehmann and Brad Hogg after our top order slumped again, this time to 6–161. I got 32 from 36 balls, another start without going on with the job, dismissed by a leading edge to mid-off as I checked my shot when the ball held up off the pitch. My score sums up our top-order problem. Once any of us gets a start, as I did here, we must convert it into a big score.

Tour match, Perth, day 1: Western Australia 1–20 trail the Pakistanis 262 (Razzaq 83*, Youhana 77) by 242 runs.

Australia announces an unchanged 12-man squad for the first Test against Pakistan in Perth.

Tour match, Perth, day 2: The Pakistanis 262 and 0–4 trail Western Australia 9–404 declared (Hussey 124, North 79) by 138 runs.

Chappell-Hadlee Trophy, Brisbane, third match: match abandoned, rain, series drawn 1–1.

The series ended in an anti-climax, with Stephen Fleming and me holding the trophy together in a small room in the bowels of the Brisbane Cricket Ground rather than in front of a full house. The equivalent of a month's rain in the past few days put paid to the match and it was called off early enough to allow me to fly home this evening.

The lack of play did not prevent a media frenzy. New Zealand coach John Bracewell apparently accused local curator Kevin Mitchell junior of switching the pitch from his original choice to a different one, to try to reduce Daniel Vettori's effectiveness.

The reality was that the rain prevented Mitchell from working on the pitch he had set aside for the match, so he was forced to repair a used pitch instead. Surely a surface already played on, with wear and footmarks, would be more use to Vettori than a new pitch, so I could not follow Bracewell's argument. Maybe he should stick to coaching and let curators look after pitches.

Tour match, Perth, day 3: Western Australia 9–404 declared and 0–34 beat the Pakistanis 262 and 174 (Dorey 5–41) by 10 wickets.

Part 7:
Pakistan home series

Thursday 16 December 2004

First Test, Perth, day 1: Australia 8–357 (Langer 181*, Gilchrist 69) v Pakistan.

We are in a strong position thanks to a brilliant innings from Justin Langer as, together with Adam Gilchrist, he rescued us from 5–78.

Langer played patiently at first then, as Pakistan wilted later in the day, he took full toll and is in sight of his second successive Test double hundred.

I love playing in Perth as, in this era where drop-in pitches that play in identical ways are being used more and more, it is one of the few venues where the pitch retains its traditional characteristics. The surface is fast and today's pitch was no exception. That means it takes time to acclimatise when you first get in and the first 15 or 20 minutes can be tough to deal with.

But once you get established it is a great place to bat, as Langer and Gilchrist showed today. The bounce may be higher than any other pitch in Australia but it is even, and that allows you to get into position to play your shot with confidence. The outfield is another bonus as it is always lightning fast.

Shoaib Akhtar operated with the wind and he bowled very quickly, at least in his opening couple of spells. He also won round one of his war of words with Matthew Hayden. The pair have clashed before, at Border Field on Pakistan's last tour in 1999, and in Sharjah and Sri Lanka when we played Pakistan at neutral venues in 2002, and this tour promises more of the same.

Hayden loves winding up fast bowlers and most times he wins as they lose their control and he capitalises. Shoaib, for his part, has said publicly that he believes Langer is a better player than Hayden, a deliberate swipe at the big Queenslander. The battle lines were drawn and Shoaib won today with a superb inswinger that trapped Hayden lbw.

I do not like wars of words. It may work for some players like Shane Warne and Glenn McGrath, but it can also be a distraction to the job of bowling and batting. Shoaib was so overjoyed to get rid of Hayden that he overstepped the mark when he pointed him

---

towards the pavilion. Match referee Ranjan Madugalle said before the series that send-offs are not permitted, so Shoaib found himself in trouble.

One positive ahead of the series was Pakistan captain Inzamam-ul-Haq's agreement with my request that batsmen should accept the word of the fielder over low catches, in contrast to New Zealand's stance on the issue. 'We want to play good cricket,' said Inzamam, which is encouraging.

Friday 17 December

First Test, Perth, day 2: Australia 381 (Langer 11, Gilchrist 69, Akhtar 5–99) and 0–15 lead Pakistan 179 (Kasprowicz 5–30) by 217 runs.

A combination of excellent bowling by our attack and some poor shot selection by Pakistan has left us in total charge of this match.

Although the visitors played a couple of matches in Perth ahead of this Test, they clearly have not come to terms with the extra bounce in the surfaces in this part of the world. Because the ball bounces more than elsewhere, forcing shots off the back foot with a straight bat are risky, but we dismissed six Pakistan batsmen caught behind the wicket.

Michael Kasprowicz bowled superbly and fully justified the decision to include him here ahead of Brett Lee. I was sorry for Lee, as he would have loved bowling on this surface and would have frightened the life out of the Pakistan batsmen, but the selectors opted to retain the same side that won so well against New Zealand and the bowlers again did the job asked of them here.

At one stage while he was batting Shoaib Akhtar asked for a runner, complaining that he had a sore ankle. I told the umpires he could have one as long as we did not then see him miraculously recover to bowl off his full run with no ill effects later on in the day. When Shoaib was told this he decided against the runner, took the field when we batted again but then left the field, apparently injured. It will be interesting to see if he appears tomorrow.

Our decision not to enforce the follow-on was in line with what happened in Adelaide against New Zealand. The pitch is still good, so there was no reason not to bat again. We want to grind Pakistan down mentally as well as on the scoreboard.

First Test, Perth, day 3: Pakistan 179 and 1–18 require another 546 runs to beat Australia 381 and 5–361 declared (Martyn 100*, Ponting 98, Langer 97).

After another successful day Pakistan look like a broken side. As we batted on today its players, apart from a few exceptions, looked as though they were going through the motions. The captain, Inzamam, was off the field for a long spell with a bad back and Shoaib Akhtar was absent with a shoulder injury to go with his earlier ankle trouble.

One of Pakistan's players who bucked that trend was leg-spinner Danish Kaneria. He stuck to his task well and always looked to spin the ball hard. He has plenty of variations with a googly, a top-spinner, a quicker ball and a leg-break, and although I was able to pick those variations out of his hand, there was the added trouble of the extra bounce he found because of the Perth pitch and his high action.

I played okay without ever being fluent and was in sight of my first Test hundred of the year when an unfortunate combination of events cost me my wicket. Trying to sweep Kaneria for two to bring up three figures, I missed the ball and suffered a cramp in my right hamstring. It caused my leg to shoot forward, taking my back foot fractionally out of the crease, and I was stumped. Thankfully, with Damien Martyn scoring a superb hundred and Justin Langer adding 97 to his first innings 191, it scarcely mattered.

First Test, Perth, day 4: Australia 381 and 5–361 declared beat Pakistan 179 and 72 (McGrath 8–24) by 491 runs.

My 30th birthday and this was the ideal present — a thumping win completed before lunch.

Pakistan batted spinelessly but that should not detract from Glenn McGrath's performance, as he claimed his best Test figures. After all, several of the Pakistan players have outstanding Test records and have made runs in Australia on previous tours. At one stage McGrath looked on course for taking all 10 wickets in the innings and when Michael Kasprowicz broke the sequence he apologised to McGrath — with a smile on his face — for ruining the chance.

Our one area of concern is our slip catching, with several chances going down over the course of the two innings. We have been fallible here for a while and that is odd because in Warne, me, Clarke and Hayden we have some excellent slip fielders and we practise every day. Confidence could be a factor, especially for someone like Clarke, who has dropped several chances since coming into the side in India. At one point during that tour, when we were chatting on the phone after he dropped a chance in Chennai, he said, 'Hurry up and get fit so you can get back into the slips.'

After last year's Perth Test against Zimbabwe, when there was disquiet among some players that our post-match celebrations broke up far too quickly, this time we settled in for a long afternoon and were joined at one point by the singer Kamahl. He still has big hair and was wearing his trademark blazer too.

This evening I had a fantastic birthday meal with Rianna at a local restaurant overlooking the water. As usual she had arranged everything, including champagne on arrival, and it was the perfect end to a perfect day of Test cricket for us.

Monday 20 December

Australia names an unchanged 12-man squad for the second Test in Melbourne.

Thursday 23 December

Justin Langer suffers a back injury during training in Melbourne and is considered doubtful for the second Test; Simon Katich is drafted into the squad as cover in case Langer does not recover in time.

Friday 24 December – Saturday 25 December

25 December: West Indies names a 14-man squad for the VB Series: Brian Lara (captain), Ian Bradshaw, Dwayne Bravo, Courtney Browne, Shivnarine Chanderpaul, Pedro Collins, Mervyn Dillon, Chris Gayle, Ryan Hinds, Wavell Hinds, Reon King, Marlon Samuels, Ramnaresh Sarwan, Xavier Marshall.

Christmas, and this year we have had the return of a tradition for the Australian squad — a party at Shane Warne's house.

It was a regular occurrence when I first played for Australia in the Boxing Day Test — Warne invited the whole squad, friends and family to his house on Christmas Eve — but the tradition died for a couple of years while he was between houses. This year it returned and he looked after everyone superbly.

The event was catered by Crown, the Melbourne casino, and there was great food, a bar fridge near the swimming pool and a terrific selection of wine, and there were also plenty of non-cricketers present, including local football celebrities Sam Newman and Rex Hunt. But even though there was plenty to drink, I did not notice any players overindulging. We are all too professional for that these days and the same applied at our Christmas Day meal for players, support staff, family and friends at Crown Casino.

Crown have catered for our Christmas Day gathering for the last few years now and do a great job, not just in supplying superb food and drink but also looking after the ever-growing numbers of children. There were arcade games, clowns and a bouncy castle to keep them amused while the adults got on with the job of relaxing and socialising.

We also had the presentation of Secret Santa gifts during Christmas lunch. Organised by Mel Gilchrist and Anna Gillespie a few days ago, everyone had to draw a name out of a hat, not tell anyone who they drew, then go and buy a present for that person costing no more than $20. I drew Darren Lehmann and got him a corkscrew and wine stopper as I reckoned it might get some use. My present was appropriate for my love of golf — a mat to putt golf balls along with an electric hole at the end which shoots the ball back to you if you get it in.

After the meal I went back to my room to relax, had a swim and then attempted to clear my head before going to sleep. I do this by visualising how I want to play and writing down those thoughts. I do not focus on the bowlers I will face but prefer to think about how I want to play, as I should then be able to cope with anything the bowlers can produce. My buzzwords this evening are:

Watch the ball

Play straight

Call loudly

Be positive in attack and defence

Bat for a long time.

Second Test, Melbourne, day 1: Pakistan 6–318 (Youhana 111, Khan 87, Butt 70) v Australia.

The first day of the Boxing Day Test, together with the start of the summer in Brisbane, is something I relish, and the chance to captain Australia today made it extra special. We did not have the best of the day thanks to some excellent batting from Pakistan's acting captain, Yousuf Youhana, but we are still very much in this match.

Youhana is standing in for the injured Inzamam and really led from the front. His battle with Shane Warne must have been a treat for the neutral, too, as he used his feet and was never afraid to hit Warne over the infield.

Our catching was again fallible, with Matthew Hayden dropping a sitter from Salman Butt from just the third ball. That would have been the perfect start, as I am sure Pakistan would have had their last effort against us — 72 all out — in mind, but we let them off the hook and their batsmen took advantage.

The outfield and the bowlers' run-ups ended up far better than anyone expected. The outfield looks parched but ran quickly, and although the bowlers were concerned before play about the area between the relaid outfield and the pitch, it held together without any problems.

The one disquieting aspect of the day was the sight on television, when we got back to the hotel, of the tsunami that has struck Asia. The horrific images we saw this evening were doubly shocking as Sri Lanka, where most of us were playing just a few months ago, is apparently one of the worst-hit countries.

Second Test, Melbourne, day 2: Australia 5–203 (Martyn 67*, Langer 50) trail Pakistan 341 (Youhana 111, Khan 87, Butt 70) by 138 runs.

Although the Test has continued, everyone's thoughts seem to be dominated by the unfolding tragedy of the tsunami disaster. The escalation of the crisis has been rapid. When we went to bed last night there were around 5000 reported casualties and by the time we got up this morning that number had risen to 35 000. We had a minute's silence as a mark of respect before play today. The whole crisis seems to be getting bigger every minute and it is rightly casting a big shadow over this match.

On the field it has been a pretty even contest so far. We started the day by disposing of the last four Pakistan wickets, but not before Abdul Razzaq played very curiously, making 4 not out from 76 balls as the tail folded around him. It made no sense as he is a dangerous striker of the ball, but it suited us fine for him to play like that.

Matthew Hayden and Shoaib Akhtar had another battle, which Shoaib won again when Hayden spooned a ball to point off the bottom of the bat. Then I fell cheaply to the same bowler, out in careless fashion caught at deep square leg hooking at a short ball.

Shoaib had banged a few balls in short and I resisted the temptation, but when he did it again I got into position, and when I found the ball did not bounce as much as I expected I looked to paddle it onto the leg-side but ended up hitting it right out of the middle of the bat. It meant it carried almost all the way to the waiting fielder on the fence. I could not believe I hit the ball so well.

Tuesday 28 December

Second Test, Melbourne, day 3: Pakistan 341 and 5–85 lead Australia 379 (Martyn 142, Gillespie 50*, Langer 50, Akhtar 5–109, Kaneria 5–125) by 47 runs.

We are in prime position to win this match, and with it the series, after a superb innings by Damien Martyn, backed up by Jason Gillespie and then some excellent bowling by our attack.

Martyn was superb against Shoaib Akhtar today. Because the pitch is uneven in bounce, Shoaib bowled like the speed of light and those factors made it difficult to play attacking or defensive shots with any certainty, but Martyn made light of the problem and I rate this innings right up there among his best Test hundreds.

He was helped by Jason Gillespie's second Test 50 of the season in a repeat of their partnership in Chennai in October. Gillespie played an excellent innings and as his confidence as a batsman grows he will get even better. His partnership with Martyn turned a large deficit into a decent lead.

The lead ended up at 38 and we took 3 wickets before Pakistan wiped it off. That included one of those moments when you look like a great captain, as I moved a fielder back to deep square leg for Imran Farhat, only to see him hook the ball down the fielder's throat two balls later. Farhat is a compulsive hooker and, rather than great captaincy, I would call it poor batting.

Second Test, Melbourne, day 4: Australia 379 and 1–127 (Ponting 62*, Hayden 50*) beat Pakistan 341 and 163 by 9 wickets.

We wrapped up the match and the series with a crushing win that has left me personally in great spirits for the final Test in Sydney in a few days' time.

I felt better and better through my time in the middle and by the end of the match, which I brought about when I drove Danish Kaneria down the ground for six, I was wishing I could start my next innings straightaway.

A major curiosity during our charge to victory was the performance of Shoaib Akhtar. The situation seemed tailor-made for him to give it all he had, as we only wanted 126 to win, so there was no point in any bowler holding anything back. Instead Shoaib seemed to go through the motions and we treated him accordingly. Maybe he was injured, but if he was not and if he had been one of my bowlers in the same situation, I would have been far from happy.

After the match I found myself very busy. First, after chatting with the media, I spoke to Tim May, the Chief Executive of the players' union, the Australian Cricketers' Association (ACA), and Michael Brown, the General Manager of Cricket Operations at Cricket Australia. They asked if I was available to play for and captain an ICC XI in a match to raise funds for tsunami relief in a couple of weeks' time. I was delighted to say yes. We had already announced we were donating our prize money from this match to relief efforts, and as the scale of the disaster has become apparent it has become more and more clear that plenty of money will be needed to rebuild lives in Asia. Among the places affected is Galle, the scene of my first Test as Australia's Test captain. The ground has been decimated while the team hotel, the Lighthouse, where the players held a pre-Test dinner for me in March, has also been badly affected. That brings the impact of the tragedy into sharp focus.

I then had a long meeting with Chairman of Selectors Trevor Hohns about the squad for the Sydney Test. The pitch is expected to help the spinners, so the selectors are keen to include Stuart MacGill to partner Shane Warne. If MacGill is included in place of a pace bowler, with the plan to leave out Michael Kasprowicz, then that would leave us with only two frontline seamers, so the plan is to include Shane Watson as a medium-paced all-rounder. Watson is a talented cricketer who almost justifies his place as a batsman alone, but he is also a handy bowler who I rate highly. The only downside of his inclusion is that a batsman has to miss out and Hohns said Darren Lehmann is favourite to be omitted.

There was still time for another meeting before I could relax and this time it was with Stephen Gough, the secretary of the Melbourne Cricket Club. He was brought to see me by James Sutherland after James was made aware of my concerns about the poor-quality practice pitches at the ground. Hopefully those concerns will now be acted upon.

Friday 31 December – Saturday 1 January

1 January: ICC Chief Executive Officer Malcolm Speed, Tim May of the ACA and James Sutherland, Cricket Australia's Chief Executive Officer, announce a game in Melbourne on 10 January to raise funds for tsunami relief and also that gate-takings from the first day of the Sydney Test will go towards that relief effort.

The build-up to this year's New Year Test is a totally new experience for me: this will be the first Test I will play in while staying at home.

With all the time we spend in hotels each year, the chance to spend a week at home while playing in a Test is something every player looks forward to, but in the past I have been the one player who has missed out, as Launceston is not on the international circuit. Even when I moved to Wollongong a couple of years ago I still had to stay in the team hotel during Sydney Tests because the 90-minute drive to and from home was just too long, but now I have moved to the outskirts of the city and have a 25-minute drive to the Sydney Cricket Ground.

I still spent the evening of New Year's Eve at the team hotel in Sydney as team manager Steve Bernard held our traditional barbecue for players, support staff and their families. Bernard gets a suite from the Quay West hotel every year that overlooks the Harbour Bridge and so everyone gets to enjoy the firework displays that bring in the New Year without the hassle of spending hours away from the hotel — an important consideration as so many of the players now have young children.

New Year's Day gave me the chance to do something nice as I told Shane Watson he will be making his Test debut tomorrow. I do not think he could quite believe it, and although he did not cry, he did get a bit emotional. He is a fantastic kid who has fought back from so many injuries to get to this point, and it was great to be able to give him the best news of his professional career.

ICC and Asian XI squads are named for the match in Melbourne on 10 January to raise funds for victims of the tsunami. They are:

ICC: Ricky Ponting (captain), Dwayne Bravo, Chris Cairns, Stephen Fleming, Chris Gayle, Adam Gilchrist, Darren Gough, Matthew Hayden, Brian Lara, Glenn McGrath, Daniel Vettori, Shane Warne. Coach/manager: Stephen Waugh.

Asia: Sourav Ganguly (captain), Sanath Jayasuriya, Virender Sehwag, Sachin Tendulkar, Marvan Atapattu, Rahul Dravid, Yousuf Youhana, Alok Kapali, Kumar Sangakkara, Chaminda Vaas, Shoaib Akhtar, Anil Kumble, Muttiah Muralitharan, Zaheer Khan.

Third Test, Sydney, day 1: Pakistan 9–292 (Butt 108, Hameed 58, MacGill 5–87) v Australia.

After a nervous start, Stuart MacGill fully justified his inclusion here. Outwardly MacGill always comes across as a confident character, but I could tell he was nervous ahead of his first Test in 10 months and it showed. He bowled poorly and was picked off by the Pakistan batsmen. My method to deal with that is to talk to the bowler, reassure him and hope things improve. Thankfully they did and he bowled beautifully during an extended spell that pulled Pakistan back after it reached 1–193.

Five frontline bowlers at my disposal was a nice problem to have after dealing with just four bowlers for so long, but being spoiled for choice was not a factor in delaying Glenn McGrath's second spell until the final session of the day. I delayed bringing him back because there was not a lot to be gained by flogging him on an easy-paced pitch while the ball was doing nothing, and I waited until there was a chance it would start to reverse-swing before reintroducing him. When he did come back he was fresh and bowled superbly.

MacGill and Shane Warne bowled for a while in tandem, and although some critics do not believe they can play together because as two leg-spinners they are too similar, I disagree. They are different types of bowlers, with Warne relying on subtle variations and flight while MacGill's main weapon is to try to spin the ball as hard as he can. They won the Test in Galle last March, and although Warne only took one wicket today they performed well together.

Shane Watson made a quiet start to his Test career, falling over in his follow-through with his first delivery but otherwise performing steadily. He swung the ball and bowled at a lively pace and went at less than 3 runs per over.

Monday 3 January

Third Test, Sydney, day 2: Australia 4–340 (Ponting 155*, Martyn 67) lead Pakistan 304 (Butt 108, Hameed 58, MacGill 5–87) by 36 runs.

It has been a long time between drinks but at last I have another Test century to reflect upon. I have never doubted my ability but there have still been understandable questions about why I have not scored a hundred as Test captain before this innings.

I am not sure what the answer is, because throughout 2004 I never felt out of touch. You know when you have lost form because you lose all sense of timing, not just with the way you strike the ball but also with your feet movement and balance, but I never felt like that. Despite that, over the past couple of weeks I have redoubled my efforts to refine my technique, making sure I left no stone unturned in the search for a big score, and this innings has justified that extra work. Assistant coach Tim Nielsen helped make sure my first movement is onto my toes so I can move again either forward or back. I also worked on driving either straight or through mid-on, getting my front foot to the pitch of the ball and not trying to hit the ball too hard. They may all seem like basic things, but sometimes going back to basics is the best way and it has worked for me here. I also believe that staying at home for this Test has relaxed me.

I was able to take full toll of the Pakistan attack because it turned out to be short-handed, as Shoaib Akhtar only bowled 10 overs all day. I do not know why but his lack of enthusiasm helped me.

Danish Kaneria again bowled well, although I did not hear the abuse he is supposed to have shouted at Michael Clarke when he dismissed him, even though I was at the non-striker's end. He was facing away from me but the umpires obviously heard something, because he was reported to the match referee for whatever he said.

Kaneria was a central figure in the final drama of the day, involving Adam Gilchrist. After Clarke was out I was desperate for us not to lose any more wickets in the day, and as Kaneria was about to start the final over of the day I walked down the pitch to Gilchrist and said, 'Just make sure you concentrate on getting through this over because if we are both here in the morning we can really press on then.'

Gilchrist's response was to waltz down the pitch and hammer Kaneria for six from a ball pitched in the footmarks outside the left-hander's off-stump. As I moved towards him to have another chat and find out what was going through his mind when he played that shot, he said, 'I know, I know, don't say a word.' With Gilchrist I have discovered over the years that it is best not to overcomplicate things. He is such an instinctive player that it is usually best just to let him get on with doing things his way. Sometimes that can mean he will fail, but if you are prepared to take the good with the bad with Gilchrist you know there will always be a lot more good.

Tuesday 4 January

Pakistan names a 16-man squad for the VB Series. It is: Inzamam-ul-Haq (captain), Abdul Razzaq, Azhar Mahmood, Iftikhar Anjum, Kamran Akmal, Mohammad Hafeez, Mohammad Khalil, Rana Naved, Salman Butt, Shahid Afridi, Shoaib Akhtar, Shoaib Malik, Taufeeq Umar, Yasir Hameed, Younis Khan, Yousuf Youhana.

Third Test, Sydney, day 3: Pakistan 304 and 1–67 trail Australia 568 (Ponting 207, Gilchrist 113, Martyn 67, Kaneria 7–188) by 197 runs.

I have watched plenty of brilliant Adam Gilchrist innings from the dressing room but I was able to watch today's masterclass in destructive batting from the non-striker's end as he monopolised our partnership and put us in a match-winning position.

He dominated our partnership not only in the number of runs he scored but also in the amount of strike he had. When we got back to the dressing room at the tea break — the first session was washed out by morning rain — I joked, 'I don't reckon I faced 20 balls in the first hour of play', and I turned out to be right. In that first hour I faced just 13 deliveries and 6 of those were a maiden I played out from Shoaib at the start of the session.

I did not mind, as with Gilchrist scoring so freely at one end my job was simple: to get a single and get him facing the bowling again. He played superbly and took the game away from Pakistan very quickly. He took the attack to Shoaib and, although he had some luck with a couple of miscued pulls that landed safely, he hit him out of the attack then did the same to Mohammad Asif.

It overshadowed my double century but that did not bother me at all. It was a significant landmark for me, my fourth, to leave me in select company as one of only three Australians, with Greg Chappell and Donald Bradman, to score that many. Of those four the one I made in Melbourne last summer against India is my favourite because it was the most important. We were 1–0 down in the series and had to win to have a hope of giving Stephen Waugh a winning send-off as captain. To deliver in such an important match made it a special innings for me, but I still enjoyed this one.

Tour match, Melbourne: Victoria 3–205 (Elliott 87, Hussey 83*) beat the West Indians 201 by 7 wickets.

Third Test, Sydney, day 4: Australia 568 and 1–62 beat Pakistan 304 and 325 (Kamal 87, Hameed 63) by 9 wickets.

Although we did not play all that well today we still sealed a very comfortable win that rounded off our home Test summer with a fifth win in five matches.

We should never have needed 62 in our final innings, but with just a couple of wickets to fall Shane Warne decided to flight the ball in the expectation he could buy the last few wickets through reckless shots. Instead Asim Kamal played well and the match lasted longer than it should have done.

That is a very minor grumble. Apart from today's short spell in the field, the first two days in Brisbane against New Zealand and the first session of the Perth Test against Pakistan, we crushed our opponents, played some entertaining cricket and only one Test has gone into the fifth day, which sums up our dominance.

Shane Watson bowled well today to pick up his first Test wicket, completing a solid first match, bowling at a lively pace, finding some reverse swing and he also batted well. Our best combination remains four frontline bowlers with Adam Gilchrist at number seven, but if conditions dictate and we need to include a second spinner, we now know we have another option thanks to Watson's efforts here.

The post-match celebrations were enjoyable but there was a sad element to them as well, as it was assistant coach Tim Nielsen's last time with us before he heads off to Brisbane to take up a post with Cricket Australia's Centre of Excellence. We made sure he got a rousing send-off after two great years with the squad and he joined Justin Langer in leading the team song.

Part 8:
Tsunami Match and
VB Series

Saturday 8 January 2005

West Indies all-rounder Ryan Hinds is ruled out of the VB Series with a groin injury; Ricardo Powell replaces him in the squad.

Tour match, Hobart: The West Indians 6–266 (Lara 116*) beat Australia A 8–263 (D Hussey 128, White 61) by 4 wickets.

Sunday 9 January – Monday 10 January

9 January, Hobart, tour match: Australia A 9–243 (M Hussey 70, White 59) beat the West Indians 192 (W Hinds 53) by 51 runs.

10 January, Melbourne, World Cricket Tsunami Appeal match: ICC World XI 8–344 (Ponting 115, Cairns 69, Lara 52) beat Asian Cricket Council Asian XI 232 (Dravid 75*) by 112 runs.

The past two days have been a fantastic experience for me. I have played with and against some of the best players in the world, scored a hundred at the Melbourne Cricket Ground and, above all, helped raise money for victims of the tsunami.

The build-up to the game helped bring home what this match was all about as I met and listened to the experiences of the Sri Lanka players who have flown in to take part in the match. Sanath Jayasuriya's mother was badly injured by the wave, while Muttiah Muralitharan could easily have been caught up in it himself had he not been running late for an appointment on the southern coast of the island. Muralitharan and some of the other Sri Lanka players have already been involved in distributing aid to the worst-affected areas and they said whole villages and towns on the coast have been washed away.

Despite that doom and gloom there was still a great atmosphere among the players, because everyone knew we had come together to enjoy ourselves, entertain and raise lots of money for the relief effort.

Not many players took the build-up to the match very seriously but most are in the middle of domestic or international series, so one more net session would not make much difference. England's Darren Gough went for a bowl but he has not turned his arm over for 10 weeks.

As captain of the ICC XI, I spoke to the players beforehand but I kept my team talk short: 'Let's make sure we do the right thing and make this a proper contest.'

* not out

I said that because I wanted to make sure the match did not degenerate into a knockabout occasion. A massive crowd and television audience were predicted, and although the event was about raising money, I wanted to make sure it was fair dinkum, especially as the game has been given official one-day international status.

That was a controversial move, because it was not a match between sides already holding full member status within the ICC, but I agree with it for commercial and cricketing reasons. Sponsors may not have been as inclined to be involved in a game without any cricketing meaning.

I need not have worried about the approach of players, because once the match started the competitive juices started flowing; players take pride in their own performance and the chance to shine alongside contemporaries is another great incentive.

I know the question marks over the match's official status resurfaced when Glenn McGrath came in at number six, ahead of Stephen Fleming and Matthew Hayden, but that was a decision that was initially taken while I was in the middle. Adam Gilchrist ran a drink out to me and asked, 'Can we pad McGrath up to face Murali?' and I agreed as long as he did not waste time trying to build an innings while quality players were kicking their heels in the dressing room.

I need not have worried. I was back in the dressing room when McGrath was out, first ball sweeping at Murali, and I predicted what would happen when he walked in: 'He'll throw his helmet down, then the bat, and curse yet another low score.' Sure enough he did, and that left everyone not used to his antics trying to hide their heads under towels so he could not see them laughing.

The overseas players on my side all lapped up the atmosphere as the crowd had a really different feel from normal. Every player, no matter where he was from, got a great reception and when Chris Cairns walked into bat he said to me, 'That's the first time I've ever got a cheer at the MCG. Am I at the right ground?'

My highlight was batting at the other end from Cairns and Brian Lara. When I have come up against Cairns I've found myself resenting his powerful hitting, but today I was awestruck. I thought I hit the ball pretty well but he managed to mishit sixes from high on the bat and the distance he hit the ball was remarkable.

Batting with Lara was a different matter. He is amazingly quick on his feet and I took the chance to try to get inside his mind to find out how he plays spin bowling — useful information when we face him later this summer. Against India's leg-spinner Anil Kumble, I asked where he looked to hit him. 'Always wide of mid-off or over cover,' said Lara.

When he carried out his plan I made a mental note to place mid-off wider than usual when Brad Hogg bowls to him in the VB Series.

When Lara hit a good shot and we met mid-pitch he tried to punch gloves with me and at first I resisted. We find that act — the 'shazam' as we call it in the Australian dressing room — pretty daft because we think it is just showing off for the sake of it when all you have done as a batsman is your job, which is to hit a four or six. I pretended I did not see his move towards me with his glove when he tried it at first, but eventually I realised it would look rude if I ignored him any longer, so I did punch gloves with him. Matthew Hayden told me afterwards that all the Australians in the dressing room picked up on it and laughed, and he promised not to let me forget it.

Shane Warne lapped up the chance to play another one-day international two years after his last appearance, and although we did not discuss it afterwards, I think he would love to come out of retirement in this form of the game, especially after the way he signed off in 2003 when a drugs ban ended his World Cup. The problem remains that he does not want to make himself available again only for the selectors to snub him in favour of someone else, and I am not sure how we get over that hurdle. While we are successful in one-day cricket I guess it will not be an issue.

Wednesday 12 January

Tour match, Adelaide: The Pakistanis 8–279 (Razzaq 89*, Mohammad 61) beat Australia A 266 (Haddin 129) by 13 runs.

Thursday 13 January

Twenty20 tour match, Adelaide: Australia A 5–185 (White 58, D Hussey 50) beat the Pakistanis 7–129 by 56 runs.

Friday 14 January

VB Series, Melbourne, match 1: Australia (6 points) 4–301 (Martyn 95*, Ponting 78, Clarke 66) beat West Indies (0 points) 185 (Lara 58, Hogg 5–32) by 116 runs.

This was a crushing win but we still have scope to get better. Our fielding is still below par, with a couple of dropped catches including one by me at slip off Michael Kasprowicz. The ball burst through my hands when I should have clung on. But apart from that, and a low chance grassed by Adam Gilchrist, we looked very impressive.

In the past we have started one-day series at home poorly because we have tried to make the change from Tests to one-day cricket too quickly, especially with the bat. I told the players that although the pace of one-day cricket may be quicker there are still 300 balls to face, so we do not have to go mad trying to hit every ball for four. We are good enough players to score at a decent rate without taking too many risks, and we showed that today.

Michael Clarke opened the batting in place of Matthew Hayden, who has been given the first two matches of the series off, and played superbly. It was a slow pitch and hard to time shots but he improvised brilliantly, using his feet to the quick bowlers and hitting over the infield. He is one reason why we are such a good one-day side, because he is so versatile, able to bat anywhere from one to seven either getting the innings off to a decent start or finishing things off.

Brett Lee bowled a rapid spell to show what we missed during the Tests this summer. He has been playing for Australia A and the way he bowled with such pace, rhythm and control shows the outings benefited him. He asked me for the first over of the innings, as he said he had taken a wicket in his previous four or five matches when he had that chance, and he did it again today with a rapid in-swinging yorker that trapped Chris Gayle lbw. Lee was desperate to show what he could do after sitting out the Test series, and although Tests and one-dayers are different forms of the game, he used this evening to remind the selectors that he is still around.

I was frustrated at my dismissal as I had a hundred for the taking before I was run out with 10 overs left. Our pre-match chat included mention that most of the West Indies squad had very poor throwing arms, but Shivnarine Chanderpaul managed to get his return right over the top of the stumps as I came back for a second run to fine leg. I gambled on the run, having lost sight of the ball and the fielder behind Damien Martyn, the non-striker, and lost.

Afterwards the West Indies players came into our dressing room for a drink and a chat. That sort of thing usually happens only after the last match but it may be smart thinking by their new coach, the former Queensland and Australian Cricket Academy coach Bennett King. He wants the West Indies players, some of them quite young, to realise that, although we are the best side in the world, we are also flesh and blood, and one way to do that is to have a drink and a chat with us.

Adam Gilchrist (left knee) and Jason Gillespie (right calf) are ruled out of Australia's next match, against Pakistan in Hobart. Brad Haddin is drafted in to replace Gilchrist.

VB Series, Hobart, match 2: Australia (5 points) 6–253 (Clarke 97) beat Pakistan (1 point) 7–272 (Inzamam 68, Butt 61, Afridi 56*) by 4 wickets (Duckworth-Lewis method).

Another good win but we still have things to work on, in this case our bowling in the final few overs of the innings. It is true that Shahid Afridi played some outrageous shots, including a six over cover point off Glenn McGrath from what appeared to be a yorker, but he has made a career of playing like that and, despite knowing the way he would play, we still failed to close him down.

We got home comfortably thanks to a calm innings from Darren Lehmann. After Michael Clarke gave us a flying start we were left wanting less than 5 runs per over, and I thought it was the perfect chance for Lehmann to go in and do what he does best in that sort of situation, to nurdle the ball into gaps and take control of the run chase. He came off with 49 not out, put his gear down, turned to me and said, 'Is that what you were after?'

Brad Haddin was also vital to our success with a run-a-ball 30 as he added 57 from 9 overs with Lehmann. Haddin made us laugh at warm-ups before play when he told us about the way he faced up to Shoaib Akhtar for Australia A. After Shoaib bowled a no-ball, the next delivery was a free hit, so Haddin went and stood behind the stumps. He said the late David Hookes had discussed the idea with him years ago when free hits were first suggested. 'I couldn't be dismissed bowled because it was a free hit,' said Haddin. 'If he bounced me it would give me more time to see the ball and hit it, and if he hit the stumps the ball might ricochet off for runs in any case.' It was innovative thinking — just what the game is all about.

Pakistan spinner Mohammad Hafeez is reported to the ICC for having a suspect bowling action.

VB Series, Brisbane, match 3: Pakistan (5 points) 4–274 (Akmal 124, Inzamam 62, Malik 60) beat West Indies (1 point) 5–273 (Gayle 82, Sarwan 76) by 6 wickets.

Jason Gillespie is passed fit to return to action after treatment on an injury to his right calf muscle.

VB Series, Brisbane, match 4: West Indies (3 points) 9–263 (W Hinds 107) v Australia (3 points) 5–43, match abandoned, rain.

The phrase 'we got out of jail' could have been invented for this match. We were heading for a thumping loss when we were saved by the rain. We were lucky and Brian Lara knew it too, as his frustration got the better of him when we came off the field for the first time after 5 overs of our innings.

That break happened when Kevin Mitchell junior, the curator, drove the covers onto the ground before the umpires called him on. Mitchell has a radar in his office and also knows the weather at The Gabba better than anyone else, so he knew rain was imminent.

The umpires took the players off but Lara was far from pleased that the curator had taken charge of the situation. 'That'll be right,' he shouted, 'always in Australia's favour here,' as he looked for match referee Chris Broad in the players' dressing room area. West Indies coach Bennett King, also a Brisbane local, calmed Lara down and 2 minutes later it was raining in any case.

Lara's mood may have been due to his dismissal. He has a reputation as a walker if he edges a catch, but when he swished at a wide Brett Lee ball and we all heard a loud nick, he stayed put and seemed very unhappy to be given out. I am not sure what else the noise could have been.

When the first rain break happened we were 2–12 but after a delay of 141 minutes we returned with our new target, 195 from 28 overs. It seemed a bit stiff to me and it got a whole lot stiffer when the ball began to swing in the humid conditions. I was lbw to a full-length inswinger and we were in tatters when the rain returned.

We bowled poorly again at the end of the innings but we felt 263 was a gettable target until we started losing wickets.

VB Series, Sydney, match 5: Australia (6 points) 1–167 (Clarke 103*) beat Pakistan (0 points) 163 (Inzamam 50) by 9 wickets.

We are back on track after Brisbane as Glenn McGrath bowled a superb spell, although I could not help thinking that Pakistan should have looked to be more positive against him. Their batsmen seemed content to survive, until Shahid Afridi played some shots late on, and it meant our eventual target was never going to test us.

Michael Clarke again got us away to a flying start and it soon became clear he could get a hundred if I played quietly at the other end, so I played out a couple of maidens to make sure he had the chance to get there. He enjoyed some amazing luck too. On 85 I thought he was out to a regulation catch at extra cover, but the fielder obviously thought the ball had not carried and just threw it back to the bowler. Then on 97 he was dropped at long-on, a simple catch at this level. But when the dust has settled all people will see in the scorebook is 103 not out to Clarke, and that is the most important fact of all.

Simon Katich is included in Australia's squad for the match against the West Indies at Adelaide Oval in place of Damien Martyn, who is rested.

Tour match, Canberra: The Pakistanis 5–192 (Khan 62*, Youhana 50) beat the Prime Minister's XI 191 by 5 wickets.

Shane Warne labels the pitch at Westpac Park, Hamilton, 'terrible' after captaining a World XI there in a one-day game against the New Zealanders. The World XI was bowled out for 81 and the home side replied with 6–83 in a match lasting just 37.1 overs. Australia is due to play a one-day international at the ground during its tour of New Zealand.

VB Series, Adelaide, match 6: Australia (6 points) 8–269 (Katich 76, Collins 5–43) beat West Indies (0 points) 196 (Chanderpaul 55) by 73 runs.

Another win for us and, in the end, a comfortable one, but once again our top order has misfired, myself included. We spoke about the need for players to put their hands up and take responsibility before play but we soon found ourselves at 4–38.

We were bailed out by Simon Katich, together with sensible batting from Brad Haddin, Brett Lee and Jason Gillespie. Katich is not always regarded as a one-day player but he is versatile because he can slot in anywhere in the order, and today he played superbly.

He summed up the situation and dug in but also kept the scoreboard ticking over by regularly hitting the gaps for singles to rotate the strike.

I thought the West Indies got their tactics all wrong all day. First, Brian Lara had Marlon Samuels, the occasional spinner, bowling with three or four attacking fielders, which created gaps for us to ease him around for runs when we should have been sweating on every run. Then, after Lee took two early wickets, one of them a screaming catch down the leg-side by Haddin, they tried to occupy the crease instead of counterattacking. It meant that when Lara came in the asking rate was already over 7 runs per over and that was too much to ask, even of him.

Friday 28 January

New Zealand Cricket opts to shift the one-day international against Australia in Hamilton, scheduled for 2 March, to another venue following criticism of the pitch.

VB Series, Adelaide, match 7: West Indies (5 points) 4–339 (Lara 156, Chanderpaul 85) beat Pakistan (1 point) 9–281 by 58 runs.

Sunday 30 January

Pakistan's Younis Khan flies home following the death of his father.

VB Series, Perth, match 8: Pakistan 7–268 (Youhana 72, Razzaq 63*) beat Australia 265 (Clarke 75*) by 3 wickets.

A disappointing loss but maybe an ideal wake-up call for us before the finals.

Once again no one in the top order went on to make a decent score and we failed to form meaningful partnerships. The 265 was still defendable but we did not bowl or field all that well either. We were maybe 5 to 10 per cent off the pace, and at this level you will get punished for that, as happened here.

Inzamam and Youhana played superbly after a rapid opening spell from Brett Lee, switching the momentum in Pakistan's favour by expertly working our spinners and medium-pacers into the gaps, and then Razzaq and Afridi played some big shots at the end to get their side over the line.

Michael Clarke played well again, this time at number six, but we have relied on him a bit too much for my liking. The result means that whichever of Pakistan or the West Indies wins Tuesday's final qualifier will face us in the final series. Both have better batting than bowling line-ups, but I would prefer to face the West Indies, because they are more of a one-man team through Brian Lara's batting than Pakistan, which has several players that can hurt us.

Monday 31 January

Michael Clarke wins the Allan Border Medal as Australia's cricketer of the year; Damien Martyn is named Test player of the year; Andrew Symonds picks up the one-day international award; Queensland's Andrew Bichel is state player of the year; Mark Cosgrove of South Australia is the young player of the year, and the woman's player of the year is Karen Rolton, also from South Australia.

Tonight's result, with Michael Clarke winning the Allan Border Medal, surprised me. He is a worthy winner and had a great 2004, but if there was any justice then the award should have gone to Damien Martyn.

It is not just that Martyn is my best mate. He came back from a poor run of form in spectacular fashion and scored six Test hundreds in the last calendar year. With form like that you wonder what else he has to do to win the Medal.

The voters — players, umpires and the media, polled after every match throughout the year — thought otherwise, and good luck to Clarke. I thought he had a chance of carrying off the one-day award but then everyone, myself included, forgot about Andrew Symonds and Michael Kasprowicz. Kasprowicz has been a model of consistency apart from his one over against New Zealand in Melbourne in December, while Symonds, although he has had a horror trot in the VB Series, was brilliant before that.

For the first time in a few years I knew I had no chance of an award. To win when you are up against the players in this Australian team, you have to have an outstanding year, and although I have done okay, my form could never be described as outstanding.

The switching of the Border Medal dinner to before rather than after the final series is one of a couple of innovations Cricket Australia has brought in this year in consultation with the players. It gives us a couple of extra days at home ahead of a tour that usually follows our domestic summer. This year has also seen a reduction in the number of matches in the VB Series. Our opponents expect us to play the same number of one-day matches as they play in Australia whenever we go on tour, so a reduction here should ease the pressure on us and make schedules less demanding when we tour in future.

Tuesday 1 February

VB Series, Perth, match 9: Pakistan (5 points) 8–307 (Youhana 105, Inzamam 74) beat West Indies 277 (Sarwan 87, Chanderpaul 58) by 30 runs.

Wednesday 2 February

Pakistan captain Inzamam-ul-Haq is fined 100 per cent of his match fee for his side's slow over rate in the match against the West Indies in Perth. As captain he is fined an additional 30 per cent and each of his players is fined 15 per cent of their match fees.

Friday 4 February

VB Series, Melbourne, first final: Australia 237 (Symonds 91, Martyn 53) beat Pakistan 219 (Malik 66, Inzamam 51) by 18 runs.

It was not a classic match and we did not play anywhere near our best, but when it comes to finals it is all about the result, and we managed to win a little more comfortably than the final margin might suggest.

After Brett Lee and Glenn McGrath bowled superbly with the new ball we were always in control, and although Malik and Afridi threatened briefly we maintained our discipline with the ball to dismiss them before they really threatened our total.

I had a tough task to announce the side to the players before the start, a side without Matthew Hayden. He has been part of the line-up for quite a while now so, as you might expect, the news hit him hard. I was in favour of retaining him despite his lean run of form because, although he only made 6 from 16 balls in Perth, I felt I spotted some good signs in his play: he left the ball well and stood tall, and defended back down the pitch rather than opening the face of the bat. The selectors disagreed and feel on current form that he is not in our best eleven in one-day cricket. Having said that, when I spoke to Trevor Hohns we both agreed this is not necessarily the end of Hayden as a one-day player. He is too good just to write off. I am hoping he will take this as a spur to bounce back because, at his best, he remains one of the best players in the world.

The foundations of our win were the innings of Damien Martyn and Andrew Symonds. Martyn showed again that he is a master at rotating the strike as he reached 50 without a single boundary, while Symonds's effort was great news after he struggled for form for most of the series. He played himself in carefully, kept the scoreboard ticking over and then played some big shots as the innings ended. The only downside was an injury he picked up to his Achilles. He has had it before and, as he is not one to usually make a fuss, I knew it was troubling him when he told me about it at the break between innings. Darren Lehmann's long-term absence last summer started with a similar niggle so I did not want Symonds to field at all. He said he was fine but bowled poorly and I think he is unlikely to play in the second final.

Sunday 6 February

VB Series, Sydney, second final: Australia 9–239 beat Pakistan 208 (Youhana 51, McGrath 5–27) by 31 runs and wins best-of-three finals series 2–0.

Not for the first time this summer the bowlers, specifically Brett Lee and Glenn McGrath, carried us to another victory. We again batted inconsistently on a painfully slow Sydney pitch and lost 3–20 in mid-innings at one point, a collapse that started when I flashed a wide ball straight to cover after taking time to play myself in.

Our final total should have been well within Pakistan's range, given its players are used to pitches of this pace back home, but McGrath and Lee again got us early wickets to increase the pressure on the batsmen and Lee also threw out Afridi from third man, just when he was threatening to take the game away from us.

The one downside of the match was another injury to poor Shane Watson, who cried his eyes out when I saw him in the dressing room. Two years ago he broke down with a fourth set of stress fractures in his back on the eve of the World Cup and today, after establishing himself in the Test and one-day squads, he tore a side muscle that is bound to rule him out of the New Zealand tour. All I could tell him was to fight back, although he has done that plenty of times already.

It is always a great feeling to win the finals series with a match to spare, because it gives us extra time to relax at home ahead of a tour and also a decent celebration, knowing we have that extra time to recover. Tonight was no different, with wives and partners joining us in the dressing room, and Rianna and I eventually staggered home at 3 a.m.

Overall I give our VB Series campaign a mark of 7/10. The bowlers were superb and deserve 9/10, while the fielding is worth 8 or 9/10, with Michael Clarke's direct hits from inside the circle a highlight. The batting rates only 5/10 as players failed to make big scores or produce big partnerships. We must improve, but the good thing for us and the bad news for the other sides is that we still won even without playing well.

Part 9:
Australia in New Zealand

Australia names a 14-man squad for the one-day series against New Zealand. It is: Ricky Ponting (captain), Michael Clarke, Adam Gilchrist (vice-captain), Jason Gillespie, Matthew Hayden, Brad Hogg, James Hopes, Michael Hussey, Michael Kasprowicz, Simon Katich, Brett Lee, Damien Martyn, Glenn McGrath, Andrew Symonds.

The big news from this squad is Darren Lehmann's absence. I fought in his corner but the selectors opted for Michael Hussey and Matthew Hayden instead. My support for him here might seem odd after I backed Simon Katich to replace him in the Test squad in November, but at that time my view was that he was not a member of our best Test line-up. Now I would love him in this one-day squad but there was not enough room and I accept that.

Lehmann's form has not been brilliant this summer but he is carrying a shoulder injury. He required cortisone injections to carry on and maybe this break will allow him to get that treated properly. Some will see his dropping as the end of his international career but I believe he has plenty to offer. It will be up to him to prove that with runs for South Australia.

Hayden has been retained on the basis that form is temporary but class is permanent. At his best he remains our strongest opener in both forms of the game but he will know he now needs to start delivering again.

Monday 14 February

James Hopes (tight hamstring) and Andrew Symonds (Achilles) are both passed fit to tour; Matthew Hayden, suffering from a chest infection, is rated a doubt.

Tuesday 15 February

Hayden is passed fit to tour.

Thursday 17 February

Twenty20 international, Auckland: Australia 5–214 (Ponting 98*) beat New Zealand 170 (Styris 66) by 44 runs.

* not out

We got the tour off to a successful start by winning the first-ever Twenty20 international, just 24 hours after flying into the country.

We had a definite advantage because most of our squad has played Twenty20 in the United Kingdom and only a couple of the NZ squad had experienced it, but we almost blew that advantage by losing the plot at the start of the match.

Like any innings you still need to get set before looking to blast the ball around — a lesson I learned from my one game for Somerset last year. Not all our top order realised that and we slipped to 4–54 before recovering.

I batted first, on the basis that it was better to set a target than chase one under constant pressure of a high asking rate, but I found it was fairly easy to score quickly because of the odd shape of the ground with short boundaries square of the wicket.

The game may have been portrayed as light-hearted, with both sides wearing 1980s-style one-day outfits and the New Zealanders replicating that era's fashion in facial hair, but it was hard cricket out in the middle and I was pleased to be able to score some points off a couple of the opposition. Daryl Tuffey conceded four sixes in his last over and he will remember that when he faces us next time.

With just 75 minutes to bowl 20 overs, the whole match flashes by, so it is tough for a captain to try to do anything on the field to influence the game. We won because of our bowlers' tactics of never bowling the same ball twice in a row. If a bowler tries to bowl nothing but yorkers, for example, a batsman can set himself accordingly. But if the bowler mixes things up — bouncer, yorker, slower ball, good length delivery and so on — the batsman loses that advantage. It worked for us with Michael Kasprowicz bowling beautifully.

The match ended with a laugh as Glenn McGrath shaped to repeat the infamous underarm ball delivered by Trevor Chappell to Brian McKechnie of New Zealand in Melbourne more than 20 years ago. We were winning easily so he asked me at the start of the over if he could bowl the last ball underarm and I said 'No', not wanting a diplomatic incident. He asked again before the fifth ball of the over and again I said 'No', but ahead of the last ball we agreed he could at least shape to do it and we told umpire Billy Bowden, so he helped make the whole thing into a joke, which was the intention. I am glad McGrath did not go through with it as, after an entertaining day of cricket, it would have been an insult given all the bad blood between our two countries that flowed following the original incident.

There was a full house for the match and the concept has taken off so well in the United Kingdom that I was asked afterwards whether Twenty20 should be played more often in future. I think so, but I am not sure international cricket is the right place for it. The need to score quickly can easily produce slogging — not ideal when you have the best players in the world on view — and I think the lower the level it is played at, the more entertaining it will be because that way there is less riding on the result. If the statistics counted towards players' international careers, the cricket might be a lot less carefree. Most of all I think too much Twenty20 could destroy the other forms of the game rather than promote them, as people will want that instant hit ahead of the subtleties of the longer games. Too much Twenty20 may even cause it to lose its appeal, because at the moment a lot of its fun is its novelty value.

Saturday 19 February

First one-day international, Westpac Stadium, Wellington: Australia 7–236 (Hayden 71, Ponting 61, Symonds 53) beat New Zealand 226 (H Marshall 76, Astle 65) by 10 runs.

We won but this match should be remembered for the crowd trouble that marred it. While we were in the field the behaviour of some spectators was disgraceful, and the action — or lack of it — by at least one steward was not much better.

The crowd were throwing plastic bottles and fruit at Glenn McGrath on the boundary, and when he cleared them off the playing area the steward just threw the items back to the crowd so they could have another go. McGrath got upset and shouted at the steward, who got fired up himself, and at one stage I saw McGrath racing around the boundary chasing after the steward to tell him exactly what he thought of him. That was no good to us because it left him out of position and he missed a catch.

On another occasion I saw Simon Katich at long-off clearing bottles off the ground while Brett Lee was running in to bowl. Some of the bottles thrown during the evening were at least half full and it just needed one player near the fence to turn round at the wrong time for some serious damage to be done.

Abuse when we travel abroad is an accepted part of life for us on tour as home supporters back their team, but we should not have to put up with things being thrown at us. The answers seem simple: people should only be allowed to drink out of plastic or paper cups, not bottles, and stewards should be more proactive and also have police back-up to stop the antics we saw tonight.

We won thanks to McGrath and Lee, who repeated their heroics from the VB Series. They just had enough runs to bowl at on a painfully slow surface after Matthew Hayden returned to form.

Tuesday 22 February

Second one-day international, Christchurch: Australia 6–314 (Hayden 114, Martyn 58, Ponting 53) beat New Zealand 208 (Vettori 83) by 106 runs.

This was our best one-day performance of the summer so far but it came at a price when Matthew Hayden, fresh from a superb hundred, went over on his right shoulder as he took a catch on the boundary.

Hayden said he heard a crack as soon as he landed and went off straightaway to get it assessed by physiotherapist Alex Kontouri. Hayden is very worried, but it was not a dislocation, and we will have to wait and see how serious the problem is.

At last most of our top order made significant scores, and I was among them before Hayden ran me out, calling me for a nonexistent run to backward point. I was less than a metre out at the striker's end but knew I was gone.

We got late impetus from Mike Hussey. He came in and did exactly what Michael Bevan made a career out of: rotating the strike, finding the gaps in the field, running well between the wickets and hitting boundaries late on in the innings. Hussey looks like he was born to play at this level.

The crowd was better behaved today after the problems in Wellington, but Simon Katich at deep square leg still copped several bottles. At least the stewards appeared to be trying to stop the trouble this time.

Saturday 26 February

Third one-day international, Auckland: Australia 5–264 (Clarke 71*, Hussey 65*, Katich 58) beat New Zealand 178 (H Marshall 55).

This was a comfortable win to seal the series, although there were elements of controversy on and off the pitch.

On the field Brett Lee beamed Brendon McCullum late on, causing a fair amount of interest among the media after the match. There was even a suggestion that Lee may have done it deliberately, but that is rubbish. Anyone who knows Lee knows he does not have a nasty bone in his body, but there are other elements in his defence too. He is battling to regain a permanent spot in the side and the only thing a deliberate beamer would do is jeopardise that — something he knows better than anyone. Also, a deliberate beamer at that stage of the match was pointless as we already had the game under lock and key, so there was no need to try and shake McCullum up. On top of that, there was heavy dew that made gripping the ball and maintaining a solid footing as Lee bowled very tricky. It all contributed to the mistake. If I thought Lee had done something like that deliberately I would come down on him hard, and I would expect the authorities to do the same, but any suggestion of that is just nonsense.

Earlier, Lee was too quick for opener Michael Papps, who was struck twice by bouncers. The first one glanced off his shoulder and helmet grille but the second hit him full on the left temple before he moved. I ran up from slip to talk to him but got no response, and when he took his helmet off there was a huge lump near his eye. Lee is clearly rattling the New Zealand batsmen and on this form must play in the first Test.

There was also controversy involving me during the day. As I waited to bat I flicked through the official New Zealand Cricket tour magazine, found an article about me and was shocked to read a paragraph that included: '... isn't this the same bloke who was embroiled in the bookmaker scandal which blew up in 1998?' I had no involvement in any such thing and I quickly showed it to team manager Steve Bernard and media manager Jonathan Rose. They got in touch with New Zealand Cricket, faxed a copy of the article to Cricket Australia and I will expect an apology at the very least. In the modern game, accusing a player of involvement in match-fixing is just about the lowest thing you can do and for that to appear in an official publication is a shocker.

I was run out again, this time by Simon Katich, who ignored my call for a single, and by the end of the night I felt a sharp pain in my right hip. Alex Kontouri was straight to work after my post-match media interviews.

Fourth one-day international, Basin Reserve, Wellington: Australia 3–236 (Martyn 65*, Gilchrist 53) beat New Zealand 233 by 7 wickets.

If there had been another day between the match in Auckland and this one — or even if the series was still alive — I could have played, but with plenty of cricket left on the trip I opted to rest my injury and make sure I am 100 per cent right.

Matthew Hayden was also still absent, and although Alex Kontouri says he is improving, he is still not fit enough to play again. I take the same approach with him as I do with myself: there is no point in rushing him back unless he is completely healed, and his priority must be the first Test.

Neither of us was missed as we cruised to victory with almost 16 overs to spare. We do not want New Zealand to win a match in this series and we also want to put an end to any chat in the media about us easing up in dead-rubber matches.

Brett Lee played as the controversy over his beamer to McCullum rumbled on. Even the match referee, Clive Lloyd, came out in his defence but that has not stopped New Zealand coach John Bracewell from keeping the subject in the public domain. I am glad we did not rest Lee, as that would have been seen as an admission that he had done something wrong the other evening. He made a mistake and is bitterly embarrassed by it, and I hope that is the end of the matter.

Australia names a 13-man squad for the three-match Test series against New Zealand. It is: Ricky Ponting (captain), Michael Clarke, Adam Gilchrist (vice-captain), Jason Gillespie, Matthew Hayden, Brad Hodge, Michael Kasprowicz, Simon Katich, Justin Langer, Brett Lee, Damien Martyn, Glenn McGrath, Shane Warne.

New Zealand names a 12-man squad for the first Test in Christchurch. It is: Stephen Fleming (captain), Nathan Astle, Craig Cumming, James Franklin, Hamish Marshall, Chris Martin, Brendon McCullum, Craig McMillan, Iain O'Brien, Daniel Vettori, Lou Vincent, Paul Wiseman.

Michael Hussey is added to the Test squad as cover as Matthew Hayden continues to recover from his shoulder injury.

Fifth one-day international, Napier: Australia 5–347 (Ponting 141*, Gilchrist 91) beat New Zealand 8–225 (McMillan 63) by 122 runs.

We put down a marker for the Test series to come with another comprehensive win that completed the whitewash.

The match marked the falling into place of a few elements that were missing in the earlier matches. I managed to make a decent score that I felt my form warranted and Adam Gilchrist, who was scratchy at the start of this series, flayed the bowling and made 91 before he was out with more than 30 overs of the innings left.

I did what I had to do: hit the bad balls for four early in the innings, keep the scoreboard ticking over through the middle overs, then exploded to find the boundary late on. My last 41 runs came from just 17 balls — exactly what should happen when you have a player in at the end who is adjusted to conditions. When I smacked the last ball for six it meant I walked off with a spring in my step while New Zealand trailed off looking beaten already.

We did not ease up in the field either. Brett Lee bowled at 160 kph and underlined why he must play in the first Test, while, not to be outdone, Michael Kasprowicz hit the bat really hard and was on a hat-trick at one stage.

It was a performance and a series that deserved to be celebrated and we certainly did that with a few drinks in the dressing room and a few more back at the hotel. I headed for bed at 1.30 a.m. but there were plenty who stayed later than me.

First Test, Christchurch, day 1: New Zealand 3–265 (Marshall 103*, Cumming 74) v Australia.

There were a few occasions today, as New Zealand made relatively comfortable progress, when I wished Brett Lee was playing.

I pushed for him with the selectors, and even dropped a hint in the media, but the selectors opted to retain the attack that has served us so well for most of the summer instead. They reasoned that it would set a bad precedent if they dropped players who were doing all that was asked of them, as the attack of McGrath, Kasprowicz, Gillespie and Warne has been doing almost nonstop ever since it was reunited against Sri Lanka in July.

I understand that, but my argument was that Lee is bowling well and quickly, and clearly has the edge over several New Zealand batsmen, and if I was one of them and saw our line-up without Lee in it, I would be relieved on current form. Those players who say they enjoy facing a bowler of Lee's pace when he is on song are lying. No one enjoys it, but some players can cope better than others.

Given that I went into bat for Lee so hard with the selectors, I made sure it was a selector — in this case, Allan Border, who is with the squad during this Test — and not me, who told Lee he was not playing. But although I disagreed with the decision, that does not mean I have any less faith in the four bowlers selected. All four can do a job but it was just our misfortune that none of them clicked today, as it highlighted Lee's absence.

The pitch did less than I expected when I put New Zealand in and whenever we found the edge we dropped the chances. Justin Langer and Shane Warne both grassed simple slip catches and, although they did not cost us many runs, they did cost us momentum. And to add to our woes Glenn McGrath started to complain of a muscle problem near his stomach in the last session.

Friday 11 March

First Test, Christchurch, day 2: Australia 3–141 trail New Zealand 433 (Marshall 146, Cumming 74, Astle 74, McGrath 6–115) by 292 runs.

We are back in this Test thanks to Glenn McGrath. He defied his stomach muscle injury to produce a superb spell of reverse-swing bowling either side of lunch.

Most bowlers only get reverse swing back into the right-hander but McGrath, helped by his great wrist position behind the ball that ensures the seam goes down the pitch perfectly upright, can swing it in either direction. That means the batsman is left guessing about the direction of the swing and today six New Zealand batsmen guessed wrong.

It was an improved display from all our bowlers but our top order failed to build on that recovery. Matthew Hayden, who is clearly not fully fit, and Justin Langer both got out to disappointing shots when set, and Damien Martyn was unluckily given out lbw just before the close even though he clearly edged the ball onto his pads. I heard the nick from the non-striker's end but umpire David Shepherd did not. When his colleague at square leg, Aleem Dar, confirmed the edge, Shepherd's response could not be printed.

Hayden had one let-off before he was eventually out, thanks to New Zealand's continuing refusal to agree that batsmen should accept the word of fielders on low catches. He pulled a short ball to square leg where Craig Cumming appeared to pull off a brilliant low catch. He thought he caught it but Hayden was not so sure and, without that agreement in place, he stayed put. Replays were inconclusive and Hayden survived.

First Test, Christchurch, day 3: New Zealand 433 and 0–9 lead Australia 432 (Gilchrist 121, Katich 118, Vettori 5–106) by 10 runs.

From our position before lunch, where we needed 33 runs to avoid the follow-on with only 4 wickets in hand, we are back on level terms thanks to two superb hundreds.

I have run out of superlatives for Adam Gilchrist, who played on pure instinct. If he thinks the ball is there to be hit for four or six he does it, and he makes the game look ridiculously simple when he is in this sort of form.

He targeted Daniel Vettori, and even though there were three men on the leg-side boundary, he still kept hitting the ball over them for six. Gilchrist's strength is his total commitment to every shot he plays and, although Vettori beat him in flight at least once that I can remember, rather than bail out of the shot — as most of us would have done — Gilchrist went through with the shot and hit the ball for six.

At the other end was Simon Katich. This was the best I have seen him play, better even than his innings against India in Sydney last year. He seemed to hit everything in the middle of the bat and between them they added 212, at better than 4 runs an over, to get us right back into the Test.

The ball is very much back in New Zealand's court. We know they will think they need at least three sessions to bowl us out and win the Test, but that leaves them with just a day to set us a target with the knowledge that we can score at 4 an over in the backs of their minds. It will be interesting to see how they respond to the pressure of setting the pace.

New Zealand names an unchanged 12-man squad for the second Test. All-rounders Jacob Oram (back) and Scott Styris (knee) are both ruled out for the rest of the series.

First Test, Christchurch, day 4: Australia 432 and 1–135 (Langer 72*) beat New Zealand 433 and 131 (Warne 5–39) by 9 wickets.

We got our answer today about New Zealand's ability to respond to our challenge. We applied the blowtorch and they crumpled in a heap, thanks in large measure to astute work by our coach, John Buchanan, backed up by the bowlers.

Buchanan said after day 3 that with the pitch lacking pace and bounce we should alter our line of attack, forget looking for catches behind the wicket and instead look to bowl full and straight and attack the stumps. The bowlers did that and we got 7 wickets lbw and 2 wickets bowled.

New Zealand did not really know how to approach today's play — whether to go hard in search of quick runs or look for a cautious safety-first approach. Craig McMillan summed it up by trying to kick away two full-tosses from Shane Warne then attempting an attacking shot against the spin as Warne pitched the next ball in the footmarks, succeeding only in giving a catch to short leg. It was poor cricket.

Warne took his 1000th first-class wicket but the pitch was still a good one, and we knocked off the runs easily before a relaxed celebration. We were joined by former team-mate Michael Slater, in New Zealand working for television, and he joined in when we sang the team song in the dressing room. It was nice for us to share the victory with him, as his Test career ended abruptly without any of us getting a chance to say thanks for all the times we shared as team-mates.

Second Test, Basin Reserve, Wellington, day 1: no play, rain.

The fog and low cloud hanging around Wellington for the past few days was frustrating in one sense today, but in another it was a welcome respite after a frantic run-up to the match.

The Pura Cup final started in Brisbane today, and with us set to retain an unchanged bowling line-up there was a growing lobby of opinion in favour of Brett Lee flying back to link up with his NSW team-mates to play in the game.

I cannot remember the last time Lee played a first-class game and I was all in favour of the move, but gradually everyone realised that the reality was harder than the theory.

We needed him here until the start of the match in case one of the starting eleven got injured. There was a private offer to provide a jet to fly him out of Wellington as soon as the Test got under way, but that still meant he would miss most of the first day at The Gabba, and in the end New South Wales thought it was too much of a risk to have to compete with ten players for that amount of time. The rain today, which would have stopped him going in any case, was the final irony.

Lee put a brave face on it but he is tearing his hair out. He is in the form of his life, but so are the other bowlers.

Saturday 19 March

Second Test, Basin Reserve, Wellington, day 2: Australia 5–337 (Martyn 106*, Hayden 61) v New Zealand.

The best way to win a shortened game is to make a big enough score quickly enough so you only have to bat once, and we have gone a long way towards that.

New Zealand put us into bat and that was the right decision, as the ball moved all over the place in the first session. But Stephen Fleming dropped Justin Langer on nought, Langer and Matthew Hayden did a great job, then Damien Martyn, Simon Katich and Adam Gilchrist cashed in during the last session as they added 163 as the bowlers tired.

Martyn and Gilchrist both had some luck against the second new ball as they edged James Franklin through the slips, but because they were blazing the ball about there were no attacking fielders there to take those chances. Fleming got that wrong: you take the new ball to take wickets, so you should support the bowlers with attacking fielders. But with the batsmen attacking he opted for caution and paid the price.

Martyn's hundred is a lesson to all players about how to remain patient even when the going is tough. He was on 24 at tea and said to me that he did not know where his next run was coming from. I told him to hang in there, as there was no way New Zealand could continue to bowl so well at him for ever. He did and he got his reward.

Second Test, Basin Reserve, Wellington, day 3: New Zealand 4–122 trail
Australia 8–570 declared (Martyn 165, Gilchrist 162, Hayden 61, Warne 50*) by 448 runs.

Today made everyone wonder why we bother getting to the ground 90 minutes before play to warm up, as Adam Gilchrist turned up 15 minutes before the start and blazed a brilliant hundred.

The reason he, together with several other players, was late was down to miscommunication with the officials at the ground. It was another foggy, drizzly morning when we were due to leave at 8.30 and at that point we were told to meet again in the hotel lobby at 9 o'clock. When we did, team manager Steve Bernard told us he had been informed there was no chance of play before lunch and we should assemble again at noon. But soon after that the drizzle stopped, the fog lifted and at 10.30 Bernard received a call that play would start in an hour. He started making frantic calls to players' rooms and Gilchrist, one of the not-out batsmen, was tracked down in the hotel pool where he was playing with his son Harrison. Gilchrist dried off, got dressed, jumped in a team minibus and walked into the dressing room at 11.15. He just had time to get his gear on when the 5-minute bell went.

For some players the lack of a warm-up would have been a problem. I have known players who do not feel relaxed on a batting day unless they have hit hundreds of balls in the nets beforehand. Gilchrist is different, as he has no set routine, so he was quite relaxed as he walked out and it showed as he and Martyn added 90 in the hour before lunch.

By mid-afternoon I felt we had enough runs to ensure that we only needed to bat once, so I declared and the bowlers got to work. Everyone performed impressively and New Zealand is already in deep trouble.

That was not the last action of the day as we had a meeting with Australian Cricketers' Association Chief Executive Tim May when we got back to the hotel. May has flown in to brief us on the latest developments concerning the negotiations of our Memorandum of Understanding with Cricket Australia (CA). In the recent past players have been paid 25 per cent of Australian Cricket Revenue but this time CA do not want to give us that much.

The gap between the two sides is about $3.2 million, which CA says it wants to plough into grassroots cricket, while we feel the money should be due to all players, state and international, in keeping with the 25 per cent figure of the previous deal.

The new agreement must be signed by 30 June and the players' only leverage is not to agree to CA's proposals, fall out of contract, then sign personal sponsorship deals with companies in direct competition with CA's sponsors. We cannot do that while under contract to CA but there would be nothing to stop us if no MoU was in place.

CA is aware of that and we, as players, do not want to resort to it, so there is a will on both sides to find a settlement. It is just a case of finding some common ground.

The evening still had its funny side. The Pura Cup final reached its climax in Brisbane, and before the meeting started Queensland's Michael Kasprowicz was in the corner of the room listening the commentary on his mobile phone as his wife held her phone next to the radio at home. Then, during the meeting, New South Wales captain Simon Katich got a call and went outside to take it. We all heard him say, 'No? Really? YOU BEAUTY!' and we knew which side had won.

Monday 21 March – Tuesday 22 March

Second Test, Basin Reserve, Wellington, days 4 and 5: Australia 8–570 declared drew with New Zealand 244 and 3–48.

We did all we could to win this game but in the end we were beaten by the return of the rain and fog, as we managed just 58.3 overs during the past two days.

It would have been easy for the bowlers to try too hard, knowing bad weather was around, but they bowled beautifully and managed 9 wickets in the time we had. We would have won easily if we had played throughout yesterday and today.

An example of that superb bowling was the way Glenn McGrath worked over Stephen Fleming this morning. McGrath had already dismissed him twice lbw in the series so the suspicion was that he would try to pitch the ball up. Instead he asked me to drop square leg back 10 yards and he then banged the first three balls in short. Before each ball I was expecting a fuller-length ball but it did not come; then, fourth ball, having driven Fleming onto the back foot, the full ball came along and he was trapped lbw again.

The other bright spot was Michael Kasprowicz's 100th Test wicket, which came when he bowled Lou Vincent just before the final stoppage for rain. Everyone knew he needed one for the landmark, and when the wicket came you would have thought each of us had taken 100 wickets, the way players were leaping about. Everyone knows how hard Kasprowicz has worked to get back into the side and the way everyone enjoyed his success it is another example of the fantastic team spirit in this side.

Third Test, Auckland, day 1: New Zealand 5–199 (H Marshall 76, Fleming 65) v Australia.

New Zealand's safety-first approach has cost them dearly already. Stephen Fleming and Hamish Marshall opted for survival rather than aggression, and that was okay as long as they both went on to make big scores; when they did not, it meant they had not hurt us and, although we did not take a wicket for more than 50 overs at one stage, we are still in control.

Marshall's dismissal was the strangest aspect of the day's play. I caught him at silly point off a thick inside edge onto the pad and appealed for the catch along with the bowler Shane Warne and Adam Gilchrist. Simon Katich at short leg and Matthew Hayden at slip were equally convinced Marshall did not hit it and went up for the lbw appeal. Umpire Jeremy Lloyds gave the batsman out and Gilchrist saw him indicate lbw to the scorers, but then the scoreboard listed Marshall as caught. To add to the confusion Lloyds then changed his decision to caught after play, presumably after he saw a replay. I do not like that as it sets a bad precedent. What happens if the last batsman is given out, we get back to the dressing room and then the umpire realises he is wrong? Do we all have to go back out? The umpire made a mistake here and, as human error is all part and parcel of the game, we should accept it and carry on as we always have in the past.

Third Test, Auckland, day 2: Australia 4–219 (Ponting 105) trail New Zealand 292 (H Marshall 76, Fleming 65) by 73 runs.

Today was satisfying and frustrating in equal measure. Satisfying because I played really well to get a Test hundred; frustrating because I got out in a soft way and my dismissal has left the game on an even keel.

I was able to score freely because New Zealand's bowlers lacked discipline against me. The fast bowlers' plan was to frustrate me by bowling full and wide outside the off-stump, trying to tempt me into a rash shot, but they served up a regular diet of half-volleys and also dropped short, easy pickings on such a slow pitch.

I drove well through mid-on and down the ground, always a sign that I am well balanced and playing well. But just when I had the bowlers at my mercy I was strangled out — cricket slang for a lucky wicket for the bowler, in this case Nathan Astle.

His plan was to bowl wide of off-stump and he brought his midwicket fielder over to cover to reinforce the offside. Next ball he slipped the ball down the leg-side by mistake, but instead of working the ball for runs I glanced it off the face of the bat straight into the wicketkeeper's gloves.

My dismissal, together with Damien Martyn's just before the close of play, means we still need two decent partnerships from here to be in command and that will be hard work on a pitch where it is not easy to score if the bowling is disciplined.

Monday 28 March

Third Test, Auckland, day 3: New Zealand 292 and 2–11 trail Australia 383 (Ponting 105, Gilchrist 60*, Franklin 6–119) by 80 runs.

Despite at least six interruptions for rain and bad light, we are in a great position thanks to some excellent batting from Simon Katich, Jason Gillespie, Adam Gilchrist and Michael Kasprowicz, and then two late wickets when we bowled a second time.

Gilchrist was once again the key figure as he and Kasprowicz regained the initiative just when New Zealand thought it was back in the game. Gilchrist had plenty of luck at first, as he began by looking like a player who had never batted before as ball after ball came off the edge. But he is that sort of player — someone who gives you a chance to dismiss him. If you do not take that chance he will hurt you, and he hurt New Zealand today as he made his runs from only 62 balls and added 74 with Kasprowicz.

Our lead of 91 looks like it's worth a lot more thanks to two late wickets from Glenn McGrath.

Third Test, Auckland, day 4: Australia 383 and 1–166 (Ponting 86*, Langer 59*) beat New Zealand 292 and 254 (Astle 69, Vettori 65) by 9 wickets.

Both sides got what they deserved today: we won the series and New Zealand got nothing.

It may sound harsh but New Zealand's tactics left a bad taste in my mouth. After we dismissed them in mid-afternoon we decided to push for a win in four days, as we knew that with bad weather around there was a chance we could be robbed by rain if we let the match drift into a fifth day. New Zealand's response was not to take the game to us and try to exploit our cavalier approach; they tried to slow the game down in the hope of getting out of the match with a draw thanks to rain, and one of their young players even shouted to me, 'It might rain all day tomorrow.'

That approach made no sense. A draw was no good to New Zealand as they would still have lost the series. Their young players will learn nothing if they are asked to play in such a negative way.

Our win was the cue for a great evening in the dressing room. With no cricket for a couple of months, pizzas were ordered, the New Zealanders came in for a drink and a chat, and any bitterness I felt about their approach on the field dissolved over a few beers. It was great to see the two sides mixing as I chatted with Brendon McCullum, Stephen Fleming and Shane Warne got together, Hamish and James Marshall shared a drink with Michael Clarke, and young fast bowler Iain O'Brien picked the brains of Michael Kasprowicz.

I had just one thing to say to the players before they relaxed too much: 'Enjoy tonight, enjoy your break, but make sure you come back in the best physical condition of your life at the start of the United Kingdom tour because I want to hit the ground running.' Hopefully the message got through before the beer and pizza took over.

My build-up to the tour has been a mix of work with Rianna, training and relaxation.

After getting back from New Zealand I had a short break from hard physical training, and I used that time to help Rianna organise two major fundraising events in support of the Children's Cancer Institute, a charity we both support.

The functions, called Cricket Rocks, took place in Melbourne and Sydney in the last week of May, and each one saw more than 600 people attending. The guests were treated to top-class entertainment from Australian music stars including Vanessa Amorosi and Diesel, there were auctions of sporting memorabilia, and players including Mark Waugh, Glenn McGrath, Michael Kasprowicz, Michael Clarke, Brett Lee and Adam Gilchrist all took the time to be there. Between them, the two events raised $415 000.

Ahead of the dinners we managed to get away for a short holiday in Spain before moving on to Portugal for the Laureus Sports Awards, a star-studded event that is patronised not only by top sports stars of the past and present — including former Olympians Edwin Moses, Michael Johnson and Sebastian Coe, tennis champion Boris Becker and England cricketer Ian Botham, to name a few — but also a host of movie stars, including Sean Connery.

The awards are designed to celebrate sporting excellence across the globe while, at the same time, the Laureus Sport for Good Foundation looks to use sport to highlight and tackle pressing social issues. For example, Botham visited Sri Lanka to assist in the relief effort following the tsunami last December.

In the past the Australian side has won the team of the year award, but this time we were not even nominated. Shane Warne received a nomination for comeback of the year for his successful return to the Test side after his drugs ban, but he was beaten by racing driver Alessandro Zanardi. As Zanardi returned to the sport after losing both legs in a horrific accident, I am sure Warne did not feel too hard done by losing out to that sort of bravery.

For the final month before we departed for the United Kingdom, I worked with Cricket Australia's fitness trainer, Jock Campbell, on what he called Project Ponting. Campbell felt I could and should improve my general fitness, power and speed, but with regular cricket year after year it was not possible to combine playing commitments with an intense physical program — it would have left me too drained to play. Now, with a two-month break between series (our longest gap for five years), Campbell felt this was the perfect time to put his plan into operation.

Campbell trained me 6 days a week, with ten sessions each week, and by the end of that program I think I am as fit as I have ever been. This was my program:

Monday
- Anaerobic interval work — this involved cricket-specific movements, for example, practising running between the wickets, an act that combines power and speed over short distances.
- Resistance training — weights working my arms and shoulders.
- Core stability work — ensuring that my abdominal muscles are strong enough to support my frame.
- Flexibility session — stretches to ensure I am as supple as I can be.

Tuesday
- Sand-hill sessions — 60 minutes of running up and down sand hills to improve aerobic fitness, specific leg strength and power, and to help reduce body fat through the high calorific energy cost.

Wednesday
- Resistance training.
- 45 minutes of cardiovascular work such as running or biking to build stamina and endurance.
- Core stability work.
- Flexibility session.

Thursday
- Speed work and flexibility session.

Friday
- Cardiovascular interval training for 60–90 minutes — this might involve running or biking for short, intense periods with small breaks in between those periods to increase both stamina and speed.
- Resistance training.
- Core stability work.
- Flexibility session.

Saturday
- Optional sand-hill session or a 60–90 minute walk.

Sunday
Rest.

I was joined for many of the sessions by the other Sydney-based members of the tour squad — Brad Haddin, Brett Lee, Glenn McGrath and Michael Clarke — as well as Campbell, and all of us improved our condition significantly. Those improvements should make us less susceptible to injury caused by lack of fitness and also, hopefully, make us that bit sharper whether we are batting or fielding at the end of a long day.

Fitness was all I worked on during this period; cricket practice could wait until I got to Brisbane for the pre-tour camp in the final week of May.

Part 10:
Australia in the UK

We arrived in Brisbane today for our pre-tour camp ahead of the Ashes series and, although it is a cliché, you could sense the feeling of excitement in everyone — players, support staff, the media, even the hotel staff at the Quay West, where we are staying.

We have had a decent break since the end of the New Zealand series, and everyone is keen to get back into action; that keenness is only heightened by the fact that we are looking forward to a 3-month stay in the United Kingdom. Even though Australia has held The Ashes since 1989, this series is still the biggest one for all the players (no disrespect to India, which have been our closest rival over the past 4 years). Australia against England is the oldest contest in the game at international level, and we have all been brought up on the traditions that flow from that, so to join the long list of players who have built that tradition is a dream come true for everyone who has been lucky enough to be selected. This is my third Ashes tour, but that does not dull the excitement — and now I have the added bonus of being captain. That obviously brings pressure and responsibility, but they are not things I am focusing on. My aim is simple: to perform to the best of my ability as a leader and a player. If everyone has that outlook, the results and our enjoyment of the tour should look after themselves.

The purpose of the camp is part administrative — handing out tour clothing and equipment, as well as the annual briefings players get on matters such as racial and religious vilification, anti-corruption and drug policy — and part fitness testing and skills work. Jock Campbell, our fitness trainer, and physiotherapist Errol Alcott gave everyone programs to follow during our break, and at this elite level it should not be necessary to monitor whether or not we have been following those programs. Also, peer pressure and on-field failure will quickly get rid of slackers. But testing helps the staff establish where each player is fitness-wise, and helps uncover any injury concerns before they get too serious.

We have one problem already: Simon Katich is complaining of a knee injury collected during an early-season stint with county side Hampshire. He returned to Australia ahead of schedule to have the injury assessed — better to be safe than sorry — but it now seems that the injury is not too serious.

The reason for having the camp in Brisbane is the climate, which allows us to get outdoors and work on our skills before the tour. No matter how much running and fitness work you do before the start of a new season or tour, once you get back into actual batting, bowling and fielding you still get stiff and sore. The idea is to get over those early-season aches before we head off, so we can hit the ground running.

Monday 30 May

Today was all about briefings and administration. For players, these sessions can be tedious — there is generally a fair degree of fidgeting in seats — but there was plenty for us to be interested in today.

Part of the day involved a long session with Tim May and Paul Marsh, from the Australian Cricketers' Association, concerning our continuing negotiations with Cricket Australia (CA) over our Memorandum of Understanding, which basically governs the employer–employee relationship. The old one runs out in the middle of this year, and during the New Zealand tour there were all sorts of suggestions that discussions were not going well.

The good news from May and Marsh was that most of the sticking points appear to have been resolved and a conclusion seems imminent. That is great news, especially for May, who has set himself the task of sorting things out before he hands over the role of leading the Association to Marsh and heads off to the United States (for family reasons).

May is also on the International Cricket Council's (ICC) Cricket Committee, and he used the session to tell us about rule changes that are likely to be adopted in one-day cricket over the next few months. One is the use of substitutes and the other is the introduction of so-called power plays, where fielding captains have to nominate 5-over periods when they are allowed only a certain number of players in defensive positions outside the fielding circle. The details of both changes are yet to be finalised, but the idea is to try to liven up the one-day game. Some critics believe it has become too formulaic, with the same pattern — a batting onslaught in the first 15 overs, steady accumulation in the middle overs and a late surge in the latter stages — being repeated in all games.

I am against the changes. The one-day game is not perfect, but I do not believe international cricket is the place to be trialling new ideas. I believe these ideas should first be trialled at domestic level; that way at least players, umpires and fans could get used to them first and a rational assessment of whether or not they work could be made before they are introduced at the elite level. I am also not convinced by the idea of trialling two new rules at once. Let us see if one works first, not try to get a grip on two at the same time.

We made these points to May, but I am not sure our voices will be heard. That is not a criticism of May; I am simply not convinced that current players get enough input into decisions that affect the game and our livelihoods. We were asked to fill out a survey during the Videocon Cup in the Netherlands last year, and it did ask about various rule changes, including the use of 5-over blocks and substitutes, but that was all I had heard on the subject until May spoke to us today. That is not ideal.

CA Chief Executive James Sutherland told us that our successes as a team — topping the Test and one-day championship ladders — have earned US$500 000 from the ICC, and he also discussed our continuing commitment to the Spirit of Cricket. This is a code which we have adopted because we recognise that we are often seen as role models, and involves behaving in a responsible way both on and off the field. We are happy to take the rewards from our status as international athletes, and we now accept that with those rewards comes the responsibility to set the right example — we really are ambassadors for both the game and our country.

As players, we used to be very reluctant to accept that our behaviour was important, or even relevant. Winning was all that mattered, and we often felt that complaints about our conduct were just the media looking for something different to write. But a couple of years ago we got a rude awakening when, during one of these administration sessions, Cricket Australia's receptionist was asked to address us. She told us about the stress she went through and the abuse she got fielding complaints on the phone if any of us stepped out of line. We also got the chance to read some of the letters CA received about our conduct. All this opened our eyes to the way we are viewed by the public.

Now we are much more conscious of the way we behave, and the upshot is that I cannot think of too many occasions over the past year when one of our players has been reported to the match referee, which is something not many other teams can claim. In January, Sutherland wrote to me to thank us for our efforts. It is now up to us to maintain those standards.

We did some fitness work at the Queensland University gym today and had a lengthy planning session with coach John Buchanan, focusing on the road to the next World Cup in 2007.

Buchanan handed us each a booklet called *ASHES 2005 (... AND BEYOND)*, which began:

WE WILL CROSS OFF EACH SERIES AS WE MARCH TOWARDS WC2007

OUR AIM IS TO NOT ONLY WIN EACH SERIES BUT ALSO TO KNOW THAT, INDIVIDUALLY AND AS A TEAM, WE ARE IMPROVING OUR TOTAL PERFORMANCE

THE VISION IS TO ARRIVE AT WC2007 THE BEST SKILLED TEAM THE WORLD HAS SEEN — TECHNICALLY, PHYSICALLY, MENTALLY, TACTICALLY & 'TEAM

THE ASCENT CONTINUES WITH THE ASHES!!

Fine words, and we all support them, but we also know that it is how we go about putting them into action that counts. We kicked around some ideas about how we can improve, starting with our first tour challenge, the NatWest Series and NatWest Challenge against England and Bangladesh.

Buchanan produced a statistic we did not know: we do not score from around 100 of the 300 balls bowled in an average one-day game. If we could score from even half of those 100 deliveries we should post formidable tallies. He also suggested we look at how we run between the wickets, and that each of us could try to practise a shot we might not normally play as a way of expanding our options when we bat.

Buchanan is like that, always challenging us to try to improve rather than simply settling for our current level of performance. I like to think all the players are on that wavelength too; that is what will keep us at the top of the game individually and collectively.

After all the talk of the past few days, today was a nice change: a lengthy training session with a focus on cricket skills. It was one of the best group sessions we have ever had.

We batted in pairs, placing a high emphasis on running between the wickets while the bowlers went through their paces against us.

Then we had a group fielding session that stretched everyone. There were high catches, reflex catches, slip catches and replicated outfield catches and ground fielding — the sorts of drills that cannot always be done on tour, as space on fields and time can be limited, and getting some rest during a busy schedule is often the highest priority.

Everyone's natural keenness at the start of a tour and desire to work hard after a good break added to the buzz around the session, and I finished feeling not just tired and sore, but also excited by what I saw. If we can maintain this level of enthusiasm for the next 3 months we should do really, really well.

During the day I also gave an interview to the Melbourne newspaper *The Age*, and one of the focus points was former Australia captain and Channel Nine commentator Ian Chappell's assessment of me as a conservative leader.

I think Ian's view is based on the way I handled the side when New Zealand's Jacob Oram hammered a hundred against us in Brisbane last summer. Oram was batting with the lower order and trying to hit sixes to maximise his side's score, and I responded by posting most of my fielders on the boundary.

Some people argue that if a player is looking to hit out, leaving gaps on the fence will encourage him to continue to play that way and sooner or later he will miscue. But Oram had already forced us to set fielders back on the boundary by looking to hit sixes, and when he kept trying to do that even after I had made those adjustments, why would you bother having those fielders anywhere else?

It is true that we have adopted slightly different tactics over the past 12 months from those employed by Stephen Waugh — using a third man fielder in India and not enforcing the follow-on a couple of times, for instance — but I like to think they were common sense measures rather than conservatism. Why give the opposition momentum by leaving a section of the boundary where the ball regularly goes unguarded? And why flog our bowlers into the ground when we can still win a game by grinding the opposition down and giving them nothing to play for? Whatever Ian thinks, and he is entitled to his opinion, we have continued to win and win well, and that has to be the bottom line.

Thursday 2 June

Today was all about fitness work, but most of it was based around cricket skills. We practised completing sets of three runs in full batting gear, and also sprinted some quick singles. Then we did six 40-metre sprints, with each sprint starting at 30-second intervals. The incentive was to run each set as quickly as possible, because the faster you completed it, the more time you had before the start of the next set.

We also did the dreaded bleep test. This involves shuttling back and forth between two fixed points, the idea being to reach each point before a recorded bleep sounds. The time between the bleeps gradually reduces, so you end up having to run faster and faster to reach the next fixed point. If you don't get there by the time the bleep sounds, you are eliminated.

It is torture that tests your stamina because, rather than slowing down as you tire, it demands that you speed up. It was no surprise that Brad Hogg was the last man standing, but John Buchanan was also impressive, as he managed to beat Stuart MacGill and Nathan Bracken. Given that Buchanan is 20 years older than them, that was not ideal, but they did have an excuse — neither is back in full training yet. MacGill is not going to join up with the tour for another month and Bracken is at the camp as a CA-contracted player rather than someone involved in the Ashes tour. I could hardly be too critical of either of them: I strained a thigh muscle during the test, but although it is tight, I do not think it is a serious problem.

Friday 3 June

Today was our final day of practice before departure, and also time to say goodbye to Rianna. We agreed that tomorrow, with the whole process of departing for the next 3 months, will be stressful enough without throwing in our goodbyes as well, so she has headed off with a friend for a few days to Margaret River, south of Perth, to take her mind off our separation. It is not an ideal situation and, as I get older, leaving family and friends behind for long periods gets harder and harder. But this is the life I have chosen. It is lucrative, and it will not last for ever, so Rianna and I have plenty of time to look forward to as a couple when cricket is no longer my job. In the short term, we will be back together in 5 weeks, when Rianna joins me in London before the first Test.

The training camp has been a great success, and I would like to see it as the beginning of a regular gathering both at the start of our international summer, and also when we go abroad out of our regular season. It has helped improve our fitness levels and allowed us to chat in detail about our plans for the tour and beyond. Brisbane has excellent weather while the southern states are shivering in winter, and has an ideal infrastructure thanks to CA's decision to base its Centre of Excellence here, so I can see no reason why Brisbane should not become Australian cricket's equivalent of the Australian rugby union team's base at Coffs Harbour.

Saturday 4 June

Departure day. This is where it really begins — except for the fact the first Test is still a month and a half away. That was one of the themes of the media conference I attended before we flew out of Brisbane to Singapore and then on to London.

We seem to have been building up to the Ashes series for ever — there were endless questions, even throughout the New Zealand tour — and although we are now finally heading to the United Kingdom, there is still the small matter of the one-day series to deal with first.

Most of the questions at the conference related to the Ashes series, but I was keen to play up the one-day matches as much as I could, because we cannot afford to take our eyes off the ball and focus on the Tests yet. It is important that we put down a marker in the one-day matches so that, by the time the Tests come around, England are already on the back foot. It would be unfair on the players who are only in the squad for the one-day series if we treated that contest as nothing more than a warm-up for the main event. Whether we are playing in white clothing or coloured, we are still playing for our country, and every international match should be played with the same intensity and carry the same importance.

For us it is a plus that the one-day series is before the Test matches. By the time the Tests come around, England will have played a fair amount of cricket — their season has been going for almost 2 months already. We should be the fresher side by the time we get to the climax of the series in early September. Another positive is that the first Test is at Lord's. We have not lost there in the longer form of the game since 1934, and England will know that.

Ideally, I would have preferred a couple fewer one-day matches — we are due to play 10 internationals plus a Twenty20 match before the first Test — but that is the itinerary we have agreed to and we must live with it.

One of our major hurdles will be to sort out the fast bowling pecking order. Brett Lee is still on the outer at Test level but I hope that he can repeat his one-day form of the New Zealand matches during the early part of the tour; if he does, he will get his Test spot back this time. Who he replaces is a tough one, and it makes me glad I am not a selector.

Official business over, it was time to board the plane, dressed in our new tour outfits: pinstripe suits and pink shirts, chosen by Adam Gilchrist in his role as head of our clothing committee. Under the suits we wore our compression garments and flight socks, all of which are designed to help prevent deep vein thrombosis, the problem that struck Stephen Waugh on his way back from the last Ashes series in 2001.

My head was racing with the excitement of the tour to come, so I found it tough to rest. It was also tough to focus on any of the in-flight entertainment available, so I ended up flicking through the golf magazines I'd bought on my way to the aircraft, as well as surfing aimlessly through the television channels available. It was lucky that I didn't feel like sleep as I was sitting next to Matthew Hayden, who is a notorious fidget, especially when he watches a film he finds boring. He watched *Phantom of the Opera* and *Sideways*, and I could tell, even before I asked him, that he hated both of them.

Sunday 5 June

After all the hype and the build-up, our arrival at London's Heathrow Airport was distinctly low-key. That may have had something to do with the time we landed — around 6 a.m. When we emerged from Customs there were just a handful of waiting photographers and camera crews, plus a few Aussie fans who had braved the early hour to welcome us.

One person who was there to meet us was Trevor Crouch, our baggage master and Mr Fix-it from the last tour, 4 years ago. Trevor's official job is to drive our baggage van from venue to venue, but he does far more than that, and established himself as an indispensable and ultra-reliable member of the tour squad on that 2001 trip. He can help with anything from boot repairs to buying birthday presents: for example, 4 years ago in Worcester he bought Stephen and Mark Waugh a pair of walking sticks to celebrate their 36th birthdays after we had a dressing room collection. Trevor is also in charge of team laundry throughout the tour. He sources laundromats at each location we visit and delivers, then collects, our gear for washing most days for a fraction of what the hotels charge. It might seem like penny-pinching, but as sportsmen we go through a massive amount of training and playing gear, not to mention street clothes, and if we put all those items into the hotel laundry we might struggle to make a profit on the tour, because some places are prohibitively expensive.

Our first bus trip of the tour was not to Lord's, or any other cricket location, but to Ashford in Kent, 120 kilometres southeast of Heathrow. From here we will catch the Eurostar train to France tomorrow to visit battlefields where Australian soldiers fought and died in World War I. The idea of visiting battlefields began with our trip to Gallipoli before the 2001 Ashes tour. That was such a success that it was decided to do something similar at the start of this tour. I am expecting it to have a similar effect on us as the visit to Gallipoli had 4 years ago — that experience made us realise how lucky we are to be able to play sport for a living, especially in comparison with those soldiers who gave their lives for their country.

After we arrived at our hotel in Ashford, Matthew Hayden and I decided to go out for a walk to loosen up after our flight. Jock Campbell also led a stretching session for all the squad in the team room before my first media conference of the tour.

Plenty was made of our squad's average age, which is over 30. We do have several players in that age bracket, but age was not a handicap last summer when we steamrolled New Zealand and Pakistan, so I cannot see how it can suddenly be a factor now, 2 months later. The players in this squad are mature, and they are here because their performances merit inclusion. I would not swap any of them for any of England's players, even though they have been impressive over the past 18 months. They know we have an awesome record in Ashes battles since 1989, and that will be a massive mental hurdle for them to get over.

Monday 6 June

Today was a real eye-opener and a thoroughly sobering experience for me — and, I think, for every member of the touring party. We travelled to Villers-Bretonneux in northern France, where Australian soldiers fought during World War I.

We caught the Eurostar train that runs under the English Channel to Lille, and when we arrived there we were met by Aaron Lord, the former Geelong and Hawthorn Australian Rules footballer, who now works for the Australian Embassy in France.

He was our chaperon for the day's events, and as we made the 2-hour bus trip from Lille to Villers-Bretonneux he talked us through what was to happen during the day and then showed us a video that detailed the scale of the battles that took place in the area we were visiting.

I joined Penelope Wensley, the Australian Ambassador to France, in laying a wreath at the Australian war memorial near the town, and we stood in the pouring rain while Adam Gilchrist read from Laurence Binyon's poem *For The Fallen*:

> They shall grow not old, as we that are left grow old
>
> Age shall not weary them, nor the years contemn.
>
> At the going down of the sun and in the morning
>
> We will remember them.

The rain was unpleasant, but as the day unfolded I realised that it was nothing compared with the suffering the soldiers must have endured during the fighting of April 1918, when Australian troops helped recapture the town from the Germans. We visited the Franco-Australian museum that celebrates links between the two countries, and at every turn we could see just how much the people of Villers-Bretonneux love Australia.

There is a Melbourne Street and an Adelaide Street, a restaurant called Le Kangaroo, and even the school has the slogan 'Never Forget Australia' in the playground. A few of us had a kick-about with a soccer ball with some local children, and although I am sure they did not know who we were, they still clamoured for our autographs.

I knew nothing of any of this part of our history before today — and I am fairly certain not many of the rest of the squad did either — and it turned out to be fantastic life-education experience. My only criticism of the day was that it ended up being a bit rushed. I would have liked a bit more time for reflection, because the more I saw, the more overwhelmed I was by the impact Australians have had on the lives of the townsfolk.

I think it had a similar effect on everyone else. The bus trip back to Lille, where we stayed the night before returning to the United Kingdom the following morning, was fairly quiet. It was a terrific way to remind us of how fortunate we are to lead the lives we do.

Tuesday 7 June

Our fitness trainer, Jock Campbell, does not like much physical activity on a travel day; he would prefer us to do some stretching and rest. But the temptation to get started on the cricketing part of the tour proved too great for a few of us today.

After a mid-morning trip by Eurostar back to England and then a 2-hour coach trip from Ashford to Brighton, the south coast city that will be our base for the next few days, I was ready to blow away the cobwebs, so I had a walk along the seafront. Then I felt the urge to have some cricket practice.

I rounded up a few others who were feeling the same way — Andrew Symonds, Glenn McGrath, Shane Watson, Damien Martyn, Matthew Hayden, Brad Hogg and Brad Haddin — and we headed to the nearby Sussex county ground, where the curator did his best to help us out.

There were no new practice pitches ready to use so we had to make do with worn surfaces, and we quickly discovered that they did not go well with the hard, new white balls, which started misbehaving when banged into the dry, dusty pitches. The bowlers quickly switched to older balls, which meant we ended up having a decent hit-out. It felt good to have a run-around, to feel bat on ball and to take a few catches — I am getting very excited about our first match on Thursday. It may only be a Twenty20 match against a mix of former and current players, but even that is a relief after all the build-up to the tour.

Wednesday 8 June

Worcestershire off-spinner Gareth Batty is drafted into England's one-day squad for the Twenty20 international against Australia and the start of the NatWest Series after Ashley Giles's failure to recover from a hip injury.

After yesterday's optional session, this afternoon's action involved everyone, again at Sussex's ground, as we got ready for the Twenty20 game.

This workout was all about perfecting specific one-day skills rather than working on the fundamentals of the game. Those fundamentals were worked on in Brisbane, so today's session was a chance to get a bit funkier and build on them.

It meant that batsmen practised specific strokes that they might not normally play other than in a run chase — shots like the reverse sweep — and bowlers tried to be unpredictable. This was the same plan we used for the Twenty20 game in New Zealand in February.

The players in our squad who have plenty of county experience at Twenty20 — Michael Kasprowicz, Mike Hussey, Andrew Symonds and a few others — are helping those of us with little or no experience of the format to come to terms with it. Although it is a compressed version of the game, I believe the basics still apply. Proper cricket shots will still get you runs and good balls will still take wickets. Each player will develop his own game plan, but the basics have always served me well, so you will not see me playing any reverse sweeps.

Thursday 9 June

Twenty20 match, Arundel: The Australians 2–170 (Hayden 79, Gilchrist 53) beat the PCA Masters XI 6–167 (Maddy 70*) by 8 wickets.

This was a fun way to start the tour. It was a reasonably light-hearted workout against a team of current and former players, but we still wanted to get off to a winning start and, thanks to the batting of Matthew Hayden and Adam Gilchrist, we did that quite comfortably.

The match gave us a first, brief look at England's latest batting hope, Kevin Pietersen, who did well on the one-day tour of South Africa at the start of the year. He did not last long today, top-edging a sweep at Michael Clarke's spin. Although the home side got a few more runs than I would have liked — thanks to some understandable rustiness with the ball and in the field on our part — the match did allow Gilchrist and Hayden time at the crease in a run-chase situation.

They played expertly before being dismissed, and it was left to me and Damien Martyn to finish off the game. When Martyn arrived at the crease and the umpire told him 'one left', he was convinced we had lost — he thought he was about to face the last ball of the game, with us still needing 10 to win — but the umpire was in fact telling him that the next ball would be the last ball of the penultimate over.

Brett Lee bowled well and continued to enjoy himself at the expense of Stephen Fleming, the New Zealand captain, who led the PCA side. Lee had dismissed Fleming regularly during the one-day series in February, but since then Fleming has scored a stack of runs for county side Nottinghamshire; it took just one ball to restore the old order — he edged the first delivery of the match straight to me at slip.

After today, my views on Twenty20 cricket have not changed. It is a great format to attract new audiences to the game, but should remain a format to attract the public to the game at domestic level, as it has done in England, South Africa and Pakistan, for example,

---

* not out

rather than a major international spectacle. I believe the higher the stakes become, the more inhibited the players will be, and that will defeat the object of the game — entertainment.

After the match we got our first chance to sample the delights of the bus that will provide our transport for the next 3 months, driven by Geoff 'Popeye' Goodwin, the same man who drove us around during last year's Champions Trophy. The bus reportedly cost £350 000, and after one look inside it is not hard to see why.

It has fridges, microwave ovens, six or seven small flat-screen televisions, DVD players, a PlayStation facility, the ability to pick up satellite television even when we are on the move, and headphone sockets at each seat so that those wanting to watch the televisions can do so without disturbing those who want peace and quiet.

At the back is a horseshoe-shaped couch which has quickly been claimed by the fast bowlers. Already, people seem to have marked out their territory. It may be part superstition, part routine, but every UK tour I have been on, people's seating positions on the tour bus rarely alter during the course of the stay. This evening I joined Hayden and Martyn at a table about halfway down the bus. Gilchrist and Shane Watson settled in at another table nearby. In front of us were other tables with Brad Haddin, Mike Hussey, Simon Katich and Jock Campbell. The other members of team management are near the front and whoever I have not mentioned is either at the back in Glenn McGrath's self-styled FBC (Fast Bowling Cartel) or happy to float about nearby in the hope of a prime spot on the couch.

As the match didn't start until 5.30 p.m. we didn't get away from the pretty Arundel ground, situated about 32 kilometres outside Brighton, until after 9 o'clock. This meant that, even allowing for our luxurious bus, everyone was still pretty tired when we arrived in Leicester, our next location and around 240 kilometres north, at about 1 o'clock in the morning.

Friday 10 June

We had an afternoon practice session at Leicestershire's Grace Road ground ahead of our one-day game against the county tomorrow, and the facilities were superb. The net pitches were brilliant, some of the best I have ever played on in this country — they reminded me of the ones at Adelaide Oval. They were that good.

This evening I attended a dinner laid on by representatives of the county club to try to generate more interest in it among the local community. The city of Leicester has a massive Asian population but very few of them are regulars at Grace Road, and the county is one of the least-supported sides in this country. It is hard to reconcile that with the passion most Asians have for cricket, and the club is trying to sort out the apparent discrepancy.

There were 70 or 80 people at the function and it was a pleasant evening. I faced a fairly relaxed question-and-answer session and signed autographs. I hope I did my bit to try to get more people involved in the game here — it would be a shame if the superb facilities at the Leicestershire club are not used by as many people as possible.

Saturday 11 June

One-day match, Leicester: The Australians 4–321 (Hayden 107, Symonds 92*, Martyn 85) beat Leicestershire 8–226 (Gibson 50) by 95 runs.

This was a comfortable outing for us, with three batsmen getting lengthy spells at the crease and the bowlers able to get some more miles in their legs under match conditions. It would have been nice to bowl Leicestershire out, but it will not do us any harm to get reacquainted with the discipline of maintaining concentration for 50 overs in the field.

I didn't get much time at the crease but still feel in decent form after my practice session yesterday. Overall, I could not be happier with our preparation so far, as I told the media afterwards. We have been working hard, and the mood among the squad is good: although everyone seems relaxed, we still have that business-like feel about us that I think typifies us at our best.

With our Twenty20 international against England just a couple of days away, the reporters I spoke to were keen to discuss which player might be a big hit in that form of the game. I nominated Andrew Symonds because he seems built for the format — he can hit boundaries, field superbly and vary his pace when he bowls. England's danger men appear to be Kevin Pietersen and Andrew Flintoff, both of whom can fill the same sorts of roles as Symonds.

After the match it was back onto the bus for another long journey, this time 240 kilometres south to Southampton, and another late arrival at our next hotel. The early part of the tour is a punishing one, with one-day matches in different locations pushing us from place to place almost every other day, making it hard to get settled and into a routine. This is one reason I did not want Rianna with me now. But we can hardly complain about the itinerary, as we did agree to it — and our luxury transport goes a long way towards softening any hardship we may be feeling.

It turns out our day at Leicester did not go as smoothly as I had first thought — at least as far as Michael Kasprowicz and Michael Clarke are concerned. Both players had kit stolen after the match.

We only found out about the theft today, when the bags were taken to the ground in Southampton for tomorrow's match, but, looking back, it is no surprise that something went missing in the chaos that followed the match.

Normally at the end of a match the players' bags are cleared from the dressing rooms straight onto the team bus, but because the bus is quite large and the entrance to the Grace Road ground is quite narrow, the bus was parked about 150 metres away. As a result, the bags were first piled up at the bottom of the steps to the dressing rooms, near a large crowd of autograph hunters, and it seems likely they were not very well supervised. Perhaps we are lucky that more bags weren't lost.

Clarke has lost all his gear, including five bats, and Kasprowicz lost the bag with his playing shirts in it. Team manager Steve Bernard has already ordered replacement clothing from Australia, but until it arrives the pair will have to play in borrowed gear. Brad Haddin has said Clarke can borrow his batting pads, and he is borrowing a pair of my shoes to bat in; he went out to a sports store to buy new batting gloves, inner gloves and even an abdominal protector, and he had to contact the Slazenger representative to get hold of some replacement bats.

To the average club player all this might not seem too much of a hardship, but at the highest level, familiarity and comfort with equipment is important. It may be partly superstition, but when a player finds a piece of equipment he likes, he tends to stick with it, especially if it is a bat or a pair of gloves. Clarke and Kasprowicz will have to get over that mental hurdle if they are going to perform tomorrow.

I gave a media conference at lunchtime at the Rose Bowl, the venue for tomorrow's match, and several questions focused on my views of the Twenty20 format. I repeated my earlier statements on the subject and was also asked about whether this match, our first against England on the tour, really marks the start of the serious business of the tour. My answer was that every match we play is serious and we want to win each one, but it would be good to put down a marker against England early on here. However, I do not believe that what happens tomorrow evening will have any bearing on the next 3 months.

Once my official duties were over, I headed to London, about 90 minutes away by car, with Adam Gilchrist for a fun afternoon at an Australian cultural festival. If we hadn't been playing a game tomorrow we could have seriously overindulged, as the place was packed with stalls full of Australian food and drink, but instead we both concentrated on looking at the produce rather than tasting it.

The highlight of the afternoon was our appearance on stage alongside television's Kath and Kim, actresses Jane Turner and Gina Riley, who are over here to promote their ABC TV show. I was paired with Kath and Gilchrist was paired with Kim, and both pairs were given a mass of ingredients — including tuna steaks, beef kebabs, a packet of marshmallows, prawns, a pineapple and garlic — with which we had to create a meal. All this was done in front of a lively crowd, with the winners to be decided by the audience's cheers.

In the end it was called a draw, which is just as well, because neither meal was edible. Hardly a surprise, given the mix of ingredients!

Monday 13 June

Twenty20 international, Southampton: England 8–179 beat Australia 79 by 100 runs.

After a promising start to our tour we crashed back to earth this evening. England got a decent score, more than they should have, but we should have got much closer than we did in reply.

We were caught out by the frantic pace of the game, and by the time we got through 6 overs the umpires told me we were 4 overs behind the required rate — the format of the game requires the fielding side to bowl its 20 overs in 75 minutes.

It forced me to bring on our spinners and try to hustle through the overs as quickly as possible, and although Andrew Symonds and Michael Clarke bowled well, it meant we ended up concentrating on the clock rather than on what tactics we should employ.

That allowed England to get away from us, and then, when we batted, it was one of those occasions when every mistake we made was capitalised on. Every time we hit the ball in the air there seemed to be an England player there to catch it, and we ended up suffering a pretty humiliating thrashing.

The evening also had an interesting postscript, as our lower order of Jason Gillespie, Brett Lee, Michael Kasprowicz and Glenn McGrath tried to bat us to respectability after we collapsed to 7–31. The England fast bowlers really gave them a fearful working over, with plenty of short-pitched bowling, and one delivery from Flintoff thumping Lee on the shoulder. The intention was clear: they wanted to make it plain to our lower order that if they intend to hang around at the crease they will need to be brave. As a statement it was impressive, but I expect our bowlers have made a note of it, and will make sure the England bowlers get plenty back when the time comes.

I described the game as a 'bit of a laugh' when I was interviewed, so I am sure we will be accused of not taking the match seriously. That is not to put down the Twenty20 format or to make out that we do not care about the loss. The format is obviously something that works in this country — the ground was full — and, more importantly, we wanted to win this game, just as we want to win every game we play. What I was trying to do was emphasise once again that I do not believe this match's result will have any bearing on the one-day internationals and the Ashes series to come, and we should treat it that way. If we win all the trophies on offer this summer, no one will remember tonight's events. That's how I want my players to think.

Although we were playing against England and there was all the hype that comes with that, I view this match as nothing more than part of our build-up to the international matches ahead. That was why we decided to play all our fast bowlers instead of including Brad Hogg, and to push Mike Hussey and Michael Clarke up the order at the expense of me and Damien Martyn. Both plans failed, but I am glad we tried them. At least now our faster bowlers have had some more match action, bowling under pressure after a lengthy lay-off, and although Clarke and Hussey scored only one run between them, at least no one can now say that they did not have a chance to bat.

Could we have done more to avoid a loss of this scale? Could we have practised more? I do not think so. I was happy with the practice and skills work we have done both before this trip and on the tour so far, and at this elite level a net session will not replicate the match situation we were in today. I prefer to think that this was a case of us being off the pace after a spell away from pressure cricket, and playing against a side that is 2 months into its domestic season. Once we adjust back to that pace we will be okay.

The English public loved our discomfort, and there was plenty of noise around the ground as we subsided to defeat. I want to use that as a positive for the rest of the tour. Everyone here wants us knocked off our pedestal at the top of the rankings, so our challenge is to shut those fans up through the quality of our cricket, as I said to my players after the match. We clearly have plenty of improving to do, as our batting, bowling and ground fielding were not up to standard this evening, but we will benefit from this first run-out.

Tuesday 14 June

We travelled the 2 hours by bus to Taunton after last night's match, and this morning we had a team meeting that included the build-up to the State of Origin rugby league match that is being played on Wednesday. Michael Clarke, a member of our social committee (it also includes Mike Hussey and Shane Watson), did some homework earlier in the trip: he found out which of the sides each member of the tour party will be barracking for and organised New South Wales or Queensland jumpers for everyone. Those jumpers were presented today. Given that I now live in Sydney, I obviously went for New South Wales. We will all have to wear them when we watch the match in Cardiff tomorrow night after playing against my old county, Somerset.

I did not dwell on last night's events. Everyone here is smart enough to know we played badly without having someone stand at the front of the room and tell them about it, so there was no table-banging speech from John Buchanan or myself today. I am a firm believer in each player taking individual responsibility for improving himself. That is what I will look for in the next match.

Our trip here is a chance for me to catch up with my team-mates from last year, and this evening I went along to a barbecue at the house of one of them, spin-bowling all-rounder Ian Blackwell. It was a relaxing evening with a 1980s theme — one of his sponsors is a website that supplies retro clothing. When I arrived, along with Adam Gilchrist, we were each given a T-shirt based on the fashions of that era, and it proved a great ice-breaker with the other people at the party, who were also wearing similar shirts.

Earlier in the day we had a practice session at the Taunton ground and, just as when I played here last season, the pitches were excellent. Tomorrow should be a good opportunity for our batsmen to find some form; it will also be a good test for our bowlers, because the surface will offer no margin for error.

One-day match, Taunton: The Australians 5–342 (Ponting 80, Hayden 76, Clarke 63*, Hussey 51) lost to Somerset 6–345 (Smith 108, Jayasuriya 101) by 4 wickets.

I might have been able to excuse Monday's loss on the basis of rustiness, but there were no such excuses today and I was furious at the end of this humiliating loss. It left me shocked by our poor standard of play.

Our bowling was woeful and our fielding was sloppy, and although we were up against two world-class batsmen — South Africa captain Graeme Smith and Sanath Jayasuriya of Sri Lanka — on an excellent pitch and a small ground, there is still no excuse for our bowlers being unable to defend a score of 342.

As I wrote yesterday, I do not believe players at this level need to be told what is expected of them, but on the evidence of this performance, maybe I am wrong; so, straight after the match I told the players exactly what I thought of our effort in the field. It was not good enough, I said. We will have to improve a heck of a lot, on this evidence, to be competitive even against Bangladesh.

In one sense I am confused by today's result, because I have been really happy with the work we have done in the lead-up to the tour. But playing in a match is a different dimension: it requires players to compete under pressure, and in the last two matches we have been found wanting really badly in that department, especially in the field.

My criticism of the bowling and fielding should not detract from the fact that Smith and Jayasuriya played sensationally well. Somerset had to score at almost 7 runs per over from the start of its innings to beat us, and with that in mind the two openers set out to dominate us. They succeeded, thrashing 197 in only a shade over 20 overs. We have played against both of them plenty of times before, but although we knew the areas where they like to hit the ball and I set fields accordingly, the bowlers failed to bowl to those fields and the result was carnage. Somerset won with more than 3 overs to spare despite the size of its target.

My mood after the match was not helped when I had to go and face the media and explain our poor performance. One reporter kept asking me whose fault it was that our bowlers had been unable to perform to the required standards. I do not want to criticise individuals, least of all in public, so I tried to avoid doing so. 'You tell me [whose fault it is],' was my first answer, but the reporter persisted: 'Is it your fault or theirs?' I resented that. I may be captain, but I cannot bowl for the bowlers. That is their job, and at this level it is up to them to get it right. If, as a bowler, someone starts to attack you, you should be good enough to think on your feet and respond. Our bowlers did not do that today and they must take responsibility for that.

I heard one comment that we got what we deserved for being arrogant. That was based on the fact that Matthew Hayden and I retired instead of waiting to be dismissed. That charge is nonsense. The key for us was to allow individual players to get the most out of the match, and our retiring meant that Damien Martyn, Michael Clarke and Mike Hussey all spent valuable time at the crease. If we were in the same situation in a practice match tomorrow, I would make the same decision.

As if the defeat was not bad enough, Brett Lee picked up an injury and is now a doubt for the weekend, when we play our opening matches against Bangladesh and England. During his opening spell he said to me that he felt something 'pop' in his right shoulder. I sent him off the field straightaway to have it looked at by Errol Alcott. Alcott will assess the extent of the problem over the next day or so.

There was at least one light-hearted aspect to the day. When we arrived at our hotel in Cardiff, the scene of our opening match on Saturday and a 90-minute drive from Taunton, we put on our State of Origin jumpers, headed for the team room and watched the match. Having something like that to take our minds off the day's events was just what was needed.

Part 11:
NatWest Series

NatWest Series, match 1, The Oval, London: England (6 points) 0–192 (Trescothick 100*, Strauss 82*) beat Bangladesh (0 points) 190 (Aftab Ahmed 51) by 10 wickets.

Errol Alcott was concerned enough about Brett Lee's shoulder to take him to London — about 3 hours' drive east of Cardiff — to have it assessed by a specialist. Though that assessment is that there is no significant damage, the area is still stiff and sore, and that means Lee is unlikely to play over the weekend. That is a major blow considering the way he has bowled in one-day cricket over the past 6 months, and I know it will be a blow to Lee as well, as he is desperate to use these one-day matches as a springboard back into the Test side. But if resting and getting treatment over the weekend means he can be fully fit for the rest of the tour, it has to be the best approach.

We wanted to have a full-scale practice session this afternoon, including fielding drills to sharpen us up after our last two displays, but it rained all day, so we held an indoor session instead at Glamorgan's excellent indoor facilities. Cardiff was our base before the 1999 World Cup, so we are pretty familiar with the place. I had a session against the bowling machine and felt in good touch.

After the session I chatted with Glamorgan batsman Michael Powell, who sought me out for some advice. At the end of last season he was playing well enough to be selected for a place in England's Academy squad, but this season he has really struggled for form, with a string of low scores. Most of his dismissals have been bowled, which is unusual, as good players very rarely miss straight balls.

When I have seen him play he has struck me as being a fairly uncomplicated player who likes to go out and hit the ball, so my advice was to not overanalyse his game technically. As long as he is doing the basics well — moving his feet, keeping his head still and watching the ball — the rest should look after itself, and he should not try to get bogged down in theory.

England and Bangladesh started the tournament today in London but I didn't watch the match. We have seen plenty of both teams on television and in the flesh over the past couple of years and have a fairly good idea of how they are going to play against us — and also of how we should play against them. England did everything expected of them today and had an easy win; as long as we show some improvement from Wednesday, we should be able to do something similar on Saturday.

This evening quite a few of the squad — me, Adam Gilchrist, Brad Haddin, Brad Hogg, Shane Watson, Andrew Symonds, Brett Lee and Simon Katich — went out for dinner to an Italian restaurant close to the team hotel. It was a regular destination for us during our time in Cardiff in 1999. Back then we also started the tour slowly but ended up lifting the World Cup. I would settle for that type of form improvement now, starting this weekend.

Friday 17 June

Fast bowler Simon Jones has been released from the England squad in order to receive treatment on an injury to his right knee at the England Cricket Academy in Loughborough; Hampshire's Chris Tremlett is called up as his replacement.

The weather cleared enough to allow us a decent workout, and John Buchanan and I placed the emphasis on fielding. We got everyone into lots of under-pressure ground fielding at pace, involving not just throwing at sets of stumps but also backing up other players' throws. I like this type of drill, with the ball going through plenty of pairs of hands in quick time. It was a high-intensity session and one where we looked sharp again, just as we did in Brisbane. Our challenge now is to take that sharpness into tomorrow's match against Bangladesh; this is something we have not done in our previous two outings.

After the session I met with match referee Jeff Crowe to go through the rules and regulations for the series. This is something that happens at every tournament, be it Tests or one-day internationals; it involves the captains, coaches, umpires and team managers.

The playing conditions are circulated for us to read beforehand, so that at the meeting we can ask the referee for clarification on any issue. Crowe had already spoken to the other teams in the tournament, so John Buchanan, Steve Bernard and I faced him alone at our hotel. The referee always talks about the standards of behaviour he expects and this conversation was no different. He also mentioned that he would be on the lookout for advertising logos that exceed the permitted size. Because playing conditions for most matches rarely change, there was not much else to discuss. We had no queries and the meeting was over within 15 minutes.

The fact that I was not with the two opposition captains for the series — Habib-ul-Bashar of Bangladesh and England's Michael Vaughan — meant I did not get the chance to discuss with them my idea of bypassing the third umpire over disputed catches, as has happened in several recent series when I have been captain. I do not believe television technology is always good enough to allow the third umpire to make a definitive ruling on whether or not a catch has carried. Knowing that, some batsmen have deliberately stood their ground after hitting a catch to a fielder, and if the catch is then referred to the third umpire, the batsman usually gets the benefit of any doubt that remains, even though most are almost certainly out. That has led to a lot of bad feeling between teams. I want to get away from that mentality and back to a situation that existed a few years ago, where a batsman accepted a fielder's word on whether or not he caught the ball cleanly. The Sri Lanka captains, Hashan Tillakaratne and Marvan Atapattu, and Pakistan's Inzamam-ul-Haq agreed with my suggestion, but Stephen Fleming of New Zealand did not.

I hope England's Michael Vaughan accepts the idea, but he benefited from just such a disputed catch when he stood his ground in Adelaide in 2002. He went on to score 177 that day. However, he knows that if his side refuses to agree to accept a fielder's word it will cut both ways: he could find himself in the field, claiming a catch, and our batsman will stand there and wait for the decision. If it goes against England then it will be on Vaughan's head, not our batsman's.

This evening we had a team meeting about tomorrow's match, but we did not go into too many specifics about the Bangladesh players. Together with Zimbabwe, the Bangladesh side are the minnows of world cricket, and we thrashed them when they toured Australia in 2003. We know that if we bat well, get the ball in the right areas when we bowl and field to the standards I expect of us, we should be far too good for them, and no amount of analysing the Bangladesh players will change that.

To lighten the mood after the formal part of the meeting, and at the end of what has been a tough week results-wise, we were entertained by a magician. He was superb. He came highly recommended by Simon Katich, who saw him perform while he was playing for county side Hampshire, and on the evidence of what we saw tonight it was no wonder Katich was impressed.

One trick he performed just blew everyone away. He took team manager Steve Bernard's credit card and somehow managed to get it hovering in mid-air, spinning as it did so. There were no wires anyone could see and none of us could figure out how he did it. The show was great value and well worth the complimentary tickets we let him have for his time.

We also used the get-together to toast Shane Watson's birthday. Some of the squad went out for a meal to celebrate with him, but I opted for room service and a quiet night before tomorrow's action. I hope we can thrash Bangladesh and get some momentum into our tour ahead of our first major test, against England on Sunday.

Saturday 18 June

NatWest Series, match 2, Cardiff: Australia (1 point) 5–249 (Martyn 77, Clarke 54) lost to Bangladesh (5 points) 5–250 (Ashraful 100) by 5 wickets.

It is difficult to know where to start in trying to sum up the events of today. It has been, for at least two reasons, my worst day as Australia captain.

To start with, we lost to Bangladesh. It was a dreadful, embarrassing defeat, as we were outplayed by a side that has never come close to beating us in any previous encounter. As a comparison, it would be like a team of Victorian Football League battlers beating my beloved Kangaroos. It should just never happen.

But, on top of that, we had to leave Andrew Symonds out of the side. He had been out partying for most of the night and he was clearly still affected by alcohol during warm-ups before the game.

I'll deal with the Symonds situation first. I first got wind that something was wrong about 75 minutes before the start of the match. When we got onto the ground we split into two groups — batsmen and bowlers — to do our warm-ups. Those warm-ups started with some gentle leg-swings, but after four or five swings in the batting group, Symonds moved away from us and headed for the other set of players. He based himself on the edge of that group and leaned against a wheelie bin that was on the edge of the field. As he did so he fell over.

I saw it all, as did Adam Gilchrist, who was next to me, and straightaway I said to him, 'Do you think he's drunk?' Neither of us could believe that he was, but we went over to him to check for ourselves.

I knew a few of the lads had gone out to celebrate Shane Watson's birthday, but surely they would not have been stupid enough to stay out late on the eve of a match, even one against a side we would be expected to beat comfortably?

When Gilchrist and I got to Symonds I did not beat around the bush. His eyes looked puffy and I could smell alcohol on his breath. 'Were you out late last night having a drink?' I said.

'Yes,' he replied.

'What time did you get back?' I responded.

'About 1.30, I think,' said Symonds.

Given the state he was in 8 hours after that, I found his claim hard to believe. My blood was beginning to boil. I did not shout, but I let Symonds know exactly what I thought of his behaviour.

'If this is the way you are going to behave, I don't want you in the side. I'm not picking you today,' I said.

'Right,' was his response, but he said it in such a casual 'see-if-I-care' way that it wound me up even more. 'Don't encourage me,' I said. I was furious at a player being so disrespectful to himself, his team-mates, his opponents and his country by turning up to play a game in that state, and I blurted out, 'He can go home then!' to Gilchrist before heading off to speak to John Buchanan. I had to let him know what was happening and what my views on the matter were.

Buchanan was Symonds's coach at Queensland, and has been a massive supporter throughout Symonds's career, so he was just as shocked as I was that something like this could have happened, although he said he had been suspicious that something out of the ordinary was going on when he went to breakfast, at around 7 o'clock.

Buchanan is one of the early risers in the tour party, and Symonds is someone who likes his sleep, so the coach was surprised to see Symonds already at breakfast when he got there. Buchanan said he did not think anything of it at the time, but thinking about it now, he had also been surprised to see that Symonds was in the clothes he had been wearing the previous evening rather than his training gear, which is usually what players wear to the ground.

The coach now went to speak to Symonds, to try to find out exactly what had happened, but, rather than apologise, Symonds sought to justify his actions. 'I've played when I've been like this before,' he said. That may have been the case at a lower level, but I was determined to make sure it was not going to happen here.

My mind had gone from thinking about the match to wondering what on earth had happened last night. I began to wonder if any other players were involved. I knew a couple of the lads had gone out with Symonds, so I turned my attention to them. Brad Haddin and Shane Watson were two of those players. The look on my face must have told them how angry I was, because when I came up to them they looked as though they had seen a ghost.

'Were you out with Symo last night?' I said.

They said nothing, which annoyed me even more, if that was possible. Looking back now, I guess their reaction was understandable. They were obviously sticking up for their mate; they realised he was in trouble and did not want him getting in any deeper than he was already. Maybe they thought I would have a go at them about being out late, but all I was interested in was getting to the bottom of what Symonds had been up to.

Having drawn a blank with those two, I suddenly realised that the toss was just 15 minutes away and I had some pressing issues to sort out, the first of them being who would replace Symonds in the side. I went to see Simon Katich, told him he was playing and then set off to deal with the next problem.

We had already announced the side to the media, and now we were changing that line-up at the eleventh hour. Quite rightly, the reporters and broadcasters would want to know why. Was the player injured or ill? If so, was it serious?

We — principally John Buchanan and I — decided that it would stir up too much of a hornets' nest to announce the real reason why Symonds had been left out at this stage, especially when we were not sure of all the facts ourselves. None of us had got much sense out of Symonds or anyone else so far, and that clearly needed to be done before we could make any statement on the situation.

I was going to be interviewed on television at the toss but still had not been able to establish the facts. So we decided to say that he had not yet fully recovered from the cold he had been suffering with during the week.

I regret that now, but at the time it seemed the right thing to do. I know that if I had said Symonds had been left out for a breach of team rules, as I should have done, all hell would have broken loose and we would have had a group of reporters outside our dressing room straightaway while we were trying to focus on the match we were about to play. In any case, the story we concocted did not wash with several reporters. A few of them had been out in the same bars as Symonds, and they were shrewd enough to guess that something other than a cold was responsible for his omission from the side. Our media manager, Belinda Dennett, was placed in an awkward situation. At that stage she had not been told the true situation and, in good faith, passed on incorrect information, initially that Symonds was injured and then that he had the flu, to the media without realising that the facts were actually different. The rumour machine cranked into full swing in the press box.

With the toss and my media interviews completed, I returned to the dressing room to try to get my mind switched on for the match. On the evidence of the result, I failed to do that very well, but though the issue did cast a massive shadow over the whole day, I do not wish to take anything away from the way Bangladesh played. We played poorly, they were good enough to take advantage of that fact, and they deserve all the credit they will get for the superb victory.

After the match I had to face the media, but I was still not totally clear about what had happened last night. We hadn't had the chance to discuss the issue either as a management group or as a team. That happened straight after I finished my media commitments.

We held a 30-minute meeting with the entire squad in the dining room on the ground floor of the pavilion. It started badly, with Buchanan tarring all the players involved — not just Symonds, but also Haddin, Watson and Brett Lee — with the same brush. They were all responsible for breaching team rules, as they were all out late at night before a game, he said. Maybe he did not want to see Symonds hung out to dry alone, but those other players then got upset at the suggestion that they had done anything wrong.

There was disagreement within the group over the role of players other than Symonds, so I had my say. It *was* wrong that they were all out late on the night before a match for their country, but only Symonds had been selected for that match, and only Symonds was clearly the worse for wear the following day. He had to expect some punishment.

Having said that, I added that this was a lesson to everyone about our commitment as a squad to the Spirit of Cricket, to behaving in a way that is appropriate for a group of individuals representing both the game of cricket and our country. Like it or not, we are role models, and the behaviour of those players out late, and Symonds specifically, was hardly in keeping with that ethic.

Although I sensed that some players still sided with Buchanan, my sentiments appeared to win over the meeting and we then separated to get ready for the trip to Bristol, about 75 minutes east along the motorway. Before we left I spoke individually to Haddin, Watson, Lee and Symonds. All of them expressed contrition over what had happened. Watson especially was down on himself, because his birthday was the reason for the evening out in the first place. Symonds, now sober, had already apologised to the group during the meeting. He realised how much he had let everyone down — especially me, because I have publicly backed him very strongly over the past 2 years.

Chatting with the players on a one-to-one basis, I began to understand some of the things I had seen this morning; things which, at the time, I had thought nothing about. I had seen Michael Clarke running from the breakfast room onto the bus with a bacon sandwich, and had joked with him: 'Bit hungry, are you?'

Clarke is usually one of the first to breakfast, especially on the day of a game, so it was uncharacteristic for him to get up so late as to miss his meal. The reality was that he had spent the previous 30 minutes trying to get Symonds out of bed and dressed so that he would not miss the bus.

After Symonds had had his early breakfast, he had gone back to his room and fallen into such a deep sleep that not even Clarke banging on his door could wake him. Clarke got a spare key from reception, let himself into the room and dragged Symonds out of bed to get him ready for the bus's departure.

Symonds knew he would face punishment over the incident, and he knew that Bernard, Buchanan and I would decide what that punishment would be when we got to Bristol. I knew he was worried about being sent home, but though I had been furious when the incident first came to light in the morning, and had blurted out that threat to Gilchrist, once I calmed down it was not something I was seriously considering.

As far as I was concerned, all the players involved had done the wrong thing, and Symonds would be punished for his excessive actions. But once that punishment was handed down, whatever it was, it was a case of everyone moving on and being better tomorrow. There was no point dwelling on the matter beyond that, and sending Symonds home would only have kept the matter bubbling — and he would have had to live with the stigma of that for the rest of his career. There are other things for us to focus on, such as the performances of individuals and the team.

When we reached Bristol, Buchanan and I headed straight for Bernard's room to discuss the punishment for Symonds. We had been appointed by CA to sit in judgment on matters of discipline on the tour, but I don't think any of us ever expected to have to do so, least of all this early in the tour.

Before we discussed the matter in detail, Bernard had rung James Sutherland to get a feel for the types of sanctions acceptable to CA. There was no point in us handing down a punishment that CA felt was unacceptable.

Even before Bernard made that call I think the three of us knew a fine would be seen as too lenient, and that sending the player home would be an over-reaction. We wanted to find some sort of middle ground, so we asked Sutherland whether a two-match ban and a fine of two match fees would fit the bill. He was content with that, and said that if that was our decision, he would support it.

Armed with that information, we came to our conclusion very quickly. We agreed that the two-game suspension was the right course of action, and that one of those suspensions had already been served. Bernard relayed that to Sutherland and also went to see Symonds to tell him the news. He was mightily relieved to remain on tour, and was determined to move on as soon as possible.

We also had to ring the Chairman of Selectors, Trevor Hohns, to apologise for changing the side without informing him. He was disappointed that none of us had called to let him know what was happening — unfortunately, with so much going on, that had been the last thing on our minds.

I am guessing that some people will draw a parallel between Symonds's actions and my own drink-related problems in 1998 in India and in Sydney the following year, with the latter incident resulting in my suspension. Were there any similarities? I think not, because when I was drunk in Sydney it was not the night before a match. Having said that, I was still in the wrong then and was suspended for my mistake.

Those experiences did not, in my opinion, make me any more or less sympathetic to Symonds's cause; and the fact that he is an integral part of the squad did not mean I was more inclined to favour suspension over sending him home. As far as I was concerned, it was simply a case of making sure the punishment fit the crime. And once that punishment was meted out, it was time to move on.

By the end of our meeting my head was swimming so much that the cricketing events of the day had almost disappeared from my thoughts. That may have been just as well, because the match itself was a disaster from start to finish, beginning with the toss.

I had it in mind to bowl first if I won that toss, because the pitch had been under cover for much of the previous 2 days and there was cloud cover first thing, which suggested to me that the pitch would give the bowlers some assistance with swing and seam early on.

But as I walked to the middle at 10.15 the sun came out, and when the coin came down in my favour I decided that conditions were not as bowler-friendly as I had originally thought. I opted to bat — and was very soon regretting the decision.

The Bangladesh bowlers may be novices in international terms, but they are still skilful enough to exploit conditions that are in their favour, and they made things extremely difficult for us in the first couple of hours. I found the going especially tough, and struggled to get my mind on the job in hand. I was soon dismissed, but the cause of my dismissal was technical rather than mental. I overbalanced towards the offside and ended up playing across a straight ball and falling plumb lbw.

Given the start we made — we were 3–57 in the 16th over — I was more than content with our final score of 5–249, but in hindsight I realised that we should have scored 20 or 30 more runs. We allowed the left-arm spinner Mohammad Rafique and the gentle medium-pacer Aftab Ahmed to operate in tandem through the middle of the innings and bowl 20 overs for just 79 runs. Martyn and Clarke, the not-out batsmen at the time, felt they needed to consolidate the innings after the early loss of those 3 wickets, but with two experienced batsmen — Hussey and Katich — still in the pavilion, we could have pressed the accelerator earlier than we did.

Having said that, the way we bowled and fielded makes me wonder whether we could have defended even 280. We were flat in the field for the whole day, and there was no real buzz out on the ground. I have to put some of that down to the disruptions of the start of the day. Even when we were batting, there were groups of players in the dressing room chatting about what had happened; it was clear minds were not wholly on the job at hand.

Maybe there was a lack of respect for the opposition as well. Bangladesh have never come close to a result of this magnitude before, so perhaps we were guilty of just waiting for the batsmen to get themselves out rather than doing something about it.

I began to fear that we were in with a chance of losing the game when we were in the field, because our bowlers made no impact at all through the middle overs of the Bangladesh innings; and the one chance we did create, when Mohammad Ashraful top-edged a hook shot to Jason Gillespie at long leg, was missed very badly.

Apart from that chance, Ashraful, together with his captain Habib-ul-Bashar and Aftab Ahmed, played superbly, and they fully deserved the victory. They made our bowling and fielding look exactly what it was — ordinary.

Our performance was definitely the worst I have been involved in, and although all I wanted to do after the match was disappear, I had to go and speak to the media to try to explain how one of the greatest shocks in the history of the game had just happened. I tried to remain upbeat — and I hope I managed it — but on the evidence of today's display there was not much to be upbeat about.

The one consolation I am clinging to at the moment is that today's results will act as a massive wake-up call to everyone in the team. I cannot believe we will play as badly as this again, or that we will suffer the level of disruption we did today before another game on this tour. It is better that this happened now rather than in the final of the tournament, but from here on we must get back to our first priority: getting to that final.

Having back-to-back matches, as we have this weekend, is not an ideal situation, especially as we are set to face a pepped-up England tomorrow. But in a strange sort of way maybe it is good that we are playing again so soon after a loss like this — perhaps it will help us put the events of the past 24 hours behind us quickly.

Sunday 19 June

NatWest Series, match 3, Bristol: Australia (1 point) 9–252 (Hussey 84, Harmison 5–33) lost to England (5 points) 7–253 (Pietersen 91*, Vaughan 57) by 3 wickets.

Another day and another defeat, but today, at least, there were some positive signs for us, and I feel a lot happier about the manner of this loss than I did after the game in Cardiff.

We lost 3 wickets in an over, including mine the first ball, but still got ourselves into a position where we were controlling the game — until the innings of a lifetime from Kevin Pietersen wrenched it out of our grasp.

He was brutal in his hitting, mostly in the arc between midwicket and long-on, and although I placed four fielders on the leg-side boundary at one stage, he still managed to hit the ball to and sometimes over the ropes.

He gave our bowlers a lesson in getting the ball in the right areas. We were trying to bowl yorkers at him in the latter stages of the match, but if we erred even slightly he was able to steady himself, get under the ball and use his fantastic strength to club it to the fence.

We definitely missed Brett Lee's extra pace against Pietersen, as he was able to ease onto the front foot in the knowledge that we did not have a bowler capable of forcing him back with a rapid short ball. Lee could also have made a difference with his reverse swinging yorkers in the late stages. But there is no point in dwelling on ifs and buts. We came up short on the day, and all credit to Pietersen for the way he played.

The fact that we had to play 2 days in a row — and today turned out very hot — was not ideal, as I have said, but it was not a factor in our loss. Opposition sides have to deal with it when they come to Australia for the VB Series, so we can hardly complain when we suffer the same fate on tour.

But, once again, our preparation was not great. We had a team meeting after breakfast, and before we left for the ground Symonds again apologised to everyone. His punishment was announced to the squad at the ground and everyone seemed to accept it. We all agreed that it was time to move on and focus on the game at hand, but when we set off for the county ground in Bristol that proved easier said than done.

The streets around the venue are very narrow, and a combination of an England–Australia match and a large bus meant that we were stuck in traffic for around 15 minutes, despite having a motorcycle outrider with us. Then, when we got to the ground, we were directed to the wrong gate and were dropped off on the other side of the ground from the dressing rooms. It meant we had to drag our kitbags through the crowds, which took time, so we were not out on the ground for warm-ups until 10 minutes before the toss. I only had time for a lap of the ground before I had to head inside to get my playing gear on.

I opted to bat and we made a great start through Gilchrist and Hayden, easing along at better than 5 runs an over. That forced Michael Vaughan to bring Stephen Harmison into the attack. That pleased us, because we know that he prefers to use Harmison later in the innings, when the fielding restrictions are relaxed and he can operate with boundary fielders on either side of the wicket.

Our pleasure at seeing Harmison come into the attack was short-lived. He dismissed Gilchrist, caught behind cutting, then me and Damien Martyn, caught upper-cutting to third man, all in the space of an over, and when he snared Hayden 2 overs later, brilliantly caught at backward point, we were in deep trouble, especially as we had left Simon Katich out and put Shane Watson in — we wanted to bolster the bowling after yesterday's effort and to rest Katich's troublesome knee.

My dismissal was similar to yesterday's: I overbalanced in the face of a full-length straight ball, ending up playing across my front pad. It is a concern that I should fall twice the same way, and I will have to work with Jamie Siddons, our assistant coach, to correct my balance and start playing straighter.

We were rescued by Mike Hussey and Michael Clarke, who played intelligent innings, accumulating runs sensibly, and ended up with a score I felt we could defend. I still believe that, even after the match. We were simply denied by Pietersen's brilliance.

Having said that, the lines we bowled to him were not great — we will have to look at bowling more outside off-stump to him in future. Katich, who played with him at Hampshire at the start of the season, said he often got out caught at second slip, so that is something we will have to look at when we face England — and Pietersen — again. We will also need to look at how we approach the contest against him. Shane Watson tried to be ultra-aggressive and let him have a few verbal volleys, but that seemed to do nothing except fire Pietersen up even more. Next time we will say nothing when he is batting.

Our bowling was disappointing today. Jason Gillespie, especially, had no rhythm at all. We left him out of the match against Somerset during the week because we felt he had been bowling well at the start of the trip and so would benefit from a rest rather than extra work ahead of the internationals, but here he was all over the place, with a succession of wides in his opening over. Pietersen tucked into him at the end of the match, when he and Michael Kasprowicz were forced to bowl — without Lee, I was short of a bowler to operate in the last few overs alongside Glenn McGrath. Kasprowicz and Gillespie can both fill that role, but neither was quick enough or accurate enough to get the ball in the right place often enough, and with Pietersen in top form their figures suffered.

Early on we were in a very strong position thanks to a great spell from Brad Hogg. The England batsmen struggled to pick what Hogg was bowling, and after he dismissed Vaughan and Geraint Jones in successive overs, the match seemed safely in our grasp — and it would have been, but for Pietersen's hitting.

Our fielding was definitely sharper than in the last few matches, and I thought I had won the game for us when I scored a direct hit on the stumps to run out Pietersen. But replays showed that he had just made his ground thanks to an uncanny sequence of events: my throw was slowed down when it bounced in some loose earth just next to the stumps, and then it hit the furthest stump away rather than the one nearest to me. The combination of those factors meant that Pietersen was just in when the bails were dislodged, and he was adept enough to take advantage of his good fortune.

My post-match media conference involved talking about another defeat, but now I can at least see some light at the end of the tunnel. We should have Lee and Symonds back for our next match; we showed a lot more fight than yesterday; and I have not seen anything from England today that makes me believe we cannot beat them.

Back at the hotel, and with no meetings to worry about, I was able to relax and try to unwind for the first time in 2 days. Luckily, the final round of the US Open golf was on television, so I was able to enjoy New Zealand's Michael Campbell securing a deserved victory.

I took the opportunity of our 480-kilometre bus trip from Bristol to Durham today to chat with our media manager, Belinda Dennett, about what has been said in the media about our performances over the weekend.

I like to be kept up to date with what the journalists are saying about us — that way I can be prepared for their questions when I have to attend a media conference — but I am not a great reader of the newspapers, especially when it comes to the opinions of ex-players and commentators. Everyone is entitled to their view, but mine is that we have enough knowledge and experience in the squad to know how we should be playing, and if it takes an outsider to point something out to us, then the players and the coaching staff are not doing their jobs properly.

Dennett said that the media reaction to our losses and the Andrew Symonds issue has been fairly predictable, with the British media gloating at our defeats and the Australian media wondering what on earth is going on. Given our run of success against England over the past two decades, I can understand those responses, but I am trying to remain level-headed about the whole thing. I saw enough signs yesterday to know that we are not too far away from a return to our winning ways, and that is something I am drilling into anyone I speak to, including my team-mates. We have not become bad players overnight, and as long as we can up our skill level by maybe 5 per cent, we can turn defeats into victories. I believe the margin is as fine as that.

Dennett seems to think everyone has been satisfied with the punishment handed down to Symonds; we are still waiting to hear from CA that there will be no further action. If the media response to the punishment has been favourable, I hope that means we will be able to continue with the rest of the tour in peace.

Different players handled our time on the tour bus in different ways. A few players watched DVDs or read magazines at the back; Jason Gillespie, Brett Lee and Brad Hogg spent the trip playing the Tiger Woods golf game on PlayStation; Shane Watson, like Lee, is someone who can sleep in almost any situation, so he was asleep for most of the time; and Adam Gilchrist tapped away on his laptop.

As well as chatting to Dennett, I listened to some music and read some golf magazines. When we arrived at our hotel in the late afternoon, I played five holes of golf before our team dinner. The golf allowed me to switch off from cricket for an hour, and that was just what I needed after the last couple of days.

Our dinner was organised by Mike Hussey, who has been playing for and captaining the Durham county side this season, and during dinner there was plenty of chat about the place where we are staying, Lumley Castle. It overlooks the ground and there are rumours that it is haunted.

I do not believe in any of that but there were a few people in our group who do — Dennett, Watson and Lucy Frostick, our massage therapist were clearly unsettled by jokes about ghosts during the evening. The hotel is a strange place: the staff are dressed in medieval costumes in keeping with the setting, the corridors are filled with suits of armour and busts, and there are some narrow and dark nooks, corners and stairways in the building. In Watson's defence, his room is gloomy and an unusual shape — his bathroom is behind a concealed door. For someone who may be nervous about ghosts, it is not an ideal spot.

Tuesday 21 June

NatWest Series, match 4, Nottingham: England (6 points) 4–391 (Strauss 152, Collingwood 112*, Trescothick 85) beat Bangladesh (0 points) 223 (Ashraful 94, Omar 59, Collingwood 6–31) by 168 runs.

I slept really well last night, but the same does not seem to have been the case for a few of the squad. Shane Watson was so unnerved by his room that he went and slept on Brett Lee's floor, and Belinda Dennett swears she saw ghosts outside her window.

It would be funny except for the fact that Watson and Dennett were genuinely concerned by their experiences. I gather it is not the first time a touring team has had these experiences at the hotel: West Indies and Bangladesh players have also reportedly been frightened by unexplained goings-on. But, as I said, I had a great night's sleep.

Ghosts were not our only concern today: Michael Clarke suffered a back injury during our training session. Everyone was very keen to work hard on our ground fielding, and perhaps Clarke overdid it, because during the session his back seized up and he had difficulty moving. He was examined by Errol Alcott. We hope the problem is something straightforward that will ease, but if it doesn't there is no way he will be fit enough to play on Thursday.

England captain Michael Vaughan is ruled out of Thursday's match with Australia after suffering a groin injury during his side's victory over Bangladesh on Tuesday.

It has not taken long for the concerns of some of our squad about ghosts at our hotel to become public knowledge.

Under the headline 'Scare dinkum', *The Sun*, Britain's leading daily tabloid newspaper, has quoted Belinda Dennett as saying that she saw spectres heading past her window on Monday night.

I feel sorry for Dennett because, having had a call from the paper about Shane Watson's sleeping arrangements yesterday, she tried to take the heat off him by talking about her own experiences instead, but it has backfired on her. The British press has tried to make her look foolish for believing in ghosts.

Having said that, it is the type of media coverage that is easy to dismiss, unlike something else we experienced today. As a few of us were heading back to the hotel after a training session at the ground, we got a call from Dennett saying there were some people waiting for us at the entrance to the hotel, hoping to get us involved in a compromising photograph. One person had a kangaroo outfit on, and there was also a young woman wearing a singlet and little else. We stopped close to the entrance and watched what they were doing, and at one stage the woman lifted up her singlet as the photographer with them took some pictures.

We sneaked around the side of the hotel to get inside and immediately reported the people to the hotel management, but when they were asked to leave the premises things got very heated — at one stage I thought it was going to turn ugly. Even as they left, the photographer was waving his camera around trying to get photographs of us.

Our practice session for tomorrow's match went well. Andrew Symonds and Brett Lee both looked fit and ready to come back into the side, and that will give us an enormous boost. Lee's extra pace and his ability to swing the ball will add a dimension to our attack, and Symonds gives our one-day line-up so much, with his hard-hitting batting, his brilliance in the field and his ability to bowl spin and seam. In every training session since his offence he has worked harder than anyone else. That is what I wanted to see: that he has put the events of last Friday and Saturday behind him.

With Michael Clarke laid low with inflammation in a disc, Symonds will come in for him. Who to leave out for Lee is a hard call. Neither Jason Gillespie nor Michael Kasprowicz is in the best of form, but I chatted with the selector on duty, Andrew Hilditch, and it is likely we will go with Gillespie because of his reputation as a big-match player over many years.

This evening I sampled the delights of Matthew Hayden's cooking. He has bought a mini gas barbecue and fired it up for myself and Damien Martyn, and it made a pleasant change from restaurant food.

Thursday 23 June

Cricket Australia Chairman Bob Merriman issues a statement confirming that no further disciplinary action will be taken against Andrew Symonds, who was handed a two-match ban and a fine because of a breach of team rules in Cardiff.

NatWest Series, match 5, Durham: Australia (6 points) 5–266 (Symonds 73, Martyn 68*) beat England (0 points) 9–209 by 57 runs.

This was a satisfying performance. I felt after Bristol that we were not far away from getting a win under our belts, and today I was proved right. We batted solidly, bowled well with the new ball, and our intensity in the field was back to the level I expect from us at all times.

It is also pleasing to see that, despite winning very comfortably, there is still plenty of room for improvement. We were sloppy with the bat in the early stages of our innings, slipping to 3–96 on a blameless pitch, and I was frustrated that we were not able to bowl England out as their last-wicket pair — Darren Gough and Stephen Harmison — added an unbroken 50. We were not helped at the end by the lack of pace in the pitch, which meant our fast bowlers were unable to rattle Gough and Harmison. A few yorkers would surely have done the job but, as in Bristol, we were unable to bowl any.

Thankfully, by that stage it did not matter too much. England were completely out of contention, as they had been ever since Glenn McGrath and Brett Lee combined with a brilliant opening burst to reduce it to 3–6. Lee gave our attack a much more menacing look than it had last weekend, swinging the new ball into the left-handed openers at pace, and he well and truly disconcerted Andrew Strauss before bowling him off the inside edge.

We were definitely helped by England's decision to bowl first, made when stand-in captain Marcus Trescothick won the toss. Having played at Durham last season with Somerset, I knew how slow the pitch was — it would be very tough to try to force the pace and chase a big total if we were batting second. And that was exactly how it turned out.

Brad Hogg again bowled well, and tied up Kevin Pietersen and Andrew Flintoff during a vital stage of the innings. The loss of early wickets meant that neither batsman could afford to look for too many big shots — there were not many capable batsmen after them — but if we had bowled a few casual overs at that stage it could still have given them some momentum. Hogg kept it tight and earned his reward when he had Flintoff caught on the boundary, and when Pietersen was caught in the deep, desperately looking for a boundary as the asking rate spiralled, I knew the game was won.

I failed again, caught at third man for, I reckon, the first time in my career. I was undone by Harmison's extra pace and bounce as I attempted to steer the ball for a single, and it flew off the leading edge, carrying all the way to the fielder running in off the boundary.

We were steadied by Andrew Symonds and Damien Martyn, with Symonds again demonstrating his value to the side. The pair assessed conditions quickly, realising that a massive score was going to be difficult to achieve, and worked the ball around cleverly to set us up for our match-winning total. Symonds was just starting to open his shoulders towards the end of the innings when he ran himself out, but he did more than enough to earn the man of the match award. I am not sure we will see him drinking the champagne that formed part of the prize for a while yet, though.

At least we have our first win on the board. Let's hope we can build on that and finally start to get some momentum.

Friday 24 June

Australia team physiotherapist Errol Alcott says Michael Clarke's back condition is improving but he is unlikely to be fit for tomorrow's game against Bangladesh at Old Trafford. 'We will continue to monitor his progress over the next couple of days,' says Alcott.

Simon Jones has rejoined the England one-day squad after a week of treatment and rehabilitation on his right knee; his replacement, Chris Tremlett, will remain with the squad.

After a 2-hour bus trip to Manchester today we had a team meeting to prepare for our next match, against Bangladesh tomorrow.

In view of the embarrassment we suffered last Saturday, there was not a lot that needed to be said, but I pointed out that it was up to us to go out and put the record straight. We have a point to prove — not only to ourselves, but also to the watching cricket world: that the events in Cardiff were a one-off that will never happen again.

I am confident they will not. We have Andrew Symonds and Brett Lee back after both missed last Saturday's debacle, and their presence makes a massive difference, as we saw against England yesterday.

Saturday 25 June

Hampshire has agreed to a request from CA that Shane Warne is rested for the next 2 weeks. Warne has experienced a slight problem in his spinning finger after bowling almost 300 overs in 8 first-class matches for the county he captains.

The news came on the same day as a joint statement by Warne and his wife, Simone, that they are to separate after almost 10 years of marriage.

NatWest Series, match 6, Manchester: Australia (6 points) 0–140 (Gilchrist 66*, Hayden 66*) beat Bangladesh (0 points) 139 (Ashraful 58, Symonds 5–18) by 10 wickets.

We gave exactly the type of performance I was after today, handing Bangladesh a comprehensive hammering.

The downside was that only two of us — Matthew Hayden and Adam Gilchrist — got to spend time at the crease, but the result was more important. I wanted us to make a statement, to let the other two sides in the tournament know that we are back and mean business. England beat Bangladesh by 10 wickets last week, so for us to do the same today will make them sit up and take notice.

We showed real intent first with the ball and then with the bat, and overcame what could have been a mistake on my part — the decision to bowl first. I thought I saw a tinge of green in the surface, but the pitch turned out to be very, very dry, and if Bangladesh had got a score of 250, as they did at Cardiff, it could have proved tough to chase.

We rolled our sleeves up and, despite some audacious strokeplay from Mohammad Ashraful, we kept our nerve. And Andrew Symonds bowled beautifully to collect a career-best return with his off-spin.

Once again we still have room for improvement. Brett Lee took a wicket with a no-ball, something that drives me mad. We have wasted hours talking about the problem in team meetings for as long as I can remember, as it is not only Lee who has been at fault: Michael Kasprowicz took the wicket of Graeme Smith with a no-ball in our match against Somerset and that, arguably, played a major part in our defeat.

When, during the meetings, it is pointed out that the bowlers always overstep in practice, their standard comeback is 'Training is all about getting some rhythm' rather than the position of their feet, and that they will not overstep in match conditions.

Well, they do, as Lee did today, and it is unacceptable, but apart from making the point again, I am not sure what else can be done. Fines are one answer, but surely at this elite level that should not be necessary. I know questions will be asked about what the captain and coach are doing to solve the problem, but my view is that it is solely the responsibility of the player who oversteps to sort it out. He is letting everyone down and, as I said to Adam Gilchrist afterwards, I do not understand why a bowler has to deliver with his heel so close to the front line in the first place.

The post-match media conference was a routine affair until, near the end, one of the Australia-based reporters on the tour came in with news of a statement that had just been issued by Shane and Simone Warne, confirming that they are separating. The newspapers in the dressing room in Bristol last Sunday apparently had some pretty lurid headlines about Shane's private life, so this latest news is not a great shock, although it is obviously very sad.

I have not been in touch with Shane either about the tour or this latest issue, but I will do so sometime over the next few days. No matter what he has gone through in his private life, during the time I have been playing alongside him he has always had the ability to focus completely on his cricket whenever he walks onto the field. And despite this new turn of events, I would not be surprised if he was able to do the same thing when he links up with us for the Test series next month.

Sunday 26 June

England and Australia are to hold discussions on whether or not to introduce new ICC regulations in the NatWest Challenge — three one-day internationals that follow the NatWest Series. The regulations, including the use of replacement fielders and new fielding restrictions, are due for worldwide implementation on 30 July for a 10-month trial period.

NatWest Series, match 7, Leeds: England (6 points) 5–209 (Strauss 98) beat Bangladesh (0 points) 7–208 (Omar 81) by 5 wickets.

After making the 2-hour trip from Manchester to Birmingham last night we had a light training session at Edgbaston today, and I did some work with assistant coach Jamie Siddons to ensure that my balance at the crease is okay. So far in the series my head has been falling over to the offside, taking me away from the line of the ball when it is bowled straight at the stumps. That, in turn, means I have ended up playing across my front pad rather than pushing straight balls back down the ground with the full face of the bat. The correction involves getting my head moving towards the ball and making sure I pick up the line of the ball before I commit to a movement. I ended the session pretty happy with the work I did, but it is what happens in the middle that counts.

I sent Shane Warne a series of text messages during the day. I wanted to find out how he is coping with the latest controversy surrounding him, and I was also keen to let him know how much we are looking forward to him linking up with the squad for the Ashes series.

Whatever the rights and wrongs of what has happened, it cannot be an easy time for him. I was encouraged when I got a text back saying he is as keen as ever to play the Test matches. He wants to put his recent problems behind him and get on with what he does best — playing cricket — and that is great news for us.

Monday 27 June

Today's training session left me with a really positive feeling about the way things are going. I know I had that feeling at the start of the tour and was proved wrong in a big way, but the buzz around the squad today was unmistakeable, and I know we are really up for tomorrow's match against England.

Bangladesh's defeat yesterday means it will be an England–Australia final at Lord's next Saturday, but I do not expect that to mean that either side will go into tomorrow's action in cruise mode; I want us to make a statement and impose ourselves on England in a way we have not done on the tour so far. I want them to have plenty to think about in the lead-up to Lord's. I am sure the England players will be thinking along the same lines.

The last time I played at Edgbaston was last September, and just about everything that could go wrong did go wrong. We lost the semi-final of the Champions Trophy, played poorly, and I broke my thumb. All that is in the past now and will have no bearing on tomorrow's match, but if we needed an added incentive, that is it.

After training, James Sutherland, who has been in London on ICC business for CA, met up with Steve Bernard, John Buchanan and a few of the senior players, including myself, Damien Martyn and Matthew Hayden, for a chat. The main topic of conversation was the incident involving Andrew Symonds.

We all get on well with Sutherland, a former first-class player with Victoria, but he took us by surprise when he asked: 'Do you feel responsible for Andrew's actions?'

His suggestion was that in a team environment, where players are meant to look out for one another, there is no way one of us should be able to go out, get drunk and stay out late on the night before a match, especially as we have all agreed to abide by the Spirit of Cricket.

I could see his point, but I couldn't agree with it. To start with, I was in bed when Symonds was out on the town, so I was not sure what I could have done to prevent him having a late night; on top of that, I am a great believer in players taking responsibility for their own actions. Symonds, as a senior player, should have known what he was doing. Instead he misbehaved, and paid the price. What happened was his fault, and trying to blame the rest of us for it was not right, in my view.

There was also the issue of the lie I told at the start of the match when I said that Symonds was ill rather than ruled out of the match for a breach of team rules. I know it was wrong, and if I had my time again I would do things differently, but, as I told Sutherland, I did not lie as a way of covering up Symonds's actions; I did it to try to buy us time to get to the bottom of what happened. Sutherland understood and accepted that, but made the point that nothing like that should be allowed to happen in the future.

Tuesday 28 June

NatWest Series, match 8, Birmingham: Australia (3 points) 9–261 (Symonds 74) v England (3 points) 1–37, match abandoned, rain.

Although today's match ended without a positive result, there was plenty to excite the crowd and the media during the day.

The major talking point seems to have been the incident involving Matthew Hayden and England's Simon Jones, which I saw from the non-striker's end. Hayden, pushing forward, defended a ball back to Jones, who gathered it and threw it in the direction of the stumps, supposedly in an attempt to run Hayden out.

The ball must have got stuck in his hand, because it came out all wrong — instead of heading toward the stumps, it bounced well short of them, then flew up and hit Hayden in the chest. Jones immediately put his hand up to apologise, but the incident fired Hayden up.

'What the hell did you do that for?' he shouted.

That seemed to take Jones by surprise, but really, if a fielder throws the ball towards the stumps, misses by almost 3 metres and hits the batsman instead, he has to expect some comeback.

Hayden's response prompted other England players to fly in and get involved. Paul Collingwood ran in and gave Hayden a few choice words, and Andrew Strauss also joined in.

I could see the incident was in danger of getting out of hand, so I moved down the pitch myself. Hayden and Collingwood were toe to toe, so I pushed Hayden away back to his crease and told Strauss and Collingwood to get on with the game. Afterwards Hayden thanked me. He said he had lost his cool and was in danger of completely over-reacting.

Looking back on the incident, I think it has been made out to be bigger than it actually was. It was something that happened in the heat of the moment, and as long as such things are treated that way and not dwelled upon — and as long as an apology is made — everyone can just get on with the game. That is what happened. There were no more incidents.

Having said all that, I wonder why Jones did it in the first place. My experience of him is of a fairly mild-mannered character. He must have known he was never going to run Hayden out, even if his throw was on target.

I suspect that he, along with the other England players, had been told to do things like that by the captain, Michael Vaughan, and the coach, Duncan Fletcher, because they think it shows they are tough cricketers, willing to stand up to us and not prepared to be bullied.

If that is the case, it is rubbish. You do not show you are tough by hurling the ball at the batsman like that; you show you are tough by being totally committed to every ball you bowl or face. I will be interested to see if they persist with that tactic, if it was indeed a tactic they had decided to use.

Once again our top order failed to fire, and we also failed to score heavily in the final 10 overs of our innings. We were bailed out again by our middle order, with Andrew Symonds and Mike Hussey once more outstanding. It was another slow surface that was going to make chasing a target tough, so we were happy to have the runs on the board.

By the time we were due to start the second innings, conditions had become unpleasant. It was dark, and although there were floodlights because it was a day–night match, they could not be put up to their full height because there were thunderstorms in the area. We were happy to be bowling in those conditions, and even happier when, after a delay for rain, England's revised target was 200 from 33 overs, something we felt would be very difficult to chase.

It was a nasty shock when England got away to a flying start when we resumed. Strauss hit 4 fours in an over from Glenn McGrath, but although McGrath came back to dismiss Strauss, so did the bad weather, and we did not bowl another ball.

There was an unpleasant postscript to the day as well. Belinda Dennett came to me in the dressing room after the match and said that some of the journalists had asked her about an allegation that Hayden swore at some children on his way to the crease. When the match gets under way the entrance to the playing arena is lined by youngsters who form an archway with flags — the players run onto the ground through that archway. The allegation was that Hayden swore at one of those children, something I found impossible to believe.

I knew something like that could be written up very unfavourably, so I immediately approached Hayden and asked him whether or not it was true. He was shocked and denied the allegation completely. 'You know what I'm like around kids,' he said. 'That is the last thing I would ever do.'

His denial was so strong that I asked Dennett to report it to the journalists who had asked about the matter; we also decided that she should try to find out the source of the claim, so that we could get to the bottom of the matter. None of that stopped me having to field questions about the allegation when I spoke the media in my post-match conference, and that angered me. It made me wonder how many times we have to deny a story before the media either believe us or present evidence to back up their claims.

Wednesday 29 June

Today's bus trip from Birmingham to Canterbury was a long one — about 5 hours, plus a motorway rest stop so we could stretch our legs and get some fresh air — and I reckon Matthew Hayden spent most of it on the phone to his management in Australia, dealing with the fallout from last night's accusations.

We have still heard nothing concrete to back up the scuttlebutt, and Belinda Dennett and Steve Bernard have so far failed to find any foundation to the story. If the source is found, I think Hayden has every right to demand an apology.

Once we got to Canterbury, Hayden was able to turn his mind to other matters: he got his gas barbecue out again and made dinner for Damien Martyn and me, cooking up a superb meal of chicken, green beans, broccoli and some salad.

We opted not to have a team meeting this evening. After the way we played against Bangladesh in our last encounter — with plenty of aggression, imposing ourselves on them — I felt it was not necessary.

We are likely to make at least one change for the match — Glenn McGrath will probably rest. He has been struggling with some fluid on his knee, and the chance for him to sit out a game that has nothing riding on it will do that problem some good, as well as giving Michael Kasprowicz another chance to impress and Jason Gillespie, who is still struggling for form, an opportunity with the new ball.

Thursday 30 June

The England & Wales Cricket Board (ECB) confirms that new ICC regulations for one-day international cricket will be trialled during the three-match NatWest Challenge between England and Australia that follows the NatWest Series: both sides will be able to introduce a substitute, and the restrictions allowing only two fielders outside the 30-yard fielding circle will be increased from one continuous block of 15 overs to three blocks of 10, 5 and 5 overs.

NatWest Series, match 9, Canterbury: Australia (5 points) 4–254 (Clarke 80*, Ponting 66) beat Bangladesh (1 point) 8–250 (Nafees 75, Mashud 71*) by 6 wickets.

This was another disappointing performance from us, especially with the ball. For the second time in the tournament, Bangladesh scored 250 against us. They should never have come close to that total after we had them at 5–75.

It was the same old problem for us on this tour: our bowlers struggled for correct execution. Lines and lengths were wrong, and they bowled no-balls and wides. It was a sloppy display, and not what we wanted 2 days before the final.

The one positive was that it gave us a decent target to chase, and that meant a couple of our batsmen got time at the crease. Michael Clarke, who has been struggling for form and fitness, played well after starting scratchily. He got his feet moving, found his timing, and by the end of his innings looked in good form, as did Andrew

Symonds, who joined him to kill off Bangladesh's dreams of a second win against us.

I spoke to the bowlers both during the Bangladesh innings and afterwards, trying to find out what problems they were having. Both Brett Lee and Michael Kasprowicz — who played in place of Glenn McGrath, who is being rested — noted that the pronounced slope that runs across the ground did not help their rhythm, but everyone in our attack has played on a sloping ground before, so that was not a great excuse. Anyone who wants to play on Saturday had better get used to a slope, because Lord's has one across the ground, just like Canterbury.

We were without Brad Hogg — he came down with food poisoning overnight. He could not keep any food down, but was still desperate to play. However, when the doctor at the ground saw him, it was obvious he was too weak and dehydrated to play.

There was one bizarre incident in the match: Adam Gilchrist walked off, under the impression that he had edged a catch to slip, only for replays to show that he'd missed the ball. Gilchrist has a policy of walking off without waiting for the umpire's decision when he has hit a catch to a fielder, and he did just that when he attempted a drive, only to see the ball balloon to the fielder.

I was at the non-striker's end when it happened, and I was fairly certain Gilchrist had not hit the ball. I turned to umpire Jeremy Lloyds at the bowler's end and said so, and he replied, 'I thought he hit the ball and the ground at the same time.'

'It just didn't look right to me,' I said. I was going to shout to Gilchrist, who by this stage was halfway back to the pavilion, and tell him to come back and let the umpire make a decision, or refer it to the television official, but I decided against it — if the replays showed it was a straightforward edge, I would look a goose for making a fuss.

When I got back to the dressing room I found out that my hunch about the dismissal was right. I asked Gilchrist about it, and he said, 'I thought I hit the ground, but I thought I felt the ball hit the outside edge too.'

I would never ask Gilchrist to change his policy of walking — every player has to be true to himself when he plays the game — but I did ask him to be absolutely certain he is out before he walks next time. There is nothing wrong with forcing the umpire to make a decision; that is what he is there to do.

I managed to make a few runs today before giving my wicket away. Bangladesh were desperate for wickets and recalled their leading bowler, Mortaza. I had no need to do anything foolish, as Clarke and I were cruising at 5 runs per over and all we had to do was see Mortaza out of the attack, but when he dropped the ball short, I instinctively went for the pull shot. The ball bounced lower than I expected and I ended up scooping it — rather than hitting it — straight to the fielder at deep square leg.

My dismissal was indicative of the type of cricket we have played over much of this tour so far: sloppy, with no big scores, no big partnerships and no consistency with the ball or in the field. I am hoping the big-match atmosphere of a final at Lord's will help us lift our game.

Friday 1 July

Several members of the squad — Andrew Symonds, Glenn McGrath, Adam Gilchrist, Jason Gillespie, coach John Buchanan, assistant coach Jamie Siddons, team manager Steve Bernard, and massage therapist Lucy Frostick — spent the afternoon at the tennis at Wimbledon, cheering on Lleyton Hewitt.

I would have loved to have been there too, but I had the more mundane duty of speaking to the media. I didn't whinge about it, but if I had, I can just imagine Damien Martyn saying, 'That's why you get paid the big bucks, Punter.'

The chat to the media about tomorrow's final was very routine — in truth, I didn't have a lot to say that was new. After all, we have played England three times already. The journalists are obviously keen to build the match up; that doesn't bother me, because I am hoping any extra hype will spur us into action after our recent lacklustre displays.

The Rest of the World squads for the one-day internationals and Tests against us in October are due to be announced tomorrow. I was given a sneak preview after the main media conference, so that I could offer my opinions at the announcement. Each squad has 20 players now, but will be whittled down to 13 or 14 for each form of the game by mid-August. Both squads look strong, and all the players have had some success against us, which is one of the criteria the selectors — Sunil Gavaskar, Michael Atherton, Sir Richard Hadlee, Clive Lloyd, Jonty Rhodes and Aravinda de Silva — used when picking them. I am excited at the prospect of playing these matches, but there is plenty of cricket to play between now and then.

At our team meeting I emphasised the fact that no matter how well or how badly we have played so far, we are now in the final. It is up to us to impose ourselves on the opposition, as we have done on so many occasions in the past. If we play as we know we can, with intent, positive body language and total commitment to every single ball of the 600-odd deliveries in the match, England will not be able to live with us — we have the skills to beat them.

I had a quiet night in preparation for tomorrow: just some room service and my now-customary scribbled note to myself. These days I write down my thoughts before most matches I play; I find it helps clear my mind, and stops me tossing those thoughts around in my head while I try to sleep. Tonight's note is a straightforward one:

Watch the ball

Play straight

Loud calls

Be positive and patient

Sometimes I focus on how I will play specific bowlers, but I did not do that tonight — I have found that in one-day cricket bowlers tend to concentrate more on containment than on how to get me out.

Saturday 2 July

NatWest Series final, Lord's, London: Australia 196 (Hussey 62*) tied with England 9–196 (G Jones 71, Collingwood 53).

After 2 weeks of travelling up and down the country playing in this one-day series, we have ended up with the ridiculous situation of sharing the trophy.

In some ways it seems appropriate, because neither side will feel it deserved to lose today — it was a high-energy match that swung both ways before finishing even.

On the other hand, for both sides to put in that effort without some form of decision seems foolish. There was a tie-breaker in the World Cup semi-final in 1999, so why not here?

Normally if there is a tie, the match is awarded to the side losing fewer wickets. That would have been England today, so I guess we should not complain. We had plenty of chances to win the match comfortably but did not take them, and I give full credit to Michael Vaughan's side for hanging in there and forcing the match to the wire.

As the match reached its dramatic conclusion I wondered whether or not I was one of the few people on the ground who knew a tie would mean a shared trophy — I had spotted that clause in the playing conditions before the series started.

I had asked match referee Jeff Crowe about it when we met him in Cardiff before our first match, and he confirmed my reading of the regulations — but I never thought we would end up with that situation actually happening. Maybe the organisers didn't see it coming either; that might explain the lack of a tie-breaker.

There was certainly an odd feeling out on the pitch immediately after the game. The players on the England balcony were cheering, but out on the field the two batsmen — Ashley Giles and Stephen Harmison — were very restrained, and none of the Australian players was very animated.

When we got back to the dressing room I found out why: some of them did not know the result. Andrew Symonds said, 'Can someone tell me what's happened? Did we win or lose? Do we have to come back tomorrow?'

The last ball of the match was a drama on its own, and a confusing one, too. England needed 2 runs to earn the tie and 3 runs to win. Glenn McGrath was bowling and Giles was on strike. Giles took a pace down the pitch as McGrath released the ball and it struck him on the pad, ballooning into a gap in the middle of four players — me, Adam Gilchrist, Brad Hogg and Brett Lee.

Giles could not have placed the ball better — he had time to scamper back for the second run comfortably, and the tie was secured.

McGrath was seething at the end. He felt certain Giles had been out lbw, and could not believe it when there was no signal for leg-byes from umpire Billy Bowden. McGrath felt Giles had missed the ball by some distance, but the lack of a signal from the umpire meant Bowden thought the batsman had touched the ball onto his pad.

As far as McGrath was concerned, an inside edge was the only thing that could have saved Giles from being lbw, so his mood was not improved when he found out later that Bowden had changed his decision after the match, after consulting with the official scorers, and the 2 runs ended up as leg-byes after all.

McGrath was also upset at the way he bowled in the final over, and blamed himself for England being able to wriggle off the hook we had them on. He bowled a no-ball in that last over, something he very rarely does, and the run that ball gave England, together with the extra delivery he had to bowl, proved crucial to the outcome.

I also take some of the blame for England scoring 18 from the final 2 overs, because I asked Brett Lee and McGrath to mix up their deliveries rather than rely on one specific type of ball, such as a yorker. I thought that if the batsmen realised they would be facing nothing but yorkers, they would be able to set themselves to play accordingly, but my plan backfired when Lee bowled a bouncer and Giles top-edged it over Gilchrist's head for a priceless boundary.

On the other hand, it should not have come down to the last 2 overs, because we had already reduced England to 5–33 thanks to outstanding opening spells from McGrath and Lee. The ball swung and seamed about all day under the cloudy skies, and at one stage it was difficult to see where England would get their next run from, so credit should go to Paul Collingwood and Geraint Jones — they dug the team out of a massive hole with a partnership of 116.

Lee was involved in the major controversy of the day when he bowled a beamer at England opener Marcus Trescothick. It was an especially nasty ball which swung back into the left-handed opener. Trescothick did well to avoid it, throwing himself backwards as it whistled past his chest.

Watching Lee's feet as he bowled his next few balls, I could see what had happened: he had been carrying moisture from the outfield on his boots, and when he banged his front foot down in delivery stride, that moisture was causing him to slip. Darren Gough had had the same trouble, but he did not bowl a beamer. Umpire Shepherd quite rightly warned Lee.

It made Lee very tentative for a few deliveries, naturally, especially as he has come in for heavy criticism for bowling beamers at other times. I considered taking him out of the attack, but quickly decided not to. I feared it would send the wrong message: that I thought he had done it deliberately and did not trust him not to do it again. I kept him on and he rewarded me with the wickets of Strauss and Pietersen in a fiery opening spell.

So maybe the tie was a fitting result, and not just because it was a thrilling final. Neither side played good enough cricket in the tournament to deserve to win it, in my opinion, but in a way that gave me some consolation. In this series we played our worst one-day cricket since I became captain, and we still earned a share of the spoils. I feel sure England are playing at almost their best already, so if we can lift our game another notch or two, I believe we can win the remaining one-day matches and the Test series comfortably.

I just hope the pitches for the rest of the tour are better than most of the surfaces we have played on in this tournament. Most have lacked pace, making fluent strokeplay difficult, and today's surface offered far too much assistance to the bowlers.

After the match we unwound over a few drinks in the dressing room before heading back to our hotel, where we met up with Bernard Fanning, lead singer with the band Powderfinger. Fanning has been a regular visitor to our dressing room in his native Brisbane, and it was good to see a familiar face at the end of a frustrating day.

Sunday 3 July

The evening in the bar with Bernard Fanning turned out to be a late one, and included a few drinks, so today turned into a bit of a write-off. I slept in, then spent the day lazing around the hotel, not doing very much apart from strolling across the road for a coffee and having lunch with Damien Martyn, who was equally fragile.

The chance to unwind after an intense last few days was just what I needed. Thinking about nothing but cricket from dawn to dusk every day is a recipe for getting stale, and there will be plenty of time to get my head around our next action — the three-match one-day series against England — once we get on the coach to Leeds tomorrow. As the series will incorporate the ICC's new playing regulations, there will be plenty to think about.

Monday 4 July

England draft Sussex wicketkeeper–batsman Matt Prior into the squad for the NatWest Challenge matches against Australia. Prior replaces bowler Kabir Ali of Worcestershire.

We did not set off on the 320-kilometre drive north to Leeds until late afternoon, because we had a lunchtime function in London at the Café Royal, which is a 2-minute walk from Piccadilly Circus.

The function — one we attend every time we have a Test tour of the United Kingdom — was run by David Willis, brother of the former England captain Bob Willis, and involved a sit-down meal with several hundred corporate guests.

There was the usual small talk, and plenty of autographs, with most of the guests wanting their menu cards signed. The compere was another former England captain, Chris Cowdrey.

Cowdrey was quite entertaining, telling everyone what a poor player he was. He can't have been too bad if he played for his country, though.

A DVD on the history of The Ashes was handed out during the function, which meant we had something to watch on the bus trip that followed. It was a long trip — four and a half hours, including a stop halfway along to allow everyone to stretch their legs — but we did not starve, thanks to the efforts of Jock Campbell, our fitness trainer, and Simon Katich.

To stop us eating junk food at motorway rest areas, Jock collects some money from all of us before we set out, then buys some bread rolls and various fillings and makes the rolls up during the journey. Katich was helping him today. Matthew Hayden did have one go at using his portable gas barbecue on the bus, earlier in the tour, but the driver, Geoff Goodwin, soon put a stop to that. With the bus worth £350 000, that is understandable.

Hayden is an injury concern for us after the Lord's final, and for a bizarre reason. After the match he slipped over and caught his shoulder blade on the corner of the large bench in the middle of the dressing room. Errol Alcott doesn't think he has broken anything, but the shoulder blade is sore, and it is hampering the movement of his arm.

Tuesday 5 July

This time of year is meant to be the height of the British summer, but it was easy to forget that at Headingley today. It was bitterly cold, with a biting wind, and although we tried to train on the ground, there were squalls of rain during our session and we had to move indoors.

In the absence of outdoor action, most of the entertainment has been provided by the coaches, Duncan Fletcher of England and John Buchanan. After the tie at Lord's on Saturday, Fletcher was quoted as saying that he felt there was some uncertainty in our play and he thought England could exploit it. Buchanan had his say today: he said he was encouraged by the way we have been dismissing England's top order. He also said some of England's fielders are 'lumbering'.

I am not sure that there is much love lost between the coaches, but the lack of friendly banter might also simply be down to mind games and a desire to give nothing away.

I know Buchanan — and the rest of us — is furious at one tactic the England team seems to have adopted: rotating players on and off the ground during matches.

The 'super sub' regulation, where a player can be replaced during a match, does not come into force until Thursday's match, but as far as we can tell England have been using a variation on that theme in all the one-day matches so far on this tour.

The playing conditions of the previous series and the laws of the game state that a substitute fielder is allowed only in the case of injury or illness, but Vikram Solanki, one of England's best fielders and someone who has not featured much in their first-choice side, seems to spend almost as much time on the field as some of the players picked ahead of him.

Either England have been suffering a rash of minor injuries or they have been indulging in gamesmanship. Presumably the match referee and umpires have been noting all the comings and goings among the England team, but nothing seems to have been done yet to curb it.

This evening I headed back to London to attend a dinner to raise funds for long-serving Somerset player Michael Burns, and for this one I travelled in style.

The prospect of making the 640-kilometre round trip by road 36 hours before our next match did not thrill me, but Burns laid on a light aircraft, and I was joined by England players Marcus Trescothick — a county team-mate of Burns — and Ashley Giles, and Glenn McGrath, for the hour-long flight.

Trescothick and Giles also attended the function in the Long Room at Lord's; for McGrath, the flight saved him the drive south to collect his wife and two children, who were due to arrive from Australia the following day. Middlesex, the London county he played for last year, arranged for a car to be available for him when he landed in London and the plan was for him to drive to meet them when they landed then drive north again tomorrow.

I slept for most of the flight, which ended up being a little longer than expected because we were kept on the plane for 15 minutes after we landed, as a jet containing a member of the Royal Family landed just behind us. It was a painless trip and we all arrived relaxed.

Graeme Smith, the South Africa captain — who took a century off us for Somerset earlier in the tour — was there too, and he joined Trescothick and me to answer some questions from the 200 or so guests. There was also an auction of cricketing memorabilia. I donated one of my old batting helmets, which I signed, but it prompted a bidding war between two people — and there was so much money on offer that I agreed to supply another signed helmet to ensure that both bidders got satisfaction for their generosity.

Having done my best to help Burns out by lending my support at his function, I headed to Heathrow to fly back to Leeds. I got to my hotel around 1 o'clock.

Wednesday 6 July

Despite my late night I felt fine this morning, and I had a great final practice session before tomorrow's match.

I did some work with assistant coach Jamie Siddons and a bowling machine, focusing on my head position and balance at the crease. Every batsman has trigger movements — small movements of the feet that are made as the bowler lets go of the ball to ensure that the feet are in the right position to play that particular delivery — and my practice was designed to groove those movements so I am not left flat-footed at the crease. My aim is to move but still be on the balls of my feet so that I can adjust my weight forward or back, depending on the length of the delivery. By the end of the session I felt in good form — it is now a matter of transferring that form into a match.

We had a team meeting to discuss the new regulations that come into force in this match. I have already stated in this diary and in public that I am against the changes, but there is no point taking a negative mind-set into the match. The regulations are here for the next 10 months, so we will have to get used to them no matter what we think.

We chatted for half an hour, but at the end of that time none of us seemed any clearer on what the regulations will mean in practice. That uncertainty is reflected in our choice of Brad Hogg as super sub, the player we will have in reserve in case we decide on a tactical switch during the match. Hogg can fill a role as a batsman or a bowler, and he is also one of our best fielders, so by naming him we are covering all bases.

We are pretty clear on what England's tactics will be. Most of their wins in recent times have come when batting second, so we expect them to name a batsman as their super sub, in the hope that they will bowl first, use all their bowlers and then replace one of them with the super sub batsman to lengthen their batting line-up for the run chase.

The problem with that tactic arises if England bat first and lose early wickets. If that happens, they may need to use the super sub batsman in order to post a decent score. However, that would leave them without one of their bowling options later on because, once replaced, a player cannot come back into the game.

Though we haven't yet played a game using this regulation, it does appear to favour the side batting second — we will have to wait and see if that turns out to be the case in reality.

Apart from our chat about these new playing conditions, I also reminded the players that, although we have not been anywhere near our best against England so far, we could — and probably should — have won every game against them apart from the Twenty20 match. If we can finally click into gear, I still think England can't get near us, despite the quality of their bowling — Andrew Flintoff and Stephen Harmison have been outstanding.

Thursday 7 July

NatWest Challenge, match 1, Leeds: Australia 7–219 lost to England 1–221 (Trescothick 104*, Vaughan 59*) by 9 wickets.

This was a worrying day in more ways than one. Not only were we thrashed on the field, but we also found out that London, our next destination on the tour, suffered a series of terrorist attacks during the morning.

I was ready to bat when the fourth umpire, Jeremy Lloyds, came into our dressing room and said there had been some explosions in the city. That set my mind racing — Rianna had been due to arrive in the country at 6.30 a.m.

For the rest of our innings the television in our dressing room was switched from the cricket coverage to a news channel, as we tried to get some more information on what was happening in London. It meant the build-up to my innings and those of the players who followed me was not ideal, but that was no excuse for our succession of low scores — once we crossed the boundary rope we were totally focused on the job at hand.

Our major problem as batsmen was the pitch, which was the most difficult I have ever batted on in one-day cricket. The ball darted around off the seam in all directions, and it swung as well. We did well to reach 219, thanks mainly to another superb innings from Mike Hussey. Given the conditions he played brilliantly, running hard between the wickets and clearly relishing the challenge. He is a great player to have around the squad, not only because of his talent but also because of the enthusiasm he brings to the dressing room.

Although conditions were tricky, we were also guilty of some loose shots. Michael Clarke missed a very extravagant drive, and I

LEFT Make the world go away. My expression says it all as I try to come to terms with our shock loss to Bangladesh in Cardiff at the start of our NatWest Series campaign. It was the most embarrassing and traumatic day of my international career.

Phil Hillyard / © Newspix

Phil Hillyard / © Newspix

Phil Hillyard / © Newspix

ABOVE Master Blaster. England's Kevin Pietersen thumped an astonishing unbeaten 91 in Bristol to deny us a morale-boosting win.

LEFT Renaissance man. Andrew Symonds, back in action after his suspension, quickly got into his stride with a man of the match performance against England at Durham.

Phil Hillyard / © Newspix

ABOVE Leap of faith. Mike Hussey leads the celebrations after Glenn McGrath bowls Michael Vaughan in the NatWest Series final at Lord's. We reduced England to 5–33 chasing 197 but could not land the killer punch.

BELOW All tied up. Michael Vaughan and I pose with the NatWest Series Trophy after the thrilling tie at Lord's.

Tom Shaw / © Getty Images

Phil Hillyard / © Newspix

LEFT Dizzy rascal. Jason Gillespie's spectacular loss of form created a huge void in our attack through the summer.

ABOVE Jump to it. Adam Gilchrist punches the air after reaching three figures against England at The Oval, his first one-day hundred since January 2004.

LEFT Satisfaction guaranteed. I show my joy after reaching a match-winning hundred against England at Lord's in the NatWest Challenge.

ABOVE The Fab Four. Australia's pace quartet recreates the famous Beatles picture outside Abbey Road recording studio in London ahead of the first Test at Lord's. Their outfits suggest that they have just recorded their own version of *The White Album*.

LEFT Let battle commence. I pose with Michael Vaughan ahead of the first Test at Lord's.

Alessandro Abbonizio/AFP/ Getty Images/© 2005 AFP

BELOW All cut up. Here I am being treated by Errol Alcott after getting hit by a Stephen Harmison bouncer during the brutal, breathless and brilliant first day of the Test series.

Phil Hillyard/ © Newspix

BELOW Pigeon flying high. Glenn McGrath acknowledges the crowd after dismissing Marcus Trescothick at Lord's to become the fourth player after Courtney Walsh, Shane Warne and Muttiah Muralitharan to take 500 Test wickets.

© AFP/NewsPix

ABOVE Balcony bliss. The celebrations are in full swing after our 239-run win in the first Test at Lord's.

RIGHT Twist of fate. Glenn McGrath's freak ankle injury during warm-ups on the first morning at Edgbaston robbed us of a vital player.

LEFT What's going on? I reflect on another boundary to England on the first day of the second Test while Shane Warne looks on. We conceded 54 fours and 10 sixes during three horrific sessions.

ABOVE LEFT Powerplay. Andrew Flintoff, here pictured pulling Brett Lee to the boundary, wrested back the initiative for England on day three of the second Test after we reduced it to 4–31.

ABOVE RIGHT Magic man. Shane Warne's 10 wickets at Edgbaston should have been the prelude to an Australian win. Here he takes wicket number nine, Stephen Harmison, thanks to my catch at silly point.

BELOW It's behind you! Brett Lee, who led our dramatic bid for victory on the final day at Edgbaston, eases away a Stephen Harmison lifter as we close in on our target.

ABOVE Winners and losers. This picture sums up the contrasting emotions for the two teams at the end of the Edgbaston Test. For England, relief and elation at its two-run win; for Australia and Brett Lee, despair and disbelief.

LEFT Well played, mate. I congratulate Michael Vaughan at the end of the pulsating second Test at Edgbaston.

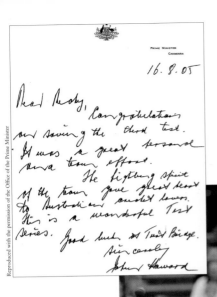

16.8.05

Dear Ricky,
Congratulations on saving the third test. It was a great personal and a team effort.
The fighting spirit of the team gave great heart to Australian cricket lovers. This is a wonderful Test series. Good luck at Trent Bridge.
Sincerely,
John Howard

LEFT A job well done. Congratulations from the Prime Minister after we saved the Old Trafford Test.

BELOW Ouch! I am in the process of being hit in the chest by a Stephen Harmison bouncer during my last-day rearguard in the third Test at Old Trafford.

ABOVE Cut away. Shane Warne made 249 runs in the series. Here he cuts during his 90 at Old Trafford that helped us save the follow-on.

RIGHT The aftermath. I am joined by Brett Lee and Glenn McGrath to reflect on our match-saving efforts at Old Trafford.

miscued a pull shot and was caught at deep square leg. After all the work I did on my technique coming into the match, the pitch did nothing for my confidence, but I still executed the pull poorly. The ball swung away, I caught it on the bottom of the bat and it lobbed up very gently to the fielder. Clarke's dismissal continues his lean pickings on this tour, but I am not concerned about his form. He would not be on the trip if he was a poor player. All he needs is to build some momentum with a few decent scores; during the early part of the tour he has been hampered by the back injury he suffered in Durham.

England cruised past our score, helped not just by an easing in conditions but also by a very lacklustre display by us in the field. As the sun came out during the afternoon, the ball stopped swinging and seaming, but even if it had continued to misbehave I am not sure we were playing well enough to take advantage of it.

We dropped an early chance when Adam Gilchrist spilled an edge from Andrew Strauss, and took a wicket from a no-ball when Marcus Trescothick carved Brett Lee to third man. From 10 overs into the England innings there was no buzz on the field; I felt we played like a beaten side and got our just desserts.

I hate opposition players scoring hundreds against us, especially someone like Trescothick, who has not scored one against us before, but we gave him the chance to do it and he took the opportunity. Mind you, he also had a massive stroke of luck: Gilchrist caught him off Andrew Symonds's bowling, but he was reprieved by umpire Rudi Koertzen, who said he did not see or hear the deflection.

There was not much chance to see how the new regulations affected the game. Both sides used their super subs — we introduced Brad Hogg to bowl and England brought in Vikram Solanki for Simon Jones once Jones had completed his bowling stint — but neither new player had much chance to make a contribution. The other new playing condition — allowing only two fielders to be placed on the boundary for 20 overs (divided into three blocks, of 10, 5 and 5 overs) rather than the previous 15 overs (in one block) — did not really come into play, because in such bowler-friendly conditions both Michael Vaughan and I kept as many fielders as we could in catching positions.

The aftermath of the match was dominated by the events in London. During the day we heard rumours of traffic chaos on the roads leading to and from the city, and there was also a question mark over whether or not it was safe to enter London even if the roads were clear.

At one point we provisionally booked accommodation in Leicester, about halfway between Leeds and the capital, but after consulting with CA — which in turn had been consulting with the ECB and, I gather, the Australian High Commission in London — we decided to head south in accordance with our original schedule.

Although I was desperate to get to London as quickly as possible to be reunited with Rianna, there was also some understandable unease on the bus as we set out. I do not think any of us have been this close to terrorism before, and no one was quite sure what to expect either on the journey or in London when we got there.

The reality was that the rumours of gridlock proved wide of the mark, and we enjoyed a trouble-free trip with barely any traffic on the road. We arrived at our hotel at 12.30 a.m. Whether or not the tour will continue after today's events remains to be seen.

Friday 8 July

After a restful day, we had a team meeting this evening to discuss the future of the tour. It took place tonight rather than this morning so that team manager Steve Bernard had a chance to discuss the situation with CA and ECB officials and establish the level of threat against the team, the security measures that would be put in place and whether or not, after assessing those factors, it was safe to proceed.

Bernard said the advice he received was that the team and sporting venues were unlikely to be targets — it seemed that the public transport system was the focus of the terrorist activity. On that basis, both he and CA had concluded that it was okay for the tour to go on. If there were other similar incidents, that position would be reviewed.

The players wanted guarantees that the level of security at playing venues would be stepped up, because we have not been happy with what we have seen so far. At Leicester we lost bags and equipment, and at Bristol, during the one-day match against England, a streaker got onto the field and none of the security staff seemed in a hurry to get him off — perhaps the next intruder on the field won't be so friendly.

Bernard said he had sought assurances that these matters would be addressed, and was told they would be, and that all bags and vehicles entering each venue would be searched thoroughly from now on. Many of us felt a bit sceptical about those assurances, but we have to take them at face value and accept them.

I know quite a few players feel that there is an element of inconsistency about our decision to continue with the tour, and I agree with that. If we were in, say, Pakistan or Sri Lanka and something like this had happened, I am sure we would have been on the first plane out. Countries like that have lost revenue as a result of tours being called off because of terrorist threats, yet here we are, staying put in the United Kingdom after terrorists didn't just threaten to do something, but in fact detonated explosives in the city where we are due to play our next two matches. I bet the officials of those other countries are wondering where the consistency is in the current situation.

It was a case of Groundhog Day for me this evening: I was back at the Lord's Long Room, the venue for the dinner I attended on Tuesday night, and the compere was Chris Cowdrey, who performed the same role at the Café Royal on Monday. This time, England captain Michael Vaughan and I were attending a dinner for the English Professional Cricketers' Association, and Cowdrey took questions for both of us from the assembled diners. We still have two one-day matches left, but the focus of all the questions was The Ashes. The public just cannot wait for the Tests to start, and after a month of one-day cricket, I think the players are feeling the same way.

Saturday 9 July

We had a fantastic team meeting today. I hope and believe it will be the turning point of this tour.

Before we practised we sat down in the dressing room at Lord's and, led by Adam Gilchrist, John Buchanan and myself, we kicked around what has gone wrong on the tour so far and how we can put it right. Everyone had a say, and at the end of it we reached the following conclusions:

OWN THE GROUND — by the time we arrive at each venue, England are usually out on the ground warming up, and their coaches have set up practice equipment, so we feel like interlopers on the playing arena. We should try to get to each venue earlier, then get out on the field and take control of the venue so that England have to make their arrangements for practice before the match around us, not the other way around.

DISCIPLINE AND ATTITUDE — we have all got to the top of our profession because our skill levels are outstanding, but we are not performing to the high standards we have set ourselves previously. A likely reason for this is that we have not been disciplined enough in executing our skills and have not been tough enough on ourselves to admit it. It is time for each of us to recapture that self-discipline, in practice and in matches, and ensure that we play to our full potential.

DO THE BASICS — our success in one-day cricket has been founded on certain basics that we have performed better than other sides: building partnerships; at least one player making a big score; building pressure in the field; forcing run-outs through direct hits; and positive body language. We need to get back to those basics.

ENJOY THE GAME — the tour so far has been hard work, with results not always going our way, but we must remember how lucky we are to be representing our country — and paid for the privilege. The rest of Australia would love to swap places with us, so we should make the most of the chance we have been given by enjoying our jobs. Tomorrow, for example, we are playing at the home of cricket, Lord's, and it does not get any better than that.

I began the meeting feeling more concerned about the team than at any time since I became captain; we have not produced the type of cricket we are capable of, and Thursday's lacklustre display in the field left me scratching my head wondering why. But after today's meeting I sense a new determination to put the record straight. We followed the get-together with a game of touch rugby and an intense fielding session that felt just like the session we had in Brisbane before the trip started. Then we headed into the practice nets. I felt superb. My feet were moving, I was striking the ball well, and afterwards I said to Matthew Hayden, 'That is as good as I have felt all tour.' Now I have to translate that into a decent score — I can think of no better place than Lord's to do that.

Security was noticeably tighter when we arrived at the ground, and all our bags were checked. It is reassuring to see that the authorities are delivering on the promises made to us yesterday.

Sunday 10 July

NatWest Challenge, match 2, Lord's, London: Australia 3–224 (Ponting 111) beat England 8–223 (Flintoff 87, Lee 5–41) by 7 wickets.

Talking is all very well, but out on the field is where it counts, so being able to put everything we discussed yesterday into action and produce perhaps our most complete performance of the tour was a superb feeling.

We hammered England in much the same way they hammered us on Thursday, and by doing so we have set up Tuesday's match at

The Oval as the one-day decider of the tour. From a personal perspective, I also had the satisfaction of seeing us to the brink of victory with my first hundred at Lord's. It was a great day for us.

My innings really allowed me to put to rest some concerns I'd had about my own form. I was really worried after I failed on Thursday: I'd felt so good in practice in the lead-up to that match, and if I could not make a decent score when I felt like that, what chance did I have at any other time? I need not have worried, though, because today everything clicked.

I rotated the strike well, played straight, felt balanced at the crease, and had time to play my shots. Best of all, by scoring the runs I did, I was able to lead from the front in achieving our standard batting targets in one-day cricket, targets which we had reaffirmed at yesterday's meeting.

I was motivated not just to reverse our loss on Thursday and turn my own form around, but also to demoralise England as they had demoralised us in the previous game. We achieved that, and my only regret was that I got out with the finish line in sight.

I was encouraged by our bowling, which was more disciplined than it has been for a while, with Glenn McGrath and Brett Lee outstanding, and we fielded impressively too.

Lee has always been in my Test line-up for the Ashes series, and after the way he bowled today I cannot see how the selectors can contemplate leaving him out. He was fast, and he swung the ball and bowled accurately, and England's batsmen never got on top of him. His pace and accuracy, combined with McGrath's accuracy at the other end, meant we built pressure from an early stage — they earned the breakthroughs that first-change bowler Michael Kasprowicz made. Marcus Trescothick and Andrew Strauss, who felt they had not scored quickly enough early on, were obliged to take risks against him, and both perished as a result.

Lee managed to complete a 5-wicket haul with his final delivery, thanks to one of my best-ever catches. I was on the edge of the fielding circle at extra cover when Ashley Giles backed away and clobbered a drive flat and hard to my right. I saw it all the way and dived, throwing out my right hand, and it stuck slap-bang in the middle of my palm. Watching the replay on the giant screen it looked spectacular, but I saw the ball all the way off the bat and always felt I was going to catch it. I should have known then that it was going to be my day with the bat.

Our one downside was Jason Gillespie's performance, and now that we have scored runs, his form has become our major concern.

He has looked out of sorts ever since we started the one-day series last month, and he shows no sign of improving. He was our only bowler who struggled to operate with consistency. He is down on pace too, and no one, least of all him, is quite sure what the problem is. He has been a top-class performer for a long time, so we have to believe he will come good again.

We altered our plan with the super sub by nominating Brad Haddin (as a batsman) instead of all-rounder Brad Hogg. Hogg was distraught when I announced the team before our warm-ups, and John Buchanan had to calm him down before he was ready to join in a jog around the ground with the rest of us, but the choice of Haddin, who had a great season with New South Wales last summer, was an obvious one in the circumstances.

The boundary on the grandstand side of the ground was very short, and England have a mix of left-handers and right-handers, so no matter which end Hogg bowled at, he would always be at risk of being hit there. Also, if we won the toss — as we did — having an extra batsman in the line-up would be a massive bonus. It would allow us to reinforce the order for the chase. Haddin eventually replaced McGrath, but in the end we did not need him.

The super sub concept does appear to favour the side batting second, in practice as well as in theory, especially if the sub is a batsman, and that suggests to me that the new regulation is not even-handed. The trial will continue for another 10 months, but on the evidence of two games I have not been convinced that it's a good move. I never believed the one-day game was so bad that it required gimmicks to liven it up: the only essential ingredients are two high-class, well-matched sides and a good pitch. For me, the fact that these new regulations have been brought in to try to spice up the format just suggests that we have not had enough of that type of match.

Rianna left early this morning for a break in New York with Helen Appleyard, Damien Martyn's former fiancée. She will meet Helen there and they will have 10 days of sightseeing before she comes back for the first Test at Lord's. Her departure reminds me how close we are to that match now.

Monday 11 July

I saw Darren Lehmann this morning, and he suggested an interesting approach to the use of the super sub.

Lehmann, who is over here working as a television commentator, suggested we name Glenn McGrath as our super sub. He feels England prefer to chase a target, and thinks that the sight of McGrath out of our original 11 might make them change that approach.

With no McGrath in the first 11 named, his theory goes, England might bat first and dare us to make the substitution straightaway. We would be happy to do that and back ourselves to win even if we replaced an original pick — probably a batsman — with McGrath, and England would be out of their comfort zone of batting second. It is a clever plan, typical of Lehmann, and worth some thought.

We had a light training session at The Oval for tomorrow's match, and were joined by members of the Test squad who have linked up with us now. Brad Hodge, Shaun Tait, Justin Langer and Stuart MacGill have all arrived — Tait, Langer and MacGill from Australia and Hodge from county commitments — and their appearance is another reminder of how close the Test series now is.

I had dinner with Matthew Hayden and Damien Martyn, and when I got back to my room there were some Titleist golf clubs waiting for me, courtesy of fellow Australian and professional golfer Peter O'Malley. O'Malley loves his cricket, and was only too happy to supply me with a set of clubs for the tour — he even put some balls and caps in the bag as well. He called to check that I had received the equipment, and joked that I would be unlikely to wear the caps.

'Why?' I said.

'Have a look at the letters on them,' he replied.

Each cap was embroidered with his initials on the back — POM. So he was right: it might not be a great look for me during an Ashes series.

Tuesday 12 July

NatWest Challenge, match 3, The Oval, London: Australia 2–229 (Gilchrist 121*) beat England 7–228 (Pietersen 74, Solanki 53*) by 8 wickets.

We signed off from the one-day leg of the tour in the most emphatic manner possible. We won with more than 15 overs to spare, and a demolition like that will give England plenty to reflect upon before the first Test at Lord's in 9 days' time.

Apart from the margin of our success, what pleased me most was that after a couple of bits of sloppiness early on we bounced back, put our feet on England's throat and never relaxed the grip for the rest of the day.

Those sloppy elements were a couple of dropped catches by Jason Gillespie and Adam Gilchrist, which followed a spell of sustained pressure from Glenn McGrath and Brett Lee with the new ball.

When the catches went down I thought, *Here we go again*, but to everyone's credit we knuckled down and pressed even harder, and although Kevin Pietersen and Vikram Solanki played well, England's eventual total was nowhere near enough to test us on what became a wonderful batting pitch.

The ball did seam a little early on for McGrath and Lee but it was by no means a minefield, and certainly did not justify England's amazing caution early on. At one point McGrath bowled 4 maidens in a row, and although he was superb, there is no way a side should allow him to do that without making any attempt to put the pressure back on him and us.

It was an example of England feeling uncomfortable batting first — I am sure the top order players would have been more positive if they'd been chasing rather than setting a target. Batting first, England obviously felt they could not afford to lose early wickets, but that caused the innings to stall, and then when the batsmen did try to press the accelerator, they lost wickets anyway.

An indication of England's problems was the fact they had to resort to using Solanki as their super sub, which meant they missed out on using Simon Jones as a bowling option later in the day. Even if Jones had been available to bowl, I am sure we would still have won easily, but it was another example of the way the regulation favours the side batting second. We did not end up trialling Darren Lehmann's theory; we opted instead for a batsman, Simon Katich, as our super sub, but we won without needing to call on him.

Pietersen's innings will have cemented his place in the first Test, but I have always felt that he should play. He has technical flaws but a good temperament, and at the top level temperament and self-belief can help overcome any technical weaknesses.

Gilchrist's blazing hundred was timely, as his form with the bat has been one of the missing pieces of the jigsaw for us on the tour so far. I was surprised to find out afterwards that it was his first one-day international hundred since January 2004 — that accounted for his extravagant celebration when he reached three figures. It was also a show of relief that, after all the pressure we have been under, we delivered when it mattered most, sealing this series win and the one-day honours against England.

Although this match marks the end of the one-day tour, our post-match celebrations were restrained. Only Brad Hogg is going back to Australia; the members of the group who are not involved in the Tests — Michael Hussey, Andrew Symonds and Shane Watson — are off to play county cricket, so we are likely to see them again during the next 2 months. We had a few drinks at the ground: in the dressing room first, and then in the committee room, where there was a reception for umpire David Shepherd, who was umpiring at international level for the last time. 'Shep' has been universally popular as an umpire, because while he is obviously in charge on the field, he is still happy to have some banter and to communicate with the players — and, most importantly of all, he gets most decisions right.

Despite the celebrations being restrained, it was late when we got back to the hotel and I was very tired. I was also hungry and I ordered room service, but by the time it arrived I was asleep.

Our performances have hardly been flawless — I'd give them no more than 5 out of 10 for most of the past month — but through a mix of skill and determination we peaked at the right time, and our last two performances have been worth 9 or 10 out of 10.

Wednesday 13 July

Channel Nine announces that it is not renewing its contract with Shane Warne.

There is no time to dwell on our one-day success: today we're on the tour bus heading 160 kilometres north to Leicester for our opening first-class match of the trip, and this time next week the first Test will be just a week away.

Already there are some tough selection issues to resolve. Brett Lee, Glenn McGrath and Shane Warne — who arrived at the team hotel last night — are inked in to play at Lord's, but that still leaves a question mark over who will occupy the slot for the third pace bowler.

Jason Gillespie and Michael Kasprowicz are vying for it, and the match at Leicester is being billed in the media as a bowl-off between the pair. Kasprowicz is well suited to bowling with the older ball, something the third pace man would have to do, as Lee and McGrath will be our opening attack. On the other hand, Gillespie at his best is a high-class operator, and his lower-order batting has been handy over the past 8 months — he has scored Test fifties against both New Zealand and Pakistan.

The selectors have tended to stick with players rather than chop and change in response to dips in form, and have been rewarded for that loyalty with excellent results. I do not expect things to be different this time, so Gillespie is likely to get the nod. I am still keen to see both players in action at Leicester, though, because both will benefit from a long bowl in wicket-taking mode with a red ball, rather than operating with a white ball to defensive fields, as they have done over the past month.

I also wanted to see Shaun Tait in action, but that is not going to be possible because we have to get Lee used to bowling with a red ball again. I don't want to over-bowl Lee, but he is a player who thrives on the rhythm that comes from match action, and if we leave him out here he would go into Lord's without having had a bowl in competitive action in the previous 9 days, and that is too long for him.

It would have been great to give Brad Hodge and Brad Haddin match time as well, but with all our first-choice Test line-up — including me — wanting time at the crease that is not going to be possible either. The itinerary for this tour means that some players spend very little time playing and can lose form as a result. On the plus side, it does give players who feature in the Tests time for recovery and rest between matches. It is not easy to maintain this fine balance, and as the tour progresses I hope we get it right.

Warne does not need to play in this match because he has bowled in eight first-class matches for Hampshire already this season, so any fine-tuning he needs can be done at practice; that means Stuart MacGill will get an early chance. MacGill, too, is someone who needs plenty of bowling to get into form, so that is a bonus. I saw the news about Warne's situation with Channel Nine when I was surfing the Internet today, but I have not heard anyone in the team mention it and I will not bring it up with him unless he mentions it — it has nothing to do with me.

McGrath will sit out the match because of a problem with his left knee that we are monitoring. He has had this injury for the past week or so, and it came about in a bizarre way. When he and I flew to London before the one-day game in Leeds, he collected a car supplied by his former county Middlesex to go and meet his wife and two children, who had just arrived in England. I gather there was a problem with the gearbox that meant he had to push quite hard with his left leg to depress the clutch, and that inflamed his knee. Then the car broke down and he ended up pushing it, which aggravated the problem. Errol Alcott, the team physiotherapist, had to get the knee drained of fluid, and although we expect McGrath to be fit again soon, it is an added concern we could well do without.

England name a 12-man squad for the first Test at Lord's, starting on 21 July. It is: Michael Vaughan (captain), Ian Bell, Andrew Flintoff, Ashley Giles, Stephen Harmison, Matthew Hoggard, Geraint Jones, Simon Jones, Kevin Pietersen, Andrew Strauss, Chris Tremlett and Marcus Trescothick.

England's squad was exactly as we expected it would be, with Ian Bell and Kevin Pietersen included and Graham Thorpe left out. We have respect for Thorpe as a battler, but the home side's selectors could hardly drop Ian Bell after he scored a century against Bangladesh in England's last Test, earlier this season, and Pietersen made an impressive case for inclusion during the one-day series.

I had a suspicion that Thorpe would be left out after a chat I had with England's most capped player, Alec Stewart, at the dinner I attended at Lord's last Friday. He suggested that Thorpe's announcement that he is quitting international cricket to move to Australia at the end of the season may mean Thorpe has lost his appetite for playing at the highest level — after all, he has played 100 Tests. The selectors obviously feel that this is the case.

John Buchanan and I sat down with each of the players who have joined the squad for the Test series to make sure he is aware of what we expect from him behaviour-wise. It was the right thing to do after what happened with Andrew Symonds at Cardiff. That issue created a bad environment within the team for a short while and we want to avoid any repeat of that during this leg of the trip.

Practice had an added air of excitement because it was our first session with red balls and white pads since March in New Zealand. Those of us involved in both forms of the game have now jettisoned the coloured clothing and equipment from our kitbags. Normally we would keep the clothing for the next series, but this tour is the last one before adidas takes over from Fila as CA's clothing supplier, so there was no reason to do that. After our final one-day game, most of the clothing was either autographed for charity or souvenirs, or given away to lucky supporters outside the dressing rooms. Most of the yellow batting pads were given to the dressing room attendant — we hope he will find local clubs that can use them.

I had several media commitments after training, including an interview for Channel Four, the broadcasters covering the Ashes series here in England, and a discussion with Andrew Ramsey of *The Australian* for my newspaper column. There were also some photos taken with me dressed in my whites, complete with my baggy green cap. Those pictures will be used in newspapers and magazines all over the world in the run-up to the series.

With all those things done I was glad to get away for a few hours in the late afternoon for a relaxing game of golf with Matthew Hayden, Damien Martyn and assistant coach Jamie Siddons. Hayden is not one of the regular golfers in the tour party, but has rediscovered a love for the game recently after having played very little in the previous few years. He plays as he bats, left-handed (Adam Gilchrist bats left-handed but plays golf right-handed), and his new-found keenness for the game has even extended to getting hold of a new set of clubs. Hayden was my partner in a best ball match-play game against Siddons and Martyn — neither of us played very well, and we ended up losing.

Friday 15 July

Tour match, Leicester, day 1: The Australians 2–169 (Hayden 75, Langer 71*) trail Leicestershire 217 (Rogers 56) by 48 runs.

Apart from a failure by Michael Clarke, this was an excellent day for us. All the bowlers had a useful workout and Justin Langer and Matthew Hayden got into Test match mode with an excellent stand that set us up for a big first innings total.

I was originally padded up to bat at number three, but Clarke begged me for the chance to go in at that spot, and because the pitch and the Leicestershire attack looked innocuous, I agreed. I thought it was the ideal chance for Clarke to play a long innings ahead of the Test — I did not reckon on him receiving a ball that kept low and bowled him out.

Clarke's failure highlighted a problem that was a result of our losing the toss. If I had won the toss I could have ensured that we got two innings in the match by batting first. Then, even if we'd bowled Leicestershire out cheaply when their chance came to bat, we could have batted again rather than enforce the follow-on if anyone needed some extra time at the crease. In a 3-day game, even if we bowled first and bowled the home side out cheaply, we were condemned to get just one innings unless we were dismissed cheaply as well.

Clarke is not under pressure for his spot at the moment, even though he has come on this tour after a run of low scores at Test level through most of this summer. He was originally picked because the selectors were looking at the long-term as well as the short-term health of the side — he is a player who should be around for many years to come, so jettisoning him now would make no sense at all.

He is working hard in practice, and if he continues to do that his form will improve. My one concern with Clarke is the number of questions he asks. He analyses his game a lot, maybe too much, and occasionally looks for too much advice. For example, he talks to me and to Hayden, but that might not be a good mix, because we have contrasting styles as batsmen and may offer conflicting advice.

Sometimes I feel that someone with Clarke's natural talent should be a bit more instinctive, like Adam Gilchrist, and a little less prepared to analyse every technical aspect of his game. Gilchrist's method is simple — he sees the ball and hits it — and there may be times when Clarke could benefit from a similar approach.

Jason Gillespie and Michael Kasprowicz both bowled steadily, but neither made a watertight case for inclusion in the Test line-up. Gillespie started the match at the other end from Brett Lee and did not enjoy operating into the wind and up the hill, but when he switched ends he improved — he found some extra pace and disconcerting bounce in his second spell.

Saturday 16 July

Tour match, Leicester, day 2: The Australians 7–582 (Martyn 154*, Ponting 119, Langer 115, Hayden 75) lead Leicestershire 217 (Rogers 56) by 365 runs.

Today was satisfying. I was able to occupy the crease and get back into the routine of building an innings in a first-class match against a red ball. The reward was just over 4 hours at the crease and three figures against my name.

The adjustment between one-day and first-class cricket is more mental than anything else. You have to retrain your mind and remove certain shots from your repertoire, such as the glide to third man. In one-day cricket, with few close catchers in place, it is a valuable tool to rotate the strike, but in the longer form of the game it is a high-risk option because the area next to the wicketkeeper is usually filled with slip fielders.

Unlike one-day cricket, where there is always a need to press on and a run of scoreless balls can put you under pressure, here it was a case of getting used to leaving any balls outside the off-stump and waiting for the bowler to stray in line or length. I played well down the ground, a sure sign that I am playing straight and am balanced at the crease, and felt in good touch throughout my innings.

The one downside of the day was Simon Katich's failure, but I am realistic enough to know that not everyone is going to make a big score in the same innings, and I have no concerns about Katich for the Lord's match. He spent the first month of the English season playing for Hampshire, so he has plenty of recent experience of conditions.

Damien Martyn and Jason Gillespie were two other players who enjoyed the chance to bat. Gillespie's contribution reinforced how useful a player he is in a Test line-up. There is nothing more dispiriting for a side than to get through the frontline batsmen only to be held up by the lower order, and Gillespie is a past master at frustrating better attacks than the one we faced here.

Sunday 17 July

Tour match, Leicester, day 3: The Australians 7–582 (Martyn 154*, Ponting 119, Langer 115, Hayden 75) drew with Leicestershire 217 (Rogers 56) and 5–363 (Rogers 209, Robinson 81).

The match ended up as a solid workout for us, and I am disappointed we did not win it.

The pitch was desperately slow, and that meant it was not easy to get batsmen out on it, but we still should have had the quality to get through a county line-up, especially as we had a whole day to do it.

The plus side of our failure was that we spent a full day in the field, something none of us has done since the New Zealand tour in March, and from that point of view it was a worthwhile exercise. It got us used to concentrating and maintaining energy levels for 6 hours instead of the 3½ hours we have become used to.

Our attempts to win the match were frustrated by Western Australia batsman Chris Rogers, who played really well. He was especially severe on Stuart MacGill's bowling, and although he had some luck when Jason Gillespie dismissed him with a no-ball just after he reached three figures, he played well enough to deserve some good fortune. It is not the first time on this trip we have taken a wicket with a no-ball, but I am hoping it is the last. I am fed up with bowlers overstepping the front line, and I reminded the side of that again. It is a basic discipline, and not something people at the elite level should have a problem with.

Leicestershire and Rogers scored freely all day, but that was partly because we maintained attacking fields. The lack of pace in the pitch meant we did not position a third man — we were trying to attack the stumps rather than the area around and outside off-stump, and most of our catchers were in front of the wicket, not in the slips. I am not sure how relevant that will be to the way we play in the Test, but conditions here dictated that approach.

Neither Gillespie nor Kasprowicz took a wicket, but Adam Gilchrist gave me some positive feedback on Gillespie's form. As wicketkeeper, Gilchrist has the best seat in the house to see how well or badly bowlers are performing, and he said Gillespie was bowling with good pace and hitting the seam regularly — something that will have been noted by watching selector David Boon.

I spoke to the media after the match, and once I had finished that we were on our way to London. During the trip, John Buchanan told me he had chatted to Michael Clarke before we left to see how he was feeling after a failure in his only innings. Buchanan agreed with me that Clarke is just one decent innings away from a return to form — I hope that innings comes at Lord's.

Part 12:
The Ashes

While the rest of the squad faced the media before Thursday's Test, I had the luxury of a sleep-in this morning. My media session will be on Wednesday, the day before the match, so instead of facing a grilling from the reporters today, I had a leisurely breakfast followed by a session in the pool to relax my muscles after 6 hours in the field at Leicester.

The idea of the team media session started 4 years ago in India. The media attention then was very much as it is on this tour, with numerous requests for interviews with every player. If some of the squad fulfilled every request, they would have little time for anything else, so CA's public affairs department came up with the idea of the single session as a focal point for all media interest. This way, the players can deal with all pre-series interview requests in one go rather than facing separate enquiries every day, and the reporters and television networks can get comments from a whole host of players at once.

Tonight we had a dinner at the National Sporting Club with several hundred paying guests, again hosted by David Willis, and with chat show host Michael Parkinson as guest speaker. Shane Warne stole the show when Willis interviewed him because, rather than being precious about his recent well-documented problems, he showed a priceless ability to laugh at himself.

As players, we are keen to be able to rest as part of our preparation immediately before an international game, but it ended up being an enjoyable evening.

I am aware of our responsibilities as a team — not just on the field, but also as ambassadors for Australia and Australian cricket — and attending functions like this, answering questions about the Test series and signing autographs come with the territory. I will never relish this part of my role, but I know it is necessary, especially in an increasingly commercial world.

We have two major injury concerns following the match at Leicester. Justin Langer experienced soreness in both his shoulders and had an injection in them to ease the pain, and Jason Gillespie reported acute soreness behind both his knees and had treatment to ease it.

Gillespie has not said much about the problem, maybe because he is under pressure coming into the Test and does not want to give anyone an excuse to leave him out. This is understandable. He will be allowed to rest during tomorrow's training session, but will be expected to bowl at full throttle on Wednesday to prove his fitness — we have other options at our disposal, and do not need to select a bowler who may break down during the match.

Tuesday 19 July

Today was all about getting settled into our surroundings and having a solid workout at Lord's.

The first task when we arrived this morning was to get our gear into the dressing room and settle in — it will be our cricketing home for the next week. After the play–pack–play–pack mentality of the one-day series, it makes a pleasant change to be able to bring gear into the room and leave it there.

The Lord's dressing room is a familiar place to most of this squad; it is also a place that has a host of great memories for us. I initially came here in 1997, on my first Ashes tour, and since then we have returned for the World Cup final in 1999, Test and one-day success in 2001, and two one-day matches against England earlier this season. If I had to pick out one special memory, it would be of our celebration of the World Cup win, which culminated in our singing the team song in the middle of the ground. I led the singing while perched on Tom Moody's shoulders.

Cricketers tend to be creatures of habit. If we get runs with a certain bat, we like to keep using it. These habits also extend to the places we occupy in a dressing room. Everyone who had played at Lord's before gravitated to the area they had changed in previously. My place is in the middle of the bench on the back wall, with a view out towards the balcony that overlooks the ground. The right-hand corner in front of me under the window is occupied by Glenn McGrath; next to him, in an armchair by the door that opens out onto the viewing balcony, is Adam Gilchrist; and on the opposite side of the room from McGrath, also under a window, is Shane Warne.

The familiar feel extends to the honours board on the wall to my left, which lists all the overseas players who have scored hundreds and taken 5-wicket hauls in a Test innings on the ground. Every bowler would like to add his name to the board during the match, but none more so than Warne, who is making what will probably be his last Test appearance here. He has played three previous matches here, but is yet to take 5 wickets in an innings.

Even our room attendant, Peter Lowe, is a familiar face, and that feeling of continuity helps make us all feel at home. That comfortable feeling is obviously something Australian sides have had here over many years, because the last time we lost a Test at Lord's was before World War II. It is not a fact that will affect the course of the match — it is how we play in this Test that counts — but if that statistic is a psychological lift to any of our players, and some unwanted baggage for the England team, that is a bonus.

Our practice session went well. I also took the opportunity to have a look at the pitch. I do not normally believe in studying pitches too closely before a match, especially 2 days out from the start, but it is difficult to avoid the surface at Lord's, as you have to walk past it on the way to and from the practice ground.

The pitch looked dry, and I was surprised at that. Curators will often leave some moisture in the surface at this stage — on the basis that it will dry out in the 48 hours leading up to the start and the moisture will help avoid cracking later on — but the pitch looked ready to play on today, apart from a decent covering of grass. Before we left that was brushed up by the ground staff so it could be cut short by the mower blades.

At this stage I would be hoping to bat first, on the basis that the pitch will spin later on, but there is plenty of time for conditions to change before the first ball on Thursday, and we saw during the NatWest Series final that cloud cover can help the ball swing here.

This evening we attended a function at the Australian High Commission attended by 450 people, most of them Australians. It made a pleasant change to hear so many familiar accents after a month of getting used to the sound of English voices.

The High Commissioner made a speech and I responded. I knew beforehand that I would have to speak, so with the help of Jonathan Rose, our media manager, I drafted a few thoughts. Most of them were based on the fact that the Prime Minister, John Howard, would be attending the function, so when he was delayed I had to make a few hurried adjustments.

The main theme of my remarks was the great side of 1948, led by Donald Bradman. A few years ago we were lucky enough to spend time with some of that squad — Bill Brown, Doug Ring and Bill Johnston — and find out more about what they had achieved on that tour, which was the first by an Australia side to England after World

War II. That team won the Ashes series 4–0, is spoken of with reverence in both the United Kingdom and Australia, and has been regarded by some as one of the best sides of all time, playing tough but always entertaining cricket. If we can follow in the footsteps of the players from that tour — by being as successful as they were on the field, and at the same time creating a lasting impression off it — we will have done our job.

Wednesday 20 July

Another hectic day, but luckily the last one involving talk about what might happen in the Ashes series. Tomorrow is where the talking finally stops and the action starts.

Rianna arrived from New York this morning, landing at 6.30. I was desperate to meet her at the airport, but as it was the day before the first Test, she said I should get some extra sleep instead. In fact, she said that if I did come to meet her she would not speak to me, so I had to be content with sending a hotel car to pick her up — she got to the hotel by 9 o'clock.

We had a team meeting at 10.30 to make sure we were all clear on our plans for tomorrow. We have played England so often already this summer that we have a good idea of how we will try to get their batsmen out and of how their bowlers will try to operate against us, so the meeting was really more of a reinforcement session than a discussion of any startling new tactics. We recapped on the England batsmen:

Andrew Strauss — loves to play square of the wicket on both sides, so make sure we bowl full and straight to him, and get him playing straight back down the ground, somewhere he does not score many runs. He can be a hooker, but it is not his strongest shot, and he tends to hook in the air either side of square leg. Do not be afraid to let him have a short ball.

Marcus Trescothick — is always a candidate to be caught behind, as he plays away from his body with little footwork. Make sure we do not offer him too much width, as his hand–eye coordination is still good enough to score freely square of the wicket on the offside.

Michael Vaughan — has a lot of movements as the bowler delivers, so aim to target a good length around off-stump early on to see if he knows where his stumps are; get him feeling for the ball. He thrives on the momentum that comes from boundaries, so try to stop him scoring freely. He hooks well, so try to bowl a full length and use the short ball only as a surprise.

Ian Bell — Shane Warne said he is a hesitant starter in county cricket and does not always get a big stride in with his front foot when he first comes to the wicket. Make sure we bowl a full length around off-stump, as he might not cover any swing and seam movement before he gets established. Warne said he fancied getting Bell out, but he tends to feel that way about most players he bowls to. Bell will be nervous, because he has played just a handful of Tests. Make sure he knows he is in a contest.

Kevin Pietersen — we saw during the one-day series how strong he is through the on-side, even playing balls from off-stump and outside through the leg-side field. Try to maintain a disciplined line on or outside off-stump to make him play in areas he is not so comfortable in. Warne, who has played county cricket with Pietersen at Hampshire, said our fast bowlers should also try to bowl full and straight at him early on, especially for the first few balls. He is a tall man with a high backlift, and until he gets used to the pace of the bowling he can struggle. Warne confirmed that he has seen Pietersen get bowled in this way during the county season.

Andrew Flintoff — loves to hit fours and sixes, so he and Pietersen are candidates to be kept quiet, maybe with defensive fields, so that they fret about getting the scoreboard moving. Flintoff is a compulsive hooker but is strong enough to hit the ball out of the ground. He also tries to force the short ball square of the wicket on the offside with a straight bat, so if the quick bowlers can maintain a tight line just outside off-stump he will bring the wicketkeeper and slip fielders into play.

Geraint Jones — loves to cut and pull. He is a compulsive hooker, so the short ball is an option to dismiss him. He is also always looking for the attacking option, so we should try to starve him of boundaries. His Australian connections — he was brought up in Brisbane — will make him especially nervous, so we must make sure we give him nothing.

Justin Langer and Matthew Hayden talked about how they thought the England bowlers would operate. We know they will rely on Stephen Harmison and Flintoff hitting the pitch hard, and expect Simon Jones and Matthew Hoggard to swing the ball. The England plan over the past year has revolved around spinner Ashley Giles keeping it tight at one end while the faster bowlers alternate at the other end. If we can get after Giles and hit him out of the attack, that will force Vaughan to use his faster bowlers in longer spells than he wants to, and in a series where five Tests are shoehorned into 7 weeks, that could work in our favour.

I ended the meeting by asking everyone to make sure they are switched on for the next 5 days, and all of the five Tests. There has been such a long build-up and so much hype surrounding the series that it will be easy for players to get caught up in that hype, lose themselves in nerves and forget about the basics that have got us to the top of the ICC's Test ladder. By just focusing on the jobs we have to do over the next few days and ignoring any side issues or personal battles, we will ensure that we start the series on the right note.

Our meeting was attended by Jonathan Wells, a junior player from Tasmania who was the beneficiary of Warne's ban from cricket 2 years ago. During that ban Warne was not paid but, rather than simply keep that money, CA and the ACA — together with Warne — came up with a novel way of using it. The money was used to allow the leading player from the annual under–17 carnival — in this case, Wells — to spend a week with us seeing how we prepare and behave before and during a Test.

I would have preferred the money to be used to fund a slightly older player to make the trip, but I hope Wells, who is here with his parents, will get a feel for what it takes to play at the highest level and be inspired to follow in our footsteps.

After the meeting I headed to Lord's for an afternoon of meetings and media briefings. It all started at 11.30 with the launch of the Compton–Miller Medal for the player of the series, named in honour of former England batsman Denis Compton and former Australia all-rounder Keith Miller (who died late last year). I attended the memorial service for Miller in Melbourne while I was recovering from my fractured thumb, and after hearing what was said about him and the way he played cricket, I was full of admiration. This medal is a fitting tribute to him and Compton, two great mates who played the game hard on the field but enjoyed life off it, and helped make cricket hugely popular in the aftermath of World War II.

From there it was on to the match referee's meeting, which was between me, England captain Michael Vaughan, coaches John Buchanan and Duncan Fletcher, and the two team managers, England's Phil Neale and Steve Bernard. These meetings can be dull affairs — the referee, in this case the Sri Lankan Ranjan Madugalle, just goes through what he expects from both sides in terms of conduct during the series and checks that we are all happy with the playing conditions. This meeting, however, was anything but dull.

The sparks began to fly when Buchanan brought up the issue of the use of substitutes. We were fed up with the way England rotated players on and off the field during the one-day series, replacing tired players with fresh — and talented — fielders, and Buchanan felt it was worth raising the matter again, especially as we have a new referee for this series.

The Laws of Cricket are quite clear on what should happen. Law 2 reads:

(a) If the umpires are satisfied that a player has been injured or become ill after the nomination of the players, they shall allow that player to have:

(i) A substitute acting instead of him in the field.

(ii) A runner when batting.

(b) The umpires shall have discretion, for other wholly acceptable reasons, to allow a substitute for a fielder, or a runner for a batsman, at the start of the match or at any subsequent time.

(c) A player wishing to change his shirt, boots, etc. must leave the field to do so. No substitute shall be allowed for him.

If a player needs to nip off for a bathroom break, that is understandable, although plenty of players in our side seem to manage to take care of that during the intervals in play that occur every couple of hours, or at the fall of a wicket or a scheduled drinks break. Our problem is that England's players seem to nip off before or after a bowling spell and spend at least 10 minutes off the field for no apparent reason.

Bringing up the subject really annoyed Fletcher, as he thought we were accusing him and his side of gamesmanship — which we were, although not directly. I thought it was going to get very heated at one point, but Madugalle and the umpires — Rudi Koertzen and Aleem Dar, who were also at the meeting — promised to monitor the comings and goings, and that calmed things down.

The meeting was also a chance for me to discuss the issue of catches with Michael Vaughan. In recent series Australia have played, I have proposed a move away from technology — which is not always good enough to determine the fairness or otherwise of disputed catches — and back to a situation where players accept each other's word on the issue. Such disputes blight a game that, years ago, prided itself on fair play and honesty. I see it as the responsibility of the players on the field to handle those matters. I spoke to Vaughan before the NatWest Challenge and he said he would speak to his players to see how they felt about the issue. Now was a chance to find out his thoughts. We ended up coming to a compromise.

Vaughan agreed that television is not always a satisfactory way to deal with the matter, but felt that the players are there to play the game, not umpire it as well. He said the on-field umpires should have a role in determining the legitimacy of a catch. After all, he said, that was what they were there for.

I accepted his point as long as the on-field umpires agreed to make the decisions themselves and not refer the matter to technology. They nodded their heads, so we had some middle ground.

After the meeting it was on to my pre-match media conferences: two separate briefings, one for television and one for the print journalists. I was asked about Matthew Hoggard's pre-match comment that Glenn McGrath may be over the hill. My response was that I did not expect any of England's top-order batsmen to share that view. Hoggard appears to have caught the disease a few of our players have had: making big comments before the series. The players in our line-up who do such things — especially McGrath and Warne — know they have to back those comments up. To their credit, they usually do. I wonder if Hoggard can do the same thing.

Talking of big comments, I was asked for my prediction of the score in the series. Unlike McGrath and Warne, I believe actions speak louder than words, so I restricted my answer to saying simply that if we play to the best of our ability, we should win.

The day involved plenty of rushing around, and though there was a team picnic in nearby Hyde Park during the afternoon — a John Buchanan idea to help the players and their families relax before tomorrow's play — I was too tired to make it. I decided to have a quiet afternoon with Rianna instead, but as we strolled across the road from our hotel we got the shock of our lives.

A massive Mercedes pulled up, the window was wound down and Hugh Jackman, the Australian actor famous for his performances in the *X-Men* films, popped his head out. His car had at this point stopped traffic on the busy Kensington High Street in central London, but he did not seem to mind. He told us he had tickets for Saturday's play and was really looking forward to being there, and I asked him to come up to the dressing rooms and meet the other players after play, something he seemed delighted about. Rianna was pretty excited about our encounter — she is a big fan of Jackman.

Rianna and I later headed out to see her family, who were staying nearby, to drop off their match tickets. When we got back we ate a room service dinner and had a relaxing evening.

I am not someone who gets particularly nervous before a match, especially if I am happy with my preparation, as I am in this case. I had a solid practice session on Tuesday and will have some throw-downs from Jamie Siddons, our assistant coach, before play tomorrow, to feel bat on ball, and make sure my feet are moving and I am balanced when I strike the ball. There is no point worrying now about what might happen; that can only be controlled when I get onto the field. And, after all the build-up, that is something I am now desperate to do.

Thursday 21 July

First Test, Lord's, London, day 1: Australia 190 (Harmison 5–43) lead England 7–92 (McGrath 5–21) by 98 runs.

It is tough to know where to start in my description of today's events. The best way to put it is that after all the hype and build-up to the series, today certainly delivered in terms of excitement and action — 17 wickets tumbled!

There was plenty of top-class bowling, but I am not convinced that all the batting was of the required standard. England bowled aggressively, but we should never have been bowled out for 190. Luckily, we hit back superbly in the final session, and with the wicket already dry and showing signs of variable bounce, we are in a very healthy position.

It was not just action on the field that concerned me. During the afternoon our security manager, Dave Woodman, pulled me aside and said there had been further terrorist acts in London. The reports we had were vague, but after everything that had been discussed lately I knew it would concern a lot of the squad, especially since many of them — myself included — have friends and family visiting for the Test.

For a while I was the only player aware of the situation, but at tea Woodman briefed the players about it and reassured them in case they had heard any rumours. The bombs did not explode this time, thank heavens, but when James Sutherland came into the dressing room after play, the issue was something we were keen to chat about with him. He promised to discuss the issue of safety and security with the ECB.

All the families and friends of the players were accounted for. We know that when they are at the ground they are as safe as they can be, because there are serious security checks in place that prevent people bringing weapons and explosives into Lord's. The potential problem for those relatives and friends — and, of course, for everyone in London — is going anywhere on public transport, as the bombers have already shown that they are targeting the transport network. Woodman's advice was to avoid public transport and travel by taxi, which is something Rianna and I have done already when we have been moving around London on our own.

The security concerns did take a little of the shine off the day but I am still content with our position.

I was awake this morning at 6.30, bouncing out of bed and pretty excited at the prospect of my first Ashes Test as captain. There was a real buzz not only among the team, but also on the streets around Lord's as we made our way to the ground. The bus took longer than usual to get there because of the volume of traffic, but we had allowed extra time for the trip so there were no problems like those on our one-day match in Bristol earlier in the tour — we still had plenty of time for warm-ups and practice.

When we first arrived at the ground the sun was out, but as the time for the toss got nearer it started to cloud over. I remembered during the one-day final at the start of the month that cloud cover meant the ball swung and seamed all day, but when I won the toss my choice was still to bat. The pitch was dry, and I thought it might become harder to bat on later in the match, becoming uneven in bounce as it dried further — this was also likely to help Shane Warne's leg-spin more and more.

We had a full-strength squad to pick from, with Jason Gillespie proving his fitness yesterday under the watchful eye of David Boon, the selector on duty for this Test. We needed to be confident that he could bowl long spells, and Errol Alcott, Boon and Gillespie himself were all satisfied with his fitness, so he got the nod over the unlucky Michael Kasprowicz.

A lot of our batting today was substandard: too many players tried to play big shots. England's bowlers did what we expected them to, with Stephen Harmison and Andrew Flintoff banging the ball into the pitch and Matthew Hoggard and Simon Jones aiming to bowl a fuller length and find some swing. Our batsmen were guilty of trying to fight fire with fire and became too aggressive.

Most of our players got out playing attacking shots, but I was undone by one from Harmison that bounced a bit more than I expected. I ended up edging it to third slip. By then I had already received treatment for a blow to the helmet, and I was not the only one struck during what was a torrid morning session. Matthew Hayden was hit on the helmet as he tried to hook and Justin Langer took a painful blow on the forearm and a few on the body.

The ball that hit me was an excellent bouncer. I am a confident hooker and puller and started to get myself into position to go for the cross-bat shot, but as I did so I could see that the ball was bouncing much higher than I had expected. I tried to pull out of the shot but made that decision too late, and the ball ended up squashing the grille of my helmet onto the right side of my face as I turned my head at the last second.

There was no pain, just a ringing feeling as the impact of the blow reverberated around in my head. I felt fine, but pretty quickly I began to feel something trickling down the side of my face, and when I looked at my shirt I could see blood dripping onto it.

I took my helmet off and could see that part of the grille was caved in — that obviously needed attention, but so did the cut on my face. Alcott, who spent most of the morning shuttling back and forth onto the field because of the blows we were taking, was quickly on the scene to inspect the damage.

He has seen plenty of blows to the head like this in the 21 years he has done the job as team physiotherapist, and was immediately concerned that I might have sustained a fracture to the jaw, eye socket or cheekbone. Luckily, the impact of the ball on the helmet and then my face seemed to have fallen between all three of those areas — I had a fortunate escape. Alcott patched me up with a plaster, and I got a new grille for my helmet and was able to continue.

I may have been helped by wearing the latest type of Albion helmet. I have always favoured the old Albion design, which fits more snugly on the head, but lately I have been forced to switch to the newer style because my favourite helmet was broken by a Shaun Tait bouncer in the nets in Colombo in March 2004. The new helmet is lighter but broader, and that has meant a degree of discomfort — sometimes I feel the grille on my left shoulder as I look down the pitch to face the bowler. On this occasion, maybe that feature — the grille being a little further away from my face — saved me from a more serious blow.

We knew England would be aggressive in the field, but one aspect of that aggression that upset me was the way they threw the ball when there was no chance of running the batsman out. A couple of those throws ended up closer to the batsman than the stumps.

Hoggard hurled one close to Hayden and Michael Vaughan only just missed Shane Warne. It was a throwback to what happened during the one-day match against England at Edgbaston, and was clearly an attempt to try to rattle us.

I don't mind the ball being thrown back to the wicketkeeper or at the stumps if a batsman is straying down the pitch, but I thought England's actions today were macho posturing and I told Vaughan as much when he came out to bat.

As he took guard from the umpire I strolled up from slip and said, 'There were a few wild throws when you fielded, eh?'

Vaughan said, 'Yes, plenty', but I thought he said, 'Yes, we meant it', and I added, 'If you hang around here for a while you can expect your fair share flying around too.'

Speaking to Brad Haddin, our reserve wicketkeeper, after play, he said that from his vantage point on the dressing room balcony he sensed Vaughan's body language visibly tailing off after my exchange with him, which is exactly the effect I wanted. If he and his team are going to dish it out, they have to take it as well. I also told our players that if any more wild throws are directed at them, they should bat the ball away to the boundary and see how the England players like that. All we would be doing is defending ourselves; the England boys need to know we will not back down in a contest.

Our bowling effort was split into two: before tea and after tea. Before the interval we only bowled a handful of overs, but I felt we bowled too short, so I pulled Glenn McGrath and Brett Lee aside at the break and told them to bowl a fuller length to get the batsmen driving, and to try to exploit any seam movement available. They followed my instructions perfectly, and the result was a 5-wicket haul for McGrath, including his 500th wicket in Tests, and good pressure from Lee at the other end.

McGrath is a great showman, and as soon as he took the wicket he needed — he started the match on 499 victims — he got twelfth man Michael Kasprowicz to bring out a new pair of white and gold boots with '500' written on them. McGrath and his manager, Warren Craig, are shrewd operators and never miss a chance to get some positive publicity, and this was another case in point — the boots will get plenty of coverage. Kasprowicz also showed his sense of humour as, after McGrath's second wicket, he brought the original boots back out with '501' on them, written in marker pen. When we got back to the dressing room after play, our room attendant, Peter Lowe, had already marked up McGrath's 5-wicket haul on the dressing room honours board using some tape and that same marker pen.

I went through the last two sessions of play with some sticking plaster on the side of my face to cover up my cut, and after play Alcott took me to get the wound stitched. I assumed it would be just a few minutes lying on a bench, but it turned out to be a bit more drawn out than that. I was put into a surgical gown, taken to theatre and given eye pads to shield my eyes from the glare of the lamps as a plastic surgeon sealed the wound with eight stitches. It meant that, after leaving the ground at 6.45 p.m. I did not get back to the hotel until 9.30 p.m., 13 hours after I'd set off in the morning.

My delayed return turned out to be an advantage, because the team had been held up by a bomb scare involving a bag on a bus outside the hotel. Everyone was allowed inside but told to stay in their rooms. That policy suited me fine — after such a long day I was going nowhere. Rianna ordered some Chinese takeaway and we had a relaxing hour or so before it was time for bed.

Friday 22 July

Graham Thorpe announces his retirement from international cricket. Thorpe, who made his Test debut against Australia in 1993, played his 100th and final Test against Bangladesh at the start of the season.

First Test, Lord's, London, day 2: Australia 190 and 7–279 (Clarke 91, Martyn 65) lead England 155 (Pietersen 57, McGrath 5–53) by 314 runs.

We are still in a very strong position, but I am disappointed with the way we finished the day. We lost 4 wickets in the last 10 overs, some of them through careless batting, and although we are still favourites to win from here, I want us to sell our wickets far more dearly tomorrow to avoid England gaining any momentum leading into their run chase in the final innings.

Michael Clarke's dismissal was the wicket that started that late slide. I was bitterly disappointed with the way he got out. England did not look like taking a wicket, and resorted to bowling a defensive line outside off-stump with seven fielders on that side of the wicket to test Clarke's patience. He tried to pierce the field to hit boundaries and get the scoreboard moving, but could not manage it, and eventually, with a hundred at Lord's for the taking, he dragged the ball onto his stumps trying to hit it too hard.

Sitting on the balcony, I could see Clarke's frustration building — I even predicted the dismissal at the start of the over in which he was out. Maybe I should have got a message to him to calm down, but I am a great believer in players doing things for themselves, and that includes learning how to play in any situation. Clarke knew straightaway that he had done the wrong thing by letting England's tactics get to him; I hope today will teach him to be more patient the next time he is in a similar position.

Clarke's dismissal was especially frustrating because it gave England a new lease of life after a period when they appeared to be just going through the motions in the field, without any real plan to get us out. We had hit the spinner, Ashley Giles, out of the attack, which forced Michael Vaughan to bowl each of his faster bowlers for longer than he would have liked, but after Clarke's dismissal Stephen Harmison and Andrew Flintoff charged in for the final 40 minutes and the result was another 3 wickets.

One of those wickets was Damien Martyn, who fell lbw to Harmison the ball after Clarke was out. The delivery kept low and cut back, and Martyn lingered at the crease for a second or so after being given out, frustrated at being dismissed after more than 3 hours of hard work. As he walked off he was told where the dressing room was by Andrew Strauss, an incident that was captured on camera. I gather no action is being taken by the match referee.

Martyn is an undemonstrative bloke, and never rants and raves when he gets out. He just returns to the dressing room and sits quietly before he takes his gear off. Out in the middle he never gets involved in any verbal exchanges with bowlers or fielders. The England boys tried to wind him up today with the same tactic they used yesterday, throwing the ball towards the stumps but also close to the batsman. Martyn had blocked a ball from Harmison back down the pitch, and the bowler picked it up and hurled it back, straight at the batsman. Martyn's response was to clip it off his toes to the fine leg boundary. That gesture had the desired effect — the England players did not throw the ball at Martyn again during his innings.

Before our late collapse, things had gone pretty much according to plan during the day. We spoke before the start about the value of a first innings lead, and we got one, albeit not as big as we'd wanted. I started with Shane Warne against Kevin Pietersen, because we felt Pietersen preferred pace on the ball; we also reckoned he might want to show Warne who was boss. Although the pair are good friends, there is fierce rivalry between them too, and I suspected that might work in our favour. It did, because Pietersen eventually got out trying to hit Warne for six. However, by that stage he had played a useful innings and reduced our lead to modest proportions.

That lead could have been much bigger if Warne had been given an lbw appeal against Pietersen in the first over of the day, but I give credit to the batsman: he played positively and well, especially against Glenn McGrath. He hit McGrath out of the attack, clobbering him into the pavilion for six, and I felt at that stage that McGrath was rattled. He said he was going to bowl short of a driving length, but then, after being hit for four on the first ball of his over, he decided to bowl a slower ball and then a fuller length than we discussed, which allowed the batsman to drive. When I decided enough was enough and it was time to look elsewhere for someone to wrap up the innings, I thought McGrath was not going to talk to me ever again — but he soon got over it.

I was frustrated with the way I was dismissed, because I did all the hard work of playing myself in only to get out to a very tame shot. The ball, from Matthew Hoggard, swung away and bounced. Looking to force it off the back foot, I lost control of the shot and ended up steering it into the hands of backward point. That summed up the way the day went: every time we looked like pulling away from England, Vaughan's side just managed to grab a wicket to stay in contention. Let's hope we can put the game completely beyond England tomorrow.

Saturday 23 July

First Test, Lord's, London, day 3: England 155 and 5–156 require another 264 runs to beat Australia 190 and 384 (Clarke 91, Katich 67, Martyn 65).

We enjoyed a great day that has left us on the verge of another win at Lord's — that would be the perfect start to this Test series. I did have one or two concerns at one point, as the England openers, Marcus Trescothick and Andrew Strauss, negotiated the new-ball spells of Glenn McGrath and Brett Lee, but in the final session Lee and Shane Warne were irresistible. The only thing that can now save the home side is bad weather.

Lee showed why, as long as he is in form, he should always be one of the first names on the team sheet. He tore in like a man on a mission, with a point to prove, and bowled with ferocious hostility. He bounced out Strauss and then bowled Michael Vaughan with a fantastic delivery that ripped his off-stump out of the ground. It was pure pace, and I can only imagine the thoughts of both Vaughan and the England dressing room when that happened.

As for Warne, his bowling was some of the best I have seen from him in years. He performed like a man inspired. He showed superb control of his line and length, and spun his leg-break sharply. Ironically, it was a ball that did not spin that produced one of the moments of the day. He dismissed Ian Bell lbw as the batsman played no shot to a ball that went straight on. We all thought Warne had bowled the straight ball deliberately after delivering a series of leg-breaks that spun across Bell. The batsman was obviously expecting another leg-spinner, which is why he didn't play a shot, but the ball held its line and cannoned into his left pad in front of all three stumps.

When we got back to the dressing room after play was called off early because of bad light, the television commentators also thought Warne had produced a well-disguised straight ball, and they were saying what a magical piece of trickery it was. At that point Warne shattered the illusion by admitting that the delivery was just a leg-break that failed to turn, but he and the rest of us were delighted that the commentators were talking it up so much. I hope the England players were listening in their dressing room. The more people start looking for things from Warne's bowling that, in reality, may not be there, the more likely he and the rest of us are to win the battle.

We were all pumped up during Warne's fantastic spell either side of tea, and we may have gone over the top with some of our appealing. The adrenaline was flowing as we sensed the kill, and with Warne bowling so well it seemed there was a chance of a wicket every ball. On reflection, we will need to watch that aspect of our conduct.

Lee was involved in a couple of moments of minor controversy as we tried to force home the advantage we'd gained by batting until after lunch and setting England a massive 420 to win. First he caught and bowled Strauss — though replays suggested he grounded the ball as he dived forward to complete the dismissal. The ball ballooned up to short cover as Strauss was beaten for pace trying to hook a short ball, and Lee sprinted forward from his follow-through to gather the ball at full stretch. He held the ball cleanly, but as he skidded across the turf the palm containing the ball rubbed along the ground. There was no doubt Lee caught the ball and had it under control, but there was also no doubt, seeing the replay, that the ball brushed the ground as he came to a stop. I felt it was out, but if I had seen that replay in the England dressing room I may have been less certain.

If Lee was lucky with that dismissal, he had some bad luck later on in another flashpoint of the day. Trying to bowl a yorker at Kevin Pietersen, he ended up bowling a knee-high full-toss which beat the batsman for pace and hit him just above the roll of the pad. It was a blisteringly quick ball and Lee, along with the rest of us, thought it was plumb lbw — I later found out that this opinion was backed up by television replays. Pietersen was furious at the delivery, which he felt was a beamer, but it was well below waist height, and I wondered if his reaction put umpire Rudi Koertzen off giving the batsman out.

Koertzen is a top umpire and a good communicator with the players, but we were left in a lot of confusion over this incident. I found out later that when Lee asked him why the lbw appeal had been turned down, Koertzen said he thought that the batsman had hit it, but when I asked him about it at the end of the over, he said he thought it was too high and drifting past leg stump. Then, when he saw the full-speed replay on the giant video screen at the ground, he said, 'Sorry, I made a mistake. I didn't see it.'

It was an example of how an umpire can dig his own grave. He does not have to justify his decision to the players, even if we ask him for an explanation. All he has to say is that he was not sure it was out, but in trying to explain his decision on this occasion, there was confusion and we were left feeling hard done by.

Although Pietersen is still there at the close and Geraint Jones is with him, we have removed the rest of the England top order, and already I hope we are establishing some sort of hold over the team. Vaughan has looked very uncomfortable during this match, and an example of his mental state came when Matthew Hayden chirped up from slip that he was under pressure. 'Show some respect,' he barked back, a sure sign that he was feeling tense — normally he says very little when he is batting, and he rarely responds to comments from fielders.

Andrew Flintoff was another player who struggled as Warne wove his magic. As I stood at silly point while Flintoff was batting with Pietersen, I started chatting with Adam Gilchrist between deliveries about how much the pitch was spinning, and at one point I made a comment about Flintoff's bat. He and Pietersen are sponsored by the same company, and I said that the company must be delighted that its two main clients were together at the crease. The comments were not directed at Flintoff, but the idea was to get his mind off the job at hand, and although he never responded to anything we said, his head was darting about as Gilchrist and I were chatting, so he was clearly taking it all in. He looked ill at ease and was quickly dismissed by Warne, caught behind cutting.

By the time we came to bowl we were in a near-impregnable position, thanks to Simon Katich, who, along with Jason Gillespie and Glenn McGrath, extended our innings past lunch. We were helped by England's fielding — they dropped several catches — and also by their approach, as their bowlers tended to bowl too short. They had some success in the first innings by banging the ball into the pitch, and we copped a few blows, as I mentioned, but rather than use that tactic as a shock weapon, it became the stock ball. This reduced the likelihood of England's bowlers getting us out, as they were no longer attacking the stumps. Our fast bowlers did not fall into the same trap.

I am not sure why England dropped catches in this match, but they put down at least seven chances, including Michael Clarke early on in his innings yesterday. We, I am happy to say, have missed nothing. Our catching, especially close to the wicket, has been a concern over the past 6 to 12 months, but we have clicked into gear in this match, and with the bowlers being so well supported it means the confidence levels of the team are rising rapidly.

Although we still have 5 wickets to take, there was almost a party atmosphere in the dressing room after play, helped by the appearance of Hugh Jackman. I am not sure who was more starstruck — Jackman at the chance to chat with the likes of McGrath and Warne, or the players in the presence of a major Hollywood star. He turned out to be a regular bloke who likes a laugh and a beer, and we ended up in the dressing room for more than an hour after play before finally heading back to the hotel. Some sides would be concerned by having players so relaxed and excited before the opposition has been beaten, but I thought it was an understandable reaction after a display in the field that was as ruthless and aggressive as anything we have produced over the past year. I know that when we come back tomorrow morning, everyone will be focused on the job at hand: taking the last 5 wickets as quickly as possible.

Sunday 24 July

First Test, Lord's, London, day 4: Australia 190 and 384 beat England 155 and 180 (Pietersen 64*) by 239 runs.

After early frustration — the whole of the first half of the day was washed out by heavy rain — we rampaged through the England lower order with amazing speed to wrap up one of the most satisfying wins of my career.

We put aside all the pre-series hype and overcame England's aggressive approach by playing our own brand of tough, dominating

---

* not out

cricket, and with Glenn McGrath and Shane Warne again outstanding, we ended up crushing England pretty ruthlessly.

I really felt we rose to the occasion, while England, after a bright start, crumpled under the weight of expectation. If we can maintain this level of performance for the rest of the series, I am not sure England will be able to live with us.

The win was a happy and unexpected contrast to the morning, when we just sat and watched the rain from the sanctuary of the dressing room. At that stage the bad weather looked set in for the day, and although I refused to believe it would last for two days, the thought that we might be denied did cross my mind.

After what happened in New Zealand — we were caught out in Wellington by a sudden improvement in conditions and Adam Gilchrist almost missed the start of play on the third day of the Test in March — we decided to go to the ground as normal and wait to see what would happen. Once there, the players split into several distinct groups. I joined McGrath, Warne and team manager Steve Bernard for a game of cards; others slept, some listened to music and others still went to the gym at the Nursery End of the ground with Jock Campbell.

Justin Langer — who has captained Middlesex, which plays its cricket here — popped down to see curator Mick Hunt and was assured we would get some play after lunch. And that is exactly what happened. The skies cleared and, thanks to the ground's excellent drainage, we were playing within an hour of the covers coming off.

I did expect England's 5 wickets to last a little longer than they did — we wrapped the match up within an hour — but on a day like this, with the bowlers fresh and the Australia players matching last night's intensity, it was never going to be easy for lower-order batsmen to survive for long. We ended up slicing through the resistance like a hot knife through butter.

Our plan was to start with Warne and McGrath, our best two bowlers, to try to suffocate the batsmen, and that is exactly what happened with Geraint Jones. He was not scoring, but when he tried to break the shackles, all he managed to do was miscue a pull shot to mid-on.

Kevin Pietersen again played well, but he could not bat at both ends, and we worked our way through the other players very quickly. The only sadness was that Shane Warne did not end up with a 5-wicket haul to make it onto the honours board in what will be his last Test here. He had an over at Simon Jones and came mighty close to bowling him, but with bad weather drifting around there was only so much room for sentiment, and rather than bowl wide of the stumps to try to give Warne another chance to get the landmark, McGrath looked for, and found, the edge of Simon Jones's bat with Warne taking the catch to secure the win.

We know we still have plenty of room for improvement, which is a real positive for us. None of our batsmen scored a hundred and Jason Gillespie went through the match without taking a wicket. If those aspects of our game click into gear, they will add an extra dimension to our play.

I threw in some comments about Michael Vaughan. He failed twice with the bat, and with us taking a lead in the series he will be feeling the pressure already. I said that I felt he was uneasy against McGrath in this match, and so McGrath would be bowling to him a lot more during the rest of the series. It is just something else for him to think about on top of his side being 1–0 down in the series.

The aftermath of the win, once I finished speaking to the media, was fantastic, with the dressing room full of friends, families and children to enjoy the success with the players. One of the perks of being captain is that it is my decision who comes into the dressing room, and, as many of our well-wishers have come from Australia to watch the match, I felt it was only right that they should share the moment with us. Prime Minister John Howard also rang (on Bernard's mobile) to offer his congratulations. The whole experience must have been like a dream come true for our under–17 player, Jonathan Wells, and I think he enjoyed himself.

I only saw one of the England players, wicketkeeper Geraint Jones, come in for a drink, and he joined our reserve wicketkeeper, Brad Haddin, for a chat. Haddin said afterwards that Jones was very down-hearted at England's loss and his own performance, which culminated in his dismissal today. It is good to know that the pressure we are trying to exert is having an effect.

Eventually everyone departed except the players and support staff, and we sang the team song, something we always do to mark a victory. Langer is in charge of that, and he came up with a superb idea for a location. He took us across the first floor of the pavilion and into the England dressing room, and it was there that we belted out the song, the final expression of our success.

It was a fitting end to a classic Test match. The intensity of both sides was high, there was a bit of needle out in the middle to add some spice, and we ended up winning in style. Now we have to make sure we maintain our intensity and do not let our foot off England's throat.

After yesterday's celebrations, today was all about relaxing, enjoying our success — and also enjoying some luxury.

During the dinner I attended at Lord's on Friday, 8 July, a representative of Rolls-Royce introduced himself and said that if I ever wanted transport around London, his company would be happy to oblige. This evening I took him up on the offer, and the result was fantastic.

At 8 o'clock, a navy blue Rolls-Royce Phantom arrived outside the hotel and it took me, Rianna, Damien Martyn and his partner to a restaurant we had booked in nearby Chelsea. The meal was great, but the journey there and back was even better.

It was like riding on a carpet of air as we glided along, and the whole experience had a classy and classical feel to it; unlike most modern cars, there was not a digital display in sight — even the clock had a dial and hands. My three companions sat in the back on a massive plush leather seat while I rode up front alongside the driver. He told me the car can accelerate from 0–96 km/h in around 5.2 seconds, so as well as luxury, it also boasts plenty of power.

The one drawback with a fantastic car like the Phantom is the price — it retails in this country for around £300 000 and costs around A$960 000 back home, a figure that got burned into my brain after I attended the car's launch in Australia in 2004. A price like that means I will have to make do with the occasional trip in one for quite a few years yet.

It was back to business today, with a decent workout. I went for a run on the treadmill in the hotel's gym and pounded out 9 kilometres in 40 minutes, then followed up with a swim and some stretches. Everyone had earned a day off on Monday thanks to our win in the Test, but I do not want us to become complacent as a result of that win. I do not believe that will happen — we have too many experienced players around to allow it — but I am still keen to set an example to the rest of the squad, as well as ensuring that I maintain my own standards when it comes to fitness and training.

I also had my stitches out today, and the surgeon was happy with the way the gash has healed. There is a noticeable scar at the top of my left cheek but the surgeon assured me that it will reduce over time. To help ensure that it does, he advised me to rub vitamin E oil into the affected area three or four times a day. He also told me that when I am outdoors, I should avoid getting the area sunburnt — I will have to cover it up with zinc cream on playing days.

Rianna caught up with her relatives for a trip to the theatre this evening while I was supposed to meet up with a mate from home, Nick Sellers from Mowbray Cricket Club. He was not able to make it, though, so I ended up having a drink with Shaun Tait and former Australia fast bowler Damien Fleming, who is in England playing some social cricket and working for satellite broadcaster Sky Sports. Fleming is great company as he has a sharp sense of humour, and we had a very enjoyable evening before I headed back to my room to pack my bags for our morning departure.

Wednesday 27 July

Even on an Ashes tour, where the emphasis is on high-pressure cricket, there is the odd day when we take our feet off the accelerator. Today was one of those days.

We visited Teddington Cricket Club, on the outskirts of London, for a day of social cricket with corporate clients, something that has happened on my two previous tours here. We had an enjoyable day, but the cricket was ruined only by the rain — we did not bowl a ball.

In the absence of any cricket, we spent most of the day in the marquee and were entertained by Geoff Miller, the England selector who is also a popular after-dinner speaker. The team split up, with one player going to sit on each corporate table, and there were plenty of autographs signed during the afternoon.

We eventually left late in the afternoon for the next stage of our tour, a 3-day game against Worcestershire starting on Friday. Worcester is about 3 hours' drive northwest of London, but we are staying around 50 kilometres away from the city, at a place called Tewkesbury. It means the journey to and from the ground will be a long one — about 40 minutes on the motorway — but the facilities at our hotel are excellent: there is a gym, and there is also a golf course, which should come in handy if we have any free time.

I spent the bus trip playing cards with team manager Steve Bernard, Shane Warne and Justin Langer. Bernard and Warne are veteran card players, but Langer is a novice. He has linked up with me while he learns the skills of card-playing, and I hope he learns quickly, because otherwise, on the evidence of today, I am going to lose a lot of games between now and the end of the trip, which is 7 weeks away.

Rianna is going to miss this leg of the tour: she left with her family this morning for a flight to Dublin. They are planning to spend some time in both Ireland and Scotland before she links up with me again before the next Test, in Birmingham.

Thursday 28 July

The plan was to have a training session at the ground, but it rained heavily overnight and during the morning, so although our kitbags made it to the ground, there was no point in us joining them.

Instead we had a good fitness session in the hotel's gym, with more running and, unlike Tuesday, some weights as well. I followed that with a few holes of golf before the rain got too heavy to carry on.

After lunch the batsmen got together to discuss what happened during the first Test — what went well, what went badly, and how we can improve during the rest of the series.

We all accepted that we played badly in the first innings, as we were bowled out for 190. We got swept along by the excitement of the first day of an Ashes series and tried to play far too many shots. In the second innings we got our tempo far better, and reached almost 400 as a result.

I was delighted with that change of approach and felt we were positive without being reckless in that innings, but added that there was still plenty of room for improvement. Most of us got established, but no one went on to reach a hundred, and that is something we need to address if we are to keep up the pressure on England.

Another positive was the way we blunted England's attack in the second innings. Because we attacked Ashley Giles, Michael Vaughan had to pull him out of the attack, which meant that Stephen Harmison and Andrew Flintoff had to bowl much more than they would have liked. By the third day they were noticeably jaded. If we can repeat that formula in the next two Tests, which are separated by just two days, it should really benefit us.

Friday 29 July

More rain meant that the facilities at Worcester were waterlogged, but we were able to get outdoors at a local cricket club which backs onto our hotel. The ground was dry enough for us to get some fielding drills done and we also had an enjoyable game of touch football, which brought out everyone's competitive instincts.

Despite the bad weather, the side for the 3-day game against Worcestershire was selected and announced. Damien Martyn and Adam Gilchrist have been given the chance to get away for a few days and have taken that chance in differing ways. Martyn has headed to Venice with his partner following a recommendation from me after I went there with Rianna in 2001, and Gilchrist has travelled to EuroDisney with his family. The policy of allowing players to forget about cricket for a few days worked well 4 years ago, so we are repeating it on this tour.

Shane Warne, Brett Lee and Glenn McGrath will stay with the squad, but all have been rested. That trio will form the core of our attack for the Test series, and we want to wrap them in cotton wool to ensure that they are fresh for each remaining match. Lee took a couple of fearful blows on his left hand while batting at Lord's and has also developed some soreness around his left ankle; missing this match should ensure that he is fully fit by the time the Test starts next week.

As several of the Test team are missing, Brad Haddin, Brad Hodge, Shaun Tait, Stuart MacGill and Michael Kasprowicz will now have a chance to find some form and press their cases for inclusion if a slot arises.

Saturday 30 July

Tour match, Worcester, day 1: The Australians 0–4 v Worcestershire.

The late evening sunshine that gave us perfect conditions for a round of golf at our hotel arrived about 12 hours too late to allow us a decent hit-out at Worcester. Instead, a combination of morning rain, a soaking wet outfield and more rain mid-afternoon restricted us to just one over of action.

One of the umpires, David Constant, wanted to start the game after lunch, only around an hour after the rain stopped, but that was not sensible or possible, because when I went out to look at conditions, water was squelching up over my shoes on parts of the ground.

For a while it looked as if Constant, a former international umpire, would get his way, but I was not willing to risk my players injuring themselves, and Worcestershire captain Vikram Solanki agreed with me. Even the curator said a county match would not start in those conditions.

Eventually Constant relented, and the curator was able to do some more drying work on the ground. We were ready to play by mid-afternoon, but the rain returned after less than 5 minutes of action.

That additional rain, on top of what had fallen over the previous few days, meant the outfield was saturated, so play was abandoned and we headed back to the hotel. By the time we got there the skies had cleared, the sun had come out and Justin Langer, Shane Warne and Brad Hodge joined me for a relaxing round of golf on the course connected to our hotel.

Off the field, physiotherapist Errol Alcott was concerned enough about Brett Lee's left ankle to send him to London for a scan. Although it showed no structural damage, the scan did reveal a minor problem that could lead to a stress fracture if Lee is overworked. It is another reason to wrap him in cotton wool between Test matches.

Sunday 31 July

England announce an unchanged 12-man squad for the second Test, at Edgbaston, starting on Thursday.

Tour match, Worcester, day 2: The Australians 9–406 (Haddin 94, Hayden 79, Langer 54, Gillespie 53*) v Worcestershire.

There were plenty of good things to come out of today's action. With the exception of Michael Clarke, everyone who made it to the crease spent a reasonable amount of time there.

Justin Langer and Matthew Hayden benefited from time in the middle before the next Test, Jason Gillespie confirmed his batting credentials, and Brad Haddin showed the type of form he displayed through much of last summer for New South Wales as he top-scored.

Haddin was rusty at first, as you might expect given that he has been on tour for almost 2 months but has barely played a match. He played at and missed four of his first five balls, but once he got over that uncertain start and came to terms with the conditions, he timed the ball sweetly and was unlucky not to score a hundred — he fell to a catch on the boundary.

I missed the latter part of his innings as I was in the practice nets with Jamie Siddons, the assistant coach, working on my footwork and technique after lasting just 35 minutes when I batted. I was caught at slip as I pushed at a ball that seamed away from me, and although Haddin, who was non-striker at the time, said there was not a lot I could have done differently, I felt I could have left the delivery alone. It was frustrating, because after all the talk in the batsmen's meeting about making the most of a start, I failed to do just that.

Monday 1 August

Paul Collingwood is added to England's squad for the second Test.

Tour match, Worcester, day 3: The Australians 9–406 declared and 2–161 (Ponting 59*, Clarke 59) drew with Worcestershire 187 (Moore 69, Kasprowicz 5–67).

We left Worcester this evening having got plenty out of this match despite the near washout on the first day.

Jason Gillespie, Shaun Tait and Michael Kasprowicz all got extended workouts, and that allowed me and Michael Clarke, two players who missed out on much time at the crease in the first innings, another chance to bat. Both of us took it by scoring unbeaten 50s, and I feel we are in good shape for Thursday's Test start.

Kasprowicz was our standout bowler, especially after lunch. Before the interval he lacked some rhythm, but afterwards he bowled with genuine pace, and also swung and seamed the ball. After we won the first Test so conclusively, it is unlikely that we will make any changes for Edgbaston, but Kasprowicz showed that he is ready to step in if we suffer any last-minute injuries; his performance also creates some competition for places in the fast-bowling department. That type of competition has helped cement our position at the top of world cricket for the past decade — every player who has a Test or one-day place knows that there are players outside the line-up ready to take their spots if they fail to perform.

Jason Gillespie also bowled well, but it was tough to get an accurate idea of how he will perform on Thursday because he filled a different role here from the one he will play at Edgbaston. Today he used the new ball and got it to seam around, dismissing former England batsman Graeme Hick with a beautiful ball that moved away, but in the Test he will be using the old ball behind Glenn McGrath and Brett Lee. I hope he can take some of the confidence he gained from today into our next match.

With the pitch helping the seam bowlers and wickets falling at regular intervals, there was little chance to give Stuart MacGill a bowl, and that was the one drawback from the match. MacGill is unlikely to play on Thursday, but if we do encounter conditions that dictate the need for a second spinner — or if Shane Warne breaks down — we need him to be ready to step in.

My post-match media conference focused more on England's problems than on our position going into the Test, which I suspected might happen if Michael Vaughan's side lost the first match of the series.

Most of the questions revolved around the ineffectiveness of Ashley Giles at Lord's and the fact that England's players are not playing any cricket between the first and second Tests. I did not get involved in commenting on England's selection policy, but my own opinion is that they would be better off picking Paul Collingwood, who has been added to their squad today, ahead of Giles. Collingwood offers England more with the bat, and if they need any overs of spin, Michael Vaughan could bowl them himself.

As for the issue of players resting between Tests, I have sympathy with England over any criticism they cop for that. We do the same with our players during a domestic season, and England's players were in action for their counties for 6 weeks before we arrived in this country. With an intense program including two Tests in the next 2 weeks, any rest they can get will be useful. Of course if England's players turn up on Thursday looking rusty, you can be sure the media's knives will be sharpened again, which will be no bad thing for us.

We made the hour-long drive to Birmingham this evening and Rianna was waiting for me when we arrived — she flew down from Scotland during the afternoon. I looked on the Internet before going to bed and saw that the Kangaroos had beaten Port Adelaide after trailing by 40 points at half-time. That terrific comeback should ensure us a spot in this season's finals; not bad for a team that was written off as also-rans at the start of the season.

Tuesday 2 August

We started the day with a team meeting, where we took a fresh look at England's batsmen and discussed whether or not we could improve on our plans against them from the first Test.

We agreed that our plans for Marcus Trescothick, Andrew Strauss, Ian Bell and Andrew Flintoff had worked well and were worth persevering with, and we also agreed that we should use Glenn

McGrath against Michael Vaughan as much as possible, to try to exploit his uncertain footwork, especially early in his innings. Vaughan loves playing seam bowling off the back foot, and McGrath's ability to bowl a full length and find seam movement looks as good a way as any of removing the England captain.

Kevin Pietersen was the one player who caused us problems in the first Test, so we revisited our approach against him. We decided that when he first comes in we should hit him with a combination of pace from Brett Lee and spin from Shane Warne — we feel he is an uncertain starter against both types of bowling.

Pietersen is a tall man with a high backlift, and Lee showed at Lord's that he could be vulnerable to fast, full-length bowling; but for an umpiring error, Lee would have trapped him lbw. We agreed to try to bluff Pietersen by posting a leg-gully to make him think we are going to bowl short at him. Warne also fancied his chances against him, as there may be an element of Pietersen wanting to show his Hampshire team-mate what a good player he is by hitting him out of the attack.

If Pietersen survives his first 10 or 15 minutes at the crease, we've decided to use McGrath against him as much as possible and look to bowl wide of the off-stump. This should keep him quiet, as his favoured area is towards the leg-side, and testing his patience might lead to him doing something rash.

This evening we discovered that Vaughan is a doubt for the Test after being hit on the right arm in practice by fast bowler Chris Tremlett. Sky News said X-rays showed no break, but from the footage I saw he was clearly in a lot of pain. The blow did not surprise me — several of our players came close to experiencing the same thing when we practised at Edgbaston after our team meeting. The net pitches were best described as lively, with the ball bouncing steeply, and I only just avoided one delivery from Michael Kasprowicz that whistled past my right shoulder.

While England have a few question marks over their line-up heading into the match, we have already settled on our line-up, retaining the same 11 who won at Lord's. Consistency of selection has been a hallmark of our success over recent years, and it is benefiting Jason Gillespie now. He is yet to fire, but is being given every chance to rediscover his form and confidence.

I had a look at the pitch and it looked damp. This is no surprise, as last week the ground reportedly suffered a torrential downpour which flooded the surface and almost washed the covers away. I expect it to assist the seam bowlers, but I am not sure it will do so at any great pace.

England's Kevin Pietersen is awarded a central contract by the ECB.

Michael Vaughan is passed fit to play in the second Test. Paul Collingwood is released from the England squad to return to play county cricket for Durham.

With no commitments until the afternoon, I took the opportunity to recharge the batteries. I had a lazy morning with a sleep-in, followed by lunch with Rianna, before heading to the ground in the mid-afternoon for my media commitments and a light training session.

The session the day before a Test is usually optional. The idea is that players should work hard 2 days out then rest on the eve of the match to conserve energy for the 5 days to follow, but I felt I wanted some extra practice — most other members of the squad also felt the need for a top-up, because virtually everyone was there.

I had a batting session against some local bowlers, then went through another workout with Jamie Siddons to ensure that we were both happy with my movement and balance at the crease. I finished that session felling confident.

My meeting with the media ended up lasting almost as long as the practice session. I spoke to the writers, then there were commitments for television, and also Jim Maxwell of ABC Radio, and after all that I chatted with Andrew Ramsey of *The Australian* about my column for the newspaper.

My message to the media was a simple one: we are confident, and if we can maintain the form we showed at Lord's, we should leave here 2–0 up. If we can get that second win, I cannot see any way back for England; they would have to win all the remaining matches to regain The Ashes.

Second Test, Edgbaston, Birmingham, day 1: England 407 (Trescothick 90, Pietersen 71, Flintoff 68) v Australia.

This was a frantic, chaotic day, but at the end of it we are still in the match, thanks to some undisciplined England batting.

Vaughan's side came out with a game plan to take the match to us, and the batsmen did just that, thrashing 55 fours and 10 sixes, but none of them went on to reach three figures, and that meant we kept the total within bounds.

We were not helped by the loss of Glenn McGrath to a freak injury less than 2 hours before the start, and in his absence we bowled with very little control for much of the day.

If I had known we would bowl as badly as we did, maybe I would not have opted to send England in after I won the toss, but hindsight is a wonderful thing, and now that day one has come and gone, there is no point looking back on what might have been. If we get a big first innings score, and there is no reason why we should not, we will still be in a good position. And it is only 4 months since we conceded more than 400 in the first innings to New Zealand in Christchurch and still won that Test in 4 days.

McGrath's injury was bizarre. We had just run out onto the ground to start our warm-ups, about 90 minutes before the match, and I headed to the middle with Adam Gilchrist for a look at the pitch. As we were standing there, Gilchrist turned around to the group away to our right and said, 'McGrath's down.'

McGrath is a practical joker, and at first neither of us thought anything of it, but when the curator moved away from the pitch to get transport to take McGrath off the field, we began to realise something was seriously wrong.

It turned out he had been exchanging hand-passes with Brad Haddin when the football went past him, and as he turned to retrieve the ball he trod on a stray cricket ball with his right foot, twisting his ankle in the process. When I got to the group of players around him, McGrath was lying on the ground being tended to by Errol Alcott, and he was white as a sheet. McGrath looked at me and said, through gritted teeth, 'I'd be surprised if it wasn't broken.'

He was helped off the ground, and although his worst-case prediction has not come true — it is a tear to ankle ligaments — he was obviously ruled out of this match. He will probably be out of the one that follows, too, as there are only 2 days between the second and third Tests.

There is a case for saying I should have changed my thinking about bowling first once McGrath was ruled out, but even without him I felt conditions would favour the faster bowlers at the start. The day was cloudy and overcast and the pitch felt cold, which is usually a sign that there is moisture within the surface, and I thought the ball would swing and seam around.

I discussed my thinking with senior players including Gilchrist, Justin Langer, Matthew Hayden, Shane Warne and also Darren Lehmann, who is working as a commentator during the series, and all of them except Warne agreed with the idea of bowling first. Warne felt we should probably bat if I won the toss, but he could see the logic behind my thoughts.

I thought the combination of Jason Gillespie, Brett Lee and Michael Kasprowicz — the latter drafted in when McGrath was ruled out — would make life tough for England's top order, but I did not allow for all of them having very ordinary days with the ball.

The pitch turned out to be very, very slow and there was no swing or seam movement, but that was no excuse for our lack of control. We conceded 20 fours before lunch alone and I think 18 of them came through cover, a sure sign that we bowled too full and with too much width. England had raced to 1–132 by lunch from just 27 overs, and that meant a radical rethink of tactics at the interval.

I chatted with John Buchanan, and we agreed we had to bowl full but also straighter and attack the stumps rather than the channel outside off-stump. But it didn't matter what plan we came up with, because a combination of our failure to execute it consistently and aggressive England batting meant that the score still raced along at 5 runs per over, even when I placed deep fielders on either side of the ground.

The one saving grace for us was that England's aggressive approach kept giving us chances to take wickets, and although we managed to drop a catch and take a wicket off a no-ball, we still maintained a foothold in the game as a result.

There was even some needle out in the middle towards the end of the England innings. Warne had an appeal for lbw against Ashley Giles, and when Giles got down to the non-striker's end he said to umpire Billy Bowden, who had ruled in his favour, 'There was no way that was out. It was heading down the leg-side.'

I was fielding at midwicket and thought that was out of order. 'Telling him [Bowden] how to do the umpiring too now, is it, mate?' I said.

We bowled England out in the final session, which left us with an awkward period to negotiate before the close, but although Hayden and Langer made it onto the ground, the umpires immediately ruled that it was too dark to start. It is never easy batting in those situations, with the light poor and against bowlers who know that with only a short session ahead of them they can go all out without the need to conserve energy for the rest of the day. It means we can start fresh tomorrow, and after seeing how the pitch behaved there is no reason why we cannot at least match England's score or even go past it.

Second Test, Edgbaston, Birmingham, day 2: England 407 and 1–25 lead
Australia 308 (Langer 82, Ponting 61) by 124 runs.

Our batting today was a mirror image of the first innings of the first
Test. Most of us got ourselves in and then tossed our wickets away.
This has left us with a difficult but not impossible mountain to climb
to get back into this match.

A lot is now resting on the shoulders of Shane Warne, who spun
the ball sharply this evening to bowl Andrew Strauss around his legs.
If Warne, together with our fast bowlers, can restrict England to a
lead of around 300, I would be happy. I feel comfortable chasing that
total in the fourth innings, as there do not appear to be too many
demons in the pitch.

I was as guilty as any player of throwing away my wicket. I
cruised to a half-century and was well set when I had a brain
explosion and miscued a half-hearted sweep straight to short fine leg.
I am not a great sweeper, but when I saw the line of the ball from
Ashley Giles, instinct took over and I set myself for the shot. That
was where my problems started. The ball was the wrong length for
the sweep — it was too short, so I could not get over the top of it —
and Michael Vaughan was placed in exactly the right position for my
miscue. As I walked off I could not believe I'd played that shot.

What was all the more galling was that, at that stage, Justin
Langer and I were going along serenely. It was a great pitch to bat on
and I felt comfortable against all the England bowlers I faced, except
Stephen Harmison. When he pitched the ball up he got some seam
movement and also made the occasional ball swing, but after hitting
Justin Langer in the ribs he started to bowl too short, which allowed
both of us to leave him with much more comfort.

Even though Langer was winded by that blow, it still gave us
something to laugh about. He was hit in the same area by Pakistan's
Rana Naved in Sydney in January, and although Rana is nowhere
near Harmison's pace, the blow had the same effect, dropping him
like a stone at the crease. He was winded this time, and as he tried to
get his breath back, unable to say anything, I walked down the pitch
to remind him of the ball from Rana. It was gallows humour, but it
managed to make Langer smile, and that was a good effort after
being hit by a ball travelling at around 150 km/h.

Langer was just about the only one to grit things out and play
what you might call a traditional Test match–type innings for us. The

rest of the batsmen got out to a combination of poor cricket and good bowling, with Andrew Flintoff and Simon Jones mopping up our lower order with some impressive reverse-swing bowling. Losing wickets at regular intervals also meant that we could not take chances to attack Ashley Giles in the way we would have done if we'd had wickets in hand, and that suited Vaughan. He was able to keep Giles going from one end while rotating his faster bowlers at the other, a plan he had not been able to put into operation at Lord's.

John Buchanan and I had planned to talk to the bowlers after the first innings mauling they suffered and come up with a strategy for the second innings, but as we kept losing wickets and were eventually bowled out, there was no chance for that before the close of play. Instead we had a meeting involving the whole squad back at the hotel.

I had some harsh things to say to get the ball rolling. 'What is the point of us having meetings and agreeing on strategies if everything goes out the window when we get out onto the field?' I asked.

'We talk about batting in partnerships, making sure we cash in and make a big score once we are set, but once again we did not deliver today. And yesterday, with the ball, we had plans and lines and lengths to bowl but we did not get the ball in the right areas anywhere near often enough.'

Buchanan was equally furious with what he has seen over the past 2 days. He is normally the moderate voice out of the two of us, and will often rein me in when I am keen to shout and bawl, but tonight he was scathing about our play.

'I have been sitting in the coaching box watching what we have done and it has been very poor,' he said.

'We have not got the basics right, and that even extends to how we look after the ball. Even that has been sloppy. We work on it to try to get swing, but we seem to stop once it gets hit. England keep working on the ball, and their reward is the reverse swing Flintoff and Jones got this evening.'

Because Buchanan so rarely blows his top, when he does it tends to have quite an impact, and no one was left in any doubt this evening that we have to lift our game for the rest of the match if we are to avoid losing the Test. Buchanan's comments reminded us all of the need to be more disciplined in all aspects of our play than we have been so far in this match.

We all agreed that Warne is likely to bowl from one end, mostly round the wicket into the footmarks he operated into this evening,

REVERSE SWING

'Reverse swing' has been one of the catch phrases of The Ashes, and our inability to cope with it has been a key factor in our failings.

The problem of coping with reverse swing comes from the fact that the ball swings in the opposite direction to the way the batsman is expecting, hence the name.

Conventional swing is achieved when the bowler shines one side of the ball and it swings away from the polished side, as that side moves quicker through the air than the rough, unpolished side.

With the phenomenon of reverse swing, the ball actually swings towards what appears to be the shiny side and that naturally creates all sorts of confusion in the minds of batsmen as they focus on the bowler's hand to try to predict which way the ball will move.

The change is effected by wetting the shiny side of the ball with spit or sweat to make it heavier and the ball naturally moves towards that heavier side.

As with conventional swing, the ball tends to swerve later the faster it is bowled, and as Andrew Flintoff and Simon Jones, England's leading exponents of the art, bowl at upwards of 150 kp/h, that can make it very difficult to deal with.

Several of Australia's bowlers are also able to generate reverse swing, but we have failed to be as effective as the England attack because either (in the case of Glenn McGrath and Michael Kasprowicz) we bowled slightly slower than they did or (in the case of Shaun Tait and Brett Lee) we did not always manage to marry swing and accuracy in the way Flintoff and Jones did.

and while he is trying to build pressure it is important for the fast bowlers to maintain control. Warne will be much less effective if runs are coming at the other end — that will mean England's batsmen will not have to take a risk against him.

As if our batting was not enough bad news for one day, Glenn McGrath's progress is also far from encouraging. Errol Alcott treated him all day, and although McGrath was putting a brave face on matters, he was still not able to put any weight on the ankle this evening and had to get around using crutches. It is difficult to see how he has any chance of being fit for the next Test, in 6 days' time.

Everyone knows the first session tomorrow is vital. If we can hit England hard and take some early wickets, this match is still very much ours for the taking.

Saturday 6 August

Second Test, Edgbaston, Birmingham, day 3: Australia 308 and 8–175 need another 107 runs to beat England 407 and 182 (Flintoff 73, Warne 6–46).

It is not all over yet, but the end seems pretty close after another disappointing batting display that followed a much-improved bowling effort.

We fought hard to bowl England out within two sessions, and all of us felt the target of 282 was within range, as the surface is still playing pretty well. However, a combination of high-quality England bowling and some more poor discipline with the bat has left us in a very deep hole.

Unlike in the first innings, I do not feel guilty about the way I was dismissed — I reckon the five balls I faced from Andrew Flintoff were among the best sequence of deliveries I have ever received in any form of cricket.

I came to the crease after Flintoff bowled Justin Langer with the second ball of his first over, and straightaway I discovered that he was moving the ball at high pace. He swung his first delivery sharply back into me and had an appeal for lbw turned down. The ball struck me above the roll of the pad, so it was too high, especially as I was jumping in the air, a reflex action to try to adjust to the late movement and extra bounce Flintoff was generating.

The next ball, rather than swinging in, held its line but still bounced more than I expected, and I edged it just short of the gully fielder; then Flintoff swung the third delivery back sharply, and again he appealed for lbw. This time I thought I was struck outside off-stump, and umpire Billy Bowden obviously agreed.

The fourth delivery I faced was outside off-stump, and although I started to try to play it, thinking it might swing back in as two of the previous three balls had done, I was able to make a late adjustment and pull my bat out of the way when I saw it carry straight on.

That would normally have been the end of the over, but that fourth delivery was also a no-ball, so it meant Flintoff had one more ball at me — and it was a beauty. From just short of a length it bounced and moved away late from a line around off-stump and as I tried to defend off the back foot I got a fine edge through to wicketkeeper Geraint Jones. It was fantastic bowling, and I am not sure there was much I could do about it.

England's bowlers maintained excellent discipline and worked their way through our line-up so well that Michael Vaughan claimed the extra half-hour available to try to finish the match off this evening. That did not surprise me: they had momentum at that stage and the adrenaline must have been flowing for them. Plus, they were backed by a sellout crowd that was baying for wickets. England needed 3 wickets in that extra time, but although they could not take them, they did strike a massive blow when Stephen Harmison dismissed Michael Clarke with a brilliant slower ball in the final over of the day.

That was the disappointing aspect of the day. On the other hand, I was pleased with the way we responded with the ball and in the field after last night's meeting. We set out to bowl aggressively, but to more defensive fields, as we did in India last year. We employed boundary fielders on both sides of the wicket and asked our faster bowlers to attack the stumps while Shane Warne wheeled away at the other end.

Brett Lee was superb. He tore in, as he had done at Lord's, and really intimidated England's top order. He suffered later on when Andrew Flintoff let fly with some big hits, but in some ways that was to be expected. Flintoff was batting with last man Simon Jones, and obviously did not expect him to last long, and Lee had bowled a lot of overs by that stage.

The fact that Lee suffered then highlighted one of our problems. Jason Gillespie looked innocuous and Michael Kasprowicz was expensive, and with those two proving ineffective I kept having to turn to Lee, even though he is at his most effective when used in short, sharp bursts. Using him for long spells obviously affected his pace and allowed Flintoff to climb into him.

Flintoff was also able to hammer our bowling because, once again, we could not execute our plans well enough. He was looking to hit sixes and fours, so the idea was to bowl yorkers, but when we failed to get those yorkers in the right place they became half-volleys and full tosses, and he was able to take advantage of them all.

We were also infuriated by an incident late in the England innings, when we were convinced Lee trapped Simon Jones lbw. From round the wicket Lee bowled a full-length delivery that knocked Jones off his feet and was so quick that the batsman did not have time to play a shot. From the angle Lee bowled the ball, my first impression was that it was going to miss leg-stump, but it swung at the last second and would have smashed into middle stump if Jones's pads had not been in the way.

It was as plumb as could be, yet Bowden said not out. As England's last-wicket pair had added 49 at this point, I was pretty agitated when the decision went against us, but I kept calm as I asked him: 'What was wrong with that?'

'Going down leg,' Bowden replied, and although I said, 'But the ball swung back ...' I knew it was useless — he was not going to change his decision.

England only added 2 runs to the total after that before they were bowled out, and I just hope those 2 runs are not going to prove costly. That looks unlikely now, because although I know Warne, Lee and Kasprowicz will fight hard, it looks like a tall order for us to win from this position.

After the day's play I met with the selector on duty, Merv Hughes, and John Buchanan in the lunch room to discuss our options after this match. No matter what the result here, we are clearly struggling in the bowling department and that is something we will need to address for the next Test, which starts on Thursday.

Hughes and Buchanan had already been talking for 5 minutes when I joined them, and they told me they felt we had three options for the third Test on the basis that McGrath is not fit, something that looks almost certain at this stage. Although he has thrown away his crutches, he can still hardly walk, so I am not sure how he could be fit for a Test match in 5 days.

The options Hughes and Buchanan outlined are:

1. keep the same side for the next Test;
2. bring in Shaun Tait for Michael Kasprowicz; or
3. play two spinners, with Stuart MacGill lining up alongside Shane Warne.

Although I knew we needed to make a change after the way the bowlers have performed here, I was not keen on any of the options being suggested.

Tait's raw pace would obviously give us some firepower, but with Brett Lee in the side I am not sure we are lacking in that area; what we need is control, and Tait will not necessarily give us that — while he is fast, he is also erratic.

The idea of playing two spinners also did not appeal to me. If we include MacGill at the expense of a fast bowler, it means we will have only two fast bowlers in the starting eleven, and that would not be ideal if the pitch starts out offering little or no assistance to spin.

Unless we are certain that the pitch at Old Trafford is going to spin from the first day, the only way MacGill can play alongside Warne is if we include him at the expense of a batsman and push Gilchrist up to number six in the order, as we did in the West Indies 2 years ago, when MacGill played as one of five specialist bowlers.

An alternative would be to call up Shane Watson, currently playing county cricket at Hampshire. He could slot into the side at number six instead of a batsman, which would give us a third seam-bowling option and allow MacGill to play, replacing one of the three fast bowlers from this match, either Kasprowicz or Gillespie. I was in favour of Watson's inclusion in the Test squad before it was announced back in March — to play exactly this role — but the selectors decided against my suggestion then.

I am a big fan of Watson, and would have no problem with him being drafted into the squad, but my ideal solution now would not involve either him or MacGill. What we have lacked is control, and the men most likely to provide it in the absence of McGrath are Stuart Clark of New South Wales and Mick Lewis of Victoria. Both are currently playing county cricket and I would draft one or both of them into the squad to play that holding role with the ball. While Warne has bowled brilliantly for us at one end, we have not been able to maintain that pressure at the other end. If we can do that, we will have much more chance of controlling the game. It would also allow me to give Lee the type of rest he needs between spells to ensure that he is capable of bowling fast throughout an whole day.

I made my points to Buchanan and Hughes, and they accepted what I had to say; it is now a question of what the other selectors say. We will find out about that over the next couple of days.

Second Test, Edgbaston, Birmingham, day 4: England 407 and 182 beat
Australia 308 and 279 by 2 runs.

We lost, and the series is tied at 1–1, but I am proud of the way we lost today.

To be realistic, we all knew winning would be tough, so my message to the remaining batsmen — Shane Warne, Brett Lee and Michael Kasprowicz — was to try to get as much out of the rest of the match as we could. 'Let's see if we can give them a fright,' I said, although I am not sure I really believed we could.

Both Lee and Warne are positive players, and they decided to take the attack to England's bowlers. In the face of that approach, it was clear that those bowlers became nervous. We scored quickly, the boundaries came at regular intervals, and suddenly the pressure was on Michael Vaughan and his players.

Reality returned when Warne trod on his stumps with 62 still needed. Kasprowicz and Lee continued to try to be positive, at the same time showing real courage, and the target kept coming down.

Cricket dressing rooms can be superstitious places at the best of times, and this morning was no exception. As our last-wicket pair whittled away at the target, everyone stayed in the same seats, no one daring to move in case it brought bad luck and the end of the innings. The drinks break arrived with us wanting 30 more for victory, and as most players bolted for the toilet, the call went up — from Justin Langer, I think — for everyone to return to the seat they had been watching from during the first hour.

I was sitting between Michael Clarke and Matthew Hayden, and as the drinks were taken onto the field Clarke said to me, 'At least it's good that we've got this close.'

'It's not finished yet,' I replied.

I did not send any instructions out to the two batsmen during that drinks break. Both Kasprowicz and Lee are experienced players who knew what had to be done, and in any case they seemed to be playing pretty well without me offering any advice from the sidelines.

As the target kept coming down, the nervous chatter in our viewing area increased. With 20 to win, Lee took a terrible blow on his top hand from an Andrew Flintoff lifter. He looked in agony as Errol Alcott went out to treat him. He took a blow on the same hand during the first Test, but we all knew there was no way he could — or would — retire hurt at this stage. He soldiered on. The tension was ratcheted up even more when Simon Jones dropped Kasprowicz just in front of us, at third man, with 15 still required.

With 4 runs needed to win, Lee faced Harmison and latched on to a superb cover drive. It was a shot worthy of winning the match — but it went straight to the fielder on the cover boundary and the batsmen picked up just 1 run. That put Kasprowicz on strike, and the rest is history.

Lee's shot is a perfect illustration of why this fantastic game called cricket can be so frustrating. If he had botched the drive and instead got a thick outside edge to the ball, the chances are it would have flown away for four and we would have won the match; instead, he got everything right with the shot and we lost by 2 runs.

Reflecting on that last ball of the match to Kasprowicz, I can see it now in my mind's eye, a bouncer which he fended at, with Geraint Jones diving forward to take the catch. I did not watch the reactions of any players, either England's fielders or Lee and Kasprowicz; instead I watched umpire Billy Bowden. Up went his crocked finger and that was it. We had lost.

I did not head into the dressing room to watch the replay, to see if the ball really had brushed Kasprowicz's glove — it would have been pointless. The decision had been made and nothing could change it now. I just sat still in my chair, trying to take in the fact that we had come so close but still lost.

I am not sure how long I sat there, but it cannot have been very long, because I had to get up pretty quickly to meet the England team as they came off the field, to shake the hands of the players after an amazing match.

They were elated, understandably, but I was quite pleased too — not that we lost, but that we showed so much fight today. We were behind in the match for much of its course, yet we came very close to pulling off a brilliant win. If we can take that fighting spirit into the next match, together with a more disciplined approach with bat and ball, I am sure we can bounce back.

I made a point of speaking to Kasprowicz, Warne and Lee before the presentation ceremony, to say how proud I was of the way they performed. Kasprowicz was calm, at least outwardly, but Warne was shattered and Lee was inconsolable. You could hardly blame Warne for his reaction, as he scored 50 runs in the match, took 10 wickets and still ended up on the losing side; Lee could not get over the fact that he had taken so many blows and come so close, yet ended up with nothing to show for it.

After the presentation ceremony I had to face the media, and one of the first questions was whether I felt my decision to bowl first had a bearing on the outcome of the match. I do not believe it did.

The pitch played well throughout, which was a factor in our lower order getting as close as they did to our target in the final innings, and with the quality of our batting line-up we should have been able to score 590 runs in the match in two innings. We could not do so through a combination of excellent England bowling and poor decision-making by our batsmen, and that, together with some wayward bowling, is something we need to put right before the next match.

We have just 3 days to do that, as the next Test begins on Thursday, but in some ways that is good. Obviously the time frame gives us less chance to get Glenn McGrath fit, but it also means there is no chance for us to dwell on our misfortune. We have an early chance to right the wrongs we committed here and I expect us to take it.

Whether or not we are going to call up any reinforcements to the squad for the next Test is still not clear. John Buchanan announced to a television crew after the match that Shane Watson will be called up, but that is not certain; my preference, as I said, is for Mick Lewis or Stuart Clark, both of whom are in this country playing county cricket, but I gather the selectors may have a phone hook-up over the next day or so to discuss the matter.

Amidst all the excitement there was an announcement during the morning that really annoyed me. England fast bowler Simon Jones, who gave Matthew Hayden a send-off by pointing him to the dressing room after dismissing him yesterday, was fined 20 per cent of his match fee, something I thought was not consistent.

Jones was found guilty of a similar offence in the West Indies last year and was fined 50 per cent of his match fee then. As this appears to me to be a repeat offence, I cannot see how he can be fined less now than he was fined before. All the players want is consistency in decision-making of this kind, and I am not sure it has happened here.

We had a team meeting before we left the ground to discuss what to do over the next few days. We cannot move onto our next destination until Tuesday morning because it would involve a mass alteration of hotel bookings, which is not possible, so we will have tomorrow in Birmingham. The batsmen and bowlers will have meetings to discuss what went wrong here and how we can put things right. The practice nets will also be available if anyone wants to use them, but with such a short time between the Tests I am keen for players to rest as much as possible before our main pre-Test session, which will be 2 days before the next match, and the match itself.

England name an unchanged 12-man squad for the third Test at Old Trafford.

We have barely had time to draw breath after yesterday's defeat, and already there is a chance we could be without Brett Lee for the next Test in 3 days' time.

Lee woke up with a sore and swollen left knee, and after he was examined by Errol Alcott he was taken to hospital, where he will stay overnight.

A cut he suffered during the first Test at Lord's has become infected, and he is on a course of antibiotics to flush out his system. Alcott is quietly confident that Lee will be fit, but with these two Tests so close together, and Glenn McGrath already on the sidelines, it will be touch and go. It is another problem we could do without.

Shaun Tait is a like-for-like replacement for Lee, but he has been nursing a sore shoulder, and although McGrath has thrown away his crutches, it is surely too much to expect him to be fit in 3 days' time. There is an obvious need for us to call another player into the squad as cover for the injury crisis that seems to have hit us since last Thursday.

I spoke with Merv Hughes, and he agreed. He will chat with his fellow selectors overnight; it is likely that either Stuart Clark or Mick Lewis will be drafted into the touring squad, at least for this match.

This afternoon the batsmen and bowlers met to discuss the Edgbaston Test. I went to both meetings to hear what my team-mates thought about our performance.

Batting-wise we underachieved in both innings, demonstrating many of the failings we exhibited in the first Test. Players got established but failed to go on with the job, and in a Test as close as this one, it would only have taken one lengthy innings to swing the balance our way.

The problem is obvious; we need to decide how to put it right. I said it will come down to ensuring that we are all as well prepared as we can be.

Preparation is an individual thing. My routine usually involves a solid net session 2 days before a match to make sure my feet are moving properly and I am hitting the ball well, and if I feel I have any problems, I will also have some throw-downs to work on specific areas of concern.

I will also do a decent amount of catching and fielding practice before a match — I find that ensures that I am watching the ball closely. So I will do all those things 2 days before a match, then spend the following day getting as much rest as I can and also thinking about how I will approach playing the bowlers I am likely to come up against.

Each player has his own approach. Matthew Hayden uses a visualisation technique where he imagines how he will deal with individual bowlers and situations, and Justin Langer hits hundreds of balls in a net session. I just want each of us to make sure we follow our own tried and tested approaches — the methods that have made us international batsmen — as thoroughly as possible, so that if things do go wrong, no one is left thinking he could and should have done more.

The bowlers accepted that we did not execute our plans well enough, especially on the first day, and that that allowed England to get away to a flying start. Everyone agreed that we have to be much better when we first head into the field at Old Trafford. We cannot afford to give England a head start again.

Tuesday 9 August

Errol Alcott gave me some amazing news today — Glenn McGrath could be fit for Thursday's Test.

It seems impossible to believe after watching him struggle to walk at Edgbaston, but Alcott believes he could make a miraculous recovery.

McGrath does have torn ligaments, but that problem can apparently be overcome by taping up the ankle to make sure it does not twist or rotate in a way that will aggravate the injury. That taping has been a feature of McGrath's routine before he bowls for as long as I can remember, so it should not be a problem for him now.

The news on McGrath is encouraging, but just because he and Alcott feel he could play does not mean we should go ahead and pick him. He will have to prove his fitness, because we need to see not only whether he can bowl with the injury, but also how it responds to the workload. He will go through his paces tomorrow.

The same is true for Brett Lee. He is spending his second night in hospital in Birmingham — even though we have now moved 2 hours' drive north to Manchester — but Alcott is happy with that situation. He thinks the longer Lee is on the course of antibiotics, the better he will feel. It will just be a question of him travelling north tomorrow morning to go through his paces alongside McGrath. I hope he too will be able to prove his fitness for the match.

The possibility of having both players available is exciting, but there are no guarantees that either will be fit, so Stuart Clark joined us at practice today, driving the 3 hours north from London (his base with county side Middlesex) after getting a call from CA's Director of Cricket Operations, Michael Brown, at 7.30 this morning. Even if McGrath and Lee enjoy good workouts, the plan is for Clark to stay around until the match starts on Thursday.

Wednesday 10 August

We will go into tomorrow's Test with a massive psychological boost after Glenn McGrath and Brett Lee both emerged from the treatment room and were judged fit.

Both men had to bowl today to be considered for selection. There is no way we could take either into the match without being sure they could bowl without ill effects. They went through their paces in the middle of the ground under the watchful eyes of Errol Alcott and selector Merv Hughes, and afterwards Hughes confirmed that both bowled with good rhythm. Alcott said they are fit to play providing neither suffers any reaction to the session overnight.

McGrath's recovery is astonishing, and is a tribute not just to his determination, but also to the skill and dedication of Alcott. He has been producing miracles like this for quite a few years now. His reputation has spread beyond cricket, and last year he was recruited by actor Russell Crowe to help him prepare for a role in a boxing film after Crowe had dislocated his shoulder. Alcott worked his magic; Crowe made the film, *The Cinderella Man*, and it is to be released here during the last week of the tour.

My main worry about McGrath is his lack of bowling over the past few weeks. He thrives on doing lots of bowling and gaining fitness and rhythm from that, but he has not bowled in match conditions since the first Test at Lord's, almost 3 weeks ago. On the other hand, he has very rarely let us down. He is an honest player, too, and if he is not ready to play he will say so.

With McGrath set to play, the selectors decided that Michael Kasprowicz would be the unlucky player to miss out. Kasprowicz was heroic with the bat in the Edgbaston Test, so leaving him out is a tough call, but when I broke the news to him after training he took the decision superbly. He said he understood, and added that it had been a bonus to play in the previous Test. I told the rest of the squad who would be in the side at a team meeting this evening.

After that meeting, as I left the team room I saw a bizarre sight at the front of the hotel. Two women were wandering around wearing T-shirts that said on the front 'I've slept with Shane Warne'.

They hung around for a short while then walked off, revealing the back of their shirts, which read, 'But Freddie bowls his maidens over', a reference to Andrew 'Freddie' Flintoff.

Just as they walked off, Warne's parents — who are over here to watch the cricket and spend time with their son — arrived. I am pretty sure that all they saw was the reference to Flintoff on the back of the shirts, which is probably just as well given Warne's recent marital problems. I wonder how they would have reacted if they had seen the other side of those T-shirts.

Thursday 11 August

Stuart Clark leaves the Australia squad to link up again with county side Middlesex.

Third Test, Old Trafford, Manchester, day 1: England 5–341 (Vaughan 166, Trescothick 63, Bell 59*) v Australia.

After all the optimism I felt coming into this Test, we managed to have one of those days when very little went right. We dropped catches, took a wicket with a no-ball, lost Michael Clarke with a back injury and ended up distinctly second best at the hands of more aggressive England batting.

Our heads dropped during the afternoon and early part of the evening session, but we managed to lift ourselves up by the bootlaces in the last hour or so to snatch three priceless wickets — and they mean we are still in the match.

Even though we lost the toss on what looked liked like an excellent pitch, I felt confident we would bowl well with Glenn McGrath back in the side. However, things started to go wrong from the second over of the innings. Clarke trotted in from cover to field a ball, threw it back to Gilchrist, and the look on his face told me he was in pain.

I have seen that look from him before, when his back has seized up, as it did earlier on this tour at Durham, and although when I ran over to see if he was okay, he said, 'I'll be right', I could tell he was not.

I watched him after the next ball, saw he was still in pain and sent him off for treatment straightaway. We did not see him on the field for the rest of the day.

That was a massive blow for us, because we missed out not just on Clarke's energy in the field but also on his bowling. The pitch played as it looked — very good — and with the fast bowlers struggling to make an impact, we could have used his left-arm spin to give us some variety. Clarke did plenty of bowling in the warm-ups for just that reason, but he obviously overdid it, and it cost us a key figure during the day.

On the other hand, if we had taken our chances we would not have needed Clarke's bowling. Adam Gilchrist missed two catches, one from Marcus Trescothick and the other from Michael Vaughan. Both chances went down with Gilchrist facing the Stretford end of the ground — in his defence, the viewing for fielders when the bowling is from that end is not ideal. I don't know why, but it was easy to lose sight of the ball against the background of the crowd; maybe that was a reason for those two dropped catches. Both were one-handed chances, but I would have backed him to take them under normal circumstances. Today, though, he appeared to move late, and both went down.

Vaughan's miss proved very expensive. He was on 41 at the time, and given that reprieve — and another to the following ball, when McGrath bowled him with a no-ball — he did what good players should do: he took advantage of his fortune and scored heavily.

He took full toll of Jason Gillespie, who once again struggled. Just after tea there was a danger that we would completely lose any semblance of control. Warne was operating from one end, Lee and McGrath had already got through a heavy workload, and with the new ball to come I needed to give them a chance to conserve some energy.

I turned to Gillespie, and we settled on the plan of bowling very straight at Vaughan, with the majority of fielders on the leg-side to try to restrict his scoring. Gillespie's line and length were completely awry, and in the end I had to take him out of the attack and throw the ball, almost in desperation, to Simon Katich. He ended up getting us the wicket of Vaughan, caught on the boundary, and Lee then picked up two late wickets with the new ball, so we are still in contention.

Gillespie's form is a massive concern. He has been a quality bowler for us for the last few years, but on this tour has looked a shadow of his former self, bowling with little pace, little seam movement and little control. With just four frontline bowlers, we need all of them firing, but Gillespie's lack of form means I am becoming reluctant to bowl him, and on that basis his place in the side must be under serious threat.

One of the few positives of the day was Shane Warne taking his 600th Test wicket. It came about through a huge slice of luck, as Trescothick gloved a sweep shot onto Gilchrist's thigh and the ball dollied up for the keeper to take it. It is a fantastic achievement by Warne and emphasises again what a massive impact he has had on the world of cricket since his debut 13 years ago. Back then, in 1992, the thought of any bowler taking 600 wickets at this level seemed pure fantasy; it seemed even more unlikely for a leg-spinner, as that style of bowling was considered an expensive luxury. Warne has turned that fantasy into reality — let's hope his latest landmark serves as an inspiration for us for the rest of this Test.

Friday 12 August

Third Test, Old Trafford, Manchester, day 2: Australia 7–214 trail England 444 (Vaughan 166, Trescothick 63, Bell 59) by 230 runs.

Even though England let us off the hook by scoring far fewer runs than I thought they would at one stage, we are still staring down the barrel of a massive first innings deficit — and maybe even the prospect of following on — after another catastrophic batting performance.

England's spinner, Ashley Giles, bowled an excellent spell at one end, allowing Michael Vaughan to use his faster bowlers in short bursts at the other, and with those fast bowlers once again finding reverse swing, we had our hands full. Our bowlers have generated reverse swing here too, but apart from Lee they are 15–20 km/h slower than the England attack. That has made our bowlers easier to play than England's attack. We have to bowl it better and play it better when we bat.

Despite the excellence of England's bowling, we have only ourselves to blame for our score. The pitch is still a good one for batting, but several of us made bad decisions when well set, and our current position is the result.

I felt I was unlucky when, first ball after tea, I received a delivery from Simon Jones that bounced much more than I expected. It could have gone anywhere but, rather than falling safely, it lobbed gently to Ian Bell in the gully and I was on my way.

Even if I was unlucky, as a group I want us to avoid feeling that nothing is going our way. If we start feeling that way, that the world is against us, that feeling can consume us. What we have to recognise is that so far we have not done the basics well enough in this match. We have bowled moderately, caught poorly and batted badly, and we have to improve.

We still have a chance to put that right, but it will be very tough from this position. For the second Test running we will have to play catch-up after a substandard first innings. The only consolation is that England did not really rub our noses in the dirt when they had the chance this morning.

Although we dismissed Bell in the fourth over of the day, Andrew Flintoff and Geraint Jones cruised along as we struggled to make another breakthrough. The pair added 87 at almost 6 runs per over, and I was not sure what to do next. But then Flintoff suddenly miscued Shane Warne to long-on, and Jones was bowled by Jason Gillespie in the next over. We took the last 4 wickets for just 11 runs, which gave us some momentum at long last, but after a promising start with the bat, England regained the ascendancy after tea.

After play Rianna and I had an Italian meal and watched the movie *Closer*, a drama with Jude Law, Clive Owen, Julia Roberts and Natalie Portman. It was a miserable film which just about summed up my feelings after 2 days of this Test.

Saturday 13 August

Third Test, Old Trafford, Manchester, day 3: Australia 7–264 (Warne 78*) trail England 444 by 180 runs.

Rain ruined the day, but in the 14 overs that were possible we did well. Shane Warne and Jason Gillespie stayed together and took us past the follow-on mark of 245. I am not sure Michael Vaughan would have enforced it, though, because he knows that our best chance of winning is to bowl last and put England under pressure, chasing a target on the last afternoon with Warne bowling on a worn surface. That cannot now happen.

With rain falling for most of the day, I used the unexpected free time to chat with John Buchanan and Errol Alcott about our trip to Edinburgh after this match. We have a one-day game to play against Scotland, which has just qualified for the 2007 World Cup in the Caribbean, but I am keen to use the few days we have there as more of a social than a cricketing exercise.

We will be coming off back-to-back Tests, which are tiring mentally as well as physically, and Scotland will be a chance for everyone to get away from the pressure of the Ashes series and recharge the batteries for the last two matches in Nottingham and London.

We have been outplayed by England at Edgbaston and here, but I told Buchanan that I do not think it is a case of needing extra practice: we have the skills, as every player in the squad has proved in the past. My gut feeling is that everyone has become a bit tense, worrying about the implications of failure rather than letting instinct take over. If we can get through that fear of failure and back into the positive mind-set that has characterised our play over the past decade, I think we will get back on track very quickly. That is easier said than done, of course, but I hope a few days relaxing in Scotland will help ease any tension we may be feeling.

Michael Clarke will not come with us — his back will not allow him to make the 6-hour bus trip. He will stay here and meet us in Northampton before our 2-day match next weekend. I hope that by then his condition will have improved.

Alcott said that Clarke is not our only fitness concern: Glenn McGrath is also struggling. It is nothing to do with his ankle, which has stood up well to the rigours of bowling in the first innings; the problem is with his general fitness, which is below his usual level. His knee problem earlier in the tour, and now the ankle injury, mean he hasn't got the bowling under his belt that he needs to be properly match fit, and his performance is suffering as a result. Errol, together with Jock Campbell, will monitor that and try to improve the situation, but it is not easy to push him when he is also recovering from injury.

This evening I had a photo shoot with Anthony Stevens, the former Kangaroos footballer, to promote our new business together, Stride Sports Management. I put on Kangaroos gear and Stevens donned whites, and I even forced him to wear my baggy green cap, though he did not want to. Stevens and fellow Kangaroo Glenn Archer approached me earlier this year to get involved, and the idea of working with and mentoring sports men and women once I finish playing was something that appealed to me. We will make an announcement about the tie-up shortly.

Sunday 14 August

Third Test, Old Trafford, Manchester, day 4: Australia 302 (Warne 90, S Jones 6–53) and 0–24 require another 399 runs to beat England 444 and 6–280 declared (Strauss 106, Bell 65, McGrath 5–115).

Although we have a chance of pulling off an amazing win, it is a very remote chance, and at this stage I am not thinking in terms of victory.

What I am thinking of is the need to consolidate through the first part of the day, lose as few wickets as possible in the first two sessions, then have a look at where we stand at tea. If we are in a sound position, then maybe we can think about pressing on for victory, but we have a lot of batting to do before we get to that point.

For much of today we found ourselves bowling for England's declaration; their batsmen played sensibly and well and we did not look like taking many wickets. Shane Warne bowled brilliantly but without any luck, and the England batsmen enjoyed the odd bit of good fortune, with several miscued shots lobbing into empty spaces — on another day, they might have gone to hand.

We did not do ourselves any favours, either, as once again we created chances but were not able to take them. Andrew Strauss, who made an increasingly assured hundred, edged Brett Lee into the slips, only for the ball to fly through the gap between me and Shane Warne, with neither of us moving to intercept it.

In that sense Strauss got lucky, but he also benefited from our poor cricket. Plenty of our past opponents have whinged about how much luck Australia have, but there are times when you create your own luck, and that is something we have not done in the last two Tests. We have been guilty of sloppy cricket and it has cost us.

The one benefit of our time in the field was that it allowed Glenn McGrath to have a lengthy bowl, and by the end of it he was starting to show signs of finding some form and rhythm. The same could not be said of Jason Gillespie, and unless we suffer a spate of injuries, he has played his last Test on this trip. I was reluctant to throw him the ball after his recent performances, and when he did bowl he went at 6 runs an over, so I had to pull him out of the attack very quickly. It meant I was reduced to three frontline bowlers: Warne at one end and McGrath and Lee alternating at the other.

Gillespie and Warne did a superb job with the bat, taking their stand to 86 before they were parted. But even allowing for his batting heroics, we can no longer carry Gillespie's bowling in this line-up. His South Australia team-mate Shaun Tait is erratic, and may also go at 6 runs per over, but he is also likely to offer more of a threat than Gillespie, so if he performs well at Northampton I think Tait will come in for the next Test. The alternative is Shane Watson, still playing county cricket at Hampshire. Using him would allow us to play Stuart MacGill as well, but I am still not sure the selectors will want to go outside the current squad.

Warne got tantalisingly close to a maiden Test hundred before he pulled Simon Jones to deep square leg. He was unlucky, because he hit the ball right out of the middle of the bat, and as he walked off I saw him mouth to his mate, Kevin Pietersen, 'I creamed that.' I said to the lads around me on our balcony, 'The first thing he says when he walks into the dressing room will be, "I creamed it"', and sure enough, I was right.

Monday 15 August

Third Test, Old Trafford, Manchester, day 5: England 444 and 6–280 declared drew with Australia 302 and 9–371 (Ponting 156).

This has been one of the most satisfying days of my career, both personally and from a team point of view. We scrambled to a draw and, against the odds, we are still level in the series.

I said to the players before a ball was bowled this morning that this was our chance to prove that we can scrap as well as dominate in Tests. One of the criticisms levelled at us in the past has been that while we may be good frontrunners, we have not always been able to save matches when the roles are reversed. The Kolkata Test of 2001 against India is one example of that; I hope today's effort will put that criticism to bed once and for all.

From my perspective, it was doubly satisfying to save the match given the amount of time I spent at the crease — almost 7 hours. It would have meant nothing to have scored 156 and then lost the match, so playing the innings I did and us getting the draw fill me with pride and a real sense of achievement.

Those feelings now are in stark contrast to the way I felt in the immediate aftermath of my dismissal. When I was out, with only 4 overs left, I felt sick, and certain that I had cost us the draw we so desperately wanted.

I decided to take responsibility for facing as many balls as I could during the closing overs, because it was one of those occasions when I felt completely at ease at the crease. I was calm, seeing the ball clearly, my feet were moving well and there was no way I was going to get out.

It was my desire to take that responsibility that cost me my wicket. Facing the last ball of a Stephen Harmison over, I knew he was going to bowl me a bouncer — that was his best chance of stopping me getting bat to ball and making it to the other end to retain the strike. In hindsight, I should have trusted my partner, Brett Lee, a little more, but he had already survived an lbw appeal I felt was out, so I thought I had to face the next over. When the bouncer I was expecting was bowled, I tried to paddle it away for a single to fine leg, but ended up getting cramped for room, and it brushed my glove on the way through to wicketkeeper Geraint Jones.

It seemed an eternity before umpire Billy Bowden gave me out, and I lingered for just a second or so before dragging myself off the ground, unable to believe what I had done. The draw was in sight and I had contrived to get myself out. I was shattered.

I headed back to the dressing room, threw my bat and helmet into my kit bag and slumped in my seat with my head in my hands. I had given myself the task of seeing us to safety and had failed. I was numb.

I could not face going out on the balcony to watch those last 4 overs. I just stayed in my seat. I could see a television in the corner of the dressing room, but it was 3 or 4 seconds behind the live action, so I heard the shouts of my team-mates outside for every remaining ball bowled before I saw each ball played.

It was agony, and every ball seemed to take an eternity, but gradually the last pair — Lee and Glenn McGrath — got down to the last ball of the match, and when Lee survived, there was a collective shout of 'Yes, Binga!' from the viewing area before I saw the evidence for myself. I threw my head back as a wave of relief washed over me. Michael Kasprowicz rushed up and hugged me, and Justin Langer said, 'That is the best innings you have ever played', but nothing sank in for a long while after the match.

My game plan throughout the day was to play naturally and not alter my normal approach. In other words, if I was bowled a half-volley I would look to hit it for four. There was no point setting out to play for a draw by blocking everything — that was not my natural game, and it would allow the bowlers to dominate me. I wanted to keep the scoreboard moving, so I was asking questions of Michael Vaughan and his bowlers, and I told the other batsmen to play the same way.

Once again luck ran against us, with Damien Martyn appearing unlucky in an lbw decision. Certainly, from my position at the non-striker's end I could see and hear that Martyn got a massive inside edge on the ball from Harmison before it cannoned into his pads, but Bucknor still put his finger up in response to the appeal. As Martyn trooped off I said to Bucknor, 'That was a diabolical decision. He's smashed that.' Bucknor's response was: 'I thought it hit his pad first.'

In all fairness, maybe Bucknor was put off by the noise of a packed stadium, something that helped create an amazing atmosphere all day. Tickets had been put on sale on the gate for £10, and the response of the public was astonishing. When we made our way to the ground 90 minutes before the start, the surrounding streets were packed and the gates were eventually closed at 10 o'clock, 30 minutes before play, with more than 20 000 fans in the ground and another 10 000 to 20 000 locked out.

As I prepared to face each ball I was able to blot out that noise and just focus on the job at hand, but between deliveries, and when standing at the non-striker's end, I was aware of the roar the crowd was making — but it was impossible to make out any specific calls or comments.

Although we lost wickets at regular intervals, John Buchanan still felt we had a chance of winning the match when I came off the ground at tea. By that stage I had been joined by Michael Clarke, now almost fully recovered from his back injury, and we needed another 207 with 42 overs and 5 wickets in hand. I was not very communicative when Buchanan was talking, as I was trying to switch off mentally after 2 hours of intense concentration — and I did not think winning was a realistic hope anyway. I preferred to continue on the path I had followed up to that point, playing each ball on its merits. If we had got to the stage of needing 100 in 16 overs with 5 wickets in hand I might have altered my approach, but it never came to that, so the idea of chasing down the 423 we needed was always just an illusion to me.

After the match I fulfilled my media commitments then headed back to our dressing room, where I found my team-mates on a high with music playing and the beers flowing. That was understandable, because we all knew we had got out of jail — thanks to a combination of bad weather on day three and today's resolute rearguard action — after having been outplayed for much of the match.

The reaction of the England players was interesting: although they must have been devastated not to finish us off, they hid that disappointment very well. By the time I got back to the dressing room, several of their players, including Andrew Flintoff and Kevin Pietersen, were sharing a drink and some banter with Shane Warne, and Flintoff, who had bowled tirelessly all day, revealed another skill he possesses — taking the tops off beer bottles with his teeth.

During the evening it seemed that everyone in the dressing room came up to me and said 'Well played', and although it was gratifying to receive the praise, it is more important to me that we use my innings and the breathing space it has earned us in a positive way. We scored almost 350 runs today against an attack that has caused us to struggle for much of the series — if we can replicate that in our next innings, we should not have to play catch-up the way we have had to do here and in Birmingham.

Tuesday 16 August

Michael Vaughan and Matthew Hoggard (Yorkshire), Kevin Pietersen (Hampshire), Ashley Giles and Ian Bell (Warwickshire) and Andrew Flintoff (Lancashire) are all ordered to rest by England coach Duncan Fletcher instead of playing for their counties in the semi-finals of the C & G Trophy on Saturday — this is the domestic knockout tournament that culminates with a final at Lord's.

My innings yesterday had a dramatic postscript this morning when we were about to set off for the drive to Scotland.

Our security manager, Reg Dickason, who has taken over from Dave Woodman for the second half of the tour, pulled me aside as I was about to board the team bus and said he wanted to chat.

'Death threats have been made against you via the enquiries email address at Cricket Australia,' he said.

Dickason explained that at around the time I was batting to try to save the match, emails suggesting I deserved a bullet in the head for my efforts were received; apparently the writer also explained that he knew people in this country who were willing to carry out the threat.

As a cricketer, I am used to facing catcalls and barracking from opposition fans, although this is an altogether new level of intimidation and I have never been threatened in this way before. Rianna was upset and quite shaken when I told her about the emails, but Dickason assured me that he and the appropriate authorities would do everything in their power to track down the perpetrator. I am sure the notes are a hoax and I will not lose any sleep over them, but until the author is located, Dickason said I should always let him know my movements.

I am never one to dwell on things I have no control over, so I quickly allowed the matter to slip to the back of my mind — I knew Dickason would let me know if there were any developments. The main issue occupying my thoughts as we journeyed north was the renewal of card-playing hostilities between me and Justin Langer on one hand and Steve Bernard and Shane Warne on the other. Langer's inexperience again cost us dearly, and we were thrashed. I am beginning to wonder how long it will be before he starts to improve. Not long, I hope.

I did have time to reflect on my innings, but I am not sure how I feel about it. I am obviously proud of what we achieved, but all I was doing was what I am paid for, nothing more. I wanted to stand up as a batsman — and the leader of this team — and do the best I could, and if we lost I wanted to make sure I was the last man standing. In the end I was not, but we did escape with a draw.

The lift that draw has given everyone is noticeable. There was a buzz around the changing rooms last night and the bus trip to Scotland was much more relaxed than it would have been if we were now 2–1 down.

We arrived in Edinburgh in the late afternoon and had a team meeting at 6 o'clock. We outlined what the next few days will involve. I emphasised that although we are playing Scotland on Thursday, a game we obviously want to and are expected to win, I also want everyone to relax and recharge their batteries after the two recent Tests.

We have plenty of time to get back into big-match mode, with a 2-day game against Northamptonshire and a few practice sessions before the Trent Bridge Test, which is 9 days away, so I said that socialising and golf are top of the agenda over the next few days — and everyone seemed happy with that.

As the day went on I felt more and more jaded. I would rather not play on Thursday, but with other players already absent for a variety of reasons, I'll have to turn up. Matthew Hayden has been given a few days away in the hope that he can switch off from cricket and his worrying form slump — he has gone fishing. Michael Clarke is resting his back in Birmingham and will join us in Northampton at the end of the week. Our key bowling assets — Glenn McGrath, Shane Warne and Brett Lee — are sitting out Thursday's action, so we have a bare 11 to play, including me.

Wednesday 17 August

Today was exactly the sort of day I wanted at this stage of the tour. We got the squad together, and everyone relaxed and had a laugh — there was no thought of cricket.

We went to Gleneagles for lunch followed by a round of golf, and even the players who did not have a hit — Stuart MacGill, Brad

Haddin and Michael Kasprowicz — enjoyed the scenery and the luxury of the clubhouse.

The golf had something for everyone, with the serious players getting a real buzz out of playing the magnificent King's Course while the less experienced had the challenge of avoiding the savage rough on either side of the fairways.

Adam Gilchrist lost 14 balls during his round and Shaun Tait took 13 at the first hole, which everyone agreed was the easiest on the course. Both players managed to laugh at their misfortune, and their tales kept us all entertained in the bar afterwards.

I shot 76, which I was delighted with, especially as I dropped 5 shots over 2 holes at one point — I found the rough and could not get my ball out without a supreme effort.

It rained for the last hour of the round, which put a slight dampener on proceedings, but otherwise it was the perfect antidote to the tiredness I had been feeling.

Thursday 18 August

One-day match, Edinburgh: Scotland v the Australians, match abandoned (rain).

It was impossible not to feel sorry for Scotland's players and officials. They had planned this match for months, sold all tickets and even persuaded the BBC to show the match live on television, but all those plans came to nothing because of the rain.

We seem to be jinxed when it comes to tour matches against Scotland or Ireland, and we play one country or the other whenever we tour the United Kingdom. In 1997 it rained when we were in Scotland, and it did the same in Belfast 4 years ago when we lined up against Ireland.

It was drizzling when I woke up, and with the weather forecast poor, a washout looked likely. The weather did clear briefly in the early afternoon, and with thousands of people packed into the ground I was happy to agree to a 20-over game. But as soon as the curator started to get the ground ready for play, the rain returned, and the match was abandoned in the late afternoon.

The rain meant that we had a fair bit of hanging around to do during the day, and many of the players spent that time signing autographs to try to keep the locals happy — I hope, and believe, we made a good impression.

This evening I went to the cinema with Justin Langer, Brad Hodge and Brad Haddin and watched the comedy *The Wedding Crashers*, which stars Owen Wilson, Vince Vaughn and Australian actress Isla Fisher. It made us all laugh.

Friday 19 August

Rather than drive from Edinburgh to Northampton, a trip of around 560 kilometres, we flew south.

The plane was obviously quicker than the bus, but by the time we travelled to Edinburgh airport, checked in, waited around, flew, landed at Heathrow and then drove to Northampton, the whole journey still ended up taking around 7 hours door to door.

We were met at Heathrow by Andrew May, who has replaced Jock Campbell as our fitness trainer for the final month of the tour. Campbell has been suffering with a longstanding shoulder injury for most of the trip and has flown home to get the problem sorted out.

We arrived in Northampton in the mid-afternoon, and players were given the option of working out in the hotel gym or practising at the ground. I opted for practice. After a few days away from the game I wanted to feel bat on ball again, especially as I plan to take this match off. I have not missed a game on tour so far, and although I will stay with the team, the fact that I will not be making decisions should allow me to switch off.

Adam Gilchrist will also miss the match to work on his fitness and his wicketkeeping — he felt the latter was sloppy at Old Trafford. He will go through some drills that he hopes will benefit him when next week's Test begins.

With Gilchrist and me both absent, someone else has to lead the side. The choosing of Australia's captain is usually done by CA's directors, but we didn't need to refer this decision back to them because this game is not a first-class match. We settled on Justin Langer, because he is one of the most senior players in the line-up.

I spoke to Chairman of Selectors Trevor Hohns this evening about the side for the match. With Warne sitting it out along with me and Gilchrist, the line-up virtually picked itself — especially as we wanted to see Shaun Tait and Michael Kasprowicz in action so we could decide which of them should replace the out-of-form Jason Gillespie for the next Test. We also wanted to give Glenn McGrath and Brett Lee some action to ensure that both remain match-fit for the Test.

The only problem we have when we include all those fast bowlers is that there is little space for Stuart MacGill, who desperately needs a long bowl after spending most of the tour on the sidelines because of Warne's excellence.

Tour match, Northampton, day 1: The Australians 6–374 declared (Hayden 136, Clarke 121) lead Northamptonshire 2–29 by 345 runs.

There was action on and off the field today. Matthew Hayden and Michael Clarke made attractive hundreds and Stuart MacGill spent most of the day getting to know the country's road network.

I'll deal with MacGill first. As the itinerary has not offered us the chance to give him the bowling he needs, John Buchanan suggested we try to place him with a county side for a few weeks. We approached the selectors with that idea before the Old Trafford Test, but it was rejected because they felt he would get some bowling against Scotland and here in Northampton.

With the Scotland game washed out and the team needing to play four fast bowlers here, he again faced the prospect of being marginalised, even though Northamptonshire agreed that both sides' twelfth men could play a full part in the match.

We approached the selectors again about MacGill playing county cricket for a short while, and this time the selectors agreed. Everything seemed set when Somerset agreed to a deal that would involve him playing two one-day games and a 4-day first-class match.

MacGill set off for Taunton ... but he never arrived, because while he was en route the ECB rejected Somerset's application to register him. The small print of the registration process said that a player had to play for a county for a minimum of 3 weeks, and MacGill was not going to be around for that long.

It was frustrating for us, and frustrating for MacGill. I would have understood if he had been furious at the turn of events, but he handled the situation very well. Rather than head back to Northampton, he made a small detour and visited relatives in Wales; he will meet up with us in Nottingham in a couple of days' time.

I chatted with Jason Gillespie before play and confirmed that he was being left out. I had the impression that it was almost a relief for him. It cannot have been any fun for him going onto the field with less and less confidence in his ability to achieve the high standards he always sets himself. The chance to step away from the spotlight seemed to be something he was happy with.

Simon Katich, who has been struggling for form since his defiant innings at Lord's, missed out again, but Matthew Hayden and Michael Clarke played very well on a very good pitch. Hayden has played county cricket for Northamptonshire, captaining the side and using his time here as a springboard back into the Australia side, and he responded superbly to being here again. Let's hope that he and Clarke, who has now fully recovered from his back trouble, can translate their fluency here into Test runs next week.

I had a relaxing day, watching the action from the viewing area and then changing into my whites to act as twelfth man when we fielded for 12 overs before the close.

Sunday 21 August

Tour match, Northampton, day 2: The Australians 6–374 declared and 2–226 (Langer 86*, Katich 63) drew with Northamptonshire 169.

I was genuinely excited by what I saw today. Our fast bowlers produced their most convincing performance of the tour, demolishing Northamptonshire — if we can repeat that sort of display at Trent Bridge, backed up by Shane Warne, there is no reason why we cannot take the lead in the Ashes series.

Shaun Tait bowled frighteningly fast at times, and together with Brett Lee created a fear factor in the home side's batting. So far in the Test series we have had Lee as our only bowler of extreme pace, and sometimes I felt England were happy to try to see him off, knowing we had no one else capable of bowling as quickly. Being able to alternate Lee and Tait from one end will offer England's batsmen less respite, and that tactic appeals to me.

I have been leaning towards Tait's inclusion at Trent Bridge ever since the opening day of the Old Trafford Test, when Jason Gillespie again failed to fire. Tait is wayward, and will go for runs, but he cannot be any more expensive than Gillespie has been, and his pace and ability to generate reverse swing mean he is more likely to pick up wickets than his South Australia team-mate.

Tait's selection would be hard on Michael Kasprowicz, who bowled beautifully today in his best display of the tour, but the extra pace Tait offers could be a handy weapon. He bounced out former England Test batsman Usman Afzaal, who could only miscue a hook shot to square leg, and then produced a superb yorker to uproot the leg-stump of the home side's captain, David Sales. He also sent opener Tim Roberts off to hospital with a bang on the head — all the batsmen who faced him after that looked apprehensive.

To complete an excellent day, Simon Katich and Justin Langer used the time that remained to get some valuable practice before we drove north to Nottingham.

Chairman of Selectors Trevor Hohns arrived last night to watch the last two Tests of the series, and this morning we had a chat about how the side is going.

It turns out we were thinking along the same lines in terms of using Shaun Tait instead of Jason Gillespie as the only change for this Test, but Hohns was still keen to see the side practice tomorrow — and also to chat to John Buchanan and the other selectors before confirming that choice.

Hohns's biggest concern was our batting. That is understandable, as we are yet to post a decent first innings score in the series. He was especially concerned about Matthew Hayden's form — Hayden has now gone 28 innings without a Test hundred — but I assured him that everyone, including Hayden, has been working hard in practice. It is not as if batsmen, including Hayden, have been getting out for single-figure scores every time. He, along with the rest of us, has usually got started, and in the practice matches he has scored heavily. The problem has been in the Tests, where most of us have failed to go on with the job.

I took a positive approach with the players when we had a team meeting this evening. 'Things *will* change,' I said, 'as long as our attitude is right, we train hard and are totally committed.

'At the same time,' I added, 'we have to make things happen in our favour; it is no good just believing that because we have practised well we have a right to do well this week.'

That was a theme Shane Warne developed. 'We have to be a lot more aggressive on the field with our body language and our attitude,' he said. 'In the past two Tests, England have been the dominant side in that area. We have been the hunted and they have been the hunters, but now we have to turn that around.

'At our best we have intimidated opposition batsmen, because when they get to the crease they are suddenly confronted by 11 Australians all over them, scrapping over every run, and that must be our approach now,' Warne concluded.

One positive for our batsmen is the anecdotal information we have about Trent Bridge, which suggests that reverse swing is not as prevalent there as at Edgbaston and Old Trafford. We have all struggled at various times to cope with it, and our left-handers especially have found it tough to handle the late swing of Andrew Flintoff and Simon Jones. If it is less of a factor here, that is a plus for us.

Tuesday 23 August

Glenn McGrath is once again a major injury doubt for the Test, this time after experiencing pain in his right elbow. The problem showed up at Old Trafford but grew significantly worse at Northampton, and it has become enough of a concern to Errol Alcott for him to travel to London with McGrath to consult a specialist.

I am keeping my fingers crossed that he will be fit to play, but just in case he is not, I spoke to Michael Kasprowicz this afternoon to ensure that he is ready to step in if required.

McGrath's absence would leave a major hole in our attack, as it did at Edgbaston, but I was encouraged by Shaun Tait's form at practice. He tore in, hitting Justin Langer in the groin with a rapid full toss then catching him on the left elbow with a sharply rising ball. It left Langer cursing the young pace bowler, and that seemed to knock the stuffing out of Tait briefly, but after the net session it was smiles all round as Langer gave him a hug.

Tait's effort confirmed the selectors' view that he should play here, and I was given the job of relaying the good news to him in the dressing room after our session. Telling a player he will make his Test debut for Australia is one of the perks of this job, and although Tait did not say much when I broke the news to him, I could tell he was bursting with pride.

That is the pleasant side of the job; the other side of the coin came when I had to tell Jason Gillespie he had been dropped. It was hardly unexpected news, and he took it well. 'Thought so,' he said.

I also took time during the day to chat with Stuart MacGill, who has rejoined us after his weekend in Wales. 'This must seem like the tour from hell,' I said, referring to the fact that he has played precious little cricket so far.

To his credit, MacGill was philosophical and also upbeat about the trip. 'I can think of worse places to be,' he said. If one of the players outside the Test squad starts to get moody, it can affect everyone in the squad, because we live in each other's pockets on a tour of this length. I am happy to say that everyone, including MacGill, has maintained enthusiasm remarkably well so far.

After we had a sharp fielding session and I batted in the practice nets, I looked at the pitch — and it reminded me of the surface at Lord's 2 days before that Test. It is white, dry, and appears ready to play on straightaway. Given that dryness, I expect it will give Shane Warne plenty of assistance as the match progresses.

Wednesday 24 August

I was happy with my preparation yesterday, which was just as well, because it hammered down with rain for most of today. We could have used the indoor facilities at the ECB's cricket academy at nearby Loughborough, but it would have involved a round trip of a couple of hours, and I felt that rest and relaxation were preferable to that.

I also had my media commitments ahead of the Test, and they took place during the morning at the team hotel in the centre of Nottingham. I was joined by Errol Alcott, who gave the journalists an update on Glenn McGrath's elbow injury, and Shaun Tait, who will make his Test debut.

Alcott had everyone chuckling when he said McGrath's problem was the presence of loose 'artefacts' around the elbow. I am not sure that he meant there was some sort of ancient treasure beneath the skin, but if he can work his magic and get McGrath ready to play, it would be a massive bonus for us. I detected signs during the second innings of the Old Trafford Test that McGrath was getting back to his best form, but if he does not play here he will be back at square one in terms of bowling fitness. He had treatment from Alcott through most of today; we will give him a chance to prove his fitness in the morning.

Tait was modest about what he will bring to the side, but I know he will bring raw pace, as he did at Northampton last weekend. He is also liable to go for a few runs, but so did his predecessor in the side, Jason Gillespie. At least with Tait there is the extra threat that pace brings, whereas Gillespie has struggled for any sort of cutting edge throughout the trip.

I was asked about Gillespie and his decline. He started the tour at number two in our fast bowlers' pecking order, and has now slipped down to number five, with no apparent way back in the immediate future. All I could say was the obvious: he has to keep working hard for the rest of this trip on the basis that he might get another chance if we suffer injuries, and when we get home he has to start taking wickets for South Australia. If he can do that, he still has a chance of a recall.

One part of touring life that can be tough, especially after more than 2 months away, is seeing the same faces every day. That is not meant as a criticism of anyone, but there are times when you just want to spent some quality time away from cricket, and that is not always easy. Rianna and I decided to leave the hotel and head into Nottingham city centre for a quiet meal during the afternoon, but our plan to avoid anything to do with cricket came unstuck when we picked the same restaurant as Andrew Flintoff, his wife, Rachael, and daughter, Holly. It still turned out to be a pleasant meal — I think they felt the same way we did. We sat together, and managed to avoid the subject of cricket all afternoon.

Thursday 25 August

Fourth Test, Trent Bridge, Nottingham, day 1: England 4–229 (Trescothick 65, Vaughan 58) v Australia.

Another frustrating day for us, with dropped catches, a wicket off a no-ball and more undisciplined bowling, but at the end of it we are still in the game. If we can pick up a couple of early wickets tomorrow we may even be in a position to take control.

We lost the toss, and for the third Test in a row gave England a flying start. Without Glenn McGrath, who failed his fitness test, we bowled with no real control, and by lunch England were scoring at around 5 runs per over with only 1 wicket down.

We should have had more than that 1 wicket, but Marcus Trescothick was bowled by a Brett Lee no-ball, something that left me furious. Lee complained to me that he was having trouble with his run-up because there was a small hill between the outfield and the square which was putting him off balance as he got into delivery stride.

That excuse cut no ice with me. 'That hill was there on Tuesday when we came down to practise and it will be there for the rest of this match,' I said. 'You knew what the conditions would be before we started, so it is no good making excuses now. You should have worked to adjust to the hill before the match, not complain about it now.'

Despite everything we have said in team meetings and in the media, we still managed to bowl 18 no-balls before lunch, and that is a disgrace for a Test side. I know John Buchanan is equally dumbfounded by the way our bowlers continue to overstep the front line, and when I walked into the dressing room at lunch I said to him, and anyone else who was listening, 'Can someone please give me some answers?'

My anger must have hit home, because after the interval we managed to tidy up the no-ball count and bowled just four more for the rest of the day. However, that problem was replaced by dropped catches — we put down two straightforward offerings. Kevin Pietersen survived a caught and bowled chance to Michael Kasprowicz, and Matthew Hayden put down Michael Vaughan at backward point.

By that stage, helped by a break for rain in the mid-afternoon, we managed to slow England's momentum. Shaun Tait overcame his early nerves and bowled an excellent spell, taking 2 wickets. He swung the ball at a lively pace and gave the attack an extra dimension that we had lacked in the previous two matches.

During the latter part of the day we played in light drizzle. This meant that the ball became a little greasy, so I could not use Shane Warne — he would have struggled to grip it in the wet conditions. That was my cue to bowl, and I took my first Test wicket for more than 6 years.

The two batsmen, Vaughan and Pietersen, were clearly unhappy at being out there in the drizzle, and at one stage Vaughan said to umpire Steve Bucknor, 'Is this fair?' It was obvious that at this stage both players were more interested in protecting their wickets than in playing each ball on its merits — they did not want to expose another batsman to the poor conditions. That meant it was the perfect time for me to bowl.

Under normal circumstances, on a fine day, both Vaughan and Pietersen would expect to score heavily off me, but my plan was to bowl to a defensive field outside off-stump and challenge their egos. They did not know whether to attack me or play defensively, because they knew that every over I was bowling was allowing my frontline bowlers to rest, and eventually Vaughan played a nondescript shot to a short ball, just guiding it into Adam Gilchrist's gloves behind the stumps.

We left the field because of bad light soon afterwards, and although I was content with our position after our ragged first session, I was not happy with the way the umpires conducted themselves when deciding whether or not conditions were fit for play. Normally, when batsmen are offered the chance to come off for bad light the umpires take a reading with light meters. The reading they get on those meters is the one they work to for the rest of the match. If the light is better than when they left the field, they will generally look to keep the players on, and if it is worse they will offer the batsmen the chance to go off. This time they offered the light to the batsmen without any reference to a light meter, and as I said to Bucknor as we walked off, I am not sure how we can now get consistency on the issue of bad light for the rest of the match.

Friday 26 August

Fourth Test, Trent Bridge, Nottingham, day 2: Australia 5–99 trail England 477 (Flintoff 102, G Jones 85, Trescothick 65, Vaughan 58) by 378 runs.

Although we did not have the rub of the green with umpiring decisions — I counted four that went against us — we have also been outplayed, and now face a massive task to try to stay in the match.

Our bowling was again not good enough, and that was put into sharp focus by the way the England attack operated when it was their turn to perform. They swung the ball, bowled good lines, got movement off the seam . . . and left our innings in tatters.

I am not sure where we go from here with our bowling attack. We have talked and talked on the tour about putting plans into operation, but time and again the bowlers have not been able to execute those plans. Today's plan, discussed before play and again at lunch, was for the fast bowlers to target off-stump so that we could try to defend one side of the wicket in order to build pressure on England's batsmen. We did it for a while just before lunch, but straightaway after the interval we started conceding runs on both sides of the wicket, and that was the cue for the wheels to come off the bowling wagon again.

Credit should still go to Andrew Flintoff and Geraint Jones for the way they played — they took advantage of our moderate bowling to add 177 — but we felt both batsmen benefited from umpiring errors. Shane Warne was convinced he had Flintoff lbw with a quicker ball that went straight on, while Jones edged a catch behind the wicket off Brett Lee's first ball after lunch, only to be reprieved by umpire Steve Bucknor.

When we batted, England benefited from two more umpiring errors — Damien Martyn and I were both given out lbw despite edging the ball onto our pads — but although it would be convenient to hide behind such things, there is no getting away from the fact that we have been second best in this match. England have looked sharper and more purposeful. It is as simple as that.

We lost a wicket in the last over of the day when Michael Clarke was lbw to Stephen Harmison. If we continue that slide tomorrow, England will have to decide whether or not to enforce the follow-on, something they have not been able to do against us for 17 years. I gather the weather forecast for Sunday is not great; that might influence Michael Vaughan's thinking, but I would expect him to bat again if he gets the choice. The pitch is still a good one, and asking us to bat a second time opens up the possibility of England facing a run chase in the fourth innings, by which time the pitch should be worn and suited to Shane Warne's spin.

That is all speculation, of course. In the immediate future, we have to scratch, kick and fight our way back — and we still have batsmen to do that: Simon Katich, Adam Gilchrist and Shane Warne. If they can make some handy contributions, backed up by Brett Lee and Shaun Tait, we can still post a decent total. That is our target now.

Before I left the ground a journalist asked me whether it had crossed my mind that we could lose The Ashes. I answered honestly that it had not, despite our position here. Even if we lose here, we will still have the chance to retain The Ashes by winning at The Oval, and there is no point in getting into a negative state of mind with so much left to play for.

There is no lack of effort from the players, but it is just not happening for us at the moment. England is putting us under pressure, more pressure than some of us have encountered at this level before, and we are struggling to cope. All we can do is try to remain positive, work hard and try our backsides off. If we do that, we have to believe our fortunes will improve.

Saturday 27 August

X-rays on the right ankle of England fast bowler Simon Jones prove 'inconclusive'. Jones was off the field for most of Australia's second innings after experiencing pain in the ankle.

Fourth Test, Trent Bridge, Nottingham, day 3: Australia 218 (S Jones 5–44) and 4–222 (Langer 61) trail England 477 by 37 runs.

This will not go down as one of my happiest days in cricket. We were forced to follow on, I got out at a crucial time, and my frustration overflowed in the form of a rant at the England balcony as I walked off the ground.

The reason for my frustration was not simply that I got out after establishing myself; it was also because I was run out by a substitute fielder.

We have discussed England's use of substitutes throughout the tour, and once again in this match they have rotated fresh reserve fielders on in place of bowlers whenever those bowlers have finished their spells. We have brought it to the attention of two match referees and the various umpires who have stood in our matches, but nothing has been done to address an issue which we believe needs re-examination.

When the substitute fielder — in this case, Durham's Gary Pratt — hit the stumps directly at the striker's end after Damien Martyn called me for a quick single, I knew I was almost certainly out, but Aleem Dar, the umpire at square leg, called for the third umpire to adjudicate, so I waited in the middle while he made his decision.

Dar came in from square leg to repair the stumps and while I was certain of the imminent decision, and accepted that it was my call to accept my partner's call, I raised the issue again and repeated our view about how substitutes are used.

Once the verdict I was expecting was delivered and I was given out, I began my walk off the field, and as I did so I was sent on my way by several of the England players. Then, once out of their earshot, I looked up at the home team's balcony. I had not seen Duncan Fletcher, the England coach, watching the game from there during the match, but now as I walked off there he was, grinning like the cat that got the cream.

Fletcher knew that the issue of substitutes had been on our agenda and when I spotted him on the England team's balcony as I walked off, it caused something inside me to call for a point to be made, and as I made my way through the crowd I looked up at him and shouted, 'Play the game properly', or words to that effect.

The irony of the situation was that Pratt, the replacement fielder, was on the field for a legitimate reason — rather than simply to allow one of the bowlers to have a rest, a toilet break, a shower, a change of shirt, a rub-down or whatever it is they have been doing. Simon Jones was absent for most of our second innings because of a foot injury, and that meant England had to try to bowl us out a second time with only four frontline bowlers.

That was a bonus for us, because Jones was England's outstanding bowler in our first innings. He bowled quickly and got the ball to swing late. Without him we had a real chance to finally post a decent score and set the home side a testing target in the final innings.

We can still do that, but a combination of good work from the remaining England bowlers and occasional sloppiness on our part, typified by my run-out, means we have a mountain to climb.

My outburst provoked plenty of interest among the media, as it was captured by the television camera positioned directly in front of our dressing room. Jonathan Rose, our media manager, received plenty of enquiries from reporters throughout the afternoon, asking for my explanation of what had happened. He asked if I would talk to the media after play. I did not want to, but at the same time, after I calmed down, I realised that my behaviour would not have looked too impressive to the viewers watching at home.

I decided that I was happy for a statement to be issued on my behalf; I would apologise for my rant, but at the same time point out what had prompted it — a combination of frustration at my dismissal and anger at England's continuing abuse of the use of substitutes. I am sure it will make the back pages of all the newspapers tomorrow and I am likely to be called a whingeing Australian, but if it highlights what we believe is an issue, then I am prepared to put up with the attention I am sure to receive.

Something positive to come out of the day was the counterattack launched by our batsmen in two stages this morning. When we discussed our tactics before play I said I wanted us to give England's bowlers something to think about, and we did that, thanks to aggressive cameos by Adam Gilchrist and Brett Lee. Gilchrist was frustrated by the way he had played at Old Trafford. He felt he had been too negative, instead of backing his instincts, so he opted to try to play his natural game this morning — he hammered 27 from 36 balls before falling to a spectacular diving catch by Andrew Strauss at slip. It was a superb, one-handed effort, but also typified the way our luck is going: Gilchrist's first mistake was also his last.

That wicket was one of four to fall in the space of 4 overs, and Lee found himself with last man Shaun Tait for company. He decided to go down swinging, and produced some spectacular hitting, with three sixes, two of them going clean out of the ground at midwicket. It was just what we needed after another dispiriting morning, but we will need more of the same to give ourselves a chance of pulling off a victory.

Sunday 28 August

Fourth Test, Trent Bridge, Nottingham, day 4: England 477 and 7–129 beat Australia 218 and 387 (Langer 61, Katich 59, Clarke 56) by 3 wickets.

Despite a fantastic effort from Shane Warne and Brett Lee, we lost a titanic battle — and Simon Katich and I are lighter in the pocket after being fined for our conduct by match referee Ranjan Madugalle.

I was handed my charge sheet after warm-ups this morning. I was charged with offence C2 in the players' and team officials' code of conduct, which reads: 'Players and/or Team Officials shall at no time engage in conduct unbecoming to their status which could bring them or the game of cricket into disrepute.'

On the charge sheet there was a space for the match referee to add his description of the alleged incident. Madugalle had written: 'Upon being given out by the 3rd umpire (over 44.1) R. Ponting was involved in a heated exchange with the England players and on leaving the playing area angrily gestured towards the England dressing room.'

Leaving aside the fact that I did not gesture at the England dressing room, a fact proven by television footage, I spent any quiet moments I had during the day reflecting on whether or not I should have issued a statement last night. By apologising, I could have been seen to be admitting that I did something wrong, and although that was true — I should not have shouted up at the England balcony — the statement almost invited the match referee to charge me.

Madugalle did so, and when I attended the hearing after play, and pleaded not guilty, I was shown the video evidence against me. It consisted of a view of my back as I spoke to the England players, then the footage from the camera in front of our dressing room as I shouted up at Duncan Fletcher.

The only thing it proved was that I shouted up at the England balcony, but Madugalle still felt it was enough to find me guilty. He fined me 75 per cent of my match fee. Although I was willing to admit I was wrong to shout at Fletcher the way I did, I was very surprised at the size of the fine, especially as it was the first time I'd had to answer a charge. It also surprised Steve Bernard and Adam Gilchrist, who attended the hearing with me.

Bernard was there in his capacity as team manager, and Gilchrist attended as vice-captain. Normally the captain attends a hearing when one of his players is charged, but as I am captain, Gilchrist was there as the second-in-command. Also present were umpires Aleem Dar, Steve Bucknor, third umpire Mark Benson and Ian Gould, the fourth official.

Bernard, Gilchrist and I all argued against the severity of the punishment, but Madugalle said he had actually been lenient — South Africa's Graeme Smith and Inzamam-ul-Haq of Pakistan had been suspended for similar offences. None of us could recall those instances, so we had to take his word for that.

We quickly realised that we were getting nowhere arguing about the size of the punishment, so we stopped, and Bernard asked if the hearing was over. When Madugalle said it was, Bernard and Gilchrist decided to use the opportunity to discuss our concern about our perceptions of consistency with the application of the code of conduct.

Gilchrist cited two recent examples. At Lord's, Andrew Strauss gestured at and verbally abused Damien Martyn after Martyn was given out, an incident that was captured on camera, but no action was taken against him. Then, at Edgbaston, when Simon Jones pointed Matthew Hayden towards the dressing room after dismissing him, Jones was fined 20 per cent of his match fee, even though he had done something similar in the Caribbean last year and been fined 50 per cent of his match fee then. Madugalle made not comment about the incident involving Strauss, but said he was referee for the previous incident involving Jones and the two offences were different, hence their different punishments.

Gilchrist then brought up the entry in the code of conduct handbook that is directly above the clause I was charged under. It reads: 'Players and/or Team Officials shall at all times conduct play within the spirit of the game as well as within the Laws of Cricket and the captains are responsible at all times for ensuring that this is adhered to.'

Gilchrist said we had done our best to adhere to that spirit for the past 18 months, but much of what we saw in return was ignorance of it. Gilchrist pointed out that we approached every opposition captain before the start of a series and asked them to respect the word of fielders over disputed catches. All of those captains, except Inzamam-ul-Haq of Pakistan and the Sri Lanka duo of Marvan Atapattu and Hashan Tillakaratne, rejected that suggestion. Meanwhile, in this series, England have rotated players on and off the ground in apparent violation of Law 2 concerning the use of substitutes, without a whimper from any match officials. Gilchrist and Bernard asked what was being done concerning the use of substitutes, but all they got was a straight bat from Madugalle. 'We are not here to discuss that,' he said.

We did not get much satisfaction out of the hearing or the discussion that followed, and there was more pain to follow, with Simon Katich charged with dissent for hanging around after he was given out lbw by Dar and then abusing spectators as he left the ground.

Katich was fined 50 per cent of his fee in what was an open-and-shut case. He had received a shocking lbw decision, as the ball had pitched well outside the line of leg-stump and would almost certainly have bounced over the stumps as well, but when he lingered before walking off he incurred the wrath not only of the umpires and match referee, but also of the crowd in front of our dressing room. They started abusing him and he snapped back. His frustration was understandable, but we all knew that in the glare of the media spotlight it could not be condoned.

It all added up to a sorry end to a sorry day. We took England to the wire, with Lee and Warne outstanding, but that was little consolation as we licked our wounds in the dressing room after the match.

If we had got a lead of 180 it might have been enough, given the way England wobbled in pursuit of their modest target of 129, but we only had ourselves to blame for not getting those extra runs. Once again, most of our batsmen got in but failed to go on and make a big score. The 30 runs we conceded in no-balls in this match also hit us hard.

I was criticised after the match by some commentators for not opening the bowling with Warne — they claimed he was always going to be the bowler most likely to win us the match. Instead, I had opted for Michael Kasprowicz alongside Lee's pace. Unfortunately he proved expensive, conceding 19 runs in 2 overs. Kasprowicz usually bowls well to left-handers, and with both England's openers fitting that description, I hoped he would get us an early breakthrough before I turned to Warne. I felt it was a gamble worth taking, but it did not pay off.

There was time during the England innings for my frustration with the officials to resurface, this time in the area of disputed catches. My preference is for the players themselves to take ownership of the issue, but Vaughan prefers to let the umpires make the decisions, so before the series we came to a compromise: we agreed, as did the officials, that the on-field umpires, not the television official, should adjudicate on any catch over which there was a question mark. The television technology is rarely good enough to offer conclusive evidence, which results in referrals usually being ruled not out, and that can create a bad atmosphere on the field.

That was the theory, but when the time came to put it into practice, the umpires backed down. When Andrew Strauss clipped Warne into Michael Clarke's hands at leg-slip and stood his ground as the catch was claimed, I expected the umpires to consult and then make a decision, but instead they got together and referred the matter to the third umpire.

As Strauss stood there he said, 'I'm waiting for the third umpire's verdict.'

'Fine,' I said as I moved towards Dar and Bucknor, 'but before the series it was agreed that the on-field umpires would make the decision themselves.'

Both umpires claimed they were unsighted, something I found hard to believe, but I had to take them at their word. Luckily, this time the third official ruled that the catch had been taken cleanly. I was disappointed that the officials had not stuck to our pre-series agreement, but at least the right decision was arrived at.

When Geraint Jones was out with 13 still needed, I thought we had a real chance of pulling off an upset, but all credit to Ashley Giles and Matthew Hoggard, who showed superb strength in a pressure situation and saw England home. At Old Trafford, when there was pressure on him to bowl us out on the last day, Giles had failed to deliver, and now he was facing Warne, who had dismissed him four times in the series already. This time he held firm, and I was happy to shake his hand and congratulate him — and Hoggard — when the winning runs were made.

We battled bravely, but the fact remains that we did the same thing we'd done at Edgbaston and Old Trafford: substandard displays in the first innings with bat and ball had left us chasing our tails for the rest of the match, and against a good side like England, that is a very tough assignment. We have to solve those issues for the final Test or we will surrender The Ashes.

Despite our performances in the past three Tests, I still believe we have the players to turn this situation around and win that match at The Oval. We will discover whether or not the selectors feel the same way over the next week or so, and I will chat with Trevor Hohns, Adam Gilchrist and John Buchanan tomorrow about where we go from here.

I think the fact that we now have to win to retain The Ashes will actually work in our favour. A draw is no good, so we have to make sure we are positive, and that might encourage our out-of-form players to come out of their shells. England, on the other hand, know that a draw is all they need for a series win. It means we are in for an intriguing final instalment of what has been a roller-coaster ride so far.

Monday 29 August

This afternoon I caught up with Trevor Hohns, John Buchanan, Jamie Siddons and Adam Gilchrist to discuss our situation and what we can do to improve it.

Hohns has watched our decline on this tour with concern, and he started the meeting with some questions: Why are we in this position? Have we trained and prepared hard enough?

I was happy to answer those queries. I confirmed that, yes, we have been training hard enough, our team meetings have had purpose and we have put some decent plans in place; our problem has been that we have not executed those plans well enough.

We agreed that once the dust has settled after the tour, we will be able to analyse our failings in detail; right now, though, what we need are short-term solutions to our problems that will ensure that we give ourselves the best chance of winning at The Oval and so retaining The Ashes.

We talked about possible line-ups for the final Test, and the subject of whether we should play four or five bowlers was raised.

My view was, and is, that our selection is entirely dependent on Glenn McGrath's fitness. If he is fit, I am happy to go into the Test with four bowlers, because he can fill two roles: as a wicket-taker with the new ball and as a stock bowler and builder of pressure later in the innings.

We also discussed whether or not there was a need to go outside the squad, and the names of Andrew Symonds, Shane Watson and Mike Hussey were all mentioned. I said I would be happy to call in either Symonds or Watson if McGrath is not fit, but that is something we will not know until much nearer the Test.

Without McGrath, my preference is for a 5-man attack, with Stuart Clark coming in for him and either Symonds or Watson also included. That would involve dropping a batsman — the likeliest candidate for the axe would be Matthew Hayden — and moving Simon Katich up to open the innings. The whole make-up of the side would be altered.

Yet another alternative would be to use Hussey instead of Hayden, but that idea was dismissed, even though he has been in excellent form for his county side, Durham, after equally impressive one-day form for Australia earlier in the tour. We wanted to give Hayden the chance to prove his form in our next game, against Essex on Saturday, and by then Hussey will be back in Australia getting ready for an Australia A tour to Pakistan.

The idea of playing two spinners was also discussed, but we agreed that we needed to see how Stuart MacGill performed against Essex before making that decision. It has been so long since he played that we need to establish whether or not he is on form.

So although we talked through plenty of options, not much was decided. I expect we will have further discussions after the match against Essex.

In the meantime, we all agreed that our basic strategy for the final 2 weeks of the tour should be all about keeping things simple.

Rather than overloading the guys with theories and plans that many have so far struggled to implement, we should focus on what has made us successful, both as individuals and as a team, over the past 6 or 7 years. Every player has enjoyed success by playing in a certain way during that time, and our best approach from now on is to try to replicate those methods and hope we can recapture some of our old magic.

Wednesday 31 August

This week has been about little else but meetings so far, and the theme continued this morning when I chatted over breakfast with Trevor Hohns, Adam Gilchrist and John Buchanan.

The previous 2 days had given us the chance to reflect on what had been discussed on Monday, and Hohns wanted us to meet again to see whether anyone had any fresh views on what was said.

Having ruled out the idea of calling up Mike Hussey, we needed a contingency plan in case we felt Matthew Hayden was not up to the job of opening in next week's Test. Simon Katich was the obvious choice, but I threw Gilchrist's name in as an extra option. We have pushed him up the order in the past to put the pressure back on opposition sides and it has often worked, most recently in Kandy against Sri Lanka last year. Everyone agreed that it was worth considering.

The one problem we had in discussing options for the Test was the fact that we do not know whether or not Glenn McGrath will be fit. My gut feeling is that he will not play, so we looked at what cricket Andrew Symonds, Shane Watson and Stuart Clark have with their respective county sides over the next week.

We contemplated calling them into the squad for the Essex match but decided that we have the resources to cope, and so can leave any decision on whether or not to draft them in until next week. Calling up one or two of them still remains an option.

Another concern emerged today when Errol Alcott let me know about an ongoing problem Shaun Tait is having with tendonitis in his right shoulder. The problem first emerged before the Old Trafford Test, and at that stage Alcott was keen to give Tait as much rest as possible to try to cure it.

That was not possible because of the injury concerns surrounding McGrath and Brett Lee ahead of that match — Tait had to bowl in the nets before that Test, and it aggravated the problem. Alcott has continued to monitor the shoulder since then, and wanted to let me know that it remains a concern, albeit a minor one. Tait told me that, although his shoulder is sore at the start of each spell, he is fine after a couple of deliveries.

After the last 3 days of meetings I was ready to try to switch off for a while, and I found the perfect excuse with a trip to Sunningdale Golf Club, on the outskirts of London. I went along with Jamie Siddons and Matthew Hayden at the invitation of television presenter Mark Nicholas, and we all had a really enjoyable and very relaxing round on a superb course.

Thursday 1 September

We made the 2-hour journey to Essex for this weekend's penultimate match of the tour, and once we arrived at our hotel, around 40 minutes' drive from the city of Chelmsford, the venue for the match, fitness trainer Andrew May put us through our paces.

The hotel, which includes a golf course, is set in extensive grounds and May used those grounds to get us running around. We did 40 minutes of warming up with soccer and rugby balls, and then played four 10-minute quarters of Australian Rules football before working on our throwing technique using cricket balls. We call May's approach to maintaining our fitness through these games 'disguised running'. The games have the same effect as running from point A to point B but are much more fun.

The throwing part of our workout showed me how far Glenn McGrath is from being fit. His elbow problem is clearly bothering him — he could barely get his arm up to throw the ball. Unless he makes a second miraculous recovery, I cannot see how he is going to be ready to play in 7 days' time.

I have been monitoring the mood of Matthew Hayden and Damien Martyn. Both were very low after the Trent Bridge Test. Team-mates have tried to speak to them at various stages to lift their spirits, and John Buchanan chatted with them individually on Tuesday to see if they are up for the challenge of the next couple of weeks.

Both said they are okay, but our approach to handling them will differ. While Hayden needs time in the middle, we will leave Martyn out of this match, giving him a break, as we did for Hayden before the previous Test. Martyn is a touch player who has never benefited from hitting hundreds of balls in practice, whereas that is exactly the type of routine Hayden has thrived on in the past.

Friday 2 September

We travelled to Chelmsford to practise for the Essex match, and although the practice nets were poor quality, we had a good run around. We also had a team meeting where John Buchanan and I addressed the players.

I started off by asking everyone to make sure that we train hard and prepare well over the next 6 days, and then moved on to the theme of what I had to say — keeping things simple.

'I know it is difficult to get this thought out of all our heads,' I said, 'but I want us to avoid thinking of next week's match as a must-win game.

'All we have to do is approach this Test in exactly the same way we approach every other match we play. Our first thought is always to go out and win, and nothing needs to change this time.

'We have got to where we are, the best side in the world, by getting the basics right, the little things, and that should be our focus both ahead of the Test and during it.

'Those basics are batting and bowling in partnerships, making big scores, having a high level of intensity in the field and looking to create chances rather than wait for them to come along.

'If we think in terms of those objectives and execute them well, we will win the Test and retain The Ashes,' I added.

Buchanan added that our situation now was no different from the one we face every year before the VB Series finals.

'Our philosophy is always just to make sure we reach the finals, then look to peak when we get there,' he said.

'We are in that finals situation now, so our objective is exactly the same — to win the match that counts,' he added.

I have decided to rest from this match. When I sat out the game at Northampton I felt fresh and in great touch, and I am looking for that same effect now. At this stage of the trip, one more innings will not benefit me, but time away from the middle might.

Glenn McGrath bowled briefly during our practice session but I am still doubtful that he will be ready for the Test. It would be nice if I am proved wrong.

Tour match, Chelmsford, day 1: Essex 4–502 (Cook 214, Bopara 135, Jefferson 64) v the Australians.

This was hardly the sort of preparation we wanted for next week's Test. We spent 7 hours getting hammered to all parts of the small Chelmsford ground, and our dressing room was a quiet place this evening.

In defence of those of our players who took the field today, the pitch was an absolute beauty, the boundaries were short and the Essex batsmen played well. However, there is still no excuse for an attack that boasts more than 600 Test wickets getting belted for over 500 runs in a day.

It was clear quite early that things were not going according to plan — by the first drinks break, Essex had already racked up more than 100 runs. I tried to lighten the mood by carrying Michael Kasprowicz's fart machine with me when I ran out the refreshments, but when I got out to the middle and let it off I soon discovered that it did not impress acting captain Adam Gilchrist one bit.

'You can turn that off,' he shouted before laying into the players. 'I'm not saying people are not trying,' he said, 'but this is embarrassing. We have to put things right.'

The pep talk worked at first, and the bowlers gained a semblance of control in the period leading up to lunch, but after the interval the batsmen re-established control and the result was carnage.

One of the batsmen, Alastair Cook, who was named England's Young Cricketer of the Year by the Cricket Writers' Club last night, played superbly — I am sure he is England's next opening batsman. Even on a pitch as good as this one he looked a well-organised player and did not allow us to dictate to him.

The day did not enhance the chances of any bowlers forcing their way into the Test squad, but if McGrath is not fit, at least two of them will have to play. It is difficult to see how one of them will be Stuart MacGill after he was flayed all round the ground on his return to competitive action.

I sat down with Gilchrist in the dressing room after play and tried to lift his spirits, but, not surprisingly, he failed to see the funny side of anything. The only positive is that although Essex have only lost 4 wickets, they cannot bat on beyond the first hour tomorrow, even if they want to, because under the playing conditions we agreed on for this 2-day match, the maximum any side can bat in its first innings is 120 overs. At least that means our batsmen will get the chance to enjoy the perfect conditions at some stage.

Lancashire's James Anderson and Paul Collingwood of Durham are named in England's squad for the final Test at The Oval; Hampshire's Chris Tremlett, who has been twelfth man for the first four Tests of the series, is left out.

Tour match, Chelmsford, day 2: The Australians 6–561 (Hodge 166, Hayden 150, Langer 87, Katich 72, Haddin 59) drew with Essex 4–502 declared.

After I acted as twelfth man yesterday, I had the chance of a relaxing morning at the hotel before heading to the ground in the afternoon.

I spent the morning with Damien Martyn. We had a leisurely breakfast, a 75-minute gym session, 9 holes of golf, and a chat about how he is feeling about the coming Test match.

Martyn seemed a lot more positive about life today than he did at Trent Bridge last week, when he was very low. Now he said he had come to terms with his run of low scores and was ready to play a major role at The Oval.

He said he has felt in pretty good form throughout the series, but knows he does not have the figures to back that up. Some of that is down to bad luck — he has received at least two very poor lbw decisions.

We all handle things differently when we fail. I rant and rave for a few minutes after being dismissed before I settle down again, but Martyn is the complete opposite. When he gets out he heads back to the dressing room, sits down and hardly says a word. That silence is his way of dealing with the disappointment.

We followed the first part of today's play by phone, and pretty quickly it was clear that we were batting just as Essex did yesterday, taking advantage of the excellent conditions. It was great to see Brad Hodge scoring some runs at the end of what has been a frustrating tour for him. The hundred for Matthew Hayden was our other plus from the day.

Hayden was the first to admit afterwards that the situation bore little relation to what he could expect at The Oval — 'It is like learning to surf in a swimming pool' was his description — but runs always breed confidence, so it should still have done him some good.

The match was our last 2-day game of the tour, and I am not sure we will continue playing matches of this length. Their shortness means that our fringe players have not had any real chance to press for higher honours, and our out-of-form players have not been given much chance to regain their touch. Also, as the matches are not first-class, they have lacked intensity, and that means they are not ideal preparation for Test matches.

Glenn McGrath had a bowl during the day after his weekly column in a British newspaper announced that he would be fit for Thursday's Test match. I remain to be convinced about that claim.

Monday 5 September

Stuart Clark is called into the Australia squad as cover for Glenn McGrath for the fifth Test, at The Oval.

Practice was optional after the 2-day match over the weekend, but I decided to head to The Oval for a workout.

I enjoyed it. The practice pitches were good, as they usually are at this ground, and it was nice to move my kit into the dressing room and settle in ahead of the next week's action.

One journalist said to me during the day that I seem to be showing no outward signs of pressure despite the importance of this Test match. I do feel very relaxed, and the main reason for that is that I have Rianna around: she keeps me grounded, and when we are together we talk about everything but cricket.

On top of that, my philosophy is to not expend energy worrying about what might happen. It is just a case of controlling the controllables — for me, that means making sure I have dome everything I can do to perform to the best of my ability. If we all do that, as a team we have nothing to worry about. Even if we lose, if each of us can look in the mirror and know that he has done his best, that is all that matters.

Tuesday 6 September

Simon Jones fails a fitness test on his injured right ankle; England are yet to decide whether to replace him with Paul Collingwood or James Anderson.

I got the first inkling today of the sort of criticism I am likely to face in Australia if we fail to win this Test match.

I held my regular pre-Test media conference for the Australian reporters on the tour, and after they asked me whether some players' careers are on the line over our failures on this tour, they moved on to my own future as captain and whether I felt my position was under threat.

That future is in the hands of the selectors, as they are the ones who will make a recommendation to CA's Board of Directors, but I like to think that my position as captain is safe, at least for the foreseeable future.

If we do not win this Test I am prepared to face some flak, and as captain I will take some responsibility for our failings on this trip, but I think it is also fair to point out that whatever shortcomings we have shown on this tour are not just down to me.

Our responsibility is always a collective one, whether we win, lose or draw, and that is how it should always be. In the same way that our World Cup win in 2003 and our 3–0 series success in Sri Lanka last year were not down to just me, so too our losses are not down to just me either. I realise that there are bound to be questions asked about our performances here, whatever the result of the final Test, but the truth is that no one person is to blame.

The questioning suggested that a degree of hysteria over our results has already started back home, but what we really need now are calm heads. The important thing to remember is that we are not 4–0 down in this series; we are 2–1 down, with a chance of retaining The Ashes.

We practised this morning, and Glenn McGrath bowled two spells during the session. The reason he bowled twice was so we could see whether his elbow would suffer any reaction after it had the chance to cool down. He did everything that was asked of him, did it with a smile on his face and even said to me afterwards, 'I'll be right.' I still have my doubts.

The selectors had a telephone hook-up overnight and decided that Matthew Hayden will retain his place. The only change from the side that lost last week will be McGrath's inclusion in place of Michael Kasprowicz; if McGrath is not fit, Stuart Clark will make his debut. This means we will go into the Test with four frontline bowlers whatever happens.

England will have to make their first change of the series, as Simon Jones has failed a fitness test. The options are fast bowler James Anderson and batting all-rounder Paul Collingwood. The brave choice would be to include Anderson, but as we need to take 20 wickets to win the Test, I suspect England will go for Collingwood, the conservative option, to shore up the batting.

We spent the afternoon playing in a corporate six-a-side cricket tournament organised by our sponsors, Travelex, with each side including one member of our squad. My side lost to the eventual winners, a team including Justin Langer, who took the whole event incredibly seriously.

Wednesday 7 September

I got the news I was hoping for today — Errol Alcott passed Glenn McGrath fit to play in the Test.

McGrath trained again and, although he felt a dull ache in his elbow, he said he was fine, and Alcott is confident McGrath will be able to make it through the 5 days without a serious risk of breaking down.

Before we confirmed McGrath's inclusion, I told him he had to be honest with us about not just his elbow, but also his general fitness. I said we could not afford a repeat of the Old Trafford Test, where his lack of bowling fitness meant he ran out of steam during England's first innings. McGrath assured me he would be fine, and that was good enough for me. He is an honest player, and I know that, although he is desperate to play, he will also not want to let his team-mates down by playing when he is not fit.

Matthew Hayden's wife, Kellie, has turned up unexpectedly. After spending the first part of the Test series — up to the end of the third Test — here, she returned home, but she is back now to lend some support to her husband in the last week of the trip. If it helps him emerge from his run drought, the journey will have been worthwhile.

With a day to go before the Test starts, John Buchanan has decorated the dressing room, covering the walls with faxes and emails wishing us luck. Reading them makes me realise both how much support we have back home, and how much this series has captured the public's imagination.

Here are just a small number of the hundreds of notes we have received:

Dear Ricky, Gilly and Boys

We are all supporting you and pray you can beat the Poms in this Test. As a cricket fan from way back I am very proud of you all. Please don't be intimidated by these people — you are the best team. Just know that although we can't be there, we are with you in spirit.

Now that you lulled the whole of England into a false sense of security the final Test is going to be one to remember. Just like the first Test, I'm sure they will choke and you guys will smash them.

I can't wait to see the English faces when the full force of the best Test team is unleashed and they are left in your wake. Go Aussie.

YOUR SKILLS HAVE NOT GONE
THEY ARE WITH YOU STILL
SO STAND TALL AND STRONG
AND THE POMMIES YOU'LL KILL!!!

We know you can do it; we are with you all the way.

Guys

I'm behind you all the way. Among some friends who think England have the edge I have become very aggressive and told them that I still believe in the Aussies. Don't relent. I absolutely love cricket, it is more than a game, it is an art. Each of you in the team has a special talent and more than that you have something more special — that is, the baggy green. When I see the baggy green my eyes light up and I think this person is a master of the art of cricket and an awfully successful one to be able to be in the Aussie team.

My eyes will continue to be glued to the TV till 2–3 a.m. every night watching you guys demoralise the English team in the Test at The Oval. Play your natural game and let your style do the talking. C'mon Aussie c'mon.

Thursday 8 September

Fifth Test, The Oval, London, day 1: England 7–319 (Strauss 129, Flintoff 72, Warne 5–118) v Australia.

We did okay today. We were not outstanding, but taking 7 wickets was a solid effort on an excellent pitch, and if we can finish off

England's innings quickly tomorrow morning we can dictate the course of the match if we post a sizeable first-innings score.

Not for the first time on this tour, our man of the day was Shane Warne. On a first-day pitch offering him very little, he almost single-handedly earned us a foothold in the match with a 5-wicket haul.

My main disappointment was that, after I lost my third successive toss, we still managed to be off the pace in the first hour of the Test, as we had been at Edgbaston, Old Trafford and Trent Bridge. With the ball running like greased lightning over the outfield, the score mounted quickly, as every error in line and length was punished. But for Warne, who brought us the priceless twin assets of control and wickets, we might be out of the match already.

The day did not start too well for me. I have never been one to worry about things that are yet to happen, but maybe I was guilty of that last night, because I slept really badly, tossing and turning and feeling really restless, and when my alarm went off at 6.45 I could not believe it was time to get up.

The journey to the ground did not help my mood — it was a long and tortuous one because of the traffic, and we did not arrive until 8.45, which was a bit later than we'd planned. It meant warm-ups and pre-match practice were a bit rushed before the 10 o'clock toss.

I called heads, as I always do, and my heart sank when match referee Ranjan Madugalle said the coin had come down tails. I thought our best chance to win was to score heavily in the first innings and then put England under pressure through Shane Warne, as we did here 4 years ago, when we made 641 and won by an innings. With the sun shining and conditions set fair today, it was no surprise that England chose to bat first — that meant we had to do things the hard way.

I have almost run out of superlatives for Warne. He was brilliant, varying his pace and flight and bowling over after over. He tired towards the end of the day, but that was hardly surprising given the amount of work he'd done.

All too often on this tour our bowlers have been unable to execute the plans we have come up with, but that is not a charge we could lay against Warne today. His first 4 wickets all came as a result of plans he executed perfectly.

For Marcus Trescothick we left the point area vacant to entice him to push at the ball in search of a single. He did so, but his failure to execute the shot correctly saw him edge to slip, where Matthew Hayden took a sharp catch.

Michael Vaughan likes to whip the ball away through the onside, against the spin of Warne, and we deliberately left that area vacant at the start of his innings to try to encourage the shot — in the hope of a miscue. His first scoring stroke was uppish in that area, but he was still keen to play it, so we stationed a man at midwicket and he obliged by chipping the ball into Michael Clarke's hands.

Ian Bell is an uncertain starter, especially against Warne, so we crowded him with close fielders. He looked nervous, and was trapped lbw playing outside a skidding delivery. When Kevin Pietersen came in, Warne consistently pitched the ball on or outside his leg-stump, trying to entice him to hit against the spin. When he could no longer resist the temptation, he was beaten by a dipping leg-break and was bowled all ends up.

If that work by Warne was impressive, the downside was Shaun Tait's first couple of spells, which were very ragged and allowed England to get away from us during the morning session. Tait redeemed himself with an excellent burst after tea — he found some reverse swing at high pace and trapped Paul Collingwood lbw with a toe-crushing yorker.

England did pick Collingwood as their replacement for Simon Jones. The choice of a batting all-rounder to replace a frontline bowler was a conservative selection, confirming my view that the draw is top of their priority list. The selection also meant they have a long batting line-up, and although we took 7 wickets, Geraint Jones — who made an excellent 85 at Trent Bridge — is still at the crease.

Warne was flexing his right shoulder more and more as the day went on, but I have no worries about his fitness for the rest of the match. If we can get England's last 3 wickets with the new ball tomorrow without having to call on him again, and then bat for 2 days, that should allow him plenty of rest before he has to bowl again later in the match. I found out this evening that he bowled 72 overs in the Test here 4 years ago; he may be required to do something similar now if we are going to win.

Glenn McGrath had a solid first day back in the side. At one stage I was worried about over-bowling him, but he seemed to get through the day pretty well. By mid-afternoon, thanks to a combination of Tait's early waywardness and my desire to use McGrath against Michael Vaughan, he had bowled 14 overs, but when I asked him if he was okay I could not get the ball out of his hands. He did not let us down, picking up the vital wicket of Andrew Flintoff, caught at slip forcing off the back foot, another dismissal we planned for.

Michael Clarke found the day in the field hard going, with his back again causing him some pain, and while the rest of the players relaxed in the dressing room after play, he headed straight back to the hotel for a session in the pool. His regime is now to swim before and after every day's play to try to ease his back condition. I hope he will not have any serious difficulties through the rest of the match.

Friday 9 September

Fifth Test, The Oval, London, day 2: Australia 0–112 (Langer 75*) trail England 373 (Strauss 129, Flintoff 72, Warne 6–122) by 261 runs.

We took a calculated gamble this evening. With Matthew Hayden and Justin Langer going well for the first time in the series, we decided to accept the offer to leave the field for bad light straight after tea, so we lost the final session of play.

We — me, Adam Gilchrist, Langer and Hayden — discussed the matter during the tea break, and we decided that, although the two batsmen at the crease were going well, it might be a different story for a new batsman if either man was dismissed.

The quality of the light was poor, Andrew Flintoff was starting to reverse swing the ball at around 150 km/h, and if a new player was required to start an innings there was no guarantee he would find it easy.

If we had lost 2 or 3 wickets in that sort of period it would have undone much of the good work Hayden and Langer had put in, and with 3 days left there was no need to put that work at risk for the sake of an extra hour's batting. We can make up much of the time lost this evening over the remaining 3 days, and with the pace of modern Test cricket it is unlikely we will have to wait until the last few minutes of the final day for a result.

If that does happen and we end up just short of a series-levelling victory, it will be apparent that we made the wrong decision this evening, but we cannot worry about that now. We decided the best way to press on to secure that victory was to bat when conditions are in our favour, and we hope that will be the case tomorrow when play resumes.

Nothing was said before we began our innings, because everyone knew how important our innings was without needing to be told. We have not scored 400 in an innings once in this series, and it was patently obvious that we had to do that — and go well beyond that — now.

As a batting group, our talk before the match was about getting back to the methods that earned us success both as individuals and as a team, and that is what Hayden and Langer set out to do today. Both played positively without being reckless, with Langer assuming the dominant role.

He was especially determined not to let Ashley Giles dictate terms to him. The left-arm spinner has dismissed him twice in this series — caught at short leg as he looked to defend — but today he adopted a more positive approach, twice hitting Giles over long-on for six, something that will pose questions for both Giles and Michael Vaughan.

If we can hit Giles out of the attack, as we did at Lord's in the first Test of the series, it will force Vaughan to turn back to his three frontline fast bowlers — Flintoff, Stephen Harmison and Matthew Hoggard — and with their workload already increased because of Simon Jones's absence, we could make England regret their decision not to select a bowler as his replacement.

Harmison was already showing signs of Jones's absence today. He bowled well within himself, maybe aware of the extra workload he was likely to face, and as a result he was much less of a threat than he has been at other times in the series.

It was great to see Hayden hang in there this afternoon. Let's hope that now he can build on the start he's made and score his first Test hundred in over a year. He looked nervous before lunch, as did Langer — both men played some ambitious shots in the first half-hour of their innings.

After the interval, Langer found his touch and played some delightful shots, and Hayden looked as solid as he ever has through the Test series, and although he did not try to crash the ball around the ground, he did not look like getting out either. His solidity must have been as ominous to England as it was reassuring to us.

England's substitute fielder, Gary Pratt — the man who ran me out at Trent Bridge — made a couple of appearances during the afternoon, but only for short periods. On one occasion the television cameras homed in on me on the dressing room balcony, watching for my reaction, but they were out of luck if they wanted me to start jumping up and down. If the reason for Pratt or any other substitute being on the ground is legitimate, or it is for just a short while during a toilet break, I don't have a problem; my complaint is when he comes on for bowlers before and after spells so they can have a shower, or a rub-down or a warm-up from the physiotherapist. That is where I draw the line. I saw on the Internet this evening that ICC

Chief Executive Malcolm Speed has accepted that point, and says he is keen to clarify the issue with all captains. I hope he does, and I look forward to his phone call.

England got a few more runs than we would have liked in the morning session, even though we managed to dismiss Geraint Jones in the second over of the day. I dropped Hoggard with a tricky catch low to my left at second slip, and Giles and Harmison mixed luck with bold strokeplay to frustrate us.

Giles was caught behind off Glenn McGrath, only to be reprieved by umpire Rudi Koertzen. This was the second time he had given an England batsman a let-off in this match. Yesterday he gave Andrew Strauss not out when the batsman edged a catch behind the wicket — on both occasions he said he did not hear the edge or see a deflection. Both edges were fine, so it is understandable that he did not see any deviation off the bat, but both were audible to fielders close to the bat — I heard a noise in the Strauss instance from cover and heard a noise from Giles from slip.

I was angry for a short while when Giles was given not out, and had a rant to myself at the end of the over. McGrath said that before the start of his next over he also heard Koertzen swearing at himself for his failure to make the correct decision. He knew he'd made a mistake, but by then, of course, it was too late to make amends.

Earpieces for the umpires that allow them to hear the sounds picked up by the stump microphones were trialled at last year's Champions Trophy in this country, and the umpires I have spoken to who used them felt they were an excellent aid to correct decision-making in issues like catches at the wicket. Despite that positive feedback, I am not aware of that technology being used since then. I am not sure why that is.

By the end of the day I was very tired, even though I'd been on the field for less than 90 minutes. I resorted to a couple of sleeping tablets last night, but still, for the second night running, I had a very poor night's sleep. I'm hoping it will be third time lucky tonight.

Saturday 10 September

Fifth Test, The Oval, London, day 3: Australia 2–277 (Hayden 110*, Langer 105) trail England 373 by 96 runs.

Matthew Hayden finally returned to form at Test level today, producing a brilliant unbeaten hundred that, together with a three-figure score from his opening partner Justin Langer, has given us a great platform to press on from tomorrow.

Hayden has been under intense pressure, and although I always felt he would score heavily again, his continued lack of success on this trip must have tested the selectors' patience.

His success today was based on doing what we talked about before the match: remembering the methods that brought us success as individuals and as a team in the past.

Hayden's success has always been based on three simple principles: showing the full face of the bat to the bowler by looking to play as straight as possible; sweeping spin hard and often; and knowing what to play at and what to leave alone outside the off-stump.

I saw examples of those principles in our practice sessions, but not in matches on this tour. Over the past 2 days, though, he has produced them with increasing assurance, and I am so happy for him and proud of the way he has come through what must have been an incredibly frustrating and worrying time in his career.

I also think his wife, Kellie, deserves some credit for this innings. She flew to London to surprise him earlier this week, maybe sensing that he needed some support, and the scoreboard shows her journey has been worth it.

At the other end for the first half of Hayden's innings was his little partner in crime over the past 4 years, Justin Langer. It was here, at The Oval, that they first opened together in Tests, adding 150, and the magic returned now as they added 185.

Langer was the more positive of the two players on a day when both passed landmarks — Langer reached 7000 Test runs and Hayden reached 6000. The fact that Hayden is the third-quickest Australia batsman of all time to that mark in terms of innings played shows the form he had been in prior to his run of modest scores in this series.

Their success, and the stand I had with Hayden — we added 79 — showcased the virtues of batsmen making hundreds and building partnerships, two elements that have been lacking for us for much of this series. We have taken advantage of England's lack of a fourth frontline seam bowler in this Test, and if we can ram home that advantage tomorrow by pressing on, we have a great chance to win the Test.

I would be the first to admit that we had the rub of the green today. Langer looked very close to lbw from the first ball of the day, Damien Martyn was given not out to a caught behind appeal when a delivery from Andrew Flintoff ran off the face of the bat as he tried to cut, and I survived a bat-pad appeal to silly point when I did edge the ball.

My bat-pad was curious, because when I got down to the non-striker's end, the umpire who gave me not out, Billy Bowden, basically asked me whether or not I nicked the ball.

'Good decision, that?' he said.

'I hit it,' I replied.

'Must have been a faint one, then,' said Bowden.

'Yes, but I did hit it.'

Soon after that exchange we headed back to the pavilion for one of the many rain interruptions that broke up play. After a few minutes, Bowden came to see me in the dressing room and continued our chat.

'Told you, you didn't hit it,' he said. 'I've seen all the slow-motion replays and spoken to the match referee and everyone agrees you didn't hit it. You hit the bottom of your pad with your bat.'

By now I had seen the replays as well, and they seemed to confirm that I *had* hit it, something I knew already.

'Sorry, Billy, but I did hit it,' I said.

A number of decisions in this series have started to convince me that technology in some form does have a part to play after all, despite my earlier misgivings on the subject.

I like the human element, but during this match there have been at least four occasions when the umpires have got caught decisions wrong, something that might not have happened if they had earpieces connected to the stump microphones to allow them to hear faint edges — and remember, this was trialled last year.

On the other side of the coin, the human element produces both good and bad decisions, and they do seem to even themselves out over time. Damien Martyn's escape came after twice being given out lbw earlier in the series when he had in fact edged the ball onto his pads, and I had suffered the same fate at Trent Bridge.

I feel no guilt about standing my ground after I offered up the bat-pad chance. My view is that the umpire is there to make the decision, not me. Adam Gilchrist thinks differently, and will always walk off if he knows he has hit the ball. As I always say, he is entitled to his approach, but that is not my way.

I felt in great form and was middling the ball really well when I got a brute of a ball from Flintoff that bounced much more than I expected, and I ended up fending it low to gully. That sort of thing can happen when you are in good touch; on the other hand, Martyn, who has been struggling for runs, played and missed at several deliveries tonight but is still there to start again tomorrow. That is the joy — and the frustration — of this great game.

Our task now is to add to the platform built for us by Hayden and Langer. Our approach will be positive, because that is the way we have played our best cricket in recent years, and if we succeed, we will give ourselves a chance to put England under pressure in their second innings.

Sunday 11 September

Fifth Test, The Oval, London, day 4: Australia 367 (Hayden 138, Langer 105, Flintoff 5–78) trail England 373 and 1–34 by 40 runs.

Another batting collapse and more bad light have loosened our grip on The Ashes still further. With just one day left in the series, we need clear skies and a miracle from our bowlers if we are to win this match.

We began the day discussing how we should try to bat during the day. Should we look to press on quickly, try to get into the lead as soon as possible and leave ourselves plenty of time to bowl England out a second time, or bat conservatively up to lunch, by which time we should have drawn level, then look to press on from there?

We settled on the latter strategy, but our plans were derailed by sustained, high-quality seam and swing bowling from Andrew Flintoff and Matthew Hoggard, together with overcast conditions.

The England duo moved the ball around, took our last 7 wickets for just 44 runs and left us trailing rather than leading after the first innings; then, with the gloomy skies persisting all day, we got precious little chance to get a crack at England's batsmen.

Conditions were not easy to bat in. The light was so poor that as early as the fourth over of the day the umpires offered Matthew Hayden and Michael Clarke the chance to leave the field. Unlike day two, this time we had to stay on the field, because we could not afford to lose any more time out of the match.

The ball moved around for the England bowlers; the Flintoff delivery that trapped Hayden lbw seamed back sharply. On the other hand, Simon Katich, Adam Gilchrist and Clarke were left to reflect on very extravagant strokes that cost them their wickets at a time when we needed major contributions from them.

Given the amount of time we have now lost in this match, I spent some of the afternoon wondering if we had made the right decisions in coming off the field on days two and three when we were offered to chance to do so. Maybe we would act differently now if we could have our time again, but no one, not even the local weather forecasters, predicted the level of disruption we have experienced in the past 3 days, and we did what we thought was right at the time. It is easy to be wise after the event.

The quality of the light was a constant issue when we took to the field after lunch for England's second innings. I opened up with Glenn McGrath, but before the second over I asked umpire Rudi Koertzen if it was bright enough for Brett Lee to bowl.

'You tell me,' he said.

'No, Rudi, I'm asking you. It's your call,' I replied.

When he answered 'Yes', I threw Lee the ball, but midway through McGrath's next over the umpires told me the light had deteriorated and we could only stay on if I replaced Lee with a slower bowler. I turned to Shane Warne, but even that was not enough to keep us on the field much longer, and we went off for an early tea.

There was precious little breeze to blow the clouds away, and it was frustrating to sit on the dressing room balcony and stare down at the ground, knowing there was nothing we could do to stop more and more time being lost from the match.

Despite those frustrations, we managed to retain our sense of humour, as we showed in the late afternoon when we got back onto the field for one brief period. McGrath suggested that we should emphasise how bright it was by wearing sunglasses. It was a decent plug for our various sponsors, but the gloom meant we all had to remove them before a ball was bowled.

Even though we were desperate to be on the field, I have no problem with the way the umpires dealt with the issue of bad light this afternoon. Using their light meters, they set a mark at which they deemed the light was unacceptable when they offered us the chance to come off on day two, and they have stuck to that mark for the rest of the match. They have been consistent and fair to both sides.

If we get a full day's play tomorrow, and that is a big if, there are 98 overs left in the match. That means, realistically, we have to bowl England out in around 50 or, at worst, 60 overs if we are to give ourselves enough time to chase down whatever runs we will need to win the match and square the series.

It is a big task, but it is by no means beyond us. We will obviously have to rely on our two biggest guns, Shane Warne and McGrath, but if we can get on a roll early on and create some panic in the England dressing room, anything is possible. And if we have a realistic chance of getting whatever the target is, I want to see us chase it to the end. If we have to risk losing the series 3–1 in order to give ourselves a chance of retaining The Ashes, that is a risk worth taking.

There was one piece of good news amid the gloom. Security manager Reg Dickason told me the authorities have apprehended a person believed to be responsible for the death threats made against me in the wake of the Old Trafford Test. I have not given the matter much thought since Dickason first briefed me, but I know it will make Rianna happy to hear that the threat against me has been dealt with.

Monday 12 September

Fifth Test, The Oval, London, day 5: Australia 367 and 0–4 drew with England 373 and 335 (Pietersen 158, Giles 59, Warne 6–124).

We have lost The Ashes. I hoped I would never have to write that, but it is a reality after a day that summed up the series for us.

We had our chances but failed to take them, and England were good enough to not just claw their way to safety but to reach it in some comfort, thanks to an amazing performance from Kevin Pietersen.

He hammered seven sixes, the most in Test history in a single innings against Australia, and together with Ashley Giles shut the door on our hopes of getting out of jail at the eleventh hour.

Pietersen is such a powerful player that he even managed to hit mistimed shots for four or six, and as he scored at an incredible rate, he took the game away from us, despite another Herculean effort from Shane Warne and brave ones from Glenn McGrath and Brett Lee.

The fact that Warne is on the losing side in this series is a travesty, as there have been large chunks of this series where he has carried the side almost single-handedly. He took another 6 wickets in this innings, for a match haul of 12, and his overall figures for the series — 40 wickets and 249 runs — are both career-best marks.

Warne is the only player from our squad who can look at himself in the mirror and know he has played to his full potential; the rest of us have just hinted at the form we are capable of, and that has cost us the series.

The hardest thing about our defeat is that we know what went wrong: we failed with the bat, lacked penetration and control with the ball (Warne and McGrath excepted), dropped catches, bowled far too many no-balls and lost Glenn McGrath to injury for the vital Edgbaston Test.

But that was *what* went wrong; the reasons *why* we failed remain a mystery. England played well, putting us under pressure with bat and ball, and that was definitely a factor in the series loss. However, despite their excellence, we should still have been able to compete far more effectively than we did.

Even now, with the series loss confirmed, I still believe we prepared as well as we could. Our meetings were constructive, our plans were sound and our practice was intense, but despite all those positives, we could not put it all together on the field on a regular basis.

The reasons for those collective failures may be hard to establish, but one thing is certain: there will be some tough questions about our performances in the days, weeks and months ahead. I discovered that this evening, just minutes after the match ended.

As soon as I sat down in my post-match media conference, a reporter I have never seen before got to his feet, announced that he was from ABC Radio and asked me, 'Would Australia have won the series with a more positive and aggressive captain?'

With a question like that, the reporter obviously knew what he was talking about, so my reply was short and sweet: 'You tell me, mate, you must be the expert.'

If the ABC reporter was suggesting that by stacking the slip cordon with fielders we would have won the series, that is clearly rubbish. Our bowlers regularly failed to bowl to the fields we originally agreed on, and that inconsistency forced us onto the defensive. Although we had attacking plans for every England player, our inability to execute those plans forced them to be torn up.

That sort of question suggests that by the time I get back to Australia on Wednesday, the media will be asking other, serious questions about my future as captain. On that same agenda, I am sure, will be John Buchanan's future as coach — his current contract ends in the next few weeks — and the positions of several players in our squad.

If those questions are asked of me, I will respond in the same way to each of them. The fact is that when we arrived in the United Kingdom we were regarded as an outstanding outfit; 3 months down the line we have lost two Tests and suddenly the captain is useless, the coach is hopeless and the players are either not good enough, too old, or both.

I do not accept that. We have had a blip, and although the margin of this series loss probably flatters us, we have not gone from world-beaters to deadbeats in one series.

We underperformed massively, but the core of players in this squad knows that, and I remain convinced that we have the right men to put the record straight. I expect us to do that over the months that will follow — and I hope we do it with me as captain.

If the powers that be — the selectors and CA's Board of Directors — decide that a change of captain is required, that is their decision. I have no plans to walk away from the leadership role and have not given the idea of returning to the ranks a second's thought. I love the job, I believe I am doing it to the best of my ability and I believe in the group of players we have at our disposal. I am sure I have the support of the players and the support staff, and that is all that matters to me; the thoughts of any critics I may have do not concern me.

While the form of the side and my role within it are two issues that are sure to be debated ad infinitum over the next few weeks, another issue is the balance of that side. That is something I am sure the selectors will be reflecting on. Throughout the series it was obvious that England had more options with the ball than we did, and today was no different — we relied on Warne, McGrath and Brett Lee for most of our overs.

The best way for us to get another bowler into the line-up is to pick an all-rounder, but I know the selectors want to ensure that the player selected is worth his place in either discipline. That sets the bar high, but it is better to do that than to have a bits-and-pieces cricketer who is not quite good enough as a batsman or as a bowler. This series has shown that a vacancy exists in that area — it is up to the likes of Shane Watson and Andrew Symonds to step up and demand selection in that role.

The day ended on a flat note, but before we left the hotel this morning I stressed to the players that we all had to believe we could win. I said that anyone who did not think we could win should not bother coming to the ground — I'm happy to say the bus was full when we left, and our play throughout the day reflected our belief.

We knew England, with one hand on the Ashes urn, would be nervous, and with Warne, Lee and McGrath outstanding before lunch, we really felt we had England on the rack.

Looking back, the timing of the lunch interval did us no favours. After going 40 minutes without a wicket at the start of the day, we got on a roll, and with Lee charging in and unsettling Pietersen just before that break, England were rocking.

After the break, Lee could not quite match the accuracy of his pre-lunch burst, Pietersen counterattacked, and the target gradually moved beyond our range as he pressed on.

I asked for us to play with smiles on our faces and to enjoy the day whatever happened, because we are all lucky to have the opportunity to play for Australia, and we managed that. Even Simon Katich remained cheerful, despite copping some fearful blows at short leg.

One of them, when Paul Collingwood pulled a ball from Warne into Katich's ribs, gave us a moment of concern followed by a laugh. Katich is as tough as teak and barely flinched as the ball ricocheted off his body, but 5 minutes later he came to me and said he was in trouble. 'I'm spitting out blood, Punter. Can I go off to get it checked out?'

I was worried that he may have cracked a rib, so I sent him off immediately. He returned just 2 overs later with a broad grin.

'False alarm,' said Katich. 'Turns out I bit my tongue as I ducked for cover and that's what caused the blood.'

After the match, as I carried out my numerous post-match interviews for television and radio on the ground, the England team did a lap of honour, and although the sight of them getting all the applause and the acclaim hurt, I have to admit that they deserved it all. They outplayed us, and they deserve their success — as the saying goes, winners can do what they like and losers can please themselves.

When I eventually got back to the dressing room there was a subdued atmosphere, with Warne in his seat by the door looking shattered — not just that we lost, but also because he had given so much for the cause. McGrath was also inconsolable, because, as he said, the two Tests he missed were the two we ended up losing.

Everyone was hurting, and that is good. Knowing what it feels like to lose is the best incentive to win, and I hope this defeat will motivate us in the same way our loss in India did in 2001. After that we went on a run of 16 series without defeat, and if this loss can be the catalyst for another run, something positive will have come out of it.

Gradually the mood lightened. Steve Bernard made presentations of signed shirts to our baggage master, Trevor Crouch, and our bus driver, Geoff Goodwin, Michael Kasprowicz cranked up his iPod and the England players came in for a beer and a chat at the end of a superb contest. The cricket has been hard on the field, but the spirit between the two sides has been excellent, and that was reflected in the scenes in the dressing room tonight.

Andrew Strauss, Stephen Harmison and Andrew Flintoff chatted with Justin Langer and Matthew Hayden, Simon Jones and Matthew Hoggard did the same with Jason Gillespie, McGrath and Kasprowicz, and there were plenty of other similar scenes for more than an hour, until at 10 o'clock we headed for our bus and the trip back to the team hotel, leaving the England players to carry on their celebrations — if we had won the Test we would have been at the ground for many more hours.

For us, all that was left to do was pack for our flight tomorrow morning. It was an anticlimactic end to a day that promised much but ultimately delivered nothing.

Tuesday 13 September – Wednesday 14 September

We left the hotel at 9.15 so it was a relatively early start to get up, pack, have breakfast and pay the bill before heading to Heathrow and the Qantas flight home.

We were all excited about the prospect of going home, as most of us had been away for more than three months, but at the same time there was a degree of uncertainty about the type of reception we would receive. England were starting out on an open-top-bus trip around London as we checked in for the flight, and we were sure there would be nothing like that in store for us as the first Australia side to lose an Ashes series in almost two decades.

A few of us chatted about the possible reaction to our defeat at home, over a few drinks at the hotel bar on Monday night. We knew we would cop some criticism — and rightly so — but we also wondered whether the public would give us some credit for our part in what has been an amazing series.

I sat next to former Test opener Michael Slater on the flight, and for the first part of the trip we shared a drink and chatted about the series. He said that the common theme in all the conversations he'd had was that it had been a fantastic series, but through it all — apart from at Lord's — we had been the side that had lost the big moments whenever they came about, something completely out of character with our previous efforts. I agreed, and although neither of us was certain why it kept happening, I thought we'd perhaps built up the series too much and put too much pressure on ourselves to perform. That in turn inhibited some of our natural attacking instincts and the result of that is now history.

After that chat I fell asleep and stayed that way for most of the journey, so I missed the chance to say a final goodbye of the tour to Jason Gillespie, Shaun Tait, Adam Gilchrist, Justin Langer, Michael Kasprowicz and John Buchanan, who all left the flight in Singapore to catch connecting flights to their respective home ports. Hopefully I will see them all sooner rather than later during the summer, and I will speak to Buchanan by phone next week to pick through the tour in more detail.

When we finally landed in Sydney I was met by Michael Brown of Cricket Australia and the media manager for the first half of our tour, Belinda Dennett, and they guided me to my final task for the trip: a media conference for the local television and newspaper reporters.

Brown told me beforehand that the feeling in Australia over the past couple of days had been a mixture of disappointment at our performance and an acceptance that we were beaten by the better side; also that we had taken part in one of the great series, which was reassuring. But the first question I faced was still a relatively hostile one, asking for my reaction to former fast bowler Dennis Lillee's call for me to be replaced by Shane Warne as captain.

Lillee is entitled to his opinion and is better qualified than most to have one, but I reiterated my desire to stay in charge. I love the job and want the chance to make amends for our defeat in this series, starting with an improved performance in the Super Series next month. During The Ashes we did not have that ruthless edge that has been one of the trademarks of this side in recent years, and although it will not be a case of waving a magic wand to get it back, it will be my job, along with Buchanan's, to try to see that we recapture it. I am hopeful that a few days at home for everyone and the chance to reflect on our failings will start us on the road to recovery.

After the media conference I was able to slip away into the night. I hailed a taxi and headed home, and it felt great to finally walk through the front door to be greeted by Rianna — who'd flown home two days ahead of me — and her family as we celebrated her sister Hayley's birthday.

I have not really had a chance to properly evaluate my performance during the Test series, but whatever conclusions I eventually come to, I know I underperformed.

Apart from my hundred at Old Trafford, I made 61 at Edgbaston, 48 at Trent Bridge and 42 at Lord's, as well as 35 in the final Test at The Oval, and that is not like me. Normally when I get established in that way I go on and make a big score, but on these occasions I did not. From the second Test onwards I always felt in good form but then got out, more often than not to poor shot selection, and as most of the rest of the squad had similar failings, it is doubly frustrating to look back on.

If I had my time again, would I change any of the decisions I made? I do not believe so, and I do not believe you can live your life thinking that way. When I made my decisions — shot selections, bowling changes, field settings, putting England into bat at Edgbaston and so on — I did so after putting a lot of thought into each one and I believed I was doing the right thing at the time. You cannot go through life with regrets, but what you can do is reflect on your decisions and if any of them produced negatives then that is something to store away for next time.

As for the future, there is very little time to draw breath. Rianna's brother is getting married in Sydney this weekend and then, next week, it is time to start training again for the Super Series. It is a tough schedule after such a draining tour, but in some ways it might be the best thing for us, to get back into action and try to exorcise the ghost of this Ashes series as quickly as possible.

Player profiles

AUSTRALIAN TEAM

Michael Clarke

Even though Michael Clarke's international career has barely started, he has already decided when he wants to retire.

It was during the final Test of the Ashes tour at The Oval that he told me: 'I'm going to retire on the same day as you.'

I hope he does not follow through on that because, as I am several years older than him and not likely to play until I am 40, it would mean Australian cricket would miss out on several extra years of a player who is overflowing with talent.

Although his first-class record with New South Wales was not stunning before he was called up for the senior international side, I was all in favour of his elevation. I saw a precocious talent that would only benefit from working with and playing against better players, and that is exactly what has happened. He has soaked up knowledge and experience like a sponge and if he stays around that will benefit Australian cricket in the long run.

His early call-up benefited him not only because it forced him to lift his game by exposing him to a higher standard of play — it also allowed him to address the major deficiency in his game at the start of his career: his fitness. He was by no means unfit, but he often found towards the end of an innings that if conditions were especially hot, he would cramp up. He worked with Australia's fitness trainer, Jock Campbell, and the results were quickly apparent. Clarke has since become one of the side's most dedicated trainers and his fitness levels have improved out of sight.

For such a talented player, it is amazing to see how nervous he gets before he plays in a game. He is always one of the first players down to breakfast in the morning, one of the first to want to go to the ground in the morning and one of the first to want to leave after play.

He has a mass of energy, which is why the back trouble he experienced in England was such a cruel blow. It disrupted his tour on two occasions and that disruption did his batting no favours.

The problem came about when he pushed himself and did a lot of bowling in the lead-up to matches, but I hope it does not encourage him to give up that part of his game. He is an effective left-arm spinner, as he has shown in India and Sri Lanka in the past 18 months, and as long as he manages his workload then I believe he should persevere, as the skill is a useful asset to himself and the team.

Another asset Clarke possesses is his flexibility, as he can bat anywhere in the top order. He opened with some success in last summer's VB Series against the West Indies and Pakistan, and he is equally at home in the middle order. In both positions his ability to hit through and over the infield means he can keep the scoreboard moving, while his temperament is rock solid. The best example of that came when he and Andrew Symonds saw us to victory in a crucial one-day game against Sri Lanka in Colombo in 2004, when Clarke played superbly against the wiles of Muttiah Muralitharan.

A former captain of the under-19 side, he has had a few nicknames even though he has been in the squad for less than three years. On the day he first played, as a late replacement for the suspended Darren Lehmann, someone in the dressing room called him 'Eminem', because at that time he had cropped blond hair in the style of the rap singer.

That name lasted as long as his hairstyle and since then he has been 'Nemo' (because when he first came into the side he was a little fish in the big pond of international cricket) and now 'Pup', the name that has stuck. It comes from the fact that he is still viewed as the young pup of the side, and I guess he will keep the name even when he becomes a senior member of the line-up in the same way Mark Waugh was always Junior, even when he had been playing for 10 years.

Clarke has definitely benefited from a spell of county cricket at Hampshire alongside Shane Warne. He did not get many runs in what were alien conditions for him, but the reports I got from team-mates and officials was that he maintained his enthusiasm and did a great job as an overseas professional in terms of the example he set.

Having said all that, I am not sure I would want Clarke to go back and play much more county cricket, especially if his back continues to trouble him. One of his major assets is the superb appetite he has for the game and I would always worry whether the treadmill of county cricket would dilute that quality.

Matthew Elliott

Matthew Elliott is an example of how fickle fate can be for even the best players.

In 1997 the tall, elegant, technically correct left-hander appeared to have the cricketing world at his feet. He made a maiden Test hundred on a tricky pitch at Lord's and followed that up with a superb 199 on an equally difficult surface at Headingley — when I made my maiden hundred in my first Ashes Test. He hit just about everything in the middle of the bat on that tour, and on the rare occasions when he did not, he either played and missed or miscued the ball into a gap.

Fast forward less than 2 years to the West Indies, and Elliott found himself up against Courtney Walsh and Curtly Ambrose on equally difficult surfaces. This time, rather than play and miss, the ball always seemed to find the edge of his bat. He had a miserable tour, and played only one more Test between then and the start of the Ashes tour of 2005.

It is not that he has been forgotten by the selectors: he earned a Cricket Australia contract in 2004 after a superb season for Victoria. It is just that opportunities for openers do not come along very often, and Elliott has been unlucky to be on the outer while Matthew Hayden and Justin Langer have piled up record after record.

On several levels, Elliott's career has been a series of 'what ifs'. If he had been born in another era, a time when the likes of Langer, Hayden, Michael Slater, Greg Blewett and Mark Taylor were not around, he may well have played more than 50 Tests. And he may have done that anyway had it not been for the chronic knee trouble that has affected him ever since he collided with Mark Waugh in Sydney during the 1996/97 Test against the West Indies, when he looked set for a century.

Fate even worked against Elliott when he was recalled to the side at the eleventh hour in 2004, when I suffered a family bereavement. He came home to Australia in the middle of his season playing county cricket for Glamorgan in the United Kingdom, and did not have any of his gear here so had to use borrowed equipment. On top of that he had to play on a poor surface at Darwin — and he made just 1 and 0.

Bad luck like that might make some people bitter, but Elliott has never come across that way to me. We have known each other for many years — we toured together with Young Australia to England in 1995. He was an intense character back then, and he has certainly mellowed since, but he has always had a very dry sense of humour and usually has a joke to tell or a funny observation to make.

As a result of his knee problems, Elliott is not as mobile in the field as he used to be, but that has not reduced his appetite for runs or his ability to score them. The lack of mobility may count against him if his name features again at the selection table, as might the fact that he is roughly the same age as Langer and Hayden. As far as I can tell, he still has the fire to play at the highest level, and if his off-season move to South Australia gets that fire burning even more fiercely, that can only be beneficial to Australian cricket.

Adam Gilchrist

In the whole history of cricket there has only been a handful of players who can be said to have changed the game, players who have altered the way it is thought of both tactically and as a spectator sport.

Donald Bradman was one such player thanks to his prolific run-scoring feats, Shane Warne is another thanks to his almost single-handed reinvention of the art of leg-spin bowling; and, thanks to his impact as a wicketkeeper–batsman, Adam Gilchrist can be added to that list.

When he came into the Test side in 1999, most teams around the world were happy if their wicketkeeper averaged 25 with the bat; if he averaged 30 then that was a bonus. Gilchrist's career average of more than 50 puts him in another dimension.

His batting skills have forced other Test sides to look around for players who can add valuable runs in the middle order, and specialist wicketkeepers with little or no batting aspirations have been consigned to the scrapheap. That is the Gilchrist influence on the modern game.

But to label Gilchrist as a batsman who keeps wicket would be unfair, because he is a genuine all-rounder whose ability with the gloves is often overlooked. Back in 1999, that ability as a 'keeper was well and truly under the microscope as he was following in Ian Healy's footsteps and faced the prospect of keeping to Warne, a skill in itself. These days, any mistakes he makes are highlighted, a sure sign that he does not make very many in the first place.

Given the impact he has made on either side of the stumps, it is amazing to think that he once contemplated giving up the gloves to concentrate on his batting. In his early days with his native New South Wales, his path was blocked by Phil Emery; but he was advised to maintain the extra string to his bow, and although he would have made it as a specialist batsman, he took that advice and, I am sure, has never regretted it.

It is easy to forget now but, throughout his career, Gilchrist has always had to deal with controversy. When he left New South Wales in search of new opportunities, he went to Western Australia and replaced Tim Zoehrer, a real fans' favourite. When he came into the Australia one-day and Test sides he displaced Ian Healy, another popular figure, and in 2000 he replaced the iconic Shane Warne as Australia's vice-captain.

Each situation created not just controversy but also pressure, because each one meant that the eyes of the cricketing world were on him, and I am sure there were people who would have liked to see him fail; to his credit, Gilchrist not only dealt with the situation but also won over the doubters.

Gilchrist's skill as a batsman is the way he plays instinctively. While some players might opt for a safety-first mentality, Gilchrist simply looks for the positive option whenever he can. If he is bowled a half-volley he tries to hit it for four or six, no matter what the situation; and he is always looking to put the pressure back on the opposition when he bats. It sometimes leads to his downfall, but it would be churlish to criticise him for his approach because it has won us so many matches over the years.

Away from the game he is shrewd, media-savvy and well-managed, and he knows his commercial value; but, like so many members of our squad, he never lets outside interests affect his cricket. He is well organised, and whenever he appears in cricket mode, he switches on instantly.

I have found him to be a superb vice-captain and he led the side superbly in my absence in India in 2004. From his position behind the stumps, he has the best seat in the house to tell how bowlers are performing and what batsmen are looking to do, and I believe we have formed a very good leadership team on the field.

We do not see eye to eye on everything, though. His policy of walking, the act of giving himself out rather than waiting for the umpire's decision when he knows he has edged the ball, is laudable but not something I agree with. He has taken his stand because he believes that the game has lost some of its old-fashioned values, while my view is that the umpires are there to make the decisions, not the players. We will agree to disagree on that one but I would never dream of ordering him to stop. All I would ever ask him to do is to not edge the ball in the first place.

How much longer we will be team-mates remains to be seen. I have no plans to pack the game in but during the Ashes series there were whispers in the media that Gilchrist was contemplating retirement in the year following the next World Cup, in the Caribbean in 2007. In one sense that is understandable, because he has a young family, and the fact he is based in Perth means that even during a domestic summer he tends to see them infrequently, because most of our cricket takes place in the eastern states.

Naturally I want him to play on as long as possible, and it is something he is physically equipped to do because he has always looked after himself. He has been helped in that regard by his wife, Mel, a dietician, but he keeps himself physically fit and handles the rigours of his dual life as a wicketkeeper–batsman exceptionally well. One of the first things any visitor to our dressing room will see on most evenings is Gilchrist sitting down, applying ice packs to his knees to soothe any inflammation, and it is a trick that has stood him in good stead throughout his career.

Players like Gilchrist only come along once in a lifetime and I am keen to ensure that we have his services for a few years yet, especially as two other players who form the foundation of our team — Shane Warne and Glenn McGrath — are likely to disappear sooner rather than later. If Gilchrist is keen on jumping off the international bandwagon and asked me for my opinion, I would advise him to play on in at least one form of the game for at least couple more years. That would allow him extra time at home while still contributing at international level, and it would also allow his successor the chance to bed down in whichever form of the game Gilchrist gives away, something Gilchrist did when he took over from Healy at one-day level two years before assuming the gloves in Tests.

Gilchrist is truly one of the all-time greats and although I know he is highly thought of by players, commentators and the public now, I am sure he will gain even more recognition when he does retire because his record will stand the test of time.

Jason Gillespie

The man nicknamed 'Dizzy' after the jazz trumpeter ended the Ashes tour with his career at a crossroads. He started the trip as one of our key assets but by the end of the tour had lost rhythm and form so completely that he was nowhere near the Test side.

I am no bowling expert so I am not sure what went so wrong for Gillespie, but if past evidence is anything to go by, it would be hasty to write him off as a force at international level just yet.

He has fought his way back from some terrible injuries throughout his career, including a stress fracture of the back and his now-infamous collision with Stephen Waugh in Sri Lanka in 1999 that saw him return home with a broken leg and wrist.

Those sorts of problems might have finished his career, but he returned to become a real force at international level and there is no reason why he cannot do that again once he has had the chance to get home, take stock of what has gone wrong and work to put things right.

Gillespie might come across as a knockabout bloke when he is interviewed in the media, but that easy-going exterior hides a player who is very ordered. He is meticulous in the way he prepares, loves routine and is the king of stretches before, during and after matches. And it is difficult to blame Gillespie for that because of the fair share of muscular and skeletal injuries he has suffered, and now he leaves nothing to chance. The reward for that thorough preparation is that these days he very rarely breaks down.

In the last few years Gillespie has definitely come out of his shell to develop a public persona, as for years he was a very private man, refusing all media interviews. He was not being rude, although it would have been easy to believe that he was; he simply hated publicity, and to an extent that is still true. When he got married a couple of years ago, the first most of us knew about it was after the event.

That gradual emergence of a public persona has gone hand in hand with his now-famous mullet. It started as a joke in a bar with Adam Gilchrist as the pair of them had a laugh about 1980s fashions, but Gillespie vowed to grow the mullet, and even though he has copped a massive amount of stick for it, he has kept it for the past couple of years.

The abuse and banter he gets because of his hair has made him even more determined to maintain it, but it has also cost him a few extra dollars in hair dye because for many years he has coloured his hair to hide premature greyness. That explains one of his lesser-used nicknames in the dressing room, 'Jamaican Brown', so called because that is the shade of dye he uses.

Gillespie's bloody-mindedness is illustrated not only by his refusal to get his hair cut but also by the way he bats. He has developed into a handy lower-order player and ended the Ashes tour on the brink of completing 1000 Test runs. But, although he is capable of expansive strokeplay, he loves blocking. When he was told last summer of a statistical study that listed him as one of the most boring batsmen in the world, he loved it; but, joking apart, the fact that he sells his wicket so dearly has helped make us an outstanding side. Last summer he made two Test 50s while his support of Damien Martyn against India in Chennai, when he batted for more than 4 hours as nightwatchman, was a key reason why we avoided defeat in that match and went on to win the series.

One of the most refreshing features of Gillespie is his total lack of airs and graces. In the dressing room environment he rarely holds back if he has something to say, and although he dresses well he is no clotheshorse or buyer of designer labels. A fan of World Wrestling Entertainment and heavy metal music, he is more at home having a beer in the dressing room after play than in a fancy restaurant.

His loss of form in the United Kingdom was inexplicable, at least to me. However, I do not believe a bowler of Gillespie's quality can suddenly lose his ability and I would never bet against him returning to the Australia side sooner rather than later.

Brad Haddin

There is little doubt in my mind Brad Haddin is probably one of the most improved cricketers in Australia in 2004/05.

His wicketkeeping and batting have come on in leaps and bounds, he benefited from the chance to lead New South Wales in the absence of Simon Katich on international duty, and he is now the clear favourite to take over from Adam Gilchrist behind the stumps for Australia when the time comes.

I was impressed with the way Haddin conducted himself right from the first time I met him. It was when he stood in for Adam Gilchrist during a VB Series match a couple of seasons ago, and when he introduced himself to me he called me Ricky. He could have called me Punter — most people do — but the fact that he took the trouble to use my first name suggested he had manners, as well as the obvious cricketing skill that earned his selection.

He has a great pair of hands, is athletic and, like Gilchrist, can bat in a variety of positions, either pinch-hitting at the top of the order or playing as a finisher towards the end of an innings. His success in either role is down to the way he strikes the ball so cleanly, something I saw at first hand a few years ago when he hammered the Tasmania side I was a part of for a quick-fire hundred at Bankstown in Sydney.

Having said all that, it would be unfair to build him up as the next Gilchrist. Our current international 'keeper–batsman is a once-in-a-lifetime cricketer, and if Haddin or whoever else eventually takes over from him is even half as good then we will be very lucky.

As a 'keeper Haddin's style is strikingly similar to that of Ian Healy, Gilchrist's predecessor behind the stumps, while as a batsman his clean striking makes it imperative to get rid of him early on. If he gets established he hits the ball hard and often.

He filled the role of reserve 'keeper during the Ashes tour with enthusiasm, which is a good effort, as that sort of position can be a tough one to occupy. There was no way he was ever going to displace Gilchrist, though, and the nature of the itinerary meant that there were limited opportunities for him to get any cricket under his belt.

The bonus for Haddin was that he was able to see at first hand how Gilchrist prepared for a Test match and he also had the chance to work with him, something he hadn't had the chance to do very much before, because usually when he was part of the squad it meant that Gilchrist was taking a break. Those factors should stand him in good stead if the selectors decide he is the man to eventually take over as the Test and one-day 'keeper.

Haddin has fitted into the Australian dressing room very easily over the past year or so, helped no doubt by the presence of several of his New South Wales team-mates, among them Michael Clarke and Brett Lee. One of his best qualities, apart from an excellent work ethic, has been his ability to laugh at himself and he cheerfully accepted the nickname 'Rockin' Rod' during the Ashes trip, which came about because some of the squad felt he had more than a passing resemblance to Rod Stewart thanks to his dyed blond hair.

Ian Harvey

When Ian Harvey finally packs cricket in, I am sure someone will write that he never reached the heights his ability suggested he should. And they would be right.

As a youngster he had it all: he was a batsman with correct technique, a full range of shots and power to match, a bowler capable of delivering outswingers at a lively pace, and a fielder who could throw equally well with either hand, something that earned him the nickname 'Freak'.

This amount of ability suggested that Harvey could become a regular at Test and one-day level for a decade, but it never quite happened for him and that is a shame — not just for Harvey, but also for Australian cricket, which has been looking for another all-rounder ever since the days of Keith Miller.

Like Miller, Harvey was also a talented Australian Rules footballer, and though he did not go on to play at the top level, I understand the West Coast Eagles were interested in signing him when he was a youngster. Anyone who has seen Harvey kick a football would have no trouble believing that.

Maybe one of the reasons he never developed into a world-class all-rounder in cricket was his spell playing county cricket. It definitely benefited him in one way: it helped him develop a well-disguised slower ball and a lethal yorker that made him one of the most effective 'death' bowlers in the county game.

On the other side of the coin, the day-in, day-out action took its toll on his body, and I am sure it contributed to making him less effective than he might otherwise have been.

Having said that, Harvey was superb for me during the World Cup campaign of 2003. He was not even supposed to be on the trip, but was drafted at the last minute when Shane Watson broke down with a back injury.

At the start of the tournament I sat him down and told him he was fortunate to be there, so he should make the most of it and be ready to play whenever the chance came along. To his credit, he did just that.

He bucked his image as a happy-go-lucky person who enjoys life by always being first to the nets and last to leave, fronting up for optional training and working harder than anyone else in the squad. He never let us down when he played, so when I had to tell him — on the morning of the final against India — that he was missing out, as Damien Martyn had been declared fit, it was one of the worst moments of my career. As I expected, he took the decision superbly, despite knowing it was probably his last chance to appear in a final — he had also missed out on selection for the final squad 4 years earlier.

He was within touching distance of a place in the Ashes squad in 2001, but I am sure that even he would admit that he didn't do quite enough to earn a Test berth. At his best, he would present a decent case for inclusion as a seam-bowling all-rounder the next time we opt to play two spinners, as we did in Sri Lanka in 2004 and against Pakistan in 2005. But it is doubtful that he will now get that chance, considering the fact that the selectors have opted for Andrew Symonds and then Watson in that role in the past 18 months.

Nathan Hauritz

Nathan Hauritz is a terrific bloke to have around the team. He has plenty of talent, and he also has a fantastic temperament, something I noticed about him as soon as we played alongside each other, in South Africa in 2002.

He was named as back-up spinner to Shane Warne on the one-day leg of that tour, my first series as captain. When Warne pulled up sore with a hamstring strain at the start of the series, Hauritz was suddenly thrust into the front line and he responded superbly.

His tidy spin kept the South African batsmen quiet and he also revealed a presentable batting technique — as well as nerves of steel, as he and Jimmy Maher earned a tie in the match at Potchefstroom by adding an unbeaten 36 inside 5 overs.

From that point, however, his career stalled. He toured again in late 2002, but with Warne fit once more and Brad Hogg jumping ahead of him in the one-day queue there were few opportunities for Hauritz. He found the door equally firmly shut in his native Queensland, where a reliance on seam restricted his chances at first-class level.

There is no doubting Hauritz's talent. A member of the Australian under-19 side that included Shane Watson and Michael Clarke, he also fitted in quickly and well to the Australian team environment. He's a nice lad with a good sense of humour, and was dubbed 'Finch' by Jason Gillespie because of his resemblance to that character in the *American Pie* films.

Hauritz may have suffered because of the increasing perception around the world that only 'unorthodox' finger spinners — people like Harbhajan Singh and Muttiah Muralitharan — can succeed on modern Test pitches. That may be true, but when Hauritz returned to the Test squad for the tour of India in 2004, I faced him in the nets and felt he was a better bowler than the one I'd seen 2 years earlier. He spun the ball more and bowled an attacking line outside off-stump. He did well when called upon in Mumbai following Warne's fractured thumb, but when he got back to Australia there was again the problem of lack of opportunity; his career may be reaching a crossroads.

Hauritz is still relatively young, especially for a spin bowler — he was not even 24 years old when the Ashes series ended — so he has time on his side. But on the other side of the coin, the emergence of Dan Cullen in South Australia must make him wonder what he has to do to press his claims for further international recognition: does he have to redouble his efforts to earn a prolonged chance at Queensland, or should he go in search of regular cricket elsewhere? Hauritz faces a testing period in his career, but if he comes through it and can again push for a Test or one-day spot, that can only benefit Australian cricket.

Matthew Hayden

I am hoping that Matthew Hayden's hundred in the final match of the Ashes series will mark the start of a new golden run of form for the giant opener.

He went 30 innings without a three-figure score at Test level but, now he has rediscovered the ability to reach that mark, I am counting on his innings at The Oval to whet his appetite for more success at the highest level.

All sorts of theories have been advanced for Hayden's loss of form, among them that he became too arrogant, that he lost his drive and had too many outside interests. I saw no evidence to support any of those claims during the period covered in this diary.

It is true he has become a published author after producing a cookbook that also includes sporting anecdotes and he has another book due out over the next year but that sort of activity is not unusual for a member of the Australia team. Most of the players have outside interests like that and we employ managers to deal with many of the issues that come from them. Hayden is no different in that regard and, like most players in the Test and one-day side, he is skilled at being able to switch onto cricket and away from any possible distractions as soon as he arrives at a ground to play or practise.

As to whether he lost his drive during that lean trot, that is nonsense. It is true he now has a young family, and that can change a player's priorities, but all through the 2004/05 season and the tour of the United Kingdom that followed, he struck me as being someone who was as hungry for runs as ever. The fact that they were not coming in massive amounts was a source of frustration for him, and us, but his desire to score them remained as strong as ever.

I definitely felt he — understandably — became more nervous as the run of low scores continued, but I never detected any slackening off of his desire to succeed. At one point during the New Zealand tour I noticed a message written on the back of his bat, so he could read it when he looked down before facing each ball. It said: 'This is worth fighting for', words that showed his continuing determination.

Earlier in his career Hayden was renowned for the amount of practising he did. He used to hit thousands of balls in the nets, and during the 2001 tour of the

United Kingdom his brother Gary arrived not just to watch the Ashes series but also to bowl at him.

These days Hayden spends less time in the nets and focuses on quality rather than quantity, as well as visualisation, where he will simply go out to the middle of the ground before a match, sit on the pitch with socks rather than shoes on and imagine how he will play each bowler.

That approach could be seen as a slackening off from his previously intense regime but I do not see it that way. If a player has scored the number of runs Hayden has over the past few years then he will know what works for him in terms of practice, and what does not, and he will prepare accordingly.

Hayden was originally rejected by the Australian Cricket Academy as a youngster and his response to that was an early illustration of his determination, as he set out to try to make himself into the perfect batsman. But although he scored mountains of runs at state level, he failed to translate that into international success until it dawned on him that, rather than trying to play every shot in the coaching manual, he only needed a few key shots to succeed. He honed them, and his outstanding record at international level is the result.

At its best, Hayden's method is very simple: he looks to drive down the ground whenever he can, he sweeps spinners hard and often, and he leaves the ball well outside the off-stump. It is often possible to tell whether or not he is in good form within a few deliveries if he shows the bowler the full face of the bat and shows good judgment over what he is playing at and what he is leaving.

There was a period in India in 2004 when bowlers got fed up with being bullied by him, and started to test his ego and his patience by bowling wide of the off-stump. They were fed up at being drilled back down the ground; they decided they would let Hayden chase the ball and they set defensive fields accordingly. For a while it worked, as Hayden looked to dominate outside his comfort zone, but his hundred at The Oval bore all the hallmarks of Hayden at his best.

Hayden's perceived arrogance is part of his make-up but I am not sure if arrogance is the right word for it. I think his love of a battle out in the middle is often perceived as arrogance when, in fact, it is simply his method of getting the adrenaline flowing, a method also favoured by Stephen Waugh and Brian Lara throughout their careers. Hayden has massive self-confidence, that is for sure, but it would have been impossible to scale the heights he has reached in the game without that.

In 2002, in the roasting hot conditions of Sharjah, he goaded Pakistan fast bowler Shoaib Akhtar into trying to bowl as fast as possible, in the knowledge that the bowler would run out of steam because of the oppressive conditions. Some might call that madness or arrogance; others might call it clever thinking. Whatever it is called, Hayden scored a century.

A practising Catholic, Hayden also discovered a love of golf in 2005, and I played several rounds with him during our tour of the United Kingdom. Golf is a perfect game for him because he loves the outdoors (hence one of his nicknames, 'Nature Boy') and is a keen surfer and fisherman. He even owned a boat with Andrew Symonds before it famously capsized a few years ago and the pair had to swim to shore through shark-infested waters.

That love of the outdoors means he can be terrible company if he is cooped up indoors and is bored, something that often seems to happen when he goes to the cinema. He is not one for movies with hidden meanings and messages, and he can be a terrible fidget if he is watching a film he does not enjoy.

I have shared many coffees with Hayden as he is one of my closest mates in the team, so maybe I am biased, but I am glad he is on our side as I would struggle to think of another player in the world I would prefer to have in my team instead of him.

Bradley Hodge

It has taken Brad Hodge more than a decade to go from a prodigy at the Commonwealth Bank Cricket Academy to the fringes of the Test side, and there must have been times when he wondered if he would ever get the chance to take that step up.

But to those of us who saw him in action as a teenager in Adelaide, his elevation to the Test squad for the tours of India — when I was injured — New Zealand and the United Kingdom came as no surprise.

I was in my second year at the Academy when 'Hodgey' arrived in 1993, and even then his talent was obvious. He had all the shots and plenty of time to play them, and when he finally made his first-class bow he exploded onto the scene with a stack of runs for Victoria, where he was affectionately known as 'Bunk' — because when he started playing for his state he still lived with his parents and slept in a bunk bed.

He was popular at the Academy, with a reputation as a good bloke who had a dry sense of humour but would never shoot his mouth off. He was a quiet guy, and maybe that aspect of his personality cost him in some ways. It meant he was not someone who was automatically thought of as captaincy material, and I reckon that is something that may have frustrated him at Victoria over the years, as more prominent players earned the chance of leadership roles ahead of him.

That quiet streak in him was never more evident than when he got a call-up for the tour of New Zealand at the start of 2005. He was happy to mix with the rest of the squad and was a popular member of the tour party, but he was equally comfortable with his own company, and I remember spotting him — on more than one occasion — lost in thought over a coffee in Cathedral Square in Christchurch ahead of the first Test of that series.

As captain of the squad, and someone who has played at international level for a decade, it is sometimes easy for me to forget how intimidating it must be for a new player to come into the Australian team, no matter how experienced he may be at state level. Looking back, maybe that was something Hodge felt in New Zealand. After all, try putting yourself in his position on that trip: you walk in as a fringe player and look around to see players with hundreds of Test wickets and thousands of Test runs under their belts, some of whom you know only by reputation. And at this point you have done little or nothing at the highest level. All we can do as a player group is try to make newcomers as welcome as possible; I think and hope we manage that pretty well.

Life as a reserve batsman, the role Hodge filled through 2004/05, can be a thankless task — especially on a short tour like ours to New Zealand, with three back-to-back Tests and no cricket in between — but I liked Hodge's dedication, and not just to his role as twelfth man, with its endless ferrying of sweaters and drinks on and off the field. He maintained his fitness with real zeal, and I even saw him head off to the gym in Auckland during the final Test of the tour, at 7 o'clock in the morning, when his last chance of a Test cap on the trip had already gone.

He has always been a natural sportsman, playing reserve grade football for the Melbourne Demons in the mid-1990s, but his obvious desire to work hard in the gym, even when there was no prospect of an immediate call-up, gave me the right signal about him. He clearly saw his tour selection as the start of something rather than an end in itself. And that hard physical conditioning work benefited him in another way, too: it meant that when he had an operation on a longstanding hernia problem at the end of the New Zealand tour, he was able to get back to full fitness quickly. That, in turn, allowed him to play the first half of the 2005 UK season for county side Lancashire before the Ashes series, and meant he was fully acclimatised at the start of the tour.

Hodge had some wilderness years, when it seemed he would never fulfil his early potential, but he has definitely benefited from time playing county cricket — he led Leicestershire with some success before moving to Lancashire. I always think players can go one of two ways when it comes to county cricket: they can either be ground down by the sheer number of matches played in the United Kingdom or (and this seems to happen to batsmen especially) take their game forward thanks to the number of innings they get to play in varying conditions and situations. Hodge has fallen into the latter category, and it really has helped him kick on. It has also given him the chance to mature by taking leadership roles he missed out on at Victoria.

Hodge is talented and ambitious, and having quality players like him constantly demanding selection can only benefit us. It keeps those players already with Test and one-day berths on their toes, and that has been one factor behind our success for the past decade at international level.

Bradley Hogg

I love having Brad Hogg around and I would say he has been a major reason for our success as a one-day side over the past 3 years.

Why? Well, first and foremost, he offers us something different with the ball. Left-arm wrist-spinners are not exactly commonplace in the international game, so there is an element of mystery about that style, which increases his effectiveness. He has a good googly, and has even bowled us to one-day wins on the subcontinent, where players are brought up on a diet of spin bowling. On top of that is his brilliance in the field, especially in the fielding circle, where his lightning pace over short distances acts as the ultimate deterrent to batsmen contemplating a stolen run. And, most of all, you know that whenever Hogg plays you will get 100 per cent from him. That might sound like an obvious requirement — everyone who plays for Australia should give it everything they have — but Hogg seems to get an extra something out of himself. I think this reflects the fact that he is especially thankful to get the chance to be a regular in the international line-up because it came relatively late in his career.

He debuted almost 10 years ago at international level when Mark Taylor was captain, but then faded away and worked for several years as a postman until the selectors resurrected him in the summer of the 2003 World Cup. It was a hunch on their part, and off-spinner Nathan Hauritz had done a good job in the one-day side in South Africa the previous season, but they were right. Hogg did not let us down, despite having to suddenly assume the role of the side's frontline spinner when Shane Warne returned home to face drugs charges. He was an unqualified success: only Sri Lanka's Muttiah Muralitharan, among the spinners, took more wickets during the tournament.

I supported that hunch, and not just for the reasons outlined above. Hogg also gave us valuable depth with the bat, and I knew his enthusiasm would be infectious. He is a fanatical trainer, a real workaholic at net practice who just runs and runs and runs — hence his nickname, 'Forrest Gump', from the film of the same name. It is not uncommon for him to ask to practise even when the team is given a day off, and occasionally coach John Buchanan and the management team have had to order him to rest. I reckon part of the reason for his boundless energy is that it is an outlet for nerves — he is quite a highly strung character. Whatever causes his hyperactivity, it rarely fails to lift others around him.

A country boy, Hogg can sometimes be guilty of opening his mouth before he engages his brain, a bit like Andrew Symonds, and that sometimes gives us all a laugh. When we were in Sri Lanka for the Champions Trophy in 2002, he was fed up with being pestered for autographs whenever he appeared in the lobby of the team hotel, and after a group of locals again pressed some paper and a pen in his hand he told us exactly what he thought of them: 'I don't mind signing autographs for most people, but these Colombians never stop bothering me,' he said.

On another trip to Sri Lanka, in 2004, we had a long bus trip from Colombo to Dambulla, and it was an occasion for another memorable 'Hogg-ism'. After we had been travelling for a couple of hours, we stopped for a refreshment break at a local roadhouse and he started chatting to team manager Steve 'Brute' Bernard.

'What's the time, Brute?' he asked.

'About 1.30, Hoggy,' came the reply.

'How much longer before we get to Dambulla then?'

'About another two hours, Hoggy.'

'So what time will we get there?'

After an exchange like that, you could not be blamed for not believing me when I say that Hogg is actually quite gifted when it comes to numbers. He has been studying for a qualification in financial management as he prepares himself for life after cricket, and during both the TVS Cup in India in 2003 and the one-day tour of the United Kingdom he took exams towards this qualification with fitness trainer Jock Campbell acting as invigilator for each 3-hour exam.

Hogg's dedication to his future career is admirable, but I personally hope it is a few years yet before he gets the chance to put his new-found skills into action. As long as he retains his sharpness and his enthusiasm for the game, I can see no reason why he should not be a part of the squad that tries to defend the World Cup he helped us win in 2003.

James Hopes

James Hopes is an example of the rewards hard work can produce. He started the summer of 2004/05 not sure whether he would get a regular slot in the Queensland side. After a series of impressive displays — not only for his state, but also for Australia A — he ended the summer with a place in the one-day side that toured New Zealand, and made a solid debut in Wellington.

It is true that he owed his place in the national squad to an injury to Shane Watson, but he would not have been selected if he had not put in performances beforehand.

I had never seen Hopes play before the tour, but as soon as I watched him in the nets and spoke to the other players and selectors, I realised that he offered us something we have not always had at one-day international level. As a batsman he can slot in anywhere: he is equally comfortable filling a pinch-hitting role at the top of the order or finishing an innings by finding the boundary under pressure, and as a bowler, his accurate medium pace can frustrate the opposition in the middle of the innings just when acceleration is needed.

Hopes is a bright lad and a talented sportsman at basketball and golf as well as cricket, and with one eye on his future and a life after cricket, he has also studied for a business degree. If his solid start at international level is anything to go by, Hopes may have to delay those plans for a while yet — he could have a role to play in Australia's one-day side if he can maintain his form.

Mike Hussey

You really have to take your hat off to Mike Hussey, because over the past 5 or 6 years he has totally transformed his game.

He started out as a solid, unspectacular opening batsman who was regarded as something of a specialist at the longer form of the game, but he has now enhanced his reputation in first-class cricket and become one of the best 'finishers' in the one-day game.

The finisher is a player who usually bats in the middle order and is adept at finding the gaps in the field in the latter stages of a one-day innings. He (or she) can rotate the strike through clever placement of the ball but also has the ability to hit boundaries to increase the scoring rate. Michael Bevan was a master at playing the role and did it with distinction for Australia for the best part of a decade.

When the selectors decided to look beyond Bevan for the future — for the 2007 World Cup, particularly — the player they chose to step into those shoes was Mike Hussey, and he has not disappointed. His performances in both New Zealand and the United Kingdom in one-day cricket were outstanding, and no less a judge than the great England all-rounder Ian Botham said publicly that he was mystified as to why Hussey was not a regular at Test level.

A call-up might not be too far away. Plenty of players in the current Test line-up have earned their chance after prolonged international exposure in the one-day side, and with Hussey a couple of years younger than both Matthew Hayden and Justin Langer, there may well come a time when he gets the chance to slot in at the top of the Australian Test order. Having said that, Hussey's versatility means he can slot in anywhere — which is also likely to count in his favour if the selectors are looking for top-order alternatives in the wake of the Ashes series.

Hussey is one player who has definitely benefited from a lengthy spell in county cricket. Playing on a day-in, day-out basis has been a key factor in allowing him to take his game to a new level, and it has also given him some experience of captaincy, at both Northamptonshire and Durham. I am sure that has also helped his development as a cricketer.

I like the versatility he brings to the one-day side, not only as a batsman who can play in a range of ways, but as someone who is capable of bowling some handy medium-pacers if conditions merit it. We have been screaming out for someone who can fill that role for us ever since Mark and Stephen Waugh retired, and while Hussey is not in their class as a bowler, he can still do a job for us in that style.

He has a dry sense of humour and is a qualified schoolteacher, which is handy, because it means he has experience in keeping order, something he often has to do in his role as a member of our social committee. 'Huss' is a lovely bloke, but he combines that with an ability to be ultra-competitive. His intensity and commitment on the field are almost legendary. Those qualities are likely to mean that we will see a lot more of Mike Hussey over the next few years, and maybe in Test as well as one-day action.

Michael Kasprowicz

Any onlooker wondering about the popularity of Michael Kasprowicz within the Australia team only had to look at the reaction of his team-mates when he took his 100th Test wicket, against New Zealand in Wellington in March 2005, to get the answer.

When he bowled Lou Vincent, the ten other Australians on the field converged on the big Queenslander and mobbed him as if he had single-handedly won The Ashes. The gesture was a genuine display of affection for a player who cannot have an enemy in the game.

One of the reasons for Kasprowicz's popularity is his sense of humour, which is extremely well developed. During the tour of India in 2004 he started the squad's own in-house newspaper, the *Mumbai Mumbler*, which poked fun at anyone and everyone, and his fart machine helps break the tension in even the most uptight situations.

If he had been playing in another era, Kasprowicz may well have had a lot more Test and one-day caps to his name, but with Glenn McGrath, Jason Gillespie and Brett Lee as his contemporaries he has often had to settle for the role of drinks waiter. The term 'fringe player' could almost have been invented for him at international level, but I have never heard him complain, and that lack of bitterness at his limited opportunities is another reason why he is so popular.

'You never know when you might be dropped for good,' he once said to me, 'so you should enjoy it all, and that way you will always have good memories.'

Beneath Kasprowicz's sunny exterior lies a pretty determined bloke, someone who has had to overcome a serious injury and reinvent himself as a bowler in order to get another chance at international level.

In 2000 he had to undergo a reconstruction of his shoulder and missed much of the 2000/01 season; then, when he was recalled for the tour of India after Brett Lee broke his elbow, he was part of the side that lost in Kolkata after we forced India to follow on.

Rather than feel sorry for himself after he missed out on the Ashes tour that followed, he simply went back to doing what he does best — taking wickets — and by 2003 the selectors could no longer ignore him. When they asked batsmen at state level who the best bowler they had faced was, the answer was always the same: Kasprowicz.

Obviously the presence of McGrath, Gillespie and Lee did not help his chances of a recall, but another reason for his time out of the Australia side may have been to do with how he has been viewed as a bowler.

When he first came into the Test and one-day line-ups he bowled outswingers, but over the years he altered his approach and now looks to run in and hit the pitch hard. Allied to that is his ability to bowl effective off-cutters and gain reverse swing when the ball gets old. This combination makes him a handful when he is at the top of his game.

His skill as a reverse-swing bowler has often seen him labelled as a subcontinent specialist, because that is where that style of bowling can be very effective. But, as he has shown not only in county cricket but also in Australia and New Zealand, he can be equally effective elsewhere. When he was picked for the 2001 tour of India, he famously joked, 'I don't just like tea; I like drinks with umbrellas in them as well', a reference to the fact that, while he was happy to tour the subcontinent, he was just as happy to tour somewhere like the Caribbean as well.

Away from cricket he is a devoted family man, and also someone who loves World Wrestling Entertainment, a passion he shares with Jason Gillespie. He is also a useful rugby union player — his brother Simon played for New South Wales in the Super 12 competition — and at one stage actively looked into combining his cricket with a rugby career before problems over insurance to play both sports put a stop to the idea.

'Kasper' is one of cricket's nice guys, a founding member of the Fast Bowlers' Cartel along with Glenn McGrath and Gillespie, and one of the blue-collar boys of the side, someone who thrives on hard work. He may have endured a disappointing Ashes tour and be nearer the end of his career than the start, but as long as he keeps taking wickets for Queensland he will never be far away from the Test or one-day side.

Simon Katich

The expressions 'hard as nails' or 'tough as teak' could easily have been invented with Simon Katich in mind. He has a sunny disposition but beneath that beats the heart of a bloke who loves a scrap, a trait that makes him a fantastic person to have around this team.

That love of a battle has helped get him where he is today, because he has not had it easy when it comes to not only breaking into the Test and one-day sides but also staying in them.

As far back as 1999 he was viewed as one of the rising stars of Australian cricket, and was picked for the Test tour of Sri Lanka and Zimbabwe as the reserve batsman, but a bout of chickenpox not only ruined his trip — it also knocked him flat for much of the season that followed.

Several members of the Western Australia side he played in back then talked of his total lack of energy that summer, and it was not unusual to go into the dressing room and find him asleep in a corner or even to wake him up so he could bat.

Katich is over that problem these days but one of the long-term side effects is that he cannot drink very much alcohol. Any more than a couple of drinks and he ends up with a shocking hangover, so much so that Stuart MacGill christened him 'Sicknote' when Katich moved to New South Wales a couple of seasons ago.

One thing that has not been affected by his illness is his appetite, and he has the reputation as one of the biggest eaters in the team. He loves his food and was once asked to select his top five lunch venues on the English county circuit. He nominated Lord's twice and his reason was simple: 'What's wrong with seconds?'

Among other lesser-known facts about Katich is his complete lack of a sense of smell. That might explain why he holds onto his cricketing equipment longer than some other members of the side, because while everyone else in the dressing room is well aware that his pads or gloves may be stinking of dried sweat, he carries on with them, blissfully unaware of their odours. He is also undoubtedly the hairiest member of the side.

Katich's move from Western Australia to New South Wales a few seasons ago — which came about after he fell out with the WACA hierarchy — has definitely taken his game forward. It gave him more of a chance to bowl at state level and that, in turn, helped bring him to the attention of the national selectors again. His bowling is rarely used at Test and one-day level because we have other options ahead of him, but it is still useful to have him available to bowl a few overs now and again, and his skills as a left-arm wrist spinner should not be underestimated. A few years ago MacGill was asked who the second-best spinner in Australia was and the assumption was that he would name himself behind Shane Warne; his answer was Katich.

His move to Sydney not only allowed Katich to develop his bowling, it also allowed him to develop his play against spin. The West is the home of pace bowling in Australia thanks to the fast, bouncy pitches that are produced on that side of the country, but spin is far more prevalent in New South Wales. His development was clear for all to see when he made his maiden Test hundred against India, in Stephen Waugh's final Test, in Sydney in January 2004.

Katich is a determined player but also a versatile one, and that is another feature of his play that appeals to the selectors. He made that maiden hundred at number six in the order, but when I was injured and missed the first three Tests of the tour to India he moved up the order, and averaged 40 batting at number three. He has also opened in one-day internationals and is equally capable of playing the finisher's role occupied for so long by Michael Bevan.

Katich has had to deal with his fair share of disappointments, but his renowned mental toughness has allowed him to cope and bounce back every time. In Sri Lanka, the tour that followed that hundred in Sydney, he was left out for the first two Tests of the series to accommodate Andrew Symonds. Some players might have complained, but he kept his head down, and when he came back into the side for the final Test in Colombo he made a crucial half-century that turned the match in our favour.

After the tour of India Katich lost his place again, this time to allow Darren Lehmann's return after injury, and although he did express his disappointment at that decision, he got on with the job of playing for New South Wales and was eventually recalled for the tour of New Zealand, marking his return with a Test-turning hundred in Christchurch.

What he has done is prove himself to be a good player in all conditions. He endured a lean tour of the United Kingdom but he was not alone in that failing during the series, and even then he still made crucial 50s at Lord's and Nottingham, the latter only ended by a shocking lbw decision when he looked immoveable.

Katich is a superbly athletic fielder but that is not always apparent, because his usual role in the Australia side is to perch under the batsman's nose at short leg or silly point. That is where spectators can get a real view of his bravery, as he will cop blow after blow in that position and still be moving forward for a bat-pad chance to the next delivery that is bowled. That takes courage and Katich has got that in abundance.

Allied to that courage is his sense of humour, which is best illustrated by his love of Richmond football club. Katich loves his Australian Rules football and whenever he is in Melbourne you can guarantee that he will never be far from Punt Road, the spiritual home of the Tigers.

He is a fantastic bloke, full of enthusiasm, a great trier, and the man Jason Gillespie calls 'Dog Scratch' (the opposite of 'Cat Itch', according to Gillespie) should be around for plenty of years to come.

Justin Langer

Justin Langer's failure to win a place in Australia's one-day side for the past eight years may have frustrated him but it has proved enormously beneficial to the health of our Test line-up.

The fact that Langer has played just one form of cricket for most of his international career has ensured that he has not been ground down by the intense nature of the current international program, and whenever he joins the squad for Test action his enthusiasm is a breath of fresh air and a wake-up call for those of us who play both forms of the game.

Langer brings real passion and a love of wearing the baggy green to the side, and it was his obvious appreciation of what it means to play for his country that led me to put him in charge of our team song which is sung whenever we win a Test match.

Part of the reason for Langer's passion might come from the fact he is determined to make the most of what has been a second chance at international level. He spent three years as a very successful player at number three in the order before losing his place when I was moved up the order, and Damien Martyn was drafted in at the start of the 2001 Ashes tour. When Langer did not play in any of the first four Tests of that series it looked odds-on that his Test career was over.

Then opportunity knocked. The selectors decided to leave Michael Slater out of the side for the final Test of the tour, and in the absence of a reserve opener in the squad they asked Langer to slot in. He responded with a century and has remained a feature alongside his great mate Matthew Hayden ever since.

He is often characterised as a determined player but he is also a very fine player and an effective one too. No one scores the volume of runs Langer has over the past four years without being an exceptional batsman, and he has made himself that way through sheer guts and determination.

Langer is a fanatical trainer, a black belt in martial arts, and has no room for shortcuts. If he fails, he wants to make sure it is never for lack of effort. He also makes an interesting character study alongside Hayden, as they really are chalk and cheese when it comes to their styles.

Langer, brought up on the bouncy pitches of Perth, is strong square of the wicket while Hayden loves to club the ball down the ground, and the contrasts also extend to their mannerisms. Before they go out to bat Langer is a bundle of energy, forever practising shadow shots and jumping around, while Hayden prefers to sit quietly, often outside the dressing room, collecting his thoughts before they walk to the crease. Whatever the contrasts, they have been a fantastic combination for Australia.

Like Hayden, Langer likes nothing better than a head-to-head contest out in the middle. He thrives on the adrenaline it generates and his battles with Shoaib Akhtar last summer made for fantastic viewing.

Langer's upbringing on those bouncy Western Australia pitches makes the fact he has been hit in the head so often while batting an oddity. It does not seem to have affected him, but a few years ago our physiotherapist Errol Alcott was so concerned about the frequency with which it was happening that he banned Langer from fielding at short leg just in case he got hit while standing there.

I know Langer has been frustrated at his lack of opportunity at one-day level, but he is also realistic enough to know the problems the selectors face in that area as Adam Gilchrist, Matthew Hayden, Michael Clarke and Simon Katich have all enjoyed success at the top of the order in the past year.

A real family man, Langer is mellow off the field and claims to have started growing roses in the garden of his home in Perth. I just hope the roses turn out better than his card-playing on the Ashes tour, because, after two months of having him as my partner on the team bus against veteran card sharks Shane Warne and team manager Steve Bernard, he showed few signs of getting any better!

Langer loves setting himself goals and one of them that's in the back of his mind is the possibility of scoring 100 first-class hundreds. He may well have to finish his career in English county cricket to try to achieve that, as he has enjoyed success there in the past and the volume of cricket played there would give him a better opportunity to complete that target rather than just by playing in Australia alone.

His hundred at the end of the Ashes series was number 71 so he still has a long way to go, and at almost 35 years of age at the start of the 2005/06 season, he is not getting any younger. But, given his determination to succeed in everything he does, I would not bet against Langer achieving the feat.

Brett Lee

There is a saying that there are lies, damned lies and statistics. In Brett Lee's case, on the 2005 Ashes tour his statistics were far from flattering, but they came nowhere near to telling the story of how well he bowled.

Both Adam Gilchrist and I agreed that his pace was back to the level it was when he first broke into Test cricket with such a bang back in December 1999, and if we can get into a position to use him in a more selective way in the future then we will see the best of Lee over the next few years, because physically he is now in his prime.

That selective use will be the key to his success, because one of the problems we had in England was that I had to bowl him for longer than I would have liked and in longer spells. The best way to use a fast bowler like Lee is in short, sharp bursts that ensure he is as fresh as possible every time I throw him the ball. In England, the regular absence of Glenn McGrath and the lack of form and control shown by Michael Kasprowicz and Jason Gillespie meant Lee ended up having to bowl for long periods, and that obviously affected his pace and also his ability to come back later in the innings.

It all added up to a reduction in his effectiveness, but despite that he still bowled like a man possessed and there was never any shortage of effort whenever he entered the attack. Lee always bowled fast and operated like a man with a point to prove — which, I guess, he was.

The Ashes series was his first Test action for 18 months and it put an end to a frustrating period in Lee's career. After playing a key role in our World Cup success in South Africa in 2003, he broke down with stomach and ankle injuries at the start of the following summer and was then over-bowled once he was fit again. That reduced his effectiveness, and when his ankle injury flared up again on the tour of Sri Lanka in early 2004, it was the start of his spell on the sidelines.

Privately he was disappointed at what he felt was inconsistency by the selectors as, having lost his place through injury, he hoped to walk straight back into the side when he was fit again. Glenn McGrath and Jason Gillespie had done just that during that period, but Lee was kept waiting while we kept winning. He could have moaned but he held his tongue and eventually his chance came again.

When Lee has played over the past year he has often courted controversy with several incidents of accidental beamers. I know that some critics felt they were far from accidental but I am convinced they were exactly that — an accident. They are dealt with in more detail elsewhere in this diary, but anyone who knows Lee will be aware that he does not have a malicious bone in his body.

Lee deserved his Test recall because his one-day form over the past year has, for the most part, been irresistible. His pace can mean that he is expensive, but when he gets it right — as he did throughout the first half of 2005 in Australia, New Zealand and the United Kingdom — then he can be lethal. He is the complete package as a bowler, with his ability to swing the new ball away and then come back later in the innings to swing the old ball back in, and he does all of it at upwards of 150 kp/h.

Lee may be a talented bowler but he is not a one-trick pony. His batting skill means he is moving closer and closer to becoming a genuine all-rounder while, away from the game, he is a guitarist and a member of a band with his brother Shane and former New South Wales team-mates Gavin Robertson, Richard Chee-Quee and Brad McNamara. They are a good enough outfit to have recorded an album and played at a past Allan Border Medal ceremony.

Lee does have a reputation as someone who is forgetful and he is also one of the best sleepers I have ever met. I have never known anyone who can fall asleep as easily as him. And he is very level-headed despite the fact that he is one of the most recognisable members of our squad, and that is probably due not only to shrewd management from his former New South Wales team-mate Neil Maxwell but also the fact that he held down a 'proper' job before he became a full-time cricketer.

Lee worked for a menswear company in Sydney and even in his first year as a Test cricketer it was possible to go into the shop and have him sell you a suit. Given that background it is maybe no surprise that he can be a bit of a clotheshorse — or a fashion victim, depending on your view of his dress sense — and his pink jumper, which appeared during the tour of New Zealand, was certainly something that caused a few light-hearted comments among some of his team-mates.

Not everything Lee does pleases me and his failure to deal with the issue of no-balls has had me tearing my hair out in the three years I have captained him at one-day and Test level. But one thing you do get from him in whatever he does, whether it is batting, bowling or fielding, is 100 per cent commitment, and in that sense he is a joy to captain and play alongside. Providing he stays fit and retains form, he will form a vital part of our attack over the next few years.

Darren Lehmann

John Howard once described himself as a 'cricket tragic', but everyone associated with the Australian team knows that one man who can out-tragic even the Prime Minister is Darren Lehmann.

He is not a great one for facts and figures, computer analysis or even bleep tests, but he does have a computer-like cricket brain, and it has been a superb resource for the side over the past few years.

He loves nothing more than to sit around over a beer and a smoke, and chat about batting and bowling techniques and fields that can be used for particular batsmen and bowlers; he also has the gift of being able to assess a batsman's strengths and weaknesses within an over or two.

A skill like that is priceless. It has made him a key figure in team meetings during our time together in the side, and on the field it has meant that he is always one of the first players I want to bounce ideas off.

It was great for me to have someone with his experience around when I first took over as one-day captain in 2002, and I like to think that we have been good for each other. He helped me get my feet under the table as captain, and I hope my belief in him was one factor in his having such a great spell in the Test and one-day line-ups from 2002 to 2004 — he finally cemented a place 13 years after first being named in an Australian squad.

His ability to analyse players and his knowledge of the game come from his upbringing, which was very much old school. He started in the days before today's fully professional environment, at a time when players learned just as much by sitting around and chatting with senior players as they did in the nets or the gym.

Lehmann's playing style could never be described as pretty. He clubs the ball rather than caresses it, and his left-arm 'nude nuts', the non-spinning slow stuff he has bowled with increasing frequency in recent years, come from a bowling arm that must be one of the lowest in world cricket.

But the lack of beauty in his cricket is more than made up for by his effectiveness. He knows his game inside out, knows how and where to score runs, and also how to bowl, especially in one-day cricket. He became an unsung all-rounder for us in the 12 months around our World Cup win in 2003, regularly rattling through an economical 6 or 7 overs in the middle of a one-day game. He even helped win a Test against Sri Lanka in Colombo in 2004, claiming 6 wickets when most of our other bowlers found the going extremely tough.

Lehmann's knowledge of the game comes not just from the era in which he started playing; it also comes from the vast amount of cricket he has played. He has played for South Australia, Victoria and Australia, and in England for Yorkshire — he had a key role in its first county championship title in 32 years. This vast experience has left him ideally placed to deal with tight run chases — he has been in those situations many times. Last summer, against Pakistan at Bellerive in Tasmania, he gave a perfect demonstration of how to pace an innings to win a match.

The downside of his year-round cricket is that it takes a heavy toll on his body. He missed a lot of the home summer of 2003/04 with an Achilles tendon injury, and then spent much of last season with a shoulder problem, playing through the pain thanks to cortisone injections.

His absence from the New Zealand and Ashes tours gave him a chance to get the shoulder injury sorted out, but with so many talented younger players around it may well have signalled the end of his international career. That would be a shame given what he brings to the squad: his analytical mind, the runs he scores and the wickets he takes, and his ability to bring clarity to most situations.

Honesty and straightforwardness are two of Lehmann's best qualities, and he is always the first to cut the waffle and prick a few ego balloons if that needs to be done. He is also generous in his praise, but on at least one occasion I thought he was too generous for his own good. His comment to the media during the India tour, that he would happily stand down if he felt he was holding a young player back, was straight from the heart, but also the wrong thing to say, at least in my opinion: as long as he was still performing he had every right to remain a part of the side, no matter who was knocking on the door for selection.

The last few years have certainly been a roller-coaster ride for Lehmann. Sandwiched between his return to the Test and one-day line-ups were two difficult events: a five-match ban — he was found guilty of racial abuse following his dismissal in a one-day game against Sri Lanka — and the tragic death of his mentor, the former South Australia captain David Hookes.

Both these events had a profound effect on Lehmann; they seem to have made him a lot more introverted. He became very withdrawn on the tour of Sri Lanka in 2004, and it took a night out with Adam Gilchrist and me in Colombo to start to bring him out of his shell again.

Looking ahead, I would like to think Lehmann can play the same role with young players today that Hookes and other veterans played with him, guiding them on the path to success in first-class cricket. I hope his skills are not lost to Australia when he finally packs the game in — there are bound to be many sides around the world that would relish the chance to employ him as a coach. He would be the ideal father figure at the newly established Centre of Excellence in Brisbane, for example. The fact that he was nominated as a national selector to replace the retiring Allan Border in 2005 is a good sign for Australian cricket.

Mike Hewitt / © 2005 Getty Images

THIS PAGE The four England fast bowlers who shared 75 wickets during the Ashes series.

Tom Shaw / © 2005 Getty Images

ABOVE The Welsh wizard. Simon Jones, the master of reverse swing, in action during the first Test at Lord's.

ABOVE RIGHT Geordie giant. Stephen Harmison, whose height generated awkward bounce throughout the series, discomfits Brett Lee during the fourth Test at Trent Bridge.

RIGHT The swing king. Matthew Hoggard, who became more effective as the series wore on, appeals successfully for lbw against Adam Gilchrist at Trent Bridge.

Hamish Blair / © 2005 Getty Images

LEFT Freddie's ready. Andrew Flintoff celebrates after dismissing Shane Warne on the dramatic final morning at Edgbaston. Earlier in the innings Flintoff dismissed me for a duck after bowling one of the best overs I have faced in Tests.

Clive Mason / © 2005 Getty Images

ABOVE Tait's turn. Australia's rising star, Shaun Tait, delivers his first ball in Tests, in the fourth match of the series at Trent Bridge.

Phil Hillyard / © Newspix

LEFT Joining the club. Tait is officially welcomed as Australia's 392nd Test player by former Test opener Michael Slater.

Phil Hillyard / © Newspix

RIGHT As rare as hen's teeth. I take my first Test wicket for more than six years and not a bad one either — England captain Michael Vaughan, caught by Adam Gilchrist.

Hamish Blair © 2005 Getty Images

Tom Shaw / © 2005 Getty Images

ABOVE Thrown out. I fear the worst as England substitute fielder Gary Pratt scores a direct hit to run me out at Trent Bridge.

Phil Hillyard / © Newspix

BELOW Power packed. Andrew Flintoff hammers Shane Warne through the offside during his first innings 102 in the fourth Test.

ABOVE Shouting match. Simon Katich reacts to spectator taunts after his controversial lbw dismissal in our second innings at Trent Bridge. His reaction earned him a 50 per cent fine from the match referee.

Tom Shaw / © 2005 Getty Images

ABOVE Knees-up. Brett Lee's blistering break-back accounted for Andrew Flintoff and gave us hope of a dramatic win at Trent Bridge.

ABOVE RIGHT Sickener. The expressions of (from left) Shaun Tait, Michael Kasprowicz and Justin Langer say it all after we went 2–1 down following defeat in the fourth Test.

ABOVE Hat stand. Shane Warne looks reflective as he leaves the field at Trent Bridge after his superb bowling came so close to winning the fourth Test.

LEFT We've done it! The relief and elation on the England balcony is obvious as they secure victory in the fourth Test to go into the lead in an Ashes series for the first time since 1997.

LEFT Run for home. I lead us out at the start of The Oval Test, followed by Adam Gilchrist, knowing that only a win would see us retain The Ashes.

Phil Hillyard / © Newspix

RIGHT You've been Warned. Bowling hero Shane celebrates with (from left) Michael Clarke, Damien Martyn and Simon Katich after dismissing Michael Vaughan at The Oval, one of 12 wickets he took in the match.

Phil Hillyard / © Newspix

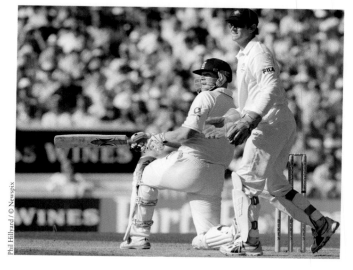

Phil Hillyard / © Newspix

LEFT Sweeping up. Andrew Flintoff hits Shane Warne for four during his first innings of 72 at The Oval, part of a series tally of 402 runs for the all-rounder.

LEFT One-man band. Shane Warne, who almost single-handedly carried our attack during the series, leaves the field on day one of the fifth Test after yet another 5-wicket haul — his 31st in Tests.

Phil Hillyard / © Newspix

RIGHT The darkness. Umpire Billy Bowden points to the pavilion after Matthew Hayden and Justin Langer controversially accepted the offer of bad light on day two at The Oval.

BELOW Frustration. My dismissal for 35 at The Oval, courtesy of an Andrew Flintoff lifter, summed up one of our failings in the series: too many batsmen did not go on to big scores after getting established.

Phil Hillyard / © Newspix

Phil Hillyard / © Newspix

LEFT Redecoration. Our dressing room during the fifth Test, with the walls covered by the many faxes and emails of support we received. My spot is in the middle of the picture, to the right of the door.

BELOW King Kevin. England hero Pietersen acknowledges the applause for his match-saving maiden Test hundred at The Oval that denied us a shot at victory — and a final chance to retain The Ashes.

BOTTOM Down — and almost out. The body language of Shane Warne (foreground) and Michael Clarke (rear) reflects our feelings as The Ashes finally slip away on the last day of the fifth Test.

TOP LEFT Our hero. Shane Warne accepts the plaudits as he is named Australia's man of the series. He did not deserve to be a loser after 249 runs and 40 wickets.

TOP RIGHT Lost in thought. I reflect on our series defeat alongside Michael Kasprowicz (left) and Stuart MacGill during the post-series presentations at The Oval.

MIDDLE LEFT We've urned it. Michael Vaughan shows what the series was all about as he holds up the replica Ashes urn alongside Marcus Trescothick and Andrew Flintoff.

LEFT Brothers in arms. The two men of the series, Andrew Flintoff and Shane Warne, relax in our dressing room after the fifth Test.

BELOW I face the press at Sydney Airport after returning from the tour.

Stuart MacGill

It cannot be easy being Stuart MacGill. In another era he would have had a long and distinguished international career but, instead, for large parts of his time in the game, he has been reduced to a walk-on part as Shane Warne's understudy.

I could have completely understood it if his frustrations had boiled over during the Ashes tour, because he quickly became one of the forgotten men of the tour party. To his credit, he took the situation well, never complained and got on with enjoying the trip as best he could.

A lot has been said in the past about the fiery side of MacGill's nature but as captain I have never had a moment's problem with him. In fact, when he came back into the Test side, against Pakistan in Sydney in January 2005, he was positively restrained. He never said as much to me but I got the impression that he was very nervous, something that seemed to be borne out by the start he made. He soon settled into his work and by the end of the Test he was bowling as well as ever.

As I see it, the problem for MacGill's Test future is our continuing lack of a genuine bowling all-rounder and until one comes along I fear his opportunities may be severely limited. Without that all-rounder, who can act as a third seamer to support the new-ball attack, MacGill's chances of playing are reduced because his inclusion would have to be in place of a pace bowler rather than Shane Warne. That would leave us with two spinners and two fast bowlers and a resultant lack of balance in the attack if we had to bowl first.

If we can find that third seamer then MacGill will always demand consideration because he is a wicket-taker, as he proved last summer with a record haul of wickets in first-class cricket. I would have no problem about playing him in the same side as Shane Warne, either. I know there are those who believe they cannot play together but I can't see why that is so as they complement each other very well. They proved that in the Galle Test of 2004 as well as the Sydney Test against Pakistan last summer, and I believe they can play together with success in the future.

MacGill is a different spinner from Warne in any case. While Warne looks to build pressure through accuracy, MacGill has one aim every time he runs in to bowl: he wants wickets and he does not care how much they cost. He looks to spin every ball hard, and although having such an attacking bowler in the line-up can be a test for a captain, it is also an asset because he has the ability to get a wicket in any situation.

The older MacGill has become, the more he has looked for interests away from the playing side of the game. During the one-day leg of the Ashes tour he spent his time in Channel Seven's studios in Sydney as a pundit, and I know that working in television is something that interests him in the longer term, although the idea of cricket commentary does not appeal.

More to his liking is the idea of making programs on wine. He discovered a passion for it a few years ago, and even took courses in wine marketing and appreciation to better understand the subject. It will be interesting to see where that takes him, but hopefully he will stay in cricket for a few years yet, because someone of his ability always has the potential to be a match-winner at Test level.

Glenn McGrath

I do not bet on cricket but if I could I would have a few dollars on Glenn McGrath being around to lead Australia's attack when it is time for us to try to regain The Ashes during the home summer of 2006/07.

McGrath took our Test series loss to England personally and I know he will want to put the record straight by beating the Poms at least once more before he heads off into international retirement.

McGrath is quite capable of being there to fill that role in the side even though he is already long in the tooth for a fast bowler. Then again, McGrath is not like most fast bowlers. As he is happy to point out, he does not bowl at express pace and does not really swing the ball, but despite that he is one of the best fast-medium bowlers to have played the game.

His success is based on several simple factors: a combination of his height and a real flick of the wrist as he releases the ball allows him to generate disconcerting bounce from a good length; he gets in close to the stumps when he delivers the ball, and that means the batsman always feels he has to play at the ball; and he is unerringly accurate and rarely bowls a bad ball. If you put all those factors together then you have pretty much the complete bowler.

McGrath also possesses something that is common in all great players: massive self-confidence. However, while some players express that self-confidence merely through acts on the field, McGrath goes one step further and loves to make predictions through the media of how well the team will do and who he will get out.

I am no great fan of it because it is stating the obvious — as a bowler you obviously want to get an opposition batsman out and as a team your side is always looking to win every match it plays — and if the prediction goes wrong there is a danger of looking foolish and arrogant. The Oval crowd were quick to remind McGrath of his pre-series prediction of a 5–0 win for Australia during the final Test of the Ashes series.

McGrath, however, seems to thrive on the pressure he puts on himself with his big calls, and in all fairness very few of his prophecies fail to come true. He loves the big occasion, loves bowling at the opposition's best batsmen — he seems to have dismissed Brian Lara and Michael Atherton as a pastime — and if those calls help him to focus on the job in hand then I suppose that is fair enough.

Physically he may be 35 but, despite his recent injury problems, he seems to be nearer 21 and in that sense he is a freak of nature. He has had a couple of major injuries through the years, but then it would difficult to find a top fast bowler who has not been sidelined at some point in their career. The irony of his injuries during the Ashes series was that they came after he started the tour in the best shape of his life. We did a fair amount of fitness work together in the lead-up to the trip and he was in outstanding physical condition.

The ankle injury he suffered in 2003 looked for some time as though it would spell the end of his career, but his comeback from that has been nothing short of amazing. I think he became so frustrated with his lengthy rehabilitation after the injury that he did consider retiring, but he persevered and his continued excellence has been the reward.

When he does eventually retire he will take several individual traits with him. Before we go into the field he always gets his ankles and feet taped up to protect the joints from twisting as he bowls. The team's long-standing physiotherapist, Errol Alcott, does the job and the way he is summoned to do it is always the same, as McGrath bellows his nickname across the dressing room. 'HOO-TER' is the cry and it will seem odd when McGrath is no longer around to make it.

In the dressing room he has taken over from former Australia fast bowler and now selector Merv Hughes as the player known as 'Fruitfly' — the great Australian pest. He is a practical joker and if someone is tapping you on the shoulder you can usually bet it is McGrath.

One of the biggest practical jokes of all used to be his batting, but although he is still hardly closing in on all-rounder status, he has worked incredibly hard on that part of his game to improve to the point where he was able to score a Test 50 against New Zealand. He loves talking about his batting and was happy to remind anyone who was willing to listen that his average for the series against England was 36.

It is still something that can give everyone else in the team a laugh, because whenever he comes back into the dressing room after being dismissed, his reaction is always the same: he throws his bat and helmet down and swears he was not really out; it was a lousy decision, a brilliant catch or a fantastic piece of bowling but rarely, if ever, was his return to the dressing room down to batsman error.

He is a paid-up member of the school of thought that believes bowlers are the workhorses of cricket while batsmen are the show ponies, and his whingeing found a dressing-room outlet during the early part of 2005 when he formed the Fast Bowlers' Cartel (or FBC for short) along with Michael Kasprowicz, Jason Gillespie and Brett Lee. I have not yet established what the FBC does, but if it keeps McGrath happy then that is a good enough reason for its existence.

McGrath's public face is that of a hard-nosed, big-talking fast bowler who rants and raves on the field, although there is no doubt he is more mellow now and in that sense he is a completely different person to the one he was even 6 years ago. He still rants and raves occasionally, but most of the time it is just with himself. He sets high standards and if he ever fails to live up to them then he is the first to be critical of his performance.

Off the field he is a doting dad and is a country boy at heart who loves his hunting. He owns a massive property in country New South Wales and I am sure that is where he will end up when his playing days are over. He was taking helicopter lessons in an effort to get ready to patrol his acreage, but I think the international schedule has made those lessons less and less frequent over the past few years. From my perspective, I hope the lessons have to be put off for a few more years yet.

Damien Martyn

When it comes to assessing the character and ability of Damien Martyn, I have a confession to make: he is probably my best mate in the Australian team, so there is no guarantee that what follows will be totally impartial.

Despite his lean Ashes series, Martyn remains an outstanding batsman and he played many crucial innings over the period covered by this diary. His hundred in Chennai played a massive part in ensuring that we regained the Border-Gavaskar Trophy; he won the McGilvray Medal, was Test player of the year and runner-up behind Michael Clarke for the Allan Border Medal.

Yet, despite all that success, I think most people would be hard pressed to remember much about a Damien Martyn innings. The blazing strokeplay of Adam Gilchrist usually sticks in the mind, but Martyn's patient accumulation tends to slip underneath the radar and that is exactly how he likes it.

Martyn never seeks out the limelight and is quite happy to let others take the glory. A journalist once described him to me as the best-kept secret in Australian cricket and I think that sums things up quite well.

The reasons for Martyn's attitude may have something to do with his first incarnation as an Australian cricketer, in the early 1990s. Back then he was hailed as the next big thing in Australian cricket, captained the under-19 side, broke into a

Test line-up still captained by Allan Border when barely out of his teens and went on an Ashes tour when he was 21.

Martyn was in the limelight, but with that increased exposure came increased expectation, and when he was a member of the side that famously lost to South Africa in Sydney in 1994 he found himself blamed for the defeat by sections of the media.

It was unfair to lay the blame for the failings of a side on one player but he copped it, lost his place and his confidence, and for a few years his career went into a steep decline. He lost the captaincy of Western Australia, a position he was probably given way too early in his career, and there was a time when he came close to being dropped from his state side altogether.

That never happened, and thanks to the guidance of Australia all-rounder Tom Moody and state coach Wayne Clark, Martyn gradually rehabilitated himself as a batsman, although it was a long process to regain his Test spot. When he finally did, in 2000, replacing me in the side on the tour of New Zealand after I broke my ankle during a fielding mishap, he had been out of the line-up for six years.

Now a settled member of the side again, he has been happy to have less exposure and content to allow the other, higher-profile members of our squad to bask in the glory. That was reflected in the way he struggled to deal with media attention during a run of low scores in 2003/04.

Martyn would much rather face a cup of coffee than a microphone and I cannot think of anyone who loves that drink as much. He is in his element when we tour the United Kingdom and stay in London, because there is a Starbucks opposite our hotel, and if they gave out a card to frequent users then Martyn's would be gold.

Technically he is quite similar to Mark Waugh because, although he is not a great mover of his feet, he remains beautifully balanced at the crease. Although he has only a small backlift, he still manages to hit the ball exceptionally hard thanks to his natural gift of timing, and there are only a handful of players — Virender Sehwag and VVS Laxman of India spring to mind — who hit the ball so well through and over extra-cover.

Like many players who rely on timing rather than pure technique, Martyn is not one for hours and hours of practice, but he is still a hard worker and someone who worked even harder once he broke back into the Australian side. Anyone who has seen photos of him five years ago would recognise instantly the work he has done to improve his condition and he has been rewarded with an excellent Test and one-day record.

On the field, he says very little. While players like Justin Langer relish some interaction with the bowler, Martyn just turns his back if anything is said to him, as he did in Melbourne last Christmas when Pakistan fast bowler Shoaib Akhtar tried to get under his skin. Martyn is pretty much unflappable.

When he does fail he tends to do so quietly, and while some players rant, rave and let off steam when they return to the sanctuary of the dressing room, he is someone who just sits in his seat without saying much. Even when he gets a bad decision, and he had a few in 2005, he is not someone who throws his bat across the dressing room.

Martyn loves watching Australian rules football and is a regular at the Grand Final. He is also a decent golfer, although his game was not helped by the horrendous fracture of his right index finger suffered during the 2003 World Cup. The injury did not stop him playing in the final against India, where we shared an unbroken double-century stand, but his willingness to play through the pain barrier did cost him a tour to the West Indies later that year when the injury did not heal properly, and he cannot now straighten the finger.

Despite his modest return in the UK, I believe Martyn is now in his prime as a batsman and I expect him to make opposition bowlers pay for that lean series for several years to come, much as he did in 2004 when he bounced back from his last run of low scores by making six Test hundreds in the calendar year.

Andrew Symonds

It seems hard to believe now, but not too long ago Andrew Symonds was so despondent at the way his cricket career was going that he seriously considered packing it in.

Despite his ability as a hard-hitting batsman, a bowler capable of operating as either a medium-pacer or an off-spinner, and a world-class fielder in any position, Symonds had been unable to convert that talent into consistent performances at the highest level. And, faced with the prospect of not fulfilling his obvious potential, he wondered whether it was worth carrying on.

The rumour on the Queensland grapevine was that he even approached the coach of the Brisbane Broncos rugby league side, Wayne Bennett, and asked whether he could try his hand at the oval ball game instead. Symonds is a gifted sportsman and as tough as teak, so I have no doubt he could have made a go of it, but Bennett, so the story goes, wisely advised him to think very carefully before taking such a massive step. Symonds decided to stick with what he knew best and Australian cricket has benefited, especially from the 2003 World Cup onwards — he has been one of the rocks of the one-day line-up since then.

So what turned him from a perennial underachiever to someone who, despite a lean trot in last summer's VB Series, still walked away with the award for the one-day cricketer of the year? As far as I am concerned, it comes down to him formulating a game plan.

His first instinct was always to try to hit the ball as hard and as far as possible, and at state level, to a large extent, he could get away with that as a plan. But at international level, where the bowlers are a lot more consistent and almost always have plans of their own, that approach was not enough. He would get out through either playing rash shots or clamming up completely.

But thanks in part to his good friend Matthew Hayden, he gradually came to terms with the need to adapt in order to succeed at the highest level, and he began to put his new game plan into action at the World Cup in southern Africa.

The plan was a simple one: early on, play each ball on its merits — don't look to belt the living daylights out of everything. It may sound like the most basic thing in the world, but it was quite an adjustment for a player whose approach had always been to try to dominate as soon as he arrived at the crease. Instead, he now made sure he was set before he tried to accelerate. I made sure he stuck to that plan when I batted with him in the first match of that tournament, against Pakistan in Johannesburg. The result was a brilliant hundred that was the best thing that could have happened to Symonds — not just because it helped us win the game, but also because it helped him see that his plan worked. He has fed off the confidence that gave him almost nonstop ever since.

Every time Symonds allows himself the luxury of playing himself in, he is likely to get you a big score, because he has the game to hurt any opposition: he hits the ball with immense power and that allows him to find the boundary regularly.

A lot has been made in the media of my support for Symonds, but I cannot claim much credit for his coming of age at international level. It is true that I lobbied for his inclusion in that 2003 World Cup squad when his figures did not make much of a case for him, but that was simply because I could see his potential. Even if you leave aside his batting, his bowling gives us options in all conditions, and as a fielder he is as good as anyone playing the game today.

Those options with the ball allowed him to earn a Test call-up in Sri Lanka in 2004 — his ability to act as a back-up seamer to Jason Gillespie and Michael Kasprowicz meant we could include both our leg-spinners, Shane Warne and Stuart MacGill, without worrying about being caught out by a lack of fast bowling options.

It was a pleasure to have him in the side during the two Tests he played. As well as his qualities as a cricketer, he also brought boundless enthusiasm to the job at hand, and his immense pride at finally getting to wear the baggy green was a reminder to all of us about what it means to play cricket for our country. He wore his cap around the team hotel after the first Test ... he even slept in it. That's how much it meant to him.

With passion for the cause like that, it would not surprise me if Symonds gets another chance at Test level to go with his regular one-day outings. In fact, he was close to replacing me when I was injured ahead of the tour of India in 2004. The lure of his off-spin was an obvious attraction, but the selectors opted at the last minute for Brad Hodge as a like-for-like replacement. The message Symonds got from the selectors when he was awarded his latest Cricket Australia contract was that he needed to score a stack of runs — I know he will do everything in his power to do just that. He has had a taste of Test cricket and wants more.

Symonds has a reputation for being a bloke who is sometimes guilty of opening his mouth before he puts his brain in gear, and his Queensland team-mate Michael Kasprowicz has a lengthy list of 'Symo-isms', but on the field it is a different story: he is one of the most street-smart cricketers I know. He understands the game and can, a bit like Darren Lehmann, dissect an opposition player's technique very quickly.

Away from cricket he has plenty of interests. That is an advantage, because it means the game does not consume him. He loves the outdoor life of shooting, hunting and fishing so, while some players might flick through *GQ* or *FHM* before they bat, Symonds will be reading a magazine about his major passion in life: hunting feral pigs. That physical outdoor life has given him a high level of fitness; that plus his natural agility means I would not fancy being a pig if he was pursuing me.

Symonds is fearless; he is also built like a tank, and sometimes appears indestructible. Maybe he believes he is, but he does need to recognise that he is human and to sometimes rein himself in, especially if he is to continue playing at the top level. Last summer was a case in point. He tried to play on through an Achilles injury he originally picked up playing in the United Kingdom in 2004. He was convinced it was only a niggle, but that was how Darren Lehmann's Achilles injury started out a year earlier, and it eventually cost Lehmann most of the 2003/04 summer. Symonds has to manage himself properly if we are to continue to see the best of him.

Shaun Tait

I have high hopes for Shaun Tait despite his modest Ashes tour, because he has that priceless commodity: pace.

Tait has real, raw pace and on top of that he has the ability to swing the ball as well, so if he can add greater control to his mix then he and Brett Lee have the potential to form a fearsome opening combination in the years ahead.

I first encountered Tait in more ways than one in Sri Lanka in 2004. He arrived as a late replacement for Lee and made an immediate impression on me when he smashed my favourite batting helmet with a bouncer that was distinctly sharp.

I like to think I am a pretty good player of short-pitched bowling, but Tait was too quick for me on that occasion, and plenty of other batsmen will encounter a similar problem in the years ahead. He has a slinging action that is very difficult to pick up when you first face him, as the ball appears from behind his back, a bit like the former great Australia fast bowler Jeff Thomson.

Through the Ashes tour I was impressed by his attitude as a wholehearted trier and I am convinced he can only get better and better with more exposure at a higher level. He has already shown his impressive temperament to come through a test early in his career. In 2004 he was signed as an overseas professional for Durham in England but the experience was a disaster, as he had no rhythm after arriving to play straight out of the Adelaide winter, and his time with Durham dissolved in a mass of no-balls, wides and shattered confidence.

Tait's response to that crisis was impressive, with 65 first-class wickets in 2004/05, and form like that demanded selection for the Ashes series. Although he did not set the world on fire in the two Tests he played, he did not disgrace himself either, and he will now have a better idea of what it takes to succeed at the highest level.

A big, rawboned country boy, I immediately spotted his abilities as a footballer whenever we warmed up ahead of practice. He was always in the thick of the action, showed plenty of skill, and it would not surprise me if he'd played a decent standard of football when he was younger. Strangely, for a South Australian lad, he barracks for the West Coast Eagles — although there is a story behind that. He was a youngster when the Eagles entered the competition and he has followed their fortunes ever since.

Tait is a natural ball-player and also has the potential to bat left-handed, as anyone who has seen him experiment in the nets will testify. Maybe he should consider giving that a go in the longer term, because he would be the first to admit that he has plenty of work to do to improve himself as a right-handed batsman!

Although most of the Ashes squad called him 'Taity', there were a few who knew him by his first nickname, picked up after he joined the squad in Sri Lanka. His nickname there was 'Sloon', a result of a hotel receptionist's failed attempts to pronounce his first name when he arrived in Colombo.

Shane Warne

It is difficult to know where to start when writing about Shane Warne, because so much has already been written about him.

In simple terms, he is a genius with the ball in his hand. His figures show that, but what they do not show is the trait all great players have: the ability to lift their level of performance when confronted with a pressure situation or when facing another outstanding performer.

What sets Warne apart for me is the way he has adapted his game as he has grown older. He no longer has the flexibility to allow him to bowl certain deliveries like the flipper, but in its place he has developed a slider, a ball that skids on and earns him countless lbws.

Zip has been replaced by guile, and even though he is still capable of spinning his leg-break a long, long way, he also seems to bowl more straight balls than anyone else in world cricket. He varies his pace, his flight and even the place on the crease he bowls from. He is the complete bowler.

In the time I have shared a dressing room with Warne over the past decade, some aspects of his life and personality have changed while others have stayed the same.

The first thing to say about Warne is that he is a generous man. Every year ahead of the Boxing Day Test in Melbourne, he has the squad around to his house for a party and he supplies everything. Nothing is too much trouble and he never quibbles about spending his own money.

He still enjoys a cigarette and a ham and pineapple pizza, but over the past couple of years wine has become his drink of choice and he has become a lot more conscious about his fitness. He always had a powerful upper body because of his bowling but he has supplemented that with weights work, and although he is not someone who enjoys running on the treadmill, he regularly uses an exercise bike.

Warne's self-image was the reason he took the now-infamous diet pill that cost him a year out of his career and a one-day farewell in the 2003 World Cup, but although that cost him a lot of time and wickets, the enforced break he endured may have benefited him in the long run.

Not only did it allow him to rest up long-term niggles and work on his overall fitness, I think it also made him appreciate the game and his love of it, so that when he came back he realised how much he had missed it and now, I believe, he wants to do everything in his power to stay at the top for as long as he can.

He was circumspect when he first rejoined the squad in Sri Lanka and that was perhaps the result of some of the public comments I made about his ban when it was first announced. I was critical of his failings but we are all grown men, that was quickly forgotten, and in the past 18 months he has returned to being an increasingly vocal and influential member of the Test side.

A lot was made in the media of Warne's role during the 2005 Ashes series, not just in terms of the 40 wickets he took or the 249 runs he scored, but also in the way he seemed active in the decision-making process on the field. I did speak with Warne about tactics on many occasions but I also did the same with several other senior players including Adam Gilchrist, Glenn McGrath and Justin Langer. I would have been a fool not to tap into Warne's experience, especially given his knowledge of the game in England thanks to his time playing county cricket for Hampshire. At the same time there was only one person in charge on the field and that was me.

Warne's captaincy credentials are obvious: he leads from the front and inspires those around him, and he has a good cricket brain. I am sure he would make an excellent Australia captain but that is not my decision; it is up to the selectors and Cricket Australia's Board of Directors. In any case, if he does still have captaincy aspirations he had better join the queue, because I am not planning on going anywhere for a while yet.

I would not rule out the idea of him coming back into the one-day side for the 2007 World Cup. I know he was upset and frustrated at the way he left the one-day arena in 2003, and I got the impression over the past year he would like to play that form of the game again. During the tsunami match in Melbourne in January 2005 he revelled in a return to the day–night atmosphere of coloured clothing, and I think it got his competitive juices flowing again.

The trouble is that I do not think he will make himself available unless he gets an assurance from the selectors that they will pick him; he will not want to go to the trouble and possible embarrassment of announcing his availability only to be overlooked. I am not sure the selectors will want to give him that assurance, because Australia has done well enough without him, and Trevor Hohns and his colleagues may even feel that his absence from the one-day line-up will extend his international career by reducing the wear and tear on his body.

The subject of Warne's retirement from Test cricket is an equally tough question. The older he gets, the more people are curious about when he will pack in the game at international level, but I am not sure he really knows the answer himself.

Warne loves the camaraderie of the dressing room environment as well as the buzz of adrenaline he gets from playing at the highest level, and I know he would miss that and find it hard to replace because he is a naturally competitive person. That is one reason why I think he will play on for as long as he can.

On the other hand, I also know he misses his children very much and the change in his marital status during 2005 obviously makes the issue of access that much harder if he is on tour a lot of the time.

I do not know what the future holds for Warne but one thing I am sure of is that, from a purely selfish point of view, I hope he stays around for a few years yet. The Australia team will be much the poorer without him and so will the whole world of cricket.

Shane Watson

If anyone warrants the tag of Australia's unluckiest cricketer, it is Shane Watson.

He has had to undergo more heartache in his relatively short career than some players go through in 20 years, but each time he has faced a setback he has bounced back stronger than before.

Before he was out of his teenage years he suffered three stress fractures of his back. Then, after becoming a regular in the one-day side during the summer of 2002/03, he broke down with another back injury on the eve of the World Cup.

Watson fought back from that, earned a recall last summer and was set to tour New Zealand when he suffered a side strain. The inability to put his case to the selectors on that trip undoubtedly cost him a berth on the Test leg of the Ashes tour that followed. He broke down in tears after that side injury — and after a catalogue of misfortune like that, you can understand why.

But one of Watson's greatest assets is his resilience and single-minded determination, so I am sure he will come back again. He has always had just one goal — to play for Australia — and now that he has had a taste of that, at both Test and one-day level, I can only see him wanting more.

That desire to represent his country was one of the reasons he moved to Tasmania in 2000 after finding his way to first-class cricket in his native Queensland blocked. It takes courage for a young bloke to leave his home and family like that but he did it, with the idea of bettering himself, and the move paid off handsomely for both him and Tasmania.

Watson got the chance to showcase his talents as a bowler and a top-order batsman with my home state, and within 2 years was part of a senior tour to South Africa, scoring a hundred on his first-class debut for Australia, against South Africa A in Port Elizabeth, reaching the milestone with a six.

I captained him during the one-day series on that trip, and if I had any criticism of him back then it was about his body language. If he bowled a bad ball he would get down on himself. I told him that sent out the wrong message to the opposition, who suddenly knew they were on top. He is a great listener, and he took that on board.

His back trouble has, in some ways, been a blessing for both him and Australian cricket in the long term. During his comeback he was still able to play, but only as a specialist batsman, and the added pressure on his batting, because of not having his bowling to fall back on, made him a better, more responsible player. His run-scoring output during that period was impressive, and he is now the closest thing we have to a genuine all-rounder in Australian cricket (with the exception of Adam Gilchrist), someone who could come close to commanding a place as a batsman or bowler alone.

Outside cricket, Watson's biggest passion, at least as far as I can see, is his love of fashion — he is a real clothes horse. And his clothes need to be large, because he is one of the most well-developed blokes I have seen in international cricket when he takes his shirt off. Another positive of his time away from the game over the past few years is that it has given him the time to develop and become stronger, and that will benefit him down the track.

I have real faith in Shane Watson. He can give our side real balance and extra options over the next few years — he is one reason why every Australian cricket fan should be optimistic for the future.

Cameron White

Cameron White — or 'Bundy Bear', as he is known in the team because of his fair hair, which gives him a passing resemblance to the character that advertises that well-known brand of rum — has bags of talent. He is a brilliant fielder, bats effectively in the middle order and is a very different leg-spinner from Shane Warne or Stuart MacGill. He relies more on skidding the ball onto the batsman — a bit like India's Anil Kumble — than on extravagant turn and, unlike Warne and MacGill, he also has a very high arm action.

Most leg-spinners with high arms tend to rely more on over-spin than side spin, and White is no exception, but I think he needs to develop his armoury to include more sideways action on the ball if he is to earn a Test call-up.

That was illustrated when he missed out — to Nathan Hauritz — on a spot in the side in Mumbai when Shane Warne was injured. White would have been the like-for-like replacement, but the selectors opted for Hauritz because they felt he did more with the ball and was the better spinner.

Unlike most leg-spinners, however, White is extremely accurate, and that, together with his abilities as a batsman and fielder, is likely to earn him a chance at one-day level if he maintains his form, especially once Brad Hogg comes to the end of his career. Hogg used the one-day side as a springboard to a Test call-up and there is no reason why White cannot do the same.

His exposure to captaincy from an early age, with the Australia under-19 side that won the World Cup in New Zealand in 2002 and then with Victoria, will help him understand the game even better. White has ambition, and I just hope his form will match that ambition.

Brad Williams

If there is one word that sums up Brad Williams, it is 'wholehearted'. In any conditions, in any circumstance, you know that if you throw the ball to 'Willo' you will get nothing but total commitment.

That type of approach has always been a Williams trademark, but it may also be the result of a desperation to make the most of every opportunity he gets. He is a player who, in another era, may have played 50 Tests; instead, he has found himself further down the pecking order, below all-time greats such as Glenn McGrath and Jason Gillespie, and top performers such as Brett Lee and Michael Kasprowicz.

When any of the above four has been injured or unavailable, the selectors have often looked to Williams to fill the breach, and although he has never enjoyed spectacular success, he has not let the side down either.

He was a stand-out performer for us in the TVS Cup in India in 2003, when we didn't have McGrath, Gillespie and Lee. We were expected to lose heavily, but Williams and Nathan Bracken played a key role in our eventual success instead. While Bracken was the man who swung the ball around corners, Williams played the role of enforcer. He charged in, and even though the surfaces were slow and offered him nothing, he still terrorised the India and New Zealand batsmen. It was impressive stuff.

His total commitment and single-minded determination to play for Australia was summed up not just by his decision to uproot his family from its Victorian base in 1999 to head to Western Australia in search of better opportunities, but also by the way he went through the pain barrier against India in Adelaide in 2003. After damaging his left shoulder when he collided with a boundary board while fielding, he left the ground that night with his arm in a sling, in considerable pain. He was not expected to take any further part in the match. But he shrugged off the pain and got out not just to bat in our second innings but also to bowl, as we strove for victory.

That type of effort is typical of the man, as I found out first on the Young Australia tour of the United Kingdom in 1995. He had a new pair of boots at the start of that trip and they gave him terrible blisters that were the size of a fist — but he kept going through the pain and bowled some frighteningly quick spells on that tour.

Williams has had his fair share of injuries, and last summer was no exception. No sooner had he recovered from the back injury that forced him home from the one-day tour of Zimbabwe than he dislocated his knee, ruining his season. That type of setback might be enough to floor some players, but not Williams. There is nothing more certain than that he will bounce back, start taking wickets again and put pressure on other players in the Australian side.

2004–2005

Statistics

COMPILED BY ROSS DUNDAS

2004–05 AUSTRALIA v SRI LANKA

SRI LANKAN TOURING PARTY

Marvan Atapattu (captain), Mahela Jayawardene (vice-captain), Sanath Jayasuriya, Kumar Sangakkara, Tillakaratne Dilshan, Thilan Samaraweera, Russel Arnold, Romesh Kaluwitharana (wk), Upul Chandana, Chaminda Vaas, Nuwan Zoysa, Dilhara Fernando, Farveez Maharoof, Lasith Malinga, Rangana Herath.

Team Management — Ajit Jayasekera (Manager), John Dyson (Coach), Ray Illangakoon (Media Manager) and Sanath Jayasundera (Cricket Analyst).

Muttiah Muralitharan withdrew from the touring team on June 15.

NORTHERN TERRITORY CHIEF MINISTER'S XI v SRI LANKANS

At Marrara Cricket Ground, Darwin, June 24,25,26,27, 2004. Sri Lankans won by five wickets. Northern Territory Chief Minister's XI 419 (J.L. Langer 151, R. Bowden 75, M.M. Brown 45, D.L. Treumer 65, G.D. McGrath 31*; M.F. Maharoof 2–73, S.L. Malinga 6–90, U.D.U. Chandana 2–118). Sri Lankans 7 dec 378 (S.T. Jayasuriya 64, K.C. Sangakkara 203*; A.C. Dent 2–51). Northern Territory Chief Minister's XI 9 dec 145 (H.M.R.K.B. Herath 4–45, U.D.U. Chandana 2–29). Sri Lankans 5 for 187 (T.T. Samaraweera 32, T.M. Dilshan 66*, R.P. Arnold 34; I. Redpath 2–22).

FIRST TEST

AUSTRALIA v SRI LANKA
Marrara Cricket Ground, Darwin, July 1,2,3, 2004.
Australia won by an 149 runs. Toss: Sri Lanka. Man of Match: G.D. McGrath.
Attendance: 13,355.

Close of play: First day, Sri Lanka (2) 3–43 (Jayawardene 12, Zoysa 8);
Second day, Australia 201 all out.

AUSTRALIA

J.L. Langer c Chandana b Samaraweera	30	–	c Sangakkara b Vaas	10
M.L. Hayden c Jayasuriya b Vaas	37	–	c Sangakkara b Zoysa	2
M.T.G. Elliott c Arnold b Vaas	1	–	c Dilshan b Vaas	0
D.R. Martyn c Arnold b Jayasuriya	47	–	c Sangakkara b Malinga	7
D.S. Lehmann lbw b Malinga	57	–	c Sangakkara b Malinga	51
S.M. Katich c Sangakkara b Vaas	9	–	c Dilshan b Chandana	15
*+A.C. Gilchrist c Sangakkara b Malinga	0	–	run out (Jayawardene)	80
S.K. Warne run out (Arnold)	2	–	lbw b Malinga	1
J.N. Gillespie lbw b Vaas	4	–	c Samaraweera b Chandana	16
M.S. Kasprowicz not out	2	–	c and b Malinga	15
G.D. McGrath c Samaraweera b Vaas	0	–	not out	0
B 2, L-B 6, W 2, N-B 8	18		L-B 3, N-B 1	4
(71.3 OVERS, 311 MINS)	207		(63.1 OVERS, 292 MINS)	201

Fall: 72 73 80 177 189 189 201 202 207 207   Fall: 12 12 14 64 77 114 127 154 201 201

Bowling: First Innings — Vaas 18.3–6–31–5; Malinga 14–3–50–2; Zoysa 13–4–24–0;
Samaraweera 9–1–43–1; Chandana 6–0–30–0; Jayasuriya 11–4–21–1.
Second Innings — Vaas 14–4–51–2; Zoysa 16–3–57–1; Malinga 15.1–3–42–4;
Jayasuriya 6–3–9–0; Chandana 11–1–30–2; Arnold 1–0–9–0.

SRI LANKA

*M.S. Atapattu b McGrath	4	–	c Warne b Kasprowicz	10
S.T. Jayasuriya lbw b McGrath	8	–	lbw b McGrath	16
+K.C. Sangakkara lbw b Gillespie	2	–	run out (Martyn)	0
D.P.M. Jayawardene c Langer b Gillespie	14	–	b McGrath	44
D.N.T. Zoysa c Gilchrist b McGrath	12	(10)	c Gilchrist b Kasprowicz	1
T.T. Samaraweera c Gilchrist b McGrath	1	(5)	c Gilchrist b Kasprowicz	32
T.M. Dilshan not out	17	(6)	c Gilchrist b Kasprowicz	14
R.P. Arnold c Elliott b McGrath	6	(7)	c Gilchrist b Kasprowicz	11
U.D.U. Chandana c Gilchrist b Warne	14	(8)	b Kasprowicz	17
W.P.U.J.C. Vaas c Hayden b Warne	5	(9)	not out	10
S.L. Malinga c Gillespie b Warne	0	–	c Gilchrist b Kasprowicz	0
L-B 7, N-B 7	14		L-B 1, W 2, N-B 4	7
(41.5 OVERS, 186 MINS)	97		(65.4 OVERS, 278 MINS)	162

Fall: 10 20 33 47 50 51 59 85 91 97   Fall: 23 23 30 109 113 132 141 152 162 162

Bowling: First Innings — McGrath 15–4–37–5; Gillespie 13–4–18–2; Kasprowicz 7–1–15–0;
Warne 6.5–1–20–3. Second Innings — McGrath 16–9–24–2; Gillespie 13–2–37–0; Kasprowicz
17.4–3–39–7; Warne 19–2–61–0.

Umpires: Aleem Dar and B.F. Bowden. TV Umpire: S.J.A. Taufel. Referee: B.C. Broad.

AUSTRALIA v SRI LANKA
Cazalys Stadium, Cairns, July 9,10,11,12,13, 2004. Match drawn. Toss: Sri Lanka.
Man of Match: M.L. Hayden. Man of the Series: S.K. Warne. Attendance: 20,102.

Close of play: First day, Australia (1) 2–370 (Langer 159, Martyn 56); Second day, Sri Lanka (1) 2–184 (Atapattu 75, Jayawardene 9); Third day, Sri Lanka (1) 5–411 (Samaraweera 53, Kaluwitharana 30); Fourth day, Australia (2) 2–194 (Hayden 68, Martyn 52).

AUSTRALIA

J.L. Langer c Jayawardene b Malinga	162	–	c Kaluwitharana b Zoysa	8
M.L. Hayden c Jayasuriya b Samaraweera	117	–	b Chandana	132
*R.T. Ponting c Atapattu b Malinga	22	–	c Jayasuriya b Zoysa	45
D.R. Martyn lbw b Chandana	97	–	st Kaluwitharana b Chandana	52
D.S. Lehmann c Sangakkara b Chandana	50	–	c Jayawardene b Chandana	21
S.M. Katich b Chandana	1	–	st Kaluwitharana b Dilshan	1
+A.C. Gilchrist c Kaluwitharana b Malinga	35	–	b Dilshan	0
S.K. Warne c Samaraweera b Chandana	2	–	c Samaraweera b Chandana	4
J.N. Gillespie c Kaluwitharana b Malinga	1	–	st Atapattu b Chandana	1
M.S. Kasprowicz c K'rana b Chandana	9	–	not out	3
G.D. McGrath not out	0			
B 7, L-B 3, W 4, N-B 7	21		L-B 20, W 1, N-B 4	25
(124.2 OVERS, 539 MINS)	517		(66.4 OVERS, 288 MINS) (9 WKTS DEC)	292

Fall: 255 291 392 454 462 469 474 476 485 517   Fall: 10 105 195 261 284 284 288 288 292

Bowling: First Innings — Vaas 27–2–102–0; Zoysa 19–5–72–0; Samaraweera 17–2–55–1; Malinga 29.2–2–149–4; Chandana 26–2–109–5; Jayasuriya 6–0–20–0. Second Innings — Vaas 13–3–52–0; Zoysa 14–6–34–2; Malinga 5–0–23–0; Samaraweera 11–0–50–0; Chandana 18.4–1–101–5; Jayasuriya 3–0–8–0; Dilshan 2–0–4–2.

SRI LANKA

*M.S. Atapattu c Hayden b McGrath	133	–	c Warne b Gillespie	9
S.T. Jayasuriya c Gilchrist b Gillespie	13	–	c Gilchrist b Warne	22
K.C. Sangakkara c Gillespie b Warne	74	–	b Warne	66
D.P.M. Jayawardene c and b Kasprowicz	43	–	c Gilchrist b McGrath	6
T.T. Samaraweera c Ponting b Gillespie	70	–	run out (Martyn)	0
T.M. Dilshan c Kasprowicz b Warne	35	–	c Warne b Gillespie	21
+R.S. Kaluwitharana c Warne b McGrath	34	–	c Lehmann b Warne	14
U.D.U. Chandana st Gilchrist b Warne	19	–	st Gilchrist b Warne	14
W.P.U.J.C. Vaas c Ponting b Gillespie	2	–	not out	11
D.N.T. Zoysa not out	0	–	not out	3
S.L. Malinga run out (Lehmann)	0			
B 3, L-B 10, W 2, N-B 17	32		B 5, L-B 3, N-B 9	17
(144.4 OVERS, 610 MINS)	455		(85 OVERS, 345 MINS) (8 WKTS)	183

Fall: 18 156 280 280 345 420 445 455 455 455   Fall: 15 49 58 64 107 136 159 174

Bowling: First Innings — McGrath 34–10–79–2; Gillespie 37.4–6–116–3; Kasprowicz 32–5–113–1; Warne 38–7–129–3; Lehmann 3–0–5–0. Second Innings — McGrath 16–7–31–1; Gillespie 18–6–39–2; Warne 37–14–70–4; Kasprowicz 11–4–34–0; Lehmann 3–2–1–0.

Umpires: Aleem Dar and B.F. Bowden. TV Umpire: R.L. Parry. Referee: B.C. Broad.

2004–05 AUSTRALIA–SRI LANKA TEST AVERAGES

Batting	M	Inn	NO	Runs	Best	50	100	Avrge	Ct/St	Stk-Rt
M.L. Hayden (Aus)	2	4	–	288	132	–	2	72.00	2/–	64.72
J.L. Langer (Aus)	2	4	–	210	162	–	1	52.50	1/–	55.85
D.R. Martyn (Aus)	2	4	–	203	97	2	–	50.75	–/–	68.12
D.S. Lehmann (Aus)	2	4	–	179	57	3	–	44.75	1/–	70.75
M.S. Atapattu (SL)	2	4	–	156	133	–	1	39.00	1/1	45.88
K.C. Sangakkara (SL)	2	4	–	142	74	2	–	35.50	7/–	46.10
R.T. Ponting (Aus)	1	2	–	67	45	–	–	33.50	2/–	49.26
T.M. Dilshan (SL)	2	4	1	87	35	–	–	29.00	2/–	40.47
A.C. Gilchrist (Aus)	2	4	–	115	80	1	–	28.75	11/2	71.43
D.P.M. Jayawardene (SL)	2	4	–	107	44	–	–	26.75	2/–	35.31
T.T. Samaraweera (SL)	2	4	–	103	70	1	–	25.75	4/–	33.44
R.S. Kaluwitharana (SL)	1	2	–	48	34	–	–	24.00	4/2	58.54
U.D.U. Chandana (SL)	2	4	–	64	19	–	–	16.00	1/–	36.16
S.T. Jayasuriya (SL)	2	4	–	59	22	–	–	14.75	3/–	47.97
M.S. Kasprowicz (Aus)	2	4	2	29	15	–	–	14.50	2/–	49.15
W.P.U.J.C. Vaas (SL)	2	4	2	28	11*	–	–	14.00	–/–	36.36
R.P. Arnold (SL)	1	2	–	17	11	–	–	8.50	2/–	44.74
D.N.T. Zoysa (SL)	2	4	2	16	12	–	–	8.00	–/–	21.05
S.M. Katich (Aus)	2	4	–	26	15	–	–	6.50	–/–	20.63
J.N. Gillespie (Aus)	2	4	–	22	16	–	–	5.50	2/–	30.99
S.K. Warne (Aus)	2	4	–	9	4	–	–	2.25	4/–	27.27
M.T.G. Elliott (Aus)	1	2	–	1	1	–	–	0.50	1/–	9.09
S.L. Malinga (SL)	2	3	–	0	0	–	–	0.00	1/–	0.00
G.D. McGrath (Aus)	2	3	2	0	0*	–	–	0.00	–/–	0.00

Bowling	Overs	Mds	Runs	Wkts	Best	5wi	10wm	Avrge	RPO
T.M. Dilshan (SL)	2.0	–	4	2	2–4	–	–	2.00	2.00
G.D. McGrath (Aus)	81.0	30	171	10	5–37	1	–	17.10	2.11
U.D.U. Chandana (SL)	61.4	4	270	12	5–101	2	1	22.50	4.38
M.S. Kasprowicz (Aus)	67.4	13	201	8	7–39	1	–	25.13	2.97
S.L. Malinga (SL)	63.3	8	264	10	4–42	–	–	26.40	4.16
S.K. Warne (Aus)	100.5	24	280	10	4–70	–	–	28.00	2.78
J.N. Gillespie (Aus)	81.4	18	210	7	3–116	–	–	30.00	2.57
W.P.U.J.C. Vaas (SL)	72.3	15	236	7	5–31	1	–	33.71	3.26
S.T. Jayasuriya (SL)	26.0	7	58	1	1–21	–	–	58.00	2.23
D.N.T. Zoysa (SL)	62.0	18	187	3	2–34	–	–	62.33	3.02
T.T. Samaraweera (SL)	37.0	3	148	2	1–43	–	–	74.00	4.00
R.P. Arnold (SL)	1.0	–	9	–	–	–	–	–	9.00
D.S. Lehmann (Aus)	6.0	2	6	–	–	–	–	–	1.00

RICKY PONTING AT SOMERSET 2004

Somerset v Yorkshire at Scarborough, July 21,22,23, 2004

Batting	How Out	Runs	Bowling	Overs	Mds	Runs	Wkts	Ct
1st Inns:	c A.W. Gale b R.K.J. Dawson	112	1st Inns:	5	2	6	0	2
2nd Inns:	did not bat	–	2nd Inns:	–	–	–	–	–

Glamorgan v Somerset at Taunton, August 3,4,5, 2004

Batting	How Out	Runs	Bowling	Overs	Mds	Runs	Wkts	Ct
1st Inns:	c S.P. Jones b S.D. Thomas	117	1st Inns:	–	–	–	–	2
2nd Inns:	not out	18	2nd Inns:	–	–	–	–	1

Durham v Somerset at Chester-le-Street, August 13,14,15,16, 2004

Batting	How Out	Runs	Bowling	Overs	Mds	Runs	Wkts	Ct
1st Inns:	c G.R. Breese b L.E. Plunkett	50	1st Inns:	–	–	–	–	1
2nd Inns:	did not bat	–	2nd Inns:	–	–	–	–	1

2004 VIDEOCON CUP — ICC CHAMPIONS TROPHY

AUSTRALIAN TOURING PARTY

Ricky Ponting (captain), Darren Lehmann (vice-captain), Michael Clarke, Jason Gillespie, Brad Haddin, Ian Harvey, Matthew Hayden, Brad Hogg, Michael Kasprowicz, Brett Lee, Damien Martyn, Glenn McGrath, Andrew Symonds, Shane Watson.

Adam Gilchrist did not tour Holland but joined the touring party for the ICC Champions Trophy in England.

Team Management — John Buchanan (Coach), Steve Bernard (Team Manager), Tim Nielsen (Assistant Coach / Performance Analyst), Errol Alcott (Physiotherapist), Jock Campbell (Physical Performance Manager), Jonathan Rose (Media Manager), Mike Young (Specialist Fielding & Throwing Consultant).

INDIA v PAKISTAN

at VRA Ground, Amstelveen, August 21, 2004. Pakistan won by 66 runs (rain rule). Pakistan 192 (Shoaib Malik 68, Abdul Razzaq 35*, L. Balaji 3-27). India 127 (V.V.S. Laxman 37, Shahid Afridi 4-20, Shoaib Malik 3-18). Man of the Match: Shoaib Malik.

AUSTRALIA v INDIA

VRA Ground, Amstelveen, August 23, 2004. No result. Toss: Australia.
Man of Match: No award.

AUSTRALIA

M.L. Hayden c Ganguly b Balaji	29	(49)
+B.J. Haddin c Balaji b Nehra	5	(13)
*R.T. Ponting lbw b Balaji	26	(28)
D.R. Martyn b Sehwag	12	(17)
A. Symonds c Dravid b Kumble	12	(12)
D.S. Lehmann c Gavaskar b Kumble	19	(29)
M.J. Clarke c Sehwag b Balaji	42	(28)
G.B. Hogg not out	17	(14)
B. Lee not out	1	(1)
B 1, L-B 4, W 6, N-B 1	12	
(31.4 OVERS)	(7 WKTS) 175	

Fall: 23 69 70 83 101 138 169

M.S. Kasprowicz, G.D. McGrath (did not bat)

Bowling: Pathan 6.4–0–34–0; Nehra 6–0–44–1; Sehwag 6–0–35–1; Balaji 6–0–20–3; Kumble 7–0–37–2.

INDIA

V. Sehwag, S.C. Ganguly (captain), V.V.S. Laxman, R.S. Dravid (wicket-keeper), Yuvraj Singh, M. Kaif, R.S. Gavaskar, IK Pathan, L. Balaji, A.R. Kumble, A Nehra.

Umpires: S.A. Bucknor and J.W. Lloyds.
TV Umpire: D.R. Shepherd.
Referee: B.C. Broad.

AUSTRALIA v PAKISTAN
**VRA Ground, Amstelveen, August 28, 2004. Australia won by 17 runs. Toss: Australia.
Man of Match: A. Symonds.**

AUSTRALIA

M.L. Hayden c Yasir Hameed b Shoaib Akhtar	59	(114)
+B.J. Haddin b Mohammad Sami	10	(30)
*R.T. Ponting c Imran Farhat b Abdul Razzaq	25	(45)
D.S. Lehmann c Moin Khan b Shabbir Ahmed	40	(66)
A. Symonds b Shoaib Akhtar	36	(41)
D.R. Martyn not out	6	(5)
M.J. Clarke c Inzamam-ul-Haq b Shoaib Akhtar	1	(2)
G.B. Hogg run out (Moin Khan)	0	(0)
B 2, L-B 4, W 5, N-B 4	15	
(50 OVERS, 196 MINS)　　　(7 WKTS)	192	

Fall: 21 65 126 183 189 192 192

B. Lee, J.N. Gillespie, G.D. McGrath (did not bat)

Bowling: Mohammad Sami 10–1–26–1; Shabbir Ahmed 8–1–25–1; Shoaib Akhtar 10–0–40–3; Abdul Razzaq 8–1–30–1; Shahid Afridi 6–0–20–0; Shoaib Malik 8–0–45–0.

PAKISTAN

Yasir Hameed b Lee	17	(43)
Imran Farhat c Hayden b Symonds	17	(49)
Shoaib Malik run out (Symonds/Lehmann)	36	(58)
*Inzamam-ul-Haq c Haddin b Symonds	7	(14)
Yousuf Youhana c Haddin b Hogg	43	(57)
Shahid Afridi run out (Symonds/Haddin)	0	(0)
Abdul Razzaq c Clarke b Lehmann	26	(33)
+Moin Khan c Haddin b Gillespie	6	(12)
Mohammad Sami b Lehmann	5	(12)
Shoaib Akhtar c Haddin b McGrath	2	(5)
Shabbir Ahmed not out	0	(2)
B 6, L-B 2, W 8	16	
(47.1 OVERS, 196 MINS)	175	

Fall: 24 47 65 93 93 154 161 171 175 175

Bowling: McGrath 7.1–1–12–1; Gillespie 9–0–22–1; Lee 7–1–29–1; Hogg 7–0–43–1; Symonds 7–1–25–2; Lehmann 10–0–36–2.

Umpires: S.A. Bucknor and D.R. Shepherd.
TV Umpire: M.R. Benson.
Referee: B.C. Broad.

ICC CHAMPIONS TROPHY

WARM-UP GAME
AUSTRALIA v PAKISTAN
Lord's Cricket Ground, Lord's, September 4, 2004. Australia won by 10 runs.
Toss: Pakistan. Man of Match: A. Symonds.

AUSTRALIA

M.L. Hayden b Shahid Afridi	52	(80)
+B.J. Haddin c Shoaib Malik b Mohammad Sami	13	(13)
*R.T. Ponting lbw b Mohammad Sami	4	(5)
D.R. Martyn c Imran Farhat b Shoaib Malik	26	(43)
A. Symonds not out	104	(103)
D.S. Lehmann run out (Shoaib Malik)	9	(21)
M.J. Clarke c Shoaib Malik b Shoaib Akhtar	31	(31)
S.R. Watson not out	7	(6)
B. Lee, M.S. Kasprowicz, J.N. Gillespie (did not bat)		
L-B 9, W 12, N-B 2	23	
(50 OVERS, 205 MINS) (6 WKTS)	269	

Fall: 19 30 99 109 148 236

Bowling: Mohammad Sami 10–1–56–2; Naved-ul-Hasan 9–0–46–0; Shoaib Akhtar 8–0–70–1; Abdul Razzaq 4–0–12–0; Shoaib Malik 10–0–36–1; Shahid Afridi 9–0–40–1.

PAKISTAN

Yasir Hameed c Hayden b Kasprowicz	47	(61)
Imran Farhat c Haddin b Lee	11	(16)
Shahid Afridi lbw b Gillespie	0	(7)
Shoaib Malik c Lee b Kasprowicz	2	(9)
*Inzamam-ul-Haq c Watson b Symonds	72	(84)
Yousuf Youhana c Watson b Kasprowicz	88	(98)
Abdul Razzaq c and b Kasprowicz	15	(8)
+Moin Khan c Martyn b Gillespie	0	(1)
Naved-ul-Hasan run out (Ponting)	2	(2)
Mohammad Sami b Kasprowicz	10	(6)
Shoaib Akhtar not out	2	(1)
L-B 4, W 2, N-B 4	10	
(48.2 OVERS, 216 MINS)	259	

Fall: 30 45 50 66 228 239 245 247 250 259

Bowling: Gillespie 8–2–26–2; Lee 10–0–67–1; Kasprowicz 9.2–1–47–5; Lehmann 5–0–24–0; Symonds 5–0–31–1; Watson 9–0–47–0; Clarke 2–0–13–0.

Umpires: S.A. Bucknor and D.R. Shepherd.
TV Umpire: J.W. Lloyds.
Referee: B.C. Broad.

AUSTRALIA v UNITED STATES OF AMERICA
The Rose Bowl, Southampton, September 13, 2004. Australia won by 9 wickets.
Toss: Australia. Man of Match: M.S. Kasprowicz.

UNITED STATES OF AMERICA

R.P. Alexander c Gilchrist b Kasprowicz	8	(28)
+M.R. Johnson b Lee	0	(1)
L.C. Romero run out (Martyn)	1	(5)
S.J. Massiah c Lehmann b Kasprowicz	23	(42)
*R.W. Staple lbw b Kasprowicz	4	(10)
C.A. Reid lbw b Kasprowicz	2	(6)
Rashid Zia lbw b Gillespie	1	(16)
Aijaz Ali c Gilchrist b Gillespie	1	(6)
Nasir Javed not out	2	(19)
D.L. Blake lbw b Gillespie	0	(2)
H.R. Johnson b Gillespie	9	(15)
L-B 2, W 7, N-B 5	14	
(24 OVERS, 116 MINS)	65	

Fall: 1 2 32 38 46 46 49 53 53 65

Bowling: Lee 5–0–21–1; McGrath 6–1–13–0; Kasprowicz 7–1–14–4; Gillespie 6–1–15–4.

AUSTRALIA

+A.C. Gilchrist not out	24	(25)
M.L. Hayden c M.R. Johnson b H.R. Johnson	23	(17)
*R.T. Ponting not out	8	(8)
L-B 1, W 6, N-B 4	11	
(7.5 OVERS, 33 MINS) (1 WKT)	66	

Fall: 41

D.S. Lehmann, A. Symonds, D.R. Martyn, M.J. Clarke, M.S. Kasprowicz, B. Lee, J.N. Gillespie, G.D. McGrath (did not bat)

Bowling: H.R. Johnson 3–0–26–1; Reid 3–0–26–0; Blake 1–0–7–0; Rashid Zia 0.5–0–6–0.

Umpires: Aleem Dar and B.F. Bowden.
TV Umpire: S.A. Bucknor.
Referee: R.S. Madugalle.

AUSTRALIA v NEW ZEALAND
The Oval, September 16, 2004. Australia won by 7 wickets.
Toss: Australia. Man of Match: A. Symonds.

NEW ZEALAND

*S.P. Fleming c Gillespie b Kasprowicz	29	(51)
N.J. Astle lbw b McGrath	18	(19)
H.J.H. Marshall lbw b McGrath	0	(2)
S.B. Styris c Clarke b McGrath	0	(11)
C.D. McMillan run out (Symonds/Kasprowicz)	18	(27)
J.D.P. Oram c and b Kasprowicz	15	(27)
C.L. Cairns lbw b Kasprowicz	0	(1)
C.Z. Harris c and b Lehmann	26	(51)
+B.B. McCullum c Kasprowicz b Gillespie	47	(68)
D.L. Vettori not out	29	(42)
K.D. Mills not out	3	(3)
L-B 4, W 7, N-B 2	13	
(50 OVERS, 204 MINS) (9 WKTS)	198	

Fall: 30 36 49 49 79 79 89 124 192

Bowling: McGrath 10–0–39–3; Gillespie 9–1–46–1; Kasprowicz 10–1–32–3; Watson 6–0–32–0; Symonds 10–2–29–0; Lehmann 5–0–16–1.

AUSTRALIA

+A.C. Gilchrist b Oram	4	(5)
M.L. Hayden c Cairns b Harris	47	(74)
*R.T. Ponting b Styris	14	(28)
D.R. Martyn not out	60	(71)
A. Symonds not out	71	(47)
L-B 1, W 1, N-B 1	3	
(37.2 OVERS, 132 MINS) (3 WKTS)	199	

Fall: 4 49 99

D.S. Lehmann, M.J. Clarke, M.S. Kasprowicz, S.R. Watson, J.N. Gillespie, G.D. McGrath (did not bat)

Bowling: Oram 9–2–34–1; Mills 5.2–0–34–0; Vettori 10–0–52–0; Styris 2–0–9–1; Cairns 3–0–17–0; Harris 7–1–36–1; McMillan 1–0–16–0.

Umpires: S.A. Bucknor and R.E. Koertzen. TV Umpire: D.R. Shepherd. Referee: R.S. Madugalle.

ENGLAND v AUSTRALIA
Edgbaston, Birmingham, September 21, 2004. England won by 6 wickets.
Toss: England. Man of Match: M.P. Vaughan.

AUSTRALIA

+A.C. Gilchrist c Trescothick b Gough	37	(50)
M.L. Hayden c Trescothick b Harmison	17	(21)
*R.T. Ponting c Gough b Giles	29	(41)
D.R. Martyn c Trescothick b Vaughan	65	(91)
D.S. Lehmann b Vaughan	38	(42)
A. Symonds run out (Vaughan)	0	(2)
M.J. Clarke b Flintoff	42	(34)
B. Lee b Gough	15	(17)
J.N. Gillespie b Gough	0	(1)
M.S. Kasprowicz not out	0	(2)
G.D. McGrath not out	0	(1)
B 3, L-B 4, W 7, N-B 2	16	
(50 OVERS, 209 MINS)　　(9 WKTS)	259	

Fall: 44 69 114 189 190 210 249 249 258

Bowling: Gough 7–1–48–3; Harmison 10–0–53–1; Flintoff 10–0–56–1; Giles 10–0–40–1; Wharf 3–0–13–0; Vaughan 10–0–42–2.

ENGLAND

M.E. Trescothick b Symonds	81	(88)
V.S. Solanki lbw b Gillespie	7	(18)
*M.P. Vaughan c Hayden b Lee	86	(122)
A.J. Strauss not out	52	(42)
A. Flintoff c Hayden b Lee	16	(9)
P.D. Collingwood not out	6	(4)
L-B 5, W 5, N-B 4	14	
(46.3 OVERS, 194 MINS)　　(4 WKTS)	262	

Fall: 21 161 227 249

+G.O. Jones, A.G. Wharf, A.F. Giles, D. Gough, S.J. Harmison (did not bat)

Bowling: McGrath 8–0–46–0; Gillespie 8–0–32–1; Kasprowicz 10–0–52–0; Lee 8.3–0–65–2; Lehmann 6–0–28–0; Symonds 6–1–34–1.

Umpires: B.F. Bowden and R.E. Koertzen.
TV Umpire: Aleem Dar.
Referee: M.J. Procter.

2004 VIDEOCON-ICC CHAMPIONS INTERNATIONAL LIMITED-OVERS AVERAGES

Batting	M	Inn	NO	Runs	Best	50	100	Avrge	Ct/St	Stk-Rt
M.L. Hayden (Aus)	6	6	–	227	59	2	–	37.83	4/–	63.94
A. Symonds (Aus)	6	5	2	223	104*	1	1	74.33	–/–	108.78
D.R. Martyn (Aus)	6	5	2	169	65	2	–	56.33	1/–	74.45
M.J. Clarke (Aus)	6	4	–	116	42	–	–	29.00	2/–	122.11
D.S. Lehmann (Aus)	6	4	–	106	40	–	–	26.50	2/–	67.09
R.T. Ponting (Aus)	6	6	1	106	29	–	–	21.20	–/–	68.39
A.C. Gilchrist (Aus)	3	3	1	65	37	–	–	32.50	2/–	81.25
B.J. Haddin (Aus)	3	3	–	28	13	–	–	9.33	5/–	50.00
G.B. Hogg (Aus)	2	2	1	17	17*	–	–	17.00	–/–	120.57
B. Lee (Aus)	5	2	1	16	15	–	–	16.00	1/–	88.89
S.R. Watson (Aus)	2	1	1	7	7*	–	–	–	2/–	116.67
M.S. Kasprowicz (Aus)	5	1	1	0	0*	–	–	–	3/–	0.00
G.D. McGrath (Aus)	5	1	1	0	0*	–	–	–	–/–	0.00
J.N. Gillespie (Aus)	5	1	–	0	0	–	–	0.00	1/–	0.00

Bowling	Overs	Mds	Runs	Wkts	Best	5wi	Avrge	RPO
M.S. Kasprowicz (Aus)	36.2	3	145	12	5–47	1	12.08	3.99
J.N. Gillespie (Aus)	40.0	4	141	9	4–15	–	15.67	3.53
B. Lee (Aus)	30.3	1	182	5	2–65	–	36.40	5.97
G.D. McGrath (Aus)	31.1	2	110	4	3–39	–	27.50	3.53
A. Symonds (Aus)	28.0	4	119	4	2–25	–	29.75	4.25
D.S. Lehmann (Aus)	26.0	–	104	3	2–36	–	34.67	4.00
G.B. Hogg (Aus)	7.0	–	43	1	1–43	–	43.00	6.14
S.R. Watson (Aus)	15.0	–	79	–	–	–	–	5.27
M.J. Clarke (Aus)	2.0	–	13	–	–	–	–	6.50

2004–05 INDIA v AUSTRALIA

AUSTRALIAN TOURING PARTY

Ricky Ponting (captain), Adam Gilchrist (vice-captain), Michael Clarke, Jason Gillespie, Matthew Hayden, Nathan Hauritz, Simon Katich, Michael Kasprowicz, Damien Martyn, Glenn McGrath, Justin Langer, Brett Lee, Darren Lehmann, Shane Warne, Shane Watson, Cameron White. Brad Hodge — added 23rd September to cover for injured Ricky Ponting.

Team Management — John Buchanan (Coach), Steve Bernard (Team Manager), Tim Nielsen (Assistant Coach / Performance Analyst), Errol Alcott (Physiotherapist), Jock Campbell (Physical Performance Manager), Jonathan Rose (Media Manager), Lucy Frostick (Massage Therapist), Kathryn Turner (Yoga and Massage Consultant), Reg Dickason (Security Consultant).

MUMBAI v AUSTRALIANS
At Brabourne Stadium, Mumbai, September 30, October 1,2, 2004. Match drawn. Australian XI 7 dec 302 (M.L. Hayden 67, S.M. Katich 30, D.R. Martyn 71, B.J. Hodge 30, A.C. Gilchrist 42*; R.R. Powar 2–104, N.M. Kulkarni 2–65). Mumbai 255 (W. Jaffer 48, A.A. Muzumdar 52, A.B. Agarkar 37; G.D. McGrath 4–25, B. Lee 2–53, S.R. Watson 2–23). Australian XI 2 for 207 (J.L. Langer 108, M.J. Clarke 52).

FIRST TEST

INDIA v AUSTRALIA

M Chinnaswamy Stadium, Bangalore, October 6,7,8,9,10, 2004. Australia won by 217 runs.
Toss: Australia. Man of Match: M.J. Clarke.

Close of play: First day, Australia (1) 5–316 (Clarke 76, Gilchrist 35); Second day, India (1) 6–150 (Patel 18, Pathan 1); Third day, Australia (2) 4–127 (Martyn 29, Clarke 11); Fourth day, India (2) 6–105 (Dravid 47, Pathan 7).

AUSTRALIA

J.L. Langer b Pathan	52	–	lbw b Pathan	0
M.L. Hayden c Yuvraj b Harbhajan Singh	26	–	run out (Harbhajan)	30
S.M. Katich b Kumble	81	–	c Dravid b Kumble	39
D.R. Martyn c Chopra b Kumble	3	–	c (sub Kaif) b Harbhajan Singh	45
D.S. Lehmann c Dravid b Kumble	17	–	c Chopra b Harbhajan Singh	14
M.J. Clarke c Patel b Zaheer Khan	151	–	c Chopra b Harbhajan Singh	17
*+A.C. Gilchrist c and b Harbhajan Singh	104	–	c Chopra b Kumble	26
S.K. Warne c Dravid b Harbhajan Singh	1	–	c Yuvraj b Harbhajan Singh	31
J.N. Gillespie not out	7	–	c Yuvraj b Harbhajan Singh	8
M.S. Kasprowicz c Yuvraj b H. Singh	3	–	c Dravid b Harbhajan Singh	8
G.D. McGrath lbw b Harbhajan Singh	0	–	not out	3
B 5, L-B 15, W 1, N-B 8	29		B 2, L-B 1, W 1, N-B 3	7
(130 OVERS, 564 MINS)	474		(78.1 OVERS, 336 MINS)	228

Fall: 50 124 129 149 256 423 427 471 474 474   Fall: 0 65 86 104 146 167 204 216 217 228

Bowling: First Innings — Pathan 21–6–62–1; Zaheer Khan 22–2–60–1; Harbhajan Singh 41–7–146–5; Kumble 39–4–157–3; Sehwag 5–0–26–0; Yuvraj Singh 2–0–3–0. Second Innings — Pathan 12–2–38–1; Zaheer Khan 13–1–45–0; Harbhajan Singh 30.1–5–78–6; Kumble 23–4–64–2.

INDIA

A. Chopra lbw b McGrath	0	–	lbw b Gillespie	5
V. Sehwag c Langer b Kasprowicz	39	–	lbw b McGrath	0
R.S. Dravid b McGrath	0	–	lbw b Kasprowicz	60
*S.C. Ganguly c Gilchrist b Kasprowicz	45	–	run out (Kasprowicz)	5
V.V.S. Laxman b Warne	31	–	lbw b Warne	3
Yuvraj Singh c Gilchrist b McGrath	5	–	c Gilchrist b McGrath	27
+P.A. Patel b Gillespie	46	–	lbw b Warne	4
I.K. Pathan c Gilchrist b Warne	31	–	c Gilchrist b Gillespie	55
A.R. Kumble b Gillespie	26	–	b Kasprowicz	2
Harbhajan Singh c Lehmann b McGrath	8	–	c McGrath b Gillespie	42
Zaheer Khan not out	0	–	not out	22
B 5, L-B 2, W 5, N-B 3	15		B 6, L-B 5, N-B 3	14
(89.2 OVERS, 396 MINS)	246		(87.4 OVERS, 383 MINS)	239

Fall: 0 4 87 98 124 136 196 227 244 246   Fall: 1 7 12 19 81 86 118 125 214 239

Bowling: First Innings — McGrath 25–8–55–4; Gillespie 16.2–3–63–2; Warne 28–4–78–2; Kasprowicz 20–4–43–2. Second Innings — McGrath 20–10–39–2; Gillespie 14.4–4–33–3; Kasprowicz 14–7–23–2; Warne 32–8–115–2; Lehmann 6–3–14–0; Clarke 1–0–4–0.

Umpires: B.F. Bowden and S.A. Bucknor. TV Umpire: A.V. Jayaprakash.
Referee: R.S. Madugalle.

SECOND TEST

INDIA v AUSTRALIA
MA Chidambaram Stadium (Chepauk), Chennai, October 14,15,16,17,18 (np), 2004.
Match drawn. Toss: Australia. Man of Match: A.R. Kumble.

Close of play: First day, India (1) 1–28 (Sehwag 20, Pathan 0); Second day, India (1) 6–291 (Kaif 34, Patel 27); Third day, Australia (2) 4–150 (Martyn 19, Gillespie 0); Fourth day, India (2) 0–19 (Yuvraj Singh 7, Sehwag 12).

AUSTRALIA

J.L. Langer c Dravid b Harbhajan Singh	71	–	c Dravid b Kumble	19
M.L. Hayden c Laxman b Harbhajan Singh	58	–	c Laxman b Kumble	39
S.M. Katich not out	36	–	(4) lbw b Zaheer Khan	9
D.R. Martyn c Yuvraj Singh b Kumble	26	–	(5) c Dravid b Harbhajan Singh	104
D.S. Lehmann c Patel b Kumble	0	–	(8) c Patel b Kumble	31
M.J. Clarke lbw b Kumble	5	–	(7) not out	39
*+A.C. Gilchrist c Yuvraj Singh b Kumble	3	–	(3) b Kumble	49
S.K. Warne c and b Kumble	4	–	(9) c Kaif b Kumble	0
J.N. Gillespie c Kaif b Kumble	5	–	(6) c Dravid b Harbhajan Singh	26
M.S. Kasprowicz c Laxman b Kumble	4	–	lbw b Kumble	5
G.D. McGrath run out (Khan)	2	–	b Harbhajan Singh	2
B 7, L-B 4, W 1, N-B 4	21		B 19, L-B 15, W 3, N-B 4	46
(71.3 OVERS, 319 MINS)	235		(133.5 OVERS, 602 MINS)	369

Fall: 136 136 189 191 204 210 216 224 228 235   Fall: 53 76 121 145 284 285 347 347 364 369

Bowling: First Innings — Pathan 12–3–29–0; Zaheer Khan 11–2–44–0; Harbhajan Singh 29–2–90–2; Kumble 17.3–4–48–7; Sehwag 2–1–8–0. Second Innings — Pathan 12–3–39–0; Zaheer Khan 22–6–36–1; Harbhajan Singh 46.5–12–108–3; Kumble 47–7–133–6; Sehwag 1–0–5–0; Yuvraj Singh 2–0–7–0; Ganguly 3–1–2–0.

INDIA

Yuvraj Singh c Gilchrist b Warne	8	–	not out	7
V. Sehwag c Clarke b Warne	155	–	not out	12
I.K. Pathan c Hayden b Warne	14			
R.S. Dravid b Kasprowicz	26			
*S.C. Ganguly c Gilchrist b Gillespie	9			
V.V.S. Laxman b Gillespie	4			
M. Kaif run out (Martyn)	64			
+P.A. Patel c Gilchrist b Warne	54			
A.R. Kumble b Warne	20			
Harbhajan Singh c and b Warne	5			
Zaheer Khan not out	0			
B 6, L-B 3, W 2, N-B 6	17			0
(134.3 OVERS, 592 MINS)	376		(3 OVERS, 12 MINS) (0 WKT)	19

Fall: 28 83 178 203 213 233 335 369 372 376   Fall:

Bowling: First Innings — McGrath 25–4–74–0; Gillespie 35–8–70–2; Warne 42.3–5–125–6; Kasprowicz 25–5–65–1; Lehmann 5–0–26–0; Katich 2–0–7–0. Second Innings — McGrath 2–0–18–0; Gillespie 1–0–1–0.

Umpires: R.E. Koertzen and D.R. Shepherd. TV Umpire: A.V. Jayaprakash.
Referee: R.S. Madugalle.

THIRD TEST

INDIA v AUSTRALIA
Vidarbha CA Ground, Nagpur, October 26,27,28,29, 2004. Australia won by 342 runs.
Toss: Australia. Man of Match: D.R. Martyn.

Close of play: First day, Australia (1) 7–362 (Clarke 73, Gillespie 4); Second day, India (1) 5–146 (Kaif 47, Patel 20); Third day, Australia (2) 3–202 (Martyn 41, Clarke 10).

AUSTRALIA

J.L. Langer c Dravid b Zaheer Khan	44	–	c Laxman b Kartik	30
M.L. Hayden c Patel b Zaheer Khan	23	–	b Zaheer Khan	9
S.M. Katich c Chopra b Kumble	4	–	lbw b Kartik	99
D.R. Martyn c Agarkar b Kumble	114	–	c Patel b Zaheer Khan	97
D.S. Lehmann c Dravid b Kartik	70			
M.J. Clarke c Patel b Zaheer Khan	91	–	(5) c Kaif b Kumble	73
*+A.C. Gilchrist c and b Kartik	2	–	(6) not out	3
S.K. Warne st Patel b Kartik	2			
J.N. Gillespie lbw b Zaheer Khan	9			
M.S. Kasprowicz c Patel b Agarkar	0			
G.D. McGrath not out	11			
B 6, L-B 13, W 1, N-B 8	28		B 1, L-B 15, W 2	18
(100.2 OVERS, 436 MINS)	398		(98.1 OVERS, 410 MINS) (5 WKTS DEC)	329

Fall: 67 79 86 234 314 323 337 376 377 398

Fall: 19 99 171 319 329

Bowling: First Innings — Agarkar 23–2–99–1; Zaheer Khan 26.2–6–95–4; Kumble 25–6–99–2; Kartik 20–1–57–3; Tendulkar 6–1–29–0. Second Innings — Zaheer Khan 21.1–5–64–2; Agarkar 21–7–68–0; Kumble 21–1–89–1; Tendulkar 8–1–12–0; Kartik 26–5–74–2; Sehwag 1–0–6–0.

INDIA

A. Chopra c Warne b Gillespie	9	–	b Gillespie	1
V. Sehwag c Gilchrist b McGrath	22	–	c Clarke b Warne	58
*R.S. Dravid c Warne b McGrath	21	–	b Gillespie	2
S.R. Tendulkar lbw b Gillespie	8	–	c Martyn b McGrath	2
V.V.S. Laxman c Clarke b Warne	13	–	c McGrath b Kasprowicz	2
M. Kaif c Warne b McGrath	55	–	c Gilchrist b Kasprowicz	7
+P.A. Patel c Hayden b Warne	20	–	c Gilchrist b Gillespie	32
A.B. Agarkar c Clarke b Gillespie	15	–	not out	44
A.R. Kumble not out	7	–	b Gillespie	2
M. Kartik c Clarke b Gillespie	3	–	c Gilchrist b McGrath	22
Zaheer Khan b Gillespie	0	–	c Martyn b Warne	25
L-B 10, W 1, N-B 1	12		L-B 2, N-B 1	3
(91.5 OVERS, 379 MINS)	185		(53.3 OVERS, 237 MINS)	200

Fall: 31 34 49 75 103 150 173 178 181 185

Fall: 1 9 20 29 37 102 114 122 148 200

Bowling: First Innings — McGrath 25–13–27–3; Gillespie 22.5–8–56–5; Kasprowicz 21–4–45–0; Warne 23–8–47–2. Second Innings — McGrath 16–1–79–2; Gillespie 16–7–24–4; Kasprowicz 7–1–39–2; Warne 14.3–2–56–2.

Umpires: Aleem Dar and D.R. Shepherd. TV Umpire: K. Hariharan. Referee: R.S. Madugalle.

FOURTH TEST

INDIA v AUSTRALIA
**Wankhede Stadium, Mumbai, November 3,4,5, 2004. India won by 13 runs. Toss: India.
Man of Match: M. Kartik. Man of the Series: D.R. Martyn.**

Close of play: First day, India (1) 2–22 (Dravid 9, Tendulkar 2); Second day, India (2) 0–5 (Gambhir 1, Sehwag 4).

INDIA

G. Gambhir lbw b Gillespie	3	–	c Clarke b McGrath	1
V. Sehwag b McGrath	8	–	lbw b McGrath	5
*R.S. Dravid not out	31	–	(5) c Gilchrist b Clarke	27
S.R. Tendulkar c Gilchrist b Gillespie	5	–	c Clarke b Hauritz	55
V.V.S. Laxman c Gilchrist b Gillespie	1	–	(3) c and b Hauritz	69
M. Kaif lbw b Gillespie	2	–	lbw b Clarke	25
+K.K.D. Karthik b Kasprowicz	10	–	c Ponting b Clarke	4
A.R. Kumble c Ponting b Hauritz	16	–	not out	13
Harbhajan Singh c Katich b Hauritz	14	–	c Hayden b Clarke	0
M. Kartik c Gilchrist b Hauritz	0	–	b Clarke	2
Zaheer Khan b Kasprowicz	0	–	lbw b Clarke	0
B 6, L-B 7, N-B 1	14		B 4	4
(41.3 OVERS, 190 MINS)	104		(68.2 OVERS, 300 MINS)	205

Fall: 11 11 29 31 33 46 68 100 102 104

Fall: 5 14 105 153 182 188 195 195 199 205

Bowling: First Innings — McGrath 16–9–35–1; Gillespie 12–2–29–4; Kasprowicz 8.3–3–11–2; Hauritz 5–0–16–3. Second Innings — Gillespie 15–1–47–0; Hauritz 22–4–87–2; McGrath 12–6–29–2; Kasprowicz 13–5–29–0; Clarke 6.2–0–9–6.

AUSTRALIA

J.L. Langer c Dravid b Zaheer Khan	12	–	c Karthik b Zaheer Khan	0
M.L. Hayden c Kaif b Kartik	35	–	b Harbhajan Singh	24
*R.T. Ponting lbw b Kumble	11	–	c Laxman b Kartik	12
D.R. Martyn b Kartik	55	–	lbw b Kartik	0
S.M. Katich c Kaif b Kumble	7	–	c Dravid b Harbhajan Singh	1
M.J. Clarke st Karthik b Kumble	17	–	b Kartik	7
+A.C. Gilchrist c Kaif b Kartik	26	–	c Tendulkar b Harbhajan Singh	5
J.N. Gillespie c Kaif b Kumble	2	–	not out	9
N.M. Hauritz c Harbhajan Singh b Kumble	0	–	lbw b Kumble	15
M.S. Kasprowicz c Kumble b Kartik	19	–	c Dravid b Harbhajan Singh	7
G.D. McGrath not out	9	–	c Laxman b Harbhajan Singh	0
B 2, L-B 4, N-B 4	10		B 8, L-B 5	13
(61.3 OVERS, 258 MINS)	203		(30.5 OVERS, 136 MINS)	93

Fall: 17 37 81 101 121 157 167 171 184 203

Fall: 0 24 24 33 48 48 58 78 93 93

Bowling: First Innings — Zaheer Khan 6–0–10–1; Harbhajan Singh 21–4–53–0; Kumble 19–0–90–5; Kartik 15.3–1–44–4. Second Innings — Zaheer Khan 2–0–14–1; Harbhajan Singh 10.5–2–29–5; Kartik 12–3–32–3; Kumble 6–3–5–1.

Umpires: Aleem Dar and R.E. Koertzen. TV Umpire: K. Hariharan. Referee: R.S. Madugalle.

2004–05 INDIA–AUSTRALIA TEST AVERAGES

Batting	M	Inn	NO	Runs	Best	50	100	Avrge	Ct/St	Stk-Rt
A.B. Agarkar (Ind)	1	2	1	59	44*	–	–	59.00	1/–	72.84
M.J. Clarke (Aus)	4	8	1	400	151	2	1	57.14	7/–	55.25
D.R. Martyn (Aus)	4	8	–	444	114	2	2	55.50	2/–	50.40
V. Sehwag (Ind)	4	8	1	299	155	1	1	42.71	–/–	68.89
S.M. Katich (Aus)	4	8	1	276	99	2	–	39.43	1/–	46.94
I.K. Pathan (Ind)	2	3	–	100	55	1	–	33.33	–/–	33.33
P.A. Patel (Ind)	3	5	–	156	54	1	–	31.20	7/1	41.38
A.C. Gilchrist (Aus)	4	8	1	218	104	–	1	31.14	16/–	78.14
M. Kaif (Ind)	3	5	–	153	64	2	–	30.60	7/–	40.26
M.L. Hayden (Aus)	4	8	–	244	58	1	–	30.50	3/–	55.58
J.L. Langer (Aus)	4	8	–	228	71	2	–	28.50	1/–	44.19
R.S. Dravid (Ind)	4	7	1	167	60	1	–	27.83	13/–	27.29
D.S. Lehmann (Aus)	3	5	–	132	70	1	–	26.40	1/–	72.93
S.C. Ganguly (Ind)	2	3	–	59	45	–	–	19.67	–/–	49.58
V.V.S. Laxman (Ind)	4	7	–	123	69	1	–	17.57	6/–	48.43
S.R. Tendulkar (Ind)	2	4	–	70	55	1	–	17.50	1/–	41.92
A.R. Kumble (Ind)	4	7	2	86	26	–	–	17.20	2/–	40.57
Yuvraj Singh (Ind)	2	4	1	47	27	–	–	15.67	6/–	34.31
Harbhajan Singh (Ind)	3	5	–	69	42	–	–	13.80	2/–	55.20
J.N. Gillespie (Aus)	4	7	2	66	26	–	–	13.20	–/–	18.23
Zaheer Khan (Ind)	4	7	3	47	25	–	–	11.75	–/–	82.46
R.T. Ponting (Aus)	1	2	–	23	12	–	–	11.50	2/–	67.65
S.K. Warne (Aus)	3	5	–	38	31	–	–	7.60	4/–	51.35
N.M. Hauritz (Aus)	1	2	–	15	15	–	–	7.50	1/–	62.50
K.K.D. Karthik (Ind)	1	2	–	14	10	–	–	7.00	1/1	40.00
G.D. McGrath (Aus)	4	7	3	27	11*	–	–	6.75	2/–	47.37
M. Kartik (Ind)	2	4	–	27	22	–	–	6.75	1/–	56.25
M.S. Kasprowicz (Aus)	4	7	–	46	19	–	–	6.57	–/–	46.94
A. Chopra (Ind)	2	4	–	15	9	–	–	3.75	5/–	20.55
G. Gambhir (Ind)	1	2	–	4	3	–	–	2.00	–/–	19.05

Bowling	Overs	Mds	Runs	Wkts	Best	5wi	10wm	Avrge	RPO
M.J. Clarke (Aus)	7.2	–	13	6	6–9	1	–	2.17	1.77
J.N. Gillespie (Aus)	132.5	33	323	20	5–56	1	–	16.15	2.43
M. Kartik (Ind)	73.3	10	207	12	4–44	–	–	17.25	2.82
N.M. Hauritz (Aus)	27.0	4	103	5	3–16	–	–	20.60	3.81
Harbhajan Singh (Ind)	178.5	32	504	21	6–78	3	1	24.00	2.82
A.R. Kumble (Ind)	197.3	29	685	27	7–48	3	1	25.37	3.47
G.D. McGrath (Aus)	141.0	51	356	14	4–55	–	–	25.43	2.52
M.S. Kasprowicz (Aus)	108.3	29	255	9	2–11	–	–	28.33	2.35
S.K. Warne (Aus)	140.0	27	421	14	6–125	1	–	30.07	3.01
Zaheer Khan (Ind)	123.3	22	368	10	4–95	–	–	36.80	2.98
I.K. Pathan (Ind)	57.0	14	168	2	1–38	–	–	84.00	2.95
A.B. Agarkar (Ind)	44.0	9	167	1	1–99	–	–	167.00	3.80
V. Sehwag (Ind)	9.0	1	45	–	–	–	–	–	5.00
S.M. Katich (Aus)	2.0	–	7	–	–	–	–	–	3.50
D.S. Lehmann (Aus)	11.0	3	40	–	–	–	–	–	3.64
S.C. Ganguly (Ind)	3.0	1	2	–	–	–	–	–	0.67
S.R. Tendulkar (Ind)	14.0	2	41	–	–	–	–	–	2.93
Yuvraj Singh (Ind)	4.0	–	10	–	–	–	–	–	2.50

2004–05 AUSTRALIA v NEW ZEALAND

NEW ZEALAND TOURING SQUAD

Stephen Fleming (captain), Nathan Astle, Ian Butler, James Franklin, Hamish Marshall, Chris Martin, Brendon McCullum, Kyle Mills, Jacob Oram, Mark Richardson, Mathew Sinclair, Scott Styris, Daniel Vettori, Paul Wiseman. Gareth Hopkins included to the squad for the NSW game only and Craig McMillan included to the touring squad on November 10.

Team management — Ross Dykes (Manager), John Bracewell (Coach), Bob Carter (Assistant Coach/Video Analyst), Daryl Shackel (Physiotherapist), Greg Owen (Fitness Conditioner) and Anthony Clearwater (Media Manager).

NEW SOUTH WALES v NEW ZEALANDERS

At Sydney Cricket Ground, Sydney, November 11,12,13,14, 2004. New South Wales won by 9 wickets. New Zealanders 213 (M.S. Sinclair 88; B. Lee 3–52, M.J. Nicholson 2–41, S.C.G. MacGill 4–57). New South Wales 286 (G.J. Mail 43, D.J. Thornely 59, J.J. Krejza 54, B. Lee 33; J.E.C. Franklin 3–70, J.D.P. Oram 2–37, I.G. Butler 3–51, P.J. Wiseman 2–76). New Zealanders 201 (M.H. Richardson 50, M.S. Sinclair 79; B. Lee 2–37, M.J. Nicholson 2–31, J.J. Krejza 2–48, S.C.G. MacGill 4–52). New South Wales 1 for 129 (P.A. Jaques 70*, M.J. Phelps 39*).

FIRST TEST

AUSTRALIA v NEW ZEALAND
Brisbane Cricket Ground, Brisbane, November 18,19,20,21, 2004.
Australia won by an innings and 156 runs. Toss: New Zealand.
Man of Match: M.J. Clarke. Attendance: 52,082.

Close of play: First day, New Zealand (1) 7–250 (Oram 63, Vettori 13); Second day, Australia (1) 4–197 (Martyn 59, Clarke 31); Third day, Australia (1) 9–564 (Gillespie 43, McGrath 54).

NEW ZEALAND

M.H. Richardson c Ponting b Kasprowicz	19	–	c Gilchrist b McGrath	4
M.S. Sinclair c Ponting b Gillespie	69	–	lbw b McGrath	0
*S.P. Fleming c Warne b Kasprowicz	0	–	c Langer b McGrath	11
S.B. Styris c Gilchrist b Kasprowicz	27	–	lbw b Warne	7
N.J. Astle run out (Clarke)	19	–	c Warne b Kasprowicz	17
C.D. McMillan c Gilchrist b Warne	23	–	lbw b Gillespie	9
J.D.P. Oram not out	126	–	c Hayden b Warne	8
+B.B. McCullum st Gilchrist b Warne	10	–	c Gilchrist b Gillespie	8
D.L. Vettori c Warne b Kasprowicz	21	–	c Hayden b Warne	2
K.D. Mills c Hayden b Warne	29	–	not out	4
C.S. Martin c Ponting b Warne	0	–	lbw b Warne	0
B 1, L-B 2, W 3, N-B 4	10		L-B 2, N-B 4	6
(117.3 OVERS, 488 MINS)	353		(36.2 OVERS, 165 MINS)	76

Fall: 26 26 77 138 138 180 206 264 317 353

Fall: 6 7 19 42 44 55 69 72 72 76

Bowling: First Innings — McGrath 27–4–67–0; Gillespie 29–7–84–1; Kasprowicz 28–5–90–4; Warne 29.3–3–97–4; Lehmann 4–0–12–0. Second Innings — McGrath 8–1–19–3; Gillespie 10–5–19–2; Kasprowicz 8–2–21–1; Warne 10.2–3–15–4.

AUSTRALIA

J.L. Langer lbw b Vettori	34
M.L. Hayden lbw b Mills	8
*R.T. Ponting c Astle b Martin	51
D.R. Martyn c McMillan b Martin	70
D.S. Lehmann c McCullum b Vettori	8
M.J. Clarke b Vettori	141
+A.C. Gilchrist c Styris b Martin	126
S.K. Warne lbw b Vettori	10
J.N. Gillespie not out	54
M.S. Kasprowicz c Mills b Martin	5
G.D. McGrath c Astle b Martin	61
B 1, L-B 7, W 1, N-B 8	17
(153.5 OVERS, 641 MINS)	585

Fall: 16 85 109 128 222 438 450 464 471 585

Bowling: First Innings — Martin 39.5–7–152–5; Mills 26–8–99–1; Styris 8–1–33–0; Oram 25–4–116–0; Vettori 50–9–154–4; McMillan 5–1–23–0.

Umpires: Aleem Dar and S.A. Bucknor. TV Umpire: P.D. Parker. Referee: M.J. Procter.

SECOND TEST

AUSTRALIA v NEW ZEALAND
Adelaide Oval, Adelaide, November 26,27,28,29,30, 2004. Australia won by 213 runs.
Toss: Australia. Man of Match: J.L. Langer. Man of the Series: G.D. McGrath.
Attendance: 60,689.

Close of play: First day, Australia (1) 3–327 (Langer 144, Lehmann 28); Second day, New Zealand (1) 2–56 (Fleming 38, Wiseman 4); Third day, Australia (2) 0–57 (Langer 31, Hayden 21); Fourth day, New Zealand (2) 5–149 (Oram 40, McCullum 34).

AUSTRALIA

J.L. Langer c Oram b Vettori	215	–	lbw b Wiseman	46
M.L. Hayden c and b Wiseman	70	–	c McCullum b Vettori	54
*R.T. Ponting st McCullum b Vettori	68	–	not out	26
D.R. Martyn c Fleming b Wiseman	7	–	not out	6
D.S. Lehmann b Wiseman	81			
M.J. Clarke lbw b Vettori	7			
+A.C. Gilchrist c and b Vettori	50			
S.K. Warne not out	53			
J.N. Gillespie c Richardson b Vettori	12			
B 4, L-B 4, N-B 4	12		L-B 6, N-B 1	7
(155.2 OVERS, 636 MINS) (8 WKTS DEC)	575		(56 OVERS, 220 MINS) (2 WKTS DEC)	139

Fall: 137 240 261 445 457 465 543 575 — Fall: 93 119

M.S. Kasprowicz, G.D. McGrath (did not bat)

Bowling: First Innings — Martin 27–4–118–0; Franklin 17–2–102–0; Oram 24–7–55–0; Vettori 55.2–10–152–5; Wiseman 32–7–140–3. Second Innings — Martin 6–1–11–0; Oram 5–1–17–0; Franklin 5–0–18–0; Wiseman 22–3–52–1; Vettori 18–2–35–1.

NEW ZEALAND

M.H. Richardson b Kasprowicz	9	–	c Langer b Kasprowicz	16
M.S. Sinclair c Warne b Gillespie	0	–	lbw b Gillespie	2
*S.P. Fleming c Gilchrist b McGrath	83	–	b McGrath	3
P.J. Wiseman lbw b Kasprowicz	11	–	(10) not out	15
N.J. Astle c Langer b McGrath	52	–	c Langer b Lehmann	38
J.D.P. Oram c Gilchrist b Gillespie	12	–	c Gilchrist b McGrath	40
+B.B. McCullum lbw b Gillespie	10	–	lbw b Gillespie	36
D.L. Vettori lbw b McGrath	20	–	c Gilchrist b Lehmann	59
J.E.C. Franklin lbw b Warne	7	–	c Gilchrist b Kasprowicz	13
S.B. Styris c Clarke b McGrath	28	–	(4) c Clarke b Warne	8
C.S. Martin not out	2	–	c Ponting b Warne	2
B 3, L-B 5, N-B 9	17		B 1, L-B 12, N-B 5	18
(88.1 OVERS, 377 MINS)	251		(82.3 OVERS, 338 MINS)	250

Fall: 2 44 80 153 178 183 190 213 242 251 — Fall: 11 18 34 34 97 150 160 206 243 250

Bowling: First Innings — McGrath 20.1–3–66–4; Gillespie 19–4–37–3; Warne 28–5–65–1; Kasprowicz 16–3–66–2; Lehmann 5–2–9–0. Second Innings — McGrath 12–2–32–2; Gillespie 16–5–41–2; Kasprowicz 14–4–39–2; Warne 27.3–6–79–2; Lehmann 13–0–46–2.

Umpires: S.A. Bucknor and D.R. Shepherd. TV Umpire: S.J. Davis. Referee: M.J. Procter.

VICTORIA INVITATIONAL v NEW ZEALANDERS
At Albert Ground, South Melbourne, December 2, 2004. New Zealanders won by 34 runs.
New Zealanders 243 (S.P. Fleming 67, N.J. Astle 66, S.B. Styris 39, M.S. Sinclair 44).
Victorian Invitation XI 7 for 277 (A.C. Blizzard 43, I.S.L. Hewett 82, G.P. Lindsay 32;
K.D. Mills 3–57, I.G. Butler 3–48, C.L. Cairns 2–20).

2004–05 AUSTRALIA–NEW ZEALAND TEST AVERAGES

Batting	M	Inn	NO	Runs	Best	50	100	Avrge	Ct/St	Stk-Rt
J.L. Langer (Aus)	2	3	–	295	215	–	1	98.33	4/–	53.54
A.C. Gilchrist (Aus)	2	2	–	176	126	1	1	88.00	9/1	76.52
M.J. Clarke (Aus)	2	2	–	148	141	–	1	74.00	2/–	68.52
R.T. Ponting (Aus)	2	3	1	145	68	2	–	72.50	4/–	65.91
J.N. Gillespie (Aus)	2	2	1	66	54*	1	–	66.00	–/–	39.29
S.K. Warne (Aus)	2	2	1	63	53*	1	–	63.00	4/–	77.78
J.D.P. Oram (NZ)	2	4	1	186	126*	–	1	62.00	1/–	57.06
G.D. McGrath (Aus)	2	1	–	61	61	1	–	61.00	–/–	66.30
D.S. Lehmann (Aus)	2	2	–	89	81	1	–	44.50	–/–	48.63
M.L. Hayden (Aus)	2	3	–	132	70	2	–	44.00	3/–	48.35
D.R. Martyn (Aus)	2	3	1	83	70	1	–	41.50	–/–	49.11
K.D. Mills (NZ)	1	2	1	33	29	–	–	33.00	1/–	45.21
N.J. Astle (NZ)	2	4	–	126	52	1	–	31.50	2/–	48.84
P.J. Wiseman (NZ)	1	2	1	26	15*	–	–	26.00	1/–	37.14
D.L. Vettori (NZ)	2	4	–	102	59	1	–	25.50	1/–	52.58
S.P. Fleming (NZ)	2	4	–	97	83	1	–	24.25	1/–	49.74
M.S. Sinclair (NZ)	2	4	–	71	69	1	–	17.75	–/–	36.41
S.B. Styris (NZ)	2	4	–	70	28	–	–	17.50	1/–	39.77
C.D. McMillan (NZ)	1	2	–	32	23	–	–	16.00	1/–	30.77
B.B. McCullum (NZ)	2	4	–	64	36	–	–	16.00	2/1	61.54
M.H. Richardson (NZ)	2	4	–	48	19	–	–	12.00	1/–	26.97
J.E.C. Franklin (NZ)	1	2	–	20	13	–	–	10.00	–/–	28.57
M.S. Kasprowicz (Aus)	2	1	–	5	5	–	–	5.00	–/–	23.81
C.S. Martin (NZ)	2	4	1	4	2*	–	–	1.33	–/–	15.38

Bowling	Overs	Mds	Runs	Wkts	Best	5wi	10wm	Avrge	RPO
G.D. McGrath (Aus)	67.1	10	184	9	4–66	–	–	20.44	2.74
J.N. Gillespie (Aus)	74.0	21	181	8	3–37	–	–	22.63	2.45
S.K. Warne (Aus)	95.2	17	256	11	4–15	–	–	23.27	2.69
M.S. Kasprowicz (Aus)	66.0	14	216	9	4–90	–	–	24.00	3.27
D.S. Lehmann (Aus)	22.0	2	67	2	2–46	–	–	33.50	3.05
D.L. Vettori (NZ)	123.2	21	341	10	5–152	1	–	34.10	2.76
P.J. Wiseman (NZ)	54.0	10	192	4	3–140	–	–	48.00	3.56
C.S. Martin (NZ)	72.5	12	281	5	5–152	1	–	56.20	3.86
K.D. Mills (NZ)	26.0	8	99	1	1–99	–	–	99.00	3.81
S.B. Styris (NZ)	8.0	1	33	–	–	–	–	–	4.13
J.D.P. Oram (NZ)	54.0	12	188	–	–	–	–	–	3.48
C.D. McMillan (NZ)	5.0	1	23	–	–	–	–	–	4.60
J.E.C. Franklin (NZ)	22.0	2	120	–	–	–	–	–	5.45

CHAPPELL–HADLEE TROPHY

AUSTRALIA v NEW ZEALAND
Docklands Stadium, Melbourne, December 5, 2004. Day/night game.
New Zealand won by 4 wickets. Toss: New Zealand. Man of Match: H.J.H. Marshall.
Attendance: 30,753.

AUSTRALIA

+A.C. Gilchrist b Cairns	68	(54)
M.L. Hayden c Sinclair b Oram	13	(21)
*R.T. Ponting lbw b Vettori	29	(49)
D.S. Lehmann c Butler b Oram	50	(73)
D.R. Martyn lbw b Vettori	1	(4)
A. Symonds c Mills b Vettori	0	(3)
M.J. Clarke b Cairns	36	(49)
S.R. Watson c McCullum b Butler	3	(7)
G.B. Hogg not out	20	(23)
B. Lee b Cairns	8	(11)
M.S. Kasprowicz not out	9	(9)
B 2, L-B 2, W 2, N-B 3	9	
(50 OVERS, 222 MINS) (9 WKTS) 246		

Fall: 64 113 121 123 123 194 198 220 236

Bowling: Mills 4–0–28–0; Butler 8–0–58–1; Oram 9–0–51–2; Cairns 10–0–39–3; Vettori 10–1–31–3; Styris 9–0–35–0.

NEW ZEALAND

*S.P. Fleming lbw b Lee	0	(2)
N.J. Astle c Ponting b Lehmann	70	(102)
M.S. Sinclair run out (Clarke)	48	(86)
S.B. Styris c Lee b Lehmann	5	(10)
H.J.H. Marshall not out	50	(52)
J.D.P. Oram c Gilchrist b Kasprowicz	24	(22)
C.L. Cairns b Lee	14	(11)
+B.B. McCullum not out	20	(13)
L-B 9, W 7	16	
(49.4 OVERS, 209 MINS) (6 WKTS) 247		

Fall: 0 128 131 140 189 208

D.L. Vettori, K.D. Mills, I.G. Butler (did not bat)

Bowling: Lee 8–0–40–2; Kasprowicz 9–1–53–1; Watson 8.4–0–42–0; Hogg 7–0–33–0; Lehmann 9–0–35–2; Symonds 8–0–35–0.

Umpires: S.J. Davis and R.E. Koertzen.
TV Umpire: R.L. Parry.
Referee: M.J. Procter.

AUSTRALIA v NEW ZEALAND
Sydney Cricket Ground, Sydney, December 8, 2004. Day/night game.
Australia won by 17 runs. Toss: Australia. Man of Match: G.B. Hogg. Attendance: 28,374.

AUSTRALIA

+A.C. Gilchrist c Astle b Styris	60	(48)
M.L. Hayden run out (Sinclair)	43	(65)
*R.T. Ponting c Fleming b Mills	32	(36)
D.R. Martyn lbw b Mills	5	(5)
A. Symonds lbw b Vettori	0	(2)
D.S. Lehmann run out (Styris/Oram)	52	(77)
M.J. Clarke c McCullum b Cairns	6	(17)
G.B. Hogg not out	41	(53)
B. Lee not out	10	(5)
L-B 2, W 2, N-B 8	12	
(50 OVERS, 229 MINS) (7 WKTS)	261	

Fall: 86 140 147 148 148 161 235

J.N. Gillespie, G.D. McGrath (did not bat)

Bowling: Mills 10–0–49–2; Oram 10–0–77–0; Cairns 10–0–60–1; Styris 10–0–37–1; Vettori 10–1–36–1.

NEW ZEALAND

*S.P. Fleming lbw b Hogg	34	(44)
N.J. Astle c Gilchrist b Lee	11	(22)
M.S. Sinclair c Hayden b Gillespie	17	(30)
S.B. Styris lbw b Symonds	5	(6)
H.J.H. Marshall b Lee	9	(24)
J.D.P. Oram lbw b Hogg	2	(8)
C.L. Cairns c McGrath b Gillespie	50	(40)
+B.B. McCullum lbw b Hogg	21	(44)
D.L. Vettori run out (Ponting)	33	(36)
K.D. Mills not out	44	(26)
C.Z. Harris b McGrath	4	(6)
L-B 5, W 6, N-B 3	14	
(47.1 OVERS, 219 MINS)	244	

Fall: 27 63 68 78 84 86 154 166 236 244

Bowling: McGrath 7.1–0–27–1; Lee 9–0–48–2; Gillespie 10–1–41–2; Symonds 10–1–47–1; Hogg 8–0–45–3; Lehmann 3–0–31–0.

Umpires: R.E. Koertzen and P.D. Parker.
TV Umpire: S.J.A. Taufel.
Referee: M.J. Procter.

AUSTRALIA v NEW ZEALAND
Brisbane Cricket Ground, Brisbane, December 11, 2004. Day/night game.
No play due to rain.

2004–05 CHAPPELL–HADLEE AVERAGES

Batting	M	Inn	NO	Runs	Best	50	100	Avrge	Ct/St	Stk-Rt
A.C. Gilchrist (Aus)	2	2	–	128	68	2	–	64.00	2/–	125.49
D.S. Lehmann (Aus)	2	2	–	102	52	2	–	51.00	–/–	68.00
N.J. Astle (NZ)	2	2	–	81	70	1	–	40.50	1/–	65.32
M.S. Sinclair (NZ)	2	2	–	65	48	–	–	32.50	1/–	56.03
C.L. Cairns (NZ)	2	2	–	64	50	1	–	32.00	–/–	125.49
G.B. Hogg (Aus)	2	2	2	61	41*	–	–	–	–/–	80.26
R.T. Ponting (Aus)	2	2	–	61	32	–	–	30.50	1/–	71.76
H.J.H. Marshall (NZ)	2	2	1	59	50*	1	–	59.00	–/–	77.63
M.L. Hayden (Aus)	2	2	–	56	43	–	–	28.00	1/–	65.12
K.D. Mills (NZ)	2	1	1	44	44*	–	–	–	1/–	169.23
M.J. Clarke (Aus)	2	2	–	42	36	–	–	21.00	–/–	63.64
B.B. McCullum (NZ)	2	2	1	41	21	–	–	41.00	2/–	71.93
S.P. Fleming (NZ)	2	2	–	34	34	–	–	17.00	1/–	73.91
D.L. Vettori (NZ)	2	1	–	33	33	–	–	33.00	–/–	91.67
J.D.P. Oram (NZ)	2	2	–	26	24	–	–	13.00	–/–	86.67
B. Lee (Aus)	2	2	1	18	10*	–	–	18.00	1/–	112.50
S.B. Styris (NZ)	2	2	–	10	5	–	–	5.00	–/–	62.50
M.S. Kasprowicz (Aus)	1	1	1	9	9*	–	–	–	–/–	100.00
D.R. Martyn (Aus)	2	2	–	6	5	–	–	3.00	–/–	66.67
C.Z. Harris (NZ)	1	1	–	4	4	–	–	4.00	–/–	66.67
S.R. Watson (Aus)	1	1	–	3	3	–	–	3.00	–/–	42.86
A. Symonds (Aus)	2	2	–	0	0	–	–	0.00	–/–	0.00
J.N. Gillespie (Aus)	1	–	–	–	–	–	–	–	–/–	–
I.G. Butler (NZ)	1	–	–	–	–	–	–	–	1/–	–
G.D. McGrath (Aus)	1	–	–	–	–	–	–	–	1/–	–

Bowling	Overs	Mds	Runs	Wkts	Best	5wi	Avrge	RPO
D.L. Vettori (NZ)	20.0	2	67	4	3–31	–	16.75	3.35
B. Lee (Aus)	17.0	–	88	4	2–40	–	22.00	5.18
C.L. Cairns (NZ)	20.0	–	99	4	3–39	–	24.75	4.95
G.B. Hogg (Aus)	15.0	–	78	3	3–45	–	26.00	5.20
J.N. Gillespie (Aus)	10.0	1	41	2	2–41	–	20.50	4.10
D.S. Lehmann (Aus)	12.0	–	66	2	2–35	–	33.00	5.50
K.D. Mills (NZ)	14.0	–	77	2	2–49	–	38.50	5.50
J.D.P. Oram (NZ)	19.0	–	128	2	2–51	–	64.00	6.74
G.D. McGrath (Aus)	7.1	–	27	1	1–27	–	27.00	3.77
M.S. Kasprowicz (Aus)	9.0	1	53	1	1–53	–	53.00	5.89
I.G. Butler (NZ)	8.0	–	58	1	1–58	–	58.00	7.25
S.B. Styris (NZ)	19.0	–	72	1	1–37	–	72.00	3.79
A. Symonds (Aus)	18.0	1	82	1	1–47	–	82.00	4.56
S.R. Watson (Aus)	8.4	–	42	–	–	–	–	4.85

2004–05 AUSTRALIA v PAKISTAN

PAKISTAN TOURING SQUAD

Inzamam-ul-Haq (captain), Yousuf Youhana (vice-captain), Abdul Razzaq, Shoaib Akhtar, Shahid Afridi, Younis Khan, Mohammad Sami, Shoaib Malik, Danish Kaneria, Yasir Hameed, Imran Farhat, Kamran Akmal, Asim Kamal, Naved-ul-Hasan, Salman Butt, Mohammad Asif, Mohammad Khalil.

Team management — Haroon Rashid (Manager), Bob Woolmer (Coach), Coertzen Hendrick (Video Analyst), Darryn Lifson (Physiotherapist), Murray Stevenson (Biokineticist) and Abdur Rauf (Masseur).

WESTERN AUSTRALIA SECOND XI v PAKISTANIS

At James Oval, Perth, December 1,2, 2004. Western Australia Second XI won by 10 runs. Western Australia Second XI 158 (S.W. Meuleman 32, L. Ronchi 66; Mohammad Sami 3–19, Mohammad Khalil 3–42, Mohammad Asif 2–52). Pakistanis 257 (Younis Khan 142; J.P. Coetzee 5–66, M.J. Petrie 4–29). Western Australia Second XI 192 (C.J. Simmons 65, J.P. Coetzee 30; Danish Kaneria 7–45). Pakistanis 83 (Yousuf Youhana 41; J.P. Coetzee 5–23, M.J. Petrie 4–29, J.R. Sprague 3–24).

WESTERN AUSTRALIA A v PAKISTANIS

At James Oval, Perth, December 3, 2004. Pakistanis won by 126 runs. Pakistanis 6 for 273 (Salman Butt 39, Imran Farhat 31, Shoaib Malik 35, Abdul Razzaq 55, Shahid Afridi 34; P.C. Worthington 2–74). Western Australia A 147 (C.J. Heron 33, A.K. Heal 53; Mohammad Khalil 2–14, Shoaib Malik 2–47, Salman Butt 2–8).

AUSTRALIAN CRICKET BOARD'S CHAIRMAN'S XI v PAKISTANIS

At Lilac Hill Park, Caversham, December 7, 2004. Pakistanis won by 43 runs. Pakistanis 9 for 256 (Salman Butt 115*; P.C. Worthington 2–46, M.E.K. Hussey 3–28). Australian Cricket Board's Chairman's XI 213 (C.J.L. Rogers 61, D.J. Thornely 38, L. Ronchi 51; Naved-ul-Hasan 3–36, Shahid Afridi 2–49, Danish Kaneria 2–40).

WESTERN AUSTRALIA v PAKISTANIS

At WACA Ground, Perth, December 9,10,11, 2004. Western Australia won by 10 wickets. Pakistanis 262 (Salman Butt 42, Yousuf Youhana 77, Abdul Razzaq 83*; S.J. Magoffin 2–68, B.R. Dorey 3–38, B.M. Edmondson 2–71, B. Casson 2–44). Western Australia 9 dec 404 (M.E.K. Hussey 124, C.J.L. Rogers 46, M.J. North 79, S.E. Marsh 39, R.J. Campbell 49; Shoaib Akhtar 2–41, Danish Kaneria 3–133, Imran Farhat 2–30). Pakistanis 174 (Salman Butt 47, Yousuf Youhana 32, Abdul Razzaq 35*; B.M. Edmondson 3–38, B.R. Dorey 5–41, S.J. Magoffin 2–52). Western Australia 0 for 34.

FIRST TEST

AUSTRALIA v PAKISTAN
WACA Ground, Perth, December 16,17,18,19, 2004. Australia won by 491 runs.
Toss: Pakistan. Man of Match: J.L. Langer. Attendance: 42,193.

Close of play: First day, Australia (1) 8–357 (Langer 181, Kasprowicz 4); Second day, Australia (2) 0–15 (Langer 3, Hayden 7); Third day, Pakistan (2) 1–18 (Salmat Butt 8, Younis Khan 7).

AUSTRALIA

J.L. Langer c Younis Khan b M. Sami	191	–	b Abdul Razzaq	97
M.L. Hayden lbw b Shoaib Akhtar	4	–	b Shoaib Akhtar	10
*R.T. Ponting b Mohammad Sami	25	–	st Kamran b Danish Kaneria	98
D.R. Martyn c Kamran Akmal b M. Sami	1	–	not out	100
D.S. Lehmann b Shoaib Akhtar	12	–	b Danish Kaneria	5
M.J. Clarke c Inzamam-ul-Haq b S. Akhtar	1	–	c Inzamam-ul-Haq b M. Sami	27
+A.C. Gilchrist b Abdul Razzaq	69	–	not out	0
S.K. Warne c Y. Youhana b A. Razzaq	12			
J.N. Gillespie c K. Akmal b S. Akhtar	24			
M.S. Kasprowicz lbw b Shoaib Akhtar	4			
G.D. McGrath not out	8			
B 1, L-B 14, W 5, N-B 10	30		L-B 15, W 2, N-B 7	24
(90.5 OVERS, 413 MINS)	381		(85.2 OVERS, 344 MINS) (5 WKTS DEC)	361

Fall: 6 56 58 71 78 230 253 333 362 381

Fall: 28 191 271 281 360

Bowling: First Innings — Shoaib Akhtar 22–1–99–5; Mohammad Sami 25.5–3–104–3; Mohammad Khalil 16–0–59–0; Abdul Razzaq 12–0–55–2; Danish Kaneria 15–2–49–0. Second Innings — Shoaib Akhtar 6.3–1–22–1; Mohammad Sami 14–1–55–1; Abdul Razzaq 12.3–1–48–1; Mohammad Khalil 9.2–0–38–0; Danish Kaneria 32–3–130–2; Imran Farhat 11–0–53–0.

PAKISTAN

Salman Butt c Gilchrist b Kasprowicz	17	–	c Hayden b McGrath	9
Imran Farhat c Gilchrist b Gillespie	18	–	lbw b McGrath	1
Younis Khan c Gillespie b Warne	42	–	c Warne b McGrath	17
*Inzamam-ul-Haq b Kasprowicz	1	–	(6) c Gilchrist b McGrath	0
Yousuf Youhana c Gilchrist b Kasprowicz	1	–	(4) c Gilchrist b McGrath	27
Abdul Razzaq b Warne	21	–	(5) c Gilchrist b McGrath	1
+Kamran Akmal b Kasprowicz	2	–	c Clarke b McGrath	0
Mohammad Sami c Clarke b Kasprowicz	29	–	b Kasprowicz	2
Mohammad Khalil b Warne	0	–	(10) c and b Kasprowicz	5
Shoaib Akhtar c Warne b McGrath	27	–	(9) c Lehmann b McGrath	1
Danish Kaneria not out	6	–	not out	0
B 1, L-B 3, W 7, N-B 4	15		L-B 7, W 2	9
(77.3 OVERS, 314 MINS)	179		(31.3 OVERS, 145 MINS)	72

Fall: 32 45 55 60 108 110 110 111 171 179

Fall: 5 34 43 49 49 61 64 66 72 72

Bowling: First Innings — McGrath 19–7–44–1; Gillespie 14–2–43–1; Kasprowicz 16.3–6–30–5; Warne 21–9–38–3; Lehmann 4–2–5–0; Ponting 3–1–15–0. Second Innings — McGrath 16–8–24–8; Gillespie 12–3–37–0; Kasprowicz 3.3–2–4–2.

Umpires: B.F. Bowden and R.E. Koertzen. TV Umpire: S.J. Davis. Referee: R.S. Madugalle.

SECOND TEST

AUSTRALIA v PAKISTAN
Melbourne Cricket Ground, Melbourne, December 26,27,28,29, 2004.
Australia won by 9 wickets. Toss: Pakistan. Man of Match: D.R. Martyn.
Attendance: 129,079.

Close of play: First day, Pakistan (1) 6–318 (Abdul Razzaq 1, Kamran Akmal 16); Second day, Australia (1) 5–203 (Martyn 67, Gilchrist 26); Third day, Pakistan (2) 5–85 (Shoaib Malik 11, Mohammad Sami 8).

PAKISTAN

Salman Butt run out (Clarke)	70	–	c Kasprowicz b McGrath	0
Imran Farhat c Ponting b Kasprowicz	20	–	c Martyn b Gillespie	5
Yasir Hameed lbw b Gillespie	2	–	c Gilchrist b McGrath	23
Younis Khan c Gilchrist b Gillespie	87	–	c Hayden b Kasprowicz	23
*Yousuf Youhana st Gilchrist b Warne	111	–	c Ponting b Warne	12
Shoaib Malik c Ponting b Gillespie	6	–	c Gillespie b Warne	41
Abdul Razzaq not out	4	–	(8) c Gilchrist b McGrath	19
+Kamran Akmal c Gilchrist b McGrath	24	–	(9) lbw b Warne	0
Mohammad Sami lbw b Warne	12	–	(7) lbw b Gillespie	11
Shoaib Akhtar st Gilchrist b Warne	0	–	b McGrath	14
Danish Kaneria run out (Clarke)	0	–	not out	9
L-B 4, W 1	5		B 4, L-B 1, N-B 1	6
(107.3 OVERS, 454 MINS)	341		(64.2 OVERS, 268 MINS)	163

Fall: 85 93 94 286 298 301 326 341 341 341   Fall: 0 13 35 60 68 98 101 140 140 163

Bowling: First Innings — McGrath 28–12–54–1; Gillespie 26–7–77–3; Kasprowicz 20–6–66–1; Warne 28.3–2–103–3; Clarke 3–0–24–0; Lehmann 2–0–13–0. Second Innings — McGrath 11.2–1–35–4; Gillespie 12–7–15–2; Kasprowicz 16–3–42–1; Warne 25–7–66–3.

AUSTRALIA

J.L. Langer c Imran Farhat b D. Kaneria	50	–	c Kamran Akmal b M. Sami	5
M.L. Hayden c Shoaib Malik b S. Akhtar	9	–	not out	56
*R.T. Ponting c Shoaib Malik b S. Akhtar	7	–	not out	62
D.R. Martyn lbw b Danish Kaneria	142			
D.S. Lehmann c Yasir Hameed b S. Akhtar	11			
M.J. Clarke c Shoaib Akhtar b D. Kaneria	20			
+A.C. Gilchrist c M. Sami b D. Kaneria	48			
S.K. Warne c and b Shoaib Akhtar	10			
J.N. Gillespie not out	50			
M.S. Kasprowicz c (sub Rana) b S. Akhtar	4			
G.D. McGrath lbw b Danish Kaneria	1			
B 1, L-B 2, W 5, N-B 19	27		L-B 2, N-B 2	4
(99.3 OVERS, 454 MINS)	379		(27.5 OVERS, 110 MINS) (1 WKT)	127

Fall: 13 32 122 135 171 230 254 347 368 379   Fall: 11

Bowling: First Innings — Shoaib Akhtar 27–4–109–5; Mohammad Sami 23–2–102–0; Abdul Razzaq 7–0–27–0; Danish Kaneria 39.3–5–125–5; Imran Farhat 3–0–13–0. Second Innings — Shoaib Akhtar 7–0–35–0; Mohammad Sami 5–0–22–1; Danish Kaneria 10.5–1–52–0; Imran Farhat 5–2–16–0.

Umpires: R.E. Koertzen and J.W. Lloyds. TV Umpire: R.L. Parry. Referee: R.S. Madugalle.

THIRD TEST

AUSTRALIA v PAKISTAN
Sydney Cricket Ground, Sydney, January 2,3,4,5, 2005. Australia won by 9 wickets.
Toss: Pakistan. Man of Match: S.C.G. MacGill. Man of the Series: D.R. Martyn.
Attendance: 105,417.

Close of play: First day, Pakistan (1) 9–292 (Kamran Akmal 35, Mohammad Asif 0); Second day, Australia (1) 4–340 (Ponting 155, Gilchrist 17); Third day, Pakistan (2) 1–67 (Yasir Hameed 40, Younis Khan 5).

PAKISTAN

Salman Butt c Gilchrist b McGrath	108	–	c Warne b MacGill	21
Yasir Hameed c Clarke b Warne	58	–	lbw b Warne	63
Younis Khan c McGrath b MacGill	46	–	lbw b Watson	44
*Yousuf Youhana c Warne b MacGill	8	–	b MacGill	30
Asim Kamal c Gillespie b MacGill	10	–	c Ponting b Gillespie	87
Shahid Afridi c McGrath b MacGill	12	–	run out (Martyn)	46
+Kamran Akmal c Warne b McGrath	47	–	c Hayden b Warne	4
Naved-ul-Hasan lbw b McGrath	0	–	lbw b Warne	9
Shoaib Akhtar b McGrath	0	–	c Martyn b Warne	0
Danish Kaneria c Gilchrist b MacGill	3	–	b MacGill	0
Mohammad Asif not out	0	–	not out	12
B 6, L-B 2, W 1, N-B 3	12		B 4, L-B 3, N-B 2	9
(86.4 OVERS, 366 MINS)	304		(89.2 OVERS, 374 MINS)	325

Fall: 102 193 209 241 241 261 261 261 280 304   Fall: 46 104 164 164 238 243 261 269 270 325

Bowling: First Innings — McGrath 16.4–5–50–4; Gillespie 14–3–47–0; Watson 10–3–28–0; Warne 24–4–84–1; MacGill 22–4–87–5. Second Innings — McGrath 16–2–53–0; Gillespie 13.2–2–39–1; Warne 26–2–111–4; MacGill 25–3–83–3; Watson 9–2–32–1.

AUSTRALIA

J.L. Langer b Naved-ul-Hasan	13	–	b Danish Kaneria	34
M.L. Hayden b Danish Kaneria	26	–	not out	23
*R.T. Ponting b Naved-ul-Hasan	207	–	not out	4
D.R. Martyn st K. Akmal b D. Kaneria	67			
M.J. Clarke st K. Akmal b D. Kaneria	35			
+A.C. Gilchrist st K. Akmal b D. Kaneria	113			
S.R. Watson c M. Asif b D. Kaneria	31			
S.K. Warne c Younis Khan b D. Kaneria	16			
J.N. Gillespie lbw b Naved-ul-Hasan	0			
G.D. McGrath c Y. Youhana b D. Kaneria	9			
S.C.G. MacGill not out	9			
B 6, L-B 13, W 3, N-B 20	42		N-B 1	1
(133.3 OVERS, 554 MINS)	568		(9.3 OVERS, 38 MINS) (1 WKT)	62

Fall: 26 83 257 318 471 529 535 537 556 568   Fall: 58

Bowling: First Innings — Shoaib Akhtar 15–2–69–0; Naved-ul-Hasan 26–3–107–3; Mohammad Asif 16–3–72–0; Danish Kaneria 49.3–7–188–7; Shahid Afridi 27–3–113–0. Second Innings — Naved-ul-Hasan 3–0–28–0; Mohammad Asif 2–0–16–0; Danish Kaneria 2.3–0–16–1; Shahid Afridi 2–0–2–0.

Umpires: B.F. Bowden and D.R. Shepherd. TV Umpire: S.J. Davis. Referee: R.S. Madugalle.

AUSTRALIA A v PAKISTANIS

At Adelaide Oval, Adelaide, January 12, 2005. Pakistanis won by 13 runs. Pakistanis 8 for 279 (Yasir Hameed 30, Mohammad Hafeez 61, Abdul Razzaq 89*; S.W. Tait 2–49, D.G. Wright 2–54). Australia A 266 (B.J. Haddin 129, B.J. Hodge 30, D.J. Hussey 45; Naved-ul-Hasan 3–42, Iftikhar Anjum 2–52, Abdul Razzaq 2–45).

AUSTRALIA A v PAKISTANIS

At Adelaide Oval, Adelaide, January 13, 2005. Australia A won by 56 runs. Australia A 5 for 185 (D.J. Hussey 50, C.L. White 58*; Shoaib Akhtar 2–37). Pakistanis 7 for 129 (Taufeeq Umar 31; D.G. Wright 2–27).

PRIME MINISTER'S XI v PAKISTANIS

At Manuka Oval, Canberra, January 25, 2005. Pakistanis won by 5 wickets. 191 (L. Ronchi 40, C.J.L. Rogers 46, S.P. Heaney 35; Azhar Mahmood 2–23, Shoaib Malik 3–29). Pakistanis 5 for 192 (Yousuf Youhana 50, Younis Khan 62*, Mohammad Hafeez 36; B.M. Edmondson 3–38).

2004–05 AUSTRALIA–PAKISTAN TEST AVERAGES

Batting	M	Inn	NO	Runs	Best	50	100	Avrge	Ct/St	Stk-Rt
D.R. Martyn (Aus)	3	4	1	310	142	1	2	103.33	2/–	60.90
R.T. Ponting (Aus)	3	6	2	403	207	2	1	100.75	4/–	60.78
A.C. Gilchrist (Aus)	3	4	1	230	113	1	1	76.67	12/2	92.33
J.L. Langer (Aus)	3	6	–	390	191	2	1	65.00	–/–	70.14
Asim Kamal (Pak)	1	2	–	97	87	1	–	48.50	–/–	56.40
Younis Khan (Pak)	3	6	–	259	87	1	–	43.17	2/–	50.49
Salman Butt (Pak)	3	6	–	225	108	1	1	37.50	–/–	56.96
J.N. Gillespie (Aus)	3	3	1	74	50*	1	–	37.00	3/–	41.34
Yasir Hameed (Pak)	2	4	–	146	63	2	–	36.50	1/–	63.20
M.L. Hayden (Aus)	3	6	2	128	56*	1	–	32.00	3/–	61.24
Yousuf Youhana (Pak)	3	6	–	189	111	–	1	31.50	2/–	63.00
S.R. Watson (Aus)	1	1	–	31	31	–	–	31.00	–/–	50.00
Shahid Afridi (Pak)	1	2	–	58	46	–	–	29.00	–/–	95.08
Shoaib Malik (Pak)	1	2	–	47	41	–	–	23.50	2/–	45.63
M.J. Clarke (Aus)	3	4	–	83	35	–	–	20.75	3/–	53.21
Abdul Razzaq (Pak)	2	4	1	45	21	–	–	15.00	–/–	20.55
Mohammad Sami (Pak)	2	4	–	54	29	–	–	13.50	1/–	27.27
Kamran Akmal (Pak)	3	6	–	77	47	–	–	12.83	3/4	55.00
S.K. Warne (Aus)	3	3	–	38	16	–	–	12.67	5/–	55.07
Imran Farhat (Pak)	2	4	–	44	20	–	–	11.00	1/–	34.11
D.S. Lehmann (Aus)	2	3	–	28	12	–	–	9.33	1/–	93.33
G.D. McGrath (Aus)	3	3	1	18	9	–	–	9.00	2/–	64.29
Shoaib Akhtar (Pak)	3	6	–	42	27	–	–	7.00	2/–	28.19
Danish Kaneria (Pak)	3	6	3	18	9*	–	–	6.00	–/–	51.43
Naved-ul-Hasan (Pak)	1	2	–	9	9	–	–	4.50	–/–	128.57

Batting (continued)	M	Inn	NO	Runs	Best	50	100	Avrge	Ct/St	Stk-Rt
M.S. Kasprowicz (Aus)	2	2	–	8	4	–	–	4.00	2/–	50.00
Mohammad Khalil (Pak)	1	2	–	5	5	–	–	2.50	–/–	21.74
Inzamam-ul-Haq (Pak)	1	2	–	1	1	–	–	0.50	2/–	6.67
Mohammad Asif (Pak)	1	2	2	12	12*	–	–	–	1/–	19.67
S.C.G. MacGill (Aus)	1	1	1	9	9*	–	–	–	–/–	90.00

Bowling	Overs	Mds	Runs	Wkts	Best	5wi	10wm	Avrge	RPO
G.D. McGrath (Aus)	107.0	35	260	18	8–24	1	–	14.44	2.43
M.S. Kasprowicz (Aus)	56.0	17	142	9	5–30	1	–	15.78	2.54
S.C.G. MacGill (Aus)	47.0	7	170	8	5–87	1	–	21.25	3.62
S.K. Warne (Aus)	124.3	24	402	14	4–111	–	–	28.71	3.23
Shoaib Akhtar (Pak)	77.3	8	334	11	5–99	2	–	30.36	4.31
J.N. Gillespie (Aus)	91.2	24	258	7	3–77	–	–	36.86	2.82
Danish Kaneria (Pak)	149.2	18	560	15	7–188	2	–	37.33	3.75
Abdul Razzaq (Pak)	31.3	1	130	3	2–55	–	–	43.33	4.13
Naved-ul-Hasan (Pak)	29.0	3	135	3	3–107	–	–	45.00	4.66
Mohammad Sami (Pak)	67.5	6	283	5	3–104	–	–	56.60	4.17
S.R. Watson (Aus)	19.0	5	60	1	1–32	–	–	60.00	3.16
Shahid Afridi (Pak)	29.0	3	115	–	–	–	–	–	3.97
D.S. Lehmann (Aus)	6.0	2	18	–	–	–	–	–	3.00
Mohammad Khalil (Pak)	25.2	–	97	–	–	–	–	–	3.83
Mohammad Asif (Pak)	18.0	3	88	–	–	–	–	–	4.89
R.T. Ponting (Aus)	3.0	1	15	–	–	–	–	–	5.00
Imran Farhat (Pak)	19.0	2	82	–	–	–	–	–	4.32
M.J. Clarke (Aus)	3.0	–	24	–	–	–	–	–	8.00

2004–05 ICC TSUNAMI MATCH

ACC ASIA WORLD XI v ICC WORLD XI
Melbourne Cricket Ground, Melbourne, January 10, 2005. Day/night game.
ICC World XI won by 112 runs. Toss: ICC World XI. Man of Match: R.T. Ponting.
Attendance: 70,101.

ICC WORLD XI

C.H. Gayle c Sangakkara b Zaheer Khan	1	(9)
+A.C. Gilchrist c Sangakkara b Zaheer Khan	24	(20)
*R.T. Ponting st Sangakkara b Kumble	115	(102)
B.C. Lara c Vaas b Kumble	52	(77)
C.L. Cairns st Sangakkara b Muralitharan	69	(47)
G.D. McGrath c Yousuf Youhana b Muralitharan	0	(1)
S.P. Fleming b Vaas	30	(28)
M.L. Hayden st Sangakkara b Muralitharan	2	(6)
D.L. Vettori not out	27	(17)
S.K. Warne not out	2	(2)
L-B 3, W 7, N-B 12	22	
(50 OVERS, 219 MINS) (8 WKTS)	344	

Fall: 1 50 172 263 264 286 292 337

D. Gough (did not bat)

Bowling: Vaas 9–1–59–1; Zaheer Khan 8–0–46–2; Abdul Razzaq 5–0–50–0; Muralitharan 10–0–59–3; Kumble 10–0–73–2; Sehwag 7–0–46–0; Jayasuriya 1–0–8–0.

ACC ASIAN XI

S.T. Jayasuriya c Fleming b Cairns	28	(29)
V. Sehwag c Gayle b Warne	45	(39)
*S.C. Ganguly c Gough b Vettori	22	(40)
R.S. Dravid not out	75	(71)
Yousuf Youhana c Ponting b Warne	4	(5)
+K.C. Sangakkara c Gilchrist b Gough	24	(24)
Abdul Razzaq st Gilchrist b Vettori	11	(12)
W.P.U.J.C. Vaas c Gayle b Vettori	7	(11)
Zaheer Khan run out (Gayle/Gilchrist)	0	(0)
A.R. Kumble b McGrath	11	(7)
M. Muralitharan run out (Vettori)	0	(2)
L-B 2, W 2, N-B 1	5	
(39.5 OVERS, 172 MINS)	232	

Fall: 59 76 107 114 156 173 197 199 226 232

Bowling: McGrath 7–0–37–1; Gough 8–0–55–1; Cairns 6–0–37–1; Warne 7–0–27–2; Vettori 10–0–58–3; Gayle 1.5–0–16–0.

Umpires: B.F. Bowden and R.E. Koertzen.
TV Umpire: R.L. Parry. Referee: B.C. Broad.

2004–05 VB SERIES

AUSTRALIAN SQUAD

Ricky Ponting (captain), Adam Gilchrist (vice-captain), Michael Clarke, Jason Gillespie, Brad Haddin, Matthew Hayden, Brad Hogg, Michael Kasprowicz, Simon Katich, Brett Lee, Darren Lehmann, Damien Martyn, Glenn McGrath, Andrew Symonds, Shane Watson.

PAKISTAN SQUAD

Inzamam-ul-Haq (captain), Yousuf Youhana (vice-captain), Abdul Razzaq, Azhar Mahmood, Iftikhar Anjum, Kamran Akmal, Mohammad Hafeez, Mohammad Khalil, Naved-ul-Hasan, Salman Butt, Shahid Afridi, Shoaib Akhtar, Shoaib Malik, Taufeeq Umar, Yasir Hameed, Younis Khan.

WEST INDIES SQUAD

Brian Lara (captain), Shivnarine Chanderpaul (vice-captain), Ian Bradshaw, Dwayne Bravo, Courtney Browne, Pedro Collins, Mervyn Dillon, Chris Gayle, Wavell Hinds, Reon King, Xavier Marshall, Ricardo Powell, Marlon Samuels, Ramnaresh Sarwan.

Team management — Anthony Howard (Manager), Bennett King (Coach), David Moore (Assistant Coach/Analyst), Stephen Partridge (Physiotherapist), Imran Khan (Media Liaison).

AUSTRALIA v WEST INDIES
Melbourne Cricket Ground, Melbourne, January 14, 2005. Day/night game.
Australia won by 116 runs. Toss: Australia. Australia 6 pts. Man of Match: G.B. Hogg.
Attendance: 51,543.

AUSTRALIA

+A.C. Gilchrist c Bravo b Bradshaw	0	(7)
M.J. Clarke b Samuels	66	(77)
*R.T. Ponting run out (Chanderpaul/Browne)	78	(92)
D.R. Martyn not out	95	(93)
A. Symonds c Gayle b Bradshaw	20	(21)
D.S. Lehmann not out	20	(14)
B 2, L-B 5, W 11, N-B 4	22	
(50 OVERS, 202 MINS) (4 WKTS)	301	

Fall: 4 119 207 254

S.R. Watson, G.B. Hogg, B. Lee, J.N. Gillespie, M.S. Kasprowicz (did not bat)

Bowling: Bradshaw 10–1–46–2; Dillon 8–0–69–0; Samuels 10–0–45–1; Hinds 3–0–20–0; Gayle 3–0–21–0; Sarwan 8–0–49–0; Bravo 8–0–44–0.

WEST INDIES

C.H. Gayle lbw b Lee	0	(3)
W.W. Hinds run out (Symonds)	5	(10)
R.R. Sarwan c Gilchrist b Lee	4	(10)
*B.C. Lara c Symonds b Hogg	58	(68)
X.M. Marshall c Gilchrist b Lee	5	(10)
S. Chanderpaul c and b Hogg	46	(73)
M.N. Samuels c and b Hogg	9	(26)
D.J.J. Bravo c Gilchrist b Hogg	3	(10)
+C.O. Browne not out	20	(39)
I.D.R. Bradshaw c Clarke b Hogg	12	(19)
M. Dillon c Ponting b Kasprowicz	6	(10)
B 1, L-B 13, W 3	17	
(46.2 OVERS, 201 MINS)	185	

Fall: 0 17 21 33 131 136 143 144 167 185

Bowling: Lee 10–1–36–3; Gillespie 8–0–29–0; Kasprowicz 6.2–0–26–1; Watson 7–0–37–0; Hogg 10–0–32–5; Symonds 5–0–11–0.

Umpires: S.J. Davis and R.E. Koertzen.
TV Umpire: R.L. Parry. Referee: B.C. Broad.

AUSTRALIA v PAKISTAN

Bellerive Oval, Hobart, January 16, 2005. Australia won by 4 wickets. Toss: Pakistan. Australia 5 and Pakistan 1 pts. Man of Match: M.J. Clarke. Attendance: 15,503.

PAKISTAN

Salman Butt c Lehmann b Hogg	61	(87)
+Kamran Akmal c Clarke b McGrath	5	(8)
Mohammad Hafeez c Hogg b Lee	0	(9)
Shoaib Malik lbw b Symonds	31	(43)
*Inzamam-ul-Haq lbw b Kasprowicz	68	(64)
Yousuf Youhana c Martyn b Kasprowicz	30	(47)
Abdul Razzaq c Clarke b McGrath	12	(14)
Shahid Afridi not out	56	(26)
Azhar Mahmood not out	3	(3)
L-B 1, W 4, N-B 1	6	
(50 OVERS, 209 MINS) (7 WKTS)	272	

Fall: 15 30 83 117 191 204 251

Shoaib Akhtar, Naved-ul-Hasan (did not bat)

Bowling: McGrath 10–2–54–2; Lee 10–0–66–1; Kasprowicz 9–0–38–2; Symonds 9–0–55–1; Hogg 7–0–28–1; Lehmann 5–0–30–0.

AUSTRALIA

M.J. Clarke c Naved-ul-Hasan b Mohammad Hafeez	97	(99)
S.M. Katich b Azhar Mahmood	38	(48)
*R.T. Ponting c Kamran Akmal b Shahid Afridi	6	(8)
D.R. Martyn b Abdul Razzaq	11	(18)
D.S. Lehmann not out	49	(57)
A. Symonds b Abdul Razzaq	0	(5)
+B.J. Haddin c Mohammad Hafeez b Naved-ul-Hasan	30	(30)
G.B. Hogg not out	3	(1)
L-B 5, W 6, N-B 8	19	
(43 OVERS, 223 MINS) (6 WKTS)	253	

Fall: 107 118 141 184 185 243

B. Lee, G.D. McGrath, M.S. Kasprowicz (did not bat)

Bowling: Shoaib Akhtar 8–0–54–0; Naved-ul-Hasan 8–0–60–1; Azhar Mahmood 6–0–33–1; Shahid Afridi 9–0–43–1; Abdul Razzaq 8–0–41–2; Mohammad Hafeez 4–0–17–1.

Umpires: B.F. Bowden and D.J. Harper. TV Umpire: P.D. Parker. Referee: B.C. Broad.

PAKISTAN v WEST INDIES

At Brisbane Cricket Ground, Brisbane, January 19, 2005. Pakistan won by 6 wickets. West Indies 273 (C.H. Gayle 82, R.R. Sarwan 76, B.C. Lara 39, Naved-ul-Hasan 2-55). Pakistan 4 for 274 (Kamran Akmal 124, Shoaib Malik 60, Inzamam-ul-Haq 62*, Bradshaw 2-49, Dillon 2-46). Man of the Match: Kamran Akmal.

AUSTRALIA v WEST INDIES

Brisbane Cricket Ground, Brisbane, January 21, 2005. Day/night game. No result. Toss: West Indies. Man of Match: No award. Attendance: 32,618.

WEST INDIES

C.H. Gayle b Gillespie	26	(22)
W.W. Hinds c Gilchrist b Watson	107	(138)
R.R. Sarwan lbw b Lehmann	27	(38)
*B.C. Lara c Gilchrist b Lee	6	(16)
S. Chanderpaul c Ponting b Kasprowicz	45	(48)
M.N. Samuels run out (Martyn/Kasprowicz)	13	(10)
D.J.J. Bravo c Kasprowicz b Gillespie	27	(22)
+C.O. Browne b Gillespie	0	(1)
M. Dillon not out	1	(3)
I.D.R. Bradshaw b Watson	1	(3)
P.T. Collins not out	0	(1)
L-B 4, W 4, N-B 2	10	
(50 OVERS, 228 MINS) (9 WKTS)	263	

Fall: 29 84 92 181 210 253 260 260 263

Bowling: Lee 7–1–30–1; Gillespie 9–1–62–3; Kasprowicz 10–1–43–1; Watson 10–0–52–2; Lehmann 7–0–34–1; Symonds 7–0–38–0.

AUSTRALIA

+A.C. Gilchrist c Browne b Bradshaw	6	(8)
M.L. Hayden c Gayle b Collins	6	(14)
*R.T. Ponting lbw b Collins	2	(10)
D.R. Martyn not out	14	(16)
A. Symonds c Browne b Collins	0	(3)
M.J. Clarke c Samuels b Dillon	2	(10)
D.S. Lehmann not out	10	(6)
L-B 1, W 1, N-B 1	3	
(11 OVERS, 54 MINS) (5 WKTS)	43	

Fall: 8 12 24 25 30

S.R. Watson, B. Lee, J.N. Gillespie, M.S. Kasprowicz (did not bat)

Bowling: Collins 4–1–8–3; Bradshaw 2–0–6–1; Dillon 3–1–15–1; Samuels 2–0–13–0.

Umpires: B.F. Bowden and S.J.A. Taufel. TV Umpire: P.D. Parker. Referee: B.C. Broad.

AUSTRALIA v PAKISTAN
Sydney Cricket Ground, Sydney, January 23, 2005. Day/night game.
Australia won by 9 wickets. Toss: Australia. Australia 6 pts. Man of Match: M.J. Clarke.
Attendance: 30,942.

PAKISTAN

Salman Butt lbw b McGrath	0	(8)
+Kamran Akmal b Lee	2	(7)
Shoaib Malik b McGrath	8	(29)
*Inzamam-ul-Haq c Clarke b Lehmann	50	(61)
Yousuf Youhana c Ponting b Kasprowicz	4	(6)
Mohammad Hafeez c Hayden b Watson	13	(36)
Abdul Razzaq run out (Clarke)	16	(21)
Shahid Afridi st Haddin b Lehmann	48	(37)
Azhar Mahmood c Hayden b Lehmann	1	(7)
Naved-ul-Hasan b Lee	6	(20)
Iftikhar Anjum not out	1	(3)
L-B 4, W 10	14	
(39.2 OVERS, 172 MINS)	163	

Fall: 2 2 38 44 68 98 103 115 161 163

Bowling: McGrath 10–3–18–2; Lee 10–0–54–2; Kasprowicz 5–0–17–1; Watson 7–2–26–1; Lehmann 7.2–0–44–3.

AUSTRALIA

M.J. Clarke not out	103	(107)
M.L. Hayden c Naved-ul-Hasan b Abdul Razzaq	27	(65)
*R.T. Ponting not out	17	(51)
B 3, L-B 5, W 7, N-B 5	20	
(36.2 OVERS, 138 MINS) (1 WKT)	167	

Fall: 79

D.R. Martyn, A. Symonds, D.S. Lehmann, +B.J. Haddin, S.R. Watson, B. Lee, M.S. Kasprowicz, G.D. McGrath (did not bat)

Bowling: Naved-ul-Hasan 6–0–20–0; Iftikhar Anjum 3–0–22–0; Abdul Razzaq 7–0–43–1; Shahid Afridi 8–0–22–0; Mohammad Hafeez 4–1–17–0; Azhar Mahmood 4.2–2–14–0; Salman Butt 4–0–21–0.

Umpires: D.J. Harper and R.E. Koertzen. TV Umpire: S.J.A. Taufel. Referee: B.C. Broad.

AUSTRALIA v WEST INDIES
Adelaide Oval, Adelaide, January 26, 2005. Day/night game. Australia won by 73 runs.
Toss: Australia. Australia 6 pts. Man of Match: B. Lee. Attendance: 26,539.

AUSTRALIA

M.J. Clarke b Collins	21	(16)
M.L. Hayden c Browne b Collins	3	(6)
*R.T. Ponting c Bravo b Collins	0	(2)
A. Symonds c Browne b Hinds	31	(49)
D.S. Lehmann c Browne b Collins	4	(6)
S.M. Katich lbw b Collins	76	(86)
+B.J. Haddin b Bravo	32	(50)
G.B. Hogg c Browne b Bravo	3	(6)
B. Lee not out	38	(44)
J.N. Gillespie not out	44	(32)
L-B 3, W 8, N-B 6	17	
(50 OVERS, 224 MINS) (8 WKTS)	269	

Fall: 24 24 34 38 85 167 182 196

G.D. McGrath (did not bat)

Bowling: Collins 10–1–43–5; Bradshaw 10–1–45–0; Dillon 6–0–37–0; Hinds 4–0–25–1; Bravo 10–0–71–2; Samuels 10–0–45–0.

WEST INDIES

C.H. Gayle c Haddin b Lee	2	(11)
W.W. Hinds c Haddin b Lee	0	(1)
R.R. Sarwan c Haddin b Hogg	39	(62)
S. Chanderpaul run out (Clarke)	55	(87)
*B.C. Lara c and b Lee	29	(38)
M.N. Samuels c Ponting b Lehmann	14	(20)
D.J.J. Bravo b McGrath	18	(24)
+C.O. Browne lbw b Lee	0	(1)
I.D.R. Bradshaw b Gillespie	15	(21)
M. Dillon b Gillespie	5	(7)
P.T. Collins not out	1	(2)
L-B 7, W 6, N-B 5	18	
(44.5 OVERS, 204 MINS)	196	

Fall: 1 3 95 110 147 153 153 185 195 196

Bowling: Lee 10–1–38–4; McGrath 8–1–18–1; Gillespie 6.5–0–25–2; Symonds 10–0–50–0; Hogg 6–0–33–1; Lehmann 4–0–25–1.

Umpires: B.F. Bowden and S.J. Davis.
TV Umpire: D.J. Harper.
Referee: B.C. Broad.

PAKISTAN v WEST INDIES
At Adelaide Oval, Adelaide, January 28, 2005. West Indies won by 58 runs. West Indies 4 for 339 (B.C. Lara 156, S. Chanderpaul 85, W.W. Hinds 30*). Pakistan 281 (Mohammad Hafeez 41, Inzamam-ul-Haq 30, Yousuf Youhana 45, Abdul Razzaq 44, Azhar Mahmood 40*, King 2-51, Hinds 2-62, Bravo 2-39). Man of the Match: B.C. Lara.

AUSTRALIA v PAKISTAN
WACA Ground, Perth, January 30, 2005. Day/night game.
Pakistan won by 3 wickets. Toss: Australia. Australia 1 and Pakistan 5 pts.
Man of Match: Abdul Razzaq. Attendance: 18,751.

AUSTRALIA

+A.C. Gilchrist b Abdul Razzaq	47	(46)
M.L. Hayden c Shahid Afridi b Naved-ul-Hasan	6	(16)
*R.T. Ponting b Abdul Razzaq	29	(45)
D.R. Martyn c Shoaib Malik b Shahid Afridi	24	(25)
A. Symonds c Shoaib Malik b Shahid Afridi	23	(41)
M.J. Clarke not out	75	(75)
S.M. Katich c Younis Khan b Mohammad Khalil	0	(3)
G.B. Hogg c Younis Khan b Mohammad Khalil	10	(13)
B. Lee c Mohammad Khalil b Abdul Razzaq	22	(35)
J.N. Gillespie c Younis Khan b Abdul Razzaq	4	(3)
G.D. McGrath b Naved-ul-Hasan	0	(1)
B 1, L-B 5, W 16, N-B 3	25	
(50 OVERS, 223 MINS)	265	

Fall: 30 63 111 113 164 167 192 246 251 265

Bowling: Naved-ul-Hasan 10–0–49–2; Iftikhar Anjum 10–0–57–0; Abdul Razzaq 10–0–53–4; Mohammad Khalil 10–0–55–2; Shahid Afridi 10–0–45–2.

PAKISTAN

Salman Butt c Gillespie b McGrath	20	(36)
Yasir Hameed c Symonds b Lee	12	(15)
+Younis Khan c Martyn b McGrath	6	(14)
Yousuf Youhana c Katich b Symonds	72	(90)
*Inzamam-ul-Haq lbw b Hogg	29	(38)
Shoaib Malik run out (Symonds)	1	(1)
Abdul Razzaq not out	63	(61)
Shahid Afridi c Lee b Symonds	30	(13)
Naved-ul-Hasan not out	20	(18)
L-B 7, W 6, N-B 2	15	
(47.2 OVERS, 204 MINS)	(7 WKTS) 268	

Fall: 27 41 49 123 125 170 223

Iftikhar Anjum, Mohammad Khalil (did not bat)

Bowling: Lee 9.2–0–63–1; McGrath 9–2–27–2; Gillespie 10–1–35–0; Hogg 10–0–71–1; Symonds 9–0–65–2.

Umpires: B.F. Bowden and P.D. Parker.
TV Umpire: S.J. Davis. Referee: B.C. Broad.

PAKISTAN v WEST INDIES
At WACA Ground, Perth, February 1, 2005. Pakistan won by 30 runs. Pakistan 8 for 307 (Yousuf Youhana 105, Inzamam-ul-Haq 74, Bradshaw 3-47). West Indies 277 (R.R. Sarwan 87, S. Chanderpaul 58, W.W. Hinds 30, C.O. Browne 36, Naved-ul-Hasan 4-29, Iftikhar Anjum 2-67, Mohammad Khalil 2-59, Shahid Afridi 2-47). Man of the Match: Yousuf Youhana.

2004–05 VB SERIES POINTS TABLE

Team	Played	Won	Lost	No Result	Bonus Points	Points	Net Run Rate
Australia	6	4	1	1	4	27	+1.0817
Pakistan	6	3	3	–	2	17	–0.2950
West Indies	6	1	4	1	2	10	–0.7176

FIRST FINAL — AUSTRALIA v PAKISTAN
Melbourne Cricket Ground, Melbourne, February 4, 2005. Day/night game.
Australia won by 18 runs. Toss: Australia. Man of Match: A. Symonds. Attendance: 27,502.

AUSTRALIA

+A.C. Gilchrist c Abdul Razzaq b Mohammad Khalil	24	(42)
M.J. Clarke lbw b Naved-ul-Hasan	9	(22)
*R.T. Ponting b Iftikhar Anjum	11	(15)
D.R. Martyn st Kamran Akmal b Shahid Afridi	53	(78)
A. Symonds c Inzamam-ul-Haq b Abdul Razzaq	91	(101)
D.S. Lehmann c Kamran Akmal b Shahid Afridi	0	(1)
S.M. Katich c (sub) Yasir Hameed b Abdul Razzaq	9	(17)
S.R. Watson c Mohammad Hafeez b Abdul Razzaq	4	(5)
B. Lee b Naved-ul-Hasan	13	(12)
J.N. Gillespie not out	3	(3)
G.D. McGrath run out (Kamran Akmal/Iftikhar)	1	(1)
B 1, L-B 8, W 7, N-B 3	19	
(49 OVERS, 199 MINS)	237	

Fall: 29 51 53 190 190 213 213 220 235 237

Bowling: Naved-ul-Hasan 9–0–50–2; Iftikhar Anjum 8–1–27–1; Mohammad Khalil 4–0–30–1; Shahid Afridi 10–0–50–2; Abdul Razzaq 10–0–33–3; Mohammad Hafeez 8–0–38–0.

PAKISTAN

Salman Butt lbw b Lee	0	(2)
+Kamran Akmal c Gillespie b McGrath	4	(4)
Mohammad Hafeez c Watson b McGrath	13	(39)
Yousuf Youhana b Lee	2	(4)
*Inzamam-ul-Haq c McGrath b Lee	51	(83)
Shoaib Malik c Lehmann b Gillespie	66	(89)
Abdul Razzaq run out (Symonds)	3	(4)
Shahid Afridi c Katich b Gillespie	26	(15)
Naved-ul-Hasan c Martyn b McGrath	29	(29)
Iftikhar Anjum not out	19	(32)
Mohammad Khalil not out	0	(0)
L-B 3, W 2, N-B 1	6	
(50 OVERS, 214 MINS) (9 WKTS)	219	

Fall: 1 7 9 27 118 123 153 171 216

Bowling: Lee 10–0–23–3; McGrath 10–3–34–3; Gillespie 10–0–47–2; Watson 9–1–38–0; Lehmann 4–0–29–0; Symonds 7–0–45–0.

Umpires: B.F. Bowden and S.J. Davis.
TV Umpire: R.L. Parry. Referee: B.C. Broad.

SECOND FINAL — AUSTRALIA v PAKISTAN
**Sydney Cricket Ground, Sydney, February 6, 2005. Day/night game.
Australia won by 31 runs. Toss: Australia. Man of Match: G.D. McGrath.
Man of the series: D.R. Martyn. Attendance: 38,279.**

AUSTRALIA

+A.C. Gilchrist c Shoaib Malik b Abdul Razzaq	40	(30)
M.J. Clarke b Mohammad Hafeez	38	(75)
*R.T. Ponting c Inzamam-ul-Haq b Shahid Afridi	41	(61)
D.R. Martyn b Abdul Razzaq	43	(60)
D.S. Lehmann b Shahid Afridi	6	(12)
S.M. Katich run out (Shoaib Malik/Kamran Akmel)	5	(8)
S.R. Watson c Shahid Afridi b Iftikhar Anjum	21	(25)
G.B. Hogg b Naved-ul-Hasan	13	(17)
B. Lee not out	14	(14)
J.N. Gillespie b Naved-ul-Hasan	0	(1)
G.D. McGrath not out	5	(2)
B 1, L-B 4, W 3, N-B 5	13	
(50 OVERS, 196 MINS) (9 WKTS)	239	

Fall: 55 118 146 156 166 203 207 230 230

Bowling: Naved-ul-Hasan 9–0–69–2; Iftikhar Anjum 10–0–33–1; Abdul Razzaq 9.5–2–51–2; Shahid Afridi 10–0–38–2; Mohammad Hafeez 10–0–34–1; Taufeeq Umar 1–0–8–0; Azhar Mahmood 0.1–0–1–0.

PAKISTAN

+Kamran Akmal c Gilchrist b McGrath	12	(19)
Taufeeq Umar c McGrath b Lee	3	(12)
Mohammad Hafeez c Clarke b McGrath	6	(25)
Yousuf Youhana b Hogg	51	(57)
*Inzamam-ul-Haq lbw b McGrath	0	(3)
Shoaib Malik c Katich b Hogg	14	(23)
Abdul Razzaq c Gilchrist b McGrath	43	(58)
Shahid Afridi run out (Lee)	31	(21)
Azhar Mahmood lbw b Gillespie	13	(14)
Naved-ul-Hasan b McGrath	19	(38)
Iftikhar Anjum not out	5	(6)
L-B 3, W 6, N-B 2	11	
(45.4 OVERS, 203 MINS)	208	

Fall: 13 17 38 38 74 97 133 153 201 208

Bowling: Lee 8–1–31–1; McGrath 7.4–0–27–5; Gillespie 10–0–35–1; Watson 3.5–0–15–0; Hogg 10–0–63–2; Lehmann 6.1–0–34–0.

Umpires: D.J. Harper and R.E. Koertzen. TV Umpire: P.D. Parker. Referee: B.C. Broad.

2004–05 VB SERIES INTERNATIONAL LIMITED-OVERS AVERAGES

Batting	M	Inn	NO	Runs	HS	50	100	Avrge	Ct/St	Stk-Rt
M.J. Clarke (Aus)	8	8	2	411	103*	3	1	68.50	5/–	85.45
Inzamam-ul-Haq (Pak)	8	8	1	364	74	5	–	52.00	4/–	91.46
Yousuf Youhana (Pak)	8	8	1	318	105	2	1	45.43	–/–	85.48
S. Chanderpaul (W.I)	6	6	1	314	85	3	–	62.80	1/–	81.35
B.C. Lara (W.I)	6	6	–	307	156	1	1	51.17	2/–	99.03
D.R. Martyn (Aus)	7	6	2	240	95*	2	–	60.00	3/–	82.76
R.R. Sarwan (W.I)	6	6	1	235	87	2	–	47.00	–/–	77.30
Shahid Afridi (Pak)	8	7	1	231	56*	1	–	38.50	2/–	167.39
W.W. Hinds (W.I)	6	6	1	201	107	–	1	40.20	–/–	76.43
Shoaib Malik (Pak)	8	8	1	195	66	2	–	27.86	4/–	72.49
Abdul Razzaq (Pak)	8	7	1	188	63*	1	–	31.33	1/–	87.04
R.T. Ponting (Aus)	8	8	1	184	78	1	–	26.29	4/–	64.79
Kamran Akmal (Pak)	7	7	–	183	124	–	1	26.14	5/2	78.54
A. Symonds (Aus)	7	6	–	165	91	1	–	27.50	2/–	75.00
S.M. Katich (Aus)	5	5	–	128	76	1	–	25.60	3/–	79.01
C.H. Gayle (W.I)	6	6	–	119	82	1	–	19.83	3/–	79.33
A.C. Gilchrist (Aus)	5	5	–	117	47	–	–	23.40	7/–	87.97
Salman Butt (Pak)	7	7	–	111	61	1	–	15.86	1/–	56.06
D.S. Lehmann (Aus)	7	6	3	89	49*	–	–	29.67	2/–	92.71
B. Lee (Aus)	8	4	2	87	38*	–	–	43.50	2/–	82.86
Naved-ul-Hasan (Pak)	8	6	1	87	29	–	–	17.40	3/–	70.73
Mohammad Hafeez (Pak)	6	6	–	75	41	–	–	12.50	4/–	47.17
B.J. Haddin (Aus)	3	2	–	62	32	–	–	31.00	3/1	77.50
Azhar Mahmood (Pak)	5	4	2	57	40*	–	–	28.50	–/–	95.00
C.O. Browne (W.I)	6	4	1	56	36	–	–	18.67	9/1	75.68
D.J.J. Bravo (W.I)	5	5	1	52	27	–	–	13.00	4/–	80.00
J.N. Gillespie (Aus)	6	4	2	51	44*	–	–	25.50	2/–	130.77
R.L. Powell (W.I)	3	3	–	46	23	–	–	15.33	–/–	73.02
M.L. Hayden (Aus)	4	4	–	42	27	–	–	10.50	2/–	41.58
Yasir Hameed (Pak)	2	2	–	36	24	–	–	18.00	–/–	78.26
M.N. Samuels (W.I)	4	3	–	36	14	–	–	12.00	1/–	64.29
Iftikhar Anjum (Pak)	6	4	4	32	19*	–	–	–	1/–	65.31
G.B. Hogg (Aus)	5	4	1	29	13	–	–	9.67	3/–	78.38
I.D.R. Bradshaw (W.I)	6	4	–	28	15	–	–	7.00	–/–	59.57
S.R. Watson (Aus)	5	2	–	25	21	–	–	12.50	1/–	83.33
M. Dillon (W.I)	4	3	1	12	6	–	–	6.00	–/–	60.00
G.D. McGrath (Aus)	6	3	1	6	5*	–	–	3.00	2/–	150.00
Younis Khan (Pak)	1	1	–	6	6	–	–	6.00	3/–	42.86
X.M. Marshall (W.I)	1	1	–	5	5	–	–	5.00	–/–	50.00
Taufeeq Umar (Pak)	1	1	–	3	3	–	–	3.00	–/–	25.00

Batting (continued)	M	Inn	NO	Runs	HS	50	100	Avrge	Ct/St	Stk-Rt
R.D. King (W.I)	2	1	1	3	3*	–	–	–	–/–	30.00
P.T. Collins (W.I)	5	3	2	2	1*	–	–	2.00	–/–	33.33
Mohammad Khalil (Pak)	3	1	1	0	0*	–	–	–	2/–	0.00
Shoaib Akhtar (Pak)	2	–	–	–	–	–	–	–	–/–	–
M.S. Kasprowicz (Aus)	4	–	–	–	–	–	–	–	1/–	–

Bowling	Overs	Mds	Runs	Wkts	Best	5wi	Avrge	RPO
Naved-ul-Hasan (Pak)	70.1	–	409	14	4–29	–	29.21	5.83
B. Lee (Aus)	74.2	4	341	16	4–38	–	21.31	4.59
G.D. McGrath (Aus)	54.4	11	178	15	5–27	1	11.87	3.26
Abdul Razzaq (Pak)	70.5	2	366	13	4–53	–	28.15	5.17
Shahid Afridi (Pak)	77.0	–	348	10	2–38	–	34.80	4.52
G.B. Hogg (Aus)	43.0	–	227	10	5–32	1	22.70	5.28
I.D.R. Bradshaw (W.I)	50.0	4	237	9	3–47	–	26.33	4.74
J.N. Gillespie (Aus)	53.5	2	233	8	3–62	–	29.13	4.33
P.T. Collins (W.I)	38.0	3	160	8	5–43	1	20.00	4.21
Mohammad Khalil (Pak)	24.0	–	144	5	2–55	–	28.80	6.00
Iftikhar Anjum (Pak)	49.0	2	256	5	2–67	–	51.20	5.22
M.S. Kasprowicz (Aus)	30.2	1	124	5	2–38	–	24.80	4.09
D.S. Lehmann (Aus)	33.3	–	196	5	3–44	–	39.20	5.85
D.J.J. Bravo (W.I)	38.0	–	209	5	2–39	–	41.80	5.50
W.W. Hinds (W.I)	25.0	–	176	4	2–62	–	44.00	7.04
Mohammad Hafeez (Pak)	39.0	1	194	4	1–17	–	48.50	4.97
R.D. King (W.I)	20.0	–	111	3	2–51	–	37.00	5.55
A. Symonds (Aus)	47.0	–	264	3	2–65	–	88.00	5.62
M. Dillon (W.I)	27.0	2	167	3	2–46	–	55.67	6.19
S.R. Watson (Aus)	36.5	3	168	3	2–52	–	56.00	4.56
Azhar Mahmood (Pak)	28.4	4	168	2	1–33	–	84.00	5.86
R.L. Powell (W.I)	4.0	–	30	1	1–30	–	30.00	7.50
M.N. Samuels (W.I)	31.0	–	175	1	1–45	–	175.00	5.65
Shoaib Akhtar (Pak)	10.5	–	61	–	–	–	–	5.63
C.H. Gayle (W.I)	12.0	–	107	–	–	–	–	8.92
Taufeeq Umar (Pak)	1.0	–	8	–	–	–	–	8.00
R.R. Sarwan (W.I)	13.0	–	80	–	–	–	–	6.15
Salman Butt (Pak)	6.0	–	42	–	–	–	–	7.00

2004–05 NEW ZEALAND v AUSTRALIA

AUSTRALIAN TOURING PARTY

Limited-Overs Touring Party

Ricky Ponting (captain), Adam Gilchrist (vice-captain), Michael Clarke, Jason Gillespie, Matthew Hayden, Brad Hogg, James Hopes, Mike Hussey, Michael Kasprowicz, Simon Katich, Brett Lee, Damien Martyn, Glenn McGrath, Andrew Symonds.

Test Match Touring Party

Ricky Ponting (captain), Adam Gilchrist (vice-captain), Michael Clarke, Matthew Hayden, Jason Gillespie, Brad Hodge, Mike Hussey, Michael Kasprowicz, Simon Katich, Justin Langer, Brett Lee, Damien Martyn, Glenn McGrath, Shane Warne.

Team Management — John Buchanan (Coach), Steve Bernard (Team Manager), Darren Holder, Jamie Siddons and Dene Hills (Assistant Coaches / Performance Analyst), Alex Kountouri (Physiotherapist), Jock Campbell (Physical Performance Manager), Jonathan Rose (Media Manager), Lucy Frostick (Massage Therapist).

TWENTY20 GAME

NEW ZEALAND v AUSTRALIA
Eden Park, Auckland, February 17, 2005. Day/night game. Australia won by 44 runs.
Toss: Australia. Man of Match: R.T. Ponting.

AUSTRALIA

+A.C. Gilchrist c McMillan b Mills	1	(3)
M.J. Clarke c McMillan b Tuffey	7	(4)
A. Symonds c McCullum b Mills	32	(13)
*R.T. Ponting not out	98	(55)
D.R. Martyn b Mills	3	(5)
S.M. Katich b Cairns	30	(25)
M.E.K. Hussey not out	31	(15)
L-B 9, W 3	12	
(20 OVERS, 83 MINS)	(5 WKTS) 214	

Fall: 10 21 46 54 137

J.R. Hopes, B. Lee, M.S. Kasprowicz, G.D. McGrath (did not bat)

Bowling: Tuffey 4–0–50–1; Mills 4–0–44–3; Cairns 4–0–28–1; Wilson 4–0–43–0; Adams 4–0–40–0.

NEW ZEALAND

+B.B. McCullum c Ponting b Kasprowicz	36	(24)
*S.P. Fleming b Kasprowicz	18	(13)
M.S. Sinclair c Katich b Kasprowicz	0	(1)
S.B. Styris b Lee	66	(39)
C.D. McMillan c Hussey b Hopes	9	(8)
C.L. Cairns c McGrath b Kasprowicz	1	(4)
H.J.H. Marshall b Symonds	8	(7)
A.R. Adams run out (McGrath/Symonds)	7	(7)
J.W. Wilson b McGrath	18	(14)
K.D. Mills c Kasprowicz b McGrath	0	(1)
D.R. Tuffey not out	5	(2)
W 2	2	
(20 OVERS)	170	

Fall: 49 49 67 93 95 105 121 161 165 170

Bowling: Lee 4–0–26–1; McGrath 4–0–48–2; Kasprowicz 4–0–29–4; Hopes 3–0–23–1; Symonds 3–0–33–1; Clarke 2–0–11–0.

Umpires: B.F. Bowden and A.L. Hill.
TV Umpire: D.B. Cowie.

NEW ZEALAND v AUSTRALIA

WestpacTrust Stadium, Wellington, February 19, 2005. Day/night game.
Australia won by 10 runs. Toss: Australia. Man of Match: G.D. McGrath.

AUSTRALIA

+A.C. Gilchrist c Sinclair b Mills	4	(5)
M.L. Hayden b Styris	71	(109)
*R.T. Ponting c Vettori b Styris	61	(84)
D.R. Martyn b Styris	7	(16)
A. Symonds b Cairns	53	(44)
M.J. Clarke c Marshall b Styris	0	(5)
S.M. Katich c McCullum b Cairns	0	(5)
G.B. Hogg not out	25	(33)
B. Lee not out	4	(3)
B 1, L-B 1, W 4, N-B 5	11	
(50 OVERS, 199 MINS) (7 WKTS)	236	

Fall: 7 140 153 158 158 160 229

M.S. Kasprowicz, G.D. McGrath (did not bat)

Bowling: Tuffey 8–0–47–0; Mills 9–1–48–1; Cairns 10–0–56–2; Styris 10–1–40–4; Vettori 10–0–33–0; Astle 3–0–10–0.

NEW ZEALAND

*S.P. Fleming lbw b Lee	5	(10)
N.J. Astle b Hogg	65	(110)
M.S. Sinclair c Gilchrist b McGrath	0	(8)
S.B. Styris c Hayden b Symonds	14	(48)
C.L. Cairns run out (Clarke/Gilchrist)	0	(3)
H.J.H. Marshall b McGrath	76	(69)
C.D. McMillan st Gilchrist b McGrath	37	(31)
+B.B. McCullum c Katich b Lee	8	(13)
D.L. Vettori b Lee	0	(1)
K.D. Mills not out	1	(1)
D.R. Tuffey b McGrath	1	(2)
L-B 6, W 8, N-B 5	19	
(48.4 OVERS, 213 MINS)	226	

Fall: 13 16 72 73 113 179 218 224 224 226

Bowling: Lee 9–1–41–3; McGrath 9.4–3–16–4; Kasprowicz 10–1–62–0; Symonds 10–0–52–1; Hogg 9–0–44–1; Clarke 1–0–5–0.

Umpires: Aleem Dar and B.F. Bowden.
TV Umpire: E.A. Watkin.
Referee: C.H. Lloyd.

NEW ZEALAND v AUSTRALIA

Lancaster Park, Christchurch, February 22, 2005. Day/night game.
Australia won by 106 runs. Toss: New Zealand. Man of Match: M.L. Hayden.

AUSTRALIA

+A.C. Gilchrist c McCullum b Tuffey	0	(2)
M.L. Hayden c Wilson b Mills	114	(124)
*R.T. Ponting run out (Marshall)	53	(57)
D.R. Martyn run out (McMillan)	58	(70)
A. Symonds c Wilson b Mills	13	(10)
M.J. Clarke c McCullum b Cairns	23	(13)
M.E.K. Hussey not out	32	(20)
G.B. Hogg not out	9	(9)
L-B 1, W 6, N-B 5	12	
(50 OVERS, 205 MINS) (6 WKTS)	314	

Fall: 0 99 232 237 254 283

B. Lee, J.N. Gillespie, G.D. McGrath (did not bat)

Bowling: Tuffey 8–1–73–1; Mills 10–0–62–2; Cairns 10–0–62–1; Vettori 10–0–31–0; Wilson 6–0–57–0; Astle 6–0–28–0.

NEW ZEALAND

*S.P. Fleming c Gilchrist b Lee	1	(4)
N.J. Astle c Gilchrist b McGrath	3	(8)
M.S. Sinclair c Gilchrist b Lee	15	(27)
H.J.H. Marshall c Gilchrist b McGrath	16	(20)
C.D. McMillan c Gilchrist b Symonds	12	(20)
C.L. Cairns c Hayden b Symonds	22	(16)
+B.B. McCullum c and b Symonds	20	(41)
D.L. Vettori c (sub) Katich b Gillespie	83	(77)
J.W. Wilson c Ponting b Gillespie	22	(27)
K.D. Mills run out (Clarke)	4	(9)
D.R. Tuffey not out	0	(0)
L-B 3, W 4, N-B 3	10	
(40.4 OVERS, 166 MINS)	208	

Fall: 4 12 28 49 72 73 135 197 208 208

Bowling: Lee 8–2–28–2; McGrath 7–0–42–2; Gillespie 9.4–1–45–2; Symonds 6–0–41–3; Hogg 10–0–49–0.

Umpires: Aleem Dar and B.F. Bowden.
TV Umpire: A.L. Hill. Referee: C.H. Lloyd.

NEW ZEALAND v AUSTRALIA
Eden Park, Auckland, February 26, 2005. Day/night game. Australia won by 86 runs.
Toss: Australia. Man of Match: M.J. Clarke.

AUSTRALIA

+A.C. Gilchrist c Astle b Cairns	18	(36)
S.M. Katich lbw b Vettori	58	(78)
*R.T. Ponting run out		
(Papps/McCullum)	11	(18)
D.R. Martyn lbw b Vettori	1	(3)
A. Symonds c Papps b Mills	21	(27)
M.J. Clarke not out	71	(75)
M.E.K. Hussey not out	65	(73)
L-B 2, W 7, N-B 10	19	
(50 OVERS, 198 MINS) (5 WKTS) 264		

Fall: 68 85 90 117 128

G.B. Hogg, B. Lee, J.N. Gillespie, M.S. Kasprowicz (did not bat)

Bowling: Tuffey 2–0–25–0; Mills 9–0–57–1; Cairns 10–1–55–1; Astle 9–0–47–0; Vettori 10–0–31–2; McMillan 10–0–47–0.

NEW ZEALAND

*S.P. Fleming b Lee	1	(6)
N.J. Astle c Gilchrist b Kasprowicz	27	(43)
M.H.W. Papps retired hurt	3	(10)
H.J.H. Marshall run out		
(Symonds)	55	(87)
C.D. McMillan c Hussey		
b Symonds	26	(43)
J.A.H. Marshall run out		
(Symonds)	14	(16)
C.L. Cairns c Hussey b Lee	12	(20)
+B.B. McCullum c Hussey b Hogg	23	(23)
D.L. Vettori c Gilchrist b Hogg	0	(1)
K.D. Mills c Kasprowicz b Hogg	1	(6)
D.R. Tuffey not out	0	(0)
L-B 8, W 4, N-B 4	16	
(41.5 OVERS, 182 MINS) (9 WKTS) 178		

Fall: 7 45 114 135 136 161 162 172 178

Bowling: Lee 7–0–25–2; Gillespie 6–0–14–0; Kasprowicz 8–1–28–1; Symonds 10–1–36–1; Hussey 3–0–22–0; Hogg 7.5–0–45–3.

Umpires: Aleem Dar and D.B. Cowie.
TV Umpire: A.L. Hill. Referee: C.H. Lloyd.

NEW ZEALAND v AUSTRALIA
Basin Reserve, Wellington, March 1, 2005. Australia won by 7 wickets.
Toss: Australia. Man of Match: A.C. Gilchrist.

NEW ZEALAND

*S.P. Fleming c Lee b Gillespie	37	(53)
N.J. Astle c Gilchrist b Kasprowicz	37	(60)
C.D. Cumming c Clarke b McGrath	10	(22)
H.J.H. Marshall c and b Clarke	23	(42)
C.D. McMillan lbw b Hopes	35	(36)
J.A.H. Marshall c Gilchrist b Gillespie	9	(21)
C.L. Cairns c Martyn b Lee	36	(35)
+B.B. McCullum c Katich b Lee	17	(21)
J.W. Wilson lbw b McGrath	1	(2)
K.D. Mills run out (K'wicz/Hussey/G'christ)	4	(7)
L.J. Hamilton not out	2	(4)
B 1, L-B 12, W 5, N-B 4	22	
(49.5 OVERS, 211 MINS)	233	

Fall: 84 90 104 145 163 173 214 220 226 233

Bowling: Lee 9–1–41–2; McGrath 9.5–1–48–2; Gillespie 10–0–46–2; Kasprowicz 8–2–34–1; Hopes 10–1–38–1; Clarke 3–0–13–1.

AUSTRALIA

*+A.C. Gilchrist c McMillan b Wilson	54	(37)
S.M. Katich c McCullum b Cairns	43	(41)
D.R. Martyn not out	65	(78)
A. Symonds c Wilson b McMillan	48	(37)
M.J. Clarke not out	10	(17)
L-B 3, W 8, N-B 5	16	
(34.2 OVERS, 146 MINS) (3 WKTS)	236	

Fall: 78 113 212

J.R. Hopes, M.E.K. Hussey, B. Lee, J.N. Gillespie, M.S. Kasprowicz, G.D. McGrath (did not bat)

Bowling: Mills 7–1–37–0; Hamilton 8–0–67–0; Wilson 9–0–68–1; Cairns 6–0–30–1; McMillan 4.2–0–31–1.

Umpires: Aleem Dar and A.L. Hill.
TV Umpire: D.B. Cowie. Referee: C.H. Lloyd.

NEW ZEALAND v AUSTRALIA

McLean Park, Napier, March 5, 2005. Australia won by 121 runs. Toss: New Zealand. Man of Match: R.T. Ponting.

AUSTRALIA

+A.C. Gilchrist c Cumming b Canning	91	(61)
S.M. Katich c McCullum b Hamilton	5	(15)
*R.T. Ponting not out	141	(127)
D.R. Martyn c Fleming b Mills	40	(46)
A. Symonds run out (Vettori/McMillan)	17	(16)
M.J. Clarke c Cumming b McMillan	43	(36)
M.E.K. Hussey not out	0	(0)
L-B 7, W 2, N-B 1	10	
(50 OVERS, 196 MINS) (5 WKTS)	347	

Fall: 37 129 204 241 335

B. Lee, G.B. Hogg, M.S. Kasprowicz, G.D. McGrath (did not bat)

Bowling: Mills 10–1–67–1; Hamilton 10–0–76–1; Canning 10–0–80–1; Vettori 10–0–37–0; McMillan 7–0–63–1; Cumming 3–0–17–0.

NEW ZEALAND

C.D. Cumming lbw b Lee	13	(24)
*S.P. Fleming c Gilchrist b Kasprowicz	35	(46)
H.J.H. Marshall run out (Clarke)	28	(41)
J.A.H. Marshall b Kasprowicz	0	(1)
C.D. McMillan c Hogg b Symonds	63	(69)
+B.B. McCullum c McGrath b Symonds	36	(60)
T.K. Canning b Kasprowicz	17	(27)
D.L. Vettori not out	16	(19)
K.D. Mills c Kasprowicz b McGrath	10	(13)
L.J. Hamilton not out	1	(2)
B 1, L-B 1, W 3, N-B 2	7	
(50 OVERS, 192 MINS) (8 WKTS)	226	

Fall: 39 60 60 103 167 196 199 223

C.L. Cairns (did not bat)

Bowling: Lee 10–0–34–1; McGrath 10–0–45–1; Kasprowicz 10–2–36–3; Hogg 10–0–53–0; Clarke 5–0–30–0; Symonds 5–0–25–2.

Umpires: A.L. Hill and D.R. Shepherd.
TV Umpire: D.B. Cowie. Referee: C.H. Lloyd.

FIRST TEST

NEW ZEALAND v AUSTRALIA
Lancaster Park, Christchurch, March 10,11,12,13, 2005. Australia won by 9 wickets.
Toss: Australia. Man of Match: A.C. Gilchrist.

Close of play: First day, New Zealand (1) 3–265 (Marshall 103, Astle 29); Second day, Australia (1) 3–141 (Ponting 41, Gillespie 0); Third day, New Zealand (2) 0–9 (Cumming 2, Fleming 7).

NEW ZEALAND

C.D. Cumming c Gillespie b Kasprowicz	74	–	lbw b Gillespie	7
*S.P. Fleming lbw b Warne	18	–	lbw b McGrath	17
H.J.H. Marshall b Warne	146	–	b Warne	22
L. Vincent lbw b Clarke	27	–	lbw b Gillespie	4
N.J. Astle lbw b McGrath	74	–	b Kasprowicz	21
C.D. McMillan c Gilchrist b McGrath	13	–	c Katich b Warne	5
+B.B. McCullum c Langer b McGrath	29	–	lbw b Gillespie	24
D.L. Vettori not out	24	–	lbw b Warne	23
J.E.C. Franklin lbw b McGrath	0	–	not out	5
I.E. O'Brien c Gilchrist b McGrath	5	–	lbw b Warne	0
C.S. Martin c Gilchrist b McGrath	1	–	lbw b Warne	0
B 4, L-B 14, W 2, N-B 2	22		B 1, L-B 1, N-B 1	3
(141 OVERS, 561 MINS)	433		(50 OVERS, 225 MINS)	131

Fall: 56 153 199 330 355 388 403 403 415 433

Fall: 20 30 34 71 78 87 121 127 131 131

Bowling: First Innings — McGrath 42–9–115–6; Gillespie 29–5–87–0; Kasprowicz 25–6–85–1; Warne 40–6–112–2; Clarke 5–0–16–1. Second Innings — McGrath 14–7–19–1; Gillespie 12–2–38–3; Kasprowicz 10–3–33–1; Warne 14–3–39–5.

AUSTRALIA

J.L. Langer b Franklin	23	–	not out	72
M.L. Hayden c Astle b O'Brien	35	–	c Cumming b Vettori	15
*R.T. Ponting c McCullum b Martin	46	–	not out	47
D.R. Martyn lbw b Vettori	32			
J.N. Gillespie c Cumming b Vettori	12			
M.J. Clarke c McCullum b Franklin	8			
S.M. Katich c Vincent b Astle	118			
+A.C. Gilchrist c O'Brien b Vettori	121			
S.K. Warne c Astle b Vettori	2			
M.S. Kasprowicz not out	13			
G.D. McGrath lbw b Vettori	0			
B 2, L-B 13, W 3, N-B 4	22		N-B 1	1
(123.2 OVERS, 486 MINS)	432		(31.3 OVERS, 126 MINS) (1 WKT)	135

Fall: 48 75 140 147 160 201 413 418 426 432

Fall: 25

Bowling: First Innings — Martin 29–6–104–1; Franklin 26–5–102–2; O'Brien 14–3–73–1; Vettori 40.2–13–106–5; Astle 14–6–32–1. Second Innings — Martin 8–0–27–0; Franklin 5–1–26–0; Vettori 13.3–0–55–1; O'Brien 5–0–27–0.

Umpires: Aleem Dar and D.R. Shepherd. TV Umpire: A.L. Hill. Referee: C.H. Lloyd.

SECOND TEST

NEW ZEALAND v AUSTRALIA
Basin Reserve, Wellington, March 18(np),19,20,21,22 2005. Match drawn.
Toss: New Zealand. Man of Match: A.C. Gilchrist.

Close of play: First day, No play (rain); Second day, Australia (1) 5–337 (Martyn 106, Gilchrist 45); Third day, New Zealand (1) 4–122 (Vincent 38, Franklin 6); Fourth day, New Zealand 244 all out.

AUSTRALIA

J.L. Langer c McCullum b Vettori	46
M.L. Hayden c Vincent b Franklin	61
*R.T. Ponting lbw b Vettori	9
D.R. Martyn c McCullum b O'Brien	165
M.J. Clarke c Fleming b Astle	8
S.M. Katich c McCullum b Franklin	35
+A.C. Gilchrist c and b Franklin	162
S.K. Warne not out	50
J.N. Gillespie b Franklin	2
M.S. Kasprowicz not out	2
B 4, L-B 8, W 2, N-B 16	30
(140 OVERS, 560 MINS) (8 WKTS DEC)	570

Fall: 82 100 146 163 247 503 557 559

G.D. McGrath (did not bat)

Bowling: First Innings — Martin 28–6–123–0; Franklin 28–4–128–4; O'Brien 24–4–97–1; Vettori 47–5–170–2; Astle 13–2–40–1.

NEW ZEALAND

C.D. Cumming b Kasprowicz	37	–	not out	10
*S.P. Fleming lbw b McGrath	0	–	lbw b McGrath	1
H.J.H. Marshall c Gillespie b McGrath	18	–	lbw b McGrath	0
L. Vincent c Gilchrist b Kasprowicz	63	–	b Kasprowicz	24
N.J. Astle c Warne b Clarke	9	–	not out	4
J.E.C. Franklin c Gilchrist b Kasprowicz	26			
C.D. McMillan b Warne	20			
+B.B. McCullum c Clarke b Warne	3			
D.L. Vettori c Martyn b Warne	45			
I.E. O'Brien b Gillespie	5			
C.S. Martin not out	0			
B 4, L-B 8, W 1, N-B 5	18	B 3, L-B 5, N-B 1		9
(81.1 OVERS, 328 MINS)	244	(17.2 OVERS, 73 MINS) (3 WKTS)		48

Fall: 9 55 78 108 166 180 184 201 212 244   Fall: 3 3 37

Bowling: First Innings — McGrath 14–3–50–2; Gillespie 20–4–63–1; Kasprowicz 16–2–42–3; Warne 28.1–7–69–3; Clarke 3–1–8–1. Second Innings — McGrath 6–3–10–2; Gillespie 5–2–5–0; Warne 3.2–0–14–0; Kasprowicz 3–0–11–1.

Umpires: R.E. Koertzen and D.R. Shepherd. TV Umpire: E.A. Watkin. Referee: C.H. Lloyd.

NEW ZEALAND v AUSTRALIA
Eden Park, Auckland, March 26,27,28,29, 2005. Australia won by 9 wickets.
Toss: New Zealand. Man of Match: R.T. Ponting. Man of the Series: A.C. Gilchrist.

Close of play: First day, New Zealand (1) 5–199 (Astle 7, McCullum 1); Second day, Australia (1) 4–219 (Clarke 18, Gillespie 1); Third day, New Zealand (2) 2–11 (H.J.H. Marshall 3, Fleming 1).

NEW ZEALAND

C.D. Cumming lbw b Gillespie	5	–	lbw b McGrath	0
J.A.H. Marshall c Hayden b McGrath	29	–	c Langer b McGrath	3
H.J.H. Marshall c Ponting b Warne	76	–	c Gilchrist b McGrath	7
*S.P. Fleming b Kasprowicz	65	–	c and b Gillespie	3
N.J. Astle c Langer b McGrath	19	–	c Katich b Warne	69
L. Vincent b Gillespie	2	–	run out (Clarke)	40
+B.B. McCullum c Gilchrist b McGrath	25	–	lbw b Warne	0
D.L. Vettori not out	41	–	c McGrath b Warne	65
J.E.C. Franklin c Katich b Warne	3	–	c Ponting b Warne	23
P.J. Wiseman c Gillespie b Warne	8	–	b McGrath	23
C.S. Martin c Clarke b Kasprowicz	0	–	not out	4
B 4, L-B 13, N-B 2	19		B 1, L-B 14, N-B 2	17
(116.2 OVERS, 480 MINS)	292		(69.2 OVERS, 301 MINS)	254

Fall: 15 53 179 183 194 228 247 262 288 292

Fall: 0 9 15 23 93 93 174 220 227 254

Bowling: First Innings — McGrath 34–20–49–3; Gillespie 25–8–64–2; Kasprowicz 30.2–7–89–2; Warne 23–4–63–3; Ponting 4–1–10–0. Second Innings — McGrath 16.2–5–40–4; Gillespie 16–4–63–1; Kasprowicz 14–2–59–0; Warne 23–5–77–4.

AUSTRALIA

J.L. Langer b Franklin	6	–	not out	59
M.L. Hayden lbw b Franklin	38	–	run out (Vettori)	9
*R.T. Ponting c McCullum b Astle	105	–	not out	82
D.R. Martyn b Wiseman	38			
M.J. Clarke run out (J.A.H. Marshall)	22			
J.N. Gillespie c McCullum b Martin	35			
S.M. Katich c Wiseman b Franklin	35			
+A.C. Gilchrist not out	60			
S.K. Warne c Fleming b Franklin	1			
M.S. Kasprowicz b Franklin	23			
G.D. McGrath c McCullum b Franklin	0			
B 4, L-B 7, N-B 9	20		L-B 14, N-B 2	16
(118.1 OVERS, 463 MINS)	383		(29.3 OVERS, 137 MINS) (1 WKT)	166

Fall: 8 84 187 215 226 297 297 303 377 383

Fall: 18

Bowling: First Innings — Martin 21–4–92–1; Franklin 26.1–3–119–6; Astle 21–7–50–1; Vettori 19–4–47–0; Wiseman 31–7–64–1. Second Innings — Martin 8–1–51–0; Franklin 7–0–40–0; Vettori 4–0–19–0; Astle 7–0–29–0; Wiseman 3.3–0–13–0.

Umpires: R.E. Koertzen and J.W. Lloyds. TV Umpire: D.B. Cowie. Referee: C.H. Lloyd.

2004–05 NEW ZEALAND–AUSTRALIA INTERNATIONAL LIMITED-OVERS AVERAGES

Batting	M	Inn	NO	Runs	HS	50	100	Avrge	Ct/St	Stk-Rt
R.T. Ponting (Aus)	4	4	1	266	141*	2	1	88.67	1/–	93.01
H.J.H. Marshall (NZ)	5	5	–	198	76	2	–	39.60	1/–	76.45
M.L. Hayden (Aus)	2	2	–	185	114	1	1	92.50	2/–	79.40
C.D. McMillan (NZ)	5	5	–	173	63	1	–	34.60	1/–	86.93
D.R. Martyn (Aus)	5	5	1	171	65*	2	–	42.75	1/–	80.28
A.C. Gilchrist (Aus)	5	5	–	167	91	2	–	33.40	11/1	118.44
A. Symonds (Aus)	5	5	–	152	53	1	–	30.40	1/–	113.43
M.J. Clarke (Aus)	5	5	2	147	71*	1	–	49.00	2/–	100.68
N.J. Astle (NZ)	4	4	–	132	65	1	–	33.00	1/–	59.73
S.M. Katich (Aus)	4	4	–	106	58	1	–	26.50	2/–	76.26
B.B. McCullum (NZ)	5	5	–	104	36	–	–	20.80	5/–	65.82
D.L. Vettori (NZ)	4	4	1	99	83	1	–	33.00	1/–	101.02
M.E.K. Hussey (Aus)	4	3	3	97	65*	1	–	–	3/–	104.19
S.P. Fleming (NZ)	5	5	–	79	37	–	–	15.80	1/–	66.39
C.L. Cairns (NZ)	5	4	–	70	36	–	–	17.50	–/–	94.59
G.B. Hogg (Aus)	4	2	2	34	25*	–	–	–	1/–	80.95
J.A.H. Marshall (NZ)	3	3	–	23	14	–	–	7.67	–/–	60.53
J.W. Wilson (NZ)	2	2	–	23	22	–	–	11.50	3/–	79.31
C.D. Cumming (NZ)	2	2	–	23	13	–	–	11.50	2/–	50.00
K.D. Mills (NZ)	5	5	1	20	10	–	–	5.00	–/–	55.56
T.K. Canning (NZ)	1	1	–	17	17	–	–	17.00	–/–	59.26
M.S. Sinclair (NZ)	2	2	–	15	15	–	–	7.50	1/–	42.86
S.B. Styris (NZ)	1	1	–	14	14	–	–	14.00	–/–	29.17
B. Lee (Aus)	5	1	1	4	4*	–	–	–	1/–	133.33
M.H.W. Papps (NZ)	1	1	1	3	3+	–	–	–	1/–	30.00
L.J. Hamilton (NZ)	2	2	2	3	2*	–	–	–	–/–	50.00
D.R. Tuffey (NZ)	3	3	2	1	1	–	–	1.00	–/–	45.45
M.S. Kasprowicz (Aus)	4	–	–	–	–	–	–	–	2/–	–
J.R. Hopes (Aus)	1	–	–	–	–	–	–	–	–/–	–
G.D. McGrath (Aus)	4	–	–	–	–	–	–	–	1/–	–
J.N. Gillespie (Aus)	3	–	–	–	–	–	–	–	–/–	–

Bowling	Overs	Mds	Runs	Wkts	Best	5wi	Avrge	RPO
B. Lee (Aus)	43.0	4	169	10	3–41	–	16.90	3.93
G.D. McGrath (Aus)	36.3	4	151	9	4–16	–	16.78	4.14
A. Symonds (Aus)	31.0	1	154	7	3–41	–	22.00	4.97
M.S. Kasprowicz (Aus)	36.0	6	160	5	3–36	–	32.00	4.44
C.L. Cairns (NZ)	36.0	1	203	5	2–56	–	40.60	5.64
K.D. Mills (NZ)	45.0	3	271	5	2–62	–	54.20	6.02
S.B. Styris (NZ)	10.0	1	40	4	4–40	–	10.00	4.00
J.N. Gillespie (Aus)	25.4	1	105	4	2–45	–	26.25	4.09
G.B. Hogg (Aus)	36.5	–	191	4	3–45	–	47.75	5.19
C.D. McMillan (NZ)	21.2	–	141	2	1–31	–	70.50	6.61
D.L. Vettori (NZ)	40.0	–	132	2	2–31	–	66.00	3.30
J.W. Wilson (NZ)	15.0	–	125	1	1–68	–	125.00	8.33
L.J. Hamilton (NZ)	18.0	–	143	1	1–76	–	143.00	7.94
J.R. Hopes (Aus)	10.0	1	38	1	1–38	–	38.00	3.80
T.K. Canning (NZ)	10.0	–	80	1	1–80	–	80.00	8.00
M.J. Clarke (Aus)	9.0	–	48	1	1–13	–	48.00	5.33
D.R. Tuffey (NZ)	18.0	1	145	1	1–73	–	145.00	8.06
M.E.K. Hussey (Aus)	3.0	–	22	–	–	–	–	7.33
C.D. Cumming (NZ)	3.0	–	17	–	–	–	–	5.67
N.J. Astle (NZ)	18.0	–	85	–	–	–	–	4.72

2004–05 NEW ZEALAND–AUSTRALIA TEST AVERAGES

Batting	M	Inn	NO	Runs	Best	50	100	Avrge	Ct/St	Stk-Rt
A.C. Gilchrist (Aus)	3	3	1	343	162	1	2	171.50	7/–	102.69
R.T. Ponting (Aus)	3	5	2	289	105	1	1	96.33	2/–	71.71
H.J.H. Marshall (NZ)	3	6	–	269	146	1	1	44.83	–/–	43.25
D.R. Martyn (Aus)	3	3	–	235	165	–	1	78.33	1/–	48.35
J.L. Langer (Aus)	3	5	2	206	72*	2	–	68.67	3/–	68.67
D.L. Vettori (NZ)	3	5	2	198	65	1	–	66.00	–/–	68.99
N.J. Astle (NZ)	3	6	1	196	74	2	–	39.20	2/–	49.87
S.M. Katich (Aus)	3	3	–	188	118	–	1	62.67	3/–	50.40
L. Vincent (NZ)	3	6	–	160	63	1	–	26.67	2/–	50.16
M.L. Hayden (Aus)	3	5	–	158	61	1	–	31.60	1/–	49.69
C.D. Cumming (NZ)	3	6	1	133	74	1	–	26.60	2/–	33.33
S.P. Fleming (NZ)	3	6	–	104	65	1	–	17.33	2/–	35.37
B.B. McCullum (NZ)	3	5	–	81	29	–	–	16.20	8/–	57.04
J.E.C. Franklin (NZ)	3	5	1	57	26	–	–	14.25	1/–	35.63
S.K. Warne (Aus)	3	3	1	53	50*	1	–	26.50	1/–	79.10
J.N. Gillespie (Aus)	3	3	–	49	35	–	–	16.33	4/–	21.68
C.D. McMillan (NZ)	2	3	–	38	20	–	–	12.67	–/–	48.10
M.S. Kasprowicz (Aus)	3	3	2	38	23	–	–	38.00	–/–	61.29
M.J. Clarke (Aus)	3	3	–	38	22	–	–	12.67	2/–	34.23
J.A.H. Marshall (NZ)	1	2	–	32	29	–	–	16.00	–/–	50.79
P.J. Wiseman (NZ)	1	2	–	31	23	–	–	15.50	1/–	72.09
I.E. O'Brien (NZ)	2	3	–	10	5	–	–	3.33	1/–	35.71
C.S. Martin (NZ)	3	5	2	5	4*	–	–	1.67	–/–	13.16
G.D. McGrath (Aus)	3	2	–	0	0	–	–	0.00	1/–	0.00

Bowling	Overs	Mds	Runs	Wkts	Best	5wi	10wm	Avrge	RPO
G.D. McGrath (Aus)	126.2	47	283	18	6–115	1	–	15.72	2.24
S.K. Warne (Aus)	131.3	25	374	17	5–39	1	–	22.00	2.84
J.E.C. Franklin (NZ)	92.1	13	415	12	6–119	1	–	34.58	4.50
M.S. Kasprowicz (Aus)	98.2	20	319	8	3–42	–	–	39.88	3.24
D.L. Vettori (NZ)	123.5	22	397	8	5–106	1	–	49.63	3.21
J.N. Gillespie (Aus)	107.0	25	320	7	3–38	–	–	45.71	2.99
N.J. Astle (NZ)	55.0	15	151	3	1–32	–	–	50.33	2.75
M.J. Clarke (Aus)	8.0	1	24	2	1–8	–	–	12.00	3.00
C.S. Martin (NZ)	94.0	17	397	2	1–92	–	–	198.50	4.22
I.E. O'Brien (NZ)	43.0	7	197	2	1–73	–	–	98.50	4.58
P.J. Wiseman (NZ)	34.3	7	77	1	1–64	–	–	77.00	2.23
R.T. Ponting (Aus)	4.0	1	10	–	–	–	–	–	2.50

2005 ENGLAND v AUSTRALIA

AUSTRALIAN TOURING PARTY

Limited-Overs Squad

Ricky Ponting (captain), Adam Gilchrist (vice-captain), Michael Clarke, Jason Gillespie, Brad Haddin, Matthew Hayden, Brad Hogg, Michael Hussey, Michael Kasprowicz, Simon Katich, Brett Lee, Damien Martyn, Glenn McGrath, Andrew Symonds and Shane Watson.

Test Squad

Ricky Ponting (captain), Adam Gilchrist (vice-captain), Michael Clarke, Jason Gillespie, Brad Haddin, Matthew Hayden, Brad Hodge, Justin Langer, Michael Kasprowicz, Simon Katich, Brett Lee, Stuart MacGill, Damien Martyn, Glenn McGrath, Shaun Tait and Shane Warne. Stuart Clark added to the squad in early August to cover Glenn McGrath.

Steve Bernard (Manager), John Buchanan (Coach), Jamie Siddons (Assistant coach/Performance Analyst), Errol Alcott (Physiotherapist), Lucy Frostick (Masseur), Jock Campbell (Physical Performance Manager), Belinda Dennett and Jonathan Rose (Media Managers).

PCA MASTERS XI v AUSTRALIANS

At Arundel Castle, Arundel, June 9, 2005. Australians won by eight wickets. PCA Masters XI 6 for 167 (D.L. Maddy 70*, P.D. Collingwood 38, M.A. Ealham 39; M.J. Clarke 3–36). Australian XI 2 for 170 (A.C. Gilchrist 53, M.L. Hayden 79, R.T. Ponting 31*).

LEICESTERSHIRE v AUSTRALIANS

At Grace Road, Leicester, June 11, 2005. Australians won by 95 runs. Australian XI 4 for 321 (M.L. Hayden 107, D.R. Martyn 85, A. Symonds 92*; O.D. Gibson 2–65). Leicestershire 8 for 226 (H.D. Ackerman 38, P.A. Nixon 43, O.D. Gibson 50; G.D. McGrath 2–33, G.B. Hogg 3–56).

ENGLAND v AUSTRALIA
Twenty/20 International
**The Rose Bowl, Southampton, June 13, 2005. England won by 100 runs. Toss: England.
Man of Match: K.P. Pietersen.**

ENGLAND

M.E. Trescothick c Hussey b Symonds	41	(37)
+G.O. Jones c Kasprowicz b McGrath	19	(14)
A. Flintoff c Symonds b Kasprowicz	6	(5)
K.P. Pietersen c Hayden b Clarke	34	(18)
*M.P. Vaughan c Ponting b Symonds	0	(1)
P.D. Collingwood c Ponting b McGrath	46	(26)
A.J. Strauss b Gillespie	18	(16)
V.S. Solanki c Hussey b McGrath	9	(5)
J. Lewis not out	0	(0)
L-B 1, W 3, N-B 2	6	
(20 OVERS, 79 MINS) (8 WKTS)	179	

Fall: 28 49 100 102 109 158 175 179

D. Gough, S.J. Harmison (did not bat).

Bowling: Lee 3–0–31–0; McGrath 4–0–31–3; Kasprowicz 3–0–28–1; Gillespie 4–0–49–1; Clarke 3–0–25–1; Symonds 3–0–14–2.

AUSTRALIA

+A.C. Gilchrist c Pietersen b Gough	15	(14)
M.L. Hayden c Pietersen b Gough	6	(4)
A. Symonds c Pietersen b Lewis	0	(2)
M.J. Clarke c Jones b Lewis	0	(1)
M.E.K. Hussey c Flintoff b Gough	1	(6)
*R.T. Ponting c Solanki b Lewis	0	(3)
D.R. Martyn c Trescothick b Lewis	4	(4)
B. Lee c Harmison b Collingwood	15	(20)
J.N. Gillespie c Trescothick b Collingwood	24	(18)
M.S. Kasprowicz not out	3	(5)
G.D. McGrath b Harmison	5	(12)
B 1, L-B 2, W 1, N-B 2	6	
(14.3 OVERS, 64 MINS)	79	

Fall: 23 23 23 24 24 28 31 67 72 79

Bowling: Gough 3–0–16–3; Lewis 4–0–24–4; Harmison 2.3–0–13–1; Flintoff 3–0–15–0; Collingwood 2–0–8–2.

Umpires: N.J. Llong and J.W. Lloyds.
TV Umpire: M.R. Benson.

SOMERSET v AUSTRALIANS

At County Ground, Taunton, June 15, 2005. Somerset won by 4 wickets. Australians 5 for 342 (M.L. Hayden 76, R.T. Ponting 80, D.R. Martyn 44, M.J. Clarke 63*, M.E.K. Hussey 51). Somerset 6 for 345 (G.C. Smith 108, S.T. Jayasuriya 101, J.C. Hildreth 38*; G.D. McGrath 2–49, M.E.K. Hussey 2–4).

NATWEST INTERNATIONAL LIMITED-OVERS SERIES

ENGLAND v BANGLADESH

At The Oval, London, June 16, 2005. England won by 10 wickets. Bangladesh 190
(Aftab Ahmed 51, Mohammad Rafique 30; D. Gough 2–33, J. Lewis 3–32,
S.J. Harmison 4–39). England 0 for 192 (M.E. Trescothick 100*, A.J. Strauss 82*).
Man of the Match: M.E. Trescothick.

AUSTRALIA v BANGLADESH

Sophia Gardens, Cardiff, June 18, 2005. Bangladesh won by 5 wickets. Toss: Australia.
Man of Match: Mohammad Ashraful.

AUSTRALIA

+A.C. Gilchrist lbw b Mashrafe Mortaza	0	(2)
M.L. Hayden b Nazmul Hossain	37	(50)
*R.T. Ponting lbw b Tapash Baisya	1	(16)
D.R. Martyn c Nafees Iqbal b Tapash Baisya	77	(112)
M.J. Clarke c Mashrafe b Tapash Baisya	54	(84)
M.E.K. Hussey not out	31	(21)
S.M. Katich not out	36	(23)
L-B 3, W 2, N-B 8	13	
(50 OVERS, 205 MINS) (5 WKTS)	249	

Fall: 0 9 57 165 183

G.B. Hogg, J.N. Gillespie, M.S. Kasprowicz, G.D. McGrath (did not bat).

Bowling: Mashrafe Mortaza 10–2–33–1; Tapash Baisya 10–1–69–3; Nazmul Hossain 10–2–65–1; Mohammad Rafique 10–0–31–0; Aftab Ahmed 10–0–48–0.

BANGLADESH

Javed Omar c Hayden b Kasprowicz	19	(51)
Nafees Iqbal c Gilchrist b Gillespie	8	(21)
Tushar Imran c Katich b Hogg	24	(35)
Mohammad Ashraful c Hogg b Gillespie	100	(101)
*Habibul Bashar run out (Gillespie)	47	(72)
Aftab Ahmed not out	21	(13)
Mohammad Rafique not out	9	(7)
B 1, L-B 11, W 6, N-B 4	22	
(49.2 OVERS, 199 MINS) (5 WKTS)	250	

Fall: 17 51 72 202 227

+Khaled Mashud, Mashrafe Mortaza, Tapash Baisya, Nazmul Hossain (did not bat).

Bowling: McGrath 10–1–43–0; Gillespie 9.2–1–41–2; Kasprowicz 10–0–40–1; Hogg 9–0–52–1; Clarke 6–0–38–0; Hussey 5–0–24–0.

Umpires: B.F. Bowden and D.R. Shepherd.
TV Umpire: M.R. Benson.
Referee: J.J. Crowe.

ENGLAND v AUSTRALIA

County Ground, Bristol, June 19, 2005. England won by three wickets. Toss: Australia.
Man of Match: K.P. Pietersen. Attendance: 15000.

AUSTRALIA

+A.C. Gilchrist c Jones b Harmison	26	(32)
M.L. Hayden c Collingwood b Harmison	31	(44)
*R.T. Ponting lbw b Harmison	0	(1)
D.R. Martyn c Pietersen b Harmison	0	(2)
M.J. Clarke b Lewis	45	(71)
M.E.K. Hussey b Harmison	84	(83)
S.R. Watson b Flintoff	25	(36)
G.B. Hogg not out	10	(13)
J.N. Gillespie c Jones b Flintoff	14	(18)
M.S. Kasprowicz b Gough	1	(3)
G.D. McGrath not out	0	(1)
L-B 6, W 6, N-B 4	16	
(50 OVERS, 216 MINS) (9 WKTS) 252		

Fall: 57 57 57 63 168 220 220 244 248

Bowling: Gough 10–0–47–1; Lewis 10–0–69–1; Harmison 10–0–33–5; Flintoff 10–1–39–2; Collingwood 2–0–11–0; Vaughan 6–0–33–0; Solanki 2–0–14–0.

ENGLAND

M.E. Trescothick b McGrath	16	(32)
A.J. Strauss b McGrath	16	(23)
*M.P. Vaughan lbw b Hogg	57	(92)
P.D. Collingwood b Kasprowicz	14	(28)
A. Flintoff c Kasprowicz b Hogg	19	(22)
K.P. Pietersen not out	91	(65)
+G.O. Jones c Martyn b Hogg	2	(5)
V.S. Solanki run out (Gilchrist)	13	(14)
J. Lewis not out	7	(15)
L-B 1, W 7, N-B 10	18	
(47.3 OVERS, 217 MINS) (7 WKTS) 253		

Fall: 39 42 82 119 150 160 214

D. Gough, S.J. Harmison (did not bat).

Bowling: McGrath 9–1–34–2; Gillespie 10–1–66–0; Kasprowicz 9–0–68–1; Watson 9.3–0–42–0; Hogg 10–1–42–3.

Umpires: Aleem Dar and J.W. Lloyds.
TV Umpire: N.J. Llong. Referee: J.J. Crowe.

ENGLAND v BANGLADESH

At Trent Bridge, Nottingham, June 21, 2005. England won by 168 runs. England 4 for 391
(M.E. Trescothick 85, A.J. Strauss 152, P.D. Collingwood 112*; Nazmul Hossain 3–83).
Bangladesh 223 (Javed Omar 59, Mohammad Ashraful 94; C.T. Tremlett 4–32,
P.D. Collingwood 6–31). Man of the Match: P.D. Collingwood.

ENGLAND v AUSTRALIA

Riverside, Chester-le-Street, June 23, 2005. Day/night game. Australia won by 57 runs.
Toss: England. Man of Match: A. Symonds.

AUSTRALIA

+A.C. Gilchrist c Jones b Tremlett	18	(31)
M.L. Hayden c Jones b Flintoff	39	(56)
*R.T. Ponting c Giles b Harmison	27	(40)
D.R. Martyn not out	68	(81)
A. Symonds run out (Trescothick)	73	(81)
M.E.K. Hussey c Collingwood b Flintoff	5	(10)
S.R. Watson not out	11	(7)
L-B 12, W 7, N-B 6	25	
(50 OVERS, 211 MINS) (5 WKTS)	266	

Fall: 44 95 96 238 247

G.B. Hogg, J.N. Gillespie, B. Lee, G.D. McGrath (did not bat).

Bowling: Gough 10–0–41–0; Tremlett 9–0–53–1; Harmison 9–2–44–1; Flintoff 10–0–55–2; Giles 9–1–44–0; Collingwood 3–0–17–0.

ENGLAND

*M.E. Trescothick c Gilchrist b McGrath	0	(15)
A.J. Strauss b Lee	3	(13)
V.S. Solanki c Ponting b Hogg	34	(69)
P.D. Collingwood b McGrath	0	(2)
A. Flintoff c Gillespie b Hogg	44	(61)
K.P. Pietersen c Hussey b Symonds	19	(28)
+G.O. Jones c Hayden b Watson	23	(31)
A.F. Giles c Symonds b Lee	4	(3)
C.T. Tremlett c Hussey b Gillespie	8	(18)
D. Gough not out	46	(47)
S.J. Harmison not out	11	(17)
L-B 8, W 6, N-B 3	17	
(50 OVERS, 217 MINS) (9 WKTS)	209	

Fall: 4 6 6 85 94 123 133 145 159

Bowling: Lee 10–2–27–2; McGrath 10–1–31–2; Gillespie 9–0–36–1; Watson 8–0–51–1; Hogg 6–0–19–2; Symonds 7–0–37–1.

Umpires: Aleem Dar and M.R. Benson.
TV Umpire: J.W. Lloyds.
Referee: J.J. Crowe.

AUSTRALIA v BANGLADESH
Old Trafford, Manchester, June 25, 2005. Australia won by 10 wickets. Toss: Australia.
Man of Match: A. Symonds.

BANGLADESH

Javed Omar lbw b Lee	3	(20)
Nafees Iqbal b Symonds	47	(57)
Tushar Imran c Gilchrist b Lee	4	(12)
Mohammad Ashraful c and b Symonds	58	(86)
*Habibul Bashar c Gilchrist b Symonds	0	(1)
Aftab Ahmed b Symonds	5	(13)
+Khaled Mashud b Hogg	4	(12)
Manjural Islam Rana st Gilchrist b Hogg	2	(5)
Mohammad Rafique b Symonds	0	(6)
Mashrafe Mortaza c Martyn b Hogg	0	(3)
Nazmul Hossain not out	0	(1)
L-B 6, W 6, N-B 4	16	
(35.2 OVERS, 154 MINS)	139	

Fall: 13 23 113 113 124 137 139 139 139 139

Bowling: Lee 6–1–36–2; McGrath 6–1–19–0;
Gillespie 3–0–17–0; Watson 4–0–14–0; Hogg
9–1–29–3; Symonds 7.2–1–18–5.

AUSTRALIA

+A.C. Gilchrist not out	66	(60)
M.L. Hayden not out	66	(54)
W 7, N-B 1	8	
(19 OVERS, 73 MINS)	(0 WKT) 140	

*R.T. Ponting, D.R. Martyn, A. Symonds,
M.E.K. Hussey, S.R. Watson, G.B. Hogg,
J.N. Gillespie, B. Lee, G.D. McGrath (did not
bat).

Bowling: Mashrafe Mortaza 6–0–32–0;
Nazmul Hossain 3–0–29–0; Mohammad
Rafique 6–0–53–0; Manjural Islam Rana
4–0–26–0.

Umpires: B.F. Bowden and J.W. Lloyds.
TV Umpire: N.J. Llong. Referee: J.J. Crowe.

ENGLAND v BANGLADESH
At Headingley, Leeds, June 26, 2005. England won by 5 wickets. Bangladesh 7 for 208
(Javed Omar 81, Tushar Imran 32, Khaled Mashud 42*; A. Flintoff 4–29). England 5 for 209
(M.E. Trescothick 43, A.J. Strauss 98; Manjural Islam Rana 3–57, Mohammad Rafique 2–44).
Man of the Match: A.J. Strauss.

ENGLAND v AUSTRALIA
Edgbaston, Birmingham, June 28, 2005. Day/night game. No result. Toss: Australia.
Man of Match: No award.

AUSTRALIA

+A.C. Gilchrist c G.O. Jones b S.P. Jones	19	(18)
M.L. Hayden lbw b S.P. Jones	14	(24)
*R.T. Ponting c G.O. Jones b Flintoff	34	(40)
D.R. Martyn c Pietersen b Harmison	36	(65)
A. Symonds run out (Collingwood)	74	(75)
M.E.K. Hussey c G.O. Jones b Harmison	45	(42)
M.J. Clarke c G.O. Jones b Gough	3	(6)
G.B. Hogg c G.O. Jones b Gough	2	(6)
B. Lee not out	21	(18)
J.N. Gillespie c Pietersen b Gough	1	(2)
G.D. McGrath not out	2	(5)
B 1, L-B 4, W 4, N-B 1	10	
(50 OVERS, 209 MINS) (9 WKTS)	261	

Fall: 34 46 95 123 224 234 236 242 254

Bowling: Gough 9–0–70–3; S.P. Jones
10–2–53–2; Harmison 10–1–38–2; Flintoff
10–0–38–1; Giles 10–1–44–0; Vaughan
1–0–13–0.

ENGLAND

M.E. Trescothick not out	11	(19)
A.J. Strauss c Gillespie b McGrath	25	(18)
*M.P. Vaughan not out	0	(0)
N-B 1		1
(6 OVERS, 25 MINS) (1 WKT)	37	

Fall: 37

A. Flintoff, K.P. Pietersen, P.D. Collingwood,
+G.O. Jones, A.F. Giles, D. Gough, S.J.
Harmison, S.P. Jones (did not bat).

Bowling: Lee 3–0–13–0; McGrath 3–0–24–1.

Umpires: B.F. Bowden and D.R. Shepherd.
TV Umpire: J.W. Lloyds.
Referee: J.J. Crowe.

AUSTRALIA v BANGLADESH
St Lawrence Ground, Canterbury, June 30, 2005. Austraia won by 6 wickets.
Toss: Australia. Man of Match: Nafees Iqbal.

BANGLADESH

Javed Omar c Gilchrist b Gillespie	0	(10)
Nafees Iqbal c Gilchrist b Watson	75	(116)
Tushar Imran b Lee	0	(1)
Mohammad Ashraful b Lee	7	(4)
*Habibul Bashar c Gilchrist b Watson	30	(24)
Aftab Ahmed c Gilchrist b Kasprowicz	7	(11)
+Khaled Mashud not out	71	(105)
Mohammad Rafique c Gilchrist b Watson	15	(13)
Khaled Mahmud c Ponting b Gillespie	22	(22)
L-B 9, W 8, N-B 6	23	
(50 OVERS, 210 MINS) (8 WKTS)	250	

Fall: 8 9 19 57 75 169 193 250

Tapash Baisya, Mashrafe Mortaza (did not bat).

Bowling: Lee 10–0–62–2; Gillespie 9–0–49–2; Watson 10–0–43–3; Kasprowicz 9–0–46–1; Symonds 10–0–36–0; Clarke 2–1–5–0.

AUSTRALIA

+A.C. Gilchrist c Khaled b Tapash Baisya	45	(36)
M.L. Hayden c Khaled b Mashrafe Mortaza	1	(4)
*R.T. Ponting c Tushar b Mashrafe Mortaza	66	(95)
D.R. Martyn c Khaled b Khaled Mahmud	9	(16)
M.J. Clarke not out	80	(104)
A. Symonds not out	42	(37)
L-B 3, W 5, N-B 3	11	
(48.1 OVERS, 187 MINS) (4 WKTS)	254	

Fall: 15 63 83 168

M.E.K. Hussey, S.R. Watson, B. Lee, J.N. Gillespie, M.S. Kasprowicz (did not bat).

Bowling: Mashrafe Mortaza 9–0–44–2; Tapash Baisya 9–0–57–1; Khaled Mahmud 10–0–54–1; Aftab Ahmed 10–0–48–0; Mohammad Rafique 10–0–44–0; Mohammad Ashraful 0.1–0–4–0.

Umpires: Aleem Dar and J.W. Lloyds.
TV Umpire: M.R. Benson.
Referee: J.J. Crowe.

ENGLAND v AUSTRALIA
Final
Lord's, London, July 2, 2005. Match tied. Toss: England. Man of Match: G.O. Jones.
Man of the Series: A. Symonds.

AUSTRALIA

+A.C. Gilchrist c Pietersen b Flintoff	27	(32)
M.L. Hayden c Giles b Gough	17	(19)
*R.T. Ponting c G.O. Jones b Harmison	7	(18)
D.R. Martyn c G.O. Jones b Harmison	11	(24)
A. Symonds c Strauss b Collingwood	29	(71)
M.J. Clarke lbw b S.P. Jones	2	(19)
M.E.K. Hussey not out	62	(81)
G.B. Hogg c G.O. Jones b Harmison	16	(22)
B. Lee c G.O. Jones b Flintoff	3	(5)
J.N. Gillespie c G.O. Jones b Flintoff	0	(1)
G.D. McGrath c Collingwood b Gough	0	(4)
B 4, L-B 5, W 7, N-B 6	22	
(48.5 OVERS, 208 MINS)	196	

Fall: 50 54 71 90 93 147 169 179 179 196

Bowling: Gough 6.5–1–36–2; S.P. Jones 8–2–45–1; Flintoff 8–2–23–3; Harmison 10–2–27–3; Collingwood 8–0–26–1; Giles 8–0–30–0.

ENGLAND

M.E. Trescothick c Ponting b McGrath	6	(16)
A.J. Strauss b Lee	2	(8)
*M.P. Vaughan b McGrath	0	(7)
K.P. Pietersen c Gilchrist b Lee	6	(10)
A. Flintoff c Hayden b McGrath	8	(9)
P.D. Collingwood runout (Symonds/Gilchrist)	53	(116)
+G.O. Jones lbw b Hogg	71	(100)
A.F. Giles not out	18	(21)
S.P. Jones b Hussey	1	(2)
D. Gough run out (McGrath)	12	(13)
S.J. Harmison not out	0	(0)
B 2, L-B 12, W 3, N-B 2	19	
(50 OVERS, 232 MINS) (9 WKTS)	196	

Fall: 11 13 19 19 33 149 161 162 194

Bowling: Lee 10–1–36–2; McGrath 10–4–25–3; Gillespie 10–1–42–0; Symonds 10–2–23–0; Hogg 6–0–25–1; Hussey 4–0–31–1.

Umpires: B.F. Bowden and D.R. Shepherd.
TV Umpire: J.W. Lloyds.
Referee: J.J. Crowe.

NATWEST CHALLENGE

ENGLAND v AUSTRALIA
Headingley, Leeds, July 7, 2005. England won by 9 wickets. Toss: England.
Man of Match: M.E. Trescothick.

AUSTRALIA

+A.C. Gilchrist c G.O. Jones b Harmison	42	(51)
M.L. Hayden c Pietersen b Flintoff	17	(47)
*R.T. Ponting c Pietersen b Collingwood	14	(30)
D.R. Martyn c G.O. Jones b Collingwood	43	(71)
A. Symonds c Trescothick b Collingwood	6	(10)
M.J. Clarke b Collingwood	2	(9)
M.E.K. Hussey not out	46	(52)
S.R. Watson c Strauss b Harmison	3	(13)
B. Lee not out	15	(19)
B 2, L-B 12, W 15, N-B 2	31	
(50 OVERS, 218 MINS) (7 WKTS)	219	

Fall: 62 68 107 116 120 159 168

G.B. Hogg, J.N. Gillespie, G.D. McGrath (did not bat)

Bowling: Gough 10–1–50–0; S.P. Jones 10–1–28–0; Harmison 10–0–39–2; Flintoff 10–0–54–1; Collingwood 10–0–34–4.

ENGLAND

M.E. Trescothick not out	104	(134)
A.J. Strauss c Gilchrist b Hogg	41	(84)
*M.P. Vaughan not out	59	(65)
B 1, L-B 2, W 3, N-B 11	17	
(46 OVERS, 197 MINS) (1 WKT)	221	

Fall: 101

V.S. Solanki, K.P. Pietersen, A. Flintoff, P.D. Collingwood, +G.O. Jones, A.F. Giles, D. Gough, S.J. Harmison, S.P. Jones (did not bat).

Bowling: Lee 9–0–48–0; McGrath 8–1–26–0; Gillespie 10–0–66–0; Watson 3–0–16–0; Symonds 10–0–32–0; Hogg 6–0–30–1.

Umpires: M.R. Benson and R.E. Koertzen.
TV Umpire: N.J. Llong.
Referee: R.S. Mahanama.

ENGLAND v AUSTRALIA

Lord's, London, July 10, 2005. Australia won by 7 wickets. Toss: Australia. Man of Match: B. Lee. Man of the Series: R.T. Ponting.

ENGLAND

M.E. Trescothick c Gilchrist b Kasprowicz	14	(36)
A.J. Strauss b Kasprowicz	11	(25)
*M.P. Vaughan lbw b McGrath	1	(3)
K.P. Pietersen b Lee	15	(23)
A. Flintoff c Hussey b Lee	87	(112)
P.D. Collingwood c Gilchrist b Lee	34	(56)
+G.O. Jones c Katich b Lee	27	(33)
A.F. Giles c Ponting b Lee	4	(6)
D. Gough not out	5	(5)
S.J. Harmison not out	6	(3)
L-B 3, W 14, N-B 2	19	
(50 OVERS, 207 MINS) (8 WKTS) 223		

Fall: 25 28 28 45 148 193 210 214

S.P. Jones (did not bat).

Bowling: Lee 10–2–41–5; McGrath 10–2–37–1; Kasprowicz 10–2–40–2; Gillespie 7–0–42–0; Symonds 7–0–31–0; Clarke 6–0–29–0.

AUSTRALIA

+A.C. Gilchrist c G.O. Jones b Flintoff	29	(20)
S.M. Katich c Harmison b Giles	30	(62)
*R.T. Ponting c Pietersen b Gough	111	(115)
D.R. Martyn not out	39	(67)
A. Symonds not out	5	(6)
L-B 2, W 4, N-B 4	10	
(44.2 OVERS, 190 MINS) (3 WKTS) 224		

Fall: 36 96 216

M.J. Clarke, M.E.K. Hussey, B. Lee, J.N. Gillespie, M.S. Kasprowicz, G.D. McGrath, B.J. Haddin (did not bat).

Bowling: Gough 6.2–0–43–1; S.P. Jones 5–0–29–0; Harmison 10–0–48–0; Flintoff 8–0–44–1; Giles 10–0–38–1; Collingwood 5–0–20–0.

Umpires: R.E. Koertzen and J.W. Lloyds. TV Umpire: M.R. Benson. Referee: R.S. Mahanama.

ENGLAND v AUSTRALIA
The Oval, London, July 12, 2005. Australia won by 8 wickets. Toss: Australia.
Man of Match: A.C. Gilchrist.

ENGLAND

M.E. Trescothick c Kasprowicz b Lee	0	(12)
A.J. Strauss c Gilchrist b Kasprowicz	36	(50)
*M.P. Vaughan run out (Ponting)	15	(30)
K.P. Pietersen b Gillespie	74	(84)
A. Flintoff c Gilchrist b Kasprowicz	5	(15)
P.D. Collingwood c Symonds b Gillespie	9	(18)
+G.O. Jones c Kasprowicz b Gillespie	1	(11)
V.S. Solanki not out	53	(63)
A.F. Giles not out	25	(19)
L-B 1, W 7, N-B 2	10	
(50 OVERS, 218 MINS) (7 WKTS) 228		

Fall: 4 44 61 74 87 93 186

S.J. Harmison, D. Gough, S.P. Jones (did not bat).

Bowling: Lee 10–0–46–1; McGrath 10–4–40–0; Kasprowicz 10–1–46–2; Gillespie 10–1–44–3; Symonds 6–1–26–0; Clarke 4–0–25–0.

AUSTRALIA

+A.C. Gilchrist not out	121	(101)
M.L. Hayden c G.O. Jones b Gough	31	(47)
*R.T. Ponting st G.O. Jones b Giles	43	(44)
D.R. Martyn not out	24	(21)
L-B 2, W 4, N-B 4	10	
(34.5 OVERS, 160 MINS) (2 WKTS) 229		

Fall: 91 185

A. Symonds, M.J. Clarke, M.E.K. Hussey, B. Lee, J.N. Gillespie, M.S. Kasprowicz, G.D. McGrath, S.M. Katich (did not bat).

Bowling: Harmison 9.5–0–81–0; Gough 4–0–37–1; Flintoff 9–0–34–0; Giles 10–0–64–1; Collingwood 2–0–11–0.

Umpires: R.E. Koertzen and D.R. Shepherd. TV Umpire: J.W. Lloyds. Referee: R.S. Mahanama.

LEICESTERSHIRE v AUSTRALIANS
At Grace Road, Leicester, July 15, 16, 17, 2005. Match drawn. Leicestershire 217 (C.J.L. Rogers 56, J.J. Krejza 38, O.D. Gibson 30, B. Lee 4-53, J.N. Gillespie 2-40, S.C.G. MacGill 2-64). Australians 7 dec 582 (J.L. Langer 115, M.L. Hayden 75, R.T. Ponting 119, D.R. Martyn 154*, J.N. Gillespie 49*, S.C.J. Broad 2-77, J.K. Maunders 3-89). Leicestershire 5 dec 363 (D.D.J. Robinson 81, C.J.L. Rogers 209, J.K. Maunders 33, S.C.G. MacGill 4-122).

FIRST TEST

ENGLAND v AUSTRALIA
Lord's Cricket Ground, London, July 21,22,23,24, 2005. Australia won by 239 runs.
Toss: Australia. Man of Match: G.D. McGrath.

Close of play: First day, England (1) 7–97 (Pietersen 29); Second day, Australia (2) 7–279 (Katich 10); Third day, England (2) 5–156 (Pietersen 42, G.O. Jones 6).

AUSTRALIA

J.L. Langer c Harmison b Flintoff	40	–	run out (Pietersen)	6
M.L. Hayden b Hoggard	12	–	b Flintoff	34
*R.T. Ponting c Strauss b Harmison	9	–	c (sub) J.C. Hildreth b Hoggard	42
D.R. Martyn c G.O. Jones b S.P. Jones	2	–	lbw b Harmison	65
M.J. Clarke lbw b S.P. Jones	11	–	b Hoggard	91
S.M. Katich c G.O. Jones b Harmison	27	–	c S.P. Jones b Harmison	67
+A.C. Gilchrist c G.O. Jones b Flintoff	26	–	b Flintoff	10
S.K. Warne b Harmison	28	–	c Giles b Harmison	2
B. Lee c G.O. Jones b Harmison	3	–	run out (Giles)	8
J.N. Gillespie lbw b Harmison	1	–	b S.P. Jones	13
G.D. McGrath not out	10	–	not out	20
B 5, L-B 4, W 1, N-B 11	21		B 10, L-B 8, N-B 8	26
(40.2 OVERS, 209 MINS)	190		(100.4 OVERS, 457 MINS)	384

Fall: 35 55 66 66 87 126 175 178 178 190   Fall: 18 54 100 255 255 274 279 289 341 384

Bowling: First Innings — Harmison 11.2–0–43–5; Hoggard 8–0–40–1; Flintoff 11–2–50–2; S.P. Jones 10–0–48–2. Second Innings — Harmison 27.4–6–54–3; Hoggard 16–1–56–2; Flintoff 27–4–123–2; S.P. Jones 18–1–69–1; Giles 11–1–56–0; Bell 1–0–8–0.

ENGLAND

M.E. Trescothick c Langer b McGrath	4	–	c Hayden b Warne	44
A.J. Strauss c Warne b McGrath	2	–	c and b Lee	37
*M.P. Vaughan b McGrath	3	–	b Lee	4
I.R. Bell b McGrath	6	–	lbw b Warne	8
K.P. Pietersen c Martyn b Warne	57	–	not out	64
A. Flintoff b McGrath	0	–	c Gilchrist b Warne	3
+G.O. Jones c Gilchrist b Lee	30	–	c Gillespie b McGrath	6
A.F. Giles c Gilchrist b Lee	11	–	c Hayden b McGrath	0
M.J. Hoggard c Hayden b Warne	0	–	lbw b McGrath	0
S.J. Harmison c Martyn b Lee	11	–	lbw b Warne	0
S.P. Jones not out	20	–	c Warne b McGrath	0
B 1, L-B 5, N-B 5	11		B 6, L-B 5, N-B 3	14
(48.1 OVERS, 227 MINS)	155		(58.1 OVERS, 268 MINS)	180

Fall: 10 11 18 19 21 79 92 101 122 155   Fall: 80 96 104 112 119 158 158 164 167 180

Bowling: First Innings — McGrath 18–5–53–5; Lee 15.1–5–47–3; Gillespie 8–1–30–0; Warne 7–2–19–2. Second Innings — McGrath 17.1–2–29–4; Lee 15–3–58–2; Gillespie 6–0–18–0; Warne 20–2–64–4.

Umpires: Aleem Dar and R.E. Koertzen. TV Umpire: M.R. Benson. Referee: R.S. Madugalle.

WORCESTERSHIRE v AUSTRALIANS
At County Ground, Worcester, July 30, 31, August 1, 2005. Match drawn.
Australians 9 dec 406 (J.L. Langer 54, M.L. Hayden 79, B.J. Hodge 38, B.J. Haddin 94,
J.N, Gillespie 53*, M.S. Mason 2-65, M.N. Malik 3-78, R.W. Price 2-68). Worcestershire 187
S.C. Moore 69, V.S. Solanki 36, J.N. Gillespie 2-45, S.W. Tait 2-51, M.S. Kasprowicz 5-67).
Australia 2 dec 161 (M.J. Clarke 59, R.T. Ponting 59*).

NEWSPAPER HEADLINES FROM THE UK

22 July 2005, *The Daily Telegraph*
McGRATH SPARKS ENGLAND FREE-FALL

24 July 2005, *The Sunday Telegraph*
AUSSIES RULE: WARNE AND LEE STRIKE TO LEAVE
ENGLAND STRUGGLING IN ASHES OPENER

25 July 2005, *The Daily Telegraph*
BRUTAL AUSTRALIA ON THE MARCH

3 August 2005, *The Independent*
VAUGHAN'S ELBOW INJURY HAS
ENGLAND FEARING THE WORST

5 August 2005, *The Independent*
ENGLAND FIREWORKS IGNITE ASHES

10 August 2005, *The Daily Telegraph*
LEE RUNNING OUT OF TIME
TO PLAY AT OLD TRAFFORD

ENGLAND v AUSTRALIA
Edgbaston, Birmingham, August 4,5,6,7, 2005. England won by 2 runs.
Toss: Australia. Man of Match: A. Flintoff.

Close of play: First day, England (1) 1–25 (Trescothick, 19, Hoggard 0); Second day, Australia (2) 8–175 (Warne 20).

ENGLAND

M.E. Trescothick c Gilchrist b Kasprowicz	90	–	c Gilchrist b Lee	21
A.J. Strauss b Warne	48	–	b Warne	6
*M.P. Vaughan c Lee b Gillespie	24	–	(4) b Lee	1
I.R. Bell c Gilchrist b Kasprowicz	6	–	(5) c Gilchrist b Warne	21
K.P. Pietersen c Katich b Lee	71	–	(6) c Gilchrist b Warne	20
A. Flintoff c Gilchrist b Gillespie	68	–	(7) b Warne	73
+G.O. Jones c Gilchrist b Kasprowicz	1	–	(8) c Ponting b Lee	9
A.F. Giles lbw b Warne	23	–	(9) c Hayden b Warne	8
M.J. Hoggard lbw b Warne	16	–	(3) c Hayden b Lee	1
S.J. Harmison b Warne	17	–	c Ponting b Warne	0
S.P. Jones not out	19	–	not out	12
L-B 9, W 1, N-B 14	24	–	L-B 1, N-B 9	10
(79.2 OVERS, 356 MINS)	407		(52.1 OVERS, 249 MINS)	182

Fall: 112 164 170 187 290 293 342 348 375 407

Fall: 25 27 29 31 72 75 101 131 131 182

Bowling: First Innings — Lee 17–1–111–1; Gillespie 22–3–91–2; Kasprowicz 15–3–80–3; Warne 25.2–4–116–4. Second Innings — Lee 18–1–82–4; Gillespie 8–0–24–0; Kasprowicz 3–0–29–0; Warne 23.1–7–46–6.

AUSTRALIA

J.L. Langer lbw b S.P. Jones	82	–	b Flintoff	28
M.L. Hayden c Strauss b Hoggard	0	–	c Trescothick b S.P. Jones	31
*R.T. Ponting c Vaughan b Giles	61	–	c G.O. Jones b Flintoff	0
D.R. Martyn run out (Vaughan)	20	–	c Bell b Hoggard	28
M.J. Clarke c G.O. Jones b Giles	40	–	b Harmison	30
S.M. Katich c G.O. Jones b Flintoff	4	–	c Trescothick b Giles	16
+A.C. Gilchrist not out	49	–	c Flintoff b Giles	1
S.K. Warne b Giles	8	–	(9) hit wicket b Flintoff	42
B. Lee c Flintoff b S.P. Jones	6	–	(10) not out	43
J.N. Gillespie lbw b Flintoff	7	–	(8) lbw b Flintoff	0
M.S. Kasprowicz lbw b Flintoff	0	–	c G.O. Jones b Harmison	20
B 13, L-B 7, W 1, N-B 10	31	–	B 13, L-B 8, W 1, N-B 18	40
(76 OVERS, 346 MINS)	308		(64.3 OVERS, 301 MINS)	279

Fall: 0 88 118 194 208 262 273 282 308 308 279

Fall: 47 48 82 107 134 136 137 175 220

Bowling: First Innings — Harmison 11–1–48–0; Hoggard 8–0–41–1; S.P. Jones 16–2–69–2; Flintoff 15–1–52–3; Giles 26–2–78–3. Second Innings — Harmison 17.3–3–62–2; Hoggard 5–0–26–1; Giles 15–3–68–2; Flintoff 22–3–79–4; S.P. Jones 5–1–23–1.

Umpires: B.F. Bowden and R.E. Koertzen. TV Umpire: J.W. Lloyds. Referee: R.S. Madugalle.

ENGLAND v AUSTRALIA
Old Trafford, Manchester, August 11,12,13,14,15, 2005. Match drawn.
Toss: England. Man of Match: R.T. Ponting.

Close of play: First day, England (1) 5–341 (Bell 59); Second day, Australia (1) 7–214 (Warne 45, Gillespie 4); Third day, Australia (1) 7–264 (Warne 78, Gillespie 7); Fourth day, Australia (2) 0–24 (Langer 14, Hayden 5).

ENGLAND

M.E. Trescothick c Gilchrist b Warne	63	–	b McGrath	41
A.J. Strauss b Lee	6	–	c Martyn b McGrath	106
*M.P. Vaughan c McGrath b Katich	166	–	c (sub) B.J. Hodge b Lee	14
I.R. Bell c Gilchrist b Lee	59	–	c Katich b McGrath	65
K.P. Pietersen c (sub) Hodge b Lee	21	–	lbw b McGrath	0
M.J. Hoggard b Lee	4			
A. Flintoff c Langer b Warne	46	–	(6) b McGrath	4
+G.O. Jones b Gillespie	42	–	(7) not out	27
A.F. Giles c Hayden b Warne	0	–	(8) not out	0
S.J. Harmison not out	10			
S.P. Jones b Warne	0			
B 4, L-B 5, W 3, N-B 15	27		B 5, L-B 3, W 1, N-B 14	23
(113.2 OVERS, 503 MINS)	444		(61.5 OVERS, 288 MINS) (6 WKTS DEC)	280

Fall: 26 163 290 333 341 346 433 434 438 444

Fall: 64 97 224 225 248 264

Bowling: First Innings — McGrath 25–6–86–0; Lee 27–6–100–4; Gillespie 19–2–114–1; Warne 33.2–5–99–4; Katich 9–1–36–1. Second Innings — McGrath 20.5–1–115–5; Lee 12–0–60–1; Warne 25–3–74–0; Gillespie 4–0–23–0.

AUSTRALIA

J.L. Langer c Bell b Giles	31	–	c G.O. Jones b Hoggard	14
M.L. Hayden lbw b Giles	34	–	b Flintoff	36
*R.T. Ponting c Bell b S.P. Jones	7	–	c G.O. Jones b Harmison	156
D.R. Martyn b Giles	20	–	lbw b Harmison	19
S.M. Katich b Flintoff	17	–	c Giles b Flintoff	12
+A.C. Gilchrist c G.O. Jones b S.P. Jones	30	–	c Bell b Flintoff	4
S.K. Warne c Giles b S.P. Jones	90	–	(9) c G.O. Jones b Flintoff	34
M.J. Clarke c Flintoff b S.P. Jones	7	–	(7) b S.P. Jones	39
J.N. Gillespie lbw b S.P. Jones	26	–	(8) lbw b Hoggard	0
B. Lee c Trescothick b S.P. Jones	1	–	not out	18
G.D. McGrath not out	1	–	not out	5
B 8, L-B 7, W 8, N-B 15	38		B 5, L-B 8, W 1, N-B 20	34
(84.5 OVERS, 393 MINS)	302		(108 OVERS, 474 MINS) (9 WKTS)	371

Fall: 58 73 86 119 133 186 201 287 293 302

Fall: 25 96 129 165 182 263 264 340 354

Bowling: First Innings — Harmison 10–0–47–0; Hoggard 6–2–22–0; Flintoff 20–1–65–1; S.P. Jones 17.5–6–53–6; Giles 31–4–100–3. Second Innings — Harmison 22–4–67–2; Hoggard 13–0–49–2; Giles 26–4–93–0; Vaughan 5–0–21–0; Flintoff 25–6–71–4; S.P. Jones 17–3–57–1.

Umpires: B.F. Bowden and S.A. Bucknor. TV Umpire: N.J. Llong. Referee: R.S. Madugalle.

NORTHAMPTONSHIRE v AUSTRALIANS

At County Ground, Northampton, August 20, 21, 2005. Match drawn. Australians 6 dec 374 (M.L. Hayden 136, M.J. Clarke 121, B.J. Hodge 34, B.J. Haddin 32*; B.J. Phillips 2–50, P.S. Jones 2–70). Northamptonshire 9 dec 169 (B.J. Phillips 37*; G.D. McGrath 3–24, B. Lee 2–30, S.W. Tait 2–52). Australians 2 for 226 (S.M. Katich 63, J.L. Langer 86*, D.R. Martyn 43*).

NEWSPAPER HEADLINES FROM THE UK

21 August 2005, *The Sunday Telegraph*
AUSTRALIA STRUGGLE WITH SWING TO THE LEFT; ENGLAND CAN REVERSE THE ASHES TREND AT TRENT BRIDGE

22 August 2005, *The Daily Telegraph*
TAIT DRAWS BLOOD IN MEAN SPELL

23 August 2005, *The Daily Telegraph*
AUSTRALIA HOPE CHANGE WILL BE GOOD AS A REST; KASPROWICZ KEEPING HIS COOL AMID THE BLOOD AND THUNDER; JONES BOYS COULD HOLD THE KEY TO UNLOCKING AUSTRALIA

24 August 2005, *The Daily Telegraph*
AUSTRALIAN MIND HAUNTED BY THE SPECTRE OF FAILURE

FOURTH TEST

ENGLAND v AUSTRALIA
Trent Bridge, Nottingham, August 25,26,27,28, 2005. England won by 3 wickets.
Toss: England. Man of Match: A. Flintoff.

Close of play: First day, England (1) 4–229 (Pietersen 33, Flintoff 8); Second day, Australia (1) 5–99 (Katich 20); Third day, Australia (2) 4–222 (Clarke 39, Katich 24).

ENGLAND

M.E. Trescothick b Tait	65	–	c Ponting b Warne	27
A.J. Strauss c Hayden b Warne	35	–	c Clarke b Warne	23
*M.P. Vaughan c Gilchrist b Ponting	58	–	c Hayden b Warne	0
I.R. Bell c Gilchrist b Tait	3	–	c Kasprowicz b Lee	3
K.P. Pietersen c Gilchrist b Lee	45	–	(6) c Gilchrist b Lee	23
A. Flintoff lbw b Tait	102	–	b Lee	26
+G.O. Jones c and b Kasprowicz	85	–	c Kasprowicz b Warne	3
A.F. Giles lbw b Warne	15	–	not out	7
M.J. Hoggard c Gilchrist b Warne	10	–	not out	8
S.J. Harmison st Gilchrist b Warne	2			
S.P. Jones not out	15			
B 1, L-B 15, W 1, N-B 25	42		L-B 4, N-B 5	9
(123.1 OVERS, 537 MINS)	477		(31.5 OVERS, 168 MINS) (7 WKTS)	129

Fall: 105 137 146 213 241 418 450 450 454 477   Fall: 32 36 57 57 103 111 116

Bowling: First Innings — Lee 32–2–131–1; Kasprowicz 32–3–122–1; Tait 24–4–97–3; Warne 29.1–4–102–4; Ponting 6–2–9–1. Second Innings — Lee 12–0–51–3; Kasprowicz 2–0–19–0; Warne 13.5–2–31–4; Tait 4–0–24–0.

AUSTRALIA

J.L. Langer c Bell b Hoggard	27	–	c Bell b Giles	61
M.L. Hayden lbw b Hoggard	7	–	c Giles b Flintoff	26
*R.T. Ponting lbw b S.P. Jones	1	–	run out ((sub) G.J. Pratt)	48
D.R. Martyn lbw b Hoggard	1	–	c G.O. Jones b Flintoff	13
M.J. Clarke lbw b Harmison	36	–	c G.O. Jones b Hoggard	56
S.M. Katich c Strauss b S.P. Jones	45	–	lbw b Harmison	59
+A.C. Gilchrist c Strauss b Flintoff	27	–	lbw b Hoggard	11
S.K. Warne c Bell b S.P. Jones	0	–	st G.O. Jones b Giles	45
B. Lee c Bell b S.P. Jones	47	–	not out	26
M.S. Kasprowicz b S.P. Jones	5	–	c G.O. Jones b Harmison	19
S.W. Tait not out	3	–	b Harmison	4
L-B 2, W 1, N-B 16	19		B 1, L-B 4, N-B 14	19
(49.1 OVERS, 247 MINS)	218		(124 OVERS, 548 MINS)	387

Fall: 20 21 22 58 99 157 157 163 175 218   Fall: 50 129 155 161 261 277 314 342 373 387

Bowling: First Innings — Harmison 9–1–48–1; Hoggard 15–3–70–3; S.P. Jones 14.1–4–44–5; Flintoff 11–1–54–1. Second Innings — Hoggard 27–7–72–2; S.P. Jones 4–0–15–0; Harmison 30–5–93–3; Flintoff 29–4–83–2; Giles 28–3–107–2; Bell 6–2–12–0.

Umpires: Aleem Dar and S.A. Bucknor. TV Umpire: M.R. Benson. Referee: R.S. Madugalle.

ESSEX v AUSTRALIANS
At County Ground, Chelmsford, September 3, 4, 2005. Match drawn. Essex 4 dec 502 (W.I. Jefferson 64, A.N. Cook 214, R.S. Bopara 135, J.S. Foster 38*; S.W. Tait 2–72, M.S. Kasprowicz 2–85). Australians 6 for 561 (J.L. Langer 87, M.L. Hayden 150, S.M. Katich 72, B.J. Hodge 166, B.J. Haddin 59; J.D. Middlebrook 2–110, T.J. Phillips 2–137).

NEWSPAPER HEADLINES FROM THE UK

25 August 2005, *The Daily Telegraph*
PRESSURE POINT AS ENGLAND GO FOR THE JUGULAR; TAIT THE HIT MAN HAPPY SOFTENING UP BATSMEN; HAVE ENGLAND BECOME AUSTRALIA?

27 August 2005, *The Daily Telegraph*
ENGLAND HUNT DOWN VICTORY; WORLD-CLASS FLINTOFF PUTS AUSTRALIANS ON THE ROPES

30 August 2005, *The Daily Telegraph*
FLINTOFF FIRED UP FOR FINAL ACT

31 August 2005, *The Daily Telegraph*
PACE ASSAULT STIRS MEMORIES OF WEST INDIES

29 August 2005, *The Daily Telegraph*
ENGLAND SHRED A NATION'S NERVES; PONTING PRIMED FOR A FIGHT AMID UNFAMILIAR PLIGHT

2 September 2005, *The Daily Telegraph*
AUSTRALIANS HOLD BREATH AS MCGRATH TESTS ELBOW

ENGLAND v AUSTRALIA
Kennington Oval, The Oval, September 8,9,10,11,12, 2005. Match drawn. Toss: England. Man of Match: K.P. Pietersen. Man of the Series: A. Flintoff.

Close of play: First day, England (1) 7–319 (Jones 21, Giles 5); Second day, Australia (1) 0–112 (Langer 75, Hayden 32); Third day, Australia (1) 2–277 (Hayden 110, Martyn 9); Fourth day, England (2) 1–34 (Trescothick, 14, Vaughan, 19).

ENGLAND

M.E. Trescothick c Hayden b Warne	43	–	lbw b Warne	33
A.J. Strauss c Katich b Warne	129	–	c Katich b Warne	1
*M.P. Vaughan c Clarke b Warne	11	–	c Gilchrist b McGrath	45
I.R. Bell lbw b Warne	0	–	c Warne b McGrath	0
K.P. Pietersen b Warne	14	–	b McGrath	158
A. Flintoff c Warne b McGrath	72	–	c and b Warne	8
P.D. Collingwood lbw b Tait	7	–	c Ponting b Warne	10
+G.O. Jones b Lee	25	–	b Tait	1
A.F. Giles lbw b Warne	32	–	b Warne	59
M.J. Hoggard c Martyn b McGrath	2	–	not out	4
S.J. Harmison not out	20	–	c Hayden b Warne	0
B 4, L-B 6, W 1, N-B 7	18		B 4, W 7, N-B 5	16
(105.3 OVERS, 471 MINS)	373		(91.3 OVERS, 432 MINS)	335

Fall: 82 102 104 131 274 289 297 325 345 373   Fall: 2 67 67 109 126 186 199 308 335 335

Bowling: First Innings — McGrath 27–5–72–2; Lee 23–3–94–1; Tait 15–1–61–1; Warne 37.3–5–122–6; Katich 3–0–14–0. Second Innings — McGrath 26–3–85–3; Lee 20–4–88–0; Warne 38.3–3–124–6; Clarke 2–0–6–0; Tait 5–0–28–1.

AUSTRALIA

J.L. Langer b Harmison	105	–	not out	0
M.L. Hayden lbw b Flintoff	138	–	not out	0
*R.T. Ponting c Strauss b Flintoff	35			
D.R. Martyn c Collingwood b Flintoff	10			
M.J. Clarke lbw b Hoggard	25			
S.M. Katich lbw b Flintoff	1			
+A.C. Gilchrist lbw b Hoggard	23			
S.K. Warne c Vaughan b Flintoff	0			
B. Lee c Giles b Hoggard	6			
G.D. McGrath c Strauss b Hoggard	0			
S.W. Tait not out	1			
B 4, L-B 8, W 2, N-B 9	23			0
(107.1 OVERS, 494 MINS)	367		(0.4 OVERS, 3 MINS)	(0 WKT) 0

Fall: 185 264 281 323 329 356 359 363 363 367

Bowling: First Innings — Harmison 22–2–87–1; Hoggard 24.1–2–97–4; Flintoff 34–10–78–5; Giles 23–1–76–0; Collingwood 4–0–17–0. Second Innings — Harmison 0.4–0–0–0.

Umpires: B.F. Bowden and R.E. Koertzen. TV Umpire: J.W. Lloyds. Referee: R.S. Madugalle.

2005 INTERNATIONAL LIMITED-OVERS

Batting	M	Inn	NO	Runs	HS	50	100	Avrge	Ct/St	Stk-Rt
A.J. Strauss (Eng)	10	10	1	466	152	2	1	51.78	3/–	87.92
A.C. Gilchrist (Aus)	10	10	2	393	121*	1	1	49.13	15/1	102.61
M.E. Trescothick (Eng)	10	10	3	379	104*	1	2	54.14	3/–	85.55
D.R. Martyn (Aus)	10	9	3	307	77	2	–	51.17	2/–	66.88
R.T. Ponting (Aus)	10	9	–	303	111	1	1	33.67	4/–	75.94
M.E.K. Hussey (Aus)	10	6	3	273	84	2	–	91.00	3/–	94.46
Mohammad Ashraful (Ban)	6	6	–	259	100	2	1	43.17	–/–	105.71
M.L. Hayden (Aus)	9	9	1	253	66*	1	–	31.63	3/–	73.33
P.D. Collingwood (Eng)	10	7	2	230	112*	1	1	46.00	4/–	73.25
A. Symonds (Aus)	8	6	2	229	74	2	–	57.25	3/–	81.79
K.P. Pietersen (Eng)	10	6	1	228	91*	2	–	45.60	8/–	96.61
A. Flintoff (Eng)	10	7	–	202	87	1	–	28.86	1/–	75.09
M.J. Clarke (Aus)	8	6	1	186	80*	2	–	37.20	–/–	63.48
Javed Omar (Ban)	6	6	–	175	81	2	–	29.17	–/–	49.16
Nafees Iqbal (Ban)	6	6	–	170	75	1	–	28.33	2/–	64.15
M.P. Vaughan (Eng)	8	7	2	132	59*	2	–	26.40	–/–	64.36
Khaled Mashud (Ban)	6	5	2	126	71*	1	–	42.00	2v	69.23
G.O. Jones (Eng)	10	7	2	126	71	1	–	25.20	24/1	68.48
Habibul Bashar (Ban)	6	6	–	122	47	–	–	20.33	1/–	70.93
V.S. Solanki (Eng)	6	4	1	108	53*	1	–	36.00	–/–	63.16
Aftab Ahmed (Ban)	6	6	1	99	51	1	–	19.80	–/–	80.49
Mohammad Rafique (Ban)	6	6	2	75	30	–	–	18.75	1/–	61.98
Tushar Imran (Ban)	6	6	–	70	32	–	–	11.67	1/–	63.64
S.M. Katich (Aus)	3	2	1	66	36*	–	–	66.00	2/–	77.65
D. Gough (Eng)	9	3	2	63	46*	–	–	63.00	–/–	96.92
A.F. Giles (Eng)	8	4	2	51	25*	–	–	25.50	2/–	104.08
B. Lee (Aus)	8	3	2	39	21*	–	–	39.00	–/–	92.86
S.R. Watson (Aus)	5	3	1	39	25	–	–	19.50	–/–	69.64
Mashrafe Mortaza (Ban)	6	4	1	30	29*	–	–	10.00	1/–	78.95
G.B. Hogg (Aus)	7	3	1	28	16	–	–	14.00	1/–	68.29
Khaled Mahmud (Ban)	2	2	–	22	22	–	–	11.00	2/–	95.65
S.J. Harmison (Eng)	9	3	3	17	11*	–	–	–	2/–	84.58
J.N. Gillespie (Aus)	10	3	–	15	14	–	–	5.00	2/–	71.43
C.T. Tremlett (Eng)	3	1	–	8	8	–	–	8.00	–/–	44.44
Nazmul Hossain (Ban)	5	3	2	8	6	–	–	8.00	–/–	26.67
J. Lewis (Eng)	3	1	1	7	7*	–	–	–	–/–	46.67
Tapash Baisya (Ban)	3	1	–	3	3	–	–	3.00	–/–	50.00
G.D. McGrath (Aus)	9	3	2	2	2*	–	–	2.00	–/–	20.00
Manjural Islam (Ban)	2	1	–	2	2	–	–	2.00	–/–	40.00
M.S. Kasprowicz (Aus)	5	1	–	1	1	–	–	1.00	3/–	33.33

Batting (continued)	M	Inn	NO	Runs	HS	50	100	Avrge	Ct/St	Stk-Rt
S.P. Jones (Eng)	6	1	–	1	1	–	–	1.00	–/–	50.00
B.J. Haddin (Aus)	1	–	–	–	–	–	–	–	–/–	–

* Denotes not out

Bowling	Overs	Mds	Runs	Wkts	Best	5wi	Avrge	RPO
S.J. Harmison (Eng)	86.5	6	404	17	5–33	1	23.76	4.65
A. Flintoff (Eng)	87.0	6	392	14	4–29	–	28.00	4.51
B. Lee (Aus)	68.0	6	309	14	5–41	1	22.07	4.54
P.D. Collingwood (Eng)	54.0	1	207	11	6–31	1	18.82	3.83
G.B. Hogg (Aus)	46.0	2	197	11	3–29	–	17.91	4.28
D. Gough (Eng)	73.3	2	416	10	3–70	–	41.60	5.66
G.D. McGrath (Aus)	76.0	15	279	9	3–25	–	31.00	3.67
J.N. Gillespie (Aus)	77.2	4	403	8	3–44	–	50.38	5.21
M.S. Kasprowicz (Aus)	48.0	3	240	7	2–40	–	34.29	5.00
A. Symonds (Aus)	57.2	4	203	6	5–18	1	33.83	3.54
C.T. Tremlett (Eng)	24.2	1	111	5	4–32	–	22.20	4.56
Nazmul Hossain (Ban)	37.0	3	281	4	3–83	–	70.25	7.59
J. Lewis (Eng)	25.0	1	124	4	3–32	–	31.00	4.96
S.P. Jones (Eng)	42.0	5	199	4	2–53	–	49.75	4.74
Tapash Baisya (Ban)	26.0	1	213	4	3–69	–	53.25	8.19
S.R. Watson (Aus)	34.3	–	166	4	3–43	–	41.50	4.81
A.F. Giles (Eng)	67.0	2	300	3	1–28	–	100.00	4.48
Manjural Islam Rana (Ban)	13.5	–	83	3	3–57	–	27.67	6.00
Mashrafe Mortaza (Ban)	50.0	3	261	3	2–44	–	87.00	5.22
Mohammad Rafique (Ban)	52.0	1	266	2	2–44	–	133.00	5.12
Aftab Ahmed (Ban)	35.5	–	188	1	1–65	–	188.00	5.25
Khaled Mahmud (Ban)	13.0	–	93	1	1–54	–	93.00	7.15
M.E.K. Hussey (Aus)	9.0	–	55	1	1–31	–	55.00	6.11
Mohammad Ashraful (Ban)	0.1	–	4	0	–	–	–	24.00
M.J. Clarke (Aus)	18.0	1	97	0	–	–	–	5.39
M.P. Vaughan (Eng)	7.0	–	46	0	–	–	–	6.57
Tushar Imran (Ban)	3.0	–	26	0	–	–	–	8.67
V.S. Solanki (Eng)	2.0	–	14	0	–	–	–	7.00

2005 ENGLAND–AUSTRALIA TEST AVERAGES

Batting	M	Inn	NO	Runs	HS	50	100	Avrge	Ct/St	Stk-Rt
K.P. Pietersen (Eng)	5	10	1	473	158	3	1	52.56	–/–	71.45
J.L. Langer (Aus)	5	10	1	394	105	2	1	43.78	2/–	58.63
M.E. Trescothick (Eng)	5	10	–	431	90	3	–	43.10	3/–	60.28
A. Flintoff (Eng)	5	10	–	402	102	3	1	40.20	3/–	74.17
R.T. Ponting (Aus)	5	9	–	359	156	1	1	39.89	4/–	59.63
A.J. Strauss (Eng)	5	10	–	393	129	–	2	39.30	6/–	57.79
M.J. Clarke (Aus)	5	9	–	335	91	2	–	37.22	2/–	54.38
G.D. McGrath (Aus)	3	5	4	36	20*	–	–	36.00	1/–	63.16
M.L. Hayden (Aus)	5	10	1	318	138	–	1	35.33	10/–	46.97
S.P. Jones (Eng)	4	6	4	66	20*	–	–	33.00	1/–	67.35
M.P. Vaughan (Eng)	5	10	–	326	166	1	1	32.60	2/–	60.82
S.K. Warne (Aus)	5	9	–	249	90	1	–	27.67	5/–	70.54
S.M. Katich (Aus)	5	9	–	248	67	2	–	27.56	4/–	46.79
B. Lee (Aus)	5	9	3	158	47	–	–	26.33	2/–	65.02
G.O. Jones (Eng)	5	10	1	229	85	1	–	25.44	15/1	57.97
A.C. Gilchrist (Aus)	5	9	1	181	49*	–	–	22.63	18/1	71.83
D.R. Martyn (Aus)	5	9	–	178	65	1	–	19.78	4/–	53.13
A.F. Giles (Eng)	5	10	2	155	59	1	–	19.38	5/–	50.64
I.R. Bell (Eng)	5	10	–	171	65	2	–	17.10	8/–	45.36
M.S. Kasprowicz (Aus)	2	4	–	44	20	–	–	11.00	3/–	67.69
S.J. Harmison (Eng)	5	8	2	60	20*	–	–	10.00	1/–	84.51
P.D. Collingwood (Eng)	1	2	–	17	10	–	–	8.50	1/–	22.08
S.W. Tait (Aus)	2	3	2	8	4	–	–	8.00	–/–	29.63
J.N. Gillespie (Aus)	3	6	–	47	26	–	–	7.83	1/–	21.56
M.J. Hoggard (Eng)	5	9	2	45	16	–	–	6.43	–/–	19.65

* Denotes not out

Bowling	Overs	Mds	Runs	Wkts	Best	5wi	10wm	Avrge	RPO
R.T. Ponting (Aus)	6.0	2	9	1	1–9	–	–	9.00	1.50
S.K. Warne (Aus)	252.5	37	797	40	6–46	3	2	19.93	3.15
S.P. Jones (Eng)	102.0	17	378	18	6–53	2	–	21.00	3.71
G.D. McGrath (Aus)	134.0	22	440	19	5–53	2	–	23.16	3.28
A. Flintoff (Eng)	194.0	32	655	24	5–78	1	–	27.29	3.38
M.J. Hoggard (Eng)	122.1	15	473	16	4–97	–	–	29.56	3.87
S.J. Harmison (Eng)	161.1	22	549	17	5–43	1	–	32.29	3.41
B. Lee (Aus)	191.1	25	822	20	4–82	–	–	41.10	4.30
S.W. Tait (Aus)	48.0	5	210	5	3–97	–	–	42.00	4.38
S.M. Katich (Aus)	12.0	1	50	1	1–36	–	–	50.00	4.17
A.F. Giles (Eng)	160.0	18	578	10	3–78	–	–	57.80	3.61
M.S. Kasprowicz (Aus)	52.0	6	250	4	3–80	–	–	62.50	4.81
J.N. Gillespie (Aus)	67.0	6	300	3	2–91	–	–	100.00	4.48
I.R. Bell (Eng)	7.0	2	20	0	–	–	–	–	2.86
M.J. Clarke (Aus)	2.0	–	6	0	–	–	–	–	3.00
P.D. Collingwood (Eng)	4.0	–	17	0	–	–	–	–	4.25
M.P. Vaughan (Eng)	5.0	–	21	0	–	–	–	–	4.20

AUSTRALIAN AVERAGES AND PLAYER STATISTICS

2004–05 AUSTRALIAN TEST AVERAGES

Batting	M	Inn	NO	Runs	HS	50	100	Avrge	Ct/St	Stk-Rt
R.T. Ponting	15	27	5	1290	207	3	6	58.64	18/–	62.68
J.L. Langer	19	36	3	1723	215	4	8	52.21	11/–	57.99
D.R. Martyn	19	31	2	1453	165	5	7	50.10	9/–	54.26
A.C. Gilchrist	19	30	4	1263	162	5	4	48.58	72/6	83.91
M.J. Clarke	17	26	1	1004	151	2	4	40.16	16/–	55.07
M.L. Hayden	19	36	3	1268	138	3	5	38.42	22/–	53.70
S.M. Katich	14	24	1	738	118	1	4	32.09	8/–	45.64
S.R. Watson	1	1	–	31	31	–	–	31.00	–/–	50.00
D.S. Lehmann	9	14	–	428	81	–	5	30.57	3/–	66.15
B. Lee	5	9	3	158	47	–	–	26.33	2/–	65.02
S.K. Warne	18	26	2	450	90	–	3	18.75	23/–	66.47
J.N. Gillespie	17	25	4	324	54*	–	2	15.43	11/–	26.47
G.D. McGrath	17	21	10	142	61	–	1	12.91	6/–	57.72
M.S. Kasprowicz	15	21	4	170	23	–	–	10.00	7/–	52.96
S.W. Tait	2	3	2	8	4	–	–	8.00	–/–	29.63
N.M. Hauritz	1	2	–	15	15	–	–	7.50	1/–	62.50
M.T.G. Elliott	1	2	–	1	1	–	–	0.50	1/–	9.09
S.C.G. MacGill	1	1	1	9	9*	–	–	–	–/–	90.00

* Denotes not out

Bowling	Overs	Mds	Runs	Wkts	Best	5wi	10wm	Avrge	RPO
M.J. Clarke	20.2	1	67	8	6–9	1	–	8.38	3.30
G.D. McGrath	656.3	195	1694	88	8–24	5	–	19.25	2.58
N.M. Hauritz	27.0	4	103	5	3–16	–	–	20.60	3.81
S.C.G. MacGill	47.0	7	170	8	5–87	1	–	21.25	3.62
S.K. Warne	845.0	154	2530	106	6–46	5	2	23.87	2.99
M.S. Kasprowicz	448.3	99	1383	47	7–39	2	–	29.43	3.08
J.N. Gillespie	553.5	127	1592	52	5–56	1	–	30.62	2.87
R.T. Ponting	13.0	4	34	1	1–9	–	–	34.00	2.62
B. Lee	191.1	25	822	20	4–82	–	–	41.10	4.30
S.W. Tait	48.0	5	210	5	3–97	–	–	42.00	4.38
S.M. Katich	14.0	1	57	1	1–36	–	–	57.00	4.07
S.R. Watson	19.0	5	60	1	1–32	–	–	60.00	3.16
D.S. Lehmann	45.0	9	131	2	2–46	–	–	65.50	2.91

2004–05 AUSTRALIA ONE-DAY AVERAGES

Batting	M	Inn	NO	Runs	HS	50	100	Avrge	Ct/St	Stk-Rt
R.T. Ponting	30	29	3	920	141*	2	4	35.38	10/–	76.10
A.C. Gilchrist	25	25	3	870	121*	1	5	39.55	37/2	103.57
M.L. Hayden	23	23	1	763	114	1	4	34.68	12/–	68.13
A. Symonds	28	24	4	769	104*	1	5	38.45	6/–	91.11
M.J. Clarke	29	25	5	902	103*	1	6	45.10	9/–	83.44
D.R. Martyn	30	27	8	893	95*	–	8	47.00	7/–	74.54
M.E.K. Hussey	14	9	6	370	84	–	3	123.33	6/–	96.83
S.M. Katich	12	11	1	300	76	–	2	30.00	7/–	77.72
D.S. Lehmann	15	12	3	297	52	–	2	33.00	4/–	73.51
J.N. Gillespie	25	8	2	66	44*	–	–	11.00	5/–	108.20
G.B. Hogg	20	13	7	169	41*	–	–	28.17	5/–	80.44
B. Lee	28	12	7	164	38*	–	–	32.80	5/–	89.13
S.R. Watson	13	7	2	74	25	–	–	14.80	3/–	74.75
M.S. Kasprowicz	19	3	2	10	9*	–	–	10.00	9/–	71.43
G.D. McGrath	25	7	4	8	5*	–	–	2.67	4/–	53.33
B.J. Haddin	7	5	–	90	32	–	–	18.00	8/1	66.18
J.R. Hopes	1	–	–	–	–	–	–	–	–	–

* Denotes not out

Bowling	Overs	Mds	Runs	Wkts	Best	5wi	Avrge	RPO
B. Lee	232.5	15	1089	49	5–41	1	22.22	4.68
G.D. McGrath	205.3	32	745	38	5–27	1	19.61	3.63
J.N. Gillespie	206.5	12	923	31	4–15	–	29.77	4.46
M.S. Kasprowicz	159.4	14	722	30	5–47	1	24.07	4.52
G.B. Hogg	147.4	2	736	29	5–32	1	25.38	4.98
A. Symonds	181.2	10	822	21	5–18	1	39.14	4.53
D.S. Lehmann	71.3	–	366	10	3–44	–	36.60	5.12
S.R. Watson	95.0	3	455	7	3–43	–	65.00	4.79
M.E.K. Hussey	12.0	–	77	1	1–31	–	77.00	6.42
J.R. Hopes	10.0	1	38	1	1–38	–	38.00	3.80
M.J. Clarke	29.0	1	158	1	1–13	–	158.00	5.45

2004–05 AUSTRALIAN INTERNATIONAL PERFORMANCES

MICHAEL CLARKE

Start Date		Opp	Venue	How Out	Runs	O	M	R	W	Ct	St
23/08/04	ODI	Ind	Amstelveen	c V. Sehwag b L. Balaji	42					–	–
28/08/04	ODI	Pak	Amstelveen	c Inzamam-ul-Haq b Shoaib Akhtar	1					1	–
04/09/04	ODI	Pak	Lord's	c Shoaib Malik b Shoaib Akhtar	31	2.0	–	13	–	–	–
13/09/04	ODI	USA	Southampton		–					–	–
16/09/04	ODI	NZ	The Oval		–					1	–
21/09/04	ODI	Eng	Birmingham	b A. Flintoff	42					–	–
06/10/04	Test	Ind	Bangalore	cwk P.A. Patel b Zaheer Khan	151					–	–
		Ind	Bangalore	c A. Chopra b Harbhajan Singh	17	1.0	–	4	–	–	–
14/10/04	Test	Ind	Chennai	lbw b A.R. Kumble	5					1	–
		Ind	Chennai	not out	39*					–	–
26/10/04	Test	Ind	Nagpur	c P.A. Patel b Zaheer Khan	91					3	–
		Ind	Nagpur	c M. Kaif b A.R. Kumble	73					1	–
03/11/04	Test	Ind	Mumbai	st K.K.D Karthik b A.R. Kumble	17					–	–
		Ind	Mumbai	b M. Kartik	7	6.2	–	9	6	2	–
18/11/04	Test	NZ	Brisbane	b D.L. Vettori	141					–	–
		NZ	Brisbane		–					–	–
26/11/04	Test	NZ	Adelaide	lbw b D.L. Vettori	7					1	–
		NZ	Adelaide		–					1	–
05/12/04	ODI	NZ	Melbourne	b C.L. Cairns	36					–	–
08/12/04	ODI	NZ	Sydney	cwk B.B. McCullum b C.L. Cairns	6					–	–
16/12/04	Test	Pak	Perth	c Inzamam-ul-Haq b Shoaib Akhtar	1					1	–
		Pak	Perth	c Inzamam-ul-Haq b Mohammad Sami	27					1	–
26/12/04	Test	Pak	Melbourne	c Shoaib Akhtar b Danish Kaneria	20	3.0	–	24	–	–	–
		Pak	Melbourne		–					–	–
02/01/05	Test	Pak	Sydney	st Kamran Akmal b Danish Kaneria	35					1	–
		Pak	Sydney		–					–	–
14/01/05	ODI	WI	Melbourne	b M.N. Samuels	66					1	–
16/01/05	ODI	Pak	Hobart	c Naved-ul-Hasan b Mohammad Hafeez	97					2	–

MICHAEL CLARKE (continued)

Start Date		Opp	Venue	How Out	Runs	O	M	R	W	Ct	St
21/01/05	ODI	WI	Brisbane	c M.N. Samuels b M. Dillon	2					–	–
23/01/05	ODI	Pak	Sydney	not out	103*					1	–
26/01/05	ODI	WI	Adelaide	b P.T. Collins	21					–	–
30/01/05	ODI	Pak	Perth	not out	75*					–	–
04/02/05	ODI	Pak	Melbourne	lbw b Naved-ul-Hasan	9					–	–
06/02/05	ODI	Pak	Sydney	b Mohammad Hafeez	38					1	–
19/02/05	ODI	NZ	Wellington	c H.J.H. Marshall b S.B. Styris	0	1.0	–	5	–	–	–
22/02/05	ODI	NZ	Christchurch	cwk B.B. McCullum b C.L. Cairns	23					–	–
26/02/05	ODI	NZ	Auckland	not out	71*					–	–
01/03/05	ODI	NZ	Wellington	not out	10*	3.0	–	13	1	2	–
05/03/05	ODI	NZ	Napier	c C.D. Cumming b C.D. McMillan	43	5.0	–	30	–	–	–
10/03/05	Test	NZ	Christchurch	cwk B.B. McCullum b J.E.C. Franklin	8	5.0	–	16	1	–	–
		NZ	Christchurch		–					–	–
18/03/05	Test	NZ	Wellington	c S.P. Fleming b N.J. Astle	8	3.0	1	8	1	1	–
		NZ	Wellington		–					–	–
26/03/05	Test	NZ	Auckland	run out (J.A.H. Marshall)	22					1	–
		NZ	Auckland		–					–	–
18/06/05	ODI	Ban	Cardiff	c Mashrafe Mortaza b Tapash Baisya	54	6.0	–	38	–	–	–
19/06/05	ODI	Eng	Bristol	b J. Lewis	45					–	–
28/06/05	ODI	Eng	Birmingham	cwk G.O. Jones b D. Gough	3					–	–
30/06/05	ODI	Ban	Canterbury	not out	80*	2.0	1	5	–	–	–
02/07/05	ODI	Eng	Lord's	lbw b S.P. Jones	2					–	–
07/07/05	ODI	Eng	Leeds	b P.D. Collingwood	2					–	–
10/07/05	ODI	Eng	Lord's		–	6.0	–	29	–	–	–
12/07/05	ODI	Eng	The Oval		–	4.0	–	25	–	–	–
21/07/05	Test	Eng	Lord's	lbw b S.P. Jones	11					–	–
		Eng	Lord's	b M.J. Hoggard	91					–	–
04/08/05	Test	Eng	Birmingham	cwk G.O. Jones b A.F. Giles	40					–	–
		Eng	Birmingham	b S.J. Harmison	30					–	–
11/08/05	Test	Eng	Manchester	c A. Flintoff b S.P. Jones	7					–	–
		Eng	Manchester	b S.P. Jones	39					–	–
25/08/05	Test	Eng	Nottingham	lbw b S.J. Harmison	36					–	–

MICHAEL CLARKE (continued)

Start Date		Opp	Venue	How Out	Runs	O	M	R	W	Ct	St
		Eng	Nottingham	cwk G.O. Jones b M.J. Hoggard	56					1	–
08/09/05	Test	Eng	The Oval	lbw b M.J. Hoggard	25					1	–
		Eng	The Oval		–	2.0	–	6	–	–	–

MATTHEW ELLIOTT

Start Date		Opp	Venue	How Out	Runs	O	M	R	W	Ct	St
01/07/04	Test	SL	Darwin	c R.P. Arnold b W.P.U.J.C. Vaas	1					1	–
		SL	Darwin	c T.M. Dilshan b W.P.U.J.C. Vaas	0					–	–

ADAM GILCHRIST

Start Date		Opp	Venue	How Out	Runs	O	M	R	W	Ct	St
01/07/04	Test	SL	Darwin	cwk K.C. Sangakkara b S.L. Malinga	0					3	–
		SL	Darwin	run out (Jayawadene/ Sangakkara)	80					5	–
09/07/04	Test	SL	Cairns	cwk R.S. Kaluwitharana b S.L. Malinga	35					1	1
		SL	Cairns	b T.M. Dilshan	0					2	1
13/09/04	ODI	USA	Southampton	not out	24*					2	–
16/09/04	ODI	NZ	The Oval	b J.D.P. Oram	4					–	–
21/09/04	ODI	Eng	Birmingham	c M.E. Trescothick b D. Gough	37					–	–
06/10/04	Test	Ind	Bangalore	c and b Harbhajan Singh	104					3	–
		Ind	Bangalore	c A. Chopra b A.R. Kumble	26					2	–
14/10/04	Test	Ind	Chennai	c Yuvraj Singh b A.R. Kumble	3					3	–
		Ind	Chennai	b A.R. Kumble	49					–	–
26/10/04	Test	Ind	Nagpur	c and b M. Kartik	2					1	–
		Ind	Nagpur	not out	3*					3	–
03/11/04	Test	Ind	Mumbai	c M. Kaif b M. Kartik	26					3	–
		Ind	Mumbai	c S.R. Tendulkar b Harbhajan Singh	5					1	–
18/11/04	Test	NZ	Brisbane	c S.B. Styris b C.S. Martin	126					2	1
		NZ	Brisbane		–					2	–
26/11/04	Test	NZ	Adelaide	c and b D.L. Vettori	50					2	–
		NZ	Adelaide		–					2	–
05/12/04	ODI	NZ	Melbourne	b C.L. Cairns	68					1	–
08/12/04	ODI	NZ	Sydney	c N.J. Astle b S.B. Styris	60					1	–

ADAM GILCHRIST (continued)

Start Date		Opp	Venue	How Out	Runs	O	M	R	W	Ct	St
16/12/04	Test	Pak	Perth	b Abdul Razzaq	69					3	–
		Pak	Perth	not out	0*					3	–
26/12/04	Test	Pak	Melbourne	c Mohammad Sami b Danish Kaneria	48					2	2
		Pak	Melbourne		–					2	–
02/01/05	Test	Pak	Sydney	st Kamran Akmal b Danish Kaneria	113					2	–
		Pak	Sydney		–					–	–
14/01/05	ODI	WI	Melbourne	c D.J.J. Bravo b IDR Bradshaw	0					3	–
21/01/05	ODI	WI	Brisbane	cwk C.O. Browne b I.D.R. Bradshaw	6					2	–
30/01/05	ODI	Pak	Perth	b Abdul Razzaq	47					–	–
04/02/05	ODI	Pak	Melbourne	c Abdul Razzaq b Mohammad Khalil	24					–	–
06/02/05	ODI	Pak	Sydney	c Shoaib Malik b Abdul Razzaq	40					2	–
19/02/05	ODI	NZ	Wellington	c M.S. Sinclair b K.D. Mills	4					1	1
22/02/05	ODI	NZ	Christchurch	cwk B.B. McCullum b D.R. Tuffey	0					5	–
26/02/05	ODI	NZ	Auckland	c N.J. Astle b C.L. Cairns	18					2	–
01/03/05	ODI	NZ	Wellington	c C.D. McMillan b J.W. Wilson	54					2	–
05/03/05	ODI	NZ	Napier	c C.D. Cumming b T.K. Canning	91					1	–
10/03/05	Test	NZ	Christchurch	c I.E. O'Brien b D.L. Vettori	121					3	–
		NZ	Christchurch		–					–	–
18/03/05	Test	NZ	Wellington	c and b J.E.C. Franklin	162					2	–
		NZ	Wellington		–					–	–
26/03/05	Test	NZ	Auckland	not out	60*					1	–
		NZ	Auckland		–					1	–
18/06/05	ODI	Ban	Cardiff	lbw b Mashrafe Mortaza	0					1	–
19/06/05	ODI	Eng	Bristol	cwk G.O. Jones b S.J. Harmison	26					–	–
23/06/05	ODI	Eng	Chester-le-St	cwk G.O. Jones b C.T. Tremlett	18					1	–
25/06/05	ODI	Ban	Manchester	not out	66*					2	1
28/06/05	ODI	Eng	Birmingham	cwk G.O. Jones b S.P. Jones	19					–	–
30/06/05	ODI	Ban	Canterbury	c Khaled Mahmud b Tapash Baisya	45					5	–
02/07/05	ODI	Eng	Lord's	c K.P. Pietersen b A. Flintoff	27					1	–

ADAM GILCHRIST (continued)

Start Date		Opp	Venue	How Out	Runs	O	M	R	W	Ct	St
07/07/05	ODI	Eng	Leeds	cwk G.O. Jones b S.J. Harmison	42					1	–
10/07/05	ODI	Eng	Lord's	cwk G.O. Jones b A. Flintoff	29					2	–
12/07/05	ODI	Eng	The Oval	not out	121*					2	–
21/07/05	Test	Eng	Lord's	cwk G.O. Jones b A. Flintoff	26					2	–
		Eng	Lord's	b A. Flintoff	10					1	–
04/08/05	Test	Eng	Birmingham	not out	49*					4	–
		Eng	Birmingham	c A. Flintoff b A.F. Giles	1					3	–
11/08/05	Test	Eng	Manchester	cwk G.O. Jones b S.P. Jones	30					2	–
		Eng	Manchester	c I.R. Bell b A. Flintoff	4					–	–
25/08/05	Test	Eng	Nottingham	c A.J. Strauss b A. Flintoff	27					4	1
		Eng	Nottingham	lbw b M.J. Hoggard	11					1	–
08/09/05	Test	Eng	The Oval	lbw b M.J. Hoggard	23					–	–
		Eng	The Oval		–					1	–

JASON GILLESPIE

Start Date		Opp	Venue	How Out	Runs	O	M	R	W	Ct	St
01/07/04	Test	SL	Darwin	lbw b W.P.U.J.C. Vaas	4	13.0	4	18	2	1	–
		SL	Darwin	c T.T. Samaraweera b U.D.U. Chandana	16	13.0	2	37	–	–	–
09/07/04	Test	SL	Cairns	cwk R.S. Kaluwitharana b S.L. Malinga	1	37.4	6	116	3	1	–
		SL	Cairns	st M.S. Atapattu b U.D.U. Chandana	1	18.0	6	39	2	–	–
28/08/04	ODI	Pak	Amstelveen		–	9.0	–	22	1	–	–
04/09/04	ODI	Pak	Lord's		–	8.0	2	26	2	–	–
13/09/04	ODI	USA	Southampton		–	6.0	1	15	4	–	–
16/09/04	ODI	NZ	The Oval		–	9.0	1	46	1	1	–
21/09/04	ODI	Eng	Birmingham	b D. Gough	0	8.0	–	32	1	–	–
06/10/04	Test	Ind	Bangalore	not out	7*	16.2	3	63	2	–	–
		Ind	Bangalore	c Yuvraj Singh b Harbhajan Singh	8	14.4	4	33	3	–	–
14/10/04	Test	Ind	Chennai	c M. Kaif b A.R. Kumble	5	35.0	8	70	2	–	–
		Ind	Chennai	c R.S. Dravid b Harbhajan Singh	26	1.0	–	1	–	–	–
26/10/04	Test	Ind	Nagpur	lbw b Zaheer Khan	9	22.5	8	56	5	–	–
		Ind	Nagpur		–	16.0	7	24	4	–	–
03/11/04	Test	Ind	Mumbai	c M. Kaif b A.R. Kumble	2	12.0	2	29	4	–	–
		Ind	Mumbai	not out	9*	15.0	1	47	–	–	–

JASON GILLESPIE (continued)

Start Date		Opp	Venue	How Out	Runs	O	M	R	W	Ct	St
18/11/04	Test	NZ	Brisbane	not out	54*	29.0	7	84	1	–	–
		NZ	Brisbane		–	10.0	5	19	2	–	–
26/11/04	Test	NZ	Adelaide	c M.H. Richardson b D.L. Vettori	12	19.0	4	37	3	–	–
		NZ	Adelaide		–	16.0	5	41	2	1	–
08/12/04	ODI	NZ	Sydney		–	10.0	1	41	2	–	–
16/12/04	Test	Pak	Perth	cwk Kamran Akmal b Shoaib Akhtar	24	14.0	2	43	1	1	–
		Pak	Perth		–	12.0	3	37	–	–	–
26/12/04	Test	Pak	Melbourne	not out	50*	26.0	7	77	3	–	–
		Pak	Melbourne		–	12.0	7	15	2	1	–
02/01/05	Test	Pak	Sydney	lbw b Naved-ul-Hasan	0	14.0	3	47	–	1	–
		Pak	Sydney		–	13.2	2	39	1	–	–
14/01/05	ODI	WI	Melbourne		–	8.0	–	29	–	–	–
21/01/05	ODI	WI	Brisbane		–	9.0	1	62	3	–	–
26/01/05	ODI	WI	Adelaide	not out	44*	6.5	–	25	2	–	–
30/01/05	ODI	Pak	Perth	cwk Younis Khan b Abdul Razzaq	4	10.0	1	35	–	1	–
04/02/05	ODI	Pak	Melbourne	not out	3*	10.0	–	47	2	1	–
06/02/05	ODI	Pak	Sydney	b Naved-ul-Hasan	0	10.0	–	35	1	–	–
22/02/05	ODI	NZ	Christchurch		–	9.4	1	45	2	–	–
26/02/05	ODI	NZ	Auckland		–	6.0	–	14	–	–	–
01/03/05	ODI	NZ	Wellington		–	10.0	–	46	2	–	–
10/03/05	Test	NZ	Christchurch	c C.D. Cumming b D.L. Vettori	12	29.0	5	87	–	1	–
		NZ	Christchurch		–	12.0	2	38	3	–	–
18/03/05	Test	NZ	Wellington	b J.E.C. Franklin	2	20.0	4	63	1	1	–
		NZ	Wellington		–	5.0	2	5	–	–	–
26/03/05	Test	NZ	Auckland	cwk B.B. McCullum b C.S. Martin	35	25.0	8	64	2	1	–
		NZ	Auckland		–	16.0	4	63	1	1	–
18/06/05	ODI	Ban	Cardiff		–	9.2	1	41	2	–	–
19/06/05	ODI	Eng	Bristol	cwk G.O. Jones b A. Flintoff	14	10.0	1	66	–	–	–
23/06/05	ODI	Eng	Chester-le-St		–	9.0	–	36	1	1	–
25/06/05	ODI	Ban	Manchester		–	3.0	–	17	–	–	–
28/06/05	ODI	Eng	Birmingham	c K.P. Pietersen b D. Gough	1					1	–
30/06/05	ODI	Ban	Canterbury		–	9.0	–	49	2	–	–
02/07/05	ODI	Eng	Lord's	cwk G.O. Jones b A. Flintoff	0	10.0	1	42	–	–	–
07/07/05	ODI	Eng	Leeds		–	10.0	–	66	–	–	–
10/07/05	ODI	Eng	Lord's		–	7.0	–	42	–	–	–

JASON GILLESPIE (continued)

Start Date	Opp	Venue	How Out	Runs	O	M	R	W	Ct	St
12/07/05	ODI Eng	The Oval		–	10.0	1	44	3	–	–
21/07/05	Test Eng	Lord's	lbw b S.J. Harmison	1	8.0	1	30	–	–	–
	Eng	Lord's	b S.P. Jones	13	6.0	–	18	–	1	–
04/08/05	Test Eng	Birmingham	lbw b A. Flintoff	7	22.0	3	91	2	–	–
	Eng	Birmingham	lbw b A. Flintoff	0	8.0	–	24	–	–	–
11/08/05	Test Eng	Manchester	lbw b S.P. Jones	26	19.0	2	114	1	–	–
	Eng	Manchester	lbw b M.J. Hoggard	0	4.0	–	23	–	–	–

BRAD HADDIN

Start Date	Opp	Venue	How Out	Runs	O	M	R	W	Ct	St
23/08/04	ODI Ind	Amstelveen	c L. Balaji b A. Nehra	5					–	–
28/08/04	ODI Pak	Amstelveen	b Mohammad Sami	10					4	–
04/09/04	ODI Pak	Lord's	c Shoaib Malik b Mohammad Sami	13					1	–
16/01/05	ODI Pak	Hobart	c Mohammad Hafeez b Naved-ul-Hasan	30					–	–
23/01/05	ODI Pak	Sydney		–					–	1
26/01/05	ODI WI	Adelaide	b DJJ Bravo	32					3	–
10/07/05	ODI Eng	Lord's		–					–	–

NATHAN HAURITZ

Start Date	Opp	Venue	How Out	Runs	O	M	R	W	Ct	St
03/11/04	Test Ind	Mumbai	c Harbhajan Singh b A.R. Kumble	0	5.0	–	16	3	–	–
	Ind	Mumbai	lbw b A.R. Kumble	15	22.0	4	87	2	1	–

MATTHEW HAYDEN

Start Date	Opp	Venue	How Out	Runs	O	M	R	W	Ct	St
01/07/04	Test SL	Darwin	c S.T. Jayasuriya b W.P.U.J.C. Vaas	37					1	–
	SL	Darwin	cwk K.C. Sangakkara b D.N.T. Zoysa	2					–	–
09/07/04	Test SL	Cairns	c S.T. Jayasuriya b T.T. Samaraweera	117					1	–
	SL	Cairns	b U.D.U. Chandana	132					–	–
23/08/04	ODI Ind	Amstelveen	c S.C. Ganguly b L. Balaji	29					–	–
28/08/04	ODI Pak	Amstelveen	c Yasir Hameed b Shoaib Akhtar	59					1	–
04/09/04	ODI Pak	Lord's	b Shahid Afridi	52					1	–
13/09/04	ODI USA	Southampton	cwk M.R. Johnson	23					–	–
16/09/04	ODI NZ	The Oval	c C.L. Cairns b CZ Harris	47					–	–

MATTHEW HAYDEN (continued)

Start Date		Opp	Venue	How Out	Runs	O	M	R	W	Ct	St
21/09/04	ODI	Eng	Birmingham	c M.E. Trescothick b S.J. Harmison	17					2	–
06/10/04	Test	Ind	Bangalore	c Yuvraj Singh b Harbhajan Singh	26					–	–
		Ind	Bangalore	run out (Harbhajan Singh)	30					–	–
14/10/04	Test	Ind	Chennai	c V.V.S. Laxman b Harbhajan Singh	58					1	–
		Ind	Chennai	c V.V.S. Laxman b A.R. Kumble	39					–	–
26/10/04	Test	Ind	Nagpur	cwk P.A. Patel b Zaheer Khan	23					1	–
		Ind	Nagpur	b Zaheer Khan	9					–	–
03/11/04	Test	Ind	Mumbai	c M. Kaif b M. Kartik	35					–	–
		Ind	Mumbai	b Harbhajan Singh	24					1	–
18/11/04	Test	NZ	Brisbane	lbw b K.D. Mills	8					1	–
		NZ	Brisbane		–					2	–
26/11/04	Test	NZ	Adelaide	c and b P.J. Wiseman	70					–	–
		NZ	Adelaide	cwk B.B. McCullum b D.L. Vettori	54					–	–
05/12/04	ODI	NZ	Melbourne	c M.S. Sinclair b J.D.P. Oram	13					–	–
08/12/04	ODI	NZ	Sydney	run out (Sinclair)	43					1	–
16/12/04	Test	Pak	Perth	lbw b Shoaib Akhtar	4					–	–
		Pak	Perth	b Shoaib Akhtar	10					1	–
26/12/04	Test	Pak	Melbourne	c Shoaib Malik b Shoaib Akhtar	9					–	–
		Pak	Melbourne	not out	56*					1	–
02/01/05	Test	Pak	Sydney	b Danish Kaneria	26					–	–
		Pak	Sydney	not out	23*					1	–
21/01/05	ODI	WI	Brisbane	c CH Gayle b P.T. Collins	6					–	–
23/01/05	ODI	Pak	Sydney	c Naved-ul-Hasan b Abdul Razzaq	27					2	–
26/01/05	ODI	WI	Adelaide	cwk C.O. Browne b P.T. Collins	3					–	–
30/01/05	ODI	Pak	Perth	c Shahid Afridi b Naved-ul-Hasan	6					–	–
19/02/05	ODI	NZ	Wellington	b S.B. Styris	71					1	–
22/02/05	ODI	NZ	Christchurch	c J.W. Wilson b K.D. Mills	114					1	–
10/03/05	Test	NZ	Christchurch	c N.J. Astle b I.E. O'Brien	35					–	–
		NZ	Christchurch	c C.D. Cumming b D.L. Vettori	15					–	–

MATTHEW HAYDEN (continued)

Start Date		Opp	Venue	How Out	Runs	O	M	R	W	Ct	St
18/03/05	Test	NZ	Wellington	c L. Vincent b J.E.C. Franklin	61					–	–
		NZ	Wellington		–					–	–
26/03/05	Test	NZ	Auckland	lbw b J.E.C. Franklin	38					1	–
		NZ	Auckland	run out (Vettori)	9					–	–
18/06/05	ODI	Ban	Cardiff	b Nazmul Hossain	37					1	–
19/06/05	ODI	Eng	Bristol	c P.D. Collingwood b S.J. Harmison	31					–	–
23/06/05	ODI	Eng	Chester-le-St	cwk G.O. Jones b A. Flintoff	39					1	–
25/06/05	ODI	Ban	Manchester	not out	66*					–	–
28/06/05	ODI	Eng	Birmingham	lbw b S.P. Jones	14					–	–
30/06/05	ODI	Ban	Canterbury	c Khaled Mahmud b Mashrafe Mortaza	1					–	–
02/07/05	ODI	Eng	Lord's	c A.F. Giles b D. Gough	17					1	–
07/07/05	ODI	Eng	Leeds	c K.P. Pietersen b A. Flintoff	17					–	–
12/07/05	ODI	Eng	The Oval	cwk G.O. Jones b D. Gough	31					–	–
21/07/05	Test	Eng	Lord's	b M.J. Hoggard	12					1	–
		Eng	Lord's	b A. Flintoff	34					2	–
04/08/05	Test	Eng	Birmingham	c A.J. Strauss b M.J. Hoggard	0					–	–
		Eng	Birmingham	c M.E. Trescothick b S.P. Jones	31					2	–
11/08/05	Test	Eng	Manchester	lbw b A.F. Giles	34					1	–
		Eng	Manchester	b A. Flintoff	36					–	–
25/08/05	Test	Eng	Nottingham	lbw b M.J. Hoggard	7					1	–
		Eng	Nottingham	c A.F. Giles b A. Flintoff	26					1	–
08/09/05	Test	Eng	The Oval	lbw b A. Flintoff	138					1	–
		Eng	The Oval	not out	0*					1	–

BRAD HOGG

Start Date		Opp	Venue	How Out	Runs	O	M	R	W	Ct	St
23/08/04	ODI	Ind	Amstelveen	not out	17*					–	–
28/08/04	ODI	Pak	Amstelveen	run out (Moin Khan)	0	7.0	–	43	1	–	–
05/12/04	ODI	NZ	Melbourne	not out	20*	7.0	–	33	–	–	–
08/12/04	ODI	NZ	Sydney	not out	41*	8.0	–	45	3	–	–
14/01/05	ODI	WI	Melbourne		–	10.0	–	32	5	2	–
16/01/05	ODI	Pak	Hobart	not out	3*	7.0	–	28	1	1	–
26/01/05	ODI	WI	Adelaide	cwk C.O. Browne b DJJ Bravo	3	6.0	–	33	1	–	–

BRAD HOGG (continued)

Start Date		Opp	Venue	How Out	Runs	O	M	R	W	Ct	St
30/01/05	ODI	Pak	Perth	cwk Younis Khan b Mohammad Khalil	10	10.0	–	71	1	–	–
06/02/05	ODI	Pak	Sydney	b Naved-ul-Hasan	13	10.0	–	63	2	–	–
19/02/05	ODI	NZ	Wellington	not out	25*	9.0	–	44	1	–	–
22/02/05	ODI	NZ	Christchurch	not out	9*	10.0	–	49	–	–	–
26/02/05	ODI	NZ	Auckland		–	7.4	–	45	3	–	–
05/03/05	ODI	NZ	Napier		–	10.0	–	53	–	1	–
18/06/05	ODI	Ban	Cardiff		–	9.0	–	52	1	1	–
19/06/05	ODI	Eng	Bristol	not out	10*	10.0	1	42	3	–	–
23/06/05	ODI	Eng	Chester-le-St		–	6.0	–	19	2	–	–
25/06/05	ODI	Ban	Manchester		–	9.0	1	29	3	–	–
28/06/05	ODI	Eng	Birmingham	cwk G.O. Jones b D. Gough	2					–	–
02/07/05	ODI	Eng	Lord's	cwk G.O. Jones b S.J. Harmison	16	6.0	–	25	1	–	–
07/07/05	ODI	Eng	Leeds		–	6.0	–	30	1	–	–

JAMES HOPES

Start Date		Opp	Venue	How Out	Runs	O	M	R	W	Ct	St
01/03/05	ODI	NZ	Wellington		–	10.0	1	38	1	–	–

MIKE HUSSEY

Start Date		Opp	Venue	How Out	Runs	O	M	R	W	Ct	St
22/02/05	ODI	NZ	Christchurch	not out	32*					–	–
26/02/05	ODI	NZ	Auckland	not out	65*	3.0	–	22	–	3	–
01/03/05	ODI	NZ	Wellington		–					–	–
05/03/05	ODI	NZ	Napier	not out	0*					–	–
18/06/05	ODI	Ban	Cardiff	not out	31*	5.0	–	24	–	–	–
19/06/05	ODI	Eng	Bristol	b S.J. Harmison	84					–	–
23/06/05	ODI	Eng	Chester-le-St	c P.D. Collingwood b A. Flintoff	5					2	–
25/06/05	ODI	Ban	Manchester		–					–	–
28/06/05	ODI	Eng	Birmingham	cwk G.O. Jones b S.J. Harmison	45					–	–
30/06/05	ODI	Ban	Canterbury		–					–	–
02/07/05	ODI	Eng	Lord's	not out	62*	4.0	–	31	1	–	–
07/07/05	ODI	Eng	Leeds	not out	46*					–	–
10/07/05	ODI	Eng	Lord's		–					1	–
12/07/05	ODI	Eng	The Oval		–					–	–

MICHAEL KASPROWICZ

Start Date		Opp	Venue	How Out	Runs	O	M	R	W	Ct	St
01/07/04	Test	SL	Darwin	not out	2*	7.0	1	15	–	–	–
		SL	Darwin	c and b S.L. Malinga	15	17.4	3	39	7	–	–
09/07/04	Test	SL	Cairns	cwk R.S. Kaluwitharana b U.D.U. Chandana	9	32.0	5	113	1	2	–
		SL	Cairns	not out	3*	11.0	4	34	–	–	–
23/08/04	ODI	Ind	Amstelveen		–					–	–
04/09/04	ODI	Pak	Lord's		–	9.2	1	47	5	1	–
13/09/04	ODI	USA	Southampton		–	7.0	1	14	4	–	–
16/09/04	ODI	NZ	The Oval		–	10.0	1	32	3	2	–
21/09/04	ODI	Eng	Birmingham	not out	0*	10.0	–	52	–	–	–
06/10/04	Test	Ind	Bangalore	c Yuvraj Singh b Harbhajan Singh	3	20.0	4	43	2	–	–
		Ind	Bangalore	c R.S. Dravid b Harbhajan Singh	8	14.0	7	23	2	–	–
14/10/04	Test	Ind	Chennai	c V.V.S. Laxman b A.R. Kumble	4	25.0	5	65	1	–	–
		Ind	Chennai	lbw b A.R. Kumble	5					–	–
26/10/04	Test	Ind	Nagpur	cwk P.A. Patel b A.B. Agarkar	0	21.0	4	45	–	–	–
		Ind	Nagpur		–	7.0	1	39	2	–	–
03/11/04	Test	Ind	Mumbai	c A.R. Kumble b M. Kartik	19	8.3	3	11	2	–	–
		Ind	Mumbai	c R.S. Dravid b Harbhajan Singh	7	13.0	5	29	–	–	–
18/11/04	Test	NZ	Brisbane	c K.D. Mills b C.S. Martin	5	28.0	5	90	4	–	–
		NZ	Brisbane		–	8.0	2	21	1	–	–
26/11/04	Test	NZ	Adelaide		–	16.0	3	66	2	–	–
		NZ	Adelaide		–	14.0	4	39	2	–	–
05/12/04	ODI	NZ	Melbourne	not out	9*	9.0	1	53	1	–	–
16/12/04	Test	Pak	Perth	lbw b Shoaib Akhtar	4	16.3	6	30	5	–	–
		Pak	Perth		–	3.3	2	4	2	1	–
26/12/04	Test	Pak	Melbourne	c (sub) Naved-ul-Hasan b Shoaib Akhtar	4	20.0	6	66	1	–	–
		Pak	Melbourne		–	16.0	3	42	1	1	–
14/01/05	ODI	WI	Melbourne		–	6.2	–	26	1	–	–
16/01/05	ODI	Pak	Hobart		–	9.0	–	38	2	–	–
21/01/05	ODI	WI	Brisbane		–	10.0	1	43	1	1	–
23/01/05	ODI	Pak	Sydney		–	5.0	–	17	1	–	–
19/02/05	ODI	NZ	Wellington		–	10.0	1	62	–	–	–
26/02/05	ODI	NZ	Auckland		–	8.0	1	28	1	1	–
01/03/05	ODI	NZ	Wellington		–	8.0	2	34	1	–	–
05/03/05	ODI	NZ	Napier		–	10.0	2	36	3	1	–

MICHAEL KASPROWICZ (continued)

Start Date		Opp	Venue	How Out	Runs	O	M	R	W	Ct	St
10/03/05	Test	NZ	Christchurch	not out	13*	25.0	6	85	1	–	–
		NZ	Christchurch		–	10.0	3	33	1	–	–
18/03/05	Test	NZ	Wellington	not out	2*	16.0	2	42	3	–	–
		NZ	Wellington		–	3.0	–	11	1	–	–
26/03/05	Test	NZ	Auckland	b J.E.C. Franklin	23	30.2	7	89	2	–	–
		NZ	Auckland		–	14.0	2	59	–	–	–
18/06/05	ODI	Ban	Cardiff		–	10.0	–	40	1	–	–
19/06/05	ODI	Eng	Bristol	b D. Gough	1	9.0	–	68	1	1	–
30/06/05	ODI	Ban	Canterbury		–	9.0	–	46	1	–	–
10/07/05	ODI	Eng	Lord's		–	10.0	2	40	2	–	–
12/07/05	ODI	Eng	The Oval		–	10.0	1	46	2	2	–
04/08/05	Test	Eng	Birmingham	lbw b A. Flintoff	0	15.0	3	80	3	–	–
		Eng	Birmingham	cwk G.O. Jones b S.J. Harmison	20	3.0	–	29	–	–	–
25/08/05	Test	Eng	Nottingham	b S.P. Jones	5	32.0	3	122	1	1	–
		Eng	Nottingham	cwk G.O. Jones b S.J. Harmison	19	2.0	–	19	–	2	–

SIMON KATICH

Start Date		Opp	Venue	How Out	Runs	O	M	R	W	Ct	St
01/07/04	Test	SL	Darwin	cwk K.C. Sangakkara b W.P.U.J.C. Vaas	9					–	–
		SL	Darwin	c T.M. Dilshan b U.D.U. Chandana	15					–	–
09/07/04	Test	SL	Cairns	b U.D.U. Chandana	1					–	–
		SL	Cairns	st R.S. Kaluwitharana b T.M. Dilshan	1					–	–
06/10/04	Test	Ind	Bangalore	b A.R. Kumble	81					–	–
		Ind	Bangalore	c R.S. Dravid b A.R. Kumble	39					–	–
14/10/04	Test	Ind	Chennai	not out	36*	2.0	–	7	–	–	–
		Ind	Chennai	lbw b Zaheer Khan	9					–	–
26/10/04	Test	Ind	Nagpur	c A. Chopra b A.R. Kumble	4					–	–
		Ind	Nagpur	lbw b M. Kartik	99					–	–
03/11/04	Test	Ind	Mumbai	c M. Kaif b A.R. Kumble	7					1	–
		Ind	Mumbai	c R.S. Dravid b Harbhajan Singh	1					–	–
16/01/05	ODI	Pak	Hobart	b Azhar Mahmood	38					–	–
26/01/05	ODI	WI	Adelaide	lbw b P.T. Collins	76					–	–
30/01/05	ODI	Pak	Perth	cwk Younis Khan b Mohammad Khalil	0					1	–

SIMON KATICH (continued)

Start Date		Opp	Venue	How Out	Runs	O	M	R	W	Ct	St
04/02/05	ODI	Pak	Melbourne	c (sub) Yasir Hameed b Abdul Razzaq	9					1	–
06/02/05	ODI	Pak	Sydney	run out (Shoaib Malik/Kamran)	5					1	–
19/02/05	ODI	NZ	Wellington	cwk B.B. McCullum b C.L. Cairns	0					1	–
26/02/05	ODI	NZ	Auckland	lbw b D.L. Vettori	58					–	–
01/03/05	ODI	NZ	Wellington	cwk B.B. McCullum b C.L. Cairns	43					1	–
05/03/05	ODI	NZ	Napier	cwk B.B. McCullum b LJ Hamilton	5					–	–
10/03/05	Test	NZ	Christchurch	c L Vincent b N.J. Astle	118					–	–
		NZ	Christchurch		–					1	–
18/03/05	Test	NZ	Wellington	cwk B.B. McCullum b J.E.C. Franklin	35					–	–
		NZ	Wellington		–					–	–
26/03/05	Test	NZ	Auckland	c PJ Wiseman b J.E.C. Franklin	35					1	–
		NZ	Auckland		–					1	–
18/06/05	ODI	Ban	Cardiff	not out	36*					1	–
10/07/05	ODI	Eng	Lord's	c S.J. Harmison b A.F. Giles	30					1	–
12/07/05	ODI	Eng	The Oval		–					–	–
21/07/05	Test	Eng	Lord's	cwk G.O. Jones b S.J. Harmison	27					–	–
		Eng	Lord's	c S.P. Jones b S.J. Harmison	67					–	–
04/08/05	Test	Eng	Birmingham	cwk G.O. Jones b A. Flintoff	4					1	–
		Eng	Birmingham	c M.E. Trescothick b A.F. Giles	16					–	–
11/08/05	Test	Eng	Manchester	b A. Flintoff	17	9.0	1	36	1	–	–
		Eng	Manchester	c A.F. Giles b A. Flintoff	12					1	–
25/08/05	Test	Eng	Nottingham	c A.J. Strauss b S.P. Jones	45					–	–
		Eng	Nottingham	lbw b S.J. Harmison	59					–	–
08/09/05	Test	Eng	The Oval	lbw b A. Flintoff	1	3.0	–	14	–	1	–
		Eng	The Oval		–					1	–

JUSTIN LANGER

Start Date		Opp	Venue	How Out	Runs	O	M	R	W	Ct	St
01/07/04	Test	SL	Darwin	c U.D.U. Chandana b T.T. Samaraweera	30					1	–

JUSTIN LANGER (continued)

Start Date		Opp	Venue	How Out	Runs	O	M	R	W	Ct	St
		SL	Darwin	cwk K.C. Sangakkara b W.P.U.J.C. Vaas	10					–	–
09/07/04	Test	SL	Cairns	c D.P.M. Jayawardene b S.L. Malinga	162					–	–
		SL	Cairns	cwk R.S. Kaluwitharana b D.N.T. Zoysa	8					–	–
06/10/04	Test	Ind	Bangalore	b IK Pathan	52					1	–
		Ind	Bangalore	lbw b IK Pathan	0					–	–
14/10/04	Test	Ind	Chennai	c R.S. Dravid b Harbhajan Singh	71					–	–
		Ind	Chennai	c R.S. Dravid b A.R. Kumble	19					–	–
26/10/04	Test	Ind	Nagpur	c R.S. Dravid b Zaheer Khan	44					–	–
		Ind	Nagpur	c V.V.S. Laxman b M. Kartik	30					–	–
03/11/04	Test	Ind	Mumbai	c R.S. Dravid b Zaheer Khan	12					–	–
		Ind	Mumbai	cwk K.K.D Karthik b Zaheer Khan	0					–	–
18/11/04	Test	NZ	Brisbane	lbw b D.L. Vettori	34					–	–
		NZ	Brisbane		–					1	–
26/11/04	Test	NZ	Adelaide	c J.D.P. Oram b D.L. Vettori	215					1	–
		NZ	Adelaide	lbw b P.J. Wiseman	46					2	–
16/12/04	Test	Pak	Perth	c Younis Khan b Mohammad Sami	191					–	–
		Pak	Perth	b Abdul Razzaq	97					–	–
26/12/04	Test	Pak	Melbourne	c Imran Farhat b Danish Kaneria	50					–	–
		Pak	Melbourne	cwk Kamran Akmal b Mohammad Sami	5					–	–
02/01/05	Test	Pak	Sydney	b Naved-ul-Hasan	13					–	–
		Pak	Sydney	b Danish Kaneria	34					–	–
10/03/05	Test	NZ	Christchurch	b J.E.C. Franklin	23					1	–
		NZ	Christchurch	not out	72*					–	–
18/03/05	Test	NZ	Wellington	cwk B.B. McCullum b D.L. Vettori	46					–	–
		NZ	Wellington		–					–	–
26/03/05	Test	NZ	Auckland	b J.E.C. Franklin	6					1	–
		NZ	Auckland	not out	59*					1	–
21/07/05	Test	Eng	Lord's	c S.J. Harmison b A. Flintoff	40					1	–
		Eng	Lord's	run out (Pietersen)	6					–	–
04/08/05	Test	Eng	Birmingham	lbw b S.P. Jones	82					–	–

JUSTIN LANGER (continued)

Start Date		Opp	Venue	How Out	Runs	O	M	R	W	Ct	St
		Eng	Birmingham	b A. Flintoff	28					–	–
11/08/05	Test	Eng	Manchester	c I.R. Bell b A.F. Giles	31					1	–
		Eng	Manchester	cwk G.O. Jones b M.J. Hoggard	14					–	–
25/08/05	Test	Eng	Nottingham	c I.R. Bell b M.J. Hoggard	27					–	–
		Eng	Nottingham	c I.R. Bell b A.F. Giles	61					–	–
08/09/05	Test	Eng	The Oval	b S.J. Harmison	105					–	–
		Eng	The Oval	not out	0*					–	–

BRETT LEE

Start Date	Opp	Venue	How Out	Runs	O	M	R	W	Ct	St
23/08/04	ODI	Ind	Amstelveen	not out	1*					–	–
28/08/04	ODI	Pak	Amstelveen		–	7.0	1	29	1	–	–
04/09/04	ODI	Pak	Lord's		–	10.0	–	67	1	1	–
13/09/04	ODI	USA	Southampton		–	5.0	–	21	1	–	–
21/09/04	ODI	Eng	Birmingham	b D. Gough	15	8.3	–	65	2	–	–
05/12/04	ODI	NZ	Melbourne	b C.L. Cairns	8	8.0	–	40	2	1	–
08/12/04	ODI	NZ	Sydney	not out	10*	9.0	–	48	2	–	–
14/01/05	ODI	WI	Melbourne		–	10.0	1	36	3	–	–
16/01/05	ODI	Pak	Hobart		–	10.0	–	66	1	–	–
21/01/05	ODI	WI	Brisbane		–	7.0	1	30	1	–	–
23/01/05	ODI	Pak	Sydney		–	10.0	–	54	2	–	–
26/01/05	ODI	WI	Adelaide	not out	38*	10.0	1	38	4	1	–
30/01/05	ODI	Pak	Perth	c Mohammad Khalil b Abdul Razzaq	22	9.2	–	63	1	1	–
04/02/05	ODI	Pak	Melbourne	b Naved-ul-Hasan	13	10.0	–	23	3	–	–
06/02/05	ODI	Pak	Sydney	not out	14*	8.0	1	31	1	–	–
19/02/05	ODI	NZ	Wellington	not out	4*	9.0	1	41	3	–	–
22/02/05	ODI	NZ	Christchurch		–	8.0	2	28	2	–	–
26/02/05	ODI	NZ	Auckland		–	7.0	–	25	2	–	–
01/03/05	ODI	NZ	Wellington		–	9.0	1	41	2	1	–
05/03/05	ODI	NZ	Napier		–	10.0	–	34	1	–	–
23/06/05	ODI	Eng	Chester-le-St		–	10.0	2	27	2	–	–
25/06/05	ODI	Ban	Manchester		–	6.0	1	36	2	–	–
28/06/05	ODI	Eng	Birmingham	not out	21*	3.0	–	13	–	–	–
30/06/05	ODI	Ban	Canterbury		–	10.0	–	62	2	–	–
02/07/05	ODI	Eng	Lord's	cwk G.O. Jones b A. Flintoff	3	10.0	1	36	2	–	–
07/07/05	ODI	Eng	Leeds	not out	15*	9.0	–	48	–	–	–
10/07/05	ODI	Eng	Lord's		–	10.0	2	41	5	–	–
12/07/05	ODI	Eng	The Oval		–	10.0	–	46	1	–	–

BRETT LEE (continued)

Start Date		Opp	Venue	How Out	Runs	O	M	R	W	Ct	St
21/07/05	Test	Eng	Lord's	cwk G.O. Jones b S.J. Harmison	3	15.1	5	47	3	–	–
		Eng	Lord's	run out (Giles)	8	15.0	3	58	2	1	–
04/08/05	Test	Eng	Birmingham	c A. Flintoff b S.P. Jones	6	17.0	1	111	1	1	–
		Eng	Birmingham	not out	43*	18.0	1	82	4	–	–
11/08/05	Test	Eng	Manchester	c M.E. Trescothick b S.P. Jones	1	27.0	6	100	4	–	–
		Eng	Manchester	not out	18*	12.0	–	60	1	–	–
25/08/05	Test	Eng	Nottingham	c I.R. Bell b S.P. Jones	47	32.0	2	131	1	–	–
		Eng	Nottingham	not out	26*	12.0	–	51	3	–	–
08/09/05	Test	Eng	The Oval	c A.F. Giles b M.J. Hoggard	6	23.0	3	94	1	–	–
		Eng	The Oval		–	20.0	4	88	–	–	–

DARREN LEHMANN

Start Date		Opp	Venue	How Out	Runs	O	M	R	W	Ct	St
01/07/04	Test	SL	Darwin	lbw b S.L. Malinga	57					–	–
		SL	Darwin	cwk K.C. Sangakkara b S.L. Malinga	51					–	–
09/07/04	Test	SL	Cairns	c K.C. Sangakkara b U.D.U. Chandana	50	3.0	–	5	–	–	–
		SL	Cairns	c DPM Jayawardene b U.D.U. Chandana	21	3.0	2	1	–	1	–
23/08/04	ODI	Ind	Amstelveen	c R.S. Gavaskar b A.R. Kumble	19					–	–
28/08/04	ODI	Pak	Amstelveen	cwk Moin Khan b Shabbir Ahmed	40	10.0	–	36	2	–	–
04/09/04	ODI	Pak	Lord's	run out (Shoaib Malik)	9	5.0	–	24	–	–	–
13/09/04	ODI	USA	Southampton		–					1	–
16/09/04	ODI	NZ	The Oval		–	5.0	–	16	1	1	–
21/09/04	ODI	Eng	Birmingham	b M.P. Vaughan	38	6.0	–	28	–	–	–
06/10/04	Test	Ind	Bangalore	c R.S. Dravid b A.R. Kumble	17					1	–
		Ind	Bangalore	c A. Chopra b Harbhajan Singh	14	6.0	3	14	–	–	–
14/10/04	Test	Ind	Chennai	cwk P.A. Patel b A.R. Kumble	0	5.0	–	26	–	–	–
		Ind	Chennai	cwk P.A. Patel b A.R. Kumble	31					–	–
26/10/04	Test	Ind	Nagpur	c R.S. Dravid b M. Kartik	70					–	–
		Ind	Nagpur		–					–	–

DARREN LEHMANN (continued)

Start Date		Opp	Venue	How Out	Runs	O	M	R	W	Ct	St
18/11/04	Test	NZ	Brisbane	cwk B.B. McCullum b D.L. Vettori	8	4.0	–	12	–	–	–
		NZ	Brisbane		–					–	–
26/11/04	Test	NZ	Adelaide	b PJ Wiseman	81	5.0	2	9	–	–	–
		NZ	Adelaide		–	13.0	–	46	2	–	–
05/12/04	ODI	NZ	Melbourne	c I.G. Butler b J.D.P. Oram	50	9.0	–	35	2	–	–
08/12/04	ODI	NZ	Sydney	run out (Styris/Oram)	52	3.0	–	31	–	–	–
16/12/04	Test	Pak	Perth	b Shoaib Akhtar	12	4.0	2	5	–	–	–
		Pak	Perth	b Danish Kaneria	5					1	–
26/12/04	Test	Pak	Melbourne	c Yasir Hameed b Shoaib Akhtar	11	2.0	–	13	–	–	–
		Pak	Melbourne		–					–	–
14/01/05	ODI	WI	Melbourne	not out	20*					–	–
16/01/05	ODI	Pak	Hobart	not out	49*	5.0	–	30	–	1	–
21/01/05	ODI	WI	Brisbane	not out	10*	7.0	–	34	1	–	–
23/01/05	ODI	Pak	Sydney		–	7.2	–	44	3	–	–
26/01/05	ODI	WI	Adelaide	cwk C.O. Browne b P.T. Collins	4	4.0	–	25	1	–	–
04/02/05	ODI	Pak	Melbourne	c Kamran Akmal b Shahid Afridi	0	4.0	–	29	–	1	–
06/02/05	ODI	Pak	Sydney	b Shahid Afridi	6	6.1	–	34	–	–	–

STUART MACGILL

Start Date		Opp	Venue	How Out	Runs	O	M	R	W	Ct	St
02/01/05	Test	Pak	Sydney	not out	9*	22.0	4	87	5	–	–
		Pak	Sydney		–	25.0	3	83	3	–	–

DAMIEN MARTYN

Start Date		Opp	Venue	How Out	Runs	O	M	R	W	Ct	St
01/07/04	Test	SL	Darwin	c R.P. Arnold b S.T. Jayasuriya	47					–	–
		SL	Darwin	cwk K.C. Sangakkara b S.L. Malinga	7					–	–
09/07/04	Test	SL	Cairns	lbw b U.D.U. Chandana	97					–	–
		SL	Cairns	st R.S. Kaluwitharana b U.D.U. Chandana	52					–	–
23/08/04	ODI	Ind	Amstelveen	b V. Sehwag	12					–	–
28/08/04	ODI	Pak	Amstelveen	not out	6*					–	–
04/09/04	ODI	Pak	Lord's	c Imran Farhat b Shoaib Malik	26					1	–
13/09/04	ODI	USA	Southampton		–					–	–
16/09/04	ODI	NZ	The Oval	not out	60*					–	–

DAMIEN MARTYN (continued)

Start Date	Opp		Venue	How Out	Runs	O	M	R	W	Ct	St
21/09/04	ODI	Eng	Birmingham	c M.E. Trescothick b M.P. Vaughan	65					–	–
06/10/04	Test	Ind	Bangalore	c A. Chopra b A.R. Kumble	3					–	–
		Ind	Bangalore	c (sub)M. Kaif b Harbhajan Singh	45					–	–
14/10/04	Test	Ind	Chennai	c Yuvraj Singh b A.R. Kumble	26					–	–
		Ind	Chennai	c R.S. Dravid b Harbhajan Singh	104					–	–
26/10/04	Test	Ind	Nagpur	c AB Agarkar b A.R. Kumble	114					–	–
		Ind	Nagpur	cwk P.A. Patel b Zaheer Khan	97					2	–
03/11/04	Test	Ind	Mumbai	b M. Kartik	55					–	–
		Ind	Mumbai	lbw b M. Kartik	0					–	–
18/11/04	Test	NZ	Brisbane	c C.D. McMillan b C.S. Martin	70					–	–
		NZ	Brisbane		–					–	–
26/11/04	Test	NZ	Adelaide	c S.P. Fleming b PJ Wiseman	7					–	–
		NZ	Adelaide	not out	6*					–	–
05/12/04	ODI	NZ	Melbourne	lbw b D.L. Vettori	1					–	–
08/12/04	ODI	NZ	Sydney	lbw b K.D. Mills	5					–	–
16/12/04	Test	Pak	Perth	cwk Kamran Akmal b Mohammad Sami	1					–	–
		Pak	Perth	not out	100*					–	–
26/12/04	Test	Pak	Melbourne	lbw b Danish Kaneria	142					–	–
		Pak	Melbourne		–					1	–
02/01/05	Test	Pak	Sydney	st Kamran Akmal b Danish Kaneria	67					–	–
		Pak	Sydney		–					1	–
14/01/05	ODI	WI	Melbourne	not out	95*					–	–
16/01/05	ODI	Pak	Hobart	b Abdul Razzaq	11					1	–
21/01/05	ODI	WI	Brisbane	not out	14*					–	–
23/01/05	ODI	Pak	Sydney		–					–	–
30/01/05	ODI	Pak	Perth	c Shoaib Malik b Shahid Afridi	24					1	–
04/02/05	ODI	Pak	Melbourne	st Kamran Akmal b Shahid Afridi	53					1	–
06/02/05	ODI	Pak	Sydney	b Abdul Razzaq	43					–	–
19/02/05	ODI	NZ	Wellington	b S.B. Styris	7					–	–
22/02/05	ODI	NZ	Christchurch	run out (McMillan)	58					–	–

DAMIEN MARTYN (continued)

Start Date		Opp	Venue	How Out	Runs	O	M	R	W	Ct	St
26/02/05	ODI	NZ	Auckland	lbw b D.L. Vettori	1					–	–
01/03/05	ODI	NZ	Wellington	not out	65*					1	–
05/03/05	ODI	NZ	Napier	c S.P. Fleming b K.D. Mills	40					–	–
10/03/05	Test	NZ	Christchurch	lbw b D.L. Vettori	32					–	–
		NZ	Christchurch		–					–	–
18/03/05	Test	NZ	Wellington	cwk B.B. McCullum b IE O'Brien	165					1	–
		NZ	Wellington		–					–	–
26/03/05	Test	NZ	Auckland	b PJ Wiseman	38					–	–
		NZ	Auckland		–					–	–
18/06/05	ODI	Ban	Cardiff	c Nafees Iqbal b Tapash Baisya	77					–	–
19/06/05	ODI	Eng	Bristol	c K.P. Pietersen b S.J. Harmison	0					1	–
23/06/05	ODI	Eng	Chester-le-St	not out	68*					–	–
25/06/05	ODI	Ban	Manchester		–					1	–
28/06/05	ODI	Eng	Birmingham	c K.P. Pietersen b S.J. Harmison	36					–	–
30/06/05	ODI	Ban	Canterbury	cwk Khaled Mashud b Khaled Mahmud	9					–	–
02/07/05	ODI	Eng	Lord's	cwk G.O. Jones b S.J. Harmison	11					–	–
07/07/05	ODI	Eng	Leeds	cwk G.O. Jones b P.D. Collingwood	43					–	–
10/07/05	ODI	Eng	Lord's	not out	39*					–	–
12/07/05	ODI	Eng	The Oval	not out	24*					–	–
21/07/05	Test	Eng	Lord's	cwk G.O. Jones b S.P. Jones	2					2	–
		Eng	Lord's	lbw b S.J. Harmison	65					–	–
04/08/05	Test	Eng	Birmingham	run out (Vaughan)	20					–	–
		Eng	Birmingham	c I.R. Bell b M.J. Hoggard	28					–	–
11/08/05	Test	Eng	Manchester	b A.F. Giles	20					–	–
		Eng	Manchester	lbw b S.J. Harmison	19					1	–
25/08/05	Test	Eng	Nottingham	lbw b M.J. Hoggard	1					–	–
		Eng	Nottingham	cwk G.O. Jones b A. Flintoff	13					–	–
08/09/05	Test	Eng	The Oval	c P.D. Collingwood b A. Flintoff	10					1	–
		Eng	The Oval		–					–	–

GLENN MCGRATH

Start Date		Opp	Venue	How Out	Runs	O	M	R	W	Ct	St
01/07/04	Test	SL	Darwin	c T.T. Samaraweera b W.P.U.J.C. Vaas	0	15.0	4	37	5	–	–
		SL	Darwin	not out	0*	16.0	9	24	2	–	–
09/07/04	Test	SL	Cairns	not out	0*	34.0	10	79	2	–	–
		SL	Cairns		–	16.0	7	31	1	–	–
23/08/04	ODI	Ind	Amstelveen		–					–	–
28/08/04	ODI	Pak	Amstelveen		–	7.1	1	12	1	–	–
13/09/04	ODI	USA	Southampton		–	6.0	1	13	–	–	–
16/09/04	ODI	NZ	The Oval		–	10.0	–	39	3	–	–
21/09/04	ODI	Eng	Birmingham	not out	0*	8.0	–	46	–	–	–
06/10/04	Test	Ind	Bangalore	lbw b Harbhajan Singh	0	25.0	8	55	4	–	–
		Ind	Bangalore	not out	3*	20.0	10	39	2	1	–
14/10/04	Test	Ind	Chennai	run out (Khan/Patel/Kumble)	2	25.0	4	74	–	–	–
		Ind	Chennai	b Harbhajan Singh	2	2.0	–	18	–	–	–
26/10/04	Test	Ind	Nagpur	not out	11*	25.0	13	27	3	–	–
		Ind	Nagpur		–	16.0	1	79	2	1	–
03/11/04	Test	Ind	Mumbai	not out	9*	16.0	9	35	1	–	–
		Ind	Mumbai	c V.V.S. Laxman b Harbhajan Singh	0	12.0	6	29	2	–	–
18/11/04	Test	NZ	Brisbane	c N.J. Astle b C.S. Martin	61	27.0	4	67	–	–	–
		NZ	Brisbane		–	8.0	1	19	3	–	–
26/11/04	Test	NZ	Adelaide		–	20.1	3	66	4	–	–
		NZ	Adelaide		–	12.0	2	32	2	–	–
08/12/04	ODI	NZ	Sydney		–	7.1	–	27	1	1	–
16/12/04	Test	Pak	Perth	not out	8*	19.0	7	44	1	–	–
		Pak	Perth		–	16.0	8	24	8	–	–
26/12/04	Test	Pak	Melbourne	lbw b Danish Kaneria	1	28.0	12	54	1	–	–
		Pak	Melbourne		–	11.2	1	35	4	–	–
02/01/05	Test	Pak	Sydney	c Yousuf Youhana b Danish Kaneria	9	16.4	5	50	4	2	–
		Pak	Sydney		–	16.0	2	53	–	–	–
16/01/05	ODI	Pak	Hobart		–	10.0	2	54	2	–	–
23/01/05	ODI	Pak	Sydney		–	10.0	3	18	2	–	–
26/01/05	ODI	WI	Adelaide		–	8.0	1	18	1	–	–
30/01/05	ODI	Pak	Perth	b Naved-ul-Hasan	0	9.0	2	27	2	–	–
04/02/05	ODI	Pak	Melbourne	run out (Kamran Akmal/Iftikhar)	1	10.0	3	34	3	1	–
06/02/05	ODI	Pak	Sydney	not out	5*	7.4	–	27	5	1	–
19/02/05	ODI	NZ	Wellington		–	9.4	3	16	4	–	–
22/02/05	ODI	NZ	Christchurch		–	7.0	–	42	2	–	–

GLENN MCGRATH (continued)

Start Date		Opp	Venue	How Out	Runs	O	M	R	W	Ct	St
01/03/05	ODI	NZ	Wellington		–	9.5	1	48	2	–	–
05/03/05	ODI	NZ	Napier		–	10.0	–	45	1	1	–
10/03/05	Test	NZ	Christchurch	lbw b D.L. Vettori	0	42.0	9	115	6	–	–
		NZ	Christchurch		–	14.0	7	19	1	–	–
18/03/05	Test	NZ	Wellington		–	14.0	3	50	2	–	–
		NZ	Wellington		–	6.0	3	10	2	–	–
26/03/05	Test	NZ	Auckland	cwk B.B. McCullum b J.E.C. Franklin	0	34.0	20	49	3	–	–
		NZ	Auckland		–	16.2	5	40	4	1	–
18/06/05	ODI	Ban	Cardiff		–	10.0	1	43	–	–	–
19/06/05	ODI	Eng	Bristol	not out	0*	9.0	1	34	2	–	–
23/06/05	ODI	Eng	Chester-le-St		–	10.0	1	31	2	–	–
25/06/05	ODI	Ban	Manchester		–	6.0	1	19	–	–	–
28/06/05	ODI	Eng	Birmingham	not out	2*	3.0	–	24	1	–	–
02/07/05	ODI	Eng	Lord's	c P.D. Collingwood b D. Gough	0	10.0	4	25	3	–	–
07/07/05	ODI	Eng	Leeds		–	8.0	1	26	–	–	–
10/07/05	ODI	Eng	Lord's		–	10.0	2	37	1	–	–
12/07/05	ODI	Eng	The Oval		–	10.0	4	40	–	–	–
21/07/05	Test	Eng	Lord's	not out	10*	18.0	5	53	5	–	–
		Eng	Lord's	not out	20*	17.1	2	29	4	–	–
11/08/05	Test	Eng	Manchester	not out	1*	25.0	6	86	–	1	–
		Eng	Manchester	not out	5*	20.5	1	115	5	–	–
08/09/05	Test	Eng	The Oval	c A.J. Strauss b M.J. Hoggard	0	27.0	5	72	2	–	–
		Eng	The Oval		–	26.0	3	85	3	–	–

RICKY PONTING

Start Date		Opp	Venue	How Out	Runs	O	M	R	W	Ct	St
09/07/04	Test	SL	Cairns	c M.S. Atapattu b S.L. Malinga	22					2	–
		SL	Cairns	c S.T. Jayasuriya b D.N.T. Zoysa	45					–	–
23/08/04	ODI	Ind	Amstelveen	lbw b L. Balaji	26					–	–
28/08/04	ODI	Pak	Amstelveen	c Imran Farhat b Abdul Razzaq	25					–	–
04/09/04	ODI	Pak	Lord's	lbw b Mohammad Sami	4					–	–
13/09/04	ODI	USA	Southampton	not out	8*					–	–
16/09/04	ODI	NZ	The Oval	b S.B. Styris	14					–	–
21/09/04	ODI	Eng	Birmingham	c D. Gough b A.F. Giles	29					–	–

RICKY PONTING (continued)

Start Date		Opp	Venue	How Out	Runs	O	M	R	W	Ct	St
03/11/04	Test	Ind	Mumbai	lbw b A.R. Kumble	11					1	–
		Ind	Mumbai	c V.V.S. Laxman b M. Kartik	12					1	–
18/11/04	Test	NZ	Brisbane	c N.J. Astle b C.S. Martin	51					3	–
		NZ	Brisbane		–					–	–
26/11/04	Test	NZ	Adelaide	st B.B. McCullum b D.L. Vettori	68					–	–
		NZ	Adelaide	not out	26*					1	–
05/12/04	ODI	NZ	Melbourne	lbw b D.L. Vettori	29					1	–
08/12/04	ODI	NZ	Sydney	c S.P. Fleming b K.D. Mills	32					–	–
16/12/04	Test	Pak	Perth	b Mohammad Sami	25	3.0	1	15	–	–	–
		Pak	Perth	st Kamran Akmal b Danish Kaneria	98					–	–
26/12/04	Test	Pak	Melbourne	c Shoaib Malik b Shoaib Akhtar	7					2	–
		Pak	Melbourne	not out	62*					1	–
02/01/05	Test	Pak	Sydney	b Naved-ul-Hasan	207					–	–
		Pak	Sydney	not out	4*					1	–
14/01/05	ODI	WI	Melbourne	run out (Chanderpaul/Browne)	78					1	–
16/01/05	ODI	Pak	Hobart	cwk Kamran Akmal b Shahid Afridi	6					–	–
21/01/05	ODI	WI	Brisbane	lbw b P.T. Collins	2					1	–
23/01/05	ODI	Pak	Sydney	not out	17*					1	–
26/01/05	ODI	WI	Adelaide	c DJJ Bravo b P.T. Collins	0					1	–
30/01/05	ODI	Pak	Perth	b Abdul Razzaq	29					–	–
04/02/05	ODI	Pak	Melbourne	b Iftikhar Anjum	11					–	–
06/02/05	ODI	Pak	Sydney	c Inzamam-ul-Haq b Shahid Afridi	41					–	–
19/02/05	ODI	NZ	Wellington	c D.L. Vettori b S.B. Styris	61					–	–
22/02/05	ODI	NZ	Christchurch	run out (Marshall)	53					1	–
26/02/05	ODI	NZ	Auckland	run out (Papps/McCullum)	11					–	–
05/03/05	ODI	NZ	Napier	not out	141*					–	–
10/03/05	Test	NZ	Christchurch	c B.B. McCullum b C.S. Martin	46					–	–
		NZ	Christchurch	not out	47*					–	–
18/03/05	Test	NZ	Wellington	lbw b D.L. Vettori	9					–	–
		NZ	Wellington		–					–	–

RICKY PONTING (continued)

Start Date		Opp	Venue	How Out	Runs	O	M	R	W	Ct	St
26/03/05	Test	NZ	Auckland	cwk B.B. McCullum b N.J. Astle	105	4.0	1	10	–	1	–
		NZ	Auckland	not out	86*					1	–
18/06/05	ODI	Ban	Cardiff	lbw b Tapash Baisya	1					–	–
19/06/05	ODI	Eng	Bristol	lbw b S.J. Harmison	0					–	–
23/06/05	ODI	Eng	Chester-le-St	c A.F. Giles b S.J. Harmison	27					1	–
25/06/05	ODI	Ban	Manchester		–					–	–
28/06/05	ODI	Eng	Birmingham	cwk G.O. Jones b A. Flintoff	34					–	–
30/06/05	ODI	Ban	Canterbury	c Tushar Imran b Mashrafe Mortaza	66					1	–
02/07/05	ODI	Eng	Lord's	cwk G.O. Jones b S.J. Harmison	7					1	–
07/07/05	ODI	Eng	Leeds	c K.P. Pietersen b P.D. Collingwood	14						
10/07/05	ODI	Eng	Lord's	c K.P. Pietersen b D. Gough	111					1	–
12/07/05	ODI	Eng	The Oval	st G.O. Jones b A.F. Giles	43						
21/07/05	Test	Eng	Lord's	c A.J. Strauss b S.J. Harmison	9						
		Eng	Lord's	c (sub) J.C. Hildreth b M.J. Hoggard	42						
04/08/05	Test	Eng	Birmingham	c M.P. Vaughan b A.F. Giles	61						
		Eng	Birmingham	c G.O. Jones b A. Flintoff	0					2	–
11/08/05	Test	Eng	Manchester	c I.R. Bell b S.P. Jones	7					–	–
		Eng	Manchester	cwk G.O. Jones b S.J. Harmison	156					–	–
25/08/05	Test	Eng	Nottingham	lbw b S.P. Jones	1	6.0	2	9	1	–	–
		Eng	Nottingham	run out (sub) G.J. Pratt	48					1	–
08/09/05	Test	Eng	The Oval	c A.J. Strauss b A. Flintoff	35					–	–
		Eng	The Oval		–					1	–

ANDREW SYMONDS

Start Date		Opp	Venue	How Out	Runs	O	M	R	W	Ct	St
23/08/04	ODI	Ind	Amstelveen	cwk R.S. Dravid b A.R. Kumble	12					–	–
28/08/04	ODI	Pak	Amstelveen	b Shoaib Akhtar	36	7.0	1	25	2	–	–
04/09/04	ODI	Pak	Lord's	not out	104*	5.0	–	31	1	–	–
13/09/04	ODI	USA	Southampton		–					–	–

ANDREW SYMONDS

Start Date		Opp	Venue	How Out	Runs	O	M	R	W	Ct	St
16/09/04	ODI	NZ	The Oval	not out	71*	10.0	2	29	–	–	–
21/09/04	ODI	Eng	Birmingham	run out (Vaughan)	0	6.0	1	34	1	–	–
05/12/04	ODI	NZ	Melbourne	c K.D. Mills b D.L. Vettori	0	8.0	–	35	–	–	–
08/12/04	ODI	NZ	Sydney	lbw b D.L. Vettori	0	10.0	1	47	1	–	–
14/01/05	ODI	WI	Melbourne	c CH Gayle b IDR Bradshaw	20	5.0	–	11	–	1	–
16/01/05	ODI	Pak	Hobart	b Abdul Razzaq	0	9.0	–	55	1	–	–
21/01/05	ODI	WI	Brisbane	cwk C.O. Browne b P.T. Collins	0	7.0	–	38	–	–	–
23/01/05	ODI	Pak	Sydney		–					–	–
26/01/05	ODI	WI	Adelaide	cwk C.O. Browne b W.W. Hinds	31	10.0	–	50	–	–	–
30/01/05	ODI	Pak	Perth	c Shoaib Malik b Shahid Afridi	23	9.0	–	65	2	1	–
04/02/05	ODI	Pak	Melbourne	c Inzamam-ul-Haq b Abdul Razzaq	91	7.0	–	45	–	–	–
19/02/05	ODI	NZ	Wellington	b C.L. Cairns	53	10.0	–	52	1	–	–
22/02/05	ODI	NZ	Christchurch	c J.W. Wilson b K.D. Mills	13	6.0	–	41	3	1	–
26/02/05	ODI	NZ	Auckland	c MHW Papps b K.D. Mills	21	10.0	1	36	1	–	–
01/03/05	ODI	NZ	Wellington	c J.W. Wilson b C.D. McMillan	48					–	–
05/03/05	ODI	NZ	Napier	run out (Vettori/McMillan)	17	5.0	–	25	2	–	–
23/06/05	ODI	Eng	Chester-le-St	run out (Trescothick)	73	7.0	–	37	1	1	–
25/06/05	ODI	Ban	Manchester		–	7.2	1	18	5	1	–
28/06/05	ODI	Eng	Birmingham	run out (Collingwood)	74					–	–
30/06/05	ODI	Ban	Canterbury	not out	42*	10.0	–	36	–	–	–
02/07/05	ODI	Eng	Lord's	c A.J. Strauss b P.D. Collingwood	29	10.0	2	23	–	–	–
07/07/05	ODI	Eng	Leeds	c M.E. Trescothick b P.D. Collingwood	6	10.0	–	32	–	–	–
10/07/05	ODI	Eng	Lord's	not out	5*	7.0	–	31	–	–	–
12/07/05	ODI	Eng	The Oval		–	6.0	1	26	–	1	–

SHAUN TAIT

Start Date		Opp	Venue	How Out	Runs	O	M	R	W	Ct	St
25/08/05	Test	Eng	Nottingham	not out	3*	24.0	4	97	3	–	–
		Eng	Nottingham	b S.J. Harmison	4	4.0	–	24	–	–	–
08/09/05	Test	Eng	The Oval	not out	1*	15.0	1	61	1	–	–
		Eng	The Oval		–	5.0	–	28	1	–	–

SHANE WARNE

Start Date		Opp	Venue	How Out	Runs	O	M	R	W	Ct	St
01/07/04	Test	SL	Darwin	run out (Arnold/Sangakkara)	2	6.5	1	20	3	–	–
		SL	Darwin	lbw b S.L. Malinga	1	19.0	2	61	–	1	–
09/07/04	Test	SL	Cairns	c T.T. Samaraweera b U.D.U. Chandana	2	38.0	7	129	3	1	–
		SL	Cairns	c T.T. Samaraweera b U.D.U. Chandana	4	37.0	14	70	4	2	–
06/10/04	Test	Ind	Bangalore	c R.S. Dravid b Harbhajan Singh	1	28.0	4	78	2	–	–
		Ind	Bangalore	c Yuvraj Singh b Harbhajan Singh	31	32.0	8	115	2	–	–
14/10/04	Test	Ind	Chennai	c and b A.R. Kumble	4	42.3	5	125	6	1	–
		Ind	Chennai	c M. Kaif b A.R. Kumble	0					–	–
26/10/04	Test	Ind	Nagpur	st P.A. Patel b M. Kartik	2	23.0	8	47	2	3	–
		Ind	Nagpur		–	14.3	2	56	2	–	–
18/11/04	Test	NZ	Brisbane	lbw b D.L. Vettori	10	29.3	3	97	4	2	–
		NZ	Brisbane		–	10.2	3	15	4	1	–
26/11/04	Test	NZ	Adelaide	not out	53*	28.0	5	65	1	1	–
		NZ	Adelaide		–	27.3	6	79	2	–	–
16/12/04	Test	Pak	Perth	c Yousuf Youhana b Abdul Razzaq	12	21.0	9	38	3	1	–
		Pak	Perth		–					1	–
26/12/04	Test	Pak	Melbourne	c and b Shoaib Akhtar	10	28.3	2	103	3	–	–
		Pak	Melbourne		–	25.0	7	66	3	–	–
02/01/05	Test	Pak	Sydney	c Younis Khan b Danish Kaneria	16	24.0	4	84	1	2	–
		Pak	Sydney		–	26.0	2	111	4	1	–
10/03/05	Test	NZ	Christchurch	c N.J. Astle b D.L. Vettori	2	40.0	6	112	2	–	–
		NZ	Christchurch		–	14.0	3	39	5	–	–
18/03/05	Test	NZ	Wellington	not out	50*	28.1	7	69	3	1	–
		NZ	Wellington		–	3.2	–	14	–	–	–
26/03/05	Test	NZ	Auckland	c S.P. Fleming b J.E.C. Franklin	1	23.0	4	63	3	–	–
		NZ	Auckland		–	23.0	5	77	4	–	–
21/07/05	Test	Eng	Lord's	b S.J. Harmison	28	7.0	2	19	2	1	–
		Eng	Lord's	c A.F. Giles b S.J. Harmison	2	20.0	2	64	4	1	–
04/08/05	Test	Eng	Birmingham	b A.F. Giles	8	25.2	4	116	4	–	–
		Eng	Birmingham	hit wicket b A. Flintoff	42	23.1	7	46	6	–	–
11/08/05	Test	Eng	Manchester	c A.F. Giles b S.P. Jones	90	33.2	5	99	4	–	–

SHANE WARNE (continued)

Start Date		Opp	Venue	How Out	Runs	O	M	R	W	Ct	St
		Eng	Manchester	cwk G.O. Jones b A. Flintoff	34	25.0	3	74	–	–	–
25/08/05	Test	Eng	Nottingham	c I.R. Bell b S.P. Jones	0	29.1	4	102	4	–	–
		Eng	Nottingham	st G.O. Jones b A.F. Giles	45	13.5	2	31	4	–	–
08/09/05	Test	Eng	The Oval	c M.P. Vaughan b A. Flintoff	0	37.3	5	122	6	1	–
		Eng	The Oval		–	38.3	3	124	6	2	–

SHANE WATSON

Start Date		Opp	Venue	How Out	Runs	O	M	R	W	Ct	St
04/09/04	ODI	Pak	Lord's	not out	7*	9.0	–	47	–	2	–
16/09/04	ODI	NZ	The Oval		–	6.0	–	32	–	–	–
05/12/04	ODI	NZ	Melbourne	cwk B.B. McCullum b I.G. Butler	3	8.4	–	42	–	–	–
02/01/05	Test	Pak	Sydney	c Mohammad Asif b Danish Kaneria	31	10.0	3	28	–	–	–
		Pak	Sydney		–	9.0	2	32	1	–	–
14/01/05	ODI	WI	Melbourne		–	7.0	–	37	–	–	–
21/01/05	ODI	WI	Brisbane		–	10.0	–	52	2	–	–
23/01/05	ODI	Pak	Sydney		–	7.0	2	26	1	–	–
04/02/05	ODI	Pak	Melbourne	c Mohammad Hafeez b Abdul Razzaq	4	9.0	1	38	–	1	–
06/02/05	ODI	Pak	Sydney	c Shahid Afridi b Iftikhar Anjum	21	3.5	–	15	–	–	–
19/06/05	ODI	Eng	Bristol	b A. Flintoff	25	9.3	–	42	–	–	–
23/06/05	ODI	Eng	Chester-le-St	not out	11*	8.0	–	51	1	–	–
25/06/05	ODI	Ban	Manchester		–	4.0	–	14	–	–	–
30/06/05	ODI	Ban	Canterbury		–	10.0	–	43	3	–	–
07/07/05	ODI	Eng	Leeds	c A.J. Strauss b S.J. Harmison	3	3.0	–	16	–	–	–